RETHINKING

THE

EAST ASIA

MIRACLE

JOSEPH E. STIGLITZ
AND
SHAHID YUSUF

Editors

A copublication of the World Bank
and Oxford University Press

Oxford University Press

Oxford • New York • Athens • Auckland • Bangkok • Bogotá • Buenos Aires • Calcutta • Cape Town • Chennai • Dar es Salaam • Delhi • Florence • Hong Kong • Istanbul • Karachi • Kuala Lumpur • Madrid • Melbourne • Mexico City • Mumbai • Nairobi • Paris • São Paulo • Singapore • Taipei • Tokyo • Toronto • Warsaw

and associated companies in

Berlin • Ibadan

Published by Oxford University Press, Inc.
198 Madison Avenue, New York, N.Y. 10016

Cover design and interior design by Naylor Design, Washington, D.C.

Manufactured in the United States of America
First printing June 2001
1 2 3 4   04 03 02 01

Library of Congress Cataloging-in-Publication Data
Rethinking the East Asian miracle/edited by Joseph Stiglitz and Shahid Yusuf.
    p. cm.
    Includes bibliographical references.
    ISBN 0-19-521600-8
    1. East Asia–Economic conditions. 2. Finance—East Asia. I. Stiglitz, Joseph E. II. Yusuf, Shahid, 1949-

HC460.5 .R48 2000
330.95'0429–dc21   00-051329

CONTENTS

Preface   v

Acknowledgements   vii

Contributors   ix

1   The East Asian Miracle at the Millennium
     Shahid Yusuf   1

2   Growth, Crisis, and the Future of Economic Recovery in East Asia
     Takatoshi Ito   55

3   Technological Change and Growth in East Asia:
     Macro versus Micro Perspectives
     Howard Pack   95

4   Chinese Rural Industrialization in the Context of the East Asian
     Miracle
     Justin Yifu Lin and Yang Yao   143

5   After the Crisis, the East Asian Dollar Standard Resurrected:
     An Interpretation of High-Frequency Exchange Rate Pegging
     Ronald I. McKinnon   197

6   Industrial and Financial Policy in China and Vietnam:
     A New Model or a Replay of the East Asian Experience?
     Dwight H. Perkins   247

7   Government Control in Corporate Governance as a Transitional
     Institution: Lessons from China
     Yingyi Qian   295

8   The Government-Firm Relationship in Postwar Japan:
    The Success and Failure of Bureau Pluralism
    Tetsuji Okazaki   323

9   Miracle as Prologue: The State and the Reform
    of the Corporate Sector in Korea
    Meredith Woo-Cumings   343

10 Trade and Growth: Import-Led or Export-Led?
    Evidence from Japan and Korea
    Robert Z. Lawrence and David E. Weinstein   379

11 Emergence of an FDI-Trade Nexus and Economic Growth in East Asia
    Shujiro Urata   409

12 Rethinking the Role of Government Policy in Southeast Asia
    K. S. Jomo   461

13 From Miracle to Crisis to Recovery:
    Lessons from Four Decades of East Asian Experience
    Joseph E. Stiglitz   509

PREFACE

Work on this book began in the late summer of 1997, when the East Asian crisis was only a small, localized cloud over Thailand. The intention was to take a fresh look at the regional experience during the 1990s and to extend and revise as necessary the findings of the World Bank's *East Asian Miracle,* published in 1993. Over the next several months the mounting seriousness of the crisis demonstrated the need not only for a new study but also for one that would bring together a number of different perspectives on key aspects of the East Asian model and its several country variants.

It was decided to approach a group of eminent scholars, each with a long-standing interest in East Asia, and task each of them to reflect on a major strand of the region's story, taking full account of the latest research and the questions raised by the crisis.

When the authors met to discuss the first drafts of the papers in the summer of 1998, both East Asia and the world economy appeared to be confronted by a bleak future. The miracle was on the ropes and few thought that the region was likely to stage a quick recovery.

With the benefit of hindsight, it is fortunate that in publishing the volume we made haste slowly—during the process much of East Asia recovered rapidly. The contributors thus both had ample time to examine the crisis and recovery and to rethink their interpretations of the miracle. They revised their papers extensively. The end result is a volume that greatly enlarges our understanding of East Asia's several and varied growth stories.

The volume assesses the evolving experience with industrial policies in the forms implemented by individual countries in East Asia. It examines in depth how the Chinese experience meshes with those of other economies in the region—a dimension that was absent in the

East Asian Miracle. The rich evidence from the 1990s also casts new light on the relative contribution of export-led policies and of import liberalization to growth, and it helps to clarify key issues influencing the choices of exchange rate policies. We now realize that an understanding of East Asian development requires that we come to grips with the political economy of change, with governance, and with the roles of key institutions. The contributors to this volume consider each of these carefully, thereby offering a reading of East Asia's economic kaleidoscope that is deep, analytically rigorous, and carefully nuanced. The findings presented will be of value to all of those who are trying to understand and learn from the extraordinary experience and record of East Asia over the last decades.

Nicholas Stern

Chief Economist and
Senior Vice President
Development Economics

Vinod Thomas

Vice President
World Bank Institute

ACKNOWLEDGMENTS

A project as large and as long running as this one accumulates many debts—perhaps too many to acknowledge in full. Our first and foremost debt is to the government of Japan for generously funding the research and publication of this volume through a Policy and Human Resources Development grant. The Asia Foundation co-hosted a workshop with us in February 1999, and their elegant facilities in San Francisco provided a fine ambience for two days of intellectual discourse. We are grateful for the foundation's support. Several persons served as discussants for selected papers at various stages of the project; in this connection we would like to thank Masahiro Kawai, Fukunari Kimura, Lawrence Lau, Tetsuji Okazaki, Masahiro Okuno-Fujiwara, Jungsoo Park, Stephen Parker, Richard Robison, Frederic Scherer, and Robert Wade. Those whose administrative contributions ensured the success of this venture include Rebecca Sugui, Chiharu Ima, Umou Al–Bazzaz, and Marc Shotten. We are deeply grateful also to Migara DeSilva, who helped organize the study and attended painstakingly to its complex logistics. Product development, book design, editing, production, and dissemination were coordinated by the World Bank Publications team. Finally, we are grateful to Farrukh Iqbal for taking the initiative to bring this study under the organizational wing of the World Bank Institute and for lending support and encouragement throughout the project.

CONTRIBUTORS

Takatoshi Ito is Professor of Economics at the Institute of Economic Research, Hitotsubashi University.

Jomo K. S. is Professor in the Applied Economics Department of the University of Malaya in Kuala Lumpur, Malaysia.

Robert Lawrence is the Albert L. Williams Professor of International Trade and Investment at Harvard University's John F. Kennedy School of Government. He is also a Senior Fellow at the Institute for International Economics.

Justin Yifu Lin is Professor and Director of China Center for Economic Research at Peking University, and Professor of Economics at Hong Kong University of Science and Technology.

Ronald I. McKinnon is the Eberle Professor of Economics and Senior Fellow at the Center for Research on Economic Development and Policy Reform at Stanford University.

Tetsuji Okazaki is Professor of Economics at the University of Tokyo and Faculty Fellow of the Research Institute of Economy, Trade, and Industry.

Howard Pack is Professor of Business and Public Policy, Economics, and Management at the Wharton School, University of Pennsylvania.

Dwight H. Perkins is the Harold Hitchings Burbank Professor of Political Economy at Harvard University.

Yingyi Qian is Professor in the Department of Economics at the University of Maryland.

Joseph E. Stiglitz is Professor of Economics at Stanford University, Senior Fellow by Courtesy at the Institute for International Studies at Stanford University, and Guest Scholar at the Brookings Institution. He was formerly the Chief Economist of the World Bank.

Shujiro Urata is Professor of Economics at Waseda University, Tokyo, Japan.

David Weinstein is the Carl Sumner Shoup Professor of the Japanese Economy at Columbia University.

Meredith Woo-Cumings is Associate Professor of Political Science at Northwestern University.

Yang Yao is Associate Professor of Economics at China Center for Economic Research, Peking University.

Shahid Yusuf is Research Manager in the Development Economics Research Group at the World Bank.

CHAPTER 1

THE EAST ASIAN MIRACLE AT THE MILLENNIUM

Shahid Yusuf

The 1990s were interesting times for East Asia in the literal sense of the term and in the more ominous sense conveyed by the famous Chinese saying. The decade started on a positive note, with most countries in the region registering high rates of growth. Rapid growth persisted for five years and then began to flag in 1996, with a slowing of exports, the emergence of excess capacity in many industries, and a decline in earnings (see tables 1.1 and 1.2). Questions surfaced about the vigor of the "tiger" economies, and these doubts turned serious in 1997, with the failure of several *chaebol* in the Republic of Korea, signs of stress in Thailand's real estate and financial sectors, and the persistent debilitating stagnation of the Japanese economy.[1]

By the year's end, the region was in the grip of a full-blown crisis, which started in Thailand and then spread to Korea, Malaysia, and Indonesia. The Philippines, Hong Kong (China), and Singapore were affected, but to a lesser degree. Growth also slowed in China and in Taiwan (China), but these two economies were the least hard-hit.[2] Earlier doubts about the future of the so-called East Asian miracle congealed into a deep gloom.

Observers who had worried about the lack of technical progress in the region; who had noted the fragility of the banking systems; who had pointed to widening current account deficits, eroding export competitiveness, meager corporate profitability, and the exposure to short-term debt; and who had criticized the pell-mell investment in real estate felt vindicated (see, for instance, Reinhardt 2000; Easterly and

Table 1.1 Annual Growth Rates of Real Gross Domestic Product Per Capita, 1973–96

Economy	Initial gross domestic product per capita (U.S. dollars)	Annual growth (percent)
United Kingdom	17,953	0.5
France	12,940	1.5
West Germany	13,152	1.8
Austria	11,308	2.0
Italy	10,409	2.1
Spain	8,739	1.8
Greece	7,779	1.5
Singapore	5,412	6.1
Hong Kong, China	6,768	5.1
Japan	11,017	2.5
Malaysia	3,167	4.0
Philippines	1,956	0.8
Korea, Rep. of	2,840	6.8
Indonesia	1,538	3.6
Thailand	1,750	5.6
China	839	5.4
United States	16,607	1.6

Source: Crafts 1999.

others 1993; and Bello and Rosenfeld 1990 for an earlier voicing of concerns). For researchers, who viewed as an anomaly the persistence of high growth in the region over three decades, the downturn and regression to an international mean seemed a natural reassertion of the force of gravity (Easterly and others 1993).

As the crisis deepened in late 1997, concern was voiced that this regional downturn could have much wider consequences. In a lead editorial, the *Economist* noted that a sharp economic slowdown affecting the Korea and Japan "took on a new seriousness. These are two of the world's largest economies which are also two of the world's largest importers as well as sending their investment all over the globe. A financial calamity there could bring on a worldwide slowdown or even a slump" (*Economist*, December 20, 1997, p. 15; on the lead up to the crisis and the aftermath, see World Bank 1999a).

Once the true magnitude of financial fragility, inadequate regulatory oversight, corporate indebtedness, failed management, and overcapacity in key manufacturing subsectors in East Asia became apparent, other countries—such as Brazil and the Russian Federation—were subjected to speculative attacks and had to cope with capital flight

Table 1.2 Percentage Change in Gross Domestic Product in East Asia, 1996–2001

Region	1996	1997	1998	1999	2000[a]	2001[b]
East Asia Five						
Indonesia	8.0	4.5	-13.7	0.5	3.0	5.0
Korea, Rep. of	6.8	5.0	-5.8	10.2	6.0	6.1
Malaysia	8.6	7.5	-7.5	5.4	6.0	6.1
Philippines	5.8	5.2	-0.5	3.2	4.0	4.8
Thailand	5.5	-1.3	-10.0	4.0	5.0	5.5
Transition economies						
China	9.6	8.8	7.8	7.1	7.0	7.2
Vietnam	9.3	8.2	5.8	4.7	4.6	4.5
Small economies						
Cambodia	7.0	1.0	1.0	4.0	5.5	6.0
Lao People's Democratic Republic	6.8	6.9	4.0	4.0	4.5	5.0
Papua New Guinea	3.5	-4.6	2.5	3.9	4.7	4.5
Fiji	3.4	-1.8	-1.3	7.8	3.5	3.0
Mongolia	2.4	4.0	3.5	3.3	4.3	4.5
Solomon Islands	0.6	-0.5	-7.0	1.0	2.0	3.0
East Asia newly industrializing economies (excluding Korea)						
Hong Kong, China	4.5	5.3	-5.1	2.0	5.2	4.4
Singapore	7.6	8.4	0.4	5.4	5.7	5.8
Taiwan, China	5.7	6.8	4.8	5.5	6.5	6.1
Industrial countries						
Japan	5.0	1.6	-2.5	0.3	0.9	1.6
United States	3.7	4.5	4.3	4.1	4.3	—

— Not available.
a. Estimate.
b. Projection.

Source: World Bank 2000a.

(Clifford and Engardio 1999; Gilpin 2000).[3] The world economy walked a tightrope through most of 1998, with the United States and some of the European economies providing much of the momentum for growth, and with the U.S. absorbing much of the capital which fled East Asia (Van Wincoop and Yi 2000). However, by early 1999 the worst was behind. Even though the Japanese economy remained weak, other East Asian countries began to rebound on the basis of export demand from the United States and Western Europe, especially for electronics, and higher domestic fiscal spending.

The pace of recovery quickened in the latter part of 1999 because of increasing intraregional trade, higher oil prices that aided the petroleum producers, and appreciation of the yen ("Southeast Asia Export Recovery," *Oxford Analytica*, December 10, 1999). In early 2000, the doubts voiced about the future of economic development in East Asia had largely dissipated.[4] Writing in the *Financial Times* (February 23, 2000), Martin Wolf saw "Asia's future burning bright." He extolled "Asia's astounding comeback" and observed that "the most important economic story of the past two decades—that of the convergence of the income levels of the advanced economies by a rising proportion of the peoples of emerging Asia—has regained its credibility." Stock market recovery throughout the region, propelled by exuberant views regarding Internet and technology stocks, provided additional impetus ("The Fear of the Internet," *Far Eastern Economic Review*, December 30–January 6, 2000).[5]

With the economies of East Asia growing by close to 6 percent in 2000, after attaining a growth rate of 4.1 percent in 1999, is there any need to rethink the East Asian miracle? Can we treat the one year of low growth—that is, 1998, when the East Asian economies expanded just 1.6 percent—as an inevitable bump on the road to globalization? Or does the crisis of 1997–98 and what it revealed about macroeconomic policy, institutions, business practices, and regulatory capability in East Asia call for a reappraisal of the East Asian model and of its underlying dynamics? Have fundamental weaknesses persisting in the East Asian economies been obscured by their undeniable strengths and by close to three decades of rapid growth?

WHY RETHINK AND WHAT?

The purpose of this volume is to cast just such a searching eye over a landscape rendered less familiar by an unforeseen event of the utmost severity. The chapters reexamine the major determinants of East Asian performance from country or regional perspectives and indicate how the experience of the 1990s has either modified or reaffirmed the mainstream views of the early 1990s, which were expressed in the *East Asian Miracle* (World Bank 1993) and many other publications (for a critical assessment of the East Asian miracle, its commissioning, and the crafting of its recommendations, especially on industrial policy, see Wade 1996).

The kind of questions motivating our inquiry were expressed with characteristic bluntness by Paul Krugman in August 1997, soon after the crisis erupted in Thailand. Krugman took as his point of departure the work of Young (1992, 1994a and b) and Kim and Lau (1994), which suggested to him that Asian growth was "mainly a matter of perspiration rather than inspiration—of working harder, not smarter." He went on to add:

> If there is one thing that believers in an Asian system admire, it is the way Asian governments promote specific industries and technologies; this is supposed to explain their economies' soaring efficiency. But if you conclude that it is mainly perspiration—that efficiency is not soaring—then the brilliance of Asian industrial policies becomes a lot less obvious. The other unwelcome implication of the perspiration theory was that the pace of Asia's growth was likely to slow. You can get a lot of economic growth by increasing labor force participation, giving everyone a basic education and tripling the investment share of GDP [gross domestic product], but these are one-time unrepeatable changes.
>
> The biggest lesson from Asia's [recent] troubles is not about economics, it is about government. When Asian economies delivered nothing but good news, it was possible to convince yourself that the alleged planners of these knew what they were doing. Now the truth is revealed, they do not have a clue. [Paul Krugman, "What Ever Happened to the Asian Miracle?" *Fortune*, August 18, 1997, p. 27.]

KEYS TO THE EAST ASIAN MIRACLE

Before rethinking the causes and dynamics of the East Asian approach to development, I summarize its main elements as perceived at the beginning of the decade of the 1990s and presented in the *East Asian Miracle* and other publications (World Bank 1993; Ohno 1998). Each country pursued its own customized variant, but a convenient stylization included four main strands.

First was the adherence to the fundamentals of macroeconomic management. This called for:

- A stable business environment with relatively low inflation that encouraged investment in long-gestation, fixed assets

- Prudent and sustainable fiscal policies to actively complement other measures aimed at equitably sharing the rewards from higher growth

- Exchange rate policies to underpin export competitiveness

- Financial development and the progressive liberalization of the sector so as to maximize domestic savings (stimulated, initially, by rapid growth) and promote efficient allocation and integration with the global financial system

- Efforts to minimize price distortions

- Actions to support the spread of primary and secondary schooling as well as the creation of a hierarchy of skills to buttress an outward-looking development push.

A second strand of the strategy stressed the need for a bureaucracy able to conceive and implement the designs of a "strong state" (meaning an authoritarian, centralized developmental state) and to make a credible commitment to long-run development. This element of the strategy, which drew selectively on the experience of Singapore, Korea, Japan, and Taiwan, called for able and well-paid administrators who were insulated to a significant degree from political pressures and empowered to take development initiatives aimed at maximizing the growth of output and employment (Campos and Root 1996; Root 1996; Ohno 1998). In this context, insulation had a particular meaning: such bureaucrats, while being embedded within the system, were less likely to be diverted from the pursuit of long-run goals by political demands that were frequently myopic (Evans 1995). It did not mean distancing government from business. In fact, the World Bank study attached much importance to the interaction between administrators and businesspeople through means such as deliberation councils so as to forge national priorities, induce an exchange of market information, and promote networking as well as coordination.[6] But the study went beyond coordination and information pooling to underscore the role of strong bureaucracies in stimulating "contests" between business groups to ensure that competition in the marketplace did not flag (Stiglitz 1996). Businessmen met with government administrators to reach an understanding on strategy and, where possible, to coordinate their activities. This did not blunt the incentives to compete against one another. On the contrary, East Asian governments adroitly employed carrots and sticks to prevent a slackening of domestic competition.

A third strand was governments' activist policies to quicken the pace of industrialization and export an increasing proportion of industrial output. Outward-oriented development, in conjunction with exchange rate policy, was a means of achieving viable external balances and generating the demand needed to accelerate GDP growth, force producers to absorb technology, and strive after competitiveness. In their efforts to industrialize, East Asian governments made selective use of tariff protection and export incentives, ranging from moral suasion to subsidies and mild financial repression, so as to provide industry with financing at lower cost. The World Bank study notes that these measures were applied sparingly and is cautious in recommending their use by other countries.

The reason for the qualified support extended to government activism was made clear by the fourth strand of the East Asian development strategy: the approach was pragmatic, and the measures were applied flexibly and abandoned if their purpose was not being fulfilled (Ohno 1998; for an East Asian perspective on industrial policy, which underscores the significance of a vision and a long-term strategy, see Yamada and Kuchiki 1997). In other words, a circumscribed dirigisme yielded good results on balance because of an overriding commitment to rapid and efficient development, combined with the ability of a strong state to abandon initiatives that were seen to be failing. The record of East Asian countries in applying this exacting pragmatic calculus was by no means perfect, and some Southeast Asian countries deviated more often than others (however, see Jomo, chapter 12 of this volume). But when certain (demanding) conditions were met, market outcomes for late developers could be improved through a clear-headed manipulation of incentives by the visible hand (see the concluding chapter of this volume, by Joseph Stiglitz; Wade 1990; Amsden 1989; and Root 1996).

QUESTIONING THE EARLIER CONSENSUS

The experience of the 1990s and research results from around the world have strongly reaffirmed the appropriateness of sound macroeconomic and sectoral policies. Nevertheless, questions have arisen regarding their execution. In particular, East Asian countries were slow to implement prudential regulations, induce banks to adopt risk management systems, strengthen banking supervision, and sharpen incentives supporting allocative efficiency prior to dismantling some of the restraints on capital flows (McKinnon 1991; Chow 2000; Flatters 2000). As a result, the authorities and banks were ill prepared to cope with the huge influx of capital or with the abrupt outflow in 1997 (Wong 1999; Furman and Stiglitz 1998; Hellman, Murdock, and Stiglitz 2000).[7] In particular, banks were guilty of currency and term mismatching, which greatly exacerbated the severity of the financial crisis (see chapter 2, by Ito, in this volume). The use of exchange rate and fiscal policies has also aroused debate, with some observers claiming that the severity of the currency crises could have been ameliorated by a different approach. Fiscal policy tended to be excessively conservative, which worsened the deflationary pressure in the immediate aftermath of the crisis.[8] The crisis underlined the advantages of public bureaucracies skilled at managing the economy and responding to shocks. But the experience of Korea and Thailand also revealed how difficult it is to sustain a meritocratic culture and insulate bureaucracies from political pressures (Haggard 2000, Heo and Kim 2000).

Moreover, the earlier "consensus" appears least settled in six areas. First, by the end of the 1980s, East Asia was rapidly converging toward the industrial countries. Growth was driven by increasing factor inputs, with total factor productivity (TFP) on an upward trend. But research during the 1990s has rendered the story much more complex. Although technical efficiency is rising, the productivity gap between middle-income East Asian countries and industrial economies is as wide as before. More seriously, the apparent contribution of technical progress to TFP remains small. This calls into question policies pertaining to industrialization, the service sector, the development of human resources, and the gains from building research capacity.

Second, the advantages of an activist and pragmatic industrial policy, which used directed credit and subsidies to build new subsectors, are far from clear. "Getting the prices wrong" and subsidizing industry for lengthy periods in an attempt to create viable exporters have entailed high costs, and they seem increasingly inappropriate in an integrated world subject to World Trade Organization (WTO) disciplines (Amsden 1989, 1991).

Third, close symbiotic relations between banks and industrial corporations, encouraged by governments, induced investment and a long-term business perspective in some East Asian countries but also resulted in misallocation of bank lending (often into real estate), the accumulation of nonperforming assets, and high corporate gearing ratios (Cho and Kim 1995, Hutchcroft 1999).[9] Moreover, even in Japan, the close links between banks and companies did not strengthen corporate governance, insulated companies from market pressures, and impeded the emergence of a competitive market for corporate control (Hall and Weinstein 2000).[10] The dominance of the banking system also may have impeded the widening of financial markets.

Fourth, the efficacy of exports as an engine of productivity and growth in East Asia has been questioned. Recent research casts doubt on the proposition that "in subsidy-dependent industrialization, growth will be faster the greater the degree to which the subsidy allocation process is disciplined and tied to performance standards—exports possibly being the most efficient monitoring device" (Amsden 1991: 285). In fact, Amsden came to view growth in Northeast Asian economies as driven more by investment and the sectoral reallocation of resources than by exports (Amsden and Singh 1994). Other researchers have also focused on investment and imports (Rodrik 1995; Lawrence and Weinstein in chapter 10 of this volume).

Fifth, the approach to governance in East Asia deserves a fresh look. Governance is about how institutions, organizations, and processes mediate relationships between principals and agents (Dyck 2000; Haggard 1999). It seeks to explain the making and implementing of collective decisions (Burki and Perry 1998). Four aspects of governance in East Asia attracted attention in the 1990s: the nature of government-business interaction to coordinate decisions, internalize externalities, and manage the market; the degree to which individual families exercised control over large business empires; the autonomy and effectiveness of regulatory agencies, especially those mandated to oversee the financial sector and shareholders; and the discipline exerted by strict rates of corporate governance on the managers of firms. East Asia's brand of governance, while occasionally criticized, was generally praised for promoting cooperation and contests that delivered good economic results (see Woo-Cumings, chapter 9 of this volume). The deterioration in performance after 1996 and the underlying problems uncovered by the crisis suggest that relationship-based governance structures, and family ownership through holding companies or complex interlocking shareholdings, must adapt as countries multiply their links with the global economy (Li 1998). By "governing the market" (Wade 1990) and relying on administrative rulings to achieve results, East Asian governments slowed the growth of legal and regulatory institutions that would strengthen the market and remedy certain types of market failure, although they promoted human resource development and the acquisition of comparative advantage in some areas (see Jomo, chapter 12 of this volume; Haggard 2000; and Heo and Kim 2000). In the East Asian institutional milieu, rules of corporate governance to solve problems of agency made little headway.

A sixth development of consequence is the progressive integration of the region as well as of the world economy because of trade and factor flows.[11] The contiguousness of the crisis revealed just how far this has progressed and the degree to which foreign investors perceive East Asia as an entity sharing certain common attributes. A decade ago, East Asian countries could pursue macroeconomic and trade policies more or less independently of their neighbors. Now they must recognize some degree of interdependence and coordinate their actions (Gilpin 2000).

The balance of this introductory chapter examines in more detail each of these facets of the East Asian miracle, indicating how an eventful decade and the latest research have qualified or altered our thinking.

MACROECONOMIC POLICY AND STABLE GROWTH

The advantages of a stable environment and low inflation remain unchallenged. Moderate rates of inflation are not necessarily harmful to growth (Bruno and Easterly 1995; Barro 1997) or to savings (Hussein and Thirlwall 1999), but business confidence, and with it investment, including foreign direct investment, thrives best under conditions of political and economic stability (Fischer 1993).[12] As East Asia becomes more closely integrated with the global economy, conducive business conditions will become even more important.

Economic stability rests on a coordinated application of fiscal, monetary, and exchange rate policies. Throughout the 1990s most East Asian countries—except Thailand—attempted to contain the growth of monetary aggregates and keep fiscal deficits to sustainable levels. When hit by the crisis, the affected countries were persuaded to follow the orthodox policy of raising interest rates to stem the outflow of capital and cut budgetary outlay so as to rebuild confidence in their finances. This proved to be harsh medicine and was diluted. However, because of policy actions, the launching of institutional reform, and strong export performance, interest rates declined, currencies subsequently strengthened, stock markets rebounded, and countries regained much of their earlier momentum. But the crisis and its aftermath indicated that in the event of a shock, which calls for a sharp rise in interest rates to restore confidence and prevent further weakening of the currency, fiscal spending may need to be increased to offset a drop in private spending and ameliorate the deflationary impact of tighter monetary policy on consumers and businesses. The desirability of such action and moderation in the use of monetary tightness become even more important when companies are highly leveraged.[13] The relatively low ratio of public debt to GDP in most East Asian countries also reduced the risks of running larger budget deficits over the medium term.[14]

The responses to the East Asian crisis indicate that the rules for dealing with shocks need to be broadened to take account of country circumstances and the possibility of contagion. Should governments continue to adhere to the fiscal fundamentals but respond to a banking-cum-currency crisis by mobilizing contingent spending plans to maintain aggregate demand, recognizing that such a move could worsen the outflow of capital? Is it the case that restricting capital movement through taxes or administrative measures may not always be suboptimal? What is the appropriate exchange rate policy for medium-sized and highly trade-oriented economies to follow? One thing is clear: a dogmatic line on either monetary or fiscal or exchange rate policies is not desirable. As Clarida, Calf, and Gertler (1999: 1703) observe, in the face of severe monetary shocks, monetary policy should not adhere to a simple rule. But on this point there is little theoretical or empirical work to guide policymakers, and it is "a fertile area for research." Furthermore, while in normal times, prudent budgetary management with low sustainable deficits is desirable, if a crisis strikes, policymakers need to examine their options carefully and weigh the tradeoff so as to avoid an unnecessary loss of output.

Fiscal action to control a deflationary spiral when the corporate sector is highly geared needs to be coordinated with monetary policy to limit interest rate spikes. In some cases, taxes on capital flows might be necessary to ensure that such policies lead to the least costly results and do not exacerbate the effects of the shock or delay adjustment.

Although the policy response to a shock has certainly become more nuanced, the East Asian crisis has not significantly altered our views on openness or on the steps toward achieving it. Banks should be well regulated. Financial management and the regulation of banks are now seen as much more critical to both growth and stability (Levine 1997). At the same time, the emergence of new products and new activities, the consolidation of financial entities, and the greater geographic scope of their activities have also confronted regulators with tougher challenges on how to attain efficiency while preserving the soundness of the financial system (Mishkin and Strahan 1999).

Banks, long accustomed to a comfortable and sheltered world of relationship banking, need to adjust to a more competitive environment in which foreign banks are a growing presence and higher-margin, consumer-oriented lending emphasizing service and new products will determine success (Wade 1998). In addition, banking cultures throughout much of East Asia are being pushed to adopt the practice of disclosure, to improve their system of evaluating credit risk, to pay greater attention to customer cash flow than collateral, to make branch offices more accountable to the head office, and to rely more on arm's-length dealing rather than on trust.[15] While the weaknesses of banks were one part of the problem, the deficiencies of non-bank financial institutions were even greater, and they exacerbated the effects of the shock (see Woo-Cumings, chapter 9 of this volume). In Japan, the housing loan corporations, or *jusen*, 70 percent of whose loans were collateralized by real estate, were at the heart of the financial crisis.

The crisis certainly revealed East Asia's deficiencies in these critical areas. But where countries achieved these objectives, an opening of the capital account did not increase the volatility of growth (Easterly, Islam, and Stiglitz 2000) and over time could promote financial development with its attendant allocative benefits.[16] Moreover, as financial sophistication rises, preventing capital outflows becomes increasingly difficult (Dooley 1995), and derivatives make it problematic for even the most skilled regulators to contain inflows of short-term capital (Garber 1998).[17] China experienced large outflows during 1998–2000, and in spite of capital controls, the restrictions imposed by Malaysia were decreasingly effective by 2000 ("Funds Leave Malaysia Despite Capital Controls," *International Herald Tribune*, December 5, 2000).

The crisis also focused attention on exchange rate policies. First it highlighted the dynamic triggered by the movements in the yen-dollar rate since the mid-1980s—the yen "carry trade" (McKinnon 2000). By putting upward pressure on the yen rate, the trading relationships between the United States and Japan pushed down interest rates in Japan and encouraged Japanese banks to seek higher—and riskier—returns in East Asia. It also encouraged other investors to borrow on the Japanese market and to place these funds in neighboring countries. The likelihood of being bailed out in the event of a crisis further emboldened banks and others and funneled large amounts of capital in what proved to be unwise investments in manufacturing as well as real estate (Overholt 1999). One lesson to be drawn is that in an integrated world, exchange rate coordination between key currencies may avoid conditions that can lead to a crisis. Unfortunately, pushing down the yen rate to enable Japan to run a large current account surplus, which accommodates its high saving and moderate investment rate, is likely to pose a serious challenge to attempts at coordination.[18]

A second and equally important lesson is that a policy regime based on a soft exchange rate peg coupled with sterilized interventions has serious drawbacks.[19] The former ultimately lacked credibility. The latter pushed up interest rates and stimulated further inflows. The crisis underscored once again the difficulties that can arise from a compromise between a fixed-rate regime—or monetary unification through dollarization or via a monetary board system with a key currency—or a freely floating exchange rate. Theory suggests that the choice of an exchange rate should be determined by the nature of expected shocks. If they are real, then a system of floating rates is advisable. If they are not, then fixed rates are more appropriate. When shocks come through the capital account and contain both real and nominal elements, the choice is unclear (Calvo and Reinhart 1999).

Recent experience has also lent weak support to theories suggesting that the likelihood of a currency crisis increases when the real exchange rate is overvalued relative to trend, credit growth is high, the ratio of M2 to GDP has risen (Berg and Pattillo 1999), the banking system is weak and undercapitalized, and countries have financed current account deficits with short-term borrowing (Dornbusch 2000).[20]

However, neither the East Asian crisis nor other currency crises in the 1990s have established the superiority of fixed or flexible rates. Although many commentators have pointed to the risks of pegging to the U.S. dollar, estimates of real appreciation of key East Asian currencies do not suggest much change in the years preceding the crisis. Only in Thailand was there any significant real appreciation. Even there, the change from peak to trough was 13 percent, and from the base value of 100, it was just 8 percent (McKibbin and Martin 1999). Moreover, some East Asian countries, notably Korea, registered a strong increase in the volume of exports.

The optimal regime ultimately depends on a range of factors peculiar to a country: size, openness, labor mobility, fiscal capacity, the size of reserves, the strength of the banking system, the credibility of legal rules and property rights, the willingness to integrate with trading partners, and, where the option is to adopt a monetary board, the political readiness to surrender control over key policy levers (Frankel 1999). For some countries, the lesson from the East Asian crisis is that a credible policy stance under conditions of openness, when much of their trade is denominated in dollars, is to opt for a fixed peg through a monetary board type of arrangement (Calvo and Reinhart 1999; McKinnon in chapter 5 of this volume). For others, the recent experience points to the advantages of greater exchange rate flexibility with an inflation target (Mishkin 1999). But exchange rate flexibility cannot be adopted after a crisis has already hit—Thailand's approach—or just before a crisis and after financial weakness is already apparent— the tack followed by Korea and Malaysia (Eichengreen 1999). It must entail a full-fledged shift to floating rates along the lines of Mexico, Brazil, and Colombia.

The future course of exchange rate policies in East Asia and other industrializing countries remains unclear, and there is bound to be a period of experimentation determined by progress with reform and the direction of political change. But the lesson emerging from the second half of the 1990s is that currency management in the region was inconsistent with the increasing vulnerability of individual countries.

PERSPECTIVES ON GROWTH IN EAST ASIA

In the early 1990s, our understanding of the determinants of growth in East Asia was assailed by contrarian evidence questioning the contribution of total factor productivity. At the start of the decade, human capital, physical capital, and labor inputs contributed about 60 percent to the growth of high-performing Asian economies (HPAEs).[21] Primary and secondary education were the largest contributors, followed by physical capital. Approximately a third of growth was derived from rising TFP. Productivity change in the East Asian countries was higher than that in other developing countries, although it was still lower than that occurring in the industrial countries. "All the HPAEs, except Singapore, [stood] up well in their ability to keep pace with the world's shifting technological frontier" (World Bank 1993: 57).

Shortly after publication of the World Bank study (1993), Young (1994b) and Kim and Lau (1994) challenged this position, finding that TFP made a negligible contribution to growth in much of industrializing East Asia. The principal drivers of growth were primarily physical capital followed by human capital, Krugman's perspiration variables.

These findings radically undermined the orthodox position and unleashed a torrent of econometric investigation (for a review of the recent literature on the sources of East Asian growth, see Crafts 1998; Felipe 1999). The results of the key research are summarized below.

This body of research has asserted the primacy of physical capital among the various sources of growth in East Asia, with labor and human capital second and TFP a distant third. Most of the East Asian economies still lag well behind the non-Asian G-7 countries (Canada, France, Germany, Italy, the United Kingdom, and the United States) and Japan in terms of TFP. Nevertheless, they do far better than other developing countries, in large part because of greater openness, better policies, and stronger institutions (Hahn and Kim 1999). They also relate to the scale economies achieved by East Asian countries through better management of capital (see Perkins in chapter 6 of this volume).

The variance in the econometric findings and the difficulty of reconciling the low TFP scores with the apparent success of East Asian countries in assimilating industrial technology have aroused a measure of skepticism and a search for other explanations (see tables 1.3 and 1.4). The skepticism derives from a resurgence of long-standing doubts about the robustness of concepts and techniques used to measure the sources of growth and about the quality of both the data as well as the deflators used to arrive at "adjusted" series (see Pack in chapter 3 of this volume).

To start with, there is the long-standing theoretical concern about finding a measure for capital as an index independent of relative prices and distribution. Growth accounting assumes that the interaction term between inputs such as physical and human capital is insignificant, whereas in practice this is unlikely to be the case.

In some cases, estimates are biased because constant returns and perfect competition are incorrectly assumed. In addition, because right-hand-side variables are measured with error, ordinary least squares

Table 1.3 Sources of Growth in Europe and Japan, 1950–73, and in East Asia, 1960–94 (percent a year)

Period and economy	Capital	Labor	Total factor productivity	Output
1950–73				
France	1.6	0.3	3.1	5.0
Italy	1.6	0.2	3.2	5.0
Japan	3.1	2.5	3.6	9.2
United Kingdom	1.6	0.2	1.2	3.0
West Germany	2.2	0.5	3.3	6.0
1960–94				
China	3.1	2.7	1.7	7.5
Hong Kong, China	2.8	2.1	2.4	7.3
Indonesia	2.9	1.9	0.8	5.6
Korea, Rep. of	4.3	2.5	1.5	8.3
Malaysia	3.4	2.5	0.9	6.8
Philippines	2.1	2.1	-0.4	3.8
Singapore	4.4	2.2	1.5	8.1
Taiwan, China	4.1	2.4	2.0	8.5
Thailand	3.7	2.0	1.8	7.5

Source: Crafts 1998.

Table 1.4 Alternative Estimates of East Asian Total Factor Productivity Growth
(percent a year)

Economy	Young (1994a and b, 1995), 1966–90	Collins and Bosworth (1996), 1960–94	Sarel (1997), 1978–96	Adjusted (Young), 1966–90[a]
China		4.6[c]		
Hong Kong, China	2.3			2.4[d]
Indonesia	1.2[b]	0.8	1.2	
Korea, Rep. of	1.7	1.5		1.3
Malaysia	1.1[b]	0.9	2.0	
Philippines		-0.4	-0.8	
Singapore	0.2	1.5	2.2	1.0
Taiwan, China	2.6	2.0		1.9
Thailand	1.5[b]	1.8	2.0	

a. Adjusted (Young) uses revised factor share weights with capital assumed to have a weight of 0.35.
b. 1970–85
c. 1984–94.
d. 1966–91.

Source: Crafts 1998.

give biased and inconsistent results, and these can be exacerbated by the choice of countries and particular data sets. Last, it is argued that unless the elasticity of substitution is known, it is not possible to assign growth accurately to changes in capital intensity as against biased technical change. In other words, "Growth accounting exercises cannot distinguish between two different explanations of growth decomposition equally consistent with the time-series data: one arising from a production function with unitary elasticity and Hicks neutral technical change and another with an elasticity of less than one and labor-using technical change" (Felipe 1999: 30).

The attempt to find additional evidence to qualify or strengthen the aggregate analysis has led to microeconomic investigations of individual industrial subsectors, R&D in East Asian countries, the national innovation systems in place, and the role of trade and foreign direct investment. Howard Pack (chapter 3 of this volume) builds on his earlier work to show how East Asian economies have successfully tackled the assimilation of technology and begun contributing fresh technological insights of their own, insights that have resulted in a stream of patents, most notably from Korea and Taiwan.[22] Pack discusses the limits of the aggregative approach and then explores, in more qualitative terms, the avenues through which technology was transferred to East Asia and absorbed by companies large and small across the region. Pack emphasizes the domestic effort that mediated the process of absorption and illuminates the enormous gains made by the East Asian countries, gains not registered by other developing countries with respectable rates of investment and stocks of human capital.

Pack also touches on the innovation systems taking root in several East Asian countries. These systems are positioning countries to contribute more actively to technical advance in a number of industries and to derive the full rents from commercially successful innovations, rents they cannot extract from borrowed technologies.

Even though the neoclassical revival in the 1990s shifted attention briefly back to capital accumulation as the primary source of growth in East Asia, the research it stimulated has again focused attention on TFP (Easterly and Levine 2000). While the industrializing countries of East Asia will continue to derive a large part of their growth from factor accumulation, over the longer term their convergence to the incomes of the advanced countries will depend on the speed of movement toward the technological frontier and eventually their ability to push this frontier outward in select areas. Thus assimilating and generating technological advances by creating the appropriate physical and institutional infrastructure will be necessary adjuncts to accumulation.[23]

How countries succeed in harnessing available technologies and then moving to the cutting edge of technological change is one of the most exciting areas of current and future research. The experience of those industrial countries that are among the most prolific producers of industrial innovation points to the intertwining of policies, institutions, industrial organization, size of market, and first-mover advantages. Although no single recipe emerges from this wealth of experience, certain common elements are also becoming sources of dynamism in some of the leading East Asian countries.

A strong, research-oriented university system, which complements vigorous research activities in corporations and other public or private institutes, appears to be a necessary condition for moving up the ladder of technology. Government policy and financial support for research activities have often proved crucial, but so has the commitment of the private sector, sharpened by competition policies pushing companies to retain or enlarge market share by way of innovation. Intellectual property rights instituted by the state have supported innovation in some sectors, as have regulatory policies in industries such as pharmaceuticals. In the United States, access to venture capital has promoted the growth of electronics and biotech industries, which derived their initial impetus from research funded by the Department of Defense and the National Institutes of Health. This abundance of venture capital arose out of institutional deepening in the financial markets, guided by a succession of government policy actions. In other countries, the banking system, vertically integrated corporations (some supporting intrapreneurial activities), or subcontracting networks have substituted for the lack of venture capital.

A large, sophisticated, and demanding market has been an asset for the United States, Japan, and some of the European countries. Such a market facilitates the launch of new products and is frequently the basis for first-mover advantages, which are responsible for the stability of firms in the chemical, pharmaceutical, and automobile industries. However, with the decline of barriers to trade, even firms in smaller countries are not overly constrained by market size if they have accumulated skills in marketing products worldwide (see Mowery and Rosenberg 1999; the papers in Mowery and Nelson 1999; Scherer 1999).

All of these lessons are being absorbed piecemeal by the East Asian countries. But the hardest step is the creation of the fundamental building block—a base of research-oriented universities and research institutes that induce creative work.[24] The importance of this has been formally recognized throughout the region and underscored by research on the role of TFP in growth. The difficult step for even the leading East Asian economies, such as Korea, Taiwan, Hong Kong, and Singapore, is to shift basic schooling away from rote learning without sacrificing their strengths in science and math. Next there is the need to encourage competition between universities and, through this, to instill a culture of excellence in research and develop the infrastructure for refereeing and disseminating research findings and strengthening the links between universities and the business sector (Lim 1999, Branscomb, Kodama, and Florida 1999). This could maximize the commercial utility of research, thereby encouraging the two-way flow of resources and talent, which has been critical to the success of Silicon Valley and the high-tech industrial networks around the Universities of Chicago and Cambridge.

INDUSTRIAL POLICY IN THE 1990S

This rethinking of the role of technology in the context of growth points to the evolution of industrial policy in an integrated world. The 1980s closed with the literature emphasizing the drawbacks of "picking winners," supporting them with directed credit from the banking system, and protecting them with trade barriers. Nevertheless, even some of the critics recognized the efficacy of industrial policy in a few East Asian countries at an early stage of their development, under special circumstances, external as well as internal. These included dynamic strategies to advance the prospects of individual sectors by enabling them to exploit economies of scale, technological spillovers, and possibilities of learning, and to coordinate their own investment with downstream producers (Stiglitz 1996).[25]

The decade of the 1990s saw the continuing retreat of industrial policy in East Asia, as countries came to recognize the advantages of openness and accepted the disciplines of the World Trade Organization.[26] Research into the merits of industrial policy, as practiced in East Asia, also focused attention on costs, in the rare instances where the presence of externalities argued for preferential treatment—as with the development of high-technology industries such as electronics and semiconductors in Malaysia, Taiwan, and Korea and auto parts in Thailand (Mathews and Cho 2000; and Jomo, chapter 12 in this volume)—and highlighted the diminished relevance of such policies in the new global environment.[27] In a world where the trend is for companies to spread the burden of R&D and gain access to markets through joint ventures, mergers, and alliances, the role of industrial policy is increasingly limited to those few cases in which countries, through skill development and research, build competitive sectors able to produce high-technology products for a global market (Jomo, chapter 12; Smith 1995; Krugman 1986).[28]

Some notable findings from the research on Japan are that subsidies had, on balance, shifted resources from high- to low-productivity uses (Noland and Bergsten 1993), and the bulk of the assistance provided through favorable tax treatment, subsidized credit, and protection had gone not to the fastest-growing subsectors, but to declining industries or mature industries with modest future prospects, such as coal, petroleum, and textiles (Beason and Weinstein 1996).[29] Industrial policies successfully assisted the growth of industries such as household sewing machines (1970s) and semiconductors and information technology (1980s). But government support was of little relevance to Japan's consumer electronics industry in the 1950s and 1960s—and at times was obstructive (Partner 1999). It was ineffective in the case of biotechnology and played a small role in the development of motorcycles, audio equipment, autos, game software, office equipment, robotics, and soy sauce (Porter and Takeuchi 1999; Porter, Takeuchi and Sakakibara 2000; Okimoto 1986; Imai 1986). Market incentives, the capacity to identify and exploit opportunities, research skills, and networking enabled these industries to thrive. They are also the ingredients that matter most in today's globalizing environment.

Research on East and Southeast Asian economies during the 1980s and 1990s has drawn attention to wasteful investment in metallurgical, chemical, and transport subsectors.[30] Such investment was made possible by directed credit to select business groups, and some of the plant was put up on the government's instruction. Directed credit and tax privileges that specifically nurtured large industrial conglomerates (called *chaebol* in Korea) also brought into existence an industrial structure where control over assets—directly or indirectly—was concentrated in the hands of a few wealthy and politically influential families (see Woo-Cumings, chapter 9 of this volume). In fact, such concentration was not peculiar to Korea. Claessens, Djankov, and Lang (2000) point out that most of East Asia's corporate assets, other than in Japan and the transition economies, are controlled by a small number of families.

By 1995, 41 percent of industrial value added and 16 percent of gross national product (GNP) were in the hands of the top 30 Korean *chaebol*. This had implications for productive efficiency, governance, and the political economy of decisionmaking, the full consequences of which became apparent at the time of the crisis in 1997 (see Woo-Cumings in chapter 9 of this volume). A study of Korean industry by McKinsey and Company (Baily and Zitzewitz 1998) shows that although Korea's ratio of capital to labor was only a third of the U.S. level, capital productivity was declining and in 1995 was only 5 percent above that of the United States. Prior to the crisis, profitability of the top 30 *chaebol* was less than the cost of debt. This story was further elaborated through an analysis of individual subsectors. For instance, food processing, with capital intensity and technology equal to that of American companies, could only achieve 50 percent of the productivity levels attained by firms in the United States. Similar results were obtained for autos, semiconductors—where Korean productivity is half that of the leading U.S. firms—and confectionery, where a poor product mix, overcapacity, and concern for sales over profits result in TFP of 42 percent, even through capital intensity exceeds that of the United States.

In part this is the outcome of rapid growth fueled by cheap credit in a protected environment. Borensztein and Lee (1999) find a negative relationship between lending and loan size, on the one hand, and average profit rates, on the other, during 1970–90. Industries with large firms were also more likely to receive credit. For example, industries with low profit rates and a few large firms, such as aircraft and shipbuilding, had good access to credit. In other words, industrial policy was instrumental in directing credit to the less efficient parts of the economy, in retarding the maturation of the financial sector, and in bringing about a steady accumulation of nonperforming assets. In 1986, the nonperforming loans on the books of the five largest commercial banks amounted to 11 percent of credit and were three times their net worth. Although the provision of directed credit began to taper off in the 1990s, the influence of the Ministry of Finance over banks remained strong (on industrial policy and the rise of the *chaebol*, see Woo-Cumings in chapter 9 of this volume).

Cho and Kim (1995) observe that the use of directed credit by the Korean government, over an extended period of time, was damaging for a number of reasons.[31] In an oligopolistic market environment, the implicit coinsurance of bank lending by the government induced banks to lend for and encouraged firms to invest in risky projects. Commercial banks in Korea functioned almost like development banks and ended up being saddled with huge nonperforming loans equal to almost 20 percent of GDP, the cost of which will be borne largely by the taxpayer. Problems faced by banks were mirrored in deteriorating industrial performance, starting with the bankruptcy of Hanbo, the 14th largest *chaebol*, in January 1997. Five others followed in quick succession—Sammi, Jinro, Dainong, Ssangyoung, and Kia (Lee 1999).[32] In 1998 Daewoo, the second-largest *chaebol*, became a victim of corporate excess and in spite of determined efforts to rescue the firm by the government and its creditors, went into liquidation in 2000. In spite of the economic rebound in 1999–2000, parts of the Hyundai and LG *chaebol* also experienced severe distress, with Hyundai Engineering and Construction teetering on the verge of bankruptcy in the last quarter of 2000.

Although Thai governments did not use directed credit to the same extent, implicit guarantees extended to the banking system because of close government-business-banking relations gave rise to almost equally serious moral hazard problems. Dollar and Hallward-Driemeier (1998) find that the financial institutions routinely extended loans without bothering about the creditworthiness of the borrower.

Southeast Asian countries used industrial policy more sparingly, but, if anything, they were even less successful in achieving desired outcomes. Indonesian agencies were unable to monitor subsidies and were susceptible to capture by business interests. Their attempts to promote the auto, aircraft, and plywood industries were expensive failures. This experience was repeated in Malaysia, where state-owned industries—basic metals, machinery, petrochemicals, paper, and building materials—did poorly (Smith 1995). And the survival of the two Malaysian car companies Proton and Perodua has depended on tariffs of 140 to 300 percent on vehicles and 42 to 70 percent on imported kits and components ("Moment of Truth," *Far Eastern Economic Review*, November 23, 2000; "Proton's Dilemma," *Oxford Analytica*, Malaysia , October 29, 2000). Thailand largely directed assistance to industries whose export performance was deteriorating.[33] And in the Philippines, preferential credit as well as other public policies were annexed by well-connected elites with the state—and the country—receiving nothing in return (Hutchcroft 1999).

The capture of industrial policy by elites is perceived more clearly now than in the past and has inflicted costs in excess of the budgetary outlays. Crony capitalism was not just a problem in the Philippines. Non-*pribumi* businesses in Indonesia (mainly owned by ethnic Chinese) connected with the Suharto family imposed large burdens on the economy (Hill 1997; Emmerson 1998). Even in Korea, the discretion enjoyed by government officials gave rise to rent-seeking opportunities that proved irresistible. For instance, the $37 billion Yulgok defense procurement program was also used as a vehicle for technology transfers to local companies being groomed as suppliers to the Korean military. As these companies evolved during the 1970s and 1980s, some of their profits found their way to defense officials managing the industrial policy. When these payments were investigated in 1993, two former defense ministers were convicted of accepting kickbacks, and 39 generals were sacked, reprimanded, or jailed (Ades and Di Tella 1997: 1024).

The power of major corporations, banks, and individual businessmen in East Asia and the close links that developed between the corporate sector and banks also affected the governments' ability to take quick and decisive action to restructure or close companies and financial entities after the crisis (Overholt 1999; Lincoln 1999).[34] The slow pace of reform is traceable, in part, to the corporate structure created by industrial policy. It has contributed to the difficulty of introducing disclosure rules, bankruptcy laws, and measures that would result in a more competitive market for corporate control, and lower the barriers to foreign direct investment in certain sectors.

Arguably, the policies introduced since 1998 reflect a widespread realization that in all but a narrow set of cases, the costs of subsidies significantly outweigh the benefits. With the exception of exports from Korea, exports of countries using export subsidies have grown no faster than those of countries that have not, and in fact subsidies can be welfare reducing (Panagariya 2000). Acceptance of WTO disciplines by East Asian countries—to be joined by China—indicates that industrial policy, as practiced prior to the mid-1980s, is seen to have outlived its usefulness, and a more market-based approach should guide future development. Such rethinking is also related to a more realistic assessment of bureaucratic capability.

The emergence and growth of a large nonstate and private industrial sector in China, starting in the late 1970s, reveal the power of market incentives to galvanize entrepreneurial initiatives and spur exports without any guidance from the central government ("Private Sector," *Oxford Analytica*, China, December 18, 2000). The share of the nonstate sector in industrial output rose from 22.4 percent in 1978 to 73.5 percent in 2000, while that of the private sector went from 2 percent in 1985 to 16 percent in 1998. Moreover, this blooming of industry in rural areas, townships, and small cities has occurred in the absence of clearly defined property rights and the still-embryonic state of infrastructure for enforcing business contracts. As Justin Lin and Yang Yao, Dwight Perkins, and Yingyi Qian show in chapters 4, 6, and 7, the dismantling of price and regulatory controls was the trigger and set the stage for the development of collective and private enterprises. The building of a market system was sustained by a succession of reforms, by investment in infrastructure, and by the easing of access to capital. What is remarkable is how the share of nonstate enterprises rose, in the face of benign neglect on the part of the government and the continuance of credit policies that direct more than 70 percent of bank lending to state enterprises. This is very much of a piece with the East Asian miracle during its later phase, beginning in the 1980s, when the emphasis on market forces was on the increase.

China was not included in the earlier World Bank study, but in many respects its performance was comparable to that of some of the other leading economies of the region. In addition, the continuing liberalization of China's economy during the 1990s is a major input in the rethinking of the East Asian experience.

THE CHANGING AUTONOMY AND ROLE OF BUREAUCRACY

Earlier views on industrial policy linked its utility to the existence of a bureaucratic apparatus committed to long-term development, yet shielded from the full force of political and corporate pressures.[35] A tiny number of countries were able to both build and use economic bureaucracies effectively. But in the majority of cases, the capacity to insulate technocrats from such pressures proved difficult. This became even more apparent in the 1990s. As democratic forces gathered momentum in East Asia, much evidence of corruption was uncovered, and the exigencies of short-term political calculation began to outweigh longer-term strategic concerns. The nature of the response of key government agencies throughout the region prior to, during, and in the aftermath of the crisis points to their susceptibility to pressure from powerful interest groups. Furthermore, the difficulty that even East Asian bureaucracies have experienced in attracting and retaining individuals of high technical caliber, as, for example, in Malaysia, indicates that in a market environment talent gravitates, as it should, to the private sector. Only Singapore, at considerable cost, has sustained a meritocratic public bureaucracy.

Clearly the circumstances have changed, and what Park Chung Hee could achieve in the 1960s and 1970s is difficult to replicate.[36]

The disarray in Korean policymaking circles during 1996–98, the tension between agencies, and the pressures impinging on regulatory bodies attempting to design and implement reforms in the postcrisis years all point to a changing political environment in which bureaucratic autonomy is neither desirable nor achievable ("Corporate Difficulties," *Oxford Analytica*, South Korea:, November 3, 2000; "Lessons Unlearned," *Far Eastern Economic Review*, September 21, 2000). Similarly, as Okazaki notes in chapter 8 of this volume, deliberation councils were an effective two-way transmission mechanism in Japan from the 1940s through the early postwar decades. But in the 1980s and 1990s, both the need for such coordinating bodies and their capacity to fulfill their earlier role have diminished, and micromanaging by public agencies is dysfunctional (see Woo-Cumings, chapter 9 of this volume).[37] The trend in Southeast Asia also suggests that the heyday of the technocratic bureaucracy at the helm of a developmental state may be past. Hal Hill described the policy inertia in Indonesia starting from the early 1990s: "The public policy agenda [was] captured by debates over irrelevant, trivial, or misleading issues—serious reform initiatives [were] hampered by these debates" (Hill 1997: 257). The governments that have come to power since 1999 are less cohesive and cannot muster a core of highly trained individuals such as the Widjojo Group, which provided economic leadership in the 1970s and 1980s. In addition, BAPENAS, the National Planning Agency, much like its Korean counterpart, has lost its influence to a political body, the National Economic Council (Hill 1999). Thai policymaking and regulatory agencies also have had to come to terms with the realities of democratic politics, which involve greater sensitivity to political concerns and more arm's-length dealings with business (Unger 1998).[38]

NATURE OF GOVERNANCE AND DEVELOPMENT OF THE LEGAL SYSTEM

A decade ago, governance was not a major concern for the East Asian region. The region was moving, along with other parts of the world, toward greater democratization and the building of legal institutions.[39] These were seen as normal accompaniments to the growing role of the market economy and increased openness. Throughout the 1990s, these developments focused attention on governance at many levels. Improved communications, the Internet, the consciousness-raising activities of many international nongovernmental organizations, and the widening acceptance of rules appropriate for democracies further underscored the significance of good governance. As a consequence, researchers began to take greater interest in the effects of corruption, nepotism, crony capitalism, and weak corporate governance and to empirically estimate their influence on development (Mauro 1995). A series of high-profile trials of past Korean presidents, of former President Ferdinand Marcos in the Philippines, the impeachment of President Estrada of the Philippines in 2000, and scandals involving politicians in Japan highlighted the magnitude of corruption in countries with apparently high standards of governance. They also revealed how a systematic pattern of bribery could seriously undermine policymaking where the rules for transparency and accountability were not in place or, even if they were, tended not to be enforced (on the relationship between banks and government in Japan, see Lincoln 1999).

Senior policymakers, specialists, and professionals questioned by David Hitchcock in June 1996 all put political problems near the top of their concerns. "Governance was a central issue everywhere. In Singapore, Malaysia, Indonesia, and China, some intellectuals, cultural figures, and activists believed governments must become more responsive to people. ... In Thailand ... respondents reported widespread disillusionment with politics ... we have the form but not the substance of democracy. In the [other countries] maintaining political stability was a prime government objective, but some thought it was being overused to keep the lid on freedom of expression and to stay in power" (Hitchcock 1997: 123–24). As Stephen Haggard observes, "Indonesia's difficulties can be attributed in part to a highly centralized regime accountable to relatively narrow constituencies and lacking both effective checks on executive authority and a succession mechanism." In many countries in the region, "close political relationships between politicians and business constituencies and particular firms have also been responsible for the crisis." Because of misguided industry policies, the moral hazard created by government intervention, "weak financial regulation, and poor systems of corporate governance were important precursors to the crisis" (Haggard 1999: 35, 37).[40]

A better understanding of governance at the key interstices of the economic system is now viewed as being at least as important as factor accumulation. It has a significant bearing on the nature of the industrial-financial policies discussed above as well as the legal system. Although a strong empirical link between democracy and growth has not been identified (Helliwell 1994; Barro 1997), prosperous countries are more likely to be democratic (with some of the effect coming from education). In addition, the vast political science literature suggests that democracy promotes good governance, especially if certain procedural and constitutional rules are in place: rules for the division of responsibility between central and subnational entities, rules for relations between the different branches of the state, rules determining representation by different groups and regions of the country on legislative bodies, and rules inducing the formation of disciplined parties and determining the timing of elections. Adapting these rules to East Asian conditions in order to raise accountability within the existing democratic frameworks calls for fresh thinking and research.

Protecting the rights of investors is a second facet of governance that acquired more prominence in the 1990s. With the majority of large companies in East Asia being closely held or controlled by families, minority shareholders have difficulty expressing themselves and safeguarding their interests. Problems of agency are serious, and the crisis showed that there is little by way of legal redress for shareholders dissatisfied with the performance of corporate managers who respond mainly to the principal owners. Corporate governance in East Asia has avoided external monitoring as well as internal oversight. "It has been characterized by ineffective boards of directors, weak internal control, unreliable financial reporting, lack of adequate disclosures, lax enforcement to ensure compliance, and poor audits" (World Bank 1999a: 67–68).

The absence of adequate investor protection through legal channels has impeded financial broadening, constrained the dispersal of share ownership, and sacrificed efficiency in the allocation of capital across firms (La Porta and others 1997, 1999). Weak minority shareholder rights are also a feature of some of the European countries, but these countries have created substitute mechanisms to counterbalance the power of managers or dominant private shareholders. These consist of banks or other institutional investors that are represented on boards of directors and wield significant power, aside from exercising surveillance over companies in which they hold a stake. Such institutional investors provide a partial solution to the agency problem and the weakness of minority investors.

East Asian countries have not yet evolved toward this model, although in the precrisis period, there was considerable interest in the Japanese main bank model.[41] Most financial or nonfinancial institutions are controlled either by the state or by corporate interests and generally have not attempted to enhance accountability and the voice of minority shareholders. The role of foreign financial entities is quite small, but it is growing in spite of domestic opposition in Thailand and Korea, and over time could affect the role of banks in corporate governance. However, until reforms and foreign investment begin to transform governance, dominant shareholders will be encouraged to seek even tighter control through direct ownership of shares and cross-shareholdings (Zingales 1994).

The crisis brought the situation to a head and exposed the true extent of mismanagement, poor investment decisions, and risk taking by enterprises. Subsequent attempts to restructure, revive, or liquidate companies in whole or in part have shown both the extent to which the rules favored the principal owners and the difficulty of changing the rules so as to give due recognition to the interests of other shareholders. The existing system, with its powerful and entrenched interests, is strongly resistant to reform that would distribute rights more fairly. However, as the East Asian economies revived in 1999–2000, the realization that lack of transparency, weak standards of accounting and auditing, and unenforceable bankruptcy laws are damaging is leading to change albeit at a slow pace (Overholt 1999).

Reform of the legal system that complements the effort to improve corporate governance has been equally sluggish and is related to the concentration of corporate ownership.[42] But change is ongoing in most East Asian countries, alongside the trend toward democracy and the increasing openness to trade as well as foreign direct investment (FDI).[43] The importance ascribed to governance in the 1990s has brought legal institutions into the mainstream of development thinking. Starting with proxy variables for institutional characteristics, economists have begun delving into the making of laws, the costs of

assigning rights, legal procedures, the infrastructure for implementing laws, the willingness to observe the law, and the legal tradition
guiding evolution in individual countries.[44] One widely noted finding
is that countries adopting the civil law tradition from continental Europe offer weaker protection to investors than those conforming to
the English common law tradition, made by judges and subsequently
incorporated into legislation. This is reflected in financial market development and the quality of corporate governance, both of which
tend to lag behind when investor protection derives from law that is
defined by scholars or legislators and is anchored in ancient Roman
law (La Porta and others 1997 and 1999).

When viewed over the span of two decades, the legal systems in
most East Asian countries have become more supportive of market-
based rules for contracting, property, and other rights. Bankruptcy
laws also are being pushed closer to the norms of industrial countries.[45]
The crisis lent urgency to this process, and some of the momentum gained
has persisted, although the opposition to corporate and financial restructuring has mounted steadily (World Bank 2000b; "South-east Asia's
Problem Trio," *Economist*, December 2, 2000; "Foreigner Friendly," *Economist Intelligence Unit*, Business Asia: October 16, 2000).

In Korea legal institutions have increasingly circumscribed government discretion since the mid-1980s. For example, enforcement of
the competition law shifted from the Ministry of Finance and Economy
to a legally independent agency in 1991. Following the onset of the
crisis in 1997 and the election of a new government later in the year,
this agency acquired greater autonomy, political clout, and ability to
challenge the state in court (Pistor and Wellons 1999: 78). By comparison, the influence of the Ministry of Finance waned, and some of
its regulatory functions were transferred to the Financial Supervisory
Commission, which has taken the lead in introducing corporate and
financial sector reform ("Power Fades at Korea's Finance Ministry,"
Wall Street Journal, June 25, 1999).[46] A measure of the change in protection afforded to investors was the aggressive stance taken by the
government against Hyundai, the largest *chaebol*, for not protecting
shareholder rights while the founder's two sons feuded over who would
control the vast conglomerate. The Ministry of Finance claimed that
Hyundai had seriously damaged transparency, responsibility, and credibility in business practices by treating management control as an in-

heritance ("Hyundai May Be Censured for Ignoring Shareholders," *Financial Times*, March 28, 2000). This came on the heels of a landmark decision by the government, Korean banks, and foreign creditors to break up Daewoo, Korea's second-biggest conglomerate.

These are major developments. Whether they will speed up Korea's convergence toward western legal systems and promote the restructuring of businesses and systems of governance will depend on domestic political and economic trends, the pressures exerted by globalization, and the greater penetration of foreign economic interests.

Such factors also will determine the direction taken by three other countries in the region: Indonesia, Malaysia, and China. The first two have no tradition of judicial autonomy. In Indonesia the Justice Ministry administers the civil and criminal courts and decides on judicial appointments, promotions, and salaries. Moreover, because of the judiciary's connections with military and business elites, there is little demand from the bench for greater autonomy. Most disputes are settled out of court, usually under the supervision of the police, whose role until recently has been larger than that of the judiciary.

The longer-run effects of the crisis, pressures to decentralize, and the declining influence of both Golkar (the former ruling party) and the military could lead to institutional changes that strengthen the judiciary. Attempts to augment the bankruptcy law in order to cope with businesses and banks hit by the crisis are a step in that direction. Academics are also calling for judicial independence. But much will depend on the government's support and a spreading demand for rules that safeguard rights. Either way this will be a live issue for some time, especially if power is dispersed away from the center through demands for greater regional autonomy ("Indonesia: Judicial Independence," *Oxford Analytica*, March 11, 2000).

Relative to Indonesia, Malaysia, with its common law system and its rule-based market economy, has a deeper-rooted and more effective judicial system. In fact, on commercial matters and on the protection of private property, the courts apply the law firmly and with little evidence of corruption. But the appearance of an independent judiciary is deceptive, and executive powers were growing in the late 1990s. Undergirding the power of the executive is the Internal Security Act, which permits a suspension of constitutionally guaranteed freedoms, as well as other statutes such as the Sedition Act and the Securities Act, giving the state latitude to charge individuals with specific political offences. In the economic sphere, the state has become increasingly assertive in allocating resources and embarking on sweeping changes, such as the move announced in September 1999 to merge the country's 58 banks initially into six groups ("Malaysia: Bank Controversy," *Oxford Analytica*, March 24, 2000). This was subsequently relaxed in the face of opposition from the banking community to permit the formation of ten groups. Although the government's actions can be subjected to judicial review, "courts seem to invoke self-restraint over cases involving the alleged executive abuses of power" (Pistor and Wellons 1999: 91) and are apparently reluctant to take an independent line when dealing with cases involving state or UMNO (United Malays National Organization)—the ruling party–managed enterprises ("Malaysia: Judicial Autonomy," *Oxford Analytica*, March 29, 2000). More troubling is the weakening protection of intellectual property rights and the use of the Internal Security Act to arrest brokers and currency traders on charges of financial sabotage.

Shifts in Malaysian politics might lend weight to the still-muted demands for judicial autonomy. Many elements of an effective judicial system are in place, but the future is still uncertain. The judiciary could emerge as a pillar of good governance, but that would require readiness on the part of the government to exercise restraint.

Whereas by the 1960s and 1970s, other East Asian countries already had the rudiments of a legal system geared to the market, China had to commence building one from scratch. In a little more than 15 years, the Chinese have greatly increased the pool of lawyers, assimilated laws, and instituted legal procedures. But the unfinished agenda of legal reform to support radical changes in governance remains vast. Rules and judicial practice still differ markedly from those of industrial countries. The state must approve all foreign investments in local business. When administrative power is misused, individuals can seek redress, but not when the Communist Party is involved. Furthermore, judges are inadequately trained, and many are drawn from a military background and susceptible to influence by the political authorities. Moreover, the courts cannot challenge the right of the police to impose administrative punishments and send people to jail ("China: Rule of Law," *Oxford Analytica*, October 25, 1999; "China: The Legal Environment," *Oxford Analytica*, July 29, 1998). There are, in addition, many areas where transparency is lacking and mechanisms of enforcement are poorly specified. Thus the absence of judicial independence and the rule of law partly vitiates the solid progress made in formulating civil and criminal laws and in engendering a social consensus on the significance of law in society ("A Slow Move to Justice," *Economist*, February 5, 2000).

From the late 1990s onward, most East Asian countries have enlarged the role of the market, pursued economic openness, adopted a more liberal political regime, and in some instances decentralized fiscal and economic decisionmaking. All these have raised the salience of governance and brought to the forefront issues pertaining to institutional development, especially in the context of the legal system. Hence, when we rethink the East Asian miracle and consider the priorities for the region, the mechanisms of governance and the assignment and enforcement of rights are among the ones deserving the closest attention.

TRADE RATHER THAN EXPORT-LED GROWTH

Earlier views on East Asia's success have frequently stressed export orientation as a major source of growth competitiveness and technology absorption. This was one of the chief lessons communicated to other countries attempting to imitate the region's performance. In fact, some recent research continues to link growth with exports.[47] But a closer look at the dynamics of growth in East Asia and changes in industrial productivity is finding that exports might have played a smaller role than was previously thought.[48]

Two kinds of results have challenged the primacy of exports. One is the finding, based on data for the United States and a handful of developing countries, that high productivity in certain industries is what leads to exports and that causation does not generally run in the other direction. Second is the finding, based on empirical tests using data for Japan and Korea and presented by Lawrence and Weinstein in chapter 10 of this volume, that imports have a stronger effect on productivity than do exports. It is also borne out by data on U.S. industries. This can be explained by the competitive pressure that imports impose on local producers, which drives some of the weakest out of business and forces the survivors to become more efficient. Imports can also influence productivity through another channel. By embodying technological gains achieved by the country of origin and other countries contributing to the product, imports are an effective vehicle for assimilating new technology (Bayoumi, Coe, and Helpman 1996). Capital investment has become a more important vehicle for technological advance because of major gains embodied in equipment—computers, telecommunications systems, and automated assembly lines. By one estimate, nearly 60 percent of recent gains in output in the United States can be traced to such investment (Greenwood, Hercowitz, and Krusell 1997). Continued protection of producers in East Asian countries has contributed to their inefficiency and is likely to be a key factor behind the slow increase in TFP (McGuire and Schuele 1999).

The relationship between openness and growth appears to be fairly robust (Sachs and Warner 1995, Edwards 1999, Frankel and Romer 1999, Irwin and Tervio 2000), and this aspect of the miracle does not need to be reconsidered. However, the balance has shifted between exports and imports as sources of growth, with imports seeming to contribute more to productivity than exports. The lowering of trade barriers during the 1990s is likely to have bolstered East Asia's performance, and future commitments to reduce tariffs should be equally advantageous, especially for countries such as China. But East Asian economies will have to cope with some transient dislocation and unemployment as a result of increased imports.

REGIONAL INTEGRATION AND POLICY

The East Asian region became more integrated in the 1990s because of intraregional trade, FDI, and labor flows in Southeast Asia. Exports among East Asian countries rose from 32 percent of total exports in 1990 to 40 percent in 1996. If Japan is included, they amounted to more than 50 percent. Nearly 78 percent of the capital inflow into China through the mid-1990s was from Hong Kong, Taiwan, and Macao. Although Southeast Asia's share was just 5 percent, it is growing steadily. Rising incomes and improvements in the quality of the goods produced are contributing to the integration. But other forces are at work as well. One is the increased migration of some Japanese industries to China and the Southeast Asian economies as the yen becomes stronger. This is enlarging Japan's FDI in the region. In the past, Japanese firms that established subsidiaries in other East Asian countries mainly sold their products on local markets or exported them to third countries. Now a rising percentage is being exported back to Japan. These changes in the pattern of FDI and associated trade flows are described by Urata in chapter 11 of this volume.

Another facet of integration is in the financial sphere, abetted by the regional Chinese network. Chinese businesses have traditionally invested a sizable part of their capital in the region, and to contain risk they have attempted to maintain a diversified portfolio of assets across countries. This has been facilitated by the opening of capital markets and the easing of regulatory controls on FDI. In fact, the volume of intraregional FDI, excluding flows from Japan, is sizable.

Apart from the intraregional circulation of capital, East Asia is the recipient of FDI, portfolio investment, and short-term capital from outside the region. Reputation, and the promise of large returns, has been a significant factor pulling in the non-FDI flows, but as the crisis of 1997–98 showed, reputation can be a two-edged sword. When the strength of one East Asian economy came under suspicion, investors poorly informed about the fundamental resilience of other economies began withdrawing funds from across East Asia. The speed and extent of the contagion revealed another side of regional integration: outsiders increasingly perceive East Asian countries as sharing many common attributes, both strengths and weaknesses.

The process of integration, real and assumed, also has implications for the conduct of policy and for institutional infrastructure. If the possibility of contagion in the event of a crisis afflicting one country is here to stay, then the advantages of undertaking regional coordination of policy and harmonizing regulatory institutions need to be explored. Continuing globalization and the greater integration of East Asian countries, both regionally and with the world economy, can enhance their development prospects. The increase in trade and capital flows during the 1990s was a source of demand, resources, and technology, fueling growth in all the regional economies. But integration also increases the risk from speculative attack under a regime of managed exchange rates.

Clearly past arrangements, which were adequate through the early 1990s, will need to be modified. One direction is to take a different approach to exchange rate policy, as discussed above. Another approach, which can be pursued in parallel, is to improve policy coordination and rely more on regional mechanisms for monitoring performance, reporting, benchmarking, and pooling resources for use in a crisis, subject to criteria that minimize moral hazard.[49] A third step, which complements the others, is to scale back trade barriers progressively, a process that was slowed by the onset of the crisis and the attendant increase in unemployment. A fourth is to harmonize key rules of business, such as auditing, accounting, and disclosure practices.

Policy coordination has a checkered and uncertain history. To yield the desired results, it must be preceded by a long spell of institution building. Some building blocks, such as the Association of Southeast Asian Nations (ASEAN) and the Asian Free Trade Area (AFTA), are in place, and bilateral negotiations are ongoing between Korea and Japan for a further easing of trade barriers in some sectors. But to make these building blocks into effective bulwarks against shocks will require converting ASEAN, for instance, from a forum of quiet and unobtrusive diplomacy based on consensus into a body capable of negotiating a coordinated set of policies and inducing members to implement them. A freeze on the membership of ASEAN to the current 10 could be the start of a process toward institutional deepening. However, ASEAN must overcome a variety of tensions before the regional approach to decisionmaking can contribute to economic management in a globalizing world. The gap between the richer and poorer countries in ASEAN is a source of friction and conflicting demands. Several members are reluctant to press ahead with tariff reduction agreed upon under the AFTA. And centrifugal pressures in Indonesia are influencing the government's ability to participate in or to make commitments on regional issues.

Other forces, such as competition with China, which may soon become a member of the WTO, are forging greater cohesion among ASEAN members, but such competition can also make it harder for all the major East Asian countries to find common ground on critical intersecting areas of policy ("ASEAN Membership Moratorium," *Oxford Analytica*, March 23, 2000).

The big shift from the late 1980s, accelerated by the crisis, is that all of East Asia is looking at the European Union, exploring the benefits of regionalization, assessing harmonization, and analyzing the benefits of adopting a single currency (Nicolas 1999). East Asian economies are also discussing the possibility of creating an Asian Monetary Fund and considering whether there might be some utility in sacrificing a degree of sovereignty on policymaking so as to buy insurance against external shocks (Sakakibara 2000).

CONCLUDING OBSERVATIONS

It would not be far-fetched to say that rethinking the East Asian miracle has been ongoing since the publication of *Asia's Next Giant* (Amsden 1989), *Governing the Market* (Wade 1990), and "A Tale of Two Cities" (Young 1992). The tempo quickened following the launch of the *East Asian Miracle* (World Bank 1993). It received a further boost when the "tigers" began slowing in the mid-1990s. The East Asian crisis confirmed the fears of the critics. But it also nudged the true believers toward a revival of the faith and a yearning for the days when authoritarian regimes with enlightened bureaucracies could pursue long-term goals through industrial policy and a tightly sequenced opening of the economy. Nineteen ninety-eight was a difficult year, when irrational pessimism, laced with glee over the humbling of the seemingly irrepressible East Asian economies, threatened a self-fulfilling prophecy that could substantially erode close to 50 years of hard-won prosperity for the entire world.

The three years of breathing room provided by the recovery in East Asia and continuing expansion in the industrial countries restored a degree of calm. We are now in a position to weigh a decade of experience more dispassionately and to marshal a wealth of research to arrive at a measured assessment of the key policies and institutions responsible for East Asia's performance.

The chapters in this volume take stock of what is arguably the most exciting development experience available to us. Measured in terms of GDP growth per capita, gains in welfare, and poverty reduction, East Asia has certainly outpaced other developing regions. Viewed from the perspective of macroeconomic policy management, most East Asian

economies have successfully pursued openness, fiscal and current account balance, and stability. A few countries effectively used industrial
policy in the early stages of development to promote the growth of
key subsectors or coordinate industrial change as shown by Okazaki.
Others deployed trade and incentive policies to attract FDI and to
build a base of export-oriented industry. In China's case, reforms created a vast rural and township industry that presently accounts for
close to half of the country's industrial product.

In other respects, East Asia's record has been mixed, with uneven
policies and gaps in institution building becoming apparent in the
1990s. In particular, the crisis of 1997–98 forced observers and
policymakers to reevaluate the approach to development that had been
broadly accepted as workable until shown to be problematic in a globalizing world.

The chapters in this volume draw attention to the revealed weakness of exchange rate policies based on a weak peg and sterilization.
They discuss the drawbacks of partial capital account liberalization in
the absence of regulatory measures ensuring financial strength and
the ability to absorb and mediate capital inflows efficiently.

Although East Asian economies gradually dismantled industrial policies during the 1990s, the effects of close government, finance, and
business relationships linger and are examined by several authors in
this volume. By inducing the accumulation of nonperforming assets
in banks and a concentration of corporate ownership, these relationships slowed financial development, impeded robust corporate governance, and hampered the emergence of legal institutions. The issue of
weak corporate governance is clearly of vital importance and is analyzed by several contributors to this volume. However, as Joseph Stiglitz
notes in the concluding chapter, we must not lose sight of the
counterfactual: Could East Asia without industrial policy have done
much better than it actually did? The experience of the 1990s and the
intense debate on the sources of East Asian growth highlighted not
only the region's continued dependence on factor inputs but also the
urgency of building capacity to participate more actively in technological advance. Research by Lawrence and Weinstein as well as others suggests that East Asia could enhance technological inflow by
matching the long-standing reliance on export growth with an equal
emphasis on import liberalization. But efforts to acquire dynamic com-

parative advantage through the accumulation of R&D capital and skills will continue to be important, at least for the Southeast Asian countries, as noted by K. S. Jomo.

Greater openness and international integration have many advantages, but they also increase risks. To manage these risks, countries will need to act on three fronts: domestic, regional, and international (Stiglitz 2000). East Asia has a good record of domestic policy, and the crisis has triggered a round of reforms that if resolutely implemented could further strengthen such policy. However, globalization may require more effort at coordinating policies and institutions at the regional and international levels, so that the gains from an integrated world can be fully realized.

NOTES

The author would like to thank Simon Evenett and Dwight Perkins for helpful comments and Marc Shotten for assistance with the research.

1. Overholt (1999) believes that Thailand's problems came into focus in June 1996, when Thai Granite's inability to service its bills made foreign lenders aware that, under Thai law, finance companies could delay payments indefinitely and the assets of debtors could not be seized.

2. The relative dynamism of Singapore and Taiwan and the factors that cushioned Taiwan against the crisis are discussed in Wang 2000. On financial reforms that reduced pressures on the Philippines see Noland 2000 and Haggard 2000. Also see "Taiwan's Trump," *Far Eastern Economic Review*, August 6, 1998, and Chow 2000.

3. See also Hamlin (1999). Industrial capacity utilization in Southeast Asia was still only 70 percent in the first quarter of 2000, compared with 85 percent prior to the crisis in 1997 ("Southeast Asia: Excess Capacity," *Oxford Analytica*, April 26, 2000).

4. However, because the tempo of reforms has slowed, the East Asian economies remain vulnerable (World Bank 1999a). Korea's gross national income grew 10.7 percent in 1999 and 9 percent in 2000 on the strength of demand in the export, industrial, consumer, and information technology sectors, and close to half of the increase was due to the rebuilding of inventories ("South Korea: Economic Exuberance," *Oxford Analytica*, April 6, 2000; Yu 2000) and fuller utilization of existing capacity.

5. The number of Internet users in East Asia rose from 13 million in 1998 to 22 million in 1999. Side by side, a new breed of entrepreneurs has emerged to exploit the opportunities extended by information technology.

6. In Japan these councils were supplemented by a large number of interest groups with a narrower focus and a strong impact on policy. Called *shingikai*, these consultative councils drew their membership from the business community and the community of scholars, journalists, and union members (Schwartz 1998).

7. Johnston and Sundarajan's (1999) review of international evidence suggests that an efficient and well-regulated financial system is more resilient than others in the face of shocks.

8. Research on the great depression of the 1930s has highlighted three major culprits: inappropriate monetary and exchange rate policies, weak banking systems, and inflexible labor markets (Crafts 2000).

9. In the 1980s Japanese banks with "the explicit support and guidance" of the Ministry of Finance invested in real estate as regulatory restrictions fell (Lincoln 1999: 59). Nonperforming loans accounted for 19, 20, 38, and 50 percent of loans in the Republic of Korea, Malaysia, Thailand, and Indonesia, respectively, in the first quarter of 2000 ("East Asia: Corporate Stress," *Oxford Analytica*, March 20, 2000).

10. Hall and Weinstein (2000) show that main bank monitoring in Japan did not reduce the riskiness of associated firms or sustain their performance following the onset of financial distress. Edwards and Ogilvie (1996) have also cast doubt on the contribution of German universal banks to industrial development prior to 1919. They show that these banks were much less important as suppliers of external finance than was previously thought. Moreover, the presence of universal banks on supervisory boards of companies did not improve either the flow of information for economic decisionmaking or coordination.

11. Portfolio capital flows rose from $40 billion a year in 1983–90 to $200 billion a year in 1992–97 ("Asia Lessons," *Oxford Analytica*, May 19, 1998).

12. The problem with estimating the effect of inflation on growth is that inflation is an endogenous variable. Barro (1997) estimates that every 10 percent increase in inflation lowers real growth per capita 0.3 to 0.4 percent a year.

13. Wade and Veneroso (1998) emphasize the danger of high real interest rates in economies with high levels of private indebtedness and low inflationary expectations. Under those circumstances, raising real interest rates can have deflationary consequences that give rise to capital outflows, regardless of the attractions of high interest rates ("The Resources Lie Within," *Economist*, pp. 19-21, November 7, 1998).

14. However, in the future several countries will have less fiscal room for maneuver, especially Japan, because of recent budget deficits and the need to service the liabilities of banks now transferred to the state ("Taxing Dilemmas," *Far Eastern Economic Review*, December 23, 1999).

15. "Culture Shock," *Far Eastern Economic Review*, April 16, 1998; "To the Ramparts," *Far Eastern Economic Review*, July 22, 1999. In Korea, the takeover of Korea First Bank by Newbridge Capital is a test of this effort to change the banking culture ("Makeover at the Bank," *Far Eastern Economic Review*, March 2, 2000).

16. Rodrik's finding that an open capital account does not enhance growth is vitiated by biases introduced by his econometric technique (Rodrik 1998; Edwards 1999).

17. Garber (1998) observes that by means of offshore swaps with call features, a long-term flow can be converted into an overnight foreign exchange loan. Rogoff (1999) makes a similar point with regard to Chilean controls on short-term borrowing, maintaining that they can be evaded by margin and call conditions. Recognizing this, Thailand further eased controls on Thai investment in overseas financial instruments (see "Thailand Eases Offshore Investment Controls," *Financial Times*, February 8, 2000).

18. Japan's rate of investment—17 percent of GDP in 1999—was higher than that of the United States—16 percent of GDP. This rate is likely to decline, whereas private savings are unlikely to fall, as individuals make provisions for retirement and anticipate the possible consequences of the swelling public sector deficit for the financing of future pension payments.

19. Sterilization proved costly because domestic debt was issued at far higher rates and higher rates pulled in more foreign capital (Folkerts-Landau and Ito 1995; Overholt 1999). As noted by Chinn and Dooley (1999), highly managed exchange rates are likely to be more vulnerable to speculative attack in an integrated global financial environment. Eichengreen has proposed a five-step process to cope with a surge in capital flows into small countries, which would have difficulty adjusting relative prices sufficiently. Countries can tighten fiscal policy, let the exchange rate appreciate somewhat to increase the exchange risk for investors, pursue a degree of sterilized intervention, increase revenue requirements for banks, and tax short-term flows (Eichengreen 1999).

20. Three financial indicators that warned of increasing vulnerability were the growing share of short-term foreign borrowing; the steep rise in bank lending to the private sector, and the dependence of the banking system on loans to the real estate sector (Miller and Luangaram 1999). Real estate lending pushed prices of commercial property and rental rates to exceedingly high levels. When the bubble burst after the start of the crisis, office rental rates fell by an average of 34 percent in dollar terms, ranging from 6 percent in Taipei to 65 percent in Bangkok (Asian Development Bank 1999).

21. Both capital as well as labor inputs have been high. Annual inputs of labor hours in East Asia still range from 2,200 to 2,400 per person as against 1,700 to 1,900 per person in Western Europe in the 1970s (Crafts 1998).

22. Between 1975 and 1992, Korea increased its output of science and engineering graduates 4.5 times. By 1990, the number engaged in research per 10,000 persons was 16 compared with 38 in the United States (Scherer 1999).

23. On research, innovation and progress up the ladder of technological innovation in East Asia, see Lim (1999), Mathews and Cho (2000)

24. On the endogeneity of technical change and the importance of investment in R&D, the evidence is by no means clear-cut. David and Hall show that innovation is not related in any well-defined linear fashion to investment in science and technology. Moreover, the effect of increased public spending on R&D de-

pends on an increase in the availability of researchers, a supply response in turn dependent on rising salaries and immigration (David and Hall 2000). The endogenous growth hypothesis also was rendered somewhat suspect by the stable growth in trend output per hour in the United States in the early and final decades of the 20th century in spite of great increases in expenditure on R&D (Jones 1995). Mills and Crafts, after yet another struggle with cross-country data, claim that some endogenous technological change must be driving endogenous growth, but that it must be small because the share of GDP devoted to R&D is also small (Mills and Crafts 2000).

25. State-directed development characteristic of some East Asian countries conformed to the pattern of late industrializers noted by Alexander Gerschenkron. It succeeded in mobilizing and investing a large volume of resources but was less successful in ensuring efficient use or promoting innovation, which is the message of theories of incomplete contracts and agency (Crafts 1999). Because governments sought to manage the markets, competition policy was generally neglected throughout East Asia, and only one member of the Association of Southeast Asian Nations—Thailand—had an antitrust law in place.

26. Data on 60 countries for the period 1975–90 (drawn from the SNA [System of National Accounts] Database) show that subsidy expenditure peaked in 1981 and declined thereafter. The trend in East Asia matched the global tendency (Schwartz and Clements 1999).

27. Baer, Miles, and Moran (1999) maintain that industrial policy was injurious to East Asian countries and was at the root of the crisis.

28. An instructive model of government assistance to industry is Taiwan's attempt to initiate semiconductor development. The government established the Electronic Research Organization under the Industrial Technology Research Institute, the United Microelectronic Company, and the Taiwan Semiconductor Manufacturing Company. However, these two publicly owned companies were run by independent managers, and after setting them up, the government did not intervene in their operation (Hong 1997).

29. There was some inconsistency in the assistance provided. Petroleum and coal received low-interest loans but also paid high indirect taxes. Textiles received protection and tax breaks, but few subsidized loans.

30. The use of a highly distortionary and protective industrial policy was particularly conspicuous in the automobile sector. It is notable that Korea succeeded in building what appears to be a viable auto industry that can compete in international markets, whereas Taiwan (China), Thailand, and to an extent Malaysia (which set up the Proton auto company) have failed in this regard (Jenkins 1995).

31. Although, as Stiglitz and Uy (1996) note, such lending might well have been promoted not only by the provision of resources but also by the benefits of signaling and risk sharing.

32. Korea First Bank was the largest creditor for Hanbo, Kia, and Daewoo. The demise of these corporations rendered the bank insolvent. Because executives of Korea First Bank received kickbacks from Hanbo, two presidents of Korea First Bank were jailed ("Makeover at the Bank," *Far Eastern Economics Review*, March 2, 2000).

33. A survey of 1,200 Thai firms in 1997–98 revealed a pervasive problem of corruption related in large part to excess regulation and the discretion enjoyed by bureaucrats. This is an outgrowth of long-standing state involvement in managing the economy (Dollar and Hallward-Driemeier 1998).

34. Commercial bankers in the Philippines regularly squandered their assets by investing in family business but the central bank never won a court case against those entities it was supervising (Hutchcroft 1999).

35. The governed interdependence between the state and business networks by an insulated but not insular bureaucracy has been forcefully argued by Linda Weiss (1995). She draws extensively on the work of Wade (1990) and Evans (1995), indicating how the latter's concept of embeddedness implies the existence of encompassing networks that span business sectors and establish links with the government.

36. See Root (1996) and Dwight Perkins in chapter 6 of this volume. The "Yushin coup" in 1972 further enhanced the executive powers enjoyed by President Park and hence the authority as well as the autonomy of the bureaucracy.

37. The papers in Carlile and Tilton (1998) analyze the process of deregulation in Japan during the 1980s and the 1990s and conclude that the earlier administrative framework for managing the economy is being dismantled. But they also note that the economic system remains state-centric and that institutions leave a good deal of discretionary power and administrative latitude in the hands of public agencies.

38. The politicization of policymaking also affects the autonomy of the central bank in Thailand. See "Passing the Baht," *Far Eastern Economic Review*, April 27, 2000.

39. This trend is discussed in the *World Development Report* (World Bank 1999b, 2000) and Dahl (1999). James Wilson (2000) views the adoption of democratic institutions as a happy accident because he thinks that the experience of the United States and England indicates that, in an earlier period, the emergence of democracy was determined by some strict conditions: physical isolation, the emergence of individual property rights, ethnic homogeneity, and traditional rules for the division of powers among levels of government. These are not easily duplicated; hence the emergence of democracy in most countries can be a difficult process.

40. Emmerson (1998) suggests that the economies that will recover most rapidly from the crisis are those enjoying the greatest political freedom. But he also maintains that electoral democracy is more likely to lead to positive outcomes when it is combined with rights and freedoms under the rule of law.

41. However, this might be dissolving in Japan itself, with banks pulling out of *keiretsu* arrangements. For example, Nissan Motor and its two main banks—Industrial Bank of Japan and Fuji Bank—are selling their cross-shareholdings. See "Disintegration of the Keiretsu," *Financial Times*, November 13–14, 1999.

42. Claessens, Djankov, and Lang (2000) indicate that the concentration of corporate ownership in East Asia may be responsible for the slow evolution of the legal system and the absence of protection for minority shareholders. Claessens and others (1999) find that higher concentration of voting rights is associated

with lower corporate market values. Thus the separation of control from ownership leads to an expropriation of minority shareholders. See also World Bank (2000b).

43. The strength of the tendency toward freer trade is being called into question by the reluctance of some members of the Asia Pacific Economic Cooperation Forum to proceed with the planned scaling down of tariff barriers and the proliferation of bilateral trade agreements ("Free Trade in Asia: Bogged Down Again," *Business Week*, December 4, 2000).

44. The absence of a tradition of judicial autonomy and even of popular sovereignty is common to all East Asian countries. When the Japanese constitution was being redrafted in 1947, the term used to denote people was *kokumin*, which does not characterize them as an independent entity but is used in the context of harmonious relations between the people and the authorities (Dower 1999).

45. Inevitably, the attempts to apply the new laws are slow, uneven, and subject to slippage. See Overholt (1999) on Thailand. On Indonesia, see "Law Set to Push Indonesian Debtors over the Edge," *Financial Times*, August 20, 1998; Linnan (1999).

46. As a result of a constitutional revision in 1997, Thailand established the National Counter Corruption Commission, which seeks to discourage bribe taking by requiring politicians to disclose sources of wealth after taking office. This agency was responsible for the resignation of Deputy Prime Minister Sanan Kachornpasart in March 2000 on charges of false declaration of assets. See "Thailand: Corruption Upheaval," *Oxford Analytica*, April 4, 1999; "Tide of Change," *Far Eastern Economic Review*, April 13, 2000.

47. The view that export-led growth was instrumental in technology transfer and assimilation by way of subcontracting, OEM (original equipment manufacturing), FDI, joint ventures, contact with foreign buyers, and licensing is supported by the work of Hobday (1996). Hill (1994) draws attention to the ostensible success of export-led strategies in promoting development. See also Begum and Shamsuddin (1998).

48. Alwyn Young also maintains that the importance of the outward orientation of East Asian countries has been exaggerated. Once crude factor accumulation is accounted for, productivity growth in even their tradable sectors is not high, and their rapid expansion should not be viewed "as evidence of the potential dynamic gains from outward-oriented policies" (Young 1994b: 965). Dani Rodrik's (1995) examination of industrial development in Korea finds growth related to high investment. In some sectors, this was aided by individual policy coordination, which orchestrated the emergence of downstream producers.

49. The proposal put forward by the Japanese authorities for a coordinated network of currency swaps with other East Asian countries is a step in this direction. See "Japan Offers Plan to Avert Financial Crisis in Asia," *Financial Times*, May 6–7, 2000.

REFERENCES

The word "processed" describes informally reproduced works that may not be commonly available through library systems.

Ades, Alberto, and Rafael Di Tella. 1997. "National Champions and Corruption: Some Unpleasant Interventionist Arithmetic." *Economic Journal* 107(July):1023–42.

Amsden, Alice H. 1989. *Asia's Next Giant: South Korea and Late Industrialization*. New York: Oxford University Press.

————. 1991. "Diffusion of Development: The Late Industrializing Model and Greater East Asia." *American Economic Review* 81(2):282–86.

Amsden, Alice H., and Ajit Singh. 1994. "Growth in Developing Countries: Lessons from East Asian Countries: The Optimal Degree of Competition and Dynamic Efficiency in Japan and Korea." *European Economic Review* 38:941–51.

Asian Development Bank. 1999. *Asian Development Outlook*. Manila.

Baer, Werner, William R. Miles, and Allen B. Moran. 1999. "The End of the Asian Myth: Why Were the Experts Fooled?" *World Development* 27(10):1735–47.

Baily, Martin N., and Eric Zitzewitz. 1998. *The East Asian Miracle and Crisis: Microeconomic Evidence from Korea*. Washington, D.C.: McKinsey and Company (June).

Barro, Robert J. 1997. *Determinants of Economic Growth*. Cambridge, Mass.: MIT Press.

Bayoumi, Tamin, David T. Coe, and Elhanan Helpman. 1996. "R&D Spillovers and Global Growth." NBER (National Bureau of Economic Research) Working Paper 5628, Cambridge Mass. (June). Processed.

Beason, Richard, and David E. Weinstein. 1996. "Growth, Economies of Scale, and Targeting in Japan (1955–1990)." *Review of Economics and Statistics* 78(2):286–95.

Begum, Shamshad, and Abul F. M. Shamsuddin. 1998. "Export and Economic Growth in Bangladesh." *Journal of Development Studies* 35(1):89–114.

Bello, Walden, and Stephanie Rosenfeld. 1990. "Dragons in Distress: The Crisis of the NICs." *World Policy* 7(Summer):431–68.

Berg, Andrew and Pattillo, Catherine. 1999. "What Caused the Asian Crises: An Early Warning System Approach." *Economic Notes/Banca Monte Dei Paschi Di Siena (Italy)* 28(3):285-334, November.

Borensztein, Eduardo, and Jong-Wha Lee. 1999. "Credit Allocation and Financial Crisis in Korea." IMF Working Paper WP /99/20. International Monetary Fund, Washington, D.C. (February). Processed.

Branscomb, Lewis M., Fumio Kodama, and Richard Florida, eds. 1999. *Industrializing Knowledge*. Cambridge, Mass.: MIT Press.

Bruno, Michael, and William Easterly. 1995. "Inflation Crises and Long-Run Growth." NBER Working Paper 5209. National Bureau of Economic Research, Cambridge, Mass. (August). Processed.

Burki, Shahid J., and Guillermo Perry. 1998. *Beyond the Washington Consensus: Institutions Matter.* Washington, D.C.: World Bank.

Calvo, Guillerno A., and Carmen Reinhart. 1999. "Capital Flow Reversals, the Exchange Rate Debate, and Dollarization." *Finance and Development* 36(September):13–15.

Campos, Edgardo, and Hilton L. Root. 1996. *The Key to the East Asian Miracle: Making Shared Growth Credible.* Washington, D.C.: Brookings Institution.

Carlile, Lonny E., and Mark C. Tilton. 1998. *Is Japan Really Changing Its Ways: Regulatory Reform and the Japanese Economy.* Washington, D.C.: Brookings Institution.

Chinn, Menzie David, and Michael P. Dooley. 1999. "International Monetary Arrangement in the Asia-Pacific Before and After." *Journal of Asian Economics* 10(3):361–82.

Cho, Yoon Je, and Joon-Kyung Kim. 1995. *Credit Policies and the Industrialization of Korea.* World Bank Discussion Paper 286. Washington, D.C.: World Bank.

Chow, Percy C.Y. 2000. "The Asian Financial Crisis and Its Aftermath." In Percy C. Y. Chow and Gill Bates, eds., *Weathering the Storm.* Washington, D.C.: Brookings Institution Press.

Claessens, Stijn, Simeon Djankov, and Larry H. P. Lang. 2000. *East Asian Corporations.* World Bank Discussion Paper 409. Washington, D.C.: World Bank.

Claessens, Stijn, Simeon Djankov, Joseph Fan, and Larry Lang. 1999. "Expropriation of Minority Shareholders in East Asia." World Bank, Washington, D.C. Processed.

Clarida, Richard, Jordi Calf, and Mark Gertler. 1999. "The Science of Monetary Policy: A New Keynesian Perspective." *Journal of Economic Literature* 37(December):1661–707.

Clifford, Mark, L., and Pete Engardio. 1999. *Meltdown: Asia's Boom, Bust, and Beyond.* New York: Prentice-Hall.

Collins, Susan M., and Barry P. Bosworth. 1996. "Economic Growth in East Asia: Accumulation versus Assimilation," *Brookings Papers on Economic Activity,* 2, pp. 135-91.

Crafts, Nicholas. 1998. "East Asian Growth Before and After the Crisis." *IMF Staff Papers* 46(2):139–66.

———. 1999. "Implications of Financial Crisis for East Asian Trend Growth." *Oxford Review of Economic Policy* 15(3):110-31.

———. 2000. "Globalization and Growth in the Twentieth Century." IMF Working Paper WP/00/44. International Monetary Fund, Washington, D.C. Processed.

Dahl, Robert A. 1999. *On Democracy.* New Haven, Conn.: Yale University Press.

David, Paul A., and Bronwyn H. Hall. 2000. "Heart of Darkness: Modelling Public-Private Funding Interactions inside the R&D Black Box." National Bureau of Economic Research, NBER Working Paper 7538, Cambridge Mass. (February). Processed.

Dollar, David, and Mary Hallward-Driemeier. 1998. "Crisis Adjustment and Reform in Thai Industry." World Bank, Development Economics Research Group, Washington, D.C. (November). Processed.

Dooley, Michael P. 1995. "A Survey of Academic Literature on Controls over International Capital Transactions." Working Paper 5347. NBER Working Paper 5347, Cambridge, Mass. Processed.

Dornbusch, Rudiger. 2000. "Asian Currency Crises." In Robert Lawrence and Sue Collins, eds., *Brookings Trade Forum 1999*. Washington, D.C. Brookings Institution.

Dower, John W. 1999. *Embracing Defeat: Japan in the Wake of World War II*. New York: W.W. Norton & Co..

Dyck, Alexander. 2000 "Privatization and Corporate Governance: Principles, Evidence, and Future Challenges." Harvard Business School, Boston, Mass. Processed.

Easterly, William, and Ross Levine. 2000. "It's Not Factor Accumulation: Stylized Facts and Growth Models." World Bank, Washington, D.C. (January). Processed.

Easterly, William, Roumeen Islam, and Joseph E. Stiglitz. 2000. "Shaken and Stirred: Explaining Growth Volatility." World Bank, Washington, D.C. (April). Processed.

Easterly, William, Michael Kremer, Lant Pritchett, and Larry Summers. 1993. "Good Policy or Good Luck? Country Growth Performance and Temporary Shocks." *Journal of Monetary Economics* 32(December):459–83.

Edwards, Sebastian. 1999 "How Effective Are Capital Controls?" *Journal of Economic Perspectives* 13(9):65–84.

Edwards, Jeremy, and Sheilagh Ogilvie. 1996. "Universal Banks and German Industrialization: A Reappraisal." *Economic History Review* 99(3):427–46.

Eichengreen, Barry. 1999. "Kicking the Habit: Moving from Pegged Rates to Greater Exchange Rate Flexibility." *Economic Journal* 109(March):C1–C14.

Emmerson, Donald K. 1998. "Americanizing Asia?" *Foreign Affairs* 77(May-June):47–56.

Evans, Peter. 1995. *Embedded Autonomy*. Princeton, N.J.: Princeton University Press.

Felipe, Jesus. 1999. "Total Factor Productivity Growth in East Asia: A Critical Survey." *Journal of Development Studies* 35(April):1–41.

Fischer, Stanley. 1993. "The Role of Macroeconomic Factors in Growth." *Journal of Monetary Economics* 32(December):485–512.

Flatters, Frank. 2000. "Thailand, the International Monetary Fund, and the Financial Crisis: First In, Fast Out?" *Weathering the Storm*. Eds. Percy C.Y. Chow and Gill Bates. Washington, D.C.: Brookings Institution Press.

Folkerts-Landau, David, and Takatoshi Ito, eds. 1995. *International Capital Markets: Development, Prospects, and Policy Issues*. Washington, D.C.: International Monetary Fund.

Frankel, Jeffrey. 1999. "Economic Forum." *IMF Survey* (July 19):238.

Frankel, Jeffrey, and David Romer. 1999. "Does Trade Cause Growth?" *American Economic Review* 89(3):279–396.

Furman, Jason, and Joseph E. Stiglitz. 1998. "Economic Crises: Evidence and Insights from East Asia." *Brookings Papers on Economic Activity 1998* (2):1–114.

Garber, Peter M. 1998. *Buttressing Capital Account Liberalization with Prudential Regulation and Foreign Entry.* Princeton Essays in International Finance 207. Princeton, N.J.: Princeton University.

Gilpin, Robert. 2000. *The Challenge of Global Capitalism.* Princeton, N.J.: Princeton University Press.

Greenwood, Jeremy, Zvi Hercowitz, and Per Krusell. 1997. "Long-run Implications of Investment-Specific Technological Change." *American Economic Review* 87(3):342–63.

Haggard, Stephen. 1999. "Governance and Growth: Lessons from the Asian Economic Crisis." *Asia Pacific Economic Literature* 13(November):30–42.

———. 2000. *The Political Economy of the Asian Financial Crisis.* Washington D.C.: Institute for International Economics.

Hahn, Chin Hee, and Jong-il Kim. 1999. "Sources of East Asian Growth: Some Evidence from Cross-Country Studies." Korea Development Institute, Seoul (November). Processed.

Hall, Brian J. and David E. Weinstein. 2000. "Main Banks, Creditor Concentration, and the Resolution of Financial Distress in Japan." *Finance, Governance, and Competitiveness in Japan.* Eds. Masahiko, Aoki, and Gary R. Saxonhouse. Oxford: Oxford University Press.

Hamlin, Kevin. 1999. "The Deflation Dragon Roars." *Institutional Investor* (February):37–90.

Helliwell, John F. 1994. "Empirical Linkages between Democracy and Economic Growth." *British Journal of Political Science* 24(2):225–48.

Hellman, Thomas F., Kevin C. Murdock, and Joseph E. Stiglitz. 2000. "Liberalization, Moral Hazard in Banking, and Prudential Regulation: Are Capital Requirements Enough?" *American Economic Review* 90(1): 142–65.

Heo, Uk, and Sunwoong Kim. 2000. "Financial Crisis in South Korea: Failure of the Government-led Development Paradigm." *Asian Survey* 40(3):492-507.

Hill, Hal. 1994. "ASEAN Economic Development: An Analytical Survey." *Journal of Asian Studies* 53(3):832–66.

———. 1997. "Myths about Tigers: Indonesian Development Policy Debates." *Pacific Review* 10(2):256–73.

———. 1999. "Indonesia's Economics Team," *Far Eastern Economic Review.* December 16, p. 30.

Hitchcock, David I. 1997. "Internal Problems in East Asia." *Washington Quarterly* 21(2):121–34.

Hobday, Mike. 1996. "Export-led Technology Development in the Four Dragons: The Case of Electronics." *Development and Change* 25(2):333–61.

Hong, Sung Gul. 1997. *The Political Economy of Industrial Policy in East Asia: The Semiconductor Industry in Taiwan and South Korea*. Cheltenham, U.K.: Edward Elgar.

Hussein, Khaled A., and A. P. Thirlwall. 1999. "Explaining Differences in the Domestic Savings Rate across Countries: A Panel Data Study." *Journal of Development Studies* 36(1):31–52.

Hutchcroft, Paul D. 1999. *Booty Capitalism*. New York: Cornell University Press.

Imai, Kenichi. 1986. "Japan's Industrial Policy for High Technology Industry." In Hugh Patrick, ed., *Japan's High Technology Industries*. Seattle: University of Washington Press.

Irwin, Douglas A., and Marko Tervio. 2000. "Does Trade Raise Income? Evidence from the Twentieth Century." National Bureau of Economic Research Working Paper W7745. Cambridge, Mass. June.

Jenkins, Rhys. 1995. "The Political Economy of Industrial Policy: Automobile Manufacture in the Newly Industrializing Countries." *Cambridge Journal of Economics* 19:625–45.

Johnston, R. B., and V. Sundarajan. 1999. "Managing Financial Liberalization: An Overview." In R. B. Johnston and V. Sundarajan, eds., *Sequencing Financial Sector Reforms: Country Experience and Issues*. Washington, D.C.: International Monetary Fund.

Jones, Charles I. 1995. "Time Series Tests of Endogenous Growth Models." *Quarterly Journal of Economics* 110(2):495–525.

Kim, Chulsoo. 1997. "Did Foreign Investors Destabilize the Korean Stock Market in 1997?" *Singapore Economic Review* 44(1).

Kim, Jong-Il, and Lawrence Lau. 1994. "The Sources of Economic Growth of the East Asian Newly Industrialized Countries." *Journal of Japanese and International Economies* 8(3):235–71.

Krugman, Paul. 1997. "What Ever Happened to the Asian Miracle?" *Fortune*, Vol. 136 (4):26–29.

Krugman, Paul, ed. 1986. *Strategic Trade Policy and the New International Economics*. Cambridge, Mass.: MIT Press.

La Porta, Rafael, Florencio Lopez-de-Silanes, Andrei Shleifer, and Robert Vishny. 1997. "Legal Determinants of External Finance." NBER Working Paper 5879. National Bureau of Economic Research, Cambridge, Mass. (January). Processed.

———. 1999. "Investor Protection: Origins, Consequences, Reform." NBER Working Paper 7428. National Bureau of Economic Research, Cambridge, Mass. (December).

Lee, Jisoon. 1999. "An Understanding of the 1997 Korean Economic Crisis." *ExIm Review* 19(2):41–87.

Levine, Ross. 1997. "Financial Development and Economic Growth: Views and Agenda." *Journal of Economic Literature* 35(2):688–726.

Li, Shuke J. 1998. "The Benefits and Costs of Relation-based Governance: An Explanation of the East Asian Miracle and Crisis." Department of Economics, City University of Hong-Kong. Processed.

Lim, Youngil.1999. *Technology and Productivity*. Cambridge, Mass.: MIT Press.

Lincoln, Edward J. 1999. "Japan's Financial Mess." *Foreign Affairs* 77(May-June):57–66.

Linnan, David K. 1999. "Insolvency Reform and the Indonesian Financial Crisis." *Bulletin of Indonesian Economic Studies* 35(August):107–37.

Martin, Will, Betina Dimaranan, and Thomas W. Hertel. 1999. "Trade Policy, Structural Change, and China's Trade Growth." World Bank, Development Research Group, Washington, D.C. (November). Processed.

Mathews, John A., and Dong-Sung Cho. 2000. *Tiger Technology*. Cambridge: Cambridge University Press.

Mauro, Paolo. 1995. "Corruption and Growth." *Quarterly Journal of Economics*. 110(3):681–713.

McGuire, G., and M. Schuele. 1999. "Restrictiveness of International Trade in Banking Services." Paper presented to the Pacific Economic Coorperation Council Trade Policy Forum, Auckland, New Zealand, June 3–4. Processed.

McKibbin, Warwick, and Will Martin. 1999. "The East Asian Crisis: Investigating Causes and Policy Responses." Policy Research Working Paper 2172. World Bank, Development Research Group, Washington, D.C. (August).

McKinnon, Ronald I. 1991. *The Order of Economic Liberalization: Financial Control in the Transition to a Market Economy*. Baltimore, Md.: Johns Hopkins University Press.

McKinnon, Ronald I. 2000. "The East Asian Dollar Standard, Life after Death?" *Economic Notes* 29(1). February.

Miller, Marcus, and Pongsak Luangaram. 1999. "Financial Crisis in East Asia: Bank Runs, Asset Bubbles, and Antidotes." *National Institute Economic Review*. Issue 165. Pp. 66–82.

Mills, Terence C., and Nicholas Crafts. 2000. "After the Golden Age: A Long-run Perspective on Growth Rates That Speeded Up, Slowed Down, and Still Differ." *Manchester School* 68(January):68–91.

Mishkin, Frederic S. 1999. "Lessons from the Asian Crisis." National Bureau of Economic Research Working Paper 7102, Cambridge, Mass. (April). Processed.

Mishkin, Fredric S. and Philip E. Strahan. 1999. "What Will Technology Do to Financial Structure?" National Bureau of Economic Research Working Paper W6892 Cambridge, Mass.

Mowery, David C., and Richard R. Nelson, ed. 1999. *Sources of Industrial Leadership*. New York: Cambridge University Press.

Mowery, David, and Nathan Rosenberg. 1999. *Paths of Innovation*. New York: Cambridge University Press.

Nicolas, Françoise. 1999. "Is There a Case for a Single Currency within ASEAN?" *Singapore Economic Review* (Singapore) 44(1):1–25.

Noland, Marcus J. 2000. "The Philippines in the Asian Financial Crisis: How the Sick Man Avoided Pneumonia." *Asian Survey*. Vol. 40(3):401-412.

Noland, Marcus, and Fred C. Bergsten. 1993. "Reconcilable Differences? United States–Japan Economic Conflict." Institute of International Economics, Washington, D.C. Processed.

Ohno, Kenichi. 1998. "Overview: Creating the Market Economy." In Kenichi Ohno and Izumi Ohno, eds., *Japanese Views on Economic Development*. London: Routledge.

Okimoto, Daniel I. 1986. "Regime Characteristics of Japanese Industrial Policy." In Hugh Patrick, ed., *Japan's High Technology Industries*. Seattle: University of Washington Press.

Overholt, William H. 1999. "Thailand's Financial and Political Systems: Crisis and Rejuvenation." *Asian Survey* 39(November-December):1009–35.

Panagariya, Arvind. 2000. Evaluating the Case for Export Subsidies. http://www.bsos.umd.edu/econ/Panagariya/cieppp.htm

Partner, Simon. 1999. *Assembled in Japan*. Berkley: University of California Press.

Pistor, Katherina, and Philip A. Wellons. 1999. *The Role of Law and Legal Institutions in Asian Economic Development, 1960–1999*. New York: Oxford University Press.

Porter, Michael E., and Hirotaka Takeuchi. 1999. "Fixing What Really Ails Japan." *Foreign Affairs* (May-June):66–81.

Porter, Michael E., Hirotaka Takeuchi, and Mariko Sakakibara. 2000. *Can Japan Compete?* London: Macmillan Press Ltd.

Reinhardt, Nola. 2000. "Back to Basics in Malaysia and Thailand: The Role of Resource-Based Exports in Their Export-led Growth." *World Development* 28(1):57–77.

Rodrik, Dani. 1994. "King Kong Meets Godzilla: The World Bank and the East Asian Miracle." In Albert Fishlow, Catherine Gwin, Stephen Haggard, Dani Rodrik, and Robert Wade, eds., *Miracle or Design? Lessons from the East Asian Experience*. Washington, D.C.: Overseas Development Council.

———. 1995. "Getting Interventions Right: How South Korea and Taiwan Grew Rich." *Economic Policy* 2(April).

———. 1998. *Who Needs Capital Account Convertibility?* Princeton Essays in International Finance. Princeton, N.J.: Princeton University.

Rogoff, Kenneth. 1999. "International Institutions for Reducing Global Financial Instability." *Journal of Economic Perspectives* 13(4):21–42.

Root, Hilton L. 1996. *Small Countries, Big Lessons*. Hong Kong: Oxford University Press.

Sachs, Jeffrey D., and Andrew Warner. 1995. "Economic Reform and the Process of Global Integration." *Brookings Papers on Economic Activity* (U.S.); No. 1: 1-118.

Sakakibara, Eisuke. 2000. "East Asian Crisis: Two Years Later." Paper prepared for the World Bank's annual conference on development economics, Washington, D.C., April. Processed.

Sarel, Michael. 1997. "Growth and Productivity in ASEAN Countries." IMF Working Paper No. 97/97.

Scherer, Frederic M. 1999. *New Perspectives on Economic Growth and Technological Change*. Washington, D.C.: Brookings Institution.

Schwartz, Frank J. 1998. *Advice and Consent*. New York: Cambridge University Press.

Schwartz, Gerd, and Benedict Clements. 1999. "Government Subsidies." *Journal of Economic Surveys* 13(2):119-148.

Smith, Heather. 1995. "Industry Policy in East Asia." *Asian-Pacific Economic Literature* 9(1):17-39.

Stiglitz, Joseph E. 1996. "Some Lessons from the East Asian Miracle." *The World Bank Research Observer* 11(2):151-77.

———. 2000. "Conclusions." *Economic Notes* 29(February):145-51.

Stiglitz, Joseph E., and Marylou Uy. 1996. "Financial Markets, Public Policy, and the East Asian Miracle." *The World Bank Research Observer* 11(2):249-76.

Unger, Danny. 1998. *Building Social Capital in Thailand: Fibres, Finance, and Infrastructure*. Cambridge, U.K.: Cambridge University Press.

Van Wincoop, Eric, and FeiMu Yi. 2000. "Asia Crisis Post-Mortem: Where Did the Money Go and Did the U.S. Benefit?" *FRBNY Economic Policy Review*, 51–70, September.

Wade, Robert. 1990. *Governing the Market*. Princeton, N.J.: Princeton University Press.

———. 1996. "Japan, the World Bank, and the Art of Paradigm Maintenance: The East Asian Miracle in Political Perspective." *New Left Review* 217:3–36.

———. 1998. "The Asian Crisis and the Global Economy: Causes, Consequences, and Cure." *Current History* 97(622):361–73.

Wang, Jiann-Chyuan. 2000. "Taiwan, and the Asian Financial Crisis: Impact and Response". In Percy C. Y. Chow and Gill Bates, eds., *Weathering the Storm*. Washington, D.C.: Brookings Institution Press.

Weiss, Linda. 1995. "Governed Interdependence: Rethinking the Government-Business Relationship in East Asia." *Pacific Review* 8(4):589–616.

Wilson, James Q. 2000. "Democracy for All." *Commentary* 109(3) (March).

Wong, Y. C. Richard. 1999. "Lessons from the Asian Financial Crisis." *Cato Journal* 18(3):391–98.

World Bank. 1993. *The East Asian Miracle: Economic Growth and Public Policy*. New York: Oxford University Press.

———. 1999a. *East Asia: The Road to Recovery*. Washington, D.C.

———. 1999b. *World Development Report 1999: Entering the Twenty-first Century*. New York: Oxford University Press.

———. 2000a. *Global Economic Prospects*. Washington, D.C.

———. 2000b. "Malaysia: Social and Structural Review Update." Washington, D.C. (August 21.)

Yamada, Katsuhisa, and Akifumi Kuchiki. 1997. "Lessons from Japan: Industrial Policy Approach and the East Asian Trial." In Louis Emmerij, ed., *Economic and Social Development in the Twenty-first Century.* Baltimore, Md.: Johns Hopkins University Press.

Young, Alwyn. 1992. "A Tale of Two Cities: Factor Accumulation and Technological Change in Hong Kong and Singapore." *National Bureau of Economic Research Macroeconomics Annual 1992.* Cambridge, Mass.: MIT Press.

————. 1994a. "Accumulation, Exports and Growth in the High Performing Asian Economies: A Comment." *Carnegie-Rochester Conference on Public Policy,* 40, pp. 237–250.

————. 1994b. "Lessons from the East Asian NICs: A Contrarian View." *European Economic Review* 38:964-973.

————. 1995. "The Tyranny of Numbers: Confronting the Statistical Realities of the East Asian Growth Experience." *Quarterly Journal of Economics* 110:641-80.

Yu, Han-Soo. 2000. "The Business Perspective." In *Korea's Economy 2000.* Vol. 16. Washington, D.C.: Korea Economic Institute of America.

Zingales, Luigi. 1994. "The Value of the Voting Right: A Study of the Milan Stock Exchange." *Review of Financial Studies* 7(1):125–48.

CHAPTER 2

GROWTH, CRISIS, AND THE FUTURE OF ECONOMIC RECOVERY IN EAST ASIA

Takatoshi Ito

The objective of this paper is threefold. First, the "miracle" of Asian economic growth before the financial crisis of 1997–98 will be reviewed. Fundamental factors that made the miracle possible will be summarized. Second, the paper will provide a view on how the financial crisis afflicted high-flying Asian economies in 1997–98. Common and idiosyncratic factors responsible for causing the problem will be identified. Most of the factors are primarily financial. Third, the paper will examine the conditions necessary for the revival of high economic growth in Asia. The contrast between the strong manufacturing sectors and the weak financial sectors will be discussed, and several suggestions for strengthening financial systems will be made.

Asia has been a focus of attention for recent decades: first as a successful model for the developing countries, and then as an epicenter of currency crises. A sudden descent into the financial crisis in 1997–98, after several decades of remarkable economic performance, was quite unexpected. During the high economic growth period, researchers tried to explain how many Asian economies had succeeded in achieving sustained economic growth or had experienced an economic miracle. The precrisis high economic growth was hailed in *The East Asian Miracle*, issued by the World Bank in 1993. Newly industrializing economies (the Republic of Korea, Taiwan [China], Singapore, and Hong Kong [China]) averaged about 7 percent growth annually between 1986 and 1997, and their per capita income levels have reached those of industrial countries. Thailand, Indonesia, Malaysia, and China also experienced nearly 10 percent growth from 1986 to 1997. Poverty in these nations has been reduced dramatically. Few predicted and warned of the coming crisis. After its onset, the spread of the crisis, if not the Thailand currency crisis, surprised observers. Other researchers, with the benefit of hindsight, have emphasized that because of weakening fundamentals a crisis was inevitable. The paper aims at providing a balanced explanation of whether and how much East Asian economies had become vulnerable to shocks and why the crisis erupted. The dramatic turn of fortune in Asia demands good explanations and a rethinking of the Asian economic growth.

Three years after the Thai currency crisis, most Asian economies seem to be growing strongly. In 2000, Korea grew by an estimated 10 percent, and China by about 8 percent. Even Indonesia's economy expanded by approximately 5 percent. However, researchers and policymakers in the region are still cautious about the sustainability of current economic growth. Problems that exacerbated the crisis, such as nonperforming loans, have yet to be satisfactorily resolved. Institutional reforms are still incomplete. As a result, the growth of financial and capital markets that would attract diverse investors has been hampered. The chapter will examine conditions that would ensure the robustness of economic growth—if not another miracle—in the Asian region.

CAUSES OF THE ASIAN MIRACLE

The World Bank study (1993) and some subsequent studies (for example, Campos and Root 1997 and Ito 1997, 2000b) have shown the world how successful Asian economies managed their economic development process. According to this literature, the "Asian miracle" was based on the following factors:

- A stable macroeconomic environment
- High saving and investment rates
- High-quality human capital (good education and a high literacy rate)
- A merit-based bureaucracy

- Low income inequality (decreasing poverty)
- Export promotion
- Successful industrialization
- The volume of foreign direct investment (FDI) and associated transfer of technological know-how.

Let me elaborate on these points.

Stable macroeconomic environment. Macroeconomic management by the monetary authorities of the Asian countries has been basically sound. None of the Asian countries—except Indonesia—experienced devastating hyperinflation over the past 40 years. For most countries, inflation rates in the 25 to 30 percent range were associated briefly with the oil crisis. These inflation records were quite comparable with those of the Organisation for Economic Co-operation and Development (OECD) countries. Monetary policies were prudent, and fiscal deficits were contained. In fact, many East Asian countries, once they reached a high economic growth phase, recorded fiscal surpluses. Thus stable macroeconomic performance distinguishes East Asian countries from many other developing countries in Latin America and Africa.

High savings and investment rates. Asian countries are noted for their high savings rates. It is not unusual for household savings rates to reach 30 percent, and when public pension plan contributions in countries such as Singapore are included, the savings rate sometimes reaches 40 percent. Domestic saving (household saving, corporate saving, and government sector saving)/gross domestic product (GDP) ratios are more than 40 percent for China, Malaysia, and Singapore; between 30 percent and 40 percent for Korea, Thailand, and Indonesia; and between 20 and 30 percent for Taiwan. See table 2.1 for a comparison of saving and investment rates. A high savings rate, accompanied by high investment, made it possible to achieve rapid economic growth without incurring current account deficits financed by capital from abroad. The savings rate is endogenous, and it has been observed that the savings rate indeed rises with the growth rate. (This was the experience in Japan during the high economic growth periods, before 1973.) There appears to be a virtuous cycle linking saving and growth.

Table 2.1. Gross Domestic Saving and Investment, 1996

Economy	Gross domestic saving	Gross domestic Investment
Hong Kong, China	30.7	32.1
Rep. of Korea	33.7	38.4
Singapore	51.2	35.3
Taiwan, China	25.1	21.2
China	40.5	39.6
Indonesia	27.3	30.7
Malaysia	42.6	41.5
Philippines	18.5	23.1
Thailand	33.7	41.7
India	24.6	25.7

High-quality human capital. The Asian economies have good educational systems and high literacy rates for their respective per capita income levels. Asian countries have better-educated populations (as measured by secondary school enrollment and the literacy rate) than many other countries at similar stages of development. This makes it possible for them to promote further industrialization without being constrained by the supply of skilled workers. Many Asian countries moved up the industrial ladder from textiles to simple assembly of machines, to electronics, and to high-tech industries.

Merit-based bureaucracy. Several of the East Asian countries have merit-based bureaucratic systems of civil service in which promotion depends on performance and not on political favors. Although there are wide variations among countries, bureaucracies in Asia have been reasonably effective, considering the countries' respective development stages. Several countries were able to create a professional bureaucracy relatively insulated from political influences, and the bureaucratic systems in these countries are less susceptible to corruption than in many other regions.

Low-income inequality and decreasing poverty. One significant characteristic of Asian development was that the middle class grew in numbers, and absolute poverty declined rapidly, especially in Indonesia and China, a fact emphasized by the World Bank study.

Export promotion. Export promotion has been a key in Asian economic development. It earns foreign currencies that are needed to import natural resources (except in Indonesia, which exports natural resources), capital goods, and parts for assembly. Because domestic markets are relatively small for many countries (except China and Indonesia), overseas markets are important in achieving minimum efficient production scales. Many countries engaged in import substitution, starting in the 1950s and 1960s, but those that moved on to export promotion were better able to strengthen economic performance. A development strategy of protecting domestic markets and nurturing domestic firms resulted in domestic firms that could not produce goods competitive in the world market. On the other hand, export promotion tested producers in the world market. Korea, Taiwan, Malaysia, and Singapore provided strong incentives for successful exporters. The composition of exports from these economies has also dramatically altered over time. Malaysia, for example, changed from a primary goods exporter to an electronics exporter within 15 years.

Successful industrialization. Any economy that sustained high economic growth for decades (say, Japan from 1950 to 1973 or Korea from 1980 to 1995, or Malaysia after 1985) experienced rapid changes in its industrial structure. Korea and Taiwan followed Japan in its industrial transformation, from light industries to heavy and chemical industries, to electronics, and to high-tech industries. Singapore and Hong Kong benefited from the deepening of commercial activities (foreign trade and finance) as well as from industrialization. Thailand, Malaysia, and Indonesia started the industrialization process with selected industries and benefited from building up physical capital and human capital through a combination of market forces and government guidance. See table 2.2 for the changes in the composition of GDP over the last three decades. Note that Asian countries industrialized quickly. It is also evident that there is a pattern of industrialization from agriculture to industry, and then to services. The industrial composition of Asian countries has also evolved in turn, namely, Japan shifted its focus away from heavy and chemical industries, enabling Korea and Taiwan to enter these subsectors and begin exporting their products. Korea and Taiwan, in turn, vacated textile and other light industries to ASEAN (Association of Southeast Asian Nations) countries (Ito 1997).

Table 2.2 Sectoral Shares of GDP

Economy	Sector	1970	1980	1991	1998
Korea	Agriculture	29.8	14.2	7.4	6.1
	Industry	23.8	37.8	46.3	43.2
	Service	46.4	48.1	46.3	50.6
Singapore	Agriculture	2.2	1.1	0.3	0.1
	Industry	36.4	38.8	36.3	34.3
	Service	61.4	60.0	63.4	65.5
Indonesia	Agriculture	35.0	24.4	18.9	17.2
	Industry	28.0	41.3	41.1	42.3
	Service	37.0	34.3	39.8	40.5
Malaysia	Agriculture		22.29	17.3	11.3
	Industry		35.8	43.8	45.8
	Service		41.3	38.9	42.9
Philippines	Agriculture	28.2	23.5	22.8	19.4
	Industry	33.7	40.5	35.0	35.5
	Service	38.1	36.0	42.2	45.1
Thailand	Agriculture	30.2	20.6	13.8	12.0
	Industry	25.7	30.8	36.4	40.4
	Service	44.1	48.6	49.8	47.6
India	Agriculture	44.5	38.1	31.0	26.2
	Industry	23.9	25.9	28.9	26.8
	Service	31.6	36.0	40.1	47.0

Notes: For Singapore, 1997 instead of 1998.

Source: Asian Development Bank. *Asian Development Outlook*, various issues.

This aspect will be elaborated in the next subsection. Whether industrialization has been achieved purely by markets or with the help of industrial policy is a controversial subject[1] . The experience of Korea, Malaysia, and Singapore suggests that export-oriented industrial policy yielded the desired results.

Foreign direct investment and technological transfer. Except for Japan and Korea, most Asian economies have succeeded in industrialization by attracting foreign direct investment. Singapore, Malaysia, and Taiwan were the early successes at doing so. Thailand and China followed a path of accelerated development through foreign direct investment. These countries tended to control the choice of which industries were to be promoted. They encouraged foreign firms not only to establish assembly plants but also to bring in parts production with them. Although establishing industrial bases is easy with foreign direct investment, how successful these operations would become depended on the rate of technological transfers, which depended on the willingness of firms to invest and the capability of management and workers of host countries to assimilate the technology.

THE FLYING GEESE HYPOTHESIS

Asian countries' success in achieving high economic growth rates is mainly based on their successful industrialization. What has been observed in Asia, and in many other countries, is a sequential industrialization from the agricultural sector to the industrial sector, with small capital requirements (light industry), to heavy and petrochemical industries, and to precision and electronics industries. These industrial changes have made it possible to maintain high economic growth. If the economy had relied on only one industry, the high growth might not have continued.

Industrialization has also led to intraregional spillover effects in Asia. Spillovers arose directly from technological transfers through direct investment from Japan, mainly, and indirectly from a "hollowing out" of the industrial economies. The latter can be explained as follows: Each shift in the industrial focus of the Japanese economy, from light to heavy to electronics and high-tech industries, created market opportunities for other economies such as Korea and Taiwan. Even within the electronics industries, midrange goods are now supplied by Korea, Taiwan, Singapore, and Malaysia, and only the most sophisticated goods are produced in Japan. More recently, as Korea, Taiwan, and Singapore in turn emphasized the heavy and high-tech goods sectors, the light industries were picked up by Thailand, the Philippines, and Indonesia. This phenomenon can be viewed in two ways. Countries move up the technology and capital-intensive ladder in industrialization. The center of gravity of industries shifts from first movers of industrialization to the second-tier group, and then to a third group of countries. This sequence of industrialization is often called the flying geese pattern.[2]

Ito and Orii (2000) examined how manufacturing subsectors in Asia have changed. First, they classified the manufacturing subsectors in three categories: Labor-intensive sectors (L-sectors), capital-intensive sectors (C-sectors), and technology-intensive sectors (T-sectors). To be more specific, these comprise:

- L-sector (International Standard Industrial Classification Code 311–332), including sectors producing food, beverage, tobacco, textile, apparel, leather products, shoes, lumber, and furniture
- C-sector (ISIC Code 341–381), including sectors producing paper, printing and publishing, petrochemicals, rubber, plastic, nonmetal (ceramic, glass, cement), steel, and nonferrous metal
- T-sector (ISIC Code 382–390), including sectors producing machinery (general, electronic, transport, and precision).

Ito and Orii observed that the L-sector shares in value added had monotonically declined over time in most countries, while the C-sectors expanded first and then declined as income rose to high levels. The T-sectors remain small when incomes are low but start to expand at a certain stage of economic development. The threshold years for the L-sector shrinkage and the T-sector expansion are shown in table 2.3.

A recurrent pattern among these three sectors is apparent, with late-comers repeating the changes in industrial composition of the leader in industrialization. In terms of the threshold ratios in Ito and Orii (2000) the evidence for the flying geese hypothesis is convincing. Asian nations seem to have succeeded in passing on comparative advantages in manufacturing from a leader to the followers, and then to the followers' followers.

Industrial policy. The use of industrial policy in East Asia has given rise to much controversy that the East Asian Miracle did nothing to quell. Proponents of industrial policy, especially in Japan, argued that for countries attempting to catch up with advanced economies, it was easy to identify which industries to promote because comparative advantage can be defined and technologies can be imported, often with foreign direct investment. The flying geese pattern can point to the "right" industries to promote, given the stages of development. Korea and Taiwan, for example, followed the pattern of Japanese industrialization, starting from light industries to heavy and chemical industries, to electronics, to high-tech industries. The heavy and chemical industries, as well as industrial infrastructure, were promoted in Korea with policy financing. The success of the electronics industry in

Table 2.3
Panel A The First Year when the L-Sector Share in Value Added Became Lower than
the Threshold Percentage

Threshold economies	50%	40%	30%	20%	10%	Recent data (year)
Singapore	Na	Na	Na	1974	1989	5.6% (1997)
Japan	Na	Na	Na	1974*		15.8% (1997)
Taiwan	Na	Na	1987	1995		19.0% (1996)
Korea	1968	1979	1987			20.1% (1996)
Malaysia	Na	1969*	1989			21.8% (1996)
China	Na	Na	Na			29.1% (1996)
Hong Kong	Na	1995				37.5% (1995)
Thailand	1990					41.3% (1996)
The Philippines	1976					44.1% (1997)
Indonesia	1985					46.8% (1997)

Na not applicable.
* indicates that the economies had crossed back above the threshold after that year.
Source: Ito and Orii (2000), based on the data of UNIDO (1999).

Panel B The First Year when the T-Sector Share in Value Added Became Higher than
the Threshold Percentage

Threshold economies	50%	40%	30%	20%	10%	Recent data (year)
Singapore	Na	1969	1970	1975	1984	62.3% (1997)
Japan	Na	Na	Na	1983		43.2% (1997)
Korea	1965	1977	1986	1995		42.0% (1996)
Malaysia	1972	1980	1990	1994		40.4% (1996)
Taiwan	Na	Na	1988			36.0% (1996)
Hong Kong	Na	Na	1993			34.7% (1995)
Thailand	Na	1987	1992			33.1% (1996)
China	Na	Na				28.3% (1996)
Indonesia	1974*					19.1% (1997)
The Philippines	Na*					16.8% (1997)

Na not applicable.
* indicates that the economies had crossed back below the threshold after year
Source: Ito and Orii (2000), based on the data of UNIDO (1999).

Malaysia is often attributed to the country's explicit policy of inviting foreign direct investment in the electronics sector.

The difficulty of industrial policy in emerging market economies lies not in identifying the industry to promote, but in designing a reward system that is less subject to moral hazard. In that sense, promoting exports by way of industrial policy, as opposed to import substitution by protection, was successful. Defenders of industrial policy point out that "crony" factors have existed during the high growth period as well as a crisis period, and they exist in many other countries too. Therefore, the "crony" factors, however detrimental and unfair from a social point of view, cannot explain the currency and financial crisis.

Opponents to the idea of industrial policy always cite the difficulty in spotting "sunrise" industries. Projects are often chosen for political reasons and can become a source of rents for favored industrialists. Governments' explicit and implicit guarantees give rise to moral hazards in borrowing and lending (by investors and foreign banks). Skeptics regarding the use of industrial policy became more convinced when they saw that "crony capitalism" contributed to the currency crisis in several Asian countries.

It is not clear at this stage whether on balance industrial policy exerted a positive influence on economic growth in the long run or whether its effect was basically negative and was responsible for overcapacity and misallocation of resources, which became apparent in 1997–98. However, if a major part of the blame for the Asian currency crisis is placed on financial factors, and not on real sectors, then the role of cronyism in Asia should be much less than commonly thought. If cronyism had been a significant drain on resources, the Asian economies would not have grown so fast in the first place.

PRELUDES TO CURRENCY CRISES

The underlying vulnerability. Industrialization requires increasing investment, and investment, in turn, requires financing. In general, funds for investment come from three sources: domestic saving, inward foreign direct investment, and portfolio capital inflows that include equities, bonds, and bank lending. Short-term bank lending, mostly denominated in U.S. dollars, was almost always intermediated by domestic financial institutions, which offered medium-term lending to domestic corporations. Thus, domestic institutions became exposed to currency and maturity risks. Although the Asian countries have relatively high domestic savings rates—mostly derived from high rates of household saving, but also complemented in certain cases by high social security saving—which can be mobilized for domestic investment, financial needs for investment exceeded domestic saving. (Recall the savings and investment numbers in table 2.1.) Some economies, most notably China, Singapore, and Malaysia, attracted foreign direct investment, while many countries have accepted portfolio investment—bond and equity investment—and bank loans. Especially in some countries, net capital inflows became very large. Table 2.4 shows the breakdown of foreign direct investment, portfolio flows, and other flows (including bank loans).

The FDI/GDP ratio, summarized in Table 2.4, Panel A, reveals the following features: China and Malaysia show high ratios, followed by Thailand, Indonesia, and the Philippines. FDI to Korea remained less than 1 percent of GDP. Table 2.4, Panel B, shows the portfolio flows/ GDP ratio for the same set of Asian countries. Korea, Indonesia, Thailand, and the Philippines received sizable portfolio capital inflows before the crisis of 1997. China and Malaysia did not. Panel C of Table 2.4 shows the other capital flow/GDP ratios. This includes bank loans. Between 1988 and 1996, Thailand received large amounts of other flows, exceeding 10 percent in 1995. Korea and the Philippines also received large amounts of other flows. The differences among the countries with respect to types of capital flows reflect partly the policy of capital controls and liberalization and partly investors' confidence in the economy.

Relying on short-term portfolio inflows, especially bonds and bank loans, is thought to increase the vulnerability of the financial and foreign exchange markets of a country. In the Mexican currency crisis of 1994–95, the large outstanding balances of Tesobonos (short-term government bonds indexed to the dollar) caused the dollar liquidity problem (or at least the perception of that problem among investors), which resulted in the sharp depreciation of the peso. In the Asian currency crisis, banking liabilities to foreigners became the source of vulnerability in Thailand and Korea. In contrast, China, which relied mostly on foreign direct investment, did not experience a currency crisis. Malaysia, which accepted a relatively large amount of foreign direct investment, also did not require an International Monetary Fund (IMF) program.

How efficiently domestic saving and foreign capital flows are allocated to various industries depends on the design and regulation of the capital and financial markets. The particular ways that some Asian

Table 2.4 Capital Flows to GDP ratios, by Types of Flows and by Country
Panel A

	FDI/GDP (%)					
Year	Korea	Thailand	Indonesia	Philippines	Malaysia	China
1976	0.28	0.46	0.00	0.00	3.45	
1977	0.25	0.54	0.00	1.01	3.09	
1978	0.18	0.23	0.00	0.42	3.06	
1979	0.05	0.20	0.00	0.02	2.70	
1980	0.01	0.59	0.00	-0.33	3.82	
1981	0.15	0.84	0.14	0.48	5.05	
1982	0.09	0.52	0.24	0.04	5.22	0.16
1983	0.08	0.87	0.34	0.32	4.18	0.22
1984	0.12	0.96	0.25	0.03	2.34	0.41
1985	0.25	0.42	0.35	0.04	2.22	0.54
1986	0.42	0.61	0.32	0.43	1.76	0.63
1987	0.45	0.70	0.51	0.92	1.34	0.72
1988	0.56	1.79	0.68	2.47	2.07	0.80
1989	0.50	2.46	0.72	1.32	4.41	0.76
1990	0.31	2.85	1.03	1.20	5.44	0.90
1991	0.40	2.04	1.27	1.20	8.31	1.08
1992	0.24	1.89	1.39	0.43	8.89	2.31
1993	0.18	1.44	1.27	2.28	7.80	4.58
1994	0.21	0.95	1.19	2.48	5.99	6.25
1995	0.39	1.23	2.16	1.99	4.73	5.14
1996	0.48	1.29	2.72	1.82		4.93
1997	0.64	1.97	2.18	1.51		4.91

financial markets and institutions developed in the 1990s became a source of problems later in the decade. With the benefit of hindsight, the following aspects, which would lead to the financial crisis, were crystallizing even during the miracle years.

Vulnerability in the financial sector. In most of the Asian countries, banking has played a major role in channeling domestic savings to investment. There are several large banks as well as many smaller deposit-taking institutions. They provided funds for various industrial firms with whom they have long-term relationships, and bank directors often served on the boards of these firms as well. The equity market was in general underdeveloped, except in Malaysia, where the market capitalization/GDP ratio was among the highest in the world.

Long-term capital needs are best provided with long-term investors' capital in the form of equities and long-term bonds. If the long-term investment is provided through banks, which take in short-term

Panel B

	Portfolio flows/GDP (%)					
Year	Korea	Thailand	Indonesia	Philippines	Malaysia	China
1976	0.26	-0.01	0.00	0.00	0.47	
1977	0.19	0.00	0.00	0.04	0.48	
1978	0.08	0.32	0.00	0.02	0.48	
1979	0.01	0.66	0.00	0.05	0.91	
1980	0.21	0.30	0.00	0.02	-0.04	
1981	0.03	0.13	0.05	0.01	4.52	
1982	-0.02	0.19	0.33	0.00	2.25	0.01
1983	0.66	0.27	0.43	0.02	2.22	0.01
1984	0.93	0.37	-0.01	0.00	3.26	0.03
1985	1.84	2.30	-0.04	0.06	6.21	0.25
1986	-0.31	-0.07	0.33	0.04	0.11	0.54
1987	-0.22	0.68	-0.12	0.06	0.44	0.37
1988	-0.33	0.86	-0.12	0.13	-1.29	0.30
1989	0.00	2.06	-0.18	0.69	-0.28	0.03
1990	0.09	-0.04	-0.09	-0.11	-0.59	0.00
1991	0.79	-0.08	-0.01	0.28	0.35	0.14
1992	1.61	0.83	-0.07	0.29	-1.92	0.08
1993	3.17	4.36	1.14	1.65	-1.10	0.61
1994	2.14	1.72	2.19	1.41	-2.28	0.73
1995	3.04	2.43	2.04	3.53	-0.50	0.10
1996	4.37	1.98	2.20	6.14		0.29
1997	2.78	2.80	-1.23	0.67		0.85

Source: IMF, *International Financial Statistics*, CD-ROM.

deposits, then "maturity mismatch" develops. Moreover, foreign bank loans are often denominated in hard currencies—the U.S. dollar, the yen, and the euro—rather than local currencies. When banks lend these foreign source funds to domestic borrowers, currency mismatch occurs. The double mismatch problem was indeed a problem in large banks and nonbanks in some of the Asian countries, most notably Thailand and Korea.

Of course, it is very easy to blame an excessive degree of maturity mismatch and currency mismatch, especially after the fact. Banks in general are supposed to engage in maturity transformation, namely, taking the risk of maturity mismatch in order to earn profits. Currency mismatch is harder to justify, especially in an economy with high domestic savings. An alternative to the banking sector is the capital market. However, creating a broad capital market infrastructure is as difficult to achieve as good banking supervision. Many Asian countries prudently maintained balanced budgets. No fiscal deficits meant

Panel C

			Other flows/GDP (%)			
Year	Korea	Thailand	Indonesia	Philippines	Malaysia	China
1976	6.94	2.65	0.00	0.00	3.30	
1977	5.81	4.73	0.00	2.97	1.80	
1978	4.38	5.19	0.00	8.22	1.33	
1979	9.30	6.54	0.00	8.25	0.95	
1980	10.06	5.50	0.00	9.79	2.49	
1981	6.68	6.28	1.83	7.17	1.98	
1982	6.50	3.06	5.38	8.58	7.03	0.26
1983	2.89	4.04	6.32	-1.83	11.27	0.17
1984	1.81	5.00	3.70	2.15	2.53	0.04
1985	1.79	1.86	1.73	1.01	-2.76	1.97
1986	-2.04	-0.49	4.56	0.02	1.91	1.11
1987	-6.33	0.78	4.19	-0.02	-4.91	1.00
1988	-1.13	3.18	2.06	-1.10	-3.43	1.17
1989	-0.64	5.12	2.55	1.20	-0.68	0.34
1990	2.17	8.17	3.29	3.56	-0.21	0.28
1991	2.38	9.77	3.62	5.00	1.03	1.11
1992	1.60	5.81	3.47	5.55	5.46	-0.85
1993	-0.44	5.38	1.38	4.52	11.59	-0.10
1994	3.58	6.82	-0.87	5.56	-2.64	-0.28
1995	4.70	11.53	1.20	4.10	3.72	0.73
1996	5.07	6.55	0.11	7.63		0.16
1997	-1.88	-13.13	-0.21	5.18		0.94

Source: IMF, International Financial Statistics, CD-ROM.

no government bonds. Without risk-free government bonds as a benchmark, it was difficult to develop a corporate bond market. The achievement in fiscal policy became a curse in funding private investment through corporate bonds.

Experience from East Asia suggests that it may be efficient to have the banking sector in low-income countries finance the industries that initiate development. Scarce financial talent may initially be allocated to the banking sector to oversee lending practices. Gradually, however, capital markets should be developed in order to attract investors with an appetite for risk. This change was slow to take place in Asia as a whole as well as in Japan.

Inadequacy of financial regulation. The regulatory and supervisory framework of financial institutions in many Asian economies was not sophisticated. It was based on the assumption that financial institutions would never fail. This is not a bad assumption in economies growing at more than 5 percent, in some cases 10 percent, every year. However, the system was vulnerable to a shock that would cause some corporations to default on bank loans. The procedure for resolving bad debts was unclear. The bankruptcy laws were inadequate in the sense that it was difficult for creditors to decide on collective actions (when opinions differ among creditors), exercise collateral rights or foreclose, or take over management of the company. Instead it was quite usual for banks just to exhibit forbearance on de facto defaulted loans, waiting for better times.

In many cases, limiting competition by restricting the number of banking licenses was considered to be enough to allow banks to earn profits. It was assumed that given profits, banks will not fail. However, once some banks accumulated large portfolios of nonperforming loans, the lack of a clear procedure for winding down financial institutions became a constraint, and much deeper costs had to be borne because of such forbearance.

In addition to a banking framework, accounting rules and disclosure practice for banks and corporations emerged as a problem in 1997–98. When the economy was growing, foreign investors did not pay much attention to accounting opaqueness, but once signs of troubles appeared, nontransparency probably accelerated the exodus of investors.

The process of financial deregulation in East Asia was also unsuccessful in displacing controls on price (interest rate) and volume (credit constraints) by prudential policies (risk management). This transformation often fails, even in industrial countries like the United States and Japan. In several of the Asian emerging economies, prudential regulation was especially weak. For example, in Thailand, the boom in real estate sectors was an outgrowth of the strong economy in the first half of the 1990s. And bank loans supported this boom. Stock prices also rose sharply, until 1994. When the bubble in asset prices burst, the quality of bank balance sheets quickly deteriorated.

In fact, a banking crisis (to be precise, a crisis in the finance company [nonbank] sector) preceded the currency devaluation in Thailand in July 1997, and a problem with some of the large *chaebol* preceded the Korean currency crisis of November-December 1997). As emphasized by Kaminsky and Reinhart (1999), banking and currency crises are like "twin crises," taking place at the same time. They most often occur sequentially, in some countries a banking crisis causing a currency crisis, and in some other countries, the other way around. It is also the case that the twin crises reinforce each other.

In the case of the Thailand currency crisis, nonperforming loans of finance companies, which are nonbank financial institutions, became one of the indicators of vulnerability that attracted selling attacks of foreign investors against the baht, from the fall of 1996 to May 1997. (See Ito and Pereira da Silva 1999 for details of the Thai banking and currency crises.) In this sense, the banking crisis preceded the currency crisis. However, after the baht depreciation of July 1997, the foreign currency liabilities of Thai corporations and banks increased the burden of repayment. Nonperforming loans of banks increased after the devaluation, and banks' balance sheets deteriorated. Thus, commercial banks in addition to finance companies became a focus of the problems in the wake of the currency crisis.

Korean financial institutions also experienced difficulties before the currency crisis. When some *chaebol* firms suffered losses in 1996–97, financial institutions, in particular merchant banks related to those weak *chaebol*, experienced sharp increases in nonperforming loans. The trouble, however, was limited to weaker *chaebol*, and the proportion of nonperforming loans to the economy was manageable up to the summer of 1997. When currency crises spread in Southeast Asia in the fall of 1997, Korea was also affected. It is not certain in the case of Korea whether the vulnerability of domestic financial institutions or contagion from other countries was a main factor in triggering the won currency crisis in December 1997.

In all countries that suffered sharp currency depreciation in Asia, banks' balance sheets were damaged. Foreign currency liabilities on banks' balance sheets became much larger in terms of local currency. That was the case in most of the Asian crisis–affected countries, including Thailand and Korea. In addition, Indonesian corporations borrowed large amounts denominated in foreign currency directly from foreign financial institutions. The rupiah depreciated most among the Asian currencies. In January 1998, the value of the rupiah became one-sixth of the precrisis level. Indonesian banks as well as foreign banks became exposed to large nonperforming loans when their borrowers became insolvent because of large loan repayment liabilities.

Sequence of liberalization. In the literature of international trade and finance, it is widely maintained that the sequence of liberalization is important. In general, trade liberalization should precede financial liberalization, domestic financial deregulation should precede external financial liberalization, and direct investment liberalization should precede portfolio and bank loan liberalization (capital account convertibility).

However, East Asian countries did not always adhere to this sequence. Indonesia liberalized the capital account a long time ago, while many goods remain subject to high tariffs. Thailand liberalized the capital account when it created the BIBF (Bangkok International Banking Facility), believing that it would serve as a platform for investment in neighboring countries. But foreign funds channeled through BIBF found their way into Thailand, thereby increasing liquidity. Korea had strict controls on inward foreign direct investment and equity investment, while banks' borrowing from abroad was liberalized. These examples represent the "wrong" order of liberalization.

It has been shown repeatedly that too hasty liberalization of capital accounts without deep domestic financial and capital markets would magnify distortions. In Thailand, high economic growth from the mid-1980s to the mid-1990s generated an increasing demand for investment financing. Since domestic bond and equities markets were not fully developed, a disproportionately large amount of financing took the form of bank loans. To accommodate demand, the authorities began easing licensing of domestic subsidiaries of foreign banks, adding to the number of foreign banks active in the domestic market. With an eye to further deregulation, the Thai government raised the possibility of granting more licenses for subsidiaries in 1994. This encouraged foreign banks to lend in the Thai market through the BIBF and through branches, so as to win favor with the Thai authorities. This added to the lending boom in 1993–94 and fueled the run-up of stock and land prices in Bangkok. Thus, deregulation indeed contributed to excess lending. The combination of all these factors—that is, a lack of deep bond and equities markets with deregulation at the height of a bubble—left the Thai banks and finance companies excessively exposed to bubbles in domestic real estate, construction, and related sectors. When the real estate bubble burst, these institutions found themselves saddled with nonperforming loans In addition, defense of the baht by high interest rates put banks that had borrowed short and lent long in a difficult position, and when the baht finally depreciated, those Thai banks that had borrowed in U.S. dollars from foreign banks and lent domestically suffered heavy currency losses. Maturity and currency mismatch thus contributed to the malaise of Thai banks in the wake of the currency crisis. In fact, what happened in Thailand in the first half of the 1990s can be regarded as an example of poorly sequenced liberalization.

Corporate governance. Many large corporations in Asian emerging markets have been controlled by family owners. Investment decisions and bank financing were often made jointly, as banks were also part of corporate groups. Independent credit analysis was generally lacking. Again, when the economy was growing at a high rate, problems remained dormant. But once the economy slowed, the misallocation of investment surfaced as a major issue. Unproductive investment was often cross-subsidized from other branches of corporate groups. These poor investment decisions were made by lending banks, and the companies and banks became vulnerable to external shocks.

In the Japanese banking system, banks often play a monitoring role in corporation management. Credit analysis for bank loans substitutes for monitoring by shareholders and board members. This system has the merit of allowing management to seek results over a long-term horizon as long as banks understand that it sometimes takes some time after physical investment to generate results, make changes in the design of products or product lines, and undertake restructuring or innovation in management. However, this banking relationship does not work if banks lack serious credit analysis. When the economy is expanding, most investment can generate adequate returns. Banks' monitoring capability is tested when the economy goes into a recession or the economy experiences a financial bubble. In many countries in Asia, bank loans ex post turned out to be risky ones, in the sense that loans were concentrated in a few sectors that either invested too much or made the wrong kind of investment.

An alternative model of corporate governance is to rely on various types of shareholder pressure and credit analysis by a credit rating agency. The U.S. type (or Anglo-Saxon type) of corporate governance uses pressure from stock markets and large shareholders such as pension funds. The stock price is a most visible indicator, and the market reacts swiftly to news including quarterly profit reports. Poor performance results often force management to resign. Corporate bonds are frequently used to finance medium- and long-term investment. Bond rating by a credit rating agency puts pressure on management to perform, since a bad rating would make financing very costly.

Many failures of banks as well as corporations in the wake of the currency crisis prompted the idea of changing from bank-based corporate governance to securities market–based corporate governance. However, a smooth transition requires adequate preparation. First, infrastructure for equities and bond market transactions, such as transactions and settlement systems of the securities markets, have to be improved. A supervisory agency to prevent insider trading also should be established. In addition, credit rating agencies must become important players in the market. (There are domestic credit rating agencies in several Asian countries, including Thailand and Malaysia, but they are not functioning the way that those in the Western countries do.) Establishing the corporate bond market is an important priority in the postcrisis economy.

An appropriate combination of equities, bond financing, and bank loans will have to be developed in Asia. That is important both for banks and for corporations. Moving toward an arms-length relationship between banks and corporations is important; moving toward market-based corporate governance is also important. Effective corporate governance in Asia will depend on structural reforms in the securities market.

Exchange rate regime. Officially, many countries, including Thailand and China, claimed to have been pegging their exchange rates to a currency, but it was clear from the actual exchange rate movements that the authorities kept the exchange rate very stable relative to the U.S. dollar. For example, the Thai baht stayed between 25 and 26 baht per U.S. dollar from 1985 to July 1997. Frankel and Wei (1994) showed that many Asian currencies, except the Singaporean dollar, had a very high correlation with the U.S. dollar. The weight of the U.S. dollar typically exceeded 90 percent if the currency movement is decomposed into correlated movements with major currencies, including the yen and the dollar. The de facto dollar peg or stability of the exchange rate was believed to have contributed to growth of tradable sectors and stimulated incoming foreign direct investment (see chapter 5 of this volume).

The de facto dollar peg gives rise to three types of problems. First, when inflation at home is higher than in the United States, the export sectors lose competitiveness in the long run. Where productivity growth compensates for the inflation differential, the real appreciation of the exchange rate can be absorbed. But, unfortunately, this was not the case for most Asian countries. For example, Indonesia had adopted a crawling peg, but it did not fully compensate for the inflation differential, and the competitiveness of the trading sectors was not maintained.

Second, Asian countries have extensive trade relationships with Japan. For many Asian countries, one-quarter to one-third of their exports and imports are to and from Japan. Even though the exchange rate was fixed to the U.S. dollar, the exchange rate relative to the yen fluctuated greatly. When the yen appreciated against the dollar, export growth from East Asian economies quickened. However, when the yen depreciated against the dollar, Asian economic performance was dampened. The period of 1994–95 was a typical boom, and 1996 was such a period of recession and export decline. Therefore, the fixed exchange rate relative to the U.S. dollar led to instability of the real effective exchange rate—the trade-weighted, inflation-adjusted exchange rate.

Third, a stable exchange rate diminished the perception of exchange rate risk in borrowing and lending short-term capital. Because of the credit risk premium and the inflation risk premium (plus possibly political risk and devaluation risk), the domestic interest rate in the local currency tended to be higher than the world interest rate, namely the dollar interest rate. Residents—banks, corporations, and in some cases individuals—were induced to borrow abroad in the U.S. dollar, because of lower interest rate costs and the apparent absence of exchange rate risk. Likewise, foreign investors came to believe that emerging markets in East Asia offered higher yields than were available in the United States. Short-term lending particularly appeared safe because in three months the likelihood of devaluation was small, and many investors were persuaded that they could anticipate exchange rate movements. It was regarded as a free lunch to borrow in the dollar and invest in the baht. Although it was good to induce FDI, presumably helped by the stability of the exchange rate, attracting portfolio investment and bank lending was problematic. Thus, the de facto exchange rate regime led to a buildup of short-term external liabilities.

This last aspect became a much larger problem when capital account transactions were gradually liberalized in the beginning of the 1990s—most notably with the establishment of the BIBF in 1994. It became much easier for domestic residents of Thailand to borrow in U.S. dollars.

Exchange rate regimes that are robust against a crisis have been extensively analyzed and debated. Mussa and others (2000) argue that the requirements for successful floating are less burdensome than for fixed exchange rate regimes. These authors recognize that ASEAN countries with diversified trading structures face risk of exchange rate volatility arising from the fluctuation of major currencies (such as the U.S. dollar, the yen, or the euro). However, they still find that an exchange rate–based stabilization (disinflation) program has been effective in many countries, provided it moves to a more binding commitment such as a currency board or to a safe exit to a flexible exchange rate (on the merits of fixed rates see chapter 5 of this volume). Eichengreen (1999) has argued in favor of a flexible exchange rate regime by pointing out the difficulty of safe exit from an exchange rate–based stabilization. The only exception is the currency board arrangement. The position that the only robust exchange rate regime is either free floating or a currency board has become known as the two-corner solution.

Williamson (2000) has questioned the efficacy of the two-corner solution. Stability of the currency board has yet to be established. Moreover, Hong Kong and Argentina experienced pressure on their exchange rates during the Asian currency crisis, and a high-cost defense was needed. A country with a freely floating rate may suffer from excess volatility of the exchange rate. Williamson recommends BBC (basket, band, crawl) for emerging market economies. Ogawa and Ito (2000) went a step further, arguing that an optimal exchange rate regime of country A (say, Thailand) depends on the exchange rate regime of country B (say, Malaysia), with which country A has a high proportion of trade. Thus, there must be coordination in selecting an exchange

rate regime among countries in the region with similar trading structures and with high intraregional trading shares.

A more suitable exchange rate regime will make it easier for a country to conduct economic policy without suffering a crisis. The selection of
an exchange rate regime will be crucial for Asian countries' further recovery and beyond. But the debate over what would be desirable exchange rate regimes for Asian countries seems likely to continue.

STRONG MANUFACTURING AND WEAK FINANCIAL SECTORS: SEPARABLE COEXISTENCE?

In the preceding subsection, we reviewed weaknesses in the precrisis
economic system. One may be puzzled over two different views: of a
strong Asia whose performance was a miracle and of a weak Asia that
plunged suddenly into a crisis. One way to resolve the puzzle is to
recognize that most of the weaknesses, except for those arising from
industrial policy, were financial matters. If the financial weakness
can be remedied by financial reform, then the strong growth led by
manufacturing sectors may resume. If "separability" holds, financial
weakness is not necessarily a sign of fundamental problems in the real
sector.

In arguing that the real sector is not beset by serious problems, one
has to overcome an objection posed by Krugman (1994) and Young
(1992). Basing his position on Young's work, Krugman maintained that
the Asian miracle was no miracle because most of the growth derived
from factor accumulation and the contribution of total factor productivity was minimal. High rates of investment and increasing labor input explain much of the economic growth, and there is little room for
technological progress, which is estimated as a residual.

Some thought that Krugman had foreseen the financial crisis. However, this was not the case. Krugman's prediction was that the high
growth rate would not continue indefinitely, as factor inputs, especially labor input, cannot go on rising. The growth rate would slow
down over time. He did not predict a sudden cessation in growth, as
experienced by the several East Asian countries in 1998.

Krugman's argument regarding long-term growth prospects can be
refuted on three different grounds. First, it is well known that the

measurement of technological progress is notoriously difficult. Since it is estimated as the difference between the actual GDP growth rate and the sum of factor contributions (that is, marginal productivity times factor increase), mismeasurement of marginal productivity or factor accumulation would show up as technological progress or a lack of it. Second, the low-income countries may not enjoy technological progress when they grow faster. It is more natural to associate their growth with high marginal productivity. Third, as development progresses, from textiles and toys to heavy and chemical industries, and to electronics, the scope for technological progress increases. Even if, according to Young's estimates, productivity growth in Singapore is lower than that of Hong Kong for the period covered, the rate for Singapore may increase for later periods.

These two concerns are partly validated by more recent studies. Table 2.5 compares Young's estimates of productivity growth for Asian countries with those of other researchers. Where Young's estimate shows that the productivity growth of Singapore was a mere 0.2 percent for 1966–90, Bosworth and Collins estimate that it was 3.1 percent for 1984–94.

In sum, several East Asian countries succeeded in industrializing and joined the ranks of middle-income, emerging market countries in the span of 30 years. This is a performance unmatched in the 19th and 20th centuries by Western countries and, for that matter, by Latin American economies.

Table 2.5 TFP Growth Comparison

Author	Young (1995)	Bosworth and Collins (1996)		Sarel (1995)	Sarel (1996)
Data period	1966–90	1960–94	1984–94	1975–90	1979–96
Hong Kong	2.3			3.8	
Korea	1.7	1.5	2.1	3.1	
Singapore	0.2	1.5	3.1	1.9	2.5
Taiwan	2.6	2.0	2.8	3.5	
Indonesia		0.8	0.9	0.9	
Malaysia		0.9	1.4	2.0	
Philippines		0.4	-0.9		-0.9
Thailand		1.8	3.3	2.0	

Source: IMF (1995), Box 9.

This success in economic development was fueled by ever-increasing investment. Funding needs were satisfied by high domestic saving, inward foreign direct investment, and foreign portfolio inflows. However, because the financial infrastructure was slow to develop or subject to distortion, countries became vulnerable to currency and banking crises. The vulnerability served as dry powder when a fire erupted in 1997. However, financial vulnerability can be separated from real factors. Once financial sectors are free of past nonperforming loans problems and supervision is enhanced, the strength of the real side will provide as strong a push as it did in the past.

CAUSES OF THE CURRENCY CRISES

Common and idiosyncratic factors. By now, there is a large literature on the Asian currency crisis. (To name a few, see Eichengreen 1999; Lane and others 1999; Radelet and Sachs 1998; Corsetti, Pesenti, and Roubini 2000; Yoshitomi and Shirai 2000; Hunter and others 1999; and Woo, Sachs, and Schwab 2000.) The following is my list of the common factors: overvaluation of currencies (all dollar-peg countries), weak bank and nonbank supervision (all countries), and the large volume of short-term capital inflows (all countries).

In addition, several factors affected only a few countries: mismanagement of foreign reserves (Thailand and Korea), the state of foreign currency–denominated borrowings among banks (Thailand and Korea), weak corporate governance (Korea and Indonesia), and contagion, which most affected countries viewed as having the weakest fundamentals.

Let me elaborate on these points.

Overvaluation of currencies (all dollar peg countries). Since Asian countries have substantial trade relationships with Japan, the yen depreciation relative to the U.S. dollar meant that some Asian countries on a de facto dollar peg became less competitive vis-à-vis Japan. Korean firms lost ground to Japanese firms as the yen depreciated in 1995–96. Thai firms also lost competitiveness when China de facto devalued its currency (formally unifying the official and market exchange rates) in

1994, and further lost competitiveness as the yen depreciated vis-à-vis the U.S. dollar in 1995–96. In general, the yen depreciation, for example, from 1993 to April 1995, produced the boom in Asia, while the yen appreciation, for example, from April 1995 to 1997, depressed economic activity. The business cycles in Asia are correlated with the yen/dollar cycle. There is a strong indication that the currency crisis of Thailand in 1997–98 was prompted by declining exports in 1995–96, partly explained by the currency overvaluation in real effective terms.

Weak bank and nonbank supervision (all countries). When an economy is growing rapidly, bankruptcy tends to be infrequent and bank portfolios tend to be stronger. However, a slowing economy can weaken the banking system. Thailand's problem with finance companies (nonbank) preceded the currency crisis. Substantial liquidity support (or bailout money) was given to finance companies between January and June 1997, but to no avail. Similarly, merchant banks in Korea accumulated a large volume of nonperforming loans prior to the currency crisis. Currency depreciation only worsened corporate and bank balance sheets. Thus the currency and banking crises occurred, and it is appropriate to view them as "twin crises" (Kaminsky and Reinhart 1999).

Too high short-term capital inflows (all countries). Capital from abroad can support economic development, as explained in the previous section. However, when capital is provided through short-term instruments, such as bank certificates of deposit, short-term securities (such as six-month government securities), and derivatives, it increases the possibility that liquidity could become a problem. This was the experience of Thailand (May-December 1997) and Korea (November-December 1997). Cross-border, short-term bank lending is one indication of the size of short-term loans to a country. The ratio of short-term bank lending to foreign reserves indicates the relative burdensomeness of the short-term liabilities. The ratio was highest in Korea (more than 2), followed by Thailand and Indonesia (more than 1). The ratios for other countries were all less than 1. China and Malaysia, the two countries that escaped IMF programs despite their high capital inflows, had a higher proportion of foreign direct investment as opposed to short-term inflows.

Then there are several idiosyncratic factors.

Mismanagement of foreign reserves (Thailand and Korea). Thailand seriously depleted its foreign reserves in defending the baht in May 1997 against speculative attacks. Since positions were taken in the forward market, the loss of reserves was not revealed until the IMF program was agreed to. Earlier, abandonment of the dollar peg would have significantly reduced the hemorrhage of reserves. Korea also encountered a similar problem. When rollovers to Korean commercial banks were refused by foreign banks, the Bank of Korea made dollar loans to Korean commercial banks to help them avoid default,. However, the foreign reserves were almost exhausted by the time the IMF and the G-7 (Canada, France, Germany, Italy, Japan, the United Kingdom, and the United States) intervened to force foreign banks to roll over (December 24, 1997, agreement).

Excessive foreign currency–denominated borrowings among banks (Thailand and Korea). The dollar peg encouraged corporations and banks to accumulate dollar-denominated liabilities. The interest rates on dollar loans were typically lower than for national currency loans. This became a major problem after the depreciation of the currencies by damaging balance sheets because of the local currency depreciation.

Weak corporate governance (Korea and Indonesia). Corporate governance was weak, particularly in Korea and Indonesia. Conglomerates in Korea expanded their businesses into sectors where they did not have competitive advantages. Overinvestment resulted in failures of several *chaebol* in the first half of 1997 before the Korean won came under pressure in November-December 1997. Indonesian firms borrowed directly from abroad, without managing currency risks.

Strong contagion. The strength of contagion was the most prominent aspect in the Asian currency crises. The crisis spread from Thailand to Indonesia to Korea. Malaysia and the Philippines were also hit hard in currency and stock markets, although they did not need IMF support. China and Hong Kong maintained the dollar peg but experienced major declines in stock price, and their growth rates declined. The extent of contagion in the Asian currency crisis was much larger than the tequila effect in the wake of the Mexican currency devaluation in December 1994. This attracted many researchers to investigate the contagion phenomenon. (See, for example, Eichengreen, Rose, and Wyplosz 1996; Masson 1999a and b; Caramazza, Ricci, and Salgado 2000; and Baig and Goldfajn 1999.)

Caramazza, Ricci, and Salgado (2000) categorized possible reasons for "contagion" of financial crises: fundamentals (common shocks), trade linkage, financial linkage, and a shift in investors' sentiment. Although fundamentals, such as the world interest rate and the U.S. business cycles, help to predict the likelihood that a country will experience a crisis, the explanatory power tends to be low. Trade linkage implies that countries that trade with, or compete in exporting markets with, a crisis-hit country that devalued its currency tend to devalue for competitiveness reasons. Financial linkage includes a situation in which investors rebalance their portfolios after they suffer losses from a crisis country and reassess the risks they incur. Sometimes investors sell assets to meet margin calls. Another factor is a shift in investor sentiment. If investors suddenly wake up from sleep (that is, with no rational calculation) and move to optimize their balance sheets, a large reallocation of assets may take place.

During the Asian currency crisis, several different factors worked to generate contagion. First, the initial baht devaluation certainly affected investors' confidence in the Asian region in general. Investors also looked for countries that looked similar to Thailand (large current account deficits, a fixed exchange rate, and loss of foreign reserves). Since the Philippines, Malaysia, and Indonesia quickly floated their currencies, an attack on the fixed exchange rate regime did not take place in these countries, but in Hong Kong. In late October, the Hong Kong dollar was under pressure. Defending the currency by increasing the interest rate caused stock prices to decline. Speculators were in fact selling short both foreign exchange and stocks—thus the appellation "double play." Although the Hong Kong Monetary Authority (HKMA) defended the peg (currency board), the linkage also induced the HKMA to later intervene in the stock market. The October shock, which originated in Hong Kong, actually went around the world, affecting stock markets in the industrial countries, such as the United Kingdom, the United States, and Japan.

Another interesting example of contagion during the Asian crisis was that the decline in the Indonesian rupiah made Korean investors suffer large losses. In order to make up the loss, Korean investors started to sell Russian and Brazilian securities, thus depressing their bond prices.

RECOVERY OF THE ASIAN ECONOMY

Economic vigor. Most Asian economies experienced negative growth rates in 1998, but by 1999 recovery had set in, and most East Asian economies performed strongly in 2000. The crisis appears to be over. Figures 2.1 and 2.2 show the degree to which Asian economies have regained growth momentum. The sharp recovery, sometimes described as a V-shape recovery, also reveals the intrinsic strength of these economies, especially in manufacturing sectors. The drop in production in 1998 should prove to be a mere blip in long-term economic growth, barring further financial turmoil. All the virtues pointed out in the miracle study—industrial competitiveness, strong exports, foreign direct investment, and high savings and investment—should propel the Asian economies' return to the earlier growth path.

When the economies in Asia were still in the trough of the recession, the World Bank (1998) mapped out a growth recovery strategy. It pointed out that structural reform, a safety net for the poor, and restoring international capital flows are the keys to recovery. The actual pace of recovery in 1999 exceeded what had been predicted in 1998.

Major factors behind the sharp recovery to a relatively high economic growth path (although not quite as high as it used to be) include strong exports, partly due to depreciated exchange rate levels; rebuilding of foreign reserves, partly because of collapsing imports in 1998; fiscal deficits and low interest rates stimulating aggregate demand; various structural reforms to strengthen the financial system; and sustained foreign direct investment inflows.

As pointed out earlier, factors that caused the Asian miracle and factors that are responsible for the Asian currency crises are somewhat different. Most development models emphasize "real factors." Financial variables have not been much emphasized in the literature, with a few exceptions. For example, one of the reasons that Asian countries focused on the real side is that their savings rates are high, so simple intermediation by banks works well. Such savings rates made it pos-

Figure 2.1 GDP Growth Rates. Four NIEs

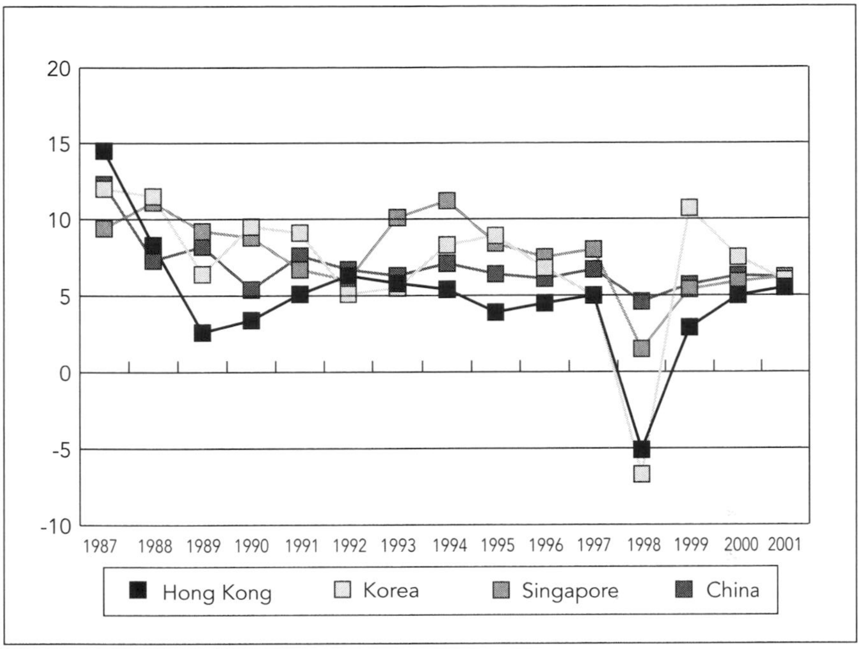

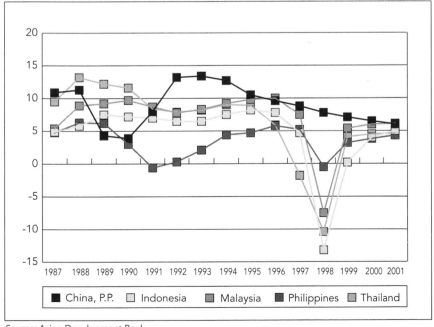

Source: Asian Development Bank.

Figure 2.2 GDP Growth Rates. Other High-Growth Rates

Source: Asian Development Bank.

sible to finance high levels of investment without much reliance on foreign financial portfolio capital. Foreign direct investment was regarded as a good way to introduce foreign technology.

On the other hand, most factors that are believed to have caused the Asian currency crises are "financial." It is of course debatable whether "real" and "financial" factors are separable, as described here. Development obviously needs both real and financial factors. If the financial sector is weakened or subject to large distortions, the real economy will be affected, and if the real economy suffers, then the financial sector will be damaged. But the crucial question is whether we can argue that Asian real economies grew *despite* the primitive state of their financial sectors and that this growth was temporarily arrested when financial institutions collapsed, either in advance of or as a result of the currency crisis.

This brings me back to the point regarding the dichotomy between the real side of the economy and the financial side. The performance of the real side—economic growth, unemployment rates, savings rates, and investment—is basically independent of the financial side: the inflation rate, monetary growth, banking performance, and so on. Most economists believe that this proposition holds true—at least in the long run. Monetarism in principle assumes this dichotomy.

However, skeptics may point out that there is strong interdependence between the real side variables and financial variables. Let us examine possible objections to the separation hypothesis.

In a modern economy a large proportion of investment is intermediated by the financial system. The question that arises is: How could East Asian countries sustain their investment rates with a weak banking system?

Foreign direct investment may have been encouraged by the dollar peg regime, since the stable exchange rate regime reduced the exchange rate risk for investors. Indeed, investors often express their preference for a fixed exchange rate regime. My interpretation, however, is that foreign direct investment has been motivated more by the long-run strength of the host country's economy and low labor costs for the skills that workers have. Fluctuations in the exchange rate can be endured by foreign direct investment firms, so long as the amplitude is not too great. The fluctuations in the exchange rate would affect the rate of short-term portfolio inflows as opposed to foreign direct investment. However, the problem that Asian countries with high savings rate had was "too much" rather than "too little" short-term capital inflows. Thus had the East Asian countries relinquished the dollar peg, short-term portfolio flows would have been smaller and foreign currency–denominated liability correspondingly less under a more flexible exchange rate regime. However, the timing of the exit would have posed a difficult decision.

CONDITIONS FOR ROBUST ECONOMIC GROWTH

Market failure. Among the lessons from the crisis that can inform future development in East Asia are the risks to stability arising from the following sources.

The first factor is herd behavior. Herd behavior suggests that investors' decisions are not always rational. The investment decisions of an individual or a company are influenced by those of others, since the individual's assessment of the yield depends on others' behavior. If others withdraw from a country, then the risk of being left with nonperforming loans increases. Hence investors are likely to move in and out together, a fact that can increase the volatility of financial markets.

Moral hazard is another factor. Suppose that some large banks in a country fail. As the government tends to protect the financial system, sometimes by rescuing financial institutions and sometimes by closing them down, investors tend to recover their investment despite their poor judgment. Support from international financial institutions (such as, for example, the IMF) can also serve to reduce the risk of losses for foreign investors.

In emerging markets, information on the financial positions of banks and corporations is far less adequate than in the markets of advanced countries. Problems associated with asymmetric information—differential information among different stakeholders—are amplified in these economies.

It seems obvious that regulating short-term capital inflows—on the basis of prudential requirements on financial institutions and regaining maneuvering room for monetary policy—is beneficial. (This was pointed out nearly six years ago in the IMF's assessment of the Mexi-

can peso crisis of 1994–95 [IMF 1995].) First, the economies that did
not experience a severe crisis during the Asian crisis had controls on
capital flows. China had extensive capital controls. Taiwan had not
attracted short-term capital inflows because of its political status.
Singapore had not internationalized its currency (because of restrictions on the usage of the Singaporean dollar and borrowing outside
Singapore), unlike Thailand. Second, considering that all severely affected countries—Korea, Thailand, and Indonesia—had extremely
large short-term borrowing from banks in industrial countries. The
ratio of short-term borrowing to foreign reserves exceeded 1 in the
three countries, while the ratio was less than 1 in other countries in
Asia (Ito 2000a). The problem is how to regulate the flows without
choking and distorting the market. Recent research has praised the
Chilean model of regulating capital inflows.

Misallocation of resources, real and financial, because of the imperfection of the markets, or because of moral hazard, asymmetric information, and herd behavior, is known as a market failure.

Optimal government intervention. Where market failures threaten,
the government has a role to play. First, reforms of the financial sector
are imperative in restoring confidence in the economy. A financial
system that is robust despite external shocks should be a key objective:
bank (and nonbank) supervision has to be strengthened, bond markets
have to be developed, and an effective way to regulate portfolio capital
inflows, if these are deemed too volatile, should be devised. Second,
the strength of "real" factors needs to be exploited. Infrastructure (such
as roads, public transportation, and public education) must be enhanced. Third, regulation has to be strengthened as an economy moves
into more developed stages. Natural monopoly needs to be replaced
with a competition policy, state banks have to be privatized or limited
in their roles, and trade protection must be dramatically lowered. Any
social protection should be done through direct subsidies instead of
through the protection of selected industrial sectors. With these reforms, the likelihood of sustained growth of the Asian economies is
much greater.

The role of the government both in creating a "miracle" and in
preventing crises cannot be overemphasized. To achieve rapid and
steady growth, the government must ensure macroeconomic and

political stability, facilitate industrialization by ensuring that the labor force is educated, and attract foreign direct investment. For crisis prevention, the government's role is to ensure that correct and standardized information is available to the public, that bank supervision is strengthened, and that some prudential regulation of capital inflows is undertaken.

The impossible trinity and resolution. It is well known—and any international finance textbook explains why—that it is impossible to have the following three regimes:

- A fixed exchange rate
- Free capital mobility
- An independent monetary policy.

This is sometimes called the impossible trinity. Without capital controls, the fixed exchange rate means that the interest rate would be equal to the world level, possibly adjusted for risk premium. Then monetary policy cannot be independent.

Policies adopted by Asian countries in the 1990s prior to the crisis can be regarded as challenging the impossible trinity. Capital inflows stimulated the domestic economy, but often to the level of overheating. Moreover, the interest rate could not be raised to dampen domestic overheating, because higher interest rates would invite more capital inflows. In the case of Thailand, easy monetary policy was blamed for causing a bubble. But in the absence of capital controls, monetary policy was bound by the world market, and offshore markets made it very easy to move money in and out of Thailand.

The crisis forced several Asian countries to adopt a floating exchange rate regime.[3] This is the case for Korea, the Philippines, Thailand, and Indonesia. These countries have retained capital mobility and attained some monetary policy independence, but they have to contend with volatility in their currency values vis-à-vis the U.S. dollar. Nevertheless, a floating exchange rate is one way out of the impossible trinity.

Another way out of the impossible trinity is to introduce capital controls and other measures to restrict capital flows. With capital controls, it is possible to regain an independent monetary policy. China has maintained strict controls on capital account transactions, although there are significant leakages. In September 1998, Malaysia adopted some controls on outflows in response to the crisis. These are examples of countries seeking to regain monetary independence with a fixed exchange rate.

Yet another way to circumvent the impossible trinity is to abandon an independent monetary policy and allow domestic interest rates to approach international rates. A currency board is a variant of a rigid regime to maintain a fixed exchange rate regime. This is the regime used by Hong Kong since 1989.

Table 2.6 shows how economies have responded to the dilemma posed by the impossible trinity.

Financial reform. Strengthening the financial system and strengthening capital markets are equally important and require government initiative.

Several East Asian countries are still having to cope with nonperforming loans that mushroomed during the financial crises. The nonperforming loan ratio among Thai banks went up to nearly 50 percent of loans in 1999 and then started to decline, slowly. Indonesian commercial banks are still significantly undercapitalized. Bad debts that have accumulated in an agency to manage assets of failed banks (IBRA) have not been sold or dealt with at the planned pace. Several investment funds in various provinces of China (ITICs) have failed. In Korea, some *chaebol* need restructuring, with important implications for

Table 2.6 How Economies Responded to the Problem of the Impossible Trinity

Response	Fixed exchange rate	Free capital mobility	Independent monetary policy	Economies
Impossible trinity	Yes	Yes	Yes	Precrisis Asia except for China and Hong Kong.
Floating	No	Yes	Yes	Korea, Philippines, Thailand, Indonesia
Capital control	Yes	No	Yes	China post-September 1998, Malaysia
Currency board	Yes	Yes	No	Hong Kong

Note: China maintains that its exchange rate regime is not a fixed exchange rate system but a flexible exchange rate system. However, the data reveal that it fluctuates very little against the U.S. dollar, and the market regards it as a de facto fixed exchange rate system. Korea, the Philippines, Thailand, and Indonesia after the crisis are categorized as "floating," not "clean floating."

banks that lend to them. Each country is taking steps to clean up bank portfolios, but it seems that a few more years will be required to bring the most seriously affected financial institutions back to health.

Once past problems have been resolved, a new regime can be introduced. It should have several components, as listed below. In East Asia, some of these components are already in place, while others remain to be put into practice in the future.

- A supervisory regime.
- A legal framework that has an explicit procedure for dealing with failing companies and seizing collateral without delay. This requires a bankruptcy law and a legal system able to implement it expeditiously.
- The development of capital markets (markets for risk capital).

First, an effective supervisory policy enforced by experienced professionals needs to be introduced to maintain robust banking, securities, and insurance businesses. In general, an independent supervisory agency is needed to avoid pressures from politicians and the fiscal authority. Which banks should be allowed to fail ought to be based solely on the health of banks. A policy of forbearance will most likely result in increasing final resolution costs.

In the aftermath of the 1997–98 crisis, the seriously affected East Asian countries introduced independent supervisory agencies. Their immediate role was to perform due diligence and evaluate the balance sheets of banks, to identify nonperforming loans and expected losses and determine whether or not banks were solvent.

Second, after identifying nonperforming loans, banks have to resolve them. Often, that involves (at least having an option of) forcing a bankruptcy and collecting collateral. Creditors, if a majority of them agree, should have a right to force bankruptcy on a firm that refuses to pay overdue interest payments. The legal procedure should be spelled out clearly and implemented. Judges must be trained for making rulings on the basis of a fair treatment of both creditors and borrowers as well as among creditors.

Third, East Asian financial markets need to acquire the depth and expertise to minimize mismatches of maturity and currency. The double mismatch at the time of the crisis was due to the weakness of capital markets. In general, long-term capital should be supplied by long-term investors via long-term investment instruments. Equity investors tend to ignore short-term volatility and keep investments through volatile periods. This kind of behavior was observed in the financial crises of Mexico and Asia. Long-term bonds can be bought and sold by many kinds of investors, including short-term investors. However, until the long-term bonds mature, the issuers will not have to face demands for payment. A liquidity shortage is far less frequent for long-term bond issuers than for short-term bond issuers. Therefore long-term bond and equity markets are good for countries that need long-term capital for investment.

Although many agree on the desirability of developing the capital market, its development requires several prerequisites. The market infrastructure, with a trading, settlement, and clearing system, should be developed, as well as securities exchange rules. An independent securities exchange commission needs to be established to monitor transactions for fairness.

Unlike bank depositors, securities investors need to be informed of the risks and prospects of corporations in which they invest. In order to disseminate investment information, credit rating agencies are essential. Another important element for disclosure is accounting rules. Accounting rules should be transparent so that domestic and foreign investors can assess balance sheets and profit-loss statements without difficulty. Toward that end, credit rating agencies and other credit analysts have a significant role to play.

CONCLUDING REMARKS

The East Asian countries have been remarkably effective in nurturing manufacturing sectors able to compete in international markets. They were less successful in developing the financial sector, hence financial vulnerability persisted even during the miracle years. This vulnerability significantly contributed to the crisis of 1997–98. In Thailand, a banking crisis preceded the currency crisis, while in Korea, large external liabilities contributed to vulnerability to contagion from Thailand and Indonesia.

Four years have passed since the onset of the Thai currency crisis. Most East Asian economies seem to be recovering strongly from a recession in 1998. Some economies are reaching a high growth path that was typical before the crisis. Others are still struggling, but mainly because of an unstable political regime. To make the current recovery more permanent and provide a buffer against external shocks in the future, East Asian countries have to strengthen their financial markets.

An important observation in this paper is that the success of the manufacturing sector and the weakness of financial sectors coexisted in the past. The currency crisis of 1997–98 was strongly affected by the latter factor. The crisis was not the result of the failure of the manufacturing sector. Therefore, once the weakness of the financial sector is addressed, East Asian economies can achieve sustainable high growth rates again. With stronger financial markets and institutions, growth is less susceptible to external shocks. In order to strengthen financial and capital markets, the adoption of an appropriate currency regime and strong financial supervision are important.

NOTES

1. For other perspectives on industrial policy in East Asia, see chapters 6, 8, 9, 10, and 12 of this volume.

2. The phrase "Flying Geese Pattern" was coined by Akamatsu (1961). But the original meaning was more like a product cycle, that is, a rise and fall of output of a particular industry in a developing country. Now it is used in a different sense, as explained in the text. Continuous economic development requires physical and human capital. Such requirement for a new industry is filled by profits from the existing industries and by trained work force and educated new graduates. A combination of product cycle theory with a hypothesis on dynamic changes in industrial structure resulted in the recent meaning of the Flying Geese Pattern. See also Murphy, Shleifer, and Vishny 1989a, b; and Matsuyama 1992, for related research in the field of new growth theory.

3. However, see chapter 5, by McKinnon.

REFERENCES

Akamatsu, Kaname. 1961. "A Theory of Unbalanced Growth in the World Economy." *Weltwirtschaftliches Archiv* 86 (2): 196–217.

Asian Development Bank. Various years. *Asian Development Outlook*. Manila, Philippines.

Baig, Taimur, and Ilan Goldfajn, 1999, "Financial Market Contagion in the Asian Crisis." *IMF Staff Papers* 46 (June): 167–95.

Campos, Jose Edgardo, and Hilton L. Root. 1997. *The Key to the Asian Miracle: Making Shared Growth Credible.* Washington, D.C.: Brookings Institution.

Caramazza, Francesco, Luca Ricci, and Ranil Salgado, 2000 "Trade and Financial Contagion in Currency Crises." IMF Working Paper WP/00/55, March. Washington, D.C.

Corsetti, Giancarlo, Paolo Pesenti, and Nouriel Roubini. 2000. "Fundamental Determinants of the Asian Crisis: The Role of Financial Fragility and External Imbalances," in T. Ito and A. O. Krueger, eds., *Regional and Global Capital Flows: Macroeconomic Causes and Consequences.* University of Chicago Press.

Eichengreen, Barry. 1999. *Toward a New International Financial Architecture: A Practical Post-Asia Agenda.* Washington, D.C.: Institute for International Economics.

Eichengreen, Barry, Andrew K. Rose, and Charles Wyplosz. 1996, "Contagious Currency Crises: First Tests." *Scandinavian Journal of Economics* 98 (4): 463–84.

Frankel, Jeffrey A., and Shang-Jin Wei. 1994. "Yen Bloc or Dollar Bloc? Exchange Rate Policies of the East Asian Economies," in T. Ito and A. O. Krueger, eds., *Macroeconomic Linkage: Savings, Exchange Rates, and Capital Flows.* University of Chicago Press.

Goldstein, Morris. 1998. *The Asian Financial Crisis: Causes, Cures, and Systemic Implications.* Washington, D.C.: Institute for International Economics.

Hunter, William C., George G. Kaufman, and Thomas H. Krueger, eds.. 2000. *The Asian Financial Crisis: Origins, Implications, and Solutions.* Boston: Kluwer Academic.

IMF (International Monetary Fund). 1995. *International Capital Markets 1995.* Washington, D.C.

———. 1997. *World Economic Outlook 1997.* Washington, D.C.

Ito, Takatoshi. 1997. "What Can Developing Countries Learn from East Asia's Economic Growth?" *Annual World Bank Conference on Development Economics 1997.* 183–200.

———. 2000a. "Capital Flows in Asia" in Sebastian Edwards, ed., *Capital Flows to Emerging Markets.* Chicago, University of Chicago Press: 255–296.

———. 2000b. "Perspectives on Asian Economic Growth: Neoclassical Growth vs. Flying Geese Growth" in Economic Planning Agency, Japan, ed., *The East Asian Economic Growth with Industrial Structural Changes,* Chapter 1, Economic Planning Agency, Tokyo.

Ito, Takatoshi, and Keisuke Orii. 2000. "Changes in Industrial Structure in East Asian Countries: Common Characteristics and Idiosyncratic Factors" in Economic Planning Agency, Japan, ed., *The East Asian Economic Growth with Industrial Structural Changes,* Chapter 1, Economic Planning Agency, Tokyo.

Ito, Takatoshi, and Luiz Pereira da Silva. 1999. "The Credit Crunch in Thailand during the 1997–98 Crisis: Theoretical and Operational Issues of the JEXIM Survey." *EXIM Review* (19) 2: 1–40.

Kaminsky, Graciela, and Carmen Reinhart. 1999. "The Twin Crises: The Causes of Banking and Balance-of-Payments problems." *American Economic Review* (89) 3: 473–500.

Krugman, Paul. 1994. "The Myth of Asia's Miracle." *Foreign Affairs* November/December: 62–78.

Lane, Timothy, Atish Ghosh, Javier Hamann, Steven Phillips, Marianne Schulze-Ghattas, and Tsidi Tsikata. 1999. "IMF-Supported Programs in Indonesia, Korea, and Thailand: A Preliminary Assessment." IMF Occasional Paper, No. 178, Washington, D.C.

Masson, Paul. 1999a. "Contagion: Macroeconomic Models with Multiple Equilibria" *Journal of International Money and Finance* (18): 587–602.

———. 1999b. "Contagion: Monsoonal Effects, Spillovers, and Jumps between Multiple Equilibria." In P. R. Agenor, M. Miller, D. Vines, and A. Weber, eds., *The Asian Financial Crisis: Causes, Contagion and Consequences.* Cambridge, U.K.: Cambridge University Press.

Matsuyama, Kiminori. 1992. "The Market Size, Entrepreneurship, and the Big Push." *Journal of the Japanese and International Economies* (6): 347–64.

Montes, Manuel F. 1998. *The Currency Crisis in Southeast Asia.* Updated Edition. Singapore: Institute of Southeast Asian Studies.

Murphy, Kevin M., Andrei Shleifer, and Robert W. Vishny. 1989a. "Industrialization and the Big Push." *Journal of Political Economy* 97 (5, October): 1003–26.

———. 1989b. "Income Distribution, Market Size, and Industrialization," *Quarterly Journal of Economics* 104 (3): 537–564.

Mussa, Michael, Paul Masson, Alexander Swoboda, Esteban Jadresic, Paolo Mauro, and Andrew Berg. 2000. "Exchange Rate Regimes in an Increasingly Integrated World Economy." IMF Occasional Paper, No. 193. Washington, D.C.

Ogawa, Eiji, and Takatoshi Ito. 2000. "On the Desirability of a Regional Basket Currency Arrangement." NBER Working Paper W8002, November (available at http://papers.nber.org/papers/W8002).

Radelet, Steven, and Jeffrey D. Sachs. 1998. "The East Asian Financial Crisis: Diagnosis, Remedies, and Prospects." *Brookings Papers on Economic Activity* (1): 1–90.

Sarel, Michael. 1995. "Growth in East Asia: What We Can and What We Cannot Infer from It." IMF Working Paper 95/98. Washington, D.C.

UNIDO (United Nations Industrial Development Organization). 1999. *Industrial Statistics Database 1999* (three-digit level of ISIC Code on diskette),Vienna, Austria.

Williamson, John. 2000. *Exchange Rate Regimes for Emerging Markets: Reviving the Intermediate Option.* Washington, D.C.: Institute for International Economics.

Woo, Wing Thye, Jeffrey D. Sachs, and Klaus Schwab. 2000. *The Asian Financial Crisis: Lessons for a Resilient Asia.* Cambridge, Mass.: MIT Press.

World Bank. 1993. *The East Asian Miracle: Economic Growth and Public Policy.* New York: Oxford University Press.

———. 1998. *East Asia: The Road to Recovery.* Washington, D.C.

Yoshitomi, Masaru, and Sayuri Shirai. 2000. "Technical Background Paper for Policy Recommendations for Preventing Another Capital Account Crisis." Tokyo: Asian Development Bank Institute.

Young, Alwyn. 1992. "A Tale of Two Cities: Factor Accumulation and Technical Change in Hong Kong and Singapore." *NBER Macroeconomic Annual 1992.* Cambridge, Mass: MIT Press.

CHAPTER 3

TECHNOLOGICAL CHANGE AND GROWTH IN EAST ASIA: MACRO VERSUS MICRO PERSPECTIVES

Howard Pack

The rapid growth in a number of Asian countries has been termed the East Asian miracle. Even before the Asian crisis began in late 1997, a contentious debate arose about whether there had indeed been any miracle or whether the entire epoch of astonishingly high growth rates in per capita income was simply the result of Soviet-style high levels of investment (Krugman 1994). Some who held the latter view now claim prescience, having argued that the rapid growth in capital was bound to encounter diminishing returns. Nevertheless, it is far from clear whether the newly industrializing economies (NIEs) in question exhibited unusually low total factor productivity (TFP) growth or whether diminishing productivity was an important contributor to the ensuing crisis. Indeed, the unexpected and remarkably rapid turnaround in gross domestic product (GDP) in 1999 and early 2000 in the Republic of Korea, Malaysia, and Thailand suggests that the accumulation of capital, skilled labor, and technological knowledge was a stable long-term phenomenon. The double-digit increases in GDP from the bottom of the 1998 trough suggest a robust supply response to changing policy parameters.[1] Although the data for evaluating TFP growth before and after the crisis will become available only slowly, it seems likely that slow TFP growth will ultimately not be seen as the major culprit in precipitating the decline, no more than it was in precipitating the Great Depression of the 1930s in the United States and Western Europe.

Liquidity problems, inadequate banking supervision, irrationally exuberant international portfolio investors, and less than stellar performance by the international financial community are all more serious candidates for the proximate cause of the decline.

Macro measures of low or zero TFP growth contradict microeconomic evidence at the firm and industry level that traces the technological mastery of individual companies. Before attempting to reconcile low TFP growth at the aggregate level with growing competence at the firm level, it is first necessary to evaluate the nature of the evidence adduced in support of the "accumulationist" view and to match this against the documentation that the successful "assimilation" of technology has been a critical dimension of success over 35 years (Nelson and Pack 1999).

Resolving these issues is fundamental to understanding the Asian financial crisis that began in 1997. If productivity growth was low throughout the period of the miracle, then the onset of diminishing returns was an inevitable consequence of rapid accumulation. Even then, if investment was financed in a responsible manner, no crisis should have occurred, only slower growth. If, on the contrary, TFP was not low, the slowing in growth was not inevitable. In either case, the search for the source of the crisis should be sought in other characteristics of the growth process such as the short-term financing of long-term projects (for extensive analysis of the causes of the Asian financial crisis, see Furman and Stiglitz 1999; World Bank 1998).

The major finding of the *East Asian Miracle* (World Bank 1993) is that in the economies considered, especially Korea and Taiwan (China), factor accumulation accounted for two-thirds to three-quarters of aggregate growth, the remainder being due to growth in total factor productivity. In addition, the World Bank study presents evidence that the performance of the Asian economies in terms of TFP was superior to that of less-developed countries. The book does not claim that most of aggregate growth was due to TFP growth or that TFP growth was unusually high by world standards, although it was greater than that in other developing countries.

In interpretations of the performance of economies such as Korea and Taiwan that had exceptionally rapid rates of capital accumulation, two issues are intertwined: the division of aggregate growth between factor accumulation and growth in productivity and the manner in which these economies avoided significant diminishing returns to capital given rapidly growing capital/labor ratios. These issues are captured in figure 3.1, which shows three production functions: oa, oa', and ob. oa is the initial production function in the developing countries, oa' is a more productive version of oa, and ob is international best practice, assumed not to change for expositional convenience. Capital accumulation that raises the capital/labor ratio from k_1 to k_2 would lead to a reduction in the marginal product of capital, F_K, if the economy moved along oa from 1 to 2. Yet many years of rapid capital accumulation did not result in significant diminishing returns. What is the explanation for this?[2]

The standard explanation, for the United States from 1900 to 1950, was proposed by Solow (1957), namely, that "technical change" shifted the function to oa' and permitted a move to 2' rather than 2, reducing or offsetting the effect of a decline in F_K along oa. Extensive microeconomic evidence from the Asian NIEs supports the Solow view, although with an interpretative twist. The NIEs, being technological laggards at the beginning of their development process, borrowed much

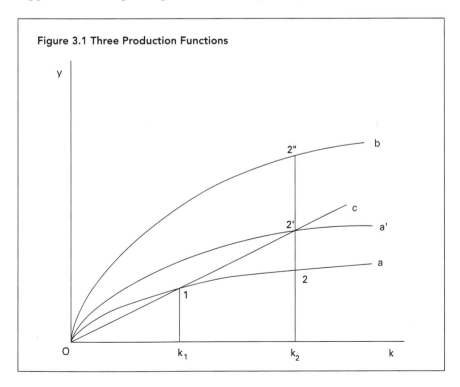

Figure 3.1 Three Production Functions

of their technology from more-advanced economies and devoted considerable effort to absorbing it productively. In contrast, Solow's interpretation depended on technological advances within the United States, then the international best-practice country, although the precise source was left open. Within the standard neoclassical production theoretic framework, the critical empirical question is the magnitude of the shift from oa to oa'.

Simply considering points such as 1 and 2' suppresses considerable knowledge about the dynamic process. The move in the NIEs was characterized by (a) a rapid growth in the relative importance of large firms that used modern technology and the parallel decline of smaller craft firms (and the agricultural and informal sector) and (b) a dramatic shift in the sectoral mix of production, away from agriculture and labor-intensive industrial products and toward increasingly complex goods (Nelson and Pack 1999). These two characteristics imply that the investment process and technological change were inextricably linked. The investment necessary to realize these changes embodied technologies new to the firms and countries, although obviously not new to the world. This was the view in the contributions of Kaldor (1957) and, in a different form, of Solow (1960). These structural shifts have important implications for interpreting some of the growth-accounting exercises that purport to demonstrate low TFP growth.

An alternate interpretation of the evolution in the Asian newly industrializing economies is given in figure 3.1, where the assumed production function is oc, which goes through points 1 and 2'; oc may be linear, as drawn, or may exhibit very little curvature, depending on the assumptions made. Endogenous growth models of the AK variety generate a linear production function, the exponent of K being unity because of a variety of hypothesized externalities. Even if the exponent of K is 0.8 rather than unity, the decline in F_K will be small relative to a standard neoclassical production function that uses the share of capital in the national accounts—about 0.25 in the United States and United Kingdom—as the relevant parameter. Because the Asian NIEs are small open economies, oc could also capture the changing composition of trade in countries that successively enter more capital-intensive sectors as their capital/labor ratios grow. Assuming that the wage/rental ratio is determined by factor price equalization, any tendency toward a decrease in F_K will be precluded by a change in the composition of trade.[3] Although each of these explanations has some power, their contribution to forestalling a decline in F_K is small relative to the diffusion and absorption of technology.

A large body of firm-level case studies finds a shift from oa to oa'. In contrast, some macro research argues that the shift was small and that accumulation was the major source of growth. This divergence between the rich description of successful learning in individual firms and macro production analyses is the core of disagreement about the experience of the NIEs.

This chapter evaluates the macro evidence that accumulation of capital was the key to development and then presents some of the micro case studies suggesting that the local production function shifted from oa to oa' due to the transfer of technology and its successful assimilation in the manufacturing sector, the major growth sector in the NIEs. I do not consider other sectors such as services, public and private organizational changes (including the provision of infrastructure), or development of the financial system (see Stiglitz 1993 for a discussion of the role of the financial sector in the development of the NIEs).

THE CONTEXT

Since the publication of Tsao's (1985) article, the extent to which growth in total factor productivity has played an important role in the development of the NIEs has been the subject of considerable research (Bosworth and Collins 1996; Hsieh 1997; Kim and Lau 1994; Nelson and Pack 1999; World Bank 1993; Young 1992, 1995). In the attempt to parse growth between capital accumulation and TFP, attention is often deflected from a major part of the success: with historically unprecedented accumulation, these economies did not encounter rapidly diminishing returns to capital, but successfully assimilated the new capital.

Table 3.1 provides comparisons for a number of economies including Japan and Germany, the star performers of the Organisation for Economic Co-operation and Development (OECD) nations in the post–World War II period. The growth rates of the capital stock alone are shown, because the growth of the labor force differs less among the countries. Korea and Taiwan experienced capital growth rates more than double that in Germany and 25 percent greater than that in Japan during their period of fastest growth.[4] Singapore's was even higher, and the new NIEs—Indonesia, Malaysia, and Thailand—with even less industrial history, absorbed capital without suffering declines in their level of TFP. German and Japanese TFP growth rates were positive in the 1950s and roughly the same as many of the estimates for Korea and Taiwan during the first two decades of their accelerated growth.

This achievement is impressive insofar as Germany and Japan had achieved very high levels of per capita income well before World War II and had extensive production experience in many complex sectors. Germany was the world leader in sectors such as chemicals during the nineteenth century, and Japan launched battleships during the Japanese-Russo war of 1905, implying a formidable array of industrial skills. In both of the Axis powers, most of their organizational and human capital survived World War II and was redeployed from military to

TABLE 3.1 Rates of Growth of Capital Stock, 1950–90

Economy	1950–60	1960–70	1970–80	1980–90
Asian newly industrializing economies				
Indonesia	0.055	0.030	0.113	0.098
Korea, Rep. of		0.125	0.147	0.108
Malaysia	—	0.097	0.109	0.082
Singapore	—	0.166	0.144	0.095
Taiwan, China	—	0.146	0.146	0.082
Thailand	0.089	0.133	0.096	0.075
Organisation for Economic Co-operation and Development				
France	0.062	0.077	0.054	0.029
Germany	0.067	0.062	0.037	0.023
Japan	0.117	0.145	0.092	0.053
Africa				
Ghana	0.032	0.067	0.024	0.011
Kenya	0.046	0.020	0.047	0.016
Nigeria	0.071	0.070	0.142	0.007
Southeast Asia				
India	0.044	0.058	0.045	0.048
Pakistan	0.078	0.138	0.052	0.057
South America				
Argentina	0.043	0.047	0.047	0.000
Brazil	0.068	0.062	0.099	0.037
Mexico	0.082	0.082	0.084	0.037

— Not available.

Note: The growth rate of capital is the fitted growth rate of the fixed capital stock from Nehru and Dhareshwar (1994).

peacetime pursuits. It was not necessary to accumulate these skills largely de nouveau as in Korea and Taiwan. New plant and equipment in Germany and Japan were invested in an organizational and technical environment in which there was considerable knowledge of how to use them effectively (on the interpretation of organization and its implications for productivity, see Stiglitz 1988). Merely restoring the physical plant lost during the war was sufficient to achieve high rates of productivity growth in the period in question.[5] Even under such favorable conditions and given the extensive productivity gains to be obtained from U.S. technology (the most advanced in the world at that time), these economies could achieve TFP growth rates no greater than 2 percent.

Contrast this with the experience of Korea and Taiwan (as well as that of the other NIEs). Both had little industrial experience and no national capacity for managing the public sector, given long periods of colonization.[6] In the 1950s, before Confucian values generated a miraculous transformation from hindrance to guarantor of economic growth, political instability, inflation, and corruption were common. In Korea virtually no buildings or equipment remained after three years of intensive fighting up and down the peninsula from 1950 to 1952, and the levels of education were relatively low compared with those of Japan and Germany. Despite such unpromising initial conditions, the huge accumulation of factors was successfully absorbed, with no decline in TFP *levels*, by even the most pessimistic assessment. Compared with this achievement, the division of the total growth rate between accumulation and TFP is a second-order question.[7] In contemporary terms, very few economists looking forward from 2000 would argue that Bangladesh, Bolivia, or Tanzania could avoid a decrease in their TFP levels if an inflow of aid increased their accumulation rates to those shown in table 3.1 for Korea and Taiwan. Indeed, Nigeria's capital growth rate in the 1970s matched those of the NIEs, yet it experienced limited growth in per capita income.

Numerous studies document that individual manufacturing firms in the Asian countries were much less productive than their OECD counterparts when they established production and then expended considerable effort to move toward OECD best practice (Enos and Pak 1987; Hobday 1995; Kim 1997; Goto and Odagiri 1997). They succeeded in raising their TFP levels toward those of the OECD countries, but remain far from parity. For example, many Korean firms and industries exhibit less than half the TFP levels of their OECD equivalents (Pilat 1994; McKinsey Global Institute 1998), a phenomenon discussed later in the chapter. Firms did not simply invest and move along a freely available, perfectly understood international best-practice production function; rather they imported technology in various forms and then systematically learned to achieve improved but not necessarily best-practice productivity with it.

A few prominent studies of aggregate productivity growth suggest that the Asian countries simply followed an updated version of primitive accumulation, their success being easy to explain if their high savings rates can be replicated (Young 1992, 1995; Kim and Lau 1994). However. a number of problems undermine confidence in their results. Understanding the problems of these studies is important for understanding the Asian experience. Both the empirical literature that claims to document the overwhelming importance of capital accumulation and many variants of endogenous growth theory that argue that there are no diminishing returns bring the discussion back to the investment-driven model of growth. As the many countries such as Algeria, Panama, Portugal, and Poland that invested more than 20 percent of GDP from 1960 to 1985 and failed to grow rapidly demonstrate, capital accumulation is necessary, but far from sufficient, for accelerating growth rates of per capita income.

In the period from 1960 to 1996, the four tigers (Hong Kong, China, Korea, Singapore, and Taiwan) did not waste investment. There were few sectors that were egregiously inefficient and few profligate investments in the nontraded goods sector. This general absence of white elephants was partly the result of the surveillance of the investment process by the relevant governments. Although it is fashionable to disparage government capacities in light of the financial problems of late 1997 and 1998, in a third of a century of massive capital accumulation, the four tigers made few reckless investments. Although some governments, for example in Korea, may have erred in promoting specific sectors, particularly the metalworking, machinery, and chemical complex, the worst that can be said is that the improvement in growth rates was small given the opportunity cost of the loss of higher returns in sectors that were not promoted. There is no evidence in the four tigers of the egregious inefficiency that prevails in many countries—

for example, negative value added at world prices. Whether such discipline was lost in the past few years remains an open question until more evidence is available about the most recent developments in productivity.

The story is not quite the same in the newer NIEs—Indonesia, Malaysia, and Thailand. All three made significant bad investment choices in the 1980s and 1990s. Perhaps reflecting the hubris of being among the "miracle" economies, all undertook investments that, ex ante, undoubtedly decreased the levels of TFP. These ranged from the fixed-wing aircraft industry in Indonesia to extensive overbuilding of office buildings in Thailand to the national car industry in Malaysia. However, even these well-documented investment errors may not have loomed large in the aggregate. For example, the Indonesian aircraft sector, initiated by President Suharto's successor, B. F. Habibie, was begun around 1980, and, despite its well-known inefficiency, Indonesia continued to prosper for the next 15 years and aggregate TFP for the entire economy continued to grow throughout the period. Although the three "follower" NIEs certainly made larger errors in investment allocations than the original tigers, their impact on aggregate productivity was not a major factor in the problems encountered in 1997 and 1998.

MACRO STUDIES OF PRODUCTIVITY GROWTH

Many TFP growth rates for a broad sample of the NIEs and other economies have been derived (Bosworth and Collins 1996; Nehru and Dhareshwar 1994). The range of calculated values is quite high, and it is not clear how one would choose the best point estimate. It is possible to adjust and refine input and output measures endlessly. The current debate on Asian TFP growth is reminiscent of that among a number of researchers in the late 1960s about whether proper measurement of inputs in the United States would show that all growth in productivity could be accounted for by properly measured inputs (Griliches and Jorgenson 1967; Denison 1979). The result of that literature is inconclusive, hinging largely on definitions.

Two forms of formal analysis have been used to examine the contribution of factor accumulation and TFP to aggregate growth, namely, growth accounting and econometric estimation of production functions. Before examining these estimates, I briefly examine the stylized facts.

Figure 3.2 shows growth rates for the capital/labor ratio and total factor productivity by regions using data from Bosworth and Collins (1996).[8] The East Asian group, largely the economies of interest here, had higher rates of capital deepening and higher rates of TFP growth than other regions for the period 1960–94. Their study, using consistent adjustments across countries, suggests that there was something different about the ability of the Asian NIEs to absorb capital productively. Although their TFP growth rates were not "miraculous," they were higher than those in other regions in which economies faced the easier task of absorbing fewer factors of production. Nehru and Dhareshwar (1994) obtain similar results. The (relatively) high TFP growth rates may have prevented diminishing returns that could have caused a decline in the very high rates of saving, the latter being a phenomenon for which no completely adequate account has been adumbrated (Deaton and Paxson 1994).

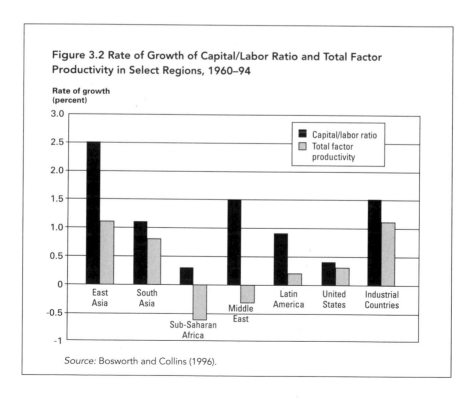

Figure 3.2 Rate of Growth of Capital/Labor Ratio and Total Factor Productivity in Select Regions, 1960–94

Source: Bosworth and Collins (1996).

Growth Accounting

Growth accounting employs observed factor shares from the national accounts to estimate partial output elasticities.[9] The change in the aggregate amount of inputs is calculated using the Tornqvist index,

$$(3.1) \quad T = \Sigma_i \left[1/2(S_{i,t} + S_{i,t-1})(\ln x_{i,t} - \ln x_{i,t-1}) \right]$$

where $S_{i,t}$ is the observed share of factor x_i in period t. This is subtracted from the log difference in output to obtain TFP growth,

$$(3.2) \quad A^* = \log(Y_t / Y_{t-1}) - T.$$

A key question is the economic behavior underlying equation 3.1 particularly, the determinants of $S_{i,t}$. But there are also important issues about the measurement of some of the $x_{i,t}$ (Hsieh 1997). Six questions arise about the measurement and interpretation of the $S_{i,t}$:

- Are all countries on the same production function?
- Are the $S_{i,t}$ affected by technical change?
- What dynamic processes generate the $S_{i,t}$?
- Are input markets distorted?
- Are Y_t and $x_{i,t}$ measured correctly?
- What are the implications of using a cost function rather than a production function?

Are countries on the same production function? Some growth-accounting studies assume that an identical international production function, with identical parameters, exists for all countries and that firms can move along it. Yet there are significant problems with this view. For example, if Korea was on the same production function as the United States in the 1980s, given the differences in capital/labor ratios and factor shares (table 3.2), the implied elasticity of substitution, σ, is 0.4, lower than most econometric estimates.[10] The difficulty with assuming a universally identical production function can be seen in a slightly different way by considering countries with roughly the same capital/labor ratio and examining their factor shares. Singapore and New Zealand had similar capital/labor ratios during the 1980s, but New Zealand's capital share was 0.38 compared with Singapore's 0.52. Figure 3.3 plots K/L against S_K for a number of countries for the 1980s. If all countries are on the same production function, the data imply either a low elasticity of substitution or wage suppression in countries with lower capital/labor ratios. Both lead to difficulties for growth accounting. As will be seen in the next section, a low value of σ combined with labor-augmenting technical change could maintain constant capital shares within a country. But this would imply that $S_{K,t}$ is itself affected by technical progress. If wages were suppressed, $S_{K,t}$ cannot be viewed as providing information about the elasticity of output with respect to capital. Yet a high value of $S_{K,t}$ is crucial to the findings

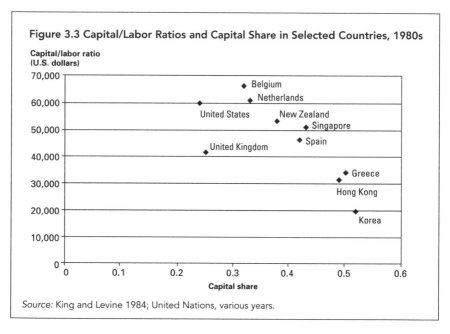

Figure 3.3 Capital/Labor Ratios and Capital Share in Selected Countries, 1980s

Source: King and Levine 1984; United Nations, various years.

Table 3.2 Share of Capital in Gross Domestic Product and Aggregate Capital/ Labor Ratios, Average for 1980s

Economies	Share of capital	Capital/labor ratio
Belgium	0.32	66,294
Netherlands	0.33	60,943
United States	0.24	60,057
New Zealand	0.38	53,461
Singapore	0.52	50,934
Spain	0.42	46,262
United Kingdom	0.25	41,672
Greece	0.5	34,123
Hong Kong	0.49	31,200
Korea, Rep. of	0.52	19,349

Source: Share of capital is calculated from United Nations (various years). Ratio of capital to labor is calculated from King and Levine (1994) and World Bank (1998).

of low TFP growth because the fastest-growing factor—capital—is weighted by a large number.

The endogenous determination of $S_{i,t}$.[11] Even ignoring the meaning of moving along an international production function when $S_{i,t}$ differs across countries, $S_{i,t}$ within a country may themselves be endogenous, reflecting technical or structural change (Nelson and Pack 1999). Existing estimates make very strong assumptions about the nature of technological change; for example, growth-accounting exercises such as Young (1992, 1995) and Bosworth and Collins (1996) assume Hicks-neutral technical change. But this assumption cannot be supported by independent production function estimates for one country, given the impossibility theorem of Diamond, McFadden, and Rodríquez (1972), which shows that, for a general neoclassical production function, the elasticity of substitution and the bias of technical change cannot be estimated simultaneously.[12]

Nelson and Pack (1999) show that $S_{i,t}$ are endogenous by assuming a neoclassical production function $Q = f(K, mL)$ in which m represents Harrod-neutral (labor-augmenting) technological advance. The rate of change of factor shares, $S_{i,t}$, is a function of the elasticity of substitution, σ, and m, or

(3.3) $S_K^* = [S_L^0 (1 - \sigma) / \sigma] (m - k^*)$

(3.4) $S_L^* = [S_K^0 (1 - \sigma) / \sigma] (k^* - m)$

where k^* is the growth rate of the capital/labor ratio. Equations 3.3 and 3.4 show that the factor shares used in calculating the Tornqvist index are affected by both technical change, in this case labor-augmenting, and changes in capital intensity. If σ is high, close to unity, a high k^* will not drive down the share of capital even if m is small. If σ is low, a high value of m could prevent a fall in S_k. In growth-accounting exercises, $S_{i,t}$ are assumed to provide information about the elasticity of output with respect to factor inputs. But $S_{i,t}$ are "uncontaminated" measures only if the *assumed* underlying production function exhibits Hicks-neutral technical change. If technical change was, in fact, labor-augmenting as in equations 3.3 and 3.4, the $S_{k,t}$ used in equation 3.1 would have been lower, hence the calculated value of T would have been smaller (as k^* was greater than 0), and the calculated value of A^* would have been greater.

Table 3.3 Effects on Factor Shares of Alternative Combinations of Capital Deepening and Technical Change

Initial share of capital (S_K)	Initial share of labor (S_L)	Elasticity of substitution (σ)	Rate of change of K/L (k^*)	Rate of labor-augmenting technical change (m)	Annual rate of change of labor share (S_K^*)	Annual rate of change of capital share (S_L^*)
0.6	0.4	0.2	0.05	0.00	0.0800	-0.1200
			0.05	0.01	0.0640	-0.0960
			0.05	0.04	0.0160	-0.0240
			0.05	0.05	0.0000	-0.0000
0.6	0.4	0.9	0.05	0.00	0.0022	-0.0033
			0.05	0.01	0.0018	-0.0027
			0.05	0.04	0.0004	-0.0007
			0.05	0.05	0.0000	-0.0000

Source: Nelson and Pack (1999).

Table 3.3 sets out alternative calculations of the evolution of factor shares to illustrate the problem. For example, if S_K^0 was 0.4, $\sigma = 0.2$, k^* = 0.05, and $m = 0$, the annual rate of decrease in S_K would have been -0.12 (line 1). This decline is reduced to -0.024 when $m = 0.04$ and is reduced to 0 when $m = 0.05$ (line 4). As can be seen in lines 5–8, when $\sigma = 0.9$, the value of S_K^* is close to 0, with any combination of parameters. If $\sigma = 0.9$, the value of m could have been from 0.01 to 0.05 and have generated little or no change in factor shares. Thus many combinations of parameters can generate the observed constancy of S_K, including ones that result from a high rate of labor-augmenting technological progress.

Given that rapid rate of growth of capital weighted by $S_{K,t}$ is employed in the calculations attempting to demonstrate the absence of high productivity growth, the precise assumptions about the nature of technical change are critical. Unless there is a strong basis for assuming the existence of Hicks-neutral technical change, calculations of TFP growth using Tornqvist indexes provide estimates that may be biased. On theoretical grounds, Hicks-neutral technical change is problematic because steady-state growth in neoclassical models can occur only if technical change is Harrod-neutral (labor-augmenting).

Dynamic processes generating $S_{i,t}$. An alternate explanation of the high value of $S_{k,t}$ takes into account the change in economic structure, including the shift from agriculture and informal sector dominance to a more important role for large industrial firms (for evidence, see Nelson and Pack 1999). Given the higher value of the capital share in large firms than in less capital-intensive farms and small firms, the rapid shift in capital toward the former leads to a maintenance of $S_{k,t}$ in the aggregate, reflecting the ability of larger firms to maintain their initial capital/output ratios despite the rapid accumulation of capital. In this interpretation, $S_{K,t}$ is the outcome of a growth process and is endogenous. It stays high due to the sectoral shift in investment and the absorption of new capital without a decline in the modern sector's capital productivity. It is not necessary to invoke a bias in technical change in the aggregate production function. Unlike the economy-wide interpretation of the previous section, this view explicitly recognizes major structural shifts within the economy and explains the relative constancy of $S_{k,t}$ by this change.

Factor and product market distortions. If input markets are distorted—for example, due to the suppression of unions—the factor shares may not yield good estimates of the elasticity of output with respect to the factor in question. If output markets are not competitive—for example, due to high rates of effective protection or high concentration—markup pricing could give rise to distorted values of $S_{i,t}$. It cannot be assumed that factor shares represent competitive imputations derived from Euler's theorem.

Factor market distortions may have been important in both Korea and Singapore, where it is widely believed that wages were suppressed during most of the period. Figure 3.4 shows the capital share in Korea from 1978 to 1994. There was a significant decrease during the political liberalization of the late 1980s when previously docile unions became more assertive. Although the decline could have been due to a very large decrease in F_K, the rapidity of the change and confluence with greater union autonomy suggest an end to wage repression. This would imply that $S_{L,t}$ was artificially low and $S_{K,t}$ was thus overstated. Given that capital was the fastest-growing factor in Korea, this would overstate the value of T and thus understate the value of A^*. Although their levels of tariff protection were lower than those in other developing countries, many of the NIEs had high rates of effective protection that increased value added at domestic prices. The precise distribution between labor and capital is unknown. If, however, it allowed firms to pursue some form of markup pricing that favored profits, then the correct value of $S_{K,t}$ is less than that observed in the national accounts, introducing another source of upward bias in T and downward bias in A^* (Hall 1990). Although domestic competition could have reduced or eliminated rents, the high levels of concentration in several of the countries militated against this.

Incorrect price and output measures. In recent years, it has become clear that the U.S. national accounts data overstate the rate of growth of prices, the primary problem being the year of introduction of new goods into the price index. Quality adjustments that might be expected on the basis of four-decade-old research on hedonic price indexes are generally not made. The rate of overstatement of the CPI is estimated to be as high as 1 percent a year (for a survey of the issues, see Nordhaus 1997). Despite extensive recalculation of some input measures, none

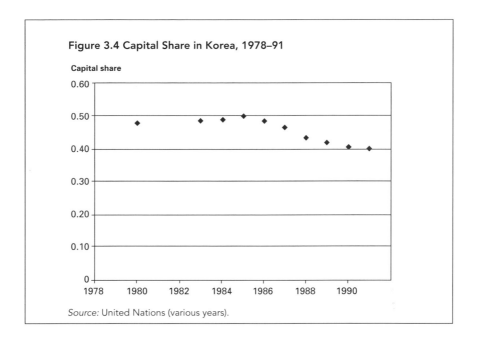

Figure 3.4 Capital Share in Korea, 1978–91

Source: United Nations (various years).

of the growth-accounting studies of the NIEs consider this issue despite the fact that all of the countries experienced exceptionally rapid changes in production and the final bill of goods entering their national accounts. This has two implications, assuming that overestimates of price growth are related to the rate of structural change. First, within the NIEs, the absolute level of TFP growth would be higher in the economies undergoing more rapid structural transformation—for example, Singapore relative to Hong Kong. Second, for the group as a whole, the price indexes are likely to be exaggerated relative to those of countries with slower growth and less rapid introduction of new products. Hence, intercountry calculations such as those of Bosworth and Collins (1996) understate TFP growth rates of the Asian NIEs relative to those of other countries, arguably by 2 percentage points a year.

Other measurement problems occur. Hsieh (1997) suggests that the imputation for housing in the national accounts is low; a correction adjusting for this raises A^* for Singapore. Other adjustments to both inputs and outputs have been suggested by various authors, a replay of the Denison-Griliches-Jorgenson debates of the 1960s. None of the existing research considers the extent to which economic rents that accrued to some of the economies affected the growth rate of output. In Hong Kong rent-earning activities were introduced during the period of observation, as local firms increasingly became brokers for China's foreign trade and generated rents. This may account for some of the discrepancy in TFP growth rates between Hong Kong and Singapore that was found by Young (1992).

Dual estimates of TFP growth. Because of the possibility of incorrectly measured physical inputs, particularly the construction of capital stock series, Hsieh (1997) estimates A^* using a cost function, the assumption being that prices are measured more accurately than quantities. He uses the following equation:

$$(3.5) \quad AC^* = \Sigma_i \left[1/2(S_{i,t} + S_{i,t-1}) \left(\ln p_{i,t} - \ln p_{i,t-1} \right) \right] - A_D^*$$

where p_i is the user cost of capital, r, and the wage rate, w. Both w and r are themselves Tornqvist aggregates of the various components of labor and capital cost. In principle, A_D^*, TFP growth measured from the dual, should equal that calculated in equation 3.2. However, this is not the case. Hsieh presents several estimates, varying with the assumed value of the interest cost used to calculate the user cost of capital. Table 3.4 presents the mean of Hsieh's results. In every case, $A_D^* > A^*$. In particular, the mean of the several calculated values of A_D^* for Singapore is considerably above Young's estimate. Although Hsieh's estimates are also subject to caveats because he assumes $S_{i,t}$ are exogenous, the exercise demonstrates the large range of estimates of economy-wide TFP growth rates calculated from growth accounting.

Table 3.4 Dual and Primal Calculations of the Growth of Total Factor Productivity

	Mean		Dual		Primal	
Country	Dual	Primal	Maximum	Minimum	Maximum	Minimum
Singapore	1.85	-0.59	2.17	1.61	-0.69	-0.3
Taiwan (China)	3.81	2.09	4.50	3.22	2.10	2.06
Hong Kong (China)	2.48	2.24	2.76	2.05	2.30	2.18
Korea, Rep. of	1.74	1.75	2.13	1.42	1.84	1.70

Source: Calculated from Hsieh (1997).

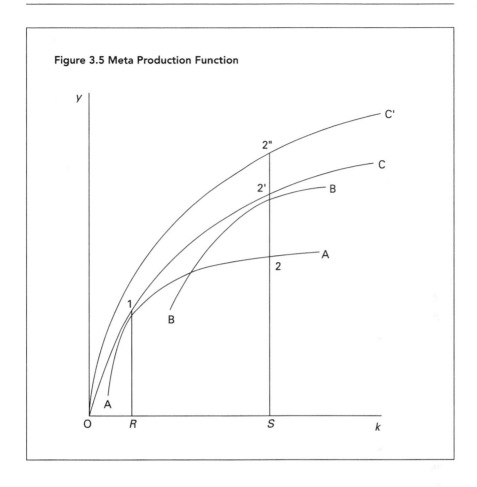

Figure 3.5 Meta Production Function

Production Function Estimates

Kim and Lau (1994) use econometric estimates of the meta production function (MPF), introduced by Hayami and Ruttan (1985), to
calculate A^*. A geometric interpretation of their framework is provided in figure 3.5. OC is the international MPF, the envelope of production functions that simultaneously exist for different capital/labor
ratios. These are known and come into use as the capital/labor ratio
increases from R to S, inducing a change in the wage/rental ratio. A
developing country, initially at 1 on AA, may move to 2' on BB, both 1
and 2' being points on the envelope. When this occurs, $A^* = 0$ when a
meta production function is estimated. A^* would exceed 0 only if the
developing country moved to a point such as 2'' along OC', the world

best-practice frontier. Kim and Lau find that the G-5 countries have been able to achieve the latter shift, but that the NIEs have only been able to move to 2'; they conclude that there has been no TFP growth. Their other key result is that technical change has been capital-augmenting, which can account for the absence of decline in the return on capital.

Their results do not suffer from the many problems of growth accounting such as the assumption of constant returns to scale and no bias in technical change. Yet the MPF approach raises questions of interpretation. In particular, it assumes that developing countries can move along OC despite extensive evidence that (a) production knowledge is imperfectly available and requires large amounts of tacit knowledge for which there may be no market;[13] (b) fear of generating future competitors makes some industrial-country firms reluctant to provide technology; (c) the existence of information asymmetries and fears on both sides may prevent the consummation of contracts for existing technology (Arrow 1969); (d) much of the successful use of knowledge requires production experience (Rosenberg 1994) and domestic absorptive efforts;[14] (e) much learning, particularly in manufacturing, is local (Evenson and Westphal 1995), and, as firms move away from their existing capital/labor ratios, their technical efficiency may decline (Atkinson and Stiglitz 1969);[15] and (f) knowledge is rarely transferred in nontraded goods, particularly services and construction. Indeed, using the MPF as a guide to production possibilities ignores many of the developments in understanding productivity, such as the emphasis on search, selection, and imitation (Nelson and Winter 1982) and the emphasis on path dependence (Arthur 1994). In a recent article Ruttan notes,

> It should now be obvious that differences in productivity levels and rates of growth cannot be overcome by the simple transfer of capital and technology. The asymmetries between firms and between countries in resource endowments and in scientific and technological capabilities are not easily overcome. The technologies that are capable of becoming the most productive sources of growth are often location specific. [Ruttan 1997: 1524.]

This view is widely shared among those who have done considerable research on the microeconomics of technology and calls into question the plausibility of the meta production function.

Kim and Lau's test of the existence of a meta production function for nine countries involves testing whether the hypothesis cannot be rejected that three parameters, β_{KK}, β_{LL}, and β_{KL} of the translog production function, equation 3.6, are equal in all countries.[16]

$$(3.6) \quad Ln\,Y_{i,t} = Ln\,Y_0 + a_k\,Ln\,K + a_L Ln + \beta_{KK}(Ln\,K_{i,t})^2/2 + \beta_{LL}$$
$$(Ln\,L_{i,t})^2\,/2 + \beta_{KL}\,(Ln\,K_{i,t})(Ln\,L_{i,t})$$

In view of the theoretical difficulties just noted and assuming an identical MPF across countries, the test of the three second-order parameters β_{KK}, β_{LL}, and β_{KL} (the first three terms are the standard Cobb-Douglas) requires great confidence in the robustness of the specification, the quality of the variables used, the impact of alternative instruments, and the role of omitted variables such as human capital. Given the large number of decisions on data, deflation, the choice of instruments, and so on, the estimates must be evaluated not only by conventional statistical criteria but also by their economic implications.

Taking the econometrics as correctly executed, there are two major implications of Kim and Lau's test that deserve comment. First, their finding that in all of the G-5 countries in their sample technological change is capital-augmenting implies that these countries could not sustain steady-state growth that requires Harrod-neutral or labor-augmenting technical change. Although a theoretical requirement cannot tell us that specific empirical estimates are incorrect, the impossibility of realizing the standard characteristics of neoclassical growth equilibrium suggests caution. Particular decisions on data or instruments might have led to anomalous results. Perhaps more important is the authors' own reconciliation of their econometric results with the considerable case study evidence that *physical* productivity per unit of combined inputs did increase in the NIEs. In the view of Kim and Lau, increases in productivity did not accrue to domestic factors but were extracted as rents by the developed-country firms providing the technology that allowed the NIEs to operate along the MPF. This view could reconcile in an elegant manner the case studies of firms discussed below with the econometric result of no TFP growth at the aggregate level.

Were charges for technology, whether embodied in equipment or disembodied in technology licensing royalties, large enough so that

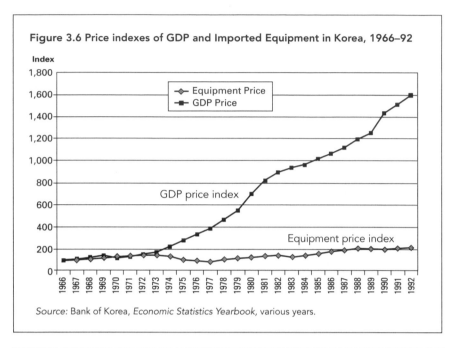

Figure 3.6 Price indexes of GDP and Imported Equipment in Korea, 1966–92

Source: Bank of Korea, *Economic Statistics Yearbook,* various years.

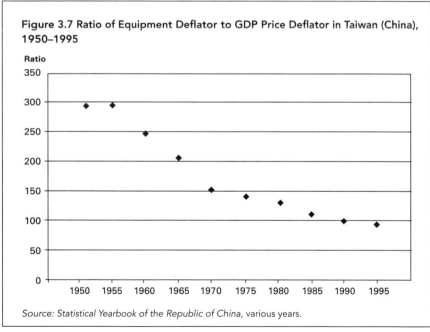

Figure 3.7 Ratio of Equipment Deflator to GDP Price Deflator in Taiwan (China), 1950–1995

Source: Statistical Yearbook of the Republic of China, various years.

Table 3.5 Korean Imports of Technology, 1962–91

Years	Imports of equipment as a share of fixed investment	Payments for importing foreign technology (millions of dollars)	Foreign direct investment (millions of dollars)
1962–66			47.6
1967–71			226.2
1972–76			894.7
1962–76	32.8[a]	113.6	1,168.5
1977–81	29.1	451.4	1,455.1
1982–86	36.3	1,184.9	2,867.9
1987–91	33.1	4,359.3	7,967.1

a. 1970–76.
Source: Sakong (1993: tables A40, A46, and A47).

payments to foreign technology purveyors could plausibly account for the absence of TFP growth? Figure 3.6 shows the price index of imported equipment prices, P_{ME}, and the GDP deflator, P_{GDP}, in Korea. The figure shows a decline in P_{ME} relative to P_{GDP} in Korea. The same is true for Taiwan, as shown in figure 3.7. Moreover, equipment investment in both economies constituted 5 to 15 percent of GDP, of which about 40 percent was of foreign origin (see table 3.5). The small share of imported equipment in GDP and its falling price imply that any extraction of rents was too small to affect TFP by any significant amount.

This still leaves the possibility that royalties from technology licenses or payments for foreign direct investment (FDI) services have been a mode for extracting large payments. However, as shown in table 3.5, in Korea, technology-licensing payments were $113 million (current prices) for the entire 1962 to 1976 period, while cumulated GDP was $147 billion. For 1987–91, total licensing payments were $4.4 billion, while comparable GDP was $1.2 trillion. Any overcharges would have been a minuscule percentage of GDP during these high-growth periods.

Given the puzzling result of finding capital-augmenting technical change (in the G-5) and the fact that rent extraction cannot be invoked to reconcile case studies with the aggregate finding of no technical progress in the NIEs, further research is needed to obtain agreement on econometric estimates of the importance of TFP growth in these economies. In contrast, the hundreds of case studies provide a consistent picture of the development process in the manufacturing sector in the NIEs, although their representativeness is questionable.[17] The case studies imply that as k grows in a typical developing country, firms will move to 2 along AA in figure 3.5. If firms succeed in achieving 2' rather than 2, then (2' − 2) / $S2$ is the appropriate measure of technological improvement.[18]

Firm case studies in the NIEs offer convincing documentation of the movement along AA, with a gradual improvement toward OC. A description of the production process in a typical firm in Korean engineering industries in the late 1970s confirms the difficulty of moving along a meta production function. The government initiated the industry in 1970, and firms invested heavily in new equipment. Yet, as late as 1977, the manufacturing processes were described as backward. According to the World Bank (1979: 33):

> The common pattern [of production] was one of machine placement that is haphazard rather than allowing for an orderly flow of work. Floor space is very crowded, and the operation of machining, fabrication of components, [and] assembly of parts are scattered in any place that happens to have available room. Too much time is spent finding work, or the next job, or material. In some cases, the men have to find their own area in which to work, perhaps make up some form of fixtures of their own, or find the means to obtain levels or measurements to work from. The almost universal characteristic is one of congestion and a mixing of operations that frequently leads to deterioration of quality because of improper floor planning. There is no adequate provision for working space around the main machines, and the aisleways that are normally used to carry the flow of work are completely congested with work in process.[19]

At the time of the description, the plant was at point 1 along OA in figure 3.5. Yet 15 years later such plants were producing high-quality machine tools for export—they had moved to 2' or 2''. The deficiencies described in 1977 were amenable to improvements through learning better practices and significant reorganization. Although it is possible to make such learning tautologically equal to moving along an international production function, it is costly, the results are uncertain, and it takes place over many years, suggesting a much more complex phenomenon not replicated in many other countries in which capital accumulation was rapid (for evidence of the role of domestic training in assimilating technology, see Gee and Chen 1990). Importing equipment was not equivalent to moving along OC (Nelson and Pack 1999).

It might be argued that FDI allowed some of these countries to move directly to the international production frontier. The importance of foreign investment in Hong Kong, Korea, and Taiwan was quite low: the ratio of accumulated FDI to GDP was 0.02 or less, while the aggregate capital/output ratio was above 2 (table 3.6). From an early period, however, Singapore depended more on foreign direct investment. The later industrializers—Indonesia, Malaysia, and Thailand—followed the Singaporean pattern. But in all of these countries, the ratio of foreign-owned capital to GDP was less than 25 percent. Given capital/output ratios of 3 or more, perhaps 8 percent of total economic activity was undertaken under foreign auspices. Paradoxically, it has been argued that there was no productivity growth in Singapore, which had the greatest dependence on FDI.

If knowledge has diffused extensively to local firms, then the FDI/GDP ratio may underestimate the extent to which the economy operates on the international frontier. However, there is no systematic evidence of spillovers of knowledge to local suppliers or purchasers of the multinationals' products, although some case studies indicate that this has occurred (Ranis and Schive 1985).[20]

Trade Theoretic Interpretations

A production relation such as oc in figure 3.1 could account for the absence of a decline in the rate of return. This relationship might arise as the result of a shift in the composition of production toward more

Table 3.6 Cumulative Stock of Foreign Direct Investment Relative to Gross Domestic Product, 1980–95

Economy	1980	1985	1990	1995
China	0.00	0.01	0.04	0.20
Hong Kong (China)	0.06	0.10	0.18	0.15
Indonesia	0.13	0.29	0.34	0.26
Korea, Rep. of	0.02	0.02	0.02	0.02
Malaysia	0.25	0.27	0.33	0.43
Singapore	0.58	0.73	0.78	0.68
Taiwan (China)	0.01	0.01	0.01	0.01
Thailand	0.03	0.05	0.04	0.10

Source: Both foreign direct investment and gross domestic product are current price values. For foreign direct investment, United Nations (1997: annex table B3); for gross domestic product, World Bank (1998).

capital-intensive sectors. In this case, diminishing returns would not set in, but this view cannot provide insight into the magnitude of technological progress. The difficulty with this interpretation is much the same as that with the meta production function approach. It assumes that technical knowledge is "out there" and, as the capital/labor ratio increases, firms simply shift sectors, using perfectly understood technologies in other industries, moving effortlessly from producing clothing to manufacturing numerically controlled machine tools. Although this convenient assumption allows the derivation of the Rybczynski theorem, it offers limited insights into the dynamic process of industrial development, in which learning in the new sectors is a major phenomenon.

Considerable effort went into learning the technologies that were required in the new industries. Some of this is shown by Korea's effort. Table 3.5 shows that Korea had relatively little FDI and few royalty payments in the early period of its development. It did import large quantities of foreign equipment to enable it to enter new sectors. Enos and Pak (1987) describe in detail the difficulties of learning to use it efficiently. As the shift to more capital- and technology-intensive sectors began, Korea, which initially limited both technology licensing and FDI, made a significant effort to tap international technology. Payments for technology, largely for licenses, in 1977–81 were four times the size for the entire 1962–76 period. FDI in 1977–81 was one-third greater than in the entire 1962–76 period. And it doubled again to 1982–86.[21] The international transfer of technology was complemented by an intensive domestic effort to understand the technology that had been purchased and to improve its performance.

Table 3.7 Research and Development and Patenting Activity in Taiwan (China), 1981, 1986, and 1991

Year	Ratio of R&D to GDP	Total patents	Domestic patents	Foreign patents
1981	0.95[a]	6,265	2,897	3,368
1986	0.98	10,526	5,800	4,726
1991	1.65[b]	27,281	13,555	13,726

a. 1984.
b. 1990.
Source: Republic of China (1992: tables 6.7, 6.8).

R&D expenditures rose enormously. Similarly, in Taiwan, local R&D increased, as an effort was undertaken to accelerate the move toward producing new products rather than simply exploiting low wages in labor-intensive sectors (see table 3.7). Between 1981 and 1991, the number of patents granted to Taiwan nationals quadrupled, being roughly equal to foreign patents in 1991. Similarly, formal R&D spending increased from 1.0 to 1.7 percent of GDP. Moreover, formal R&D is likely to constitute a minor part of domestic technological effort.

In sum, the difficulties with the Rybczynski interpretation are similar to those with the meta production function—it assumes an ease of switching techniques and products that is belied by extensive microeconomic evidence. Domestic learning, both formal and informal, is required to put a new sector's potential isoquants into efficient operation.

Were Scale Economies and Externalities Important?

The measured residual in either growth-accounting or production function estimates could be the result of scale economies or externalities. Endogenous growth theory puts the latter at the core of its explanation of the absence of diminishing returns.

There have been extensive attempts in the growth-accounting literature, beginning with Denison (1962), to determine the importance of economies of scale. It is not easy to reconcile the existence of economy-wide scale economies with growth accounting—the possibility of invoking Euler's theorem to explain factor shares and using the latter as output elasticities loses its logic. Denison and others simply guess their importance but do not explicitly note the theoretical inconsistency. Estimates of returns to scale can be obtained from production function estimates, but there have been few such exercises in the NIEs.

Is it likely that economy-wide increasing returns to scale constitute a major explanation of the TFP that has been measured? There are two potential sources of these—namely, technical engineering ones such as the 0.6 rule and Marshallian economies (for careful estimates of technical scale economies by industry in many sectors, see Pratten 1971). The 0.6 rule—$TC = AQ^{.6}$ (where TC is total firm cost, and Q is total output)—applies largely to the chemical and some basic metal sectors. In all of the tigers, these sectors constituted too small a share of GDP to exert the necessary quantitative impact. Moreover, A^* was high even during the period of labor-intensive growth, when growth was based on textiles, clothing, wigs, sneakers, and so on, which are not subject to significant scale economies.

Real external economies could provide the required boost in TFP. Marshallian economies have been measured largely in efforts to calculate urban agglomeration impacts. Most empirical studies suggest relatively weak effects (Henderson 1988). If agglomeration effects were industry-specific, higher concentration ratios would be observed in developing countries than have been found (Lee 1992).

Endogenous growth theory has suggested several mechanisms to explain the absence of decreasing returns to capital accumulation, arguing that a variety of externalities associated with investment lead to the coefficient of K in a production function being unity, $Y = AK$ in one formulation, rather than $Y = K^{\alpha}$ as in the Cobb-Douglas. Although some of these arguments have existed since Arrow's formal presentation in 1962, there is no empirical evidence at the aggregate level to support them, intriguing as they may be (Arrow 1962; Pack 1994). If such evidence did exist, the externalities associated with investment would have to be substantial, given observed capital shares of 0.25–0.30 in the OECD countries.

THE TRANSFER AND ABSORPTION OF TECHNOLOGY

I now turn to a discussion of the transfer and absorption of technology that allowed the eventual movement from 1 to 2' in figure 3.5. The import of machinery and some of the software of production was supplemented by an intense domestic effort to obtain the best use of the imported knowledge. The imports served as a template on which local skills were exercised to improve productivity levels. Other countries that have imported equipment have achieved much less growth. In each of the Asian NIEs, one or more modes of technology transfer were employed. All imported equipment. Some obtained knowledge from FDI, some from licenses, others from consultants. Yet all of the micro evidence finds that the transfer by itself was not sufficient to allow firms to move to 2' along OC in figure 3.5. Significant local effort was required as a complement.[22]

Local R&D increased, as noted in the previous section. Firms also learned as they undertook production as original equipment manufacturers for companies with brand names, at other times on their own initiative. They acquired equipment and incomplete production engineering knowledge—it was impossible to write contracts with suppliers, which would have led to full disclosure of all the relevant knowledge, much of which was not codified. This pattern necessitated their own efforts at learning to operate a technology. Kim (1997) describes one such effort to develop an auto engine. A short excerpt provides a flavor of the learning process and the importance of local efforts to build on the foundations provided by international technology transfer.

> Despite the training and consulting services of experts, Hyundai engineers repeated trials and errors for 14 months before creating the first prototype. But the engine block broke into pieces at its first test. New prototype engines appeared almost every week, only to break in testing. No one on the team could figure out why the prototypes kept breaking down, casting serious doubts, even among Hyundai management, on its capability to develop a competitive engine. The team had to scrap 11 more broken prototypes before one survived the test. There were 2,888 engine design changes . . . Ninety-seven test engines were made before Hyundai refined its natural aspiration and turbocharger engines. . . . In addition, more than 200 transmissions and 150 test vehicles were created before Hyundai perfected them in 1992. [Kim 1997: 122.]

Enos and Pak (1987), Gee and Chen (1990), Hobday (1995), and Kim (1997) provide scores of examples of the magnitude and the vicissitudes of the domestic efforts required to master technologies in the NIEs.[23]

The Interaction of High Education and Technology Imports

As is well known, the Asian NIEs were characterized by high levels of general education at the beginning of their rapid growth and spent considerable resources on technical education (see table 3.8). By the late 1970s the percentages of tertiary school graduates majoring in computer science, mathematics, and engineering were comparable to OECD levels, indeed above many of the latter (table 3.9). It seems plausible that growth in productivity and the efficient transition among sectors were greatly facilitated by the presence of a large group of technically educated members of the labor force. Typically, growth accounting calculates the stock of education or skill-adjusted labor, imputes a share to education, and calculates the percentage of output growth due to improved education.[24] "Education" is simply another multiplicative factor in the production function. The rapid increase in education levels thus explains a significant part of growth, reducing the size of A^*.

A more compelling approach is that of Nelson and Phelps (1966) and Schultz (1975), who argue that education has a payoff only in the presence of rapid technological change. A Korean cotton spinner in 1960 who was a high school graduate but tended spindles not much different in design from those of 1900 would not have benefited much from his education. In contrast, his education would have led to an increase in productivity relative to a less-educated spinner if he had to adjust to the complexities of open-end spinning, which had been developed only recently. Flexibility and problem-solving abilities conferred by more education yield a reward when technology is changing, but education may have little payoff in the absence of technological change. The rapid growth of imports, facilitated by export growth, was important because it provided both new intermediate and capital goods. High education without the imports that provided new challenges would not have had as high a return. High levels of education in the absence of imported technology, whether equipment, intermediates, or production engineering knowledge, often lead to the expensive local replication of knowledge that is already present abroad (Katz 1987; Lall 1987).

Table 3.8 Level of Education in Asia, 1960

Economy	Literacy rate	Percentage enrolled in primary school	Percentage enrolled in secondary school
Hong Kong (China)	0.70	0.87	0.24
Korea, Rep. of	0.71	0.94	0.27
Singapore	0.50	1.11	0.32
Taiwan (China)		0.63	0.38
Indonesia	0.39	0.67	0.06
Malaysia	0.53	0.96	0.19
Thailand	0.68	0.83	0.12

Source: For all economies, except Taiwan (China), Levine and Renelt (1992); for Taiwan, Republic of China (1992).

**Table 3.9 Percentage of Tertiary Graduates in Computer
Science, Mathematics, Engineering, Various Years**

Economy and year	Share
Hong Kong (China)	
1981	0.34
1992	0.34
Korea, Rep. of	
1981	0.34
1993	0.28
Singapore	
1980	0.51
Indonesia	
1992	0.12
Malaysia	
1981	0.27
1990	0.25
Thailand	
1992	0.21
India	
1978	0.18
1990	0.16
Israel	
1979	0.33
1992	0.28
Brazil	
1993	0.12
Mexico	
1993	0.26
Japan	
1979	0.19
1991	0.20
France	
1992	0.31
Germany	
1979	0.16
1990	0.29
Greece	
1991	0.23

Source: UNESCO (1995: table 3.12; 1983: table 3.14).

Schultz (1975) emphasizes the role that education plays in monitoring new technologies and efficiently allocating resources among sectors. It is unlikely that the exceptionally rapid industrial transformation among sectors in the NIEs could have occurred without growing levels of higher education. Had the economies expanded largely in their initial sectors as new competitors arose, it is likely that the growth impact of capital accumulation and technical change would have been weakened by declining prices in those sectors.

Public Sector Support

The public sector provided a supportive environment for achieving the transfer and assimilation of technology. Both the macro environment and specific micro interventions were important. A major contribution was the limited rate of inflation, which allowed firms to anticipate that their major source of profit growth would be efficient operation rather than the management of financial assets, as was often the case in Latin America. In Korea, the setting of export targets and preferential treatment to exporters provided strong incentives to improve productivity. Even where domestic markets were substantially protected, as in Korea and Taiwan, incentives to export provided a competitive environment (Pack and Westphal 1986). Otherwise, it would have been possible to replicate the situation that prevailed in Latin American firms in the 1970s and 1980s, in which considerable technological ingenuity was employed to improve productivity in sectors that had no prospects for long-term profitability without high continuing rates of effective protection.

Explicit public actions supporting technical change included the encouragement of the acquisition of foreign knowledge. FDI was not restricted in Indonesia, Malaysia, Singapore, and Thailand. Although Korea and Japan (and Taiwan to a smaller extent), limited FDI, they encouraged other means of technology acquisition such as technology licensing. The licensing of foreign technology was not restricted in any of the countries. In contrast, the northern Latin American countries that are members of the Andean Pact engaged in a microscopic inspection of each technology contract despite the near impossibility of preventing firms from attempting to live up to the agreements (Mytelka 1978).

A number of indirect public activities supported technological improvement. The most important was the building of a very good education system that placed increasing emphasis on technical subjects. By itself, this would not have been a major contributor had economic policies not encouraged the growth of activities that provided a demand for graduates and provided new inputs, as discussed above. In several countries, publicly supported institutions sought to enhance the capacities of the private sector. These included the Korean Institute for Science and Technology, the Institute for Technology Research for Industry, and the China Productivity Center in Taipei.

Through the late 1970s, some government agencies such as the Economic Planning Board in Korea undertook efforts to monitor world product markets and technologies and to diffuse this information to individual firms. Lall and Teubal (1998) list many incentives designed to encourage local technological effort as well as the acquisition of international knowledge. There has been no systematic testing of the impact of policies explicitly designed to promote technology transfer and development, although there are well-documented case studies of their importance—for example, the role of the Industrial Technology and Research Institute in the development of Taiwan's computer chip sector (Dahlman and Sananikone 1997).

The Role of International Trade

The export orientation in the Asian countries had two benefits apart from financing the importation of inputs that embodied improved technology. First, unlike firms fostered by import-substituting industrialization policies, firms could not spend a long time using equipment inefficiently. Governments offered substantial economic incentives (low-interest loans) and pressures (export targets in Korea) to enter the international market. Second, firms derived knowledge from their purchasers in the OECD countries, an important source of knowledge especially in the earliest stages of industrialization.[25] Importers provided specifications for new products that the local firms manufactured as original equipment manufacturers. To maintain their contracts, they were forced to constantly reduce costs by improving productivity, as the purchasers were constantly seeking newer, lower-cost sources. The process thus provided a strong learning environment in which firms not able to meet quality and cost specifications in short-term opportunistic relationships could easily lose their markets. To quote from a case study of a Taiwan computer peripherals supplier,

> Foreign buyers are an important source of technological enhancement. Their rigorous specifications are seen as a challenge for the firm to meet. Equipped with different viewpoints and accumulated experience, they criticize a lot and suggest other ways of doing things. Although they do not provide exact blue prints, their suggestions are invaluable in upgrading the technology level of the firm. *Still, our own research and development is the most important source of technology. Without this capability, the firm would not be able to evaluate research proposals, technology contracts, licenses, or buyers' suggestions.* [Emphasis added; Pack, Wang, and Westphal 1996: 12.]

This illustrates a typical interaction between foreign knowledge and local capability. Although knowledge was obtained from the rest of the world, and the need to meet export requirements served as a focusing mechanism, any knowledge transferred was improved on by local efforts, which were themselves dependent on the rapid growth in educational levels. The cost of assimilating knowledge was quite high in the more advanced sectors, even when the basic template was provided by foreign equipment and technology licensing agreements. Incurring such expenses would have been less likely if firms had anticipated that they could be recouped solely in domestic markets, which were relatively small. Hence, the greater anticipated market due to export orientation was an important contributor to undertaking the effort necessary to improve productivity.

THE LIMITS OF LEARNING

Despite the considerable learning that has occurred, many firms and sectors in the NIEs remain below OECD best practice. For example, as late as 1987, manufacturing-wide TFP levels in Korea were about a quarter of those in the United States (see table 3.10). Even in the most advanced sectors—basic and fabricated metals—the TFP level was 41 percent of that in the United States. For individual Korean companies, TFP levels calculated in 1997 show that most manufacturing and service firms achieved no more than 60 percent of the TFP level of U.S. firms (McKinsey Global Institute 1998).[26]

Table 3.10 Sectoral Total Factor Productivity in Korea Relative to the United States, 1975 and 1987

Sector	1975	1987
Food, beverages, tobacco	0.17	0.14
Textile mill products	0.34	0.30
Wearing apparel	0.16	0.19
Leather and footwear	0.38	0.31
Wood, furniture, fixtures	0.19	0.14
Paper, printing, publishing	0.14	0.32
Chemicals, petroleum, coal	0.22	0.25
Rubber and plastic products	0.14	0.23
Nonmetallic mineral products	0.30	0.35
Basic and fabricated metals	0.20	0.41
Machinery and transport equipment	0.11	0.35
Electrical machinery and equipment	0.28	0.39
Other manufacturing	0.15	0.20
Total manufacturing	0.18	0.26

Source: Pilat (1994: table 7.9).

What do such results indicate? First, in historic context, this situation is not unusual. Western Europe exhibited much lower labor productivity and TFP levels than the United States from 1870 to 1950. Only in the period from 1950 to 1973 did convergence take place, and then to levels that remained 20 to 30 percent below those in the United States. Second, current Korean shortfalls in TFP (and probably those in other countries) are not due to the inability to acquire modern equipment, but to the difficulty of developing efficient networks of suppliers, establishing appropriate labor relations that allow rationalization of production, and achieving greater product specialization (McKinsey Global Institute 1998). Deficiencies in these areas underline the problematic nature of employing a meta production function. These skills are only acquired slowly, and they cannot be imported. Even sophisticated firms cannot easily duplicate foreign methods—the U.S. auto industry in the 1980s lagged behind that in Japan in inventory control and speed of new design, despite its longer history (Clark and Fujimoto 1992).

Nevertheless, despite the shortfall relative to the United States and Japan, these TFP levels are surprisingly high. In semiconductors, calculations of the McKinsey Global Institute find that Korean plants have TFP that is 65 percent of that of plants in the United States. Given its relatively late entry into a technologically demanding sector, it is extraordinary that Korea has been able to achieve such levels. Similar relative TFP is found in autos. It is unlikely that European companies such as Volvo and Saab would have greater relative TFP even given their long histories.

If one looks for the source of Korea's crisis in levels of *aggregate* TFP or its growth rate, they are not likely to provide a major clue to the crisis. Some answers begin to emerge at the sectoral level. In automobiles, semiconductors, and a few other sectors, there was a substantial increase in investment and production in the 1990s. The government encouraged investment and production through a variety of policies. A very large share of investment in semiconductors occurred after 1993. Although TFP levels were surprisingly high, given the technological complexity of the sectors, firms were unprofitable for reasons that differ among the sectors (McKinsey Global Institute 1998). For example, the semiconductor firms specialized in d-rams whose price collapsed in 1997.[27] They did not possess design abilities necessary to compete in more profitable microprocessors. In autos, Korean firms produced too many models, were incapable of developing effective supplier relationships, and were not able to achieve greater labor efficiency given union rules (McKinsey Global Institute 1998). Although both sectors had, within relatively short periods, achieved high TFP levels (compared to the United States and Japan), this was not enough, given the price collapse in one sector and the higher costs, even after extensive learning, compared with international competitors. The well-known problems in both industries were attracting attention in the first half of 1997, before the crisis in Thailand catalyzed the East Asian crisis. Several *chaebol* were known to be in a weak financial position. These problems were widely discussed in the Korean and international financial press and may have contributed to the doubts on the part of lenders and portfolio investors. Panics can be catalyzed not only by low ratios of foreign exchange reserves to short-term debt but also by a few instances of low profits from which generalizations are drawn. The rebound of chip prices in 1998 and 1999 underlines the danger of drawing conclusions about long-term productivity failures from an episode of temporary decline in an industrial price.

In some sectors, such as automobiles, these relatively low TFP levels may be partly attributable to the continuing protection received by

Korean firms, largely from nontariff measures. The exclusion of foreign direct investment and the competition it offers in the domestic market have reduced competitive pressures. Finally, the absence of shareholder pressure to increase company profitability, partly a result of the intricate cross-holdings among firms that prevent an accurate assessment of performance, decreases the incentive of firms to seek more efficient production. Although learning has occurred as the result of technological effort and exporting has necessitated increasing productivity, the growth in TFP may have been limited by the absence of conventional disciplining institutions. Although government export targets and low-interest loans and other benefits contingent on meeting these targets provided a strong incentive to learn, Korean industrial sectors were still 30 percent or more less efficient than those in the United States in 1975, 1987, and 1997 (McKinsey Global Institute 1998). The year 1975 roughly demarcates the end of the labor-intensive growth phase; by 1987, most of the learning that had occurred during the encouragement of heavy and chemical industries begun in the early 1970s should have been revealed in the data. These figures suggest that Korea's success in export markets still depended on lower wage rates and, to a smaller extent, cross-subsidization of exports by the profitable domestic market. The 1997 productivity shortfalls are probably not very different from those that would be calculated in other OECD countries relative to the United States. Although there is scope for improvement, the last 30 percentage points between locally achieved and U.S. TFP are difficult to remove. The figures in table 3.10 indicate that Korea continued to enter new sectors before fully exploiting potential productivity gains in older sectors. Learning is not solely a function of cumulated output but is affected by incentive structures that, in recent years, may have led firms to pay insufficient attention to improving productivity.

There also was a problem in allocative efficiency that was unrelated to TFP levels or growth in individual sectors. For a considerable period, Korea encouraged investment in manufacturing while discouraging investment in nontraded goods such as construction and services. However, rates of return on capital in untraded goods were higher, despite public restrictions that reduced their profitability. Although it is not clear that this was a new problem, the economy did not avail itself of one option to maintain high returns, which would have reduced vulnerability. However, such a disequilibrium may have existed for a long time without noticeable effects on the aggregate growth rate.

In sum, the levels of Korean productivity relative to that of the United States were never high, but there is nothing to suggest either a slowing in the rate of growth of TFP or a downturn before the crisis began. Moreover, Korea's productivity levels relative to those of the United States were probably not much below those of Western Europe.

TFP GROWTH AND RATES OF RETURN IN THE ASEAN COUNTRIES

Much of the discussion has concentrated on Korea and Taiwan because there has been more research on productivity at both the aggregate and firm level. However, several of the ASEAN countries were severely affected by the financial crisis. In these countries as well, it does not appear that the crisis was preceded by a sustained slowing of conventionally measured TFP. For example, Sarel (1997) presents calculations of TFP growth for 1978–96 and 1991–96 for five ASEAN economies. The figures shown in table 3.11 indicate sustained growth in all of the countries during the former period and higher growth in the 1990s than over the entire period. Although the absolute values of A^* are likely to be understated in both periods, there is no basis for concluding that the figures in the latter period are more subject to bias. However, Sarel's figures do suggest that a decline could have occurred in the rate of return on capital.

Table 3.11 Total Factor Productivity in ASEAN Economies, 1978–96

Country	Rate of growth of the capital/labor ratio (k')		Rate of growth of total factor productivity (A')	
	1978–96	1991–96	1978–96	1991–96
Indonesia	9.0	7.0	1.16	2.20
Malaysia	6.9	8.3	2.00	2.00
Philippines	1.8	1.2	-.78	.67
Singapore	6.5	5.6	2.23	2.46
Thailand	7.3	11.1	2.03	2.25

Source: Sarel (1997: table 2).

The change in the rate of return on capital can be written as:

(3.7) $r^* = - (SL /\sigma) k^* + A^*$

where, for simplicity, A^* is the Hicks-neutral rate of technical change. If the value of S_L is 0.25, and assuming that $\sigma = 0.8$, then an increase in k^* of 1 percent requires an increase in A^* of roughly 0.3 to preclude a decline in r^*. In the 1990s, in both Malaysia and Thailand, the values of k^* were 1.4 and 3.8 points above their average for the entire 1978–96 period, while the value of A^* was constant in one case and 0.22 higher in the other. This suggests the possibility that there was some decline in rates of return in the early 1990s. Such calculations are necessarily tentative because the value of A^* calculated by Sarel is subject to the problems discussed earlier and the correct value of σ is only a guess.

The possibility of a decline in r depends critically on the value of σ and any bias in technical change. For example, if technical change was Harrod-neutral, then equation 3.7 should be rewritten as

(3.8) $r^* = - (S_L /\sigma) (m - k^*)$.

If $m = 0.05$ and $k^* = 0.08$, then the annual rate of decline of r^* would have been 0.01 a year. If the rate of return had been 20 percent in 1990, this would imply a decline to roughly 18.5 by 1997, hardly a change to generate a collapse. Without independent knowledge of the nature of bias and magnitude of technical change, it is quite possible that the best interpretation of the maintenance of high investment levels is that high levels of k^* were largely offset by high values of m.

A firm-level survey in Thailand by Dollar and Hallward-Driemeier (1998) finds that the value of A^* was not decreasing but that rates of return were declining, implying a value of k^* considerably greater than m in the period immediately preceding the crisis. In almost all countries, low, but not declining, rates of return prevailed throughout the entire period of rapid growth. McKinsey Global Institute (1998) documents this for individual Korean firms. There is little systematic evidence that it suddenly declined in 1997. TFP growth rates were not the precipitating factor. Using constant price value added, TFP growth was not slowing. But profits are based on current prices. Declining goods prices, short-term financing, and panic may have brought down robust sectors.

CONCLUSIONS

Over the past 35 years, the Asian NIEs accumulated enormous amounts of capital and skilled labor and were successful at deploying them productively, particularly within the manufacturing sector. Although a considerable part of such growth was due to capital accumulation, much of it also was due to its productive assimilation. A large corpus of case studies supports the view that firms in many of the countries successfully absorbed international knowledge, whether in the form of new equipment, intermediates, or disembodied knowledge, and improved on it. Within all of the NIEs, a strong industrial base exists, with modern equipment, good organization at the firm and industry level, strong marketing abilities, a considerable pool of efficient workers, and a demonstrated record of flexibility in response to vicissitudes ranging from oil price increases to tumultuous changes of political regime.

In the crisis-of-the-day atmosphere in late 1997 through 1998, these fundamental achievements were often forgotten. A view became prevalent that the decline was inevitable and that both governments and firms had always been incompetent. Like the stock and foreign exchange markets, the intellectual fashion market often overshoots. Although some laxity in financial regulation and questionable targeting within manufacturing and service sectors occurred, this may have been due partly to hubris brought about by the very success that is now too often forgotten. But there were also intrinsically difficult transitions to accomplish, particularly as the earlier closed financial markets were prematurely opened, partly at the urging of international agencies.

Recent problems have not brought into question the major achievement in industrialization. Undoubtedly, there was too much expansion in some sectors; for example, capacity in the Korean auto industry is certainly too large given prospective sales, and Malaysian steel and Indonesian aircraft were clearly bad choices. This provides a cautionary tale about the volatility of animal spirits and, occasionally, political choices that were perverse, not unlike the British-French Concorde. It does not provide a basis for asserting that most of the growth was based solely on high investment rates in these countries. To the contrary, an extraordinary effort was generally made to absorb new capital in a productive manner, precluding a dramatic fall in rates of return and encouraging continuing high saving. If investment rates were the only variable that mattered in explaining growth, the Iron Curtain would still be with us.

Looking forward, there are major issues, discussed elsewhere in this volume, about corporate governance and the financial sector. On the real side, two interrelated lessons may not have been learned. First, the successful execution of sectoral industrial targeting is likely to bring relatively limited benefits—although choosing sectoral champions was not the pernicious influence, for the entire economy, that some analysts now claim it was; neither was it a magic elixir of growth (Pack 2000). Second, there is still an obsession with further industrial development, if only the right sectors can be identified. The difficulty with this view, apart from the great difficulties in identifying future leading industrial sectors, is the changing comparative advantage of the countries and the need to diversify to high-value-added service sectors ranging from insurance to investment banking. Hong Kong, one of the success stories, has already made this transition, its manufacturing share of GDP being about 7 percent. The other NIEs still exhibit ratios well above 20 percent. Engel's law and the evolving set of endowments suggest that these ratios are likely to decrease rapidly. Institutions to encourage an efficient transition should be high on the agenda.

NOTES

This chapter was written while the author was a consultant to the Development Research Group at the World Bank. The author benefited from comments of participants in two conferences sponsored by DECRG on Rethinking the East Asia Miracle. Many of the views in this chapter were developed in earlier research conducted with Richard R. Nelson. Mark Gersovitz provided helpful comments on an earlier draft.

1. Preliminary estimates of the percentage change in real GDP in 1998 and 1999 for the nations most affected by the crisis are Indonesia (-13.2, 0.2), Korea (-6.7, 10.7), Malaysia (-7.5, 5.4), and Thailand (-10.4, 4.4).

2. One simple explanation—namely, the existence of capital-augmenting technical change—has limited empirical confirmation, although an exception is Kim and Lau (1994).

3. More precisely, assuming that factor price equalization holds, the Rybczynski theorem implies growth in capital-intensive sectors and an absolute decline in the size of labor-intensive sectors.

4. Korea and Taiwan did, in fact, have increasing labor force participation rates so that their labor force growth also was greater than that in Germany and Japan in the relevant periods.

5. The Marshall Plan in Germany and the American occupation in Japan provided macroeconomic conditions suitable for rapid growth.

6. In both economies, there had been limited experience with industrialization during the Japanese occupation. See Ranis (1979) on Taiwan and Kuznets (1977) on Korea.

7. It could be argued that the new capital embodied technical improvements that helped to accelerate productivity growth. However, the same could be said for other countries with high investment rates. The key ingredient for realizing higher productivity with new capital was sustained domestic effort. New equipment provided no guarantee that such benefits would be realized.

8. Although their calculations are open to many of the same criticisms of growth accounting that I present below, it is unlikely that the qualitative pattern of their findings would be reversed with revisions of their procedure.

9. Some analysts adjust the shares to correct various deficiencies such as those dealing with the remuneration of unpaid family members (see, for example, Young 1995).

10. The value of σ is derived from $S_L/S_K = (\delta/[1 - \delta])(K/L)^\rho$ (where $\rho = (1/\sigma - 1)$.

11. This subsection and the following are condensed from Nelson and Pack (1999).

12. Kim and Lau (1994) estimate production functions and solve this problem by using several countries in their pooled cross-section, time-series analysis.

13. On these and other questions related to interpretation of the production function, see Nelson and Winter (1982). For evidence that firms in some developing countries do not possess the same production knowledge, see Pack (1987).

14. Hayami and Ruttan (1985) postulate the MPF for agriculture and argue that, as factor prices changed secularly, induced innovation would occur, reducing the demand for more expensive factors. They envision the process as one in which new isoquants would be developed by research rather than be chosen from a menu available across the world. Moreover, even in agriculture, the successful adoption of new technologies such as the green revolution required long and expensive domestic efforts (Evenson and Westphal 1995). Farms in India could not move toward the world frontier without considerable research in each region. In nonagricultural activities, the world frontier may be even more difficult to achieve, lessening the plausibility of the MPF metaphor.

15. These factors also underlie the considerable diversity in productivity among firms in the same industry in industrial countries. Estimates of frontier production functions have demonstrated the very large range of productivity achieved within industrial countries among firms in which relatively similar equipment is employed (Caves and others 1992). The existence of such divergences even within developed countries is one more reason for doubting that all firms throughout the developing and developed world produce along the same production function.

16. The United States, England, France, Germany, Japan, Hong Kong, Korea, Singapore, and Taiwan.

17. For example, it is possible that, despite the many manufacturing case studies suggesting positive growth in TFP, other sectors were regressing, thus leading

to zero aggregate TFP growth. But given the growing share of manufacturing in value added, and no a priori reason to believe that TFP was declining in other sectors, I doubt that the problem is one of aggregation.

18. Nishimizu and Page (1982) define technological progress as including both the shift in best-practice frontier and the move toward it by firms off the frontier, terming the latter efficiency gains. They find that this accounted for most of measured TFP growth in Yugoslavia.

19. Although the production process described could be interpreted as a cost-minimizing response to the relative cost of labor and space, the engineers observed that the same amount of space could have been reorganized in order to achieve much better work flow.

20. See, for example, Lim and Fong (1991) and Goh (1996). A complete survey of the literature is given in Blomstrom and Kokko (1997), who find mixed results on the existence of external effects of FDI. Unfortunately, much of the econometric research on the topic suffers from serious problems of specification that preclude strong inferences.

21. These figures are in current prices and overstate the changes in constant prices.

22. This parallels the well-known result that successful absorption of the green revolution required substantial local research to obtain full benefits from the new seed. See Evenson and Westphal (1995).

23. Rich descriptions of the same process in Japan are provided in Goto and Odagiri (1997), Hayashi (1990), Minami (1995), and Ozawa (1974).

24. The share used may also have biases of the type discussed earlier.

25. Pack and Saggi (forthcoming) analyze the process and provide references to the now-extensive literature documenting the phenomenon.

26. As these calculations use the same method as growth accounting—namely, assuming that observed factor shares represent elasticities of output with respect to factors—some of the same qualifications discussed earlier apply. These figures also should be viewed as approximations.

27. For a good summary of many of the relevant issues on industrial prices, see World Bank (1998).

REFERENCES

The word "processed" describes informally reproduced works that may not be commonly available through library systems.

Arrow, Kenneth. 1962. "The Economic Implications of Learning-by-Doing." *Review of Economic Studies* 29(June):155–73.

———. 1969. "Classificatory Notes on the Production and Transmission of Technological Knowledge." *American Economic Review* 59(May):29–35.

Arthur, Brian. 1994. *Increasing Returns and Path Dependence in the Economy.* Ann Arbor: University of Michigan Press.

Atkinson, A. B., and Joseph E. Stiglitz. 1969. "A New View of Technological Change." *Economic Journal* 59(September):46–69.

Blomstrom, Magnus, and Ari Kokko. 1997. "How Foreign Investment Affects Host Countries." Policy Research Working Paper 1745. World Bank, International Economics Department, International Trade Division, Washington, D.C. Processed.

Bosworth, Barry, and Susan Collins. 1996. "Economic Growth in East Asia: Accumulation vs. Assimilation." *Brookings Papers on Economic Activity* 2:135–203.

Caves, Richard, and others. 1992. *Industrial Efficiency in Six Nations.* Cambridge, Mass.: MIT Press.

Clark, Kim, and Takahiro Fujimoto. 1992. "Product Development and Competitiveness." *Journal of the Japanese and International Economies* 6(June):101–43.

Dahlman, Carl, and Ousa Sananikone. 1997. "Taiwan, China: Policies and Institutions for Rapid Growth." In Danny M. Leipziger, ed., *Lessons from East Asia.* Ann Arbor: University of Michigan Press.

Deaton, Angus, and Christina Paxson. 1994. "The Effects of Economics and Population Growth on National Saving." *Demography* 34(1):97–114.

Denison, Edward. 1962. *Sources of Economic Growth and the Alternatives before Us.* New York: Committee for Economic Development.

————. 1979. *Accounting for Slower Economic Growth: The United States in the 1970s.* Washington, D.C.: Brookings Institution.

Diamond, Peter, Daniel MacFadden, and Miguel Rodríguez. 1972. "Identification of the Elasticity of Substitution and the Bias of Technical Change." In Daniel MacFadden, ed., *An Econometric Approach to Production Theory.* Amsterdam: North-Holland.

Dollar, David, and Mary Hallward-Driemeier. 1998. "Crisis, Adjustment, and Reform: Results from the Thailand Industrial Survey." World Bank, Development Research Group, Washington, D.C. Processed.

Enos, John L., and U-hui Pak. 1987. *The Adoption and Diffusion of Imported Technology: The Case of Korea.* London: Croom Helm.

Evenson, Robert E., and Larry E. Westphal. 1995. "Technological Change and Technology Strategy." In Jere Behrman and T. N. Srinivasan, eds., *Handbook of Development Economics.* Vol. 3a. Amsterdam: North-Holland.

Furman, Jason, and Joseph E. Stiglitz. 1999. "Economic Crises: Evidence and Insight from East Asia." *Brookings Papers on Economic Activity 1998* 2:1–114.

Gee, San, and Chao-nan Chen. 1990. "In-Service Training in Taiwan, Republic of China." Chunghua Institution for Economic Research. Chunghua, Taiwan. Processed.

Gee, San, and Wen-jeng Kuo. 1994. "Export Success and Technological Capabilities: The Case of Textiles and Electronics in Taiwan Province of China." UNCTAD, Geneva. Processed.

Goh, Keng Swee. 1996. "The Technology Ladder in Development: The Singapore Case." *Asian Pacific Economic Literature* 10(201):1–11.

Goto, Akira, and Hiroyuki Odagiri. 1997. *Innovation in Japan.* New York: Oxford University Press.

Griliches, Zvi, and Dale Jorgenson. 1967. "The Explanation of Productivity Change." *Review of Economic Studies* 34(July):229–48.

Hall, Robert. 1990. "Invariance Properties of Solow's Productivity Residual." NBER Working Paper 3034. National Bureau of Economic Research, Cambridge, Mass. Processed.

Hayami, Yujiro, and Vernon Ruttan. 1985. *Agricultural Development: An International Perspective.* Baltimore, Md.: Johns Hopkins University Press.

Hayashi, Takeshi. 1990. *The Japanese Experience in Technology.* Tokyo: United Nations University.

Henderson, Vernon. 1988. *Urban Development: Theory, Fact, and Illusion.* New York: Oxford University Press.

Hobday, Mike. 1995. *Innovation in East Asia: The Challenge to Japan.* Aldershot: Edward Elgar.

Hsieh, Chang-Tai. 1997. "What Explains the Industrial Revolution in East Asia? Evidence from Factor Markets." University of California, Berkeley, Department of Economics. Processed.

Kaldor, Nicholas. 1957. "A Model of Economic Growth." *Economic Journal* 57(December):591–624.

Katz, Jorge. 1987. *Technology Generation in Latin American Manufacturing Industries.* London: Macmillan.

Kim, J. I., and L. J. Lau. 1994. "The Sources of Economic Growth in the East Asian Newly Industrialized Countries." *Journal of Japanese and International Economics* 8(2):235–71.

Kim, Linsu. 1997. *From Imitation to Innovation: Dynamics of Korea's Technological Learning.* Cambridge, Mass.: Harvard Business School Press.

King, Robert, and Ross Levine. 1994. "Capital Fundamentalism, Economic Development, and Economic Growth." *Carnegie Rochester Conference Series on Public Policy* 40(June):259–300.

Krugman, Paul. 1994. "The Myth of Asia's Miracle." *Foreign Affairs* (December): 62–78.

Kuznets, Paul. 1977. *Economic Growth and Structure in the Republic of Korea.* New Haven, Conn.: Yale University Press.

Lall, Sanjaya. 1987. *Learning to Industrialize.* London: Macmillan.

Lall, Sanjaya, and Morris Teubal. 1998. "Market Stimulating Technology Policies in Developing Countries: A Framework with Examples from East Asia." *World Development* 26(August):1369–85.

Lee, Norman. 1992. "Market Structure and Trade in Developing Countries." In Gerald K. Helleiner, ed., *Trade Policy, Industrialization, and Development: New Perspectives.* Oxford: Clarendon Press.

Levine, Ross, and David Renelt. 1992. "A Sensitivity Analysis of Cross-Country Growth Regressions." *American Economic Review* 82(September):942–63.

Lim, Linda Y. C., and Pang Eng Fong. 1991. *Foreign Direct Investment and Industri-*

alization in Malaysia, Singapore, Taiwan, and Thailand. Paris: Organisation for Economic Co-operation and Development.

McKinsey Global Institute. 1998. "Productivity-Led Growth in Korea." McKinsey and Company, Washington, D.C.. Processed.

Minami, Ryoshin. 1995. *Acquiring, Adapting, and Developing Technologies.* New York: St. Martin's Press.

Mytelka, L. K. 1978. "Licensing and Technology Dependence in the Andean Group." *World Development* 6(April):447–61.

Nehru, Vikram, and Ashok Dhareshwar. 1994. "New Estimates of Total Factor Productivity Growth for Developing and Industrial Countries." World Bank, Development Research Group, Washington D.C. Processed.

Nelson, Richard R., and Howard Pack. 1999. "The Asian Growth Miracle and Modern Growth Theory." *Economic Journal* 109(July):1–21.

Nelson, Richard R., and Edmund Phelps. 1966. "Investment in Humans, Technological Diffusion, and Economic Growth." *American Economic Review* 56(May):69–75.

Nelson, Richard R., and Sidney Winter. 1982. *An Evolutionary Theory of Economic Change.* Cambridge, Mass.: Harvard University Press.

Nishimizu, Mieko, and John M. Page. 1982. "Total Factor Productivity Growth, Technological Progress, and Technical Efficiency: Dimensions of Productivity Change in Yugoslavia 1965–78." *Economic Journal*: 92(December):920–36.

Nordhaus, William. 1997. "Traditional Productivity Estimates are Asleep at the (Technological) Switch." *Economic Journal* 107(September):1548–59.

Ozawa, Terutomo. 1974. *Japan's Technological Challenge to the West, 1950–74: Motivation and Accomplishment.* Cambridge, Mass.: MIT Press.

Pack, Howard. 1987. *Productivity, Technology, and Industrial Development.* New York: Oxford University Press.

———. 1994. "Endogenous Growth Theory: Intellectual Appeal and Empirical Shortcomings." *Journal of Economic Perspectives* 8(Winter):55–72.

———. 2000. "Industrial Policy: Growth Elixir or Poison?" *The World Bank Research Observer* 15(1):47–67.

Pack, Howard, and Kamal Saggi. 1999. "Exporting, Externalities, and Technology Transfer." Policy Research Paper. World Bank, Policy Research Department, Washington, D.C. Processed.

———. Forthcoming. "Vertical Technology Transfer, Diffusion, and Competition." *Journal of Development Economics.*

Pack, Howard, and Larry E. Westphal. 1986. "Industrial Strategy and Technological Change: Theory vs. Reality." *Journal of Development Economics* 22(January):87–128.

Pack, Howard, Fang-yi Wang, and Larry E. Westphal. 1996. "Acquisition of Technical Knowledge in the Taiwanese Electronics Sector." Swarthmore College, Department of Economics, Swarthmore, Penn. Processed.

Pilat, Dirk. 1994. *The Economics of Rapid Growth: The Experience of Japan and Korea.* Brookfield, Vt.: Edward Elgar.

Pratten, C. F. 1971. *Economies of Scale in Manufacturing Industry.* Cambridge, Mass.: Cambridge University Press.

Ranis, Gustav. 1979. "Industrial Development." In Walter Galenson, ed., *Economic Growth and Structural Change in Taiwan.* Ithaca, N.Y.: Cornell University.

Ranis, Gustav, and Chi Schive. 1985. "Direct Foreign Investment in Taiwan's Development." In Walter Galenson, ed., *Foreign Trade and Investment: Economic Development in the Newly Industrializing Asian Countries.* Madison: University of Wisconsin Press.

Republic of China. 1992. *Taiwan Statistical Data Book 1992.* Taipei: Council for Economic Planning and Development.

Rhee, Yung, Bruce Ross-Larson, and Gary Pursell. 1984. *Korea's Competitive Edge: Managing Entry into World Markets.* Baltimore, Md.: Johns Hopkins University Press.

Rosenberg, Nathan. 1994. "Uncertainty and Technological Advance." Stanford University, Department of Economics, Palo Alto, Calif. Processed.

Ruttan, Vernon. 1997. "Induced Innovation, Evolutionary Theory, and Path Dependence: Sources of Technical Change." *Economic Journal* 107(September):1520–29.

Sakong, Il. 1993. *Korea in the World Economy.* Washington, D.C.: Institute for International Economics.

Sarel, Michael. 1997. "Growth and Productivity in ASEAN Countries." IMF Working Paper 97/97. International Monetary Fund, Washington D.C. Processed.

Schultz, Theodore W. 1975. "The Value of the Ability to Deal with Disequilibria." *Journal of Economic Literature* 13(September):827–46.

Solow, Robert M. 1957. "Technical Change and the Aggregate Production Function." *Review of Economics and Statistics* 39(May):312–20.

———. 1960. "Investment and Technical Progress." In Kenneth Arrow, Samuel Karlin, and Patrick Suppes, eds., *Mathematical Methods in the Social Sciences.* Palo Alto, Calif.: Stanford University Press.

———. 1987. "On the Microeconomics of Technical Progress." In Jorge Katz, ed., *Technology Generation in Latin American Manufacturing Industries.* New York: Macmillan.

Stiglitz, Joseph. 1987. "Learning to Learn, Localized Learning, and Technological Progress." In Partha Dasgupta and Paul Stoneman, eds., *Economic Policy and Technological Performance.* New York: Cambridge University Press.

———. 1988. "Economic Organization, Information, and Development." In Hollis B. Chenery and T. N. Srinivasan, eds., *Handbook of Development Economics.* Vol 1. Amsterdam: North-Holland.

———. 1993. "The Role of the State in Financial Markets." *Proceedings of the World Bank Annual Conference on Development Economics.* Washington, D.C.: World Bank.

Tsao, Yuan. 1985. "Growth without Productivity: Singapore Manufacturing in the 1970s." *Journal of Development Economics* 19(1):25–39.

UNESCO (United Nations Educational, Scientific, and Cultural Organization). 1983. *Statistical Yearbook.* New York.

United Nations. 1997. *World Investment Report 1997.* New York.

———. Various years. *Yearbook of National Accounts Statistics.* New York.

———. 1995. *Statistical Yearbook.* New York.

World Bank. 1979. "Korea: Development of the Machinery Industries." World Bank, Industrial Development and Finance Department, Washington, D.C. Processed.

———. 1993. *The East Asian Miracle: Economic Growth and Public Policy.* New York: Oxford University Press.

———. 1998. *East Asia: The Road to Recovery.* Washington, D.C.

Young, Alwyn. 1992. "Tale of Two Cities: Factor Accumulation and Technical Change in Hong Kong and Singapore." *NBER Macroeconomics Annual: 1992.* Cambridge, Mass.: MIT Press.

———. 1995. "The Tyranny of Numbers: Confronting the Statistical Realities of the East Asian Growth Experience." *Quarterly Journal of Economics* 110(August):641–80.

CHAPTER 4

CHINESE RURAL INDUSTRIALIZATION IN THE CONTEXT OF THE EAST ASIAN MIRACLE

Justin Yifu Lin and Yang Yao

Rural industrialization has been exclusively an East Asian phenomenon and has constituted an indispensable part of the East Asian miracle. As the largest economy in the region, China has kept up with, if not exceeded, the neighboring economies in industrializing its countryside. China's economic development in the past 20 years has been supported largely by the rapid growth of its rural industrial sector, which is composed of numerous small-scale rural enterprises (REs) established by townships, villages, and individuals.[1] China's unique feature is its unprecedented scale. In 1978, less than 10 percent of the rural labor force was engaged in industrial activities, and the nonfarm sector contributed only 8 percent of rural income; by 1996, 30 percent of the rural labor force was working in local industry, and nonfarm income accounted for 34 percent of total rural income. This remarkable growth, although its role in regional income disparity remains controversial, has brought more equal income distribution at the local level.

The magnitude and speed of China's rural industrialization have attracted wide attention in the international academic community. Several competing theories have been developed to explain the success. Culture theory has been applied to emphasize the role of cooperative culture in the Chinese village in enhancing the development of rural enterprises. The new growth theory has been applied to emphasize the positive externality created by the accumulation of knowledge, and recently of social capital, in promoting sustainable growth. Fascinated by the existence of public firms owned by local governments, a large body of the literature focuses on the positive functions of vaguely defined property rights in promoting the rapid growth of rural enterprises. This body of literature emphasizes the positive role of local governments—noticeably those at the township and village levels—in helping rural enterprises to obtain access to precious financial and material resources as well as to walk through the mazelike bureaucratic hierarchy. Yet another theory points to the alignment of rural enterprises with the comparative advantage of rural China. This explanation, classical as it is, is often overlooked in economists' search for new and exotic theories, yet it may explain China's successful rural industrialization as well as the wide regional disparity in its vast territory.

The aim of this chapter is to evaluate the different explanations as well as to present an overview of the development and characteristics of China's rural enterprises. An econometric analysis is conducted to test various competing theories explaining their success. The history of rural industrialization in the Chinese provinces in the past 30 some years is analyzed.

We also place the Chinese experience in the context of East Asia and compare it to that of other East Asian countries, notably Thailand. The Chinese experience has unique features that are specific to its recent historical events and background. Nevertheless, there also are commonalties between the experience of China and that of some of the other East Asian countries. In the light of the Asian financial crisis, the Chinese experience could provide a useful lesson for other developing countries. Although the crisis was triggered by capital flight, the economies hit most by the crisis might have had some fundamental faults that could not withstand serious financial shocks. Governments in Korea, Thailand, and other East and Southeast Asian countries encouraged the development of large-scale industrial establishments in the hope of competing in the world markets. However, this development strategy largely deviated from these countries' comparative advantage as revealed in the world division of labor. This deviation, together with these countries' weak but closely directed financial systems, constituted the fundamental cause of the crisis. As such, the proposition of the developmental state postulated in World Bank (1993) could not stand the test even in Korea, which was regarded as having the right institutional and cultural context for the proposition to succeed. By presenting the experience of China and that of Taiwan (China) and early Japan as successful cases of aligning policy with the country's comparative advantage, this chapter seeks to improve the understanding of the Asian financial crisis as well as of the mechanism of development in general.

CONTRIBUTION OF RURAL ENTERPRISES TO CHINA'S NATIONAL ECONOMY

After more than 20 years of growth, rural enterprises have changed the economic landscape in China's rural areas. In the period 1978 to 1997, the number of rural enterprises increased from 1.5 million to 20.2 million, and the number of workers hired increased from 28.3 million to 130.5 million, or from 9 to 28 percent of the rural labor force. The share of rural enterprises in the total value of gross rural output increased more remarkably. In 1978, rural enterprises created only 24 percent of total gross rural output; by 1995, their contribution had increased to 79 percent (table 4.1).

Equally remarkable, rural enterprises became one of the major forces behind China's overall sustained growth. The output value of rural enterprises in the industrial sectors accounted for only 9 percent of the national total in 1978. After almost 20 years, this figure was 58 percent in 1997. Rural industry is no longer merely a supplement to agricultural production; it is now an indispensable source of growth nationwide. It is widely acknowledged that exports are one of the leading factors contributing to China's recent success. Rural enterprises have done equally well in exporting, especially in the past 10 years, a period in which their exports increased much faster than the national average. In 1986, the RE share of total exports was only 9 percent; by 1997, the figure was 46 percent (table 4.2).

When the comparison comes down to the provincial level, there clearly is a close correlation between RE development and per capita gross domestic product (GDP). The data presented in table 4.3 show that the provinces with higher levels of RE development are also those with high per capita GDP. This leads to the question of whether the

Table 4.1 The Development of Rural Enterprises in China, 1978-97 (current prices)

Year	Labor force			Gross output[a]		Industrial output		Rural income	
	Number of firms (millions)	Amount millions of (persons)	Percent of total rural labor	Value (100 million yuan)	Percent of total rural output[b]	Value (100 million yuan)	Percent of national output	Per capita income[b]	Contribution of rural enterprises (percent)
1978	1.52	28.27	9.2	495.1	24.2	385.3	9.1	122.9	7.6
1979	1.48	29.09	9.4	552.3	—	425.3	9.1	—	—
1980	1.42	30.00	9.4	656.9	23.5	515.1	10.0	166.4	10.1
1981	1.34	29.70	9.1	736.7	—	567.9	10.5	194.5	—
1982	1.36	31.13	9.2	846.3	30.4	636.0	12.0	—	—
1983	1.35	32.35	9.3	1,007.9	24.4	744.3	11.5	272.91	—
1984	6.07	52.08	14.5	1,697.8	33.7	1,240.0	16.3	315.06	—
1985	12.22	69.79	18.8	2,755.0	43.5	1,845.9	19.0	350.1	24.6
1986	15.15	79.37	20.9	3,583.3	47.7	2,443.5	21.8	374.68	—
1987	17.50	88.05	22.6	4,947.7	52.4	3,412.4	24.7	418.4	28.1
1988	18.88	95.45	23.8	7,017.8	56.0	4,992.9	27.4	494	30
1989	18.69	93.67	22.9	8,401.8	58.0	6,144.7	27.9	540.3	31.2
1990	18.50	92.65	22.1	9,581.1	57.7	7,097.1	29.7	623.1	26.8
1991	19.08	96.09	22.3	11,611.7	61.1	8,708.6	32.7	638.9	27.9
1992	20.92	106.25	24.2	17,695.7	69.7	13,193.4	38.1	746	27.1
1993	24.53	123.45	27.9	31,776.9	74.3	23,558.6	48.7	873	32.5
1994	24.95	120.18	26.9	45,378.5	74.2	34,688.0	49.4	1,144.8	31.8
1995	22.03	128.61	28.6	68,915.2	77.2	51,259.2	55.8	1,479.5	32.6
1996	23.36	135.08	29.8	77,903.5	76.9	55,901.1	56.1	1,813.3	34.2
1997	20.15	130.50	28.4	89,900.6	78.5	65,851.5	57.9	1,987.27	—

— Not available.

a. Gross output is the total of all kinds of rural enterprises as defined in the text.

b. The values of total rural gross output after 1991 only include the output of agricultural and rural enterprises, whereas the values for other years include outputs (such as household sideline products) that are not covered by the two categories. Rural income is income net of transfer and remittance income.

Source: State Statistical Bureau (SSB) China Statistical Yearbook, 1997, 1998; The Yearbook of Chinese Township and Village Enterprises, 1995, 1997, 1998; China Economic Yearbook, 1997, 1998.

Table 4.2 Export Performance of Rural Enterprises in China, 1986–97
(100 million U.S. dollars in current prices)

Year	Total exports	Rural enterprise exports	Ratio of rural enterprise exports to total exports	Ratio of rural enterprise exports to total output
1986	309.42	28.45	9.19	0.03
1987	394.37	43.45	11.02	0.03
1988	475.40	72.31	15.21	0.04
1989	525.38	99.77	18.99	0.04
1990	620.91	96.07	15.47	0.05
1991	719.10	148.27	20.62	0.07
1992	849.40	216.66	25.51	0.07
1993	917.44	380.70	41.50	0.07
1994	1,210.38	394.64	32.60	0.07
1995	1,487.70	644.58	43.33	0.08
1996	1,510.66	723.86	47.92	0.08
1997	1,827.00	836.93	45.81	0.08

Sources: SSB. *China Statistical Yearbook, 1995, 1997, 1998; The Yearbook of Chinese Township and Village Enterprises, 1995, 1997, 1998.*

development of rural enterprises has exacerbated China's regional economic disparity (see, for example, Lin, Cai, and Li 1997; Rozelle 1994). Ignoring interprovincial equality for a moment, let us first look at how RE development has affected income disparity inside a province.

Table 4.3 shows the shares of nonagricultural output in total rural output in China's 30 provincial units and their Gini coefficients of income per capita for both urban and rural areas together and for rural areas alone in 1992.[2] The 30 provincial units are divided into two groups according to their nonagricultural shares, using the median as the cutoff point. The group with higher nonagricultural shares (averaging 65 percent) consisted of all the coastal provinces and municipalities and several resource-rich inland provinces, while the group with lower shares (averaging 30 percent) were all inland provinces. Contrary to the general belief, income distribution on average was more equitable in the first group than in the second group. The average of the provincial Gini coefficients was 0.25 for the first group, whereas it was 0.28 for the second group. The gap between the averages of the rural Gini coefficients was also 0.03, with the average of the first group being 0.14 and that of the second group being 0.16. This seemingly small gap of 0.02 was actually quite significant, as the

Table 4.3 Share of Nonagricultural Output and Income Disparity of China's Provinces, 1992

| | Share of rural enterprise output in total rural output (percent) | Gini coefficient | |
		Whole region	Rural areas
Whole country	60	0.35	0.20
Provinces with higher levels			
Shanghai	86	0.12	0.09
Tianjin	85	0.14	0.03
Beijing	78	0.04	0.13
Jiangsu	76	0.30	0.16
Zhejiang	76	0.30	0.23
Shandong	67	0.31	0.13
Shanxi	66	0.32	0.15
Hebei	63	0.30	0.17
Liaonin	63	0.24	0.15
Guangdong	61	0.40	0.12
Henan	59	0.25	0.13
Fujian	54	0.24	0.10
Sichuan	49	0.30	0.18
Anhui	48	0.26	0.13
Shannxi	47	0.30	0.13
Submean	65	0.25	0.14
Provinces with lower levels			
Hubei	46	0.31	0.16
Jiangxi	44	0.22	0.16
Hunan	43	0.23	0.12
Jilin	43	0.20	0.05
Gansu	42	0.38	0.24
Heilongjiang	38	0.21	0.12
Ninxia	35	0.43	0.30
Guangxi	30	0.25	0.17
Guizhou	27	0.34	0.18
Inner Mongolia	27	0.23	0.13
Yunnan	27	0.39	0.25
Qinhai	21	0.31	0.15
Xingjiang	15	0.31	0.15
Hainan	14	0.29	0.08
Tibet	04	0.16	0.16
Submean	30	0.28	0.16

Sources: Figures of the shares of nonagricultural income are from SSB. 1993. *Rural Statistical Yearbook of China*, China Statistical Press, Beijing.; Gini coefficients are from Lin, Cai, and Li (1997: table 11).

Gini coefficient of income per capita for the whole country was only raised from 0.13 in 1978 to 0.18 in 1995 (Lin, Cai, and Li 1997).

The remarkable role of Chinese rural enterprises in bringing equitable income distribution inside a province is achieved by their small, indigenous, and labor-intensive nature. This is very much like Taiwan and in contrast to the Republic of Korea. In Korea, industrialization was accomplished by drawing rural migrants into cities where a few fairly large firms were concentrated. Although the country was industrialized as rapidly as Taiwan was, its rural areas, until very recently, were much less developed than those of Taiwan (Saith 1987). China, by coincidence or intention, followed Taiwan's road to industrialization by establishing labor-intensive and low-tech firms in rural areas. The labor-intensive and indigenous nature of rural enterprises enabled a wide range of the population to share the benefits created by them, which reduced the income disparities both between and within urban and rural areas. In addition, as the demand for RE products increased, the return to labor—the factor that is used most intensively—was raised faster than the return to capital, the factor used less intensively. This added benefit to labor accelerated the equalization of income between urban and rural areas.

However, there is also a debate about whether the uneven development of rural enterprises among China's provinces exacerbated regional income disparity. Although no study provides direct empirical evidence, Lin, Cai, and Li (1997) show that the most significant factor contributing to China's income disparity is the income gap between rural and urban residents, whereas the gap between coastal and inland areas is not a significant factor. Therefore, the regional income disparity is likely related to the contrast between a large rural population in the inland provinces and a smaller rural population in the coastal provinces. By raising incomes in rural areas, therefore, the development of rural enterprises attacks the most important factor in China's income inequality.

A BRIEF HISTORICAL PERSPECTIVE

In the period of the People's Republic before the 1970s, China's industrialization overwhelmingly favored large establishments in heavy industries. As a result, rural areas were largely left out of the industrialization process. Ironically, steady growth in the RE sector started in the early 1970s as a response to a call for mechanizing Chinese agriculture, a policy that was not in touch with Chinese reality. Responding to the call, some rural areas began to set up commune- and brigade-owned factories for manufacturing agricultural machinery and repairing farm tools. As the urban factories were paralyzed by factional divisions during the Cultural Revolution, a large market opened for the products of rural enterprises. As a result, the value of their output increased from 9.5 billion yuan in 1970 to 27.2 billion yuan in 1976, with an average annual growth rate of 26 percent.[3] After the fall of the Gang of Four in 1976, the development of the commune and brigade enterprises accelerated. By 1978, the value of their output reached 49.3 billion yuan in 1970 constant prices, with employment of 28.3 million. However, the output value of commune and brigade enterprises only accounted for 24 percent of the total value of rural gross output, and their employment constituted less than 10 percent of total agricultural labor (table 4.1).

The development of the commune and brigade enterprises in the 1970s laid a solid foundation for RE development in the 1980s. In fact, the many publicly owned rural enterprises that have attracted wide academic interest were a continuum of these firms (Putterman 1997). In addition, the commune system, although it was proven a dysfunctional economic organization, resulted in considerable investments in rural infrastructure building, notably roads. Nevertheless, the strongest factor determining the geographic distribution of rural enterprises in the 1970s was the endowment of land and labor, as shown by their concentration in the coastal provinces.

The rural reform carried out at the end of the 1970s and beginning of the 1980s opened a new chapter for China's rural areas. In accordance, rural industrialization embarked on a fast track to success. From 1978 to 1984, the family farming system, which had been abandoned for 20 years, was restored. As a result of the reform, the real value of agricultural output increased at an annual rate of 6 percent in this period. By one estimation, the reform contributed 60 percent of this agricultural growth (Lin 1992). The fast growth of agricultural output, although occupying the major efforts of the rural areas, accumulated crucial initial capital for the takeoff of rural enterprises.

The period 1984 to 1988 was the takeoff period of China's rural industrialization and witnessed the fastest growth of rural enterprises. This can be attributed to several institutional and market reforms, notably the dismantling of the commune system and price reform, as well as to the increased income in rural areas. In 1984, 4.7 million new firms were set up, and the total number of firms reached 6.1 million, four and a half times the number in 1983. In the next year, the number of firms more than doubled again, reaching 12.2 million (table 4.1). Most of the newly established firms were privately owned or operated. In 1984, 69 percent out of the total of 6.1 million rural enterprises were private or cooperative enterprises, and the ratio increased to 89 percent in 1986 (see Chen 1988).

In the 1990s, the RE sector continued to expand at a robust pace. In addition, privatization was launched to correct the disincentives in publicly owned firms. By the end of 1998, more than 80 percent of the public firms owned by county- or lower-level governments had been privatized (Zhao 1999). This completely changed China's economic landscape at the grassroots level. In recent years, the number of firms has declined, but this may be only a correction to the overinvestment made after Deng's 1992 speech calling for continuation of the reform efforts. Indeed, unlike the number of firms, the RE output continued to expand throughout the period. This may indicate a structural adjustment by which inefficient firms were eliminated or consolidated with efficient firms.

DETERMINANTS OF RURAL ENTERPRISE DEVELOPMENT IN THE REFORM ERA

Several salient features characterize RE development in the reform era. First, much of the capital supporting RE development came initially from agricultural surplus and later from the accumulation of rural enterprises themselves. Credits provided by the formal banking system were minimal. Second, rural enterprises were overwhelmingly concentrated in labor- and resource-intensive industries, although those in the coastal areas recently began to enter capital-intensive and sophisticated consumer product industries. Third, Chinese rural enterprises were characterized by a wide range of ownership types; nevertheless, the trend was toward private ownership in the 1990s. Fourth, rural enterprises were tied to urban industry in various ways, ranging from obtaining technologies, equipment, personnel, and market channels from urban enterprises to engaging heads-on competition with them. Lastly, RE development was distributed unevenly across the country, but the pattern can be explained mostly by differences in the initial conditions, location, and factor endowments possessed by different regions. In the rest of this section, we review these five major characteristics in detail. The objective of the review is to demonstrate the complexities and dynamics of China's rural industrialization as well as to present the competing theories that try to explain the success of China's rural enterprises.

Capital Accumulation

Two factors contributed to the initial capital accumulation of rural enterprises in rural China during the early reform period. First, the heavy industry–oriented development strategy gradually weakened, and the price ceilings on agricultural products were reduced in relative terms (Feng and Li 1993). Second, the household responsibility system that was implemented in the rural areas restored farmers' work incentives and drastically raised agricultural output and income in the first half of the 1980s (Lin 1992). These two factors combined have resulted in large increases in rural savings. Table 4.4 shows the deposits received by rural credit cooperatives between 1978 and 1993. Rural credit cooperatives are the only type of financial institution that is officially allowed to exist below the county level, so the amount of deposits received by them is a good proxy for the total amount of savings in rural areas. The total amount of deposits made in 1993 was 26 times that in 1978.

The initial growth and capital accumulation of rural enterprises were also facilitated by a large market for basic consumer goods that was left unfilled as a result of the catch-up development strategy pursued before 1978. The Chinese industrial structure was strongly oriented toward heavy industry at the outset of the reform. Table 4.5 shows the amount of fixed capital investment allocated to light and heavy industries and their shares of the industrial total in different periods from 1952 to 1978. As less than 10 percent of the investment was directed

Table 4.4 Deposits Received by Rural Credit Cooperatives in China, 1978–93
(100 million yuan in current prices)

Year	Total	By collectives		By rural enterprises		By households		
		Amount	Share	Amount	Share	Amount	Share	Other
1978	166.0	93.8	0.57	—	—	55.7	0.34	16.5
1979	215.9	98.3	0.46	21.9	0.10	78.4	0.36	17.3
1980	272.3	105.5	0.39	29.5	0.11	117.0	0.43	20.3
1981	319.6	113.2	0.35	29.7	0.09	169.6	0.53	7.1
1982	389.9	121.1	0.31	33.7	0.09	228.1	0.59	7.0
1983	487.4	91.8	0.19	62.3	0.13	319.9	0.66	13.4
1984	624.9	89.9	0.14	81.1	0.13	438.1	0.70	15.8
1985	724.9	71.9	0.10	72.1	0.10	564.8	0.78	16.1
1986	962.3	83.9	0.09	91.7	0.10	766.1	0.80	20.6
1987	1,225.2	89.9	0.07	104.7	0.09	1,005.7	0.82	24.9
1988	1,399.8	98.4	0.07	128.3	0.09	1,142.3	0.82	30.8
1989	1,669.5	92.3	0.06	126.2	0.08	1,412.1	0.85	38.9
1990	2,144.5	106.5	0.05	149.9	0.07	1,841.6	0.86	47.0
1991	2,709.5	135.9	0.05	191.7	0.07	2,316.7	0.86	65.2
1992	3,477.7	215.2	0.06	301.8	0.09	2,867.3	0.82	93.4
1993	4,297.3	245.8	0.06	362.1	0.08	3,576.2	0.83	113.2

— Not available.

Source: SSB, Financial Press, Beining, China Financial Yearbook. 1990–93

to light industry in most of the period, a shortage of consumer goods was evident, symbolized by rationing coupons covering products ranging from basic foods to a limited number of luxury goods. With the adoption of the reform and open-door policy in the late 1970s and early 1980s, income in both urban and rural areas was raised. In the period 1978 to 1992, rural and urban consumption expenditure grew at an average annual rate of 6.5 and 5.8 percent, respectively, much higher than their growth rates in the period 1952 to 1977 (1.8 and 3.0 percent, respectively; see Lin, Cai, and Li 1994: 155). After two decades of stagnation, the high growth in the demand for consumer goods created a perfect opportunity for rural industry to occupy the niche of labor-intensive consumer goods left by the heavy industry–oriented state-run enterprises.

As for the channels of finance, rural enterprises rely heavily on household savings and borrowing from the informal financial market, and credits in the form of formal bank loans are limited. Table 4.6 compares the amount of formal bank loans obtained by rural enterprises and state-owned enterprises (SOEs) in recent years. The state banks (including rural credit cooperatives) overwhelmingly favor the SOEs, which received nearly 90 percent of their loans from 1993 to 1996.

Table 4.5 Industrial Fixed Capital Investment in China, 1952–78
(billion yuan in current prices)

Period	Light industry		Heavy industry	
	Amount	Share (percent)	Amount	Share (percent)
First Five-Year Plan (1952–57)	3.75	15.0	21.28	85.0
Second Five-Year Plan (1957–62)	7.66	10.1	65.17	89.9
Adjustment Period (1963–65)	1.65	7.8	19.37	92.2
Third Five-Year Plan (1966–70)	4.26	7.9	49.89	92.1
Fourth Five-Year Plan (1971–75)	10.30	10.5	87.49	89.5
Fifth Five-Year Plan (1976–78)	7.48	10.6	62.45	89.4

Source: Lin, Cai, and Li (1994: 62).

Foreign direct investment (FDI) has been playing an increasingly important role in financing China's rural industrialization. In 1978, the amount of realized FDI was only US$263 million. By 1997, it reached US$64.4 billion. Although data on the amount of FDI received by rural firms are not available, it is believed that a large part of FDI has gone to firms in the rural areas of coastal provinces. This assessment is especially pertinent to capital from the Great China regions, namely, Hong Kong, Taiwan, Macao, and Singapore. Studies show that FDI from this group of investors is more likely to enter labor-intensive sectors that are dominated by rural enterprises (Wang 1997). In 1995, 28 percent of the output of firms at the township and village level was created by FDI firms, which include firms solely owned by foreign investors and joint ventures.

Industrial Structure

The industrial structure of rural enterprises reflects the comparative advantage of China's rural areas. At the international level, comparative advantage in international trade is still dominated by each country's factor endowments (Song 1993). With abundant labor and limited land, natural resources, and capital, China's comparative advantage clearly rests in labor-intensive industries. Table 4.7 compares China with several developed and Asian developing countries in their nonresidential capital stocks per worker in 1975 and 1990. China was at the lower end of capital endowment per worker in both years (only India was lower), making clear that its comparative advantage in the international division of labor rests in labor-intensive industries.

Inside China, rural areas are obviously endowed with far less capital and far more labor and resources than cities. Table 4.8 shows the industrial structure of township and village-owned enterprises from 1987 to 1996. At the early stage of development, these enterprises were heavily resource-based. In 1987, 61 percent of their light industrial output and 93 percent of their heavy industrial output were generated by resource-based enterprises. In 1996, these enterprises were still largely resource-based, but light industries have been departing from this pattern over the years. In 1996, the share of resource-based output dropped to 53 percent of the light industrial total. This trend is consistent with changes in the factor endowments. In addition, Lu

Table 4.6 Access of Rural Enterprises and State-Owned Enterprises to Formal Bank Loans in China, 1993–96 (billions of yuan in current prices)

Year	Rural enterprises			State-owned enterprises		
	Loan (billion yuan)	Share (percent)	Loan/profit (yuan)	Loan (billion yuan)	Share (percent)	Loan/profit (yuan)
1993	2,198	9.08	1.24	22,014	90.02	8.97
1994	3,686	12.37	1.61	26,104	87.63	9.08
1995	4,823	13.41	1.48	31,149	86.59	10.84
1996	5,191	13.14	1.34	34,324	86.86	12.54

Note: Loan is the total liability at the end of each year. Profit is measured in before-tax terms.
Source: SSB, China Statistical Year Book: 1995, 1997; The Yearbook of Chinese Township and Village Enterprises: 1995, 1997.

Table 4.7 International Comparison of Nonresidential Capital Stocks per Worker in China, 1975 and 1990 (U.S. dollars in 1985 international prices)

Year	United States	United Kingdom	France	Japan	Republic of Korea	Taiwan (China)	Thailand	Philippines	India	China
1975	26,109	14,618	24,242	16,400	6,533	8,451	2,385	3,314	1,259	1,869
1990	34,705	21,179	35,600	36,480	17,995	25,722	4,912	3,698	1,946	3,260

Source: International data are from Penn World Tables, Mark 5.6. Chinese data are calculated based on figures published in The Statistical Yearbook of Chinese Industries: 1991. Chinese Statistical Press, Beijing. The producer price index is used to convert the values into 1985 constant prices. The official exchange rate in 1985, 2.94 yuan to the U.S. dollar, is used to convert Chinese yuan into dollars.

(1998) shows that China is losing comparative advantage in grain production. Therefore, it is unwise for rural enterprises to stick to food and related industries whose relative input prices are rising.

Rural enterprises use much more labor and much less capital than SOEs in the cities. Table 4.9 compares the capital intensities of rural enterprises and SOEs from 1978 to 1996. Net capital stock per worker of rural enterprises has never passed 20 percent of that of SOEs, and the number of workers hired by rural enterprises per 10,000 yuan of output has been several times that of the number hired by SOEs for most years. However, the gap between SOEs and rural enterprises in their capital intensities has narrowed through the years. This catch-up can be explained by rural enterprises' adjustment to changes in the factor endowments (and thus the comparative advantages) in the economy. One indicator of this change is that the gap between the average annual wage per worker of rural enterprises and that of SOEs has narrowed.

The labor-intensive nature of Chinese rural enterprises has enhanced their position in China's exports. As table 4.2 shows, the RE share of China's exports was only 9 percent in 1986; but after that year, it grew at an average annual rate of 21 percent for the next 10 years, reaching 48 percent in 1996. From 1986 to 1995, the percentage of exports in the total output of rural enterprises was raised from 3 to 8 percent, a 1.6 times increase, as rural enterprises shifted from domestic to international markets and the growth rate of their output outpaced the national average.

Ownership and Its Dynamics

Unlike its urban industry, which is dominated by public ownership, China's rural industry is characterized by a plurality of ownership. There is a heavy presence of local government ownership among the rural enterprises. Together with the extraordinary performance of Chinese rural enterprises, this has spurred wide academic interest in the relationship between local government ownership and the success of rural enterprises. Several theories have emerged to explain why local government ownership emerged and why it was successful. Most of them treat public ownership as a second-best choice in an imperfect institutional and market environment (Fan 1988; Chang and Wang

Table 4.8 Output Distribution of Township and Village-Owned Enterprises in China, 1987–96
(billions of yuan in current prices unless otherwise noted)

Year	Light industries			Heavy industries		
	Total value (billions of yuan in current prices)	Resource-based firms (percent)	Manufacturing firms (percent)	Total value (billions of yuan in current prices)	Resource-based firms (percent)	Manufacturing firms (percent)
1987	134.93	61.21	38.79	126.09	93.10	6.90
1988	182.69	58.39	41.61	161.09	92.88	7.12
1989	237.98	59.93	40.07	223.47	93.19	6.81
1990	282.17	59.93	40.07	241.85	93.31	6.69
1991	354.49	59.47	40.53	297.34	93.36	6.64
1992	523.17	57.34	42.66	462.11	93.20	6.80
1993	864.00	56.05	43.95	832.23	93.16	6.84
1994	1,292.40	57.41	42.59	1,260.08	93.22	6.78
1995	1,846.11	55.95	44.05	1,628.26	93.33	6.67
1996	1,851.75	52.91	47.09	1,702.12	93.47	6.53

Source: SSB, Yearbook of Township and Village Enterprises, 1995, 1997; China Statistical Yearbook, 1995, 1997.

Table 4.9 Capital Intensity and Wages of State-Owned Enterprises and Rural Enterprises in China, 1978–96

Year	Capital per worker (yuan)			Workers per 10,000 yuan of output			Annual wage (yuan)		
	State-owned enterprises	Rural enterprises	Ratio of rural to state-owned enterprises	State-owned enterprises	Rural enterprises	Ratio of rural to state-owned enterprises	State-owned enterprises	Rural enterprises	Ratio of rural to state-owned enterprises
1978	7,090	643	0.09	0.92	5.71	6.21	681	307	0.45
1979	—	777	—	0.86	5.27	6.11	755	357	0.47
1980	7,582	887	0.12	0.85	4.57	5.38	852	398	0.47
1981	—	1,024	—	0.86	4.03	4.69	851	440	0.52
1982	—	1,100	—	0.83	3.68	4.46	863	493	0.57
1983	—	1,153	—	0.76	3.21	4.20	877	544	0.62
1984	9,255	856	0.09	0.71	3.07	4.32	1,070	601	0.56
1985	10,435	—	—	0.65	2.53	3.88	1,239	676	0.55
1986	11,489	—	—	0.64	2.22	3.47	1,448	738	0.51
1987	12,830	—	—	0.50	1.78	3.59	1,601	836	0.52
1988	14,283	—	—	0.41	1.36	3.33	1,931	1,009	0.52
1989	16,460	—	—	0.35	1.11	3.22	2,177	1,126	0.52
1990	18,534	2,254	0.12	0.33	0.97	2.89	2,409	1,219	0.51
1991	21,259	2,484	0.12	0.30	0.83	2.77	2,627	1,358	0.52
1992	24,293	2,964	0.12	0.25	0.60	2.37	3,161	1,445	0.46
1993	29,578	4,164	0.14	0.20	0.39	1.96	3,912	1,898	0.49
1994	31,282	5,539	0.18	0.17	0.26	1.59	5,165	2,499	0.48
1995	39,741	7,933	0.20	0.14	0.19	1.33	6,343	3,406	0.54
1996	51,767	9,254	0.18	0.15	—	—	7,069	3,957	0.56

— Not available.

Note: Capital is the average net fixed capital stock in each year. Figures are measured in current prices. Figures of rural enterprises before 1984 do not account for private firms.

Source: SSB, *China Statistical Yearbook, 1995, 1997; The Yearbook of Chinese Township and Village Enterprises, 1995, 1997.*

1994; D. Li 1994; Che and Qian 1998; S. Li 1997; Zhao 1997). Some of them point to the cooperative culture in Chinese villages (Weitzman and Xu 1994). Although these theories have some merit, the past two decades have shown that their applicability might be limited to specific periods of time.

In the planning era, there were no private firms in China. In the early stage of the rural reform, although private firms were not encouraged by the government, their number still increased drastically. The official abolishment of the commune system and the beginning of the urban reform in 1984 further accelerated the development of private rural enterprises. Table 4.10 shows the development of private rural enterprises from 1984 to 1997. In 1984, 69 percent of rural enterprises were privately owned. In 1997, that figure had grown to 94 percent; that is, private firms had become the vast majority of rural enterprises. In terms of employment and output, private firms accounted for 59 percent of total RE employment and 51 percent of total RE output in 1997. Therefore, although individual private firms are generally smaller than publicly owned firms, they had become as important as public firms. Overly emphasizing the functions of publicly owned firms is misleading because the majority of rural enterprises are privately owned, and they account for more than half of total RE employment and output.

Entering the 1990s, privatization programs have spread widely throughout the country. In the process of their development, rural public firms began to share the same soft-budget constraints as their urban counterparts (Zhang 1997). They also shouldered other functions such as employment generation. As a result, they operated much less efficiently than private firms (Yao 1998). These problems provided the impetus for the privatization programs (Zhao 1999). Although China has experienced problems similar to those common in Eastern Europe and Russia, where embezzlement of public assets has been widespread, the demand for clarifying the property rights of rural enterprises is high, and the results have been generally good (Zhao 1999).

The theoretical models at best describe why government ownership survived, given its existence in the first place. In addition, all of these models fail to explain the huge regional diversity in RE development, although all of them claim to have found the reasons for successful RE development. In explaining the success and regional diver-

Table 4.10 The Development of Private Rural Enterprises in China, 1984–97

Year	Number of firms		Labor force		Gross output	
	Amount (million)	Percent of all rural enterprises	Amount (millions)	Percent of total rural enterprise labor	Value (100 million yuan)	Percent of total rural enterprise output
1984	4.20	69.28	12.26	23.54	244.01	14.37
1985	10.37	84.87	26.52	38.00	681.41	24.73
1986	13.43	88.60	33.96	42.78	1,026.98	28.66
1987	15.92	90.95	40.87	46.42	1,587.95	32.11
1988	17.29	91.58	46.52	48.73	2,282.94	32.53
1989	17.15	91.78	46.47	49.61	2,819.55	33.56
1990	17.05	92.14	46.72	50.43	3,327.34	34.73
1991	17.64	92.44	48.42	50.39	3,901.87	33.57
1992	19.39	92.70	54.49	51.28	5,883.15	33.31
1993	22.84	93.13	65.78	53.28	11,355.42	35.73
1994	23.29	93.38	61.19	50.91	14,712.41	32.42
1995	20.41	92.65	68.01	52.88	5,236.00	35.88
1996	21.81	93.37	75.55	55.93	7,401.00	41.91
1997	18.86	93.59	77.24	59.19	46,056.46	51.23

Note: Private firms include solely individually owned and shareholding firms.

Source: SSB; China Statistical Yearbook, 1997; The Yearbook of Chinese Township and Village Enterprises, 1995, 1998; China Economic Yearbook: 1998.

sities of Chinese rural enterprises, the old theory of comparative advantage seems to have more power.

Relationships with Urban Industry

From the very beginning of its development, rural industrialization in China has been tied to urban industry. In the early days, the tie was only one way: technologies were only transferred from urban industry to rural industry. In this respect, the lightness of industrial structure of the urban industries in a particular region had positive externalities for the development of rural enterprises in that region because most rural industries were labor-intensive. We return to this point in the next section when we examine the regional disparity of RE development.

After the late 1980s, technical transfers from urban to rural industry began to take another route. Cooperation with urban firms began to emerge as the major channel through which rural enterprises obtained new technologies. Yan and Zhang (1995), in a survey study of a group of rural enterprises, show that firms engaged in outside cooperation had more standardized products, higher labor productivity, a more qualified labor force, and more investment in technical innovations than firms of the same size not engaged in outside cooperation (table 4.11). In addition, these firms were keener to use middle technologies.

As the size of rural industry increased, urban industry began to feel the pressure in the late 1980s. Before the urban reform was initiated in the middle of the 1980s, urban industry was insulated by a plan that allocated material supplies, credits, and product sales channels. As table 4.12 shows for one city, large firms, state firms, and firms affiliated with higher levels of government clearly had more access to planned resources (Jia and others 1994). With loose financial discipline, the SOEs have performed much less efficiently in their use of financial resources. As table 4.6 shows, the amount of loans per unit of pretax profit of the SOEs is seven to ten times that of rural enterprises.

In contrast, limited or no access to planned resources has proved to be a blessing as well as a constraint to rural enterprises. Under the harsh environment, rural enterprises learned to survive in the real market. Meanwhile, the industrial and urban reforms begun in 1984

Table 4.11 Comparison of Firms with and without Outside Cooperation in China, 1990

Characteristic	Firms with cooperation	Firms without cooperation	Ratio of firms with to firms without cooperation
Number of workers	228	211	1.08
With high school education or above (percent)	25.9	24.5	1.06
Technicians (percent)	4.6	3.1	1.48
Trained workers	8.0	4.5	1.77
Contracted outside technical and management personnel	4.9	2.2	2.25
Spending on innovation (thousands of yuan)	127.5	16.2	7.87
Standardized products (percent)	50.5	31.3	1.61
Equipment made in 1980s (percent)	69.0	71.0	0.97
Pretax profit per worker (thousands of yuan)	2.83	2.6	1.06

Source: Yan and Zhang (1995).

gradually dismantled the plans and enlarged the scope for RE activities. The result of the initial urban reform was a dual price system that maintained a planned price and a market price for every industrial product. Although rent seeking was rampant, this system greatly enlarged the allocative role of the market and served as a bridge for the smooth transition to a market economy. The rural industry benefited from this transition. Now rural enterprises could buy production materials in the market and break into markets originally monopolized by state enterprises such as textile and garment markets. Entering the 1990s, almost all industrial products were priced in the market, and rural enterprises and SOEs alike now have equal access to materials and product markets.

It is true that most of the rural enterprises are technically inferior to the SOEs, but this gap has narrowed with time. Table 4.13 shows the total factor productivity (TFP) indexes and the growth rates of the SOEs and rural enterprises in the 1980s. On average, rural enterprises were 49 percent less technically efficient than the SOEs. However, the TFP growth rates of rural enterprises were much higher than those of SOEs. As a result, the gap in technical efficiency narrowed quickly. Rural enterprises were 61 percent less efficient than the SOEs in 1980,

Table 4.12 Access to Planned Resources by Type of Firm in China, 1980s

Resource	By scale			By ownership		By affiliation			
	Large	Medium	Small	State	Collective	Central	Municipal	County	Township
Planned production	26.3	21.9	17.2	24.2	10.6	14.8	21.6	0	0
Planned material supply	58.5	19.6	21.4	21.0	24.5	54.0	21.0	17.9	0
Investment									
Allocated by plan	22.2	5.6	3.7	6.9	2.1	31.5	3.1	6.7	7.5
Bank loans	46.2	48.3	50.6	51.5	47.9	24.6	53.0	27.7	45.0
By firm itself	31.5	46.2	42.2	41.6	43.6	43.9	41.6	65.7	47.5
Sales through the plan	18.6	3.6	12.8	9.0	11.2	8.3	10.5	0	0

Source: Jia and others (1994: 37–39).

but the gap narrowed to 41 percent by 1988. Although direct calculations for the 1990s have not emerged, Wang and Yao (1998) show that the gap between large firms, most of which are SOEs, and small firms, most of which are rural enterprises, was 35 percent in 1995.

Regional Diversity

As one expects, China's RE development is quite uneven across regions. As table 4.3 shows, the share of RE output in total rural output varied from 86 percent in Shanghai to 4 percent in Tibet, and the average of the group with higher shares was 35 percent more than that of the group with lower shares. Several factors may have contributed to the huge regional diversity in China's RE development. Here we discuss the three most important: initial conditions, location, and factor endowments.

China's coastal provinces had two advantages over their counterparts in inland areas in the late 1970s. One is that commercialization took place much earlier in coastal provinces than in others following

Table 4.13 Total Factor Productivity Indexes and Growth Rates of the State-Owned Enterprises and Rural Enterprises in China, 1980s

	Total factor productivity indexes			Total factor productivity growth rates (percent)	
Year	State-owned enterprises	Rural enterprises	Ratio of rural to state-owned enterprises	State-owned enterprises	Rural enterprises
1980	1.102	0.431	0.39	-2.4	5.3
1981	1.029	0.451	0.44	-6.9	4.4
1982	1.036	0.466	0.45	0.7	3.7
1983	1.073	0.509	0.47	3.7	9.6
1984	1.156	0.591	0.51	7.9	19.8
Submean				0.6	8.6
1985	1.174	0.638	0.54	1.5	8.7
1986	1.160	0.659	0.57	-1.2	3.6
1987	1.175	0.663	0.56	1.3	0.5
1988	1.137	0.668	0.59	-3.5	0.8
1989	—	0.663		—	-1.0
Submean				-0.5	2.5
Total mean	1.116	0.574	0.51	0.1	5.5

— Not available.

Source: Y. Wu (1992: table 4).

their partial colonization by the world powers in the late nineteenth century. Before 1949, the economy of the coastal regions was centered in several large commercial cities, such as Tianjin, Shanghai, and Guangzhou, that linked China with the rest of the world. In the Yangtze River delta, the rural economy was closely tied with Shanghai, and rural nonfarm income, coming mostly from raising silkworms—and, to a less extent, from other sideline activities and local silk factory jobs—surpassed farm income even in the 1930s (Cao 1996). This long history of engagement in commercial activities nurtured entrepreneurship, which was a vital ingredient in the late stages of RE development.

The other advantage that many coastal provinces had over other provinces was that they had a lighter industrial structure in the late 1970s. In the planning era, a large proportion of national investment was placed in central and western regions (the so-called second and third fronts) due to the consideration of balanced development and, more important, of preparation for war. Most of the factories thus established were in heavy industry. As a result, the industrial structure of the inland areas was biased toward heavy industry, unlike the coastal areas. A lighter industrial structure, however, was more consistent with China's comparative advantage and made the diffusion of technology to rural enterprises much easier in the coastal areas.

A good location means better access to markets, information, and foreign capital. In this regard, the coastal provinces have an overwhelming advantage over the inland provinces. The most prominent example is Guangdong, whose proximity to Hong Kong and Macao gave a big lift to its RE development (Zhe 1997).

Factor endowments may be the most significant element in explaining the regional diversity of RE development in China. The provinces that started earlier and have been taking the lead in RE development are those located in the coastal areas where labor is much more abundant relative to land and other natural resources than it is in the inland areas. The last three columns of table 4.14 show the amount of arable land per capita in all the provinces in 1987 and 1995 and their percentage change. Specifically, the provinces are divided into a group of coastal provinces and municipalities and a group of others. The average arable land per capita of the first group was only 51 percent—54 percent of that of the second group. The division of labor based on regional comparative advantage thus requires that the inland areas specialize in agriculture and resource-related industries and that the coastal areas specialize in labor-intensive industries in which rural enterprises have considerable comparative advantage. This largely explains why coastal provinces had more successful rural enterprises than inland provinces.

The different factor endowment ratios of the coastal and inland provinces resulted in different capital intensities of their rural enterprises. Table 4.15 lists data for two years to show the differences. The average capital stock per worker of the inland provinces was 65 percent of that of the coastal provinces in 1987. Between 1987 and 1995, the capital stock of coastal provinces increased 154 percent on average, but that of inland provinces increased only 108 percent. As a result, capital stock per worker of the inland provinces as a percentage of that of the coastal provinces was reduced to 54 percent. This shift was consistent with the dynamic changes in the comparative advantage of these two regions.

ECONOMETRIC ANALYSIS OF RURAL ENTERPRISE DEVELOPMENT

Empirical studies on China's rural enterprises are flourishing. Some of them are general descriptions of the features of RE development (Putterman 1997; Ronnas 1996; Zweig 1997). More of them are concerned with the interaction of the RE sector, agriculture, and urban industry (Byrd and Lin 1990; Y. Wu 1990; H. Wu 1992a; Zhang 1993; Lim 1994), efficiency measurements (Y. Wu 1992, 1993; H. Wu 1992b; Jefferson, Rawski, and Zheng 1996), and wage and employment determination (Byrd and Lin 1990). In the early 1990s, the probing of ownership issues generated fruitful results (see, for example, Byrd and Lin 1990; Dong and Putterman 1997). A few studies analyze the determinants of the rapid development of rural enterprises (Chen, Watson, and Findley 1990; H. Wu 1992b; Zweig 1997), but none of them alone constitutes a comprehensive study that either examines the huge regional diversity or tests the various theories emerging in the literature.[4] Lin and Yao (1999) study how the degree of alignment with their comparative advantage has led Chinese provinces to different performances in RE development. In this section, we use the same

Table 4.14 Gross Domestic Product per Capita and Arable Land per Capita of China's Provinces, 1987 and 1995

Region	GDP per capita (1990 yuan)			Arable land per capita (hectares)		
	1987	1995	Change (percent)	1987	1995	Change (percent)
Whole country	1,741	3,010	72.9	0.154	0.161	4.3
Coastal provinces						
Liaoning	2,511	3,959	57.7	0.179	0.183	1.9
Tianjin	3,795	5,665	49.3	0.119	0.125	4.5
Beijing	4,730	6,467	36.7	0.077	0.062	-19.1
Hebei	1,307	2,568	96.4	0.147	0.135	-8.6
Shandong	1,491	3,333	123.6	0.103	0.093	-10.3
Jiangsu	2,011	4,232	110.4	0.096	0.087	-9.0
Shanghai	6,243	10,094	61.7	0.077	0.069	-10.3
Zhejiang	1,990	4,733	137.9	0.060	0.061	1.1
Fujian	1,322	3,871	192.8	0.065	0.057	-12.4
Guangdong	1,980	4,842	144.5	0.070	0.077	10.5
Submean	2,738	4,976	81.8	0.099	0.095	-4.6
Inland provinces						
Heilongjiang	1,838	3,157	71.8	0.447	0.539	20.6
Jilin	1,729	2,527	46.2	0.320	0.372	16.3
Inner Mongolia	1,228	2,115	72.2	0.439	0.487	11.1
Shanxi	1,296	2,059	58.9	0.199	0.208	4.7
Henan	1,094	1,914	75.0	0.109	0.103	-5.5
Anhui	1,122	1,933	72.2	0.106	0.097	-8.2
Hubei	1,464	2,403	64.2	0.099	0.103	3.4
Jiangxi	1,052	1,777	69.0	0.091	0.132	45.6
Hunan	1,161	1,992	71.6	0.079	0.083	5.9
Guangxi	860	2,051	138.4	0.079	0.080	1.7
Hainan		2,917			0.087	
Shannxi	1,080	1,642	52.0	0.199	0.187	-6.0
Gansu	1,085	1,316	21.4	0.217	0.214	-1.5
Ninxia	1,249	1,919	53.7	0.221	0.274	23.8
Qinhai	1,449	1,993	37.5	0.182	0.166	-8.8
Xingjiang	1,493	2,881	93.0	0.265	0.305	14.8
Sichuan	1,007	1,810	79.8	0.076	0.083	9.6
Guizhou	776	1,010	30.2	0.081	0.079	-3.3
Yunnan	858	1,754	104.4	0.099	0.117	18.9
Tibet	1274	1,353	6.2	0.157	0.158	0.4
Submean	1,217	2,026	66.6	0.182	0.194	6.2

Source: SSB, *China Statistical Yearbook: 1988, 1996*

Table 4.15 Capital Stocks per Worker of Rural Enterprises, 1987 and 1995 (original value at 1990 prices)

Region	1987	1995	Change (percent)
Whole country	2,604	5,790	122.3
Coastal provinces			
Liaoning	3,445	5,942	72.5
Tianjin	4,119	11,071	168.8
Beijing	5,299	11,033	108.2
Hebei	1,972	5,704	189.3
Shandong	3,007	6,464	115.0
Jiangsu	3,086	9,341	202.7
Shanghai	5,463	14,523	165.9
Zhejiang	3,175	9,112	187.0
Fujian	2,396	6,644	177.3
Guangdong	3,129	7,814	149.7
Submean	3,509	8,765	153.6
Inland provinces			
Heilongjiang	3,222	4,786	48.5
Jilin	2,926	3,644	24.6
Inner Mongolia	2,577	3,430	33.1
Shanxi	3,256	4,562	40.1
Henan	1,801	5,117	184.1
Anhui	1,590	4,977	213.0
Hubei	2,563	4,142	61.6
Jiangxi	1,828	2,881	57.6
Hunan	2,154	3,237	50.2
Guangxi	1,546	6,399	313.8
Hainan		9,417	
Shannxi	2,067	3,121	51.0
Gansu	1,894	2,673	41.1
Ninxia	2,682	7,269	171.0
Qinhai	2,221	5,842	163.1
Xingjiang	3,115	7,014	125.2
Sichuan	1,980	3,041	53.6
Guizhou	1,330	4,571	243.6
Yunnan	2,517	4,260	69.2
Submean	2,293	4,757	108.0

Source: SSB, *China Statistical Yearbook: 1988, 1996.*

data set used in Lin and Yao (1999) to test the various theories and assessments surveyed in the previous two sections. Every province in China is equivalent to a medium- or large-size country in terms of both territory and population, and tremendous variations exist among them. This provides us with a good opportunity to conduct the tests.

From the discussions carried out in the last two sections, several testable hypotheses can be formed:

1. *Initial conditions.* The provinces with favorable initial conditions in rural industry, state industry, and structure or close proximity to markets, especially to foreign markets, and foreign capital will have a larger rural industrial sector.

2. *Market conditions.* The provinces with higher income, more urban population, a larger population density, and more transportation facilities will have a larger rural industrial sector.

3. *Human capital.* The provinces with a more educated labor force will have a larger rural industrial sector.

4. *Interaction with SOEs.* An SOE sector biased toward light industry will help RE development.

5. *Economic reforms.* Economic reforms will accelerate rural industrialization nationwide.

6. *Factor endowments.* The provinces with more arable land and less capital relative to labor will have a smaller rural industrial sector.

7. *Public ownership.* Provinces with more publicly owned firms will have a larger rural industrial sector.

Regarding the main theme of this chapter, the last two hypotheses are the most important. In the next subsection, we define the variables to be used in our tests.

Variables

We conduct our tests based on two sets of data. In the appendix, we present a detailed description of how the two data sets are constructed. The first data set is compiled on 28 provinces in the period 1978–97, and the second data set is compiled on 15 provinces in the period 1970–97. In both data sets, the year 1996 is excluded because only value added RE output is recorded, while in other years gross output is recorded. The number of provinces drops to 15 for the period 1970–97 because the rest of the provinces do not have data on the output of rural industry in the period 1970–77. Even for the remaining 15 provinces, we lack data on some key variables in this period and have to drop them. We run our regressions separately on the two sets of data. While the data set of 1978–97 captures a relatively normal development path and is enough to test most of our hypotheses, the data set of 1970–97 provides more information on the factors that determine long-run economic development. In what follows, we discuss the variables used in the regressions.

For the period 1978–97, the dependent variable is the value of RE output per rural population (yuan per capita) of each province.[5] The year 1978 is used as the starting point. The initial conditions in that year include three variables and several regional dummies. The three variables are value per capita of RE output (yuan per capita), value per capita of SOE output in the whole province (yuan per capita), and SOE capital per worker (yuan per worker). The meaning of the first variable is obvious—it accounts for the initial condition of the RE sector itself. The second and third variables account for possible impacts of the size and capital structure of the SOE sector. A larger state sector may have more by way of appropriate technologies to provide to the rural area, and a lighter state sector (with less capital per worker) may have more technologies that are suitable for labor-intensive rural firms. Both factors set a favorable stage for later RE development. To preserve the impacts of the three variables, we do not use province dummies. Instead, following Jin and Qian (2000), we divide the 28 provinces into six regions: large cities (Beijing, Shanghai, and Tianjin), coastal, south, southwest, northwest, and north. The three large cities are quite different from the rest of the regions because they have much smaller agricultural populations. The coastal region has a longer history of industrial development and commerce. It is also close to foreign capital and markets. South and north are two interim regions, and southwest and northwest are the two most underdeveloped. In the regressions, south is used as the reference region.

Variables accounting for market conditions are lagged provincial GDP per capita (yuan per capita), urbanization rate (ratio of urban to total population), population density (persons per square kilometer), and density of roads, paved roads, and railroads (kilometers per square kilometer). The first three variables account for the purchasing power in a province, and the last three account for the convenience of transportation. Roads include paved and unpaved roads. As RE products are mainly sold in the same province, purchasing power in a province is an important factor determining the development of rural enterprises. GDP is lagged to avoid the problem of reversed causality because rural enterprises contribute to current GDP.

We add two variables indicating the openness of a province: exports per capita (yuan per capita) and FDI per capita (yuan per capita). Export is lagged because RE exports consist of a major part of total exports. FDI is not only a measure of openness but also a measure of the availability of capital in a province. We do not have data on the amount of FDI going to rural areas; otherwise, we would have added it to the amount of capital available in the rural area.

For human capital, we use the ratio of certified technicians in the RE sector. For the interaction with the state sector, as in the case of accounting for the initial conditions, we use SOE value per capita and SOE capital per worker in a province. Most economic reforms have been carried out uniformly across the country, so their effects are mixed with the time dummies that we add into the regressions. One exception is the household responsibility system (HRS) that was implemented gradually and unevenly across the country in the period from 1978 to 1983. Therefore, we include a variable measuring the ratio of villages adopting the HRS in each year to account for the effect of this reform. Two other major reforms and policy changes happened in 1984 and 1992. Their effects can only be determined by looking at the time dummies.

Two variables are used to measure a province's relative endowments. One is arable land per capita (mu per capita: one mu = one-fifteenth of a hectare); the other is lagged capital per capita (yuan per capita), both for rural areas only. We do not have good labor data, so rural population is used instead. Capital per capita is lagged to avoid the endogeneity of this variable. For public ownership, we use the share of output produced by firms owned by townships and villages in a province's total RE output.

Finally, time dummies are included for the years, with 1979 being the reference year. Although these time dummies carry a lot of information ranging from government policy changes to technological progress, we use them mainly to gauge the effects of major economic reforms, especially the two in 1984 and 1992.

For the period 1970 to 1997, we cannot construct a complete series for the three transportation variables, ratio of technicians, and SOE capital per worker. Although we have to drop the first four variables, we use the lagged output share of light industry in total industrial output to substitute for the last variable. Compared with the original variable, the new variable has two drawbacks. One is that the share of light industry is a measure for all industry in a province, not just for the SOE sector. The other is that light industry in Chinese statistics is based on products and does not reflect capital intensity in the production process.

The categorizations for RE output before and after 1978 are different. Before 1978, only industrial firms were recorded, while after 1978, all kinds of firms (manufacturing, construction, transportation, and services) are recorded. To get a unified measurement for RE output, we add the output of industrial firms and the output of sideline activities for the years before 1978 and add the output of all firms and the output of sideline activities for 1978 and after. Although the statistical scope of the two periods still has not reached a perfect match, we believe the difference is small.

Regression Results

We run two models for each data set, one without the regional dummies and one with them. The results of the four models are presented in table 4.16. We first discuss the results based on the 1978–97 data set.

Results based on the 1978–97 data set. Except for the value of RE output in 1978, all the other variables have similar results in the two regressions without (model 1) and with (model 2) the regional dummies. In model 1, where no regional dummies are present, initial RE output has a significantly positive impact on future RE development. However, when the regional dummies are included, this positive impact vanishes, indicating that the initial variations in the size of the rural industrial sector have a strong regional pattern. As the five regional dummies show, while the rest of the three regions are not sig-

Table 4.16 Regression Results

Variables	1978–97		1970–97	
	(1)	(2)	(3)	(4)
Constant	1,468.90*	1,330.4*	-914.45**	112.23
	(294.29)	(378.27)	(496.00)	(543.53)
Lagged gross domestic product	1.69*	1.70*	0.48*	0.74*
	(0.14)	(0.14)	(0.15)	(0.16)
Urbanization	659.80	-383.97	-537.65	-6176.3*
	(588.93)	(679.89)	(606.89)	(1,576.9)
Population density	0.04	-0.24	-0.12	-1.4*
	(0.27)	(0.35)	(0.30)	(0.45)
Road	-1,723.9*	-1,285.2**		
	(581.52)	(716.19)		
Paved road	1,528.6*	1,371.2*		
	(516.19)	(516.87)		
Railroad	1,631.3*	4,404.1*		
	(668.08)	(1,092.6)		
Lagged export per capita	-0.93*	-1.08*	1.34*	1.08*
	(0.16)	(0.17)	(0.28)	(0.28)
Foreign direct investment per capita	3.43*	3.49*	2.37*	2.44*
	(0.50)	(0.50)	(0.52)	(0.51)
Ratio of technicians	-2,458.2	-117.62		
	(2,687.4)	(2,724.6)		
SOE value per capita	0.25*	0.24*	-0.16**	-0.07
	0.09	(0.09)	(0.87)	(0.08)
SOE capital per worker (share of light industry)	-0.02*	-0.02*	14.94	-229.81
	(0.006)	(0.006)	(122.48)	(150.89)
HRS	-14.31	-23.56	105.46	67.33
	(241.91)	(236.19)	(300.28)	(292.72)
Land per capita	-46.23	-15.94	6.64	143.97*
	(33.70)	(45.56)	(38.96)	(59.027)
Lagged capital per capita	0.70*	0.86*	1.01*	0.92*
	(0.20)	(0.20)	(0.16)	(0.16)
Share of public firm output	-723.81*	-855.06*	407.73	287.02
	(240.60)	(242.12)	(304.58)	(307.50)
Initial RE value per capita	7.23*	3.83	3.74	3.70
	(1.50)	(2.07)	(6.25)	(6.15)
Initial SOE value per capita	0.64	0.43	-0.03	1.10*
	(0.42)	(0.47)	(0.26)	(0.36)
Initial SOE capital per worker (initial share of light industry)	-4.52*	-2.64*	303.27*	236.97**
	(0.78)	(0.97)	(100.66)	(123.86)
Large cities		-1,019.3*		1,129.2*
		(406.56)		(519.94)
Coastal provinces		175.03**		412.74*
		(97.45)		(132.17)
Southwest		-85.10		-282.47*
		(111.51)		(94.69)
Northwest		-164.96		-587.79*
		(125.08)		(161.00)
North		-192.87		-415.52*
		(133.38)		(131.67)

* Significant at the 5 percent significance level.
** Significant at the 10 percent significance level.
Note: Standard errors are reported in the parentheses.
Source: Authors' calculations.

nificantly different from the south, large cities fall far behind, and coastal provinces lead all the others. The leading position of the coastal provinces is not surprising, because they generally have more advantageous historical backgrounds as well as better access to foreign capital and markets. Nonetheless, the difference between the south and other regions is not large in an economic sense (only 175 yuan per person), indicating that the contribution of intrinsic characteristics that are not taken into account is not substantial. The finding that the two western regions (southwest and northwest) are not different from the two central regions (south and north) shows that the backwardness of RE development in the west is not caused by its intrinsic "backward" characteristics, such as the lack of entrepreneurship or the lack of a commercial tradition; rather, it is caused by inferior market and transportation conditions and other factors explicitly accounted for in our regressions. The finding that the three large cities fall far behind the south (the difference is 1,019 yuan per capita) is somewhat surprising. One explanation is that they have much more favorable conditions, as accounted for by the variables used in our regressions, yet these conditions have not yielded a comparable success.

For the two variables accounting for a province's SOE sector in 1978, the size of the sector does not have a significant impact on future RE development, but the dominance of light industry significantly improves a province's prospect of RE development. The initial conditions of the SOE sector set the stage for technological transfers to the RE sector. These results show that the initial size of the SOE sector does not matter in this respect; the important factor is its weight. This conclusion lends support to the comparative advantage argument that emphasizes rural China's position in low-capital-intensity industries.

We now turn to the results of the market and transportation conditions. Lagged GDP per capita is the most important and powerful indicator of the market demand for RE products. One yuan increase in GDP per capita will induce about a 1.70 yuan increase in RE output per capita in the following year. Transformed into elasticity, this means that a 1 percent increase in GDP per capita brings a 1.89 percent increase in RE output (evaluated at the variable means). In contrast, urbanization and population density do not play a significant role. For transportation facilities, the densities of paved roads and railroads increase RE output significantly. However, RE output is negatively correlated with the density of all roads, a result that is hard to comprehend. When this variable is taken out of the regression, the positive effect of paved roads vanishes. This shows that the two variables are highly correlated (their correlation coefficient is 0.74). Although the effects of both kinds of roads are not large, we learn from the regression that paved roads are more important than ordinary roads in providing better transportation facilities to the rural industrial sector.

For the two variables measuring a province's openness, lagged exports have a negative effect, while FDI has a positive effect; both are significant. The negative effect of exports seems to suggest that more foreign demand suppresses the growth of the RE sector. Nevertheless, this puzzling result is reversed in the regressions based on the 1970–97 data set. As exports in the 1970s were quite small, adding these years in the analysis enables us to capture the significant increase in exports in the 1980s. The positive effect of FDI verifies the importance of foreign capital in financing China's rural industrialization. The elasticity of this positive effect is 0.12 (model 2); that is, a 1 percent increase in FDI per capita in a province will bring a 0.12 percent increase in RE output per rural population.

The variable measuring the stock of human capital in the RE sector—the ratio of technicians in the labor force—has a significant impact on the size of the sector. This result may arise for two reasons. First, we only have a measure for certified technicians, whereas many technicians in rural areas do not have formal certifications. That is, the variable we use in our regression underestimates the number of technicians in the rural industrial sector. Second, because rural firms are mainly engaged in labor-intensive industries that do not demand a sophisticated labor force, more technicians do not necessarily mean higher output.

Now we turn to a discussion of the link between the RE and SOE sectors. Not only does the light manufacturing bias of the SOE sector have a positive impact on the size of the RE sector, but so does its size. The elasticity is about 0.24 (model 2). Although it is not relevant whether a province starts with a large SOE sector, the RE sector benefits from a larger SOE sector in subsequent development.

The adoption of the HRS is highly insignificant. The variable HRS has variations only for the period 1978 to 1983, because after 1983 almost all the villages adopted HRS. The period of HRS reform was marked by relative stagnation of RE development. The reform raised agricultural productivity and facilitated the accumulation of the initial capital for the rural enterprises' takeoff; nonetheless, its effect on immediate RE development was weak because the rural areas were occupied in increasing agricultural production.

For the two variables representing a province's factor endowments, arable land per capita has no significant impact, although its sign is negative, and rural capital per capita has a significantly positive impact. Although we find a difference in land endowments between the two groups of provinces that have different levels of RE development, this difference vanishes in multivariate analysis. Capital endowment makes a strong difference in the size of a province's RE sector.

Lastly, we come to the function of public firms. The share of the output value generated by public firms has a significantly negative impact on the size of the RE sector. According to the estimate in model 2, a 1 percent increase in the SOE share means a 0.61 percent decrease in overall RE output.

Results based on the 1970–97 data set. In the regressions based on the 1970–97 data set, the estimates for GDP per capita, FDI per capita, HRS, capital per capita, and the initial size of the RE sector are qualitatively the same as in the regressions on the 1978–97 data set. We skip these results here and concentrate on the variables that show different results. These different results are mainly brought about by adding the data before 1978 into our regression analysis.

China in the 1970s was still pursuing a development strategy geared toward heavy industrialization, and many irrational decisions were being made regarding firm locations. In the 1960s and early 1970s, in addition to the pressure from Western countries, China was traumatized by the prospect of a war with the Soviet Union. Therefore, many factories were deliberately located in remote inland provinces, in many cases in mountains that were not readily accessible via any modern means of transportation. Many of the results shown in our regressions based on the 1970–97 data set reflect this irrationality.

The most significant results are for urbanization, population density, and arable land per capita. The first two variables have significantly negative impacts on the size of the RE sector in a province, and the last variable has a strong positive impact. These results contrast sharply with those obtained with the 1978–97 data but match perfectly with the firm-locating strategy in the 1970s, which put firms in sparsely populated rural provinces. In addition, the positive link between the SOE and RE sectors disappears, although the initial size of the SOE sector and the share of light manufacturing in 1970 have a positive impact on future RE development. Despite the irrational firm-locating strategy, however, the two inland regions plus the north are still behind the south, which is, in turn, behind the coastal provinces and large cities.

The new regressions also show several interesting results that deserve more discussion. As opposed to the regressions based on the 1978–97 data set, lagged exports have a significantly positive effect on RE output in the next year. This is mainly because the new data set captures the fast export growth after 1978. In addition, the share of public firms becomes irrelevant to the size of the RE sector. This result could reflect the fact that only public firms were allowed before 1978 and that the differentiation only began after the reform was initiated.

Most important, the new regressions reveal the long-term trend in RE development. Although the regressions based on the 1978–97 data set show no clear time pattern, the new regressions show a clear time pattern by which the whole period 1970–97 can be divided into three subperiods: 1970–83, 1984–91, and 1992–97. The beginning years of the last two periods—1984 and 1992—marked important reforms and policy changes. In 1984, the commune system was formally dismantled, private firms were officially sanctioned, and urban reform was launched. In 1992, Deng Xiaoping paid a visit to the south and called for continuation of the reform efforts, ending three year-long repressive measures toward rural enterprises. The effects of these reforms and policy changes are reflected in the year dummies as estimated in model 4. Although the year dummies before 1984 are insignificantly different from the starting year 1971, those in the period 1984–91 are weakly significant, and those in the period 1992–97 are all highly significant. With 1984 as the dividing point, the average of the year dummies before 1984 is 135.5, and the average after 1984 (1984 included) is 771.6. The F-statistic for the test that the two averages are different is 4.01, larger than the critical value at the 5 percent significance level. With 1992 as the dividing point, the average of the year dummies before that year is 282.5, and the average after that year (1992 itself included) is 116.58. The F-statistic for the test that the two averages are different is 16.72, larger than the critical value at the 1 percent significance level. Although the year dummies carry a lot more than just the impacts of policy changes, the match of the estimated time pattern and the timing of the reforms and policy changes cannot be explained as merely a coincidence.

The Hypothesis

With the discussions of the regression results concluded, we are in a position to assess the validity of the hypotheses proposed at the outset of this section. We have verified most of the claims in hypothesis 1 except that the initial size of the RE sector is shown not to matter very much. Instead, we have found strong regional variations, with the coastal provinces being in a clearly more advantageous position than the rest of the country. For hypothesis 2, we have found that income is the most powerful demand factor that drives faster RE development. Transportation facilities are also shown to make a significant contribution. Related to this hypothesis, we have found that engaging in world trade and receiving foreign direct investment help RE development in a province. We do not find supporting evidence for hypothesis 3, partly because we do not have adequate data with which to measure human capital stock in the RE sector. For hypothesis 4, we find strong evidence in the period 1978–97 that a larger and a lighter SOE sector helps a province to develop a larger RE sector. The positive effects of the economic reforms, as stated in hypothesis 5, are verified in the case of the reforms in 1984 and 1992. For the hypothesis concerning factor endowments, hypothesis 6, strong evidence is found to support the claim concerning capital endowment, but only weak evidence is found for the claim concerning land endowment in the period 1978–97. For the last hypothesis on the role of public ownership, we find strong evidence that more public ownership in a province has a negative impact on the RE sector for the period 1978–97. However, this negative role vanishes when we extend our data set to include the period 1970–77. This latter finding could be explained by the fact that only public firms were allowed before 1978.

CHINESE RURAL INDUSTRIALIZATION FROM AN
EAST ASIAN PERSPECTIVE

To what extent can the Chinese experience of rural industrialization fit into the broad picture of East Asia? China surely has unique features that are rooted in its planning past as well as related to its current transition to a market economy. More important, however, it has broad commonality with the initial industrialization processes of two East Asian economies, Japan and Taiwan. Common to these three economies, rural industrialization took the road of establishing small, labor-intensive, and indigenous firms in rural areas. In addition, rural industrialization started at the very beginning of the three economies' takeoff period. This is sharply contrasted with the experience of other East Asian economies such as Korea, Thailand, Malaysia, and Indonesia that adopted government policies advocating the establishment of large urban firms. Starting in early 1980s, some of the countries such as Korea and Thailand began to disperse urban industry into rural areas. Korea seems to have succeeded in this regard (Otsuka and Reardon 1998), but the situation in Thailand remains largely unchanged (Poapongsakorn 1995).[6] For categorization purposes, we dub the strategy adopted by China, Taiwan, and Japan the indigenous strategy, and the strategy adopted by the other countries the push strategy. Many studies have compared the East Asian experiences with the rest of the developing world as well as among themselves (besides World Bank 1993, see also White 1988; Hughes 1988; Amsden 1989; Ranis, Hu, and Chu 1998; Hayami 1998; Hayami and Aoki 1998, to name a few). Two schools are emerging from the literature. The neoclassical school treats the East Asian success as the triumph of the free market and a limited government; the developmental state school emphasizes the role of government interventions (White and Wade 1988). The neoclassical school ignores the heavy government interventions present in the East Asian economies; the developmental state school fails to explain why government interventions did not succeed in other developing countries, notably those in Latin America. Lin (1996) tries to reconcile the two schools by arguing that the East Asian success was brought about because the industrial-technological structure at each stage of development was better aligned with the comparative advantage in each economy. In this section, we extend Lin's argument by examining the two development strategies adopted by the East Asian countries. It is not our intention to provide yet another complete comparison. Instead, we only present a selective comparison that is pertinent to the topic of rural industrialization, taking Taiwan and China as the representatives of the indigenous strategy and Korea and Thailand as the representatives of the push strategy.

The contrast between Taiwan and Korea has received especially strong attention (Ho 1979; Saith 1987; Kuznets 1988; Otsuka and Reardon 1998), partly because they are among the first four East Asian economies that attained the status of newly industrialized economies in a short period of time. While the neoclassical school emphasizes the function of the free market and a limited government in the two economies' rapid growth, the developmental state school emphasizes their commonalties in successful government interventions. However, besides export orientation, the two economies share few common attributes.

Although both economies experienced a period of import substitution in the 1950s when both of them adopted very similar policies— low interest rates, overvalued currency, taxation on agriculture—government interventions in subsequent years diverged widely in the two economies. In Korea, the government pursued an active industrial policy, directing private investment to certain industries that it thought were vital for the whole economy (see the chapters by Perkins and Woo-Cumings in this volume and Luedde-Neurath 1988). While acknowledging Korea's gradual move from labor-intensive industries to capital-intensive industries, Amsden (1989) emphasizes the government's role in bringing about the leap between two consecutive stages of development, in many cases by deliberately setting the relative prices "wrong." Large conglomerates were encouraged in steel, shipbuilding, heavy chemicals, and auto industries. To ensure that these large firms got enough capital, the government tightly controlled the financial system (Luedde-Neurath 1988). As a result, Korean industrialization was overwhelmingly concentrated in and around two cities, Seoul and Pusan, and the development of the rural areas was retarded.

In contrast with Korea, Taiwan took a relatively decentralized strategy. Although it also used selective policies to promote certain industries (such as heavy chemicals in the 1960s), government interventions were much less than, and the form was much different from, those adopted by the Korean government. Instead of economywide control of private investment, the Taiwanese government adopted government ownership in key industries such as heavy chemicals and steel. The private sector was left largely intact. This created ample room for rural indigenous industrialization. One indicator of the two development strategies is the different size of firms in the two countries. In 1981, the average urban firm in Korea hired 67.8 workers, and the average rural firm hired 51.5 workers. In the same year, the average urban firm in Taiwan only hired 31.8 workers, and the average rural firm only hired 18.1 workers (Otsuka and Reardon 1998).

Why did the two economies adopt different strategies of industrialization? Saith (1987) provides an answer by tracing the initial conditions faced by the two economies. Both were colonies of Japan before World War II, but Taiwan enjoyed a much higher level of rural infrastructure development than Korea. This had much to do with Japan's strategy of developing Taiwan as an agricultural colony complementary to its own industrial development. In addition, Taiwan enjoyed a favorable agroclimate that allowed it to have a much more diversified and profitable agriculture, whose surplus provided vital initial capital for rural industrialization. Korea had no such luck. It maintained a monoagriculture centered on expensive rice production. Lastly, although both implemented land reforms, Taiwan gave much more initiative to the locals than Korea did. However, although these factors definitely played a role in setting the two economies' initial development paths, subsequent government policies in Korea aggravated the problem and created new ones. In what follows, we compare China and Thailand to put forward some new insights on the government's role as well as to further Saith's arguments.

Both China and Thailand are still engaged in rural industrialization, yet their approaches are quite different. While China largely takes the indigenous strategy, Thailand takes the push strategy. The word "takes," though, is somewhat misleading, as it seems to suggest that the two governments consciously selected the different strategies. This was not the case for China, at least, because the fast development of rural industry in the 1980s came as a total surprise to its leadership.[7] In Thailand, the government was more conscious of adopting deliberate policies encouraging the development of large firms and geographical concentration. Although this difference is consistent with the initial conditions and factor endowments of the two countries, government policies have reinforced the trend toward large establishments and geographical concentration in Thailand.

Both China and Thailand were predominantly agricultural at the outset of their rural industrialization in the 1960s and 1970s. Rural population accounted for 80 percent of China's total population for a long period of time before the 1980s. In 1960, rural employment accounted for 90 percent of Thailand's national labor force (Krongkaew 1995). However, two significant factors differentiated the two countries.

One is that China had more favorable initial conditions in terms of infrastructure and initial accumulation. This had much to do with more than 20 years of collective economy in rural China. The collective economy, despite its well-documented inefficiency, accumulated a considerable amount of public goods in roads, electricity, and basic health care. In addition, the commune and brigade enterprises that thrived in the 1970s laid a firm foundation in parts of rural China. Lastly, the existence of a large state sector, especially in provinces with lighter industrial structures favoring light manufacturing, provided the rural industrial sector with needed technologies and human capital. In contrast, Thai rural industrialization started almost from scratch. Even the import substitution strategy pursued in the 1960s did not improve the situation in the rural areas. This contrast of initial conditions is parallel to that between Taiwan and Korea, as suggested by Saith (1987).

The other factor is that China and Thailand had, and still have, different land endowments. While China is well known for its limited arable land, land is relatively abundant in Thailand. Until the mid-1980s, the average area cultivated per farm household in Thailand was increasing because of land abundance (Poapongsakorn 1995). Most of the new land came from encroachment on forestland that nominally belonged to the king but was de facto open land until very recently. The abundance of land gives Thailand a comparative advantage in agricultural production, especially in its traditional product, rice. This largely explains why Thailand remains a major rice exporter in the world market. Land abundance contains labor outflow from the sector. In addition, because to claim marginal land as private was illegal, squatters had to stay on their newly claimed land by building a household. This further retarded the development of rural industry as well as permanent migration to the cities.

The development strategies adopted in China and Thailand are largely consistent with their initial conditions and land endowments. In China, land is scarce relative to labor in almost every province, giving provinces an incentive to develop nonagricultural activities, albeit to various extents, depending on their land scarcity compared with that of other provinces. In addition, relatively favorable initial conditions in the rural areas facilitated the establishment of indigenous industrial firms. Together, these two factors made decentralized rural industrialization possible in China. This was by no mean a conscious choice of the Chinese government. Although it was reversing the heavy-industrialization strategy at the beginning of the 1980s, the government never expected the rural industrial sector to become a major contributor to the national economy. Rather, as in the case of many rural reforms, rural industrialization was spontaneously initiated by the localities in a spontaneous way.

In Thailand, the lack of solid infrastructure in rural areas and the abundance of land were conducive to industrial concentration, at least at the early stage of industrialization, when higher labor costs around Bangkok were more than offset by urban agglomeration economies. However, the differences in initial conditions and land endowments are not the end of the story. Although China has also maintained financial and other policies that discriminate against small rural firms, these policies have not halted the growth of the rural industrial sector. This should be attributed to local public accumulation in the planning era and private accumulation that benefited from agricultural reform. The situation in Thailand is quite different. Without solid capital accumulation in rural areas, biased government policies aggravated the concentration of large firms.

Before 1960, the Thai government pursued a development strategy that was characterized by state capitalism. Accepting the World Bank's then state-of-the-art advice of import substitution centered on private investment, the Thai government gave up the state capitalism approach and enacted an investment law encouraging private and foreign investment (Falkus 1995). Under the law, large firms engaged in import substitution enjoyed tariff exemptions on imported capital goods and raw materials and permission to export manufactured products, repatriate profits, and so on. In addition, a minimum-wage law discouraged employment. As a result, large and capital-intensive firms emerged and dominated their respective industries (Tinakorn 1995). In addition, large firms needed better infrastructure, so industrial concentration in and around Bangkok was reinforced. Apparently, this trend deviated from Thailand's comparative advantage at that time. As a natural result, the import substitution strategy encountered problems at the end of the 1960s because of a persistent trade deficit and an insufficient domestic market. Government policy shifted to the promotion of exports. The size limit for preferential treatments was lowered, and a spatial industrial policy was adopted to disperse industries away from Bangkok. However, several factors still hinder the development of small firms in rural areas. First, the Thai fiscal system is still highly centralized, depriving local provinces of the capacities to improve their investment environments. Second, there is still a size limit and a substantial application fee to be eligible for the privileges. Third, firms located in industrial estates are better able than other firms to obtain privileges. Because the price of land on the industrial estates is usually two to three times the price elsewhere, the policy clearly discriminates against small firms. Lastly, the minimum-wage law raises labor costs, discouraging the establishment of new firms in rural areas. Consequently, industrial dispersion has not occurred, because 35 percent of the enterprises were still located in Bangkok in 1995 (Poapongsakorn 1995).

Although the development records of both the indigenous and push strategies are remarkable, there are considerable gaps between them in specific areas. The most prominent is income distribution. While China's Gini coefficient of 0.20 could be attributed to its long history of egalitarian distribution in the planning era, the information presented in table 4.17 on eight East Asian newly industrializing economies is illuminating. The table shows the ranks of the eight economies in a comparison of 34 developing economies in terms of growth and income distribution in 1985 (Riedel 1988). The ranks are based on border count, a rule that aggregates multiple criteria into a single rank ordering. The ranks of income growth alone and income growth and distribution together are much more compact than the rank of income distribution alone. While Taiwan occupies the first place for all three rankings, Korea is fourth for income growth, but eighth for income distribution. Other countries following Korea's strategy are

even worse. For example, in terms of income growth alone, Thailand
and Indonesia stand tenth and eighth, but in terms of income distribution, they are sixteenth and fifteenth, respectively. Some authors
(for example, Wade 1988) argue that the more equitable income distribution in Taiwan was a result of Chinese cultural sensitivities, which
regard income inequality as a more serious problem than poverty. If
that were true, we would see more redistributive measures being
adopted by Taiwan than by other economies such as Korea, yet no
such evidence is found. We contend that the more equal income distribution in Taiwan, as in China, was the result of the indigenous nature of its industrialization.

In addition to income distribution, the two industrialization strategies also have long-lasting effects on the adopters' economic performance. It is not a coincidence that Taiwan is the only economy in East
Asia that had a convertible currency, yet was not affected by the East
Asian financial crisis.[8] Although the crisis was triggered by and, in
most countries, confined to the financial sector, the development strategy of encouraging the establishment of large firms and conglomerates should take the blame for the resulting unbalanced industrial structure and weak financial system. First, many of the large firms, especially
in Korea, were established to explore the so-called dynamic comparative advantage—that is, the comparative advantage that a country would
possess in the future. However, any planned development runs the
risk of making the wrong prediction about the future. As a result, the

Table 4.17 Ranking in Growth and Equity of Eight East Asian Newly Industrializing
Economies among 34 Countries

Economies	Income distribution	Growth of income and gross domestic product	Income distribution and growth of income per capita
Taiwan (China)	1	1	1
Singapore	5	2	2
Korea, Rep. of	8	4	3
Hong Kong	11	5	4
Indonesia	15	8	8
Thailand	16	10	9
Malaysia	26	16	14
Philippines	22	17	17

Source: Riedel (1988: 20).

widening of comparative advantage may never be realized. The contrast between Taiwan's and Korea's approaches to the automobile industry is illuminating. Taiwan specializes in making auto parts, and firms enjoy a large margin of profits. Korea produces whole cars, but profit margins are minimal. Yet, before the financial crisis, the government, with its control of the banking system, kept pumping credits into those large firms. The government support also sent a wrong signal to foreign lenders that these large firms would not fail easily. This encouraged irresponsible borrowing. As a result, the average debt/ equity ratio of the 30 largest conglomerates reached 350 percent, and some even reached 1,200 percent. A similar situation prevailed in Thailand, where the country's biased policies encouraged large, capital-intensive firms to dominate the economy with high debt/equity ratios that contributed to corporate vulnerability in the years leading to the crisis.

CONCLUSIONS

Rural industrialization is a phenomenon unique to East Asia, and rural industrialization in China has been the most significant by far. Several conclusions can be drawn from our analysis. First, Chinese rural industrialization has been largely an unintended consequence that is mainly induced by China's land, capital, labor endowment, and relatively good rural infrastructure, the result of its recent history of collectivization. Second, the rapid growth of the RE sector has been facilitated by the market-oriented reforms carried out in the past 20 years. Specifically, the sector has benefited from the abandonment of the heavy industry–oriented development strategy that strongly favored large establishments. Third, urban light manufacturing industry helped the growth of the RE sector in the early years. Fourth, in the course of its development, the RE sector has gradually abandoned public ownership and hardened the financial discipline on firms.

To what extent is the Chinese experience applicable to other developing countries? Rural industrialization has resulted in more equal income distribution within a region because the benefits of development are accessible to a larger portion of the population. It also eases social tension that could arise from widening income disparity. However, to the extent that it is an unintended consequence arising from its endowments and history, the Chinese experience may have very limited direct implications for land- and capital-abundant countries such as those in Latin America. Nevertheless, even these countries can derive the lesson that government policies should not encourage deviation from a country's comparative advantage. However, for countries in Asia whose endowments are similar to those of China, the Chinese experience has more direct implications. Besides emphasizing the need to align a country's choice of industrial-technological structure with its comparative advantage, the Chinese experience also shows that investment in rural infrastructure is a key factor in promoting RE development.

APPENDIX. DESCRIPTION OF THE DATA

In this appendix, we present a detailed description of our data. We have constructed two data sets: one for 28 provinces in the period 1978–97 and one for 15 provinces in the period 1970–97. In the first data set, Hainan and Tibet are excluded, and Chongqing is added into Sichuan. The second data set includes Beijing, Tianjin, Hebei, Shanxi, Shanghai, Jiangshu, Zhejiang, Anhui, Jiangxi, Hubei, Hunan, Guangxi, Sichuan, Shannxi, and Ningxia. All of the data on rural enterprises are taken from *Rural Statistical Yearbook of China* (from 1987 to 1997) and the Ministry of Agriculture. Other data, such as population, the share of light industry, cultivated land, exports, foreign direct investment, and so on, are taken from *Chinese Domestic Production: 1952–95, Quanguo Ge Sheng Zizhiqu Zhixiashi Lishi Tongji Ziliao Huibian: 1949–1989 [Historical Records of Chinese Provinces, Autonomous Regions, and Municipals: 1949–1989], China Agricultural Yearbook* from 1978 to 1990, *China Rural Statistical Yearbook* from 1986 to 1997, and *The Statistical Yearbook of China* from 1983 to 1998. All the financial measures are in 1978 prices. Two kinds of price deflators are used for various variables. One is the price index for specific items such as the retail price index for industrial products and the price index for fixed capital. We construct the other. For example, we construct a GDP deflator for each province by comparing the province's real GDP and nominal GDP. This deflator is used to deflate exports per capita and other variables. In what follows, we describe how some of the variables used in our regressions are constructed (for the variables not discussed, the description in the text is enough).

- *Value of RE output per capita.* For the period 1985–97, it is the value of gross output of all rural enterprises. For the period 1977–84, data on private firms are not available, so we only account for the output of collective enterprises. For the period 1970–76, the figure is the sum of the output value of rural industrial enterprises and the value of sidelines. The data set for 1970–97 includes the value of sidelines to the output value of rural enterprises for the years after 1976 to obtain a more consistent measure. The deflator we use for this variable is the rural retail price index of industrial products in each province.

- *Paved roads.* Starting in 1996, the official statistical publications no longer publish data on paved roads. We use the sum of class one and two roads and highways for 1996 and 1997.

- *Share of technicians.* Data for 1987, 1990, and 1991 are not available. The 1987 data are fit in by the average of 1986 and 1988. To recover the data for the other two years, we assume that the number of technicians grew at a constant annual rate from 1989 to 1992.

- *Share of light industry.* For the period 1978–97, the share is based on the value of gross output of industrial enterprises at the township level and above. For the period 1970–77, it is based on the value of gross output of all the industrial enterprises in a province.

- *Export and foreign direct investment.* Both are converted into Chinese renminbi. From 1970 to 1986, the official exchange rates are used; from 1995 to 1997, the weighted averages of the official and swap exchange rates are used. Export is deflated by the GDP deflator of each province, FDI is deflated by the price index of fixed assets.

- *SOE output value.* It is deflated by the industrial GDP deflator of each province.

- *Capital per capita in rural areas.* From 1985 to 1997, it is the sum of productive fixed assets owned by rural enterprises and rural households. From 1977 to 1980, it is the fixed assets of the communes.

Data before 1977 are not available. To get a complete series of data, we use the smoothing method used by Fan and Pardey (1997) to fill the missing data. For the years before 1977, we assume that the growth rate of the productive fixed assets in each province is constant from 1970 to 1980. So the average growth rate from 1977 to 1980 is used to backward recover the data of each province before 1977, using 1977 as the starting point. For the years between 1980 and 1985, we assume that the growth rate is constant from 1980 to 1985. The missing data are filled by referring to the data in these two years. The price index of the fixed assets in each province is used to convert the data into 1978 prices.

- *Share of public firms.* For the years before 1985, the share is assumed to be 1. For 1995 and 1996, the share is based on the value added instead of gross value.

NOTES

We are indebted to Shahid Yusuf and the February 1999 San Francisco workshop participants for their insightful comments. Mingxing Liu provided very capable assistance in data collection and processing.

1. In Chinese literature and statistics, rural enterprises include all the enterprises at or below township level, regardless of their type of ownership. These enterprises include not only those operating in industrial sectors but also those in construction, transportation, commerce, and food services. We adopt this definition here.

2. The Gini coefficients are calculated based on county-level income data rather than on household income data. For a description of the methodology and data issues, see Lin, Cai, and Li (1997).

3. The numbers cited in this section, if not otherwise noted, are from Byrd and Lin (1990: 9–10).

4. The study by Jin and Qian (2000) is close to such a study, but their panel is too short (from 1986 to 1994) to make their study comprehensive because many policy changes happened before 1986.

5. All the monetary measurements are normalized to 1978 yuan. For a detailed discussion of the normalization, see the appendix.

6. Nugent (1996) shows that the reversal was made possible by changes in the Korean government's financial policies toward a friendly environment for smaller firms.

7. The Chinese former leader Deng Xiaoping once told a reporter, "Generally

speaking, our rural reforms have proceeded very fast, and farmers have been enthusiastic. What took us by surprise completely was the development of township and village industries. The diversity of production, commodity economy, and all sorts of small enterprises boomed in the countryside, as if a strange army appeared suddenly from nowhere. This is not the achievement of our central government. Every year township and village industries achieved 20 percent growth. This was not something I thought about. Nor had the other comrades. This surprised us." (*People's Daily*, June 13, 1987).

8. Certainly, Taiwan has been more prudent in opening its financial markets. For example, it still maintains quite restrictive regulations toward short-term foreign loans and the operation of foreign banks in its territory. Recently, its currency was also devalued, but not as a direct result of the financial crisis; rather, it was caused by sluggish demand in the other East Asian countries.

REFERENCES

The word "processed" describes informally reproduced works that may not be commonly available through library systems.

Amsden, Alice. 1989. *Asia's Next Giant: South Korea and Late Industrialization.* New York: Oxford University Press.

Byrd, William, and Qingsong Lin. 1990. *China's Rural Industry: Structure, Development, and Reform.* New York: Oxford University Press.

Cao, Xinshui. 1996. *Traditional Chinese Peasant Economy in Southern Jiangsu.* Beijing: Central Translation Press.

Chang, Chun, and Yijiang Wang. 1994. "The Nature of the Township Enterprises." *Journal of Comparative Economics* 19:434–52.

Che, Jiahua, and Yingyi Qian. 1998. "Insecure Property Rights and Government Ownership of Firms." *Quarterly Journal of Economics* 113(2):467–96.

Chen, Chunlai, Andrew Watson, and Christopher Findley. 1990. "One State–Two Economies: Current Issues in China's Rural Industrialization." Working Paper series 1990004. University of Adelaide, Chinese Economic Research Unit, Adelaide. Processed.

Chen, Jiyuan. 1988. *A Study of the Models of the Township and Village Enterprises.* Beijing: Chinese Social Sciences Press.

Dong, Xiao-yuan, and Louis Putterman. 1997. "Productivity and Organization in China's Rural Industries: A Stochastic Frontier Analysis." *Journal of Comparative Economics* 24(2):181–201.

Falkus, Malcolm. 1995. "Thai Industrialization: An Overview." In Medhi Krongkaew, ed., *Thailand's Industrialization and Its Consequences.* New York: St. Martin's Press.

Fan, Gang. 1988. "A Theory of Grey Markets." *Economic Research* (8):3–12.

Fan, Shenggen, and Philip Pardey. 1997. "Research, Productivity, and Output Growth in Chinese Agriculture." *Journal of Development Economics* 53(1):115–37.

Feng, Haifa, and Wei Li. 1993. "A Study on the Surplus Provided by Agriculture to Industry in China." *Economic Research* (9):60–64.

Hayami, Yujiro, ed. 1998. *Rural-Based Development of Commerce and Industry: Selected Experience from East Asia*. Washington, D.C.: World Bank, Economic Development Institute.

Hayami, Yujiro, and M. Aoki, eds. 1998. *The Institutional Foundation of East Asian Economic Development*. London: Macmillan Press.

Ho, Samuel. 1979. "Decentralized Industrialization and Rural Development." *Economic Development and Cultural Change* 28(1):77–96.

Hughes, Helen, ed. 1988. *Achieving Industrialization in East Asia*. Cambridge, U.K.: Cambridge University Press.

Jefferson, Gary, Thomas Rawski, and Yuxin Zheng. 1996. "Chinese Industrial Productivity: Trends, Measurement Issues, and Recent Development." *Journal of Comparative Economics* 23:146–80.

Jia, W., Wei Li, Yanghong Li, and Qichang Zhan. 1994. *Technical Innovations*. Beijing: Zhongguo Jinji Press.

Jin, Hehui, and Yingyi Qian. 2000. "Public vs. Private Ownership of Firms: Evidence from Rural China." *Quarterly Journal of Economics* 113(3):773–808.

Krongkaew, Medhi. 1995. "Introduction: The Making of the Fifth Tiger: Thailand's Industrialization and Its Consequences." In Medhi Krongkaew, ed., *Thailand's Industrialization and Its Consequences*. New York: St. Martin's Press.

Kuznets, Paul. 1988. "An East Asian Model of Economic Development: Japan, Taiwan, and South Korea." *Economic Development and Cultural Change* 36(3):S11–43.

Li, David. 1994. "Ambiguous Property Rights in Transition Economies." *Journal of Comparative Economics* 23(1):1–19.

Li, Shuhe. 1997. "The Institutional Foundation of Self-Enforcing Contracts: The Township Enterprises." Department of Finance and Economics, City University of Hong Kong. Processed.

Lim, Steve. 1994. "Rural Industry: Interactions with Agricultural and State Industry." University of Adelaide, Chinese Economic Research Unit, Adelaide. Processed.

Lin, Justin Y. 1992. "Rural Reforms and Agricultural Growth in China." *American Economic Review* 82(1):34–51.

———. 1996. "Comparative Advantage, Development Policy, and the East Asian Miracles." Processed.

Lin, Justin Y., Fang Cai, and Zhou Li. 1994. *The China Miracle: Development Strategy and Economic Reform*. Hong Kong: Chinese University Press.

———. 1997. "The Social Outcomes of China's Economic Reform." Beijing University, China Center for Economic Research, Beijing. Processed.

Lin, Justin Y., and Yang Yao. 1999. "Alignment with Comparative Advantage and RE

Development in China's Provinces." China Center for Economic Research, Beijing University. Processed.

Liu, Shouying, Michael Carter, and Yang Yao. 1998. "Dimensions and Diversity of Property Rights in Rural China: Dilemmas on the Road to Further Reform." *World Development* 26(10):1799–806.

Lu, Feng. 1998. "The Change of Comparative Advantage of Chinese Agriculture." *Economic Research* (3):3–11.

Luedde-Neurath, Richard. 1988. "State Intervention and Export-Oriented Development in South Korea." In Gordon White, ed., *Developmental States in East Asia*. New York: Macmillan Press.

Nugent, Jeffery. 1996. "What Explains the Trend Reversal in the Size Distribution of Korean Manufacturing Establishments?" *Journal of Development Economics* 48(2):225–51.

Otsuka, Keijiro, and Thomas Reardon. 1998. "Lessons from Rural Industrialization in East Asia: Are They Applicable to Africa?" Paper 13. Prepared for the conference Strategies for Stimulating Growth of the Rural Nonfarm Economy in Developing Countries, International Food Policy Research Institute, Washington, D.C. May 17–21, 1998. Processed.

Poapongsakorn, Nipon. 1995. "Rural Industrialization: Problems and Prospects." In Medhi Krongkaew, eds., *Thailand's Industrialization and Its Consequences*. New York: St. Martin's Press.

Putterman, Louis. 1997. "On the Past and Future of China's Township and Village-owned Enterprises." *World Development* 25(10):1639–55.

Ranis, Gustav, Sheng-Cheng Hu, and Yun-Peng Chu, eds. 1998. *The Economics and Political Economy of Comparative Development into the 21st Century*. London: Edward Elgar.

Riedel, James. 1988. "Economic Development in East Asia: Doing What Comes Naturally?" In Helen Hughes, ed., *Achieving Industrialization in East Asia*. Cambridge, U.K.: Cambridge University Press.

Ronnas, Per. 1996. *Rural Industries in Post-reform China*. New Delhi: International Labour Organization.

Rozelle, Scott. 1994. "Rural Industrialization and Increasing Inequality: Emerging Patterns in China's Reforming Economy." *Journal of Comparative Economics* 19(3):362–91.

Saith, Ashwani. 1987. "Contrasting Experiences in Rural Industrialization: Is the East Asian Success Transferable?" In Rizwanul Islam, ed., *Rural Industrialization and Employment in Asia*. New Delhi: International Labour Organization.

Song, Ligang. 1993. *Sources of International Comparative Advantage: Further Evidence*. Ph.D. diss., Department of Economics. Australian National University. Canberra.

Tinakorn, Pranee. 1995. "Industrialization and Welfare: How Poverty and Income Distribution Are Affected?" In Medhi Krongkaew, ed., *Thailand's Industrialization and Its Consequences*. New York: St. Martin's Press.

Wade, Robert. 1988. "State Intervention in 'Outward-looking' Development: Neo-classical Theory and Taiwanese Practice." In Gordon White, ed., *Developmental States in East Asia*. New York: Macmillan Press.

Wang, Yueping. 1997. "FDI and Industrial Development in China." Working Paper 1997-013. Beijing University, China Center for Economic Research, Beijing. Processed.

Wang, Yueping, and Yang Yao. 1998. "Technological Capacities and Development China's Small Enterprises." Paper prepared for a World Bank comparative study of small firms in developing countries. World Bank, World Bank Institute. Washington, D.C. Processed.

Weitzman, Martin, and Chenggang Xu. 1994. "Chinese Township Village Enterprises as Vaguely Defined Cooperatives." *Journal of Comparative Economics* 23(1):121–45.

White, Gordon, ed. 1988. *Developmental States in East Asia*. New York: Macmillan Press.

White, Gordon, and Robert Wade. 1988. "Development States and Markets in East Asia: An Introduction." In Gordon White, ed., *Developmental States in East Asia*. New York: Macmillan Press.

World Bank. 1993. *The East Asian Miracle: Economic Growth and Public Policy*. New York: Oxford University Press.

Wu, Harry. 1992a. "The Industrialization of China's Rural Labor Force since the Economic Reform." Working Paper series 1992010. University of Adelaide, Chinese Economic Research Unit, Adelaide. Processed.

———. 1992b. "China's Rural Economic Performance during the Reform Decade: Estimate and Assessment." Working Paper series 1992011. University of Adelaide, Chinese Economic Research Unit, Adelaide. Processed.

Wu, Yanrui. 1990. "Rural Industrialization in China: A General Equilibrium Analysis." Working Paper series 1992009. University of Adelaide, Chinese Economic Research Unit, Adelaide. Processed.

———. 1992. "Productivity Performance of Chinese Rural Enterprises: A Comparative Study." Working Paper series 1993014. University of Adelaide, Chinese Economic Research Unit, Adelaide. Processed.

———. 1993. "One Industry, Two Regimes: The Chinese Textile Sector Growth, Reforms, and Efficiency." Working Paper series. University of Adelaide, Chinese Economic Research Unit, Adelaide. Processed.

Yan, Y., and S. Zhang. 1995. *Technical Advancement of Chinese Res*. Beijing: Nongye Keji Press.

Yao, Yang. 1998. "Non-state Factors and Technical Efficiency of the Chinese Industry." *Economic Research* (in Chinese) (12):29–35.

Zhang, Gang. 1997. *Chinese Rural Enterprises between Plan and Market*. Ph.D. diss., Stockholm School of Economics.

Zhang, Xiaohe. 1993. "Modeling China's Rural Economy." Working Paper series 1993011. University of Adelaide, Chinese Economic Research Unit, Adelaide. Processed.

Zhao, Yaohui. 1997. "Property Rights of Chinese REs and Their Influence on Rural Employment." In Wen Hai, ed., *Chinese Township Village Enterprises: Nature, Experience, and Reforms.* Beijing, Zhonghua Gongshang Lianghe Press.

Zhao, Xiao. 1999. "Political Competition and Privatization in China." CCER Working Paper series no. C1999002.

Zhe, Xiaoye. 1997. *The Remaking of a Village.* Beijing: China Social Sciences Press.

Zweig, David. 1997. *Free China's Farmers: Restructuring in the Reform Era.* Hong Kong: The Chinese University of Hong Kong.

CHAPTER 5

AFTER THE CRISIS, THE EAST ASIAN DOLLAR STANDARD RESURRECTED: AN INTERPRETATION OF HIGH-FREQUENCY EXCHANGE RATE PEGGING

Ronald I. McKinnon

For more than a decade before the crisis of June 1997 to December 1998, East Asian currencies were pegged to the U.S. dollar. With the important exception of Japan, the crisis economies of Indonesia, the Republic of Korea, Malaysia, the Philippines, and Thailand as well as the noncrisis economies of Hong Kong (China), Singapore, and Taiwan (China) organized their domestic monetary policies to keep their dollar exchange rates remarkably stable. In effect, their mutual link to the dollar was the nominal anchor for their domestic price levels—the East Asian dollar standard (McKinnon 2000). Although exchange rate policies have been comprehensively reviewed following the crisis, it is notable that East Asian countries appear to have resumed formal or informal pegging to the dollar, reaffirming the attractiveness of the rule followed through the nineties.

In 1994, as China moved to full current account but not capital account convertibility, the government unified its exchange rate regime and then kept the rate virtually unchanged at 8.3 yuan to the dollar through the crisis to the present. After a net 50 percent devaluation of the ringgit, the Malaysian government imposed capital controls and announced, in September 1998, a fixed exchange rate of 3.8 ringgits to the dollar, which it still maintains.

Of all these economies, only Hong Kong declared an official exchange rate *parity* against the dollar. (The others remained noncommittal on parity obligations.) Since 1983, Hong Kong's parity of 7.8 Hong Kong dollars to the U.S. dollar has been the anchor of domestic monetary policy based on a currency board—the only one in East Asia. And despite continual attacks during 1997–98, Hong Kong sustained this exchange rate without the aid of capital controls.

In this chapter, I first analyze what happened to the East Asian dollar standard during the crisis. In the period of wildly fluctuating exchange rates from mid-1997 through 1998, how did the dollar fare as nominal anchor? The collective importance of the East Asian dollar standard as a regional monetary anchor was revealed by the massive deflationary pressure in dollar terms that was unleashed throughout East Asia.

Second, I consider how the postcrisis exchange rate regime has evolved since 1998. The precrisis pegged-rate regime has been judged a failure because of its moral hazard in inducing short-term hot money flows. Fischer (1999) suggests that greater exchange rate flexibility would be desirable in the future, while others suggest that a zone of more stable exchange rates against the yen might be preferable (Kwan 2001; Kawai and Akiyama 2000; Ohno 2000). Except for Indonesia, however, the East Asian dollar standard seems to be resurrecting itself. Dollar exchange rates, particularly when observed on a high-frequency (daily) basis, have become as stable as they were before the crisis. This "fear of floating" identified by Calvo and Reinhart (2000a, 2000b) is shown at higher frequencies to be a rational response to capital market conditions in emerging markets.

Third, I explore the "honeymoon" effect. After a major crisis with sharp devaluations and some exchange rate overshooting, hot money inflows are naturally somewhat muted. But this calm since 1998 is deceptive. To prevent the cycle of international overborrowing from repeating itself, the banking and foreign exchange authorities must still put proper prudential regulations in place; these regulations, in turn, affect the nature of the optimal exchange rate regime.

I conclude by discussing how the informal rules of the game under which the East Asian dollar standard operates could be modified to curb hot money flows. One objective is to lengthen the term to maturity of finance in the smaller East Asian debtor economies. But in order for Japan—the largest creditor—to have less of a destabilizing effect on the others while promoting its own economic recovery, a somewhat different set of rules is appropriate.

THE COLLECTIVE NOMINAL ANCHOR

Using precrisis data, McKinnon (2000) presents evidence that international trade in the region was overwhelmingly invoiced in dollars and that, in the 1990s, the domestic American price level was quite stable. This price level of the "center" country was considered to be the "anchor" to which any individual East Asian country could attach itself. However, this earlier view substantially oversimplifies how the East Asian dollar standard actually works.

First, this nominal anchor argument rests more on low- than on high-frequency pegging. To stabilize and protect domestic price levels from (inadvertent) beggar-thy-neighbor devaluations, the monetary authorities need only be concerned with stabilizing the exchange rate on a monthly or quarterly basis. Figures 5.1 and 5.2 indicate that monthly exchange rates against the dollar were quite stable before the 1997–98 crisis—albeit sometimes with drift—and, in 1999–2000, showed signs of stabilizing once more. But this nominal anchor argument fails to explain the much tighter pegging on a *daily* basis, which is discussed below.

Second, for any one member country of the East Asian dollar standard, the stability of this nominal anchor depends more on having all or most East Asian countries jointly stabilizing their dollar exchange rates than on the American price level alone. The 1997–98 crisis throws strong light on the issue. The sharp currency devaluations of Indonesia, Korea, Malaysia, Philippines, and Thailand—and the collapse in their demand for imports—imparted severe deflationary pressure on those countries that did not devalue or that devalued by considerably less than did these crisis economies. This deflationary effect was further aggravated by the earlier fall of the yen from 80 to the dollar in April 1995 to a bottom of 147 to the dollar in June 1998 (figure 5.2). For 9 of the 10 countries (Indonesia is omitted because of problems with vertical scaling) and the United States itself, figures 5.3 and 5.4 plot consumer price indexes from January 1995 to April 2000. With the U.S. consumer price index (CPI) as the benchmark, two features stand out:

- The domestic inflationary impact in each of the four crisis economies from their deep devaluations was surprisingly muted. Their price levels increased by less than half of whatever devaluation against

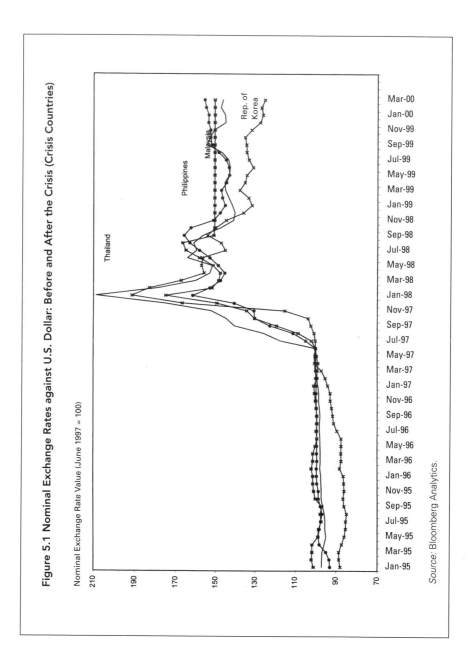

Figure 5.1 Nominal Exchange Rates against U.S. Dollar: Before and After the Crisis (Crisis Countries)

Nominal Exchange Rate Value (June 1997 = 100)

Source: Bloomberg Analytics.

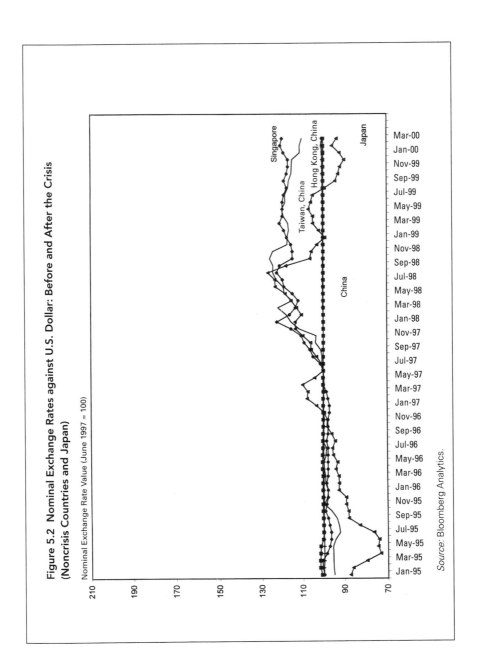

Figure 5.2 Nominal Exchange Rates against U.S. Dollar: Before and After the Crisis (Noncrisis Countries and Japan)

Nominal Exchange Rate Value (June 1997 = 100)

Source: Bloomberg Analytics.

the dollar was sustained into the year 2000. Even the earlier substantial fall in the yen in 1997–98 did not impart any inflation in
Japan's CPI (figure 5.4).

- The deflationary pressure imparted to the noncrisis, nondevaluing,
  economies was quite severe. Figure 5.4 shows the CPIs of Hong
  Kong and China falling about 10 percent relative to the U.S. CPI,
  but also falling absolutely from late 1997 to 2000. Even Singapore
  and Taiwan, with 10 to 15 percent devaluations against the dollar,
  saw modest falls in their internal CPIs from mid-1997 to 2000.

Of course, these two features are related. The sharp devaluations
and falls in aggregate demand in the five crisis economies imposed
strong downward pressure on the *dollar*-invoiced prices of most goods
traded in the region. This fall in the general dollar price level then
muted the increases in the internal price levels of the devaluing economies, while contributing to the serious absolute deflationary pressure
in China and Hong Kong, which did not devalue at all. Even the United
States itself was affected. A broad tradable goods price index, the
American producer price index (PPI; not shown) fell about 5 percent
from mid-1997 to early 1999.

What is the lesson from this regional deflation? East Asian countries are now highly integrated in their trading relationships with each
other (see chapter 11, by Urata, and Bergsten 2000). Indeed, C. H.
Kwan (2001) shows that, for the last two decades, intra-Asian trade
(including Japan) rose much faster than trade with the United States.
Now about 50 percent of gross East Asian exports go to other East
Asian countries and only 25 percent go to the United States. The 1997–
98 crisis revealed how the success of any one country pegging to the
dollar as a nominal anchor depends heavily on having its trading partners and competitors securely anchored as well. From this collective
"nominal anchor" perspective, East Asia has become a natural currency area over which it is desirable for exchange rates to be stable.

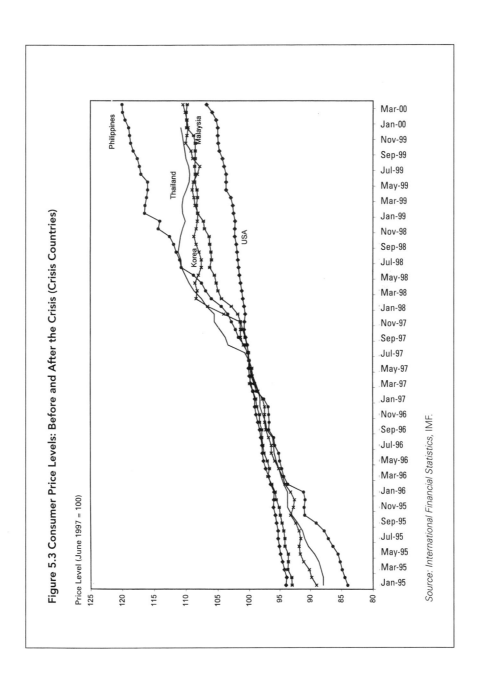

Figure 5.3 Consumer Price Levels: Before and After the Crisis (Crisis Countries)

Price Level (June 1997 = 100)

Source: International Financial Statistics, IMF.

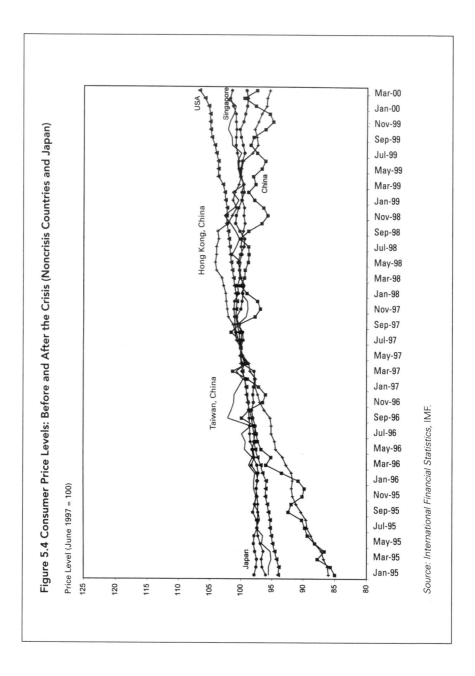

Figure 5.4 Consumer Price Levels: Before and After the Crisis (Noncrisis Countries and Japan)

Price Level (June 1997 = 100)

Source: International Financial Statistics, IMF.

OPTIMUM CURRENCY AREAS VERSUS THE COLLECTIVE NOMINAL ANCHOR

Are there other perspectives? Some might object that the East Asian countries, with or without Japan, do not constitute an optimum currency area in the sense of Mundell (1961) because they experience macroeconomic shocks "asymmetrically." For East Asia, C. H. Kwan (2001: 11, 12) states Mundell's 1961 argument this way:

> The major cost associated with monetary integration arises from the abandonment of an independent monetary policy. By fixing its exchange rate to other members of the monetary union, a country joining a union automatically gives up control over its own monetary policy. When its economy is subject to an external shock, it has no choice but to follow the common monetary policy of the monetary union. Countries with similar economic structures can respond to a common shock with a common monetary policy, and the costs of giving up an independent monetary policy are relatively small. In contrast, countries with heterogeneous economic structures require different policy responses to common shocks, and the costs of sharing a common monetary policy are relatively large. For example, Japan and Korea, both oil importers, can respond to a surge in oil prices with the same monetary policy. This, however, would not apply to Japan and Indonesia, where the latter is an oil exporter. . . .
>
> In view of the diversity among these countries, it is unlikely that Japan, the Asian NIEs [newly industrializing economies], the ASEAN [Association of South East Asian Nations] countries, and China together and at once have formed an optimum currency area. Higher-income countries such as those of the Asian NIEs have trade structures similar to that of Japan, while lower-income countries such as lower-income members of ASEAN and China have trade structures very different from that of Japan.

Based on Mundell's 1961 analysis, Kwan concludes that East Asian economies collectively do not form an optimal currency area. Kwan's careful analysis is in line with a huge volume of similar literature showing that continental Europe before the euro was not an optimum currency area either (see Eichengreen 1997). In his 1961 paper, "A Theory of Optimum Currency Areas," Mundell (1961: 511) illustrated his argument thus:

> If demand shifts from the products of country B to the products of country A, a depreciation by country B or an appreciation by country A would correct the external imbalance and also relieve unemployment in country B and restrain inflation in country A. This is the most favorable case for flexible exchange rates based on national currencies.

But Mundell's narrow interpretation of asymmetric shocks does not make much sense for industrially diversified economies, each producing hundreds or thousands of commodities. Private demand would not suddenly shift away from French goods collectively toward German—or even from Thai goods toward Korean.[1]

To make more empirical sense out of Mundell's traditional analysis, writers like C. H. Kwan stress the problems for countries with different industrial structures facing a common external shock. This common shock could be a change in the price of some primary commodity, such as a rise in the price of oil. (For the smaller East Asian economies pegged to the dollar, fluctuations in the yen/dollar exchange rate have been the most important common external shock; McKinnon 2000). Or national business cycles could simply be out of phase. To better preserve national monetary autonomy, the early Mundell tradition stressed the advantage of keeping currency areas small and separated by flexible exchange rates.

Was the early Mundell right? At a conference in Madrid in 1970, Mundell essentially changed his mind (Mundell 1973a, 1973b; McKinnon 2001)! In these 1973 papers, he showed that heterogeneous economies could share the risks from asymmetric shocks better *within* a common currency area. For this later Mundell, the key was international portfolio diversification in both assets and liabilities. Full diversification and risk sharing were possible only if future exchange rates were certain. Then a country suffering an adverse shock could easily draw down its claims on, or borrow from, other countries in the common currency area. By not having to devalue, domestic money would be as good as foreign money.

> A harvest failure, strikes, or war in one of the countries causes a loss of real income, but the use of a common currency (or foreign exchange reserves) allows the country to run down its currency holdings and cushion the impact of the loss, drawing on the resources of the other country until the cost of the adjustment has been efficiently spread over the future. If, on the other hand, the two countries use separate monies with flexible exchange rates, the whole loss has to be borne alone; the common currency cannot serve as a shock absorber for the nation as a whole except insofar as the dumping of inconvertible currencies on foreign markets attracts a speculative capital inflow in favor of the depreciating currency. [Mundell 1973b: 115.]

Even before the 1997–98 crisis, however, the East Asian economies were a long way from establishing a truly diversified capital market among themselves. Exchange rates were insufficiently pinned down *in the longer run* for insurance companies, well-behaved banks, trust funds, and other fiduciaries in any one country to hold claims on the other countries denominated in their currencies. True, Japan was the largest net creditor. But even in the absence of crises, there was insignificant diversification of gross assets and liabilities within the East Asian region. Indeed, substantial portfolio diversification within Europe had to wait for the advent of the euro on January 1, 1999 (McKinnon 2001). And complete monetary unification in East Asia, with the introduction of an "Asian euro," is certainly not imminent.

A COMMON MONETARY STANDARD VERSUS A COMMON CURRENCY

Although not as good as a common currency, a common monetary standard among close trading partners is still preferable to (unrestricted) exchange rate flexibility. For our purposes, a common monetary standard is one where participating countries keep, with some success, their exchange rates fixed against a common nominal anchor, possibly provided externally. Although exchange rates may remain fixed for many years (as in some East Asian countries before the crisis), longer-term exchange rate uncertainty remains. In comparison, a "common currency" provides a common anchor *and* full long-run exchange rate certainty.

However, a common monetary standard among countries that trade extensively with each other is still better than floating exchange rates for mitigating asymmetric shocks. Indeed, the common nominal anchor itself becomes more stable if business cycles across member countries are *not* synchronized. If country A experiences a cyclical downturn, then the common price level provided by the nominal anchor will be more stable as long as country B does not experience the same shock. With a series of such random shocks affecting each country differentially, there will be a natural tendency toward business cycle smoothing for the region as whole.

If countries A and B have synchronized business cycles with upturns and downturns experienced in unison, this amplifies the common business cycle. The extreme case was the East Asian crisis, with devaluations and downturns in several member economies simultaneously imposing a deflationary slump on other members. Each crisis economy's own downturn was thereby aggravated.

Why, then, did interpreters of the early Mundell (1961) lean toward grouping similar countries or regions together—for example, those with synchronous business cycles—in defining an "optimum" currency area, as in Kwan's analysis quoted above? Like most macro economists in the early 1960s, Mundell still had a postwar Keynesian mind-set in believing that national governments could successfully fine-tune aggregate demand to offset private sector shocks on the supply or demand sides. As a modeling strategy, he assumed stationary expectations: people acted as if the current domestic price level, interest rate, and exchange rate would hold indefinitely (even when the exchange rate was floating). Both his theory of optimum currency areas (Mundell 1961) and the standard textbook Mundell-Fleming model (Mundell 1968) of how monetary and fiscal policy work themselves out in an open economy depend on stationary expectations.

We now realize that expectations are not stationary. Asset markets in general, and the foreign exchange market in particular, are forward-looking—a fact appreciated by the later Mundell (1973b). They become very volatile if the government just might take discretionary action to fine-tune the domestic macroeconomy: the well-known time-consistency problem (Kydland and Prescott 1977). Risk premiums in bond markets increase. Thus modern macroeconomic thinking leans toward constraining and limiting what governments might try. If the inflation tax is not needed for revenue (which has been true of East Asia except for Indonesia), central banks everywhere are more narrowly mandated to stabilize the domestic price level.

In industrial economies, this mandate is interpreted as direct inflation targeting. With a well-developed, long-term domestic bond market, the central bank can use open-market operations to control the monetary base. Continual adjustments in short-term interest rates for controlling domestic inflation become feasible—as per Taylor's rule (Taylor 1993). In a rules-based environment, industrial economies can credibly fashion their own nominal anchor. This limits the moral hazard of governments trying to take markets by surprise.

But in emerging markets, and those in East Asia in particular, finance is too short-term for something like Taylor's rule to be operational. Increases in short-term interest threaten bankruptcy much more because banks and firms have such short-term liquid liabilities relative to their longer-term, less liquid assets. Whence came the importance of targeting the exchange rate as (a) an instrument of monetary policy for stabilizing the domestic price level in an area where most trade is invoiced in dollars and (b) a highly visible rule that, if followed in a consistent fashion by subordinating domestic monetary policy to the international standard, constrains erratic behavior by the government itself.

The East Asian crisis has shown that even if the time-consistency problem is "solved" for any one country, monetary stability itself is not ensured unless trading partners and competitors are also pegged to the dollar. Indeed, relying on an outside country to provide the nominal anchor has risks of its own should that center country's monetary authority misbehave.

EXCHANGE RATE TARGETING: YEN VERSUS DOLLAR

Why not choose the yen rather than the dollar as the central currency around which the common monetary standard is organized? In East Asia, Japan by some measures is a slightly bigger trader, and certainly a more important source of capital, than is the United States. C. H. Kwan (2001) has estimated that intra-Asian exports (including Japan) rose from about 30 percent of total Asian exports in 1986 to 50 percent by the late 1990s. Similarly, Asian exports to the United States fell from about 35 to 25 percent of all Asian exports. When the smaller East Asian economies are pegged to the dollar, as the yen/dollar rate fluctuates, Japan's real exchange rate varies not only against that of the United States but also against all those of Japan's East Asian trading partners.

Thus it is not surprising that the Japanese government has long sought to create a yen zone in Asia. Japan's exchange risk would be greatly reduced if the other East Asian nations pegged collectively to the yen instead of the dollar. Less drastic would be for each of the smaller economies simply to weigh the yen more heavily in pegging to a currency basket. This basket would be trade-weighted to reflect the importance of that country's exports to, or its imports from, Japan relative to the importance of its trade with the United States, euroland, other East Asian economies, and so on. For variants of this alternative, see Williamson (2000), Kwan (2001), Kawai and Akiyama (2000), and Ito, Ogawa, and Sasaki (1998).

If the trade weights in any one country's currency basket are picked appropriately, this basket approach also minimizes the variance in that country's similarly trade-weighted real exchange rate arising from external sources, as with fluctuations in the yen/dollar or euro/dollar exchange rates. (One still has to adjust separately for the effect of internal inflation on the real exchange rate.) So, the welfare criterion underlying the currency-basket approach is one of minimizing variance in the effective real exchange rate of the country in question. Should this welfare criterion, advocated by so many authors, be the dominant one for the smaller East Asian countries?

First, targeting the real exchange rate, however measured, by continually moving the nominal rate means that the exchange rate cannot anchor the domestic price level. A "random" increase in domestic inflation would require an offsetting devaluation that accommodates the ongoing inflation. And before the 1997–98 crisis, the smaller East Asian economies—with the possible exception of Indonesia—had good fiscal balance so that revenue from the inflation tax was unnecessary. China had ongoing fiscal deficits but could finance these in a noninflationary manner by allowing the government to borrow from China's huge banking system (McKinnon 1993: ch. 13). In countries such as these, in contrast to countries with chronic inflation, as in Latin America, targeting the real exchange rate introduces monetary instability, that is, greater persistence in inflation rates, when none need exist.

Second, because the trade weights in each country's basket would differ from those of its neighbors, the commonality of the East Asian monetary standard would be lost. Country A would be continually moving its exchange rate differently from country B, requiring further exchange rate adjustment in country B. Worse, if a calamitous devaluation occurred in any one Asian economy (as in Thailand in June 1997), the rules of the currency-basket game would require neighboring countries to devalue as well. So contagious devaluations would be built into the rules of the currency-basket regime.

Third, the appropriate trade weights are necessarily ambiguous. For a group of countries that compete in third markets, as the East Asian countries do, conventional trade weights based on the size of bilateral trade between any pair might seriously understate the importance of movements in either country's exchange rate for the other. Also, trade weighting does not reflect the preponderance of dollar invoicing of trade in East Asia. In normal times, these dollar prices may be quite sticky, reflecting the pricing-to-market competition among firms in the area. For primary commodities, where producers have no market power, dollar prices are given in world markets independently (McKinnon 1979). Thus, even using this basket technique, the dollar should receive a much higher weight than suggested by simple bilateral trade with the United States.

Fourth, the simplest conceptual solution for stabilizing effective real exchange rates in East Asia is to fix the yen to the dollar. Being part of the dollar zone would dramatically reduce the variance in real exchange rates that Japanese producers and overseas investors now face. It also would reduce residual exchange risk in the other East Asian economies as well.

Such a drastic change in Japan's foreign exchange policy—and necessarily in its monetary policy—would have to be argued on domestic grounds as well. Fortunately, no conflict between internal and external balance exists. Kenichi Ohno and I have shown (McKinnon and Ohno 1997, 2000) that a long-term fix of the yen against the dollar (requiring American cooperation to be credible) is the key for Japan to escape from the low-interest liquidity trap and deflationary expectations in which its economy is now mired.

RESURRECTION: THE RETURN OF HIGH-FREQUENCY PEGGING

A priori, one can rehash indefinitely the debate over fixed versus flexible exchange rates or whether East Asia is a natural yen zone or dollar zone. However, the outcome has already been decided by a "natural experiment." In 2000, both the crisis and noncrisis countries of East Asia (with Japan remaining the important exception) returned to formal or informal dollar pegging, which is statistically indistinguishable from what they were doing before the crisis.

Except for Indonesia, figures 5.1 and 5.2 plot the dollar exchange rates of the East Asian countries on a monthly basis. Figure 5.1 shows the crisis economies—Korea, Malaysia, Philippines, and Thailand—

stabilizing their dollar rates after about a 25 to 50 percent net devaluation against the dollar from mid-1997 to 2000. Figure 5.2 shows the noncrisis economies of Taiwan and Singapore stabilizing their exchange rates after about a 10 percent devaluation; China and Hong Kong show no change in their dollar exchange rates throughout the crisis. The figure also shows greater fluctuations of the yen against the dollar and the marked (if temporary) depreciation of the yen from July 1995, when the rate was 80 yen to the dollar, to June 1998, when the yen bottomed out at 147 to the dollar.

However, these low-frequency—that is, monthly—plots, which the eye can easily follow, are deceptive. In some important sense, they understate the degree to which the East Asian dollar standard has been, or is on its way to being, resurrected. To understand better what is going on, one must consider higher-frequency—that is, weekly and daily—data. Then the hypothesis cannot be rejected that the East Asian countries from January 1999 to May 2000 returned to a dollar standard like the pre-1997 regime.

Weekly and daily exchange rate data were taken from Bloomberg Analytics for nine East Asian economies—China, Hong Kong, Indonesia, Korea, Malaysia, Philippines, Singapore, Thailand, and Taiwan. The data were broken up into three periods—precrisis from January 1994 to the last week of May 1997, the crisis from June 1997 to December 1998, and postcrisis from January 1999 to May 2000.

The basic regression model draws from the work of Frankel and Wei (1994). A relatively independent currency, such as the Swiss franc, was chosen as an arbitrary *numéraire* for measuring variations in the exchange rate. The simple regression model is multivariable ordinary least squares for each country and time period.

The basic regression model draws from the work of Frankel and Wei (1994). A relatively independent currency, such as the Swiss franc, was chosen as an arbitrary *numéraire* for measuring variations in the exchange rate. Based on the first difference of logarithms (percentage changes), the simple regression model is multivariate ordinary least squares for each country and time period.

(5.1)   Local Currency/SWF = β_1 + β_2 USD/SWF + β_3 JPY/SWF + β_4 DEM/SWF + ε

where SWF is the Swiss franc, USD is the U.S. dollar, JPY is the Japanese yen, DEM is the German mark, and D is an operator denoting the percentage rate of change, e is assumed to be a well-behaved error term, following $N(0,\sigma^2)$.

According to Frankel and Wei, if the local currency is tightly fixed to some particular value of the dollar, then the regression coefficient β_2 in equation 5.1 should approximate unity, while β_3 and β_4 are close to 0. If it tracked the Japanese yen, then β_3 should be close to 1 and the others close to 0.

Daily Data

Tables 5.1, 5.2, and 5.3 summarize the regression results before, during, and after the crisis. All three are based on daily observations of exchange rates.

Table 5.1 summarizes the tightness of the exchange rate band around the U.S. dollar during the precrisis time period from January 1994 to May 1997. The β_2 coefficients were all very close to 1 and always statistically significant. The coefficients for the other two potential anchor currencies (the yen and the mark) were typically close to 0 and were not statistically significant. Judging from the high R^2, the statistical model captures most of the exchange rate variance of each East Asian country. These precrisis data suggest that East Asian countries kept their dollar exchange rates remarkably stable week-to-week.

More specifically, China and Hong Kong had β_2 coefficients and R^2 of almost exactly 1. Their extremely small standard errors suggest that the authorities ensured that the exchange rate fluctuated very little. Although Hong Kong had an official exchange rate parity, China did not. But they were statistically indistinguishable.

Next, Indonesia and Philippines had β_2 coefficients very close to 1, but with somewhat larger standard errors, suggesting that their authorities allowed some exchange rate movements on a weekly basis. Singapore and Thailand pegged most loosely to the dollar, with β_2 coefficients of 0.85 and 0.89, respectively. Even these coefficients were remarkably high: a 1 percent change in the U.S. dollar to Swiss franc exchange rate implies a 0.85 percent change in the Singapore dollar to Swiss franc exchange rate.

Table 5.1: Daily Observations: Precrisis Period, January 1994–May 1997
Observations: 889

Currency	β Constant	β₁ U.S. dollar	β₂ Japanese yen	β₃ German mark	R square	Adj R square	F statistic
Chinese yuan	0.000	0.996	0.000	0.012	0.99563	0.99561	67,142.17
	(0.000)	(0.003)	(0.003)	(0.007)			
Hong Kong dollar	0.000	1.000	-0.002	0.002	0.99811	0.99810	155,457.53
	(0.000)	(0.002)	(0.002)	(0.005)			
Indonesian rupiah	0.000	0.999	-0.014	-0.021	0.96058	0.96045	7,188.77
	(0.000)	(0.008)	(0.009)	(0.022)			
Korean won	0.000	1.021	0.006	-0.032	0.88348	0.88308	2,236.68
	(0.000)	(0.016)	(0.017)	(0.041)			
Malaysian ringgit	0.000	0.886	0.062	0.039	0.88911	0.88873	2,365.31
	(0.000)	(0.014)	(0.015)	(0.036)			
Philippine peso	0.000	0.987	-0.009	-0.012	0.83598	0.83543	1,503.58
	(0.000)	(0.018)	(0.021)	(0.049)			
Singapore dollar	0.000	0.817	0.114	0.037	0.90524	0.90492	2,818.02
	(0.000)	(0.012)	(0.013)	(0.032)			
Thai baht	0.000	0.955	0.070	-0.087	0.92323	0.92297	3,547.57
	(0.000)	(0.012)	(0.013)	(0.031)			
Taiwan dollar	0.000	1.015	0.015	-0.067	0.92799	0.92775	3,801.82
	(0.000)	(0.012)	(0.013)	(0.031)			

Note: Standard errors are in parentheses.
Source: Bloomberg Analytics and International Monetary Fund.

Table 5.2 shows that in the crisis period, from June 1997 to December 1998 only China and Hong Kong continued with unwavering dollar pegs; the others gave up. The β_2 coefficients for Indonesia, Malaysia, Philippines, Singapore, and Thailand differed from 1 with large standard errors. Although the Korean β_2 coefficient remained slightly more than 1, its standard error was very high. The goodness-of-fit (R^2) for these regressions fell completely apart.

Table 5.2 also shows that the noncrisis economies of Taiwan and Singapore pegged more weakly to the dollar during the crisis than they did before mid-1997. Still, these two creditor economies maintained their dollar pegs somewhat more strongly than the neighboring debtor economies in crisis, but not as strongly as China and Hong Kong.

The β_3 coefficients of the Japanese yen increased a bit in the crisis. The yen became significant for Malaysia, Philippines, Singapore, and Thailand, but the goodness-of-fit of these equations was poor.

Dating the postcrisis period is necessarily somewhat arbitrary. Indonesia still seems to be in a quasi-crisis mode. For the other four crisis economies, 1998 was still a bad year, with high risk premiums in interest rates associated with the troubles of the Russian Federation and Brazil. However, by the beginning of 1999, recovery seemed at hand, and private foreign capital began to return; whence came the choice of January 1999 to May 2000 for the postcrisis period.

In table 5.3, the postcrisis equations show a tremendous improvement in all the goodness-of-fit (R^2) coefficients compared with the crisis equations. Except for Indonesia, the β_2 coefficients were now again close to 1, although not quite so tightly as the precrisis coefficients. For China, Hong Kong, and now Malaysia, the coefficients were identically 1. The fact that Hong Kong and China held their fixed dollar exchange rates throughout the crisis, and that Malaysia fixed its dollar exchange after September 1998, augurs well for the future robustness of the dollar-based system.

But a formal statistical test of this postcrisis return to the dollar standard is in order. For each country equation, I hypothesize that the degree of fixity to the dollar was the same after as before the crisis. More formally, I hypothesize that

Ho: (β_2) precrisis = (β_2) postcrisis

Table 5.2 Daily Observations: Crisis Period, June 1997–Dec 1998
Observations: 412

	β	β_1	β_2	β_3			
Currency	Constant	U.S. dollar	Japanese yen	German mark	R square	Adj R square	F statistic
Chinese yuan	0.000	1.001	0.000	0.000	1.000	1.000	1289001.652
	(0.000)	(0.000)	(0.000)	(0.001)			
Hong Kong dollar	0.000	1.000	0.000	0.003	0.998	0.998	57485.443
	(0.000)	(0.003)	(0.002)	(0.005)			
Indonesian rupiah	0.004	0.550	0.615	0.716	0.038	0.031	5.321
	(0.002)	(0.388)	(0.239)	(0.710)			
Korean won	0.001	1.086	0.160	0.179	0.087	0.080	12.951
	(0.001)	(0.226)	(0.139)	(0.413)			
Malaysian ringgit	0.001	0.755	0.244	0.506	0.161	0.155	26.233
	(0.000)	(0.138)	(0.085)	(0.252)			
Philippine peso	0.001	0.788	0.318	0.240	0.196	0.190	33.176
	(0.000)	(0.125)	(0.077)	(0.229)			
Singapore dollar	0.000	0.727	0.265	0.157	0.447	0.443	110.177
	(0.000)	(0.061)	(0.037)	(0.111)			
Thai baht	0.000	0.688	0.216	0.588	0.107	0.101	16.366
	(0.000)	(0.165)	(0.102)	(0.302)			
Taiwan dollar	0.000	0.930	0.036	0.077	0.552	0.548	167.72
	(0.000)	(0.050)	(0.031)	(0.091)			

Note: Standard errors are in parentheses.
Source: Bloomberg Analytics and International Monetary Fund.

This test was unnecessary in the cases of China, Hong Kong, and Malaysia, which now have fixed their exchange rates against the dollar. For the rest of the countries, one could reject this hypothesis if

$$\frac{(\beta_2) \text{ postcrisis} - (\beta_2) \text{ precrisis} \mid > 2}{\text{Standard Error (postcrisis)}}$$

These results suggest that the East Asian countries have made a clandestine return to their old pegged regimes—in fact to the same tightness of the peg that they had in the precrisis period. With weekly data, it is just barely possible to reject the null hypothesis for Thailand. However, using the daily data shown in tables 5.1 and 5.3, one cannot reject the null hypothesis even for Thailand.

An important caveat concerns Indonesia. Because of the large standard error on the U.S. dollar coefficient, one cannot reject the null hypothesis that (β_2) postcrisis = 0. More generally, the Indonesian economy still seems to be out of control.

Figure 5.5 presents a more dramatic picture of Korea's and Thailand's return to the dollar standard. Based on daily data, rolling 30-day β_2 regression coefficients are plotted over the precrisis, crisis, and postcrisis periods.

What can one conclude from this statistical analysis? At high data frequencies—weekly and even more so daily—the peg to the dollar was remarkably robust in noncrisis periods; whereas, at lower frequencies—monthly or quarterly—exchange rates drifted more. The exceptions were the Chinese renminbi , Hong Kong dollar, and Malaysian ringgit, which are now firmly pegged for any frequency of measurement.

THE "ORIGINAL SIN" HYPOTHESIS AND HIGH-FREQUENCY PEGGING

What could be the motivation for emerging-market governments to damp these very short-term movements in their exchange rates?

Guillermo Calvo and Carmen Reinhart (2000a, 2000b) show that this short-term rigidity, which they measure on a monthly basis, is quite general in emerging-market economies in Latin America, East Asia, and elsewhere. Since the collapse of Bretton Woods exchange parities in 1971, the apparent move to more flexible exchange rates has been a mirage for much of the developing world. In the industrial

Table 5.3 Daily Observations: Postcrisis Period, Jan 1999–May 2000
Observations: 350

		β_1	β_2	β_3			
Currency	Constant	U.S. dollar	Japanese yen	German mark	R square	Adj R square	F statistic
Chinese yuan	0.000	1.000	0.000	-0.001	0.99992	0.99992	1,492,141.09
	(0.000)	(0.000)	(0.000)	(0.001)			
Hong Kong dollar	0.000	0.998	0.001	0.002	0.99977	0.99976	493,579.34
	(0.000)	(0.001)	(0.000)	(0.002)			
Indonesian rupiah	0.000	0.848	0.299	0.063	0.18162	0.17452	25.59
	(0.000)	(0.163)	(0.111)	(0.329)			
Korean won	0.000	0.957	0.070	0.147	0.70585	0.7033	276.75
	(0.000)	(0.045)	(0.030)	(0.090)			
Malaysian ringgit	0.000	1.000	0.000	-0.001	1	1	1,960,427.44
	(0.000)	(0.000)	(0.000)	(0.001)			
Philippine peso	0.000	0.945	0.067	0.042	0.74064	0.73839	329.35
	(0.000)	(0.040)	(0.027)	(0.080)			
Singapore dollar	0.000	0.818	0.124	0.026	0.84805	0.84674	643.71
	(0.000)	(0.026)	(0.018)	(0.053)			
Thai baht	0.000	0.858	0.128	0.014	0.63936	0.63623	204.47
	(0.000)	(0.049)	(0.033)	(0.098)			
Taiwan dollar	0.000	0.986	-0.005	-0.051	0.88334	0.88232	873.26
	(0.000)	(0.024)	(0.016)	(0.048)			

Note: Standard errors are in parentheses.
Source: Bloomberg Analytics and International Monetary Fund.

Figure 5.5 Thirty-Trading-Day Rolling Coefficients for U.S. Dollar: Before and After the Crisis

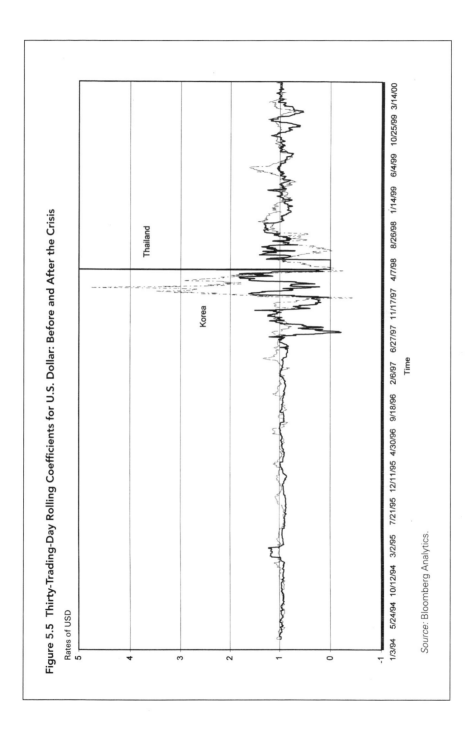

Source: Bloomberg Analytics.

world, only Great Britain, Japan, and now euroland have freely floating currencies, where their central banks do not react to daily movements in exchange rates, with Australia approximating this state of
bliss. In the appendix, figures 5A.1 to 5A.4 show that the Japanese yen
is much more volatile against the dollar on a daily basis than are the
currencies of other East Asian countries. In the short term, only the
yen floats "freely."

In contrast, countries on the periphery of the industrial center have
formally or informally pegged exchange rates through direct or indirect foreign exchange intervention—what Calvo and Reinhart call "fear
of floating" or "soft pegs."

> The root causes of the marked reluctance of emerging markets to float
> their exchange rates are multiple. When circumstances are favorable (i.e.,
> there are capital inflows, positive terms of trade shocks, etc.) many emerg-
> ing markets are reluctant to allow the nominal (and real) exchange rate to
> appreciate.... When circumstances are adverse, the fear of a collapse in the
> exchange rate comes from pervasive liability dollarization. Devaluations
> are associated with recessions and inflation, and not export-led growth.
> [Reinhart 2000: 69.]

Reinhart helps to explain exchange rate stickiness at lower frequencies, for example, using monthly or quarterly observations. Her explanation is consistent with the argument here that linking to the dollar
provides a common nominal anchor for domestic price levels in East Asia.
But this nominal anchor argument does not carry much weight at higher
frequencies. Stability of the domestic price level is not significantly
affected by dampening day-to-day movements in the exchange rate.

Why should governments in less-developed countries be so anx-
ious to stabilize their exchange rates against the dollar from one day to
the next? One explanation attributes this to incomplete domestic financial markets: the "original sin" hypothesis:

> "Original sin" ... is a situation in which the domestic currency cannot be
> used to borrow abroad or to borrow long term, even domestically. In the
> presence of this incompleteness, financial fragility is unavoidable because
> all domestic investments will have either a currency mismatch (projects
> that generate pesos will be financed with dollars) or a maturity mismatch
> (long-term projects will be financed by short-term loans).
>   Critically, these mismatches exist not because banks and firms lack the
> prudence to hedge their exposures. The problem rather is that a country

whose external liabilities are necessarily denominated in foreign exchange is by definition unable to hedge. Assuming that there will be someone on the other side of the market for foreign currency hedges is equivalent to assuming that the country can borrow abroad in its own currency. Similarly, the problem is not that firms lack the foresight to match the maturity structure of their assets and liabilities; it is that they find it impossible to do so. The incompleteness of financial markets is thus at the root of financial fragility. [Eichengreen and Hausmann 1999: 3.]

Why original sin exists in most emerging markets, including the debtor economies of East Asia, is an important stylized fact whose implications will become clearer. Not only is private foreign borrowing denominated in foreign exchange, typically dollars, but it is mostly short term, as are domestic currency credits. Markets in medium- or longer-term domestic bonds bearing fixed rates of interest are absent. Although still denominated in foreign exchange, only sovereign bond issues in international bond markets and government borrowing from official international agencies are somewhat longer term. But even these often have variable interest rates—that is, so many points above the London interbank offered rate—tied to yields on short-term assets.

These incomplete markets make it difficult and expensive to hedge foreign exchange risk. Importers more than exporters find it difficult to cover forward commercial transactions, including ordinary trade credit, which must be continually repaid within a few days or weeks.

Consider first the case of a Thai importer who is *not* liquidity constrained but must repay dollar trade credit in 30 days. If foreign exchange regulations permit, the cheapest way to hedge would be to buy dollars today to hold on deposit for 30 days. But consider the opportunity cost of doing so. Figure 5.6 shows that, before the crisis of 1997–98, interest rates in baht deposits averaged about 5 percentage points higher than interest rates on dollar deposits. Relative to going unhedged by holding higher-interest baht deposits for 30 days, this (annualized) 5 percentage point margin is the importer's cost of hedging.

Second, consider the case of an *illiquid* Thai importer, one who does not yet have ready liquid assets for repaying the debt. To fashion the same kind of hedge, he must first borrow baht from the bank, and in 1995–96 the prime loan rate in Thailand was 13.5 percent. By investing in a dollar deposit at 5 percent, he is hedged, but the opportunity cost of doing so has risen to 8.5 percentage points.

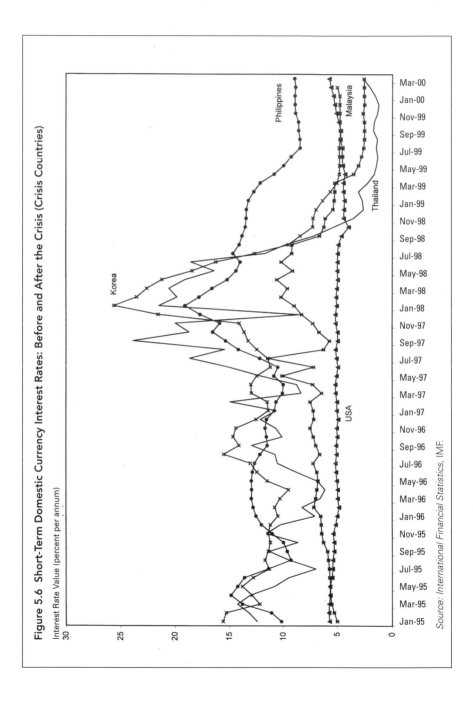

Figure 5.6 Short-Term Domestic Currency Interest Rates: Before and After the Crisis (Crisis Countries)

Source: International Financial Statistics, IMF.

True, the illiquid Thai importer is more likely to resort to the futures market to buy dollars forward on an organized exchange if it exists. However, the cost of this forward cover (not including brokerage fees) would be roughly the forward premium on dollars over baht, which will be somewhere between the opportunity cost of the liquid importer and the illiquid, for example, between 5 and 8.5 percentage points in the example (McKinnon 1979: ch. 5). With large interest differentials between the center country and the periphery, merchants and manufacturers find the opportunity cost of hedging to be correspondingly high.

Now consider the problem facing financial institutions. Suppose banks accept short-term deposits in dollars to finance their longer-term domestic loan portfolio in baht. Then, in the forward market, the cost of buying dollars forward to hedge the foreign exchange risk over 30 days will be between 5 and 8.5 percentage points. (Having banks themselves hold extra dollars on deposit for 30 days defeats the whole idea of accepting low-interest dollar deposits to make high-yield baht loans!) In financing the bank's portfolio of baht loans, having to hedge dollar deposits would be virtually equivalent (though perhaps a bit more expensive) to bidding directly for high-cost baht deposits.

However, banks whose motivation is one of simply servicing or facilitating the foreign exchange needs of their nonbank customers may well be willing to hedge. Suppose a "good" retail customer contracts with the bank to buy dollars 30 days forward. The bank will then charge the customer the prevailing forward premium on dollars over baht, but then cover itself by buying a low-interest 30-day dollar deposit in exchange for a high-interest baht deposit—likely in the domestic interbank market.

What are the implications for bank regulation? If the regulatory authorities strictly limited any net direct or indirect foreign exchange exposure on the part of banks, this would drive them out of the business of accepting low-cost foreign exchange deposits to finance higher-yield domestic currency loans. The inflow of *short-term* foreign capital into the economy would be reduced. But such strict regulation would not impair the banks' role of servicing and facilitating foreign exchange transactions by domestic merchants and manufacturers.

Strict regulation against foreign exchange exposure could severely limit the ability of banks to act collectively as dealer-speculators to "make" the foreign exchange market. "Stabilizing" speculation by banks—the most natural foreign exchange traders and dealers—would not be possible.

Consider the implications for optimal short-term foreign exchange management, first when capital controls are absent and second when they are effectively applied.

- *Case 1: No capital controls, imperfect bank regulation.* Either because regulatory weakness leaves too many banks (and possibly importers) with exposed foreign exchange positions, or because the government does not want to impose Draconian rules prohibiting institutions from assuming *any* open foreign exchange position, an informal hedge is provided by keeping the exchange rate steady in the short term. The short time frame over which foreign currency debts—largely in dollars—are incurred, and then repaid on a day-to-day or even a week-to-week basis, defines the same time frame over which the dollar exchange rate is (and should be) kept stable in noncrisis periods.

- *Case 2: Direct capital controls.* Suppose the government prevents banks, other financial institutions, and individuals from holding any foreign exchange assets or liabilities. Nonbank firms engaged in foreign trade cannot take positions in foreign exchange except for the minimum necessary in their particular trade. Importers are prevented from building up undue foreign currency debts except for ordinary trade credit, and exporters are required to repatriate their dollar earnings quickly. In particular, banks cannot accept foreign currency deposits or hold foreign currency deposits abroad, or make foreign currency loans. Then private agents in general, and banks in particular, cannot act as dealer-speculators to make the foreign exchange market (McKinnon 1979: ch. 6). The exchange rate will become indeterminate unless the government steps in as a dealer to clear international transactions. Thus the government must take open positions, which determine the level of the exchange rate, and assume the exchange risk. If the government is determining the exchange rate anyway, why not keep it stable?

China and Malaysia more or less correspond to case 2 in imposing capital controls (although not as rigidly as described under case 2).

Their governments have wisely fixed their dollar exchange rates—certainly in the short run and maybe longer. Because Korea and Thailand have pretty well rid themselves of the last vestiges of the capital controls they once had, they correspond more to case 1. And the Korean and Thai governments are indeed reducing exchange risk in their economies by keeping their rates virtually pegged in the short run, even if they cannot prevent some medium- and longer-term movement, particularly in the unsettled aftermath of the 1997–98 crisis.

Although such soft short-term pegs reduce foreign exchange risk for "well-behaved" merchant traders and financial institutions, this regime may be exploited by financial institutions (and some traders) with moral hazard. Poorly regulated and undercapitalized banks with deposit insurance may be more willing to gamble by accepting short-term unhedged foreign currency deposits to finance their domestic loan portfolios.

With or without capital controls, high-frequency pegging is optimal when there is original sin. Beyond the nominal anchor argument for stabilizing exchange rates in the medium and longer terms, there is a risk-reducing argument for very short-term pegging.

Except in a crisis, pervasive direct capital controls on the gross foreign exchange positions of banks (as under case 2) are unlikely to be the first-best way of controlling exchange risk when private financial markets are incomplete (original sin).

First, preventing banks from accepting any foreign currency deposits, or making any foreign currency loans, disrupts banks' traditional role of clearing foreign payments and settling accounts. On any trading day, the enormous flow of foreign payments would have to be cleared directly by the central bank.

Second, such capital controls make it impossible for banks to do the covered interest arbitrage necessary to make the forward market in foreign exchange (McKinnon 1979: ch. 5). Either the private sector is left with no mechanism for hedging international transactions, or the government (central bank) is dragged into writing forward exchange contracts for private traders—a process open to abuse around the world.

So, keeping the assumption of original sin, the first-best way of controlling risk in the foreign exchanges is encapsulated in case 3:

• *Case 3: Net foreign exchange exposure of banks regulated to be zero.* The domestic banking authorities let "authorized" banks acquire gross foreign exchange assets and liabilities, but their net position, perhaps defined at the end of one trading day, must be zero. In making this calculation, the regulators also consider indirect as well as direct foreign exchange liabilities. For example, if a bank accepts dollar deposits but then on-lends to domestic firms in dollars, its balance sheet may look square. But the nonbank domestic borrower may now be exposed to currency risk and could default if the domestic currency is devalued. Exchange risk is translated into default risk and then into banking risk. Similarly, banks may undertake off-balance-sheet transactions in derivatives that increase their foreign exchange exposure and are hard to detect.

Although necessarily only approximate in practice, forcing banks to (near) zero net foreign exchange exposure is nevertheless a valuable regulatory principle. It counters the various margins of temptation not to hedge. In particular, it prevents banks from accepting foreign currency deposits to make domestic currency loans. But even if applied quite strictly, this regulatory principle leaves enough flexibility for the commercial banking system as a whole to perform its normal facilitating role in the foreign exchanges. For any given spot exchange rate, the clearing of international payments and settling of accounts can devolve from the central bank. Commercial banks can still undertake covered interest arbitrage and so create a market in forward exchange to service the hedging needs of their nonbank "retail" customers.

That said, however, imposing the rule of no net foreign exchange exposure means that the banks still cannot act as (stabilizing) speculators to determine the level of the exchange rate. In this one important respect, case 3 is similar to case 2. With either capital controls or a rule of no net foreign exchange exposure, the exchange rate is indeterminate unless the government itself enters the market to act as a stabilizing speculator. So with "first-best" bank regulation for controlling risk in place—case 3—the government is still forced to determine the equilibrium exchange rate.

These cases represent three quite different foreign exchange regimes. All three are consistent with the high-frequency pegging to the dollar observed in the "original sin" economies of East Asia.

THE HONEYMOON IN THE INTEREST DIFFERENTIAL:
A SIMPLE MODEL

In postcrisis East Asia, do governments have much time to establish a better system of financial regulation for managing exchange risk? Without such regulatory reforms (case 3), the cycle of short-term over-borrowing, by weakly regulated banks and other financial institutions, might happen again.

However, in the aftermath of the crisis, there is a "honeymoon" effect. In 1999–2000, the differential in short-term interest rates between the peripheral East Asian debtor economies and the indus-trial center, as represented by the United States, was narrower than normal, and even negative. Figure 5.6 shows the dramatic fall in the short-term interest rates of Korea, Malaysia, the Philippines, and Thailand after 1998, that is, after the crisis and exchange rate devalu-ations. Figure 5.7 shows the more modest fall in short-term rates in the noncrisis economies. Correspondingly, the margin of temptation to accept unhedged foreign currency deposits to make loans denomi-nated in the domestic currency in debtor economies has almost vanished. Thus bank regulators have some temporary—but only tem-porary—breathing space in which to reform the system.

To understand this honeymoon effect, consider some interest rate identities for a very short term to maturity. Suppose that there are no government controls on foreign exchange transacting so a well-orga-nized market in currency futures can exist. By covered interest arbi-trage among "liquid" banks, the (deposit) interest differential is equal to the forward premium:

(5.2) $i - i^* = f > 0$ where

   i = the domestic nominal (deposit) interest rate

   i^* = the dollar (deposit) interest rate in the international capi-tal market

   f = the forward premium on dollars in domestic currency.

If domestic banks accepting dollar deposits at the low-interest rate i^* cover by buying dollars forward, the cost of the forward cover per dollar so borrowed is simply f. Thus the effective interest rate on hedged dollar deposits is $i^* + f$.

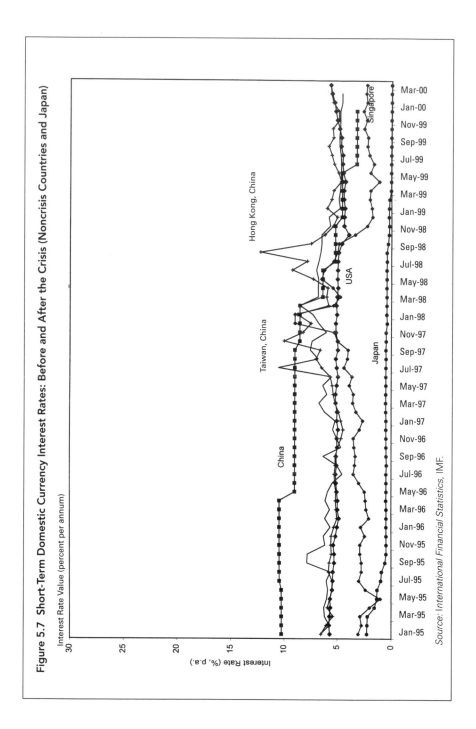

Figure 5.7 Short-Term Domestic Currency Interest Rates: Before and After the Crisis (Noncrisis Countries and Japan)

Source: International Financial Statistics, IMF.

$$(5.3) \quad i_{hedged} = i^* + f = i$$

With forward covering, there is no net interest gain from accepting dollar deposits over accepting higher-interest deposits in domestic currency. Liquid hedged borrowers in foreign exchange see the same cost of capital as do domestic banks accepting deposits denominated in the domestic currency.

Banks without moral hazard would voluntarily cover the exchange risk. They may well have accepted dollar deposits simply for convenience in clearing international payments. In contrast, poorly capitalized banks prepared to gamble on the basis of government deposit insurance might well accept low-cost dollar deposits as an ongoing source of finance for loans denominated in the domestic currency—unless a vigilant regulatory authority forces them to hedge.

But how much of the interest differential in equation 5.2 represents a margin of temptation where banks with (latent) moral hazard try to avoid regulatory sanctions and borrow in dollars anyway? Let the interest differential be partitioned into

$$(5.4) \quad i - i^* = E\hat{e} + \rho_{currency}$$

$\rho_{currency}$ is the currency risk premium as ordinarily defined. Apart from any unidirectional expected movement in the exchange rate, it represents the extra return that investors require to hold domestic rather than foreign currency assets. In the specific East Asian context, it represents the cost of domestic financial volatility—in interest rates or domestic price levels—measured against similar risk(s) prevailing in the markets of the center country, for example, the United States. Thus $\rho_{currency}$ increases with that country's exchange rate volatility against the U.S. dollar.

In the peripheral Asian debtor countries, $\rho_{currency}$ is (was before 1997) normally greater than zero. But it can be reduced toward zero if there is financial convergence with the United States; that is, the dollar exchange rate has been credibly stabilized so that interest rate volatility also approaches U.S. levels (McKinnon 2000). Indeed, one motivation for high-frequency pegging is to reduce the risk premium in domestic short-term interest rates; that is, to reduce $\rho_{currency}$.

The other component of the interest differential—the expected depreciation of the domestic currency, $E\hat{e}$—can be decomposed into two parts. First, the exchange rate can change predictably and smoothly according to the government's policy announcements and commitments, such as the downward crawl in the Indonesian rupiah before the 1997 crash. Second is the small probability of a "regime change": a large, sudden devaluation whose timing is unpredictable.

$$(5.5) \quad E\hat{e} = E\hat{e}_{predictable} + E\hat{e}_{regime\ change}$$

Both types of expected change in the exchange rate in equation 5.5 widen the nominal interest differential in equation 5.4. However, $E\hat{e}_{regime\ change}$ is part of the margin of temptation for banks with moral hazard to overborrow, while $E\hat{e}_{predictable}$ is not. If the exchange rate were expected to depreciate smoothly through time, even banks with very short time horizons would account for the higher domestic currency costs of repaying short-term foreign currency deposits. Therefore, $E\hat{e}_{predictable}$ is excluded from the *super risk premium*:

$$(5.6) \quad \rho_{super} = \rho_{currency} + E\hat{e}_{regime\ change} = i - i^* - E\hat{e}_{predictable}$$

The super risk premium, ρ_{super}, represents the margin of temptation for banks to overborrow in foreign exchange beyond what they might do if forced to hedge. (Even if banks were required to hedge their foreign exchange exposure, international overborrowing could still occur because banks with moral hazard assume too much domestic credit risk; see McKinnon and Pill 1996, 1997.) ρ_{super} has two components: the currency risk premium, as defined, and the possibility that the regime could change through a discrete devaluation. The latter source of upward pressure on the interest rate on assets denominated in the domestic currency is sometimes called "the peso problem."

The basic idea is that the decisionmaking horizon of the bank with moral hazard is sufficiently short that it ignores unpredictable changes in the exchange rate. The managers of the bank simply hope that anything drastic, if it happens at all, will not happen on their watch. The super risk premium in the interest differential then defines their margin of temptation to gamble and accept foreign currency deposits unhedged.

How does this super risk premium vary through time, specifically through the precrisis, crisis, and then postcrisis episodes? Figure 5.6 plots the short-term interest rates of Korea, Malaysia, Philippines, and Thailand against that of the United States over these three episodes from 1995 into 2000. In the precrisis period, their super risk premiums were virtually the whole of the interest differential: up to May 1997, the differential was anywhere between 2 and 10 percentage points.

Empirically, it is hard to partition this differential between $\rho_{currency}$ and $E\hat{e}_{regime\ change}$ except to note that the possibility of a discrete devaluation was an important component, even though none of the four countries had an obviously overvalued exchange rate (McKinnon 2000). Indeed, the system of soft pegs had gone on for a decade or more. This interest differential contributed to the unhedged overborrowing observed before the crash.

Then, from June 1997 to December 1998, a virtually complete loss of confidence occurred in one or another of the four currencies. In the crisis, these interest differentials widened to between 5 and 25 percentage points (figure 5.6). In effect, there were extrapolative expectations: exchange rate depreciation led to expectations of further depreciation. In these panic conditions, the problem was rapid capital outflows and not more overborrowing, as in the precrisis period. (Still, importers in this period had terrific incentive not to hedge their exchange risks.)

Finally, the postcrisis honeymoon took place from January 1999 to June 2000. Figure 5.6 shows short-term interest rates in the four crisis economies falling sharply, with Thailand and Malaysia's rates even falling to 2 or so percentage points less than the U.S. benchmark rate of 5 to 6 percent. At these low short-term interest rates, East Asian importers had no incentive not to hedge their exchange risks, nor did banks have an incentive to accept short-term dollar deposits to expand their loans in domestic currency. Whence came the honeymoon for bank regulators.

The proximate cause of this remarkable fall in short-term interest rates was the change in the $E\hat{e}_{regime\ change}$ component of the interest differential. After the dramatic overshooting of the exchange rates of the devaluing countries, as confidence returned and the fear of another speculative attack became much more remote, the market began to anticipate the near-term appreciations of 1999 and 2000 (figure 5.1). However, these appreciations remained erratic and difficult to predict, as if the $E\hat{e}_{regime\ change}$ component had changed sign, that is, from positive to negative. And this change could (more than) offset the effect of the ordinary currency risk premium, $\rho_{currency}$, on the interest differential. For this reason, *short-term* interest rates in the former crisis economies fell to levels sometimes even below those prevailing in the United States (figure 5.6). The corresponding falls in short-term rates in the noncrisis economies were not nearly as marked (figure 5.7).

This is not the end of the story. From precrisis to postcrisis, *long-term* expectations of future devaluations and other risks did not change all that much. True, these long-term expectations are difficult to measure because of the absence of truly long-term bond markets in domestic currency within each of our affected economies. Korea came closest to having a bond market, but really for just three years out. In August 2000, when Korean short-term interest rates were about 5 percent, three-year bond rates were up at 9.5 percent—and 10- or 20-year bond rates, if they existed, were much higher still.

At moderately longer terms (six to eight years), sovereign bond issues denominated in dollars existed for each of our crisis economies. Because these carry default risk, but not currency risk, these dollar interest rates were very much a lower-bound estimate of what hypothetical domestic currency bonds would carry at the same term to maturity. Interest rates on these dollar-denominated bonds remained up at 8 to 10 percent in the postcrisis period (figures 5.8 and 5.9). More important, in the postcrisis period, interest rates on sovereign bonds seem to have been somewhat higher than their precrisis equivalents. Because long rates are an average of expected future short rates plus a liquidity premium, the market seemed to be betting that—within three years or so—short rates would rise back to where they were before the crisis and maybe higher.

So the honeymoon for the regulators will end like most honeymoons.

LENGTHENING THE TERM STRUCTURE OF FINANCE

Is there a general lesson about the feasibility of freely floating exchange rates among different classes of economies? In his chapter titled "The Confidence Game," Paul Krugman (1999) identifies the differences thus:

> It seems, in other words, that there is a sort of double standard enforced by the markets. The common view among economists that floating rates are

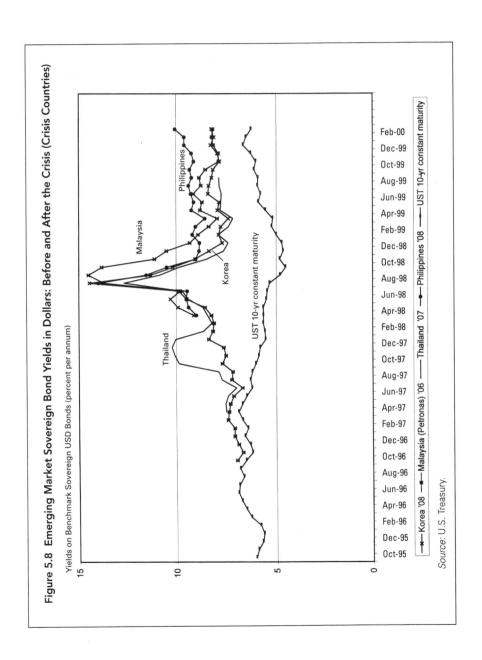

Figure 5.8 Emerging Market Sovereign Bond Yields in Dollars: Before and After the Crisis (Crisis Countries)

Yields on Benchmark Sovereign USD Bonds (percent per annum)

Source: U.S. Treasury.

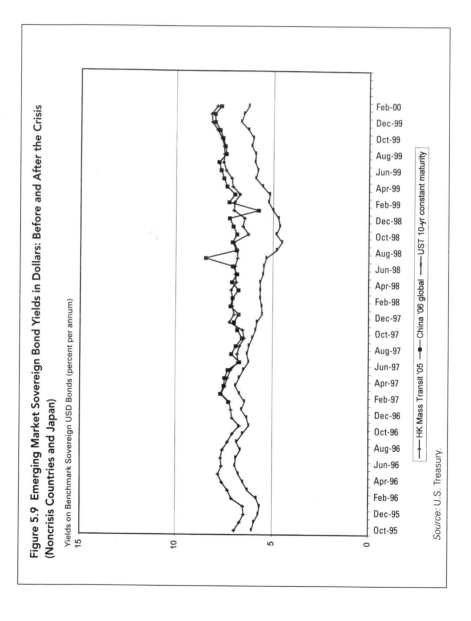

Figure 5.9 Emerging Market Sovereign Bond Yields in Dollars: Before and After the Crisis (Noncrisis Countries and Japan)

Yields on Benchmark Sovereign USD Bonds (percent per annum)

Legend: HK Mass Transit '05 — China '06 global — UST 10-yr constant maturity

Source: U.S. Treasury.

the best, if imperfect, solution to the international monetary trilemma was based on the experience of countries like Canada, Britain, and the United States. And sure enough, floating exchange rates work pretty well for First World countries, because markets are prepared to give those countries the benefit of the doubt. But since 1994 one Third World country after another—Mexico, Thailand, Indonesia, Korea, and, most recently, Brazil—has discovered that it cannot expect the same treatment. Again and again, attempts to engage in moderate devaluations have led to a drastic collapse in confidence. And so now markets believe that devaluations in such countries are terrible things; and because markets believe this, they are. [Krugman 1999: 111.]

He makes an important distinction. To cushion the effects of the fall in prices of primary products as a result of the Asian crisis, Australia and Canada could let their currencies float downward without capital controls and not be attacked. Why? Because exchange rate expectations for Australian and Canadian dollars were already fundamentally regressive: during the course of the downward float, people generally expected the rate to come back. Both were mature market economies with (a) credible internal monetary mechanisms (independent central banks) for targeting their domestic price levels over the long run and (b) relatively long terms to maturity for their internal and external debts. (In Asia, the noncrisis creditor economies of Taiwan and Singapore were—are—more like mature capitalist ones in these respects.)

Of course, both features are complementary. Only with long-term confidence in the purchasing power of domestic money (against the center country's) would exchange rate expectations be naturally regressive and long-term bond and mortgage markets be possible to organize—both domestically and for commercial (nonsovereign) international borrowing. And having longer-term finance bolsters the credibility of the central bank to hit its inflation targets over the longer term.

Now return to the emerging-market debtor economy with original sin. The term structure of finance is short, and there is no history of central bank independence. Indeed, in most developing economies, including the Asian Five, the central bank often has been commandeered to provide cheap credit for promoting exports, subsidizing commercial banks, and otherwise directing credit in line with the government's development program. Sometimes, this strategy has been facilitated by ringing the country with capital controls. Correspondingly, there is a potential lack of confidence in the long-term exchange rate *unless* the government can effectively restrain itself.

During their "miracle" growth phases before 1997, the East Asian economies successfully pegged to the dollar as the nominal anchor for their domestic price levels. With the benefit of hindsight, however, we now know that this policy was seriously incomplete. First, and most obvious, was the failure to properly regulate the financial system, including the central bank itself in some cases, against undue risk taking, including short-term foreign exchange exposure.

Second, and more subtle, the East Asian debtor economies were not committed to a long-term exchange rate parity in the mode of the nineteenth-century gold standard (Goodhart and Delargy 1998), even though they seemed to be securely pegged in the short and medium terms. Because of the short-term structure of finance, each was vulnerable to a speculative attack on its currency, but none had a long-run exchange rate strategy in place to mitigate the worst consequences of any such attack. Postcrisis, there was no well-defined tradition of returning to the precrisis exchange rate. In contrast, under the classical gold standard, if a government was forced to suspend its gold parity in a crisis, it was obligated to return to its precrisis parity (McKinnon 1996: ch. 2, 4). This restoration rule kept exchange rate expectations regressive.

Besides original sin itself, the problem was aggravated because the pre-1997 East Asian dollar standard was informal rather than formal. With the exception of Hong Kong, none of the countries involved had formally declared a dollar parity, and each had been classified by the International Monetary Fund as following some variety of "managed floating" rather than as being pegged to the dollar. Thus with the forced suspension of these dollar pegs in the 1997–98 crisis, there was no traditional dollar parity (gold parity, in the nineteenth-century sense) to which the government was bound to return. In the crisis, the absence of regressive expectations led to a very inefficient tradeoff: the East Asian Five suffered from both deep devaluations and very high (short-term) interest rates (McKinnon 2000).

Thus emerging-market economies whose macroeconomic fundamentals are sound so as to permit a "good fix" for their exchange rates should extend the maturity of that commitment to the distant future (McKinnon and Pill 1999). If the East Asian Five had, before the 1997 crisis, adopted a restoration rule explicitly—and, ideally, collectively— they could have moderated the high interest rates and deep devaluations, which bankrupted so much of their economies, once the attacks began. (Of course, countries that must rely on the inflation tax and cannot credibly commit to long-run exchange rate stability should not try it.) The benefits of having the exchange rate pinned down in the long run exceed those of having a hard short-term fix.

Without going to complete dollarization Latin American style, redemption from original sin is possible. Even though the domestic monetary regime and note-issuing authority remain independent, the good record of fiscal balance in the East Asian economies suggests that a longer-term commitment to maintain their dollar exchange rates could be credible. Then, with regressive exchange rate expectations and the future price level more secure in the face of any mishap forcing the (temporary) suspension of the commitment to a fixed exchange rate, the authorities could seriously encourage lengthening the term structure of domestic and foreign finance in the bond market. An appropriate accounting framework with full disclosure for bond issuers and a legal framework for securing the rights of bond holders now become more relevant.

To escape from original sin, Eichengreen and Hausmann (1999) discuss, very perceptively, the need to lengthen the term to maturity of domestic markets for bonds and bank loans. However, their approach is the inverse of what I am suggesting here. They want to start encouraging longer-term bond finance by domestic institutional and legal changes and hope that this would lead to greater (long-term) stability of the exchange rate. I would start with a long-run exchange rate commitment—the restoration rule—to create a friendlier environment for strengthening the institutions governing bond markets. The emphasis of the two approaches is different, but they are not in conflict.

There is a virtuous circle. When long-term bond issues in the nineteenth-century mode begin to displace short-term bank finance, the government's commitment to long-term exchange rate stability is naturally reinforced. On the one hand, lengthening the term structure of finance makes the economy less vulnerable to currency attacks in the foreign exchanges; on the other hand, the domestic banking system becomes less vulnerable to internal runs. In countries with original sin, the empirical evidence suggests that currency attacks and commercial bank runs are strongly correlated (Kaminsky and Reinhart 1999). Finally, with a more vigorous domestic bond market, the central bank can better conduct domestic open-market operations to defend the currency and secure the domestic price level over the longer run.

NEW RULES FOR THE DOLLAR STANDARD GAME: A CONCLUDING COMMENT

Recent experience suggests that the informal rules under which the East Asian dollar standard operates can be modified to make this common monetary standard more robust and efficient in the presence of original sin and also to lengthen the term structure of finance for achieving redemption.[2] The most significant new or modified rules for the peripheral countries in the system would be the following:

1. Avoid net foreign exchange exposure by banks or other financial institutions with short-term assets or liabilities. Comprehensive capital controls are a second-best alternative. In either case, the government must then make the dollar-based foreign exchange market on a day-to-day basis.

2. Move from informal dollar pegging to official dollar parities. Treat these parities as long-term obligations to which the government is committed after any crisis.

3. Make other institutional changes—improving legal recourse of creditors, achieving greater accounting transparency, and so on— to lengthen the term structure of domestic finance by encouraging the development of bond and mortgage markets.

4. Rationalize the position of Japan within the dollar-based East Asian system, having the United States and Japan jointly commit to a benchmark parity for the yen/dollar rate over the long term, but let the yen/dollar rate float freely on a day-to-day or week-to-week basis.

To create a viable, longer-term bond market in the "emerging-market" economies of East Asia, rules 1, 2, and 3 offer both a carrot and a stick. To lengthen the term structure of both domestic and foreign finance, rule 1 is the stick, and rules 2 and 3 are the carrot.

Because of their special position in clearing domestic and international payments, commercial banks have been overly subsidized as short-term financial intermediaries. Formal or informal deposit insurance, special discount privileges with the central bank, and internationally organized bailouts by the International Monetary Fund or similar international agencies have all been designed to prevent systemic breakdowns in the payments mechanism for economies in distress. Although all of this may be well and good, the incidental effect tilts the whole structure of finance toward the short term. It reinforces original sin because international and domestic bond markets at longer terms have not been similarly subsidized. Thus rule 1 is a stick designed to force banks out of the business of being international short-term intermediaries—that is, accepting foreign currency deposits to make domestic currency loans.[3]

Rules 2 and 3 hold out carrots to encourage longer-term domestic and international bond markets for the private sector. In particular, rule 2 gives *long-term* assurance that the moneys of the peripheral countries will not be willingly devalued against the dollar. This is important because U.S. Treasury bonds are the "risk-free" asset in international bond markets. Thus risk premiums in the interest rates on bonds of the peripheral countries, particularly at longer term, would be reduced.

The analysis of Japan's position in the system is quite different. Japan is by far the largest creditor country with long-term bond markets of its own. Nevertheless, since the 1970s, the fear of yen *appreciation* has generated a parallel fear of ongoing domestic deflation with nominal interest rates approaching zero (McKinnon and Ohno 1997, 2000). Thus by rule 4 quashing the fear of yen appreciation, Japan itself would be the main beneficiary, realizing an end to deflation and an increase in nominal (although not real) interest rates on yen assets.

Over the past decade, Japan's unnaturally low nominal interest rates have had an unfortunate side effect on the rest of East Asia. Except in honeymoon periods, such low rates provoke banks and other institutions in the smaller East Asian economies to overborrow. Because of the (temporary) interest differential between, say, baht and yen assets, the margin of temptation to undertake unhedged short-term borrowing is accentuated. Thus if Japanese nominal interest rates rose to more normal international levels, short-term capital flows in East Asia would become less volatile.

APPENDIX 5

Exchange Rate Volatility: Japan versus Other East Asian Economies

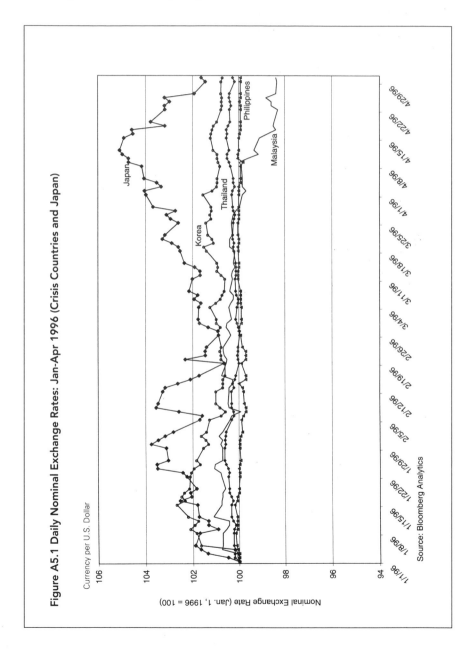

Figure A5.1 Daily Nominal Exchange Rates: Jan-Apr 1996 (Crisis Countries and Japan)

Source: Bloomberg Analytics

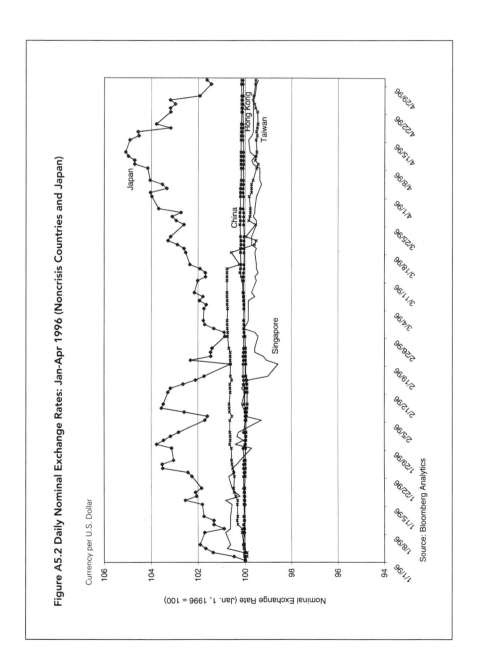

Figure A5.2 Daily Nominal Exchange Rates: Jan-Apr 1996 (Noncrisis Countries and Japan)

Source: Bloomberg Analytics

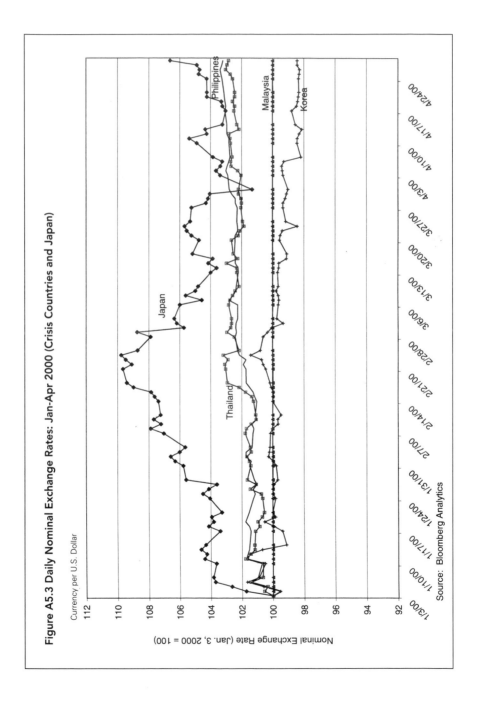

Figure A5.3 Daily Nominal Exchange Rates: Jan-Apr 2000 (Crisis Countries and Japan)

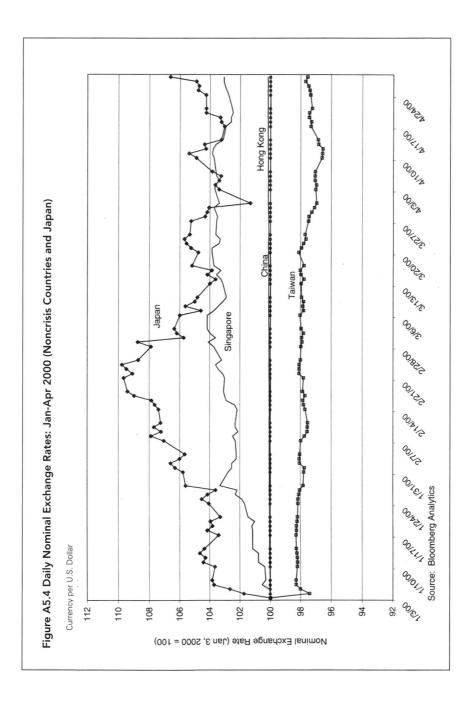

Figure A5.4 Daily Nominal Exchange Rates: Jan–Apr 2000 (Noncrisis Countries and Japan)

NOTES

I would like to thank Sumit Khedekar for his enormous input in setting up all the statistical tests and Masahiro Kawai for his own valuable statistical work, which parallels that presented here, although some of his conclusions on optimum exchange rate strategies may differ. Rishi Goyal provided invaluable general research assistance.

1. Although shocks imposed by national governments would be quite asymmetric. This issue of disciplining governments is taken up below.

2. If the sin is truly "original," then of course there is no escape!

3. Within the purely domestic part of the system, transformation of maturity by banks has also been (inadvertently) overly subsidized. Thus there is a case for domestic regulation to limit transformation of maturity by banks, but issues of purely domestic bank regulation are not treated here.

REFERENCES

The word "processed" describes informally reproduced works that may not be commonly available through library systems.

Bergsten, C. Fred. 2000. "East Asian Regionalism: Toward a Tripartite World." *The Economist*, July 15, pp. 23–26.

Calvo, Guillermo, and Carmen Reinhart. 2000a. "Fear of Floating." University of Maryland Economics Department, College Park, Md. (January). Processed.

———. 2000b. "Fixing for Your Life." University of Maryland Economics Department, College Park, Md. (April). Processed.

Eichengreen;, Barry. 1997. *European Monetary Unification: Theory, Practice, Analysis.* Cambridge, Mass.: MIT Press.

Eichengreen, Barry, and Ricardo Hausmann. 1999. "Exchange Rates and Financial Fragility." NBER Working Paper 7418. National Bureau of Economic Research, Cambridge, Mass. (November). Processed.

Fischer, Stanley. 1999. "On the Need for a Lender of Last Resort." Address to the American Economic Association, New York, January 3. Processed.

Frankel, Jeffrey A., and S. J. Wei. 1994. "Yen Bloc or Dollar Bloc? Exchange Rate Policies in the East Asian Economies." In Takatoshi Ito and Anne Krueger, eds., *Macroeconomic Linkage: Savings, Exchange Rates, and Capital Flows.* NBER–East Asia Seminar on Economics 3. Chicago: University of Chicago Press.

Goodhart, Charles, and P. J. R. Delargy. 1998. "Financial Crises: Plus ça Change, plus c'est la Même Chose." *International Finance* 1(2, December): 261–88.

Ito, Takatoshi, Eiji Ogawa, and Yuri Sasaki. 1998. "How Did the Dollar Peg Fail in Asia?" NBER Working Paper 6729. National Bureau of Economic Research, Cambridge, Mass. Processed.

Kaminsky, Graciela, and Carmen Reinhart. 1999. "The Twin Crises: Balance of Payments and Banking Crises in Developing Countries." *American Economic Review* 89(3, June):473–500.

Krugman, Paul. 1999. *The Return of Depression Economics.* New York: W.W. Norton.

Kawai, Masahiro, and Shigeru Akiyama. 2000. "Implications of the Currency Crisis for Exchange Rate Arrangements in Emerging East Asia." World Bank, East Asia Department. Washington, D.C. (May). Processed.

Kwan, Chi Hung. 1999. "Towards a Yen Bloc in Asia," *Nomura Research Institute Quarterly* 8(2, Summer):2–13.

———. 2001. "The Economics of a Yen Bloc." Brookings Institution, Washington, D.C., and Nomura Research Institute, Tokyo (June). Processed.

Kydland, Finn E., and Edward Prescott. 1977. "Rules Rather than Discretion: The Inconsistency of Optimal Plans." *Journal of Political Economy* 85(3):473–91.

McKinnon, Ronald I. 1979. *Money in International Exchange: The Convertible Currency System.* New York: Oxford University Press.

———. 1993. *The Order of Economic Liberalization: Financial Control in the Transition to a Market Economy.* Baltimore, Md.: Johns Hopkins University.

———. 1996. *The Rules of the Game: International Money and Exchange Rates.* Cambridge, Mass.: NBER Press.

———. 2000. "The East Asian Dollar Standard, Life after Death?" *Economic Notes* 29(1, February):31–82.

———. 2001. "Euroland and East Asia in a Dollar-Based International Monetary System: Mundell Revisited," In G. A. Calvo, R. Dornbusch, and M. Obstfeld, eds., *Money, Capital Mobility, and Trade: Essays in Honor of Robert Mundell.* Cambridge, Mass: MIT Press.

McKinnon, Ronald I., and Kenichi Ohno. 1997. *Dollar and Yen: Resolving Economic Conflict between the United States and Japan* [Japanese translation, Nihon Keizai Shimbun, 1998]. Cambridge, Mass.: NBER Press.

———. 2000. "The Foreign Exchange Origins of Japan's Economic Slump and Low Interest Liquidity Trap." Forthcoming in *The World Economy.* Now available at http://www-econ.stanford.edu/faculty/workp/index.html.

McKinnon, Ronald I., and Huw Pill. 1996. "Credible Liberalizations and International Capital Flows: The Overborrowing Syndrome." In Takatoshi Ito and Anne Krueger, eds., *Financial Deregulation and Integration in East Asia*, pp. 7–48. Chicago: National Bureau of Economic Research and University of Chicago Press.

———. 1997. "Credible Liberalizations and Overborrowing." *American Economic Review* (May) 87, 2: 189–93.

———. 1999. "Exchange Rate Regimes for Emerging Markets: Moral Hazard, and International Overborrowing." *Oxford Review of Economic Policy* 15(3) autumn:19–38.

Mundell, Robert A. 1961. "A Theory of Optimum Currency Areas." *American Economic Review* 51(November):509–17.

———. 1968. *International Economics.* New York: Macmillan.

————. 1973a. "A Plan for a European Currency." In Harry G. Johnson and Alexander K. Swoboda, eds., *The Economics of Common Currencies: Proceedings of the Madrid Conference on Optimum Currency Areas*, pp. 143–72. London: Allen and Unwin.

————. 1973b. "Uncommon Arguments for Common Currencies." In Harry G. Johnson and Alexander K. Swoboda, eds., *The Economics of Common Currencies: Proceedings of the Madrid Conference on Optimum Currency Areas*, pp. 114–32. London: Allen and Unwin.

Ohno, Kenichi. 2000. "Exchange Rate Management in Developing Asia: Reassessment of the Precrisis Soft Dollar Zone." ADBI Working Paper 1. Asian Development Bank Institute, Tokyo (January). Processed.

Reinhart, Carmen. 2000. "The Mirage of Floating Exchange Rates." *American Economic Review* 90, 2(May):65–70.

Taylor, John. 1993. "Discretion versus Policy Rules in Practice." *Carnegie Rochester Conference Series on Public Policy* 29(December):195–214.

Williamson, John. 2000. "Exchange Rate Regimes for Emerging Markets: Reviving the Intermediate Option." Institute for International Economics, Washington, D.C. (July). Processed.

CHAPTER 6

INDUSTRIAL AND FINANCIAL POLICY IN CHINA AND VIETNAM: A NEW MODEL OR A REPLAY OF THE EAST ASIAN EXPERIENCE?

Dwight H. Perkins

From the beginning of their economic reforms, China and Vietnam have labored to become part of the East Asian economic success story. The Asian financial crisis of 1997–98 led some of the leadership of the two countries to have second thoughts, but the basic goal of achieving rapid economic growth with an economic system something like that of their neighbors did not really change. China and Vietnam, however, began at a very different starting point from that of their neighbors. Both countries for a period of three decades had followed an economic development model patterned on the Soviet-style system of a command economy run by a central plan. The effort to move toward an East Asian economic system, therefore, involved much more than a few changes in policy from import-substituting industrialization to export-led growth or from distorted prices to market-determined prices. To become more like the rest of East Asia, China and Vietnam had to fundamentally change the way their economies were organized from top to bottom. The Chinese and Vietnamese economic stories of the past one to two decades, therefore, involve two different, but closely related, strands. There was the transition away from a command to a market economy, but there also was the effort to learn from, and to some degree to pattern themselves after their conception of, what made their East Asian neighbors economic successes.

By the end of the 1990s, however, it was no longer clear whether what made other East Asian economies successful had much relevance to what would determine the success of China and Vietnam in the future. The international economic environment in which China and Vietnam operated at the turn of the century was very different from the environment that existed in the 1950s and 1960s, when Japan, Korea, and the other East Asian early developers conceived their industrial policies. The Uruguay Round and the rapid globalization of the economy had changed the rules of the game. What was possible in the middle of the twentieth century was no longer acceptable at the beginning of the twenty-first. In the 1950s through the 1970s, for example, the economic managers of Japan, the Republic of Korea, and Taiwan Province (China) could use tariffs and quotas widely to promote particular industries. The role of foreign direct investment (FDI) was severely circumscribed. Japan and the Republic of Korea were welcomed as members of the General Agreement on Tariffs and Trade (GATT), even though much of what they were doing violated the free trade principles of GATT.

In contrast, China's negotiations to join GATT and its successor, the World Trade Organization (WTO), dragged on through the 1990s, and China was still negotiating with the European Union in 2000. As China's trade agreement with the United States indicated, to become a member of the WTO, China would have to open to trade and foreign investment to a degree never dreamed of in the 1950s through the 1970s. Quantitative restrictions on trade, domestic content requirements, and other such instruments of industrial policy were to be eliminated quickly. Foreign investors were to receive "national treatment" in sectors that previously had been wholly closed to foreign ownership. Vietnam could not even get most favored nation status or normal trading relations without agreeing to similar conditions. Vietnam initially refused to sign the agreement it had negotiated, but that could not be a long-term solution for either Vietnam or China. The two economies, as a number of studies have shown, had too much to gain from normal trading relations with the United States, in the case of Vietnam, and from membership in the WTO, in both cases.

The question facing Chinese and Vietnamese policymakers is to learn from the economic development experience of their East Asian neighbors. The earlier East Asian model is still very appealing to the former planners who now preside over economic policy in the two countries. The Asian financial crisis of 1997–98 led many leaders in China and Vietnam to doubt the applicability of the Korean or Japanese model of industrial policy, but did not kill the idea. A decade of stagnation in Japan in the 1990s, a stagnation that is widely perceived to result from the industrial and financial approaches of the past, has also led some to rethink their views. Many hope, nevertheless, that an activist industrial-financial policy model can be reconciled somehow with the demands of the global trading system and the rules of the WTO. But that may not be realistic. Complete laissez-faire on the Hong Kong model probably is not realistic either. Clearly, China and Vietnam will have to develop their own approach to industrial and financial development over the coming decades, but just what is that approach likely to look like? What are the real choices facing the two countries?

It is not just the new external environment that is forcing China and Vietnam to come up with a new approach. The simpler parts of the transition to a market economy have been accomplished. Agriculture and commerce have been reorganized into small competitive units that are, for all practical purposes, private and that respond mainly to market forces. Many of the so-called township and village enterprises in China and some of the joint ventures with foreign firms in both China and Vietnam also behave in accordance with market rules. But the large and medium state-owned enterprises together with the state-owned banks remain in a twilight zone between a command and a market system. In both China and Vietnam, this failure to complete the reform appears to have contributed to the slowdown in economic growth in 1998 and 1999. Just continuing with the policies of the past decade, therefore, is likely to exact a higher and higher economic cost. A new approach is needed.

DEVELOPMENT STRATEGY AND INDUSTRIAL POLICY CHOICES

When the transition to a market-based system began, several components of the East Asian approach to economic development were not controversial within the leadership of China and Vietnam, and these components were put in place at the beginning of the reform period in both countries. Foremost among these elements was an outward orientation with a particularly strong emphasis on the growth of exports. Exports in the Chinese case, as in the cases of the four East Asian tigers (Hong Kong, Korea, Singapore, and Taiwan Province) plus Japan, meant the export of manufactures rather than of minerals and agricultural products. In the Vietnamese case, the goal was to expand manufactured exports, but the immediate reality was that export expansion depended more on the growth of agricultural exports and petroleum. Over the longer run, however, Vietnam will have to rely increasingly on manufactured exports for much the same reason as China will. Both countries have 0.1 hectare of cultivated land per capita, and countries with limited land endowments of this sort usually become net importers of food and other agricultural products, not net exporters.

Nations with huge populations relative to their total land area generally become net importers of minerals as well. During the first years of rapid industrial growth, natural resource–based products may make up a substantial share of exports, but as per capita incomes rise, the domestic demand for these products soon outstrips supply. In China, primary products of all kinds (agriculture plus minerals) still constituted 50 percent of all exports in 1980, but this percentage fell rapidly to 26 percent in 1990 and 11 percent in 1998. In 1995, for the first time, China became a net importer of primary products. In Vietnam, primary products made up more than 90 percent of all exports as late as 1992, but manufactured exports rose from 9 percent of total exports in 1992 to 29 percent in 1996.

The turn outward in China and Vietnam involved more than just a rejection of the Soviet-style autarchic policies of the past. The emphasis on the export of manufactures meant that the whole industrial system had to be reoriented. An inward-looking system could produce low-quality goods for a captive market, but an outward-oriented industry had to compete in both quality and cost with the most able manufacturers around the world. Marketing skills are almost unknown in an autarchic system with central planning and are not very important in the export of minerals, but they are an essential part of any manufactured export strategy. An inward-focused system also had to produce its own machinery and steel, because development required producer goods and the system did not generate enough foreign exchange to pay for the import of these items. An outward-oriented industry could export consumer manufactures and import many of the producer goods required, at least in the early stages of rapid growth.

Chinese and Vietnamese enterprise managers did not suddenly acquire the marketing and quality control skills needed to compete in international markets. Success in expanding manufactured exports was achieved by relying on people outside of China and Vietnam who already had the necessary skills. In China's case, turning mainly to the skilled trading companies of Hong Kong solved the marketing problem. The share of Chinese exports that went first to Hong Kong and then were reexported rose steadily throughout the 1980s, and most of these reexports were manufactures (for a detailed discussion of the role of Hong Kong, see Sun 1991). Foreign direct investment also played a central role both in marketing and in the restructuring of Chinese and Vietnamese industry to produce quality products for international markets. Most of this foreign direct investment came from ethnic Chinese in Hong Kong, Taiwan Province, and Southeast Asia. Not only was FDI from the United States, Europe, and even Japan small relative to that of the Chinese, but also much of that FDI went to offshore petroleum development or to large import-substituting efforts such as automobiles.

It is interesting to speculate whether China and Vietnam could have sustained a manufactured export drive if overseas Chinese had not been willing to play such an active role. Conceivably, China and Vietnam could have relied directly on help from buyers in the United States and Europe or on the big trading companies of Japan. In effect, that was how Korea and Taiwan learned what foreign markets required, doing so for the most part without much foreign direct investment. If FDI from the industrial countries had been necessary for rapid export development, China and Vietnam would have had to move more quickly to create an environment satisfactory to industrial-country investors. That would have required making far more progress toward establishing an economic system based on the rule of law than what in fact occurred.

The overseas Chinese community, in contrast, had long experience using family and more extended personal relationships to provide a secure environment for their investments and had little trouble transferring those skills to the Chinese mainland. American and European investors relied instead on contracts and a strong legal system to stand behind those contracts. If China had been forced to develop its legal system more rapidly, it would have had considerable difficulty doing so. A Confucian tradition followed by the outright abolition of China's legal system during the Cultural Revolution (1966–76) left China at the beginning of the reform era with little foundation on which to build. China could and did pass volumes full of new laws after the reform period began in 1978, but a Communist Party and government used to making decisions only partially constrained by law did not surrender that discretionary authority easily. Much the same could be said about Vietnam. China's and Vietnam's turn outward forced the two nations to make fundamental changes in the way they approached industrial development. In one respect, however—the creation of a system based on the rule of law—these two countries did not have to make as much progress as many western analysts frequently argued was necessary.

The decision to turn outward was not an inevitable result of the decision to move toward a market economy, particularly in the case of China. China, after all, has a huge domestic market, and many analysts have argued that China will have to rely mainly on that market if it is to grow rapidly. China, like all very large countries, which typically have low foreign trade ratios, could not expect export growth to pull the whole economy along indefinitely. Exports between 1978 and 1998 did grow at nearly 16 percent a year in nominal U.S. dollars and 25 percent a year in current Chinese renminbi, to some degree pulling the rest of the economy along with them (China, State Statistical Bureau 1998: 620). But by 1999, total exports had reached US$194.9 billion and could not be expected to continue rising at the rates of the past. China would have to rely more on domestic demand for its products. Even at a 10 percent annual rate of growth, Chinese exports would total more than US$700 billion in less than 15 years, and there are serious doubts that the rest of the world could absorb Chinese exports of this magnitude in such a short time span.

Could Chinese gross domestic product (GDP) continue to grow at 8 or 9 percent a year if exports did not make a major contribution to that growth rate? The years 1998 and 1999 provided a partial answer to this question. Exports grew only 0.5 percent in 1998, then fell during the first part of 1999, in large part because of the Asian financial crisis, before ending up with a 6.1 percent rate of growth for the year as a whole (China, National Bureau of Statistics 1999b: 19; 2000: 21). Private consumption and public and private enterprise investment also grew slowly, leaving government expenditure on domestic infrastructure with the task of maintaining a high rate of growth in aggregate demand and hence in GDP. China, as a result, struggled to keep GDP growth above 7 percent, and many feel that the official rate of almost 8 percent in 1998 was inflated by false reporting from the provinces. GDP growth in 1999 was reported to be 7 percent. For reasons that are poorly understood, but that probably have something to do with the productivity-enhancing influence of foreign competition, growth based mainly on domestic demand may not be able to sustain the high GDP growth rates enjoyed while exports were surging. Clearly, China needs to keep exports growing as rapidly as possible, but it also needs to generate a more rapid increase based on domestic demand.

Vietnam is still a very small exporter, and a high growth rate of exports from Vietnam could be sustained for a long time without facing markets unable to absorb what Vietnam could produce. The problem for Vietnam is to initiate the boom in manufactured exports. The lack of export growth in Vietnam in 1998 and 1999 was due to the Asian financial crisis, together with Vietnamese policies that discouraged foreign investors, the main exporters of manufactures. That slowdown was not due to the long-term saturation of Vietnam's export markets.

Industrial Organization and Industrial Policy

Given the importance of exports and foreign investment to the economic development of China and Vietnam, it becomes all the more important for those two economies to abide by the rules of the international economic system, as embodied in organizations such as the WTO. Since the WTO rules explicitly disallow many critical aspects of government interventions to restrict imports and control foreign investment, it would seem to follow almost automatically that China and Vietnam will have to forgo any attempt to direct the development of industry and the financial sector along lines pioneered by the government planners of Japan and Korea from the 1950s through the 1970s.

But rules imposed by an external body, even an international body such as the WTO that is led by the economically most powerful nations in the world, are not as compelling as a nation's own internal logic. Nowhere is that more true than in China and Vietnam, with their long history of resistance to foreign domination. If China's and Vietnam's economic decisionmakers are persuaded that an activist Korean- or Japanese-style industrial policy would not work even if it were allowed, they are likely to focus systematically on making a less interventionist, more market-dominated system work. If they are not so convinced, they are more likely to circumvent the strictures of the global economic rules, just as Japan and Korea did in the 1970s and 1980s.

It is not just a country's orientation toward the rules of the international marketplace that shapes how its industrial sector should be organized and led. In the cases of both China and Vietnam, the inherited structure of industry and the financial sector itself has considerable bearing on how industry should be organized and the role that the government should play in the direction and control of industry and finance. China, in particular, experienced nearly three decades of industrial development before the reform era began—nearly nine decades, if one goes back to the first modern factories established during the 1890s. Vietnam in 1986 or 1989 had a much smaller industrial sector than did China, but there was some industry, and that industry had been developed in the context of war and a Soviet-style economic system.

The nature of the issue that faces industrial policymakers in China irrespective of the rules of the WTO is illustrated by the data in table 6.1 and figure 6.1. To begin with, the industrial sector is large. Industrial value added in 1999 was a sizable RMB3.5 trillion (US$427 billion). Any industrial policymaker inclined to rely on government directions over market forces had to direct an industrial sector larger than that of France and roughly three times the size of industry in the Republic of Korea in the mid-1990s.

Size of output was only the beginning of the problem. China in 1996 had nearly 8 million industrial enterprises. Of these, 6 million were individual proprietorships with at most a few workers. Only 506,000 enterprises (in 1996) were classified as being "independent accounting units," a term that is roughly equivalent to an incorpo-

Table 6.1 The Ownership Structure of Industry in China, 1996

Type of firm	Number of enterprises (thousands)	Gross value of output (millions of renminbi)
All industrial units	7,986.5	9,959,500
Independent accounting units	506.4	6,274,016
Large-scale	7.1	2,475,665
State-owned	113.8	2,836,100
Collective	1,591.8	3,923,200
Township	202.3	1,173,000
Village	678.4	1,590,000
Other	518.6	338,700
Individual	6,210.7	1,542,000
Other	70.2	1,658,200
Shareholding	7.8	328,103
Foreign-funded	19.4	658,146
Hong Kong/Taiwan (China)	24.0	538,136

Source: China, State Statistical Bureau (1997: 411, 415–18).

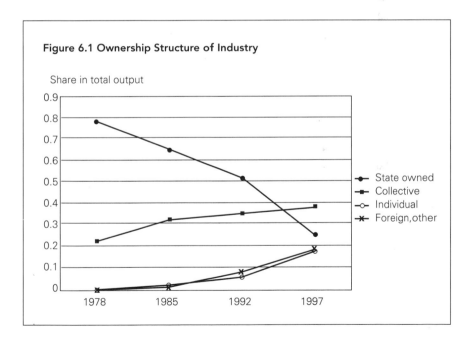

Figure 6.1 Ownership Structure of Industry

Share in total output

rated enterprise in the industrial world.[1] It is easy to dismiss the 7.48 million industrial units that were not independent accounting units as being small and therefore unimportant, but these firms produced 37 percent of all industrial output (measured in gross value terms) in 1996. It made no more sense to attempt to direct this portion of industrial activity through nonmarket channels than to attempt to control farm households in that way. No policymaker in Beijing or even in the provincial capitals could possibly have enough timely information to give meaningful guidance to the daily activities of small industrial firms.

The 506,000 enterprises that were independent accounting units also presented a problem for prospective industrial policy activists. A total of 43,000 of these firms, producing 19 percent of the gross output of independent accounting units and a much larger share of exports, were owned by foreign firms or firms based in Hong Kong or Taiwan. Another 352,000 were the more developed of the township and village enterprises (TVEs) or the urban, collectively owned firms. These collective independent accounting units taken together accounted for another 30 percent of the gross value of output of all industrial independent accounting units.

There is now a large literature on the nature of the ownership of TVEs, but one point on which almost everyone agrees is that these firms are not owned or controlled by the central government or by provincial governments. Local governments, townships, and occasionally counties have a major role in TVEs, but these governments do not behave primarily as taxers and regulators with respect to the TVEs. In the regions where TVEs have enjoyed the greatest success, governments actively promote their local enterprises. It is not much of an exaggeration to say that many local governments behave like small business conglomerates. Property rights are reasonably well defined in the sense that the locality clearly controls the activities of the enterprise, receives the benefits, and does not share these benefits with higher-level government units, except that the TVEs do pay taxes. TVEs face hard budget constraints, buy their inputs on the market, sell their output on the market, and enter into contractual relationships with other firms, including both state-owned and foreign-owned firms. (See also the chapters by Qian and Lin and Yao.)

Thus 114,000 state-owned enterprises in 1996 only produced 50 percent of the output of independent accounting units and 29 percent of total gross industrial output. This contrasts with the state enterprise share of 78 percent in 1978 and 65 percent in 1985, although the 1978 figure is not precisely comparable to that for either 1985 or 1996.[2] In these calculations, the state enterprise share has been reduced to less than a third of industrial output, and there are still more than 100,000 firms. This number is still far too large to be efficiently directed by the central government, especially given the weak accounting systems of many of these enterprises.

In China, 7,000 industrial firms are classified as large-scale. The majority of these enterprises are state-owned, but the figure includes some foreign joint ventures and even a few township enterprises. Together, these large firms produce 25 percent of all industrial output, less if only large state-owned firms are included in the total. From 1996 on, there was much talk in Beijing of the government only playing an active role in the management of 1,000 to 2,000 state-owned enterprises. After the Fifteenth Party Congress in 1997 and the National People's Congress in early 1998, the figure being bandied about was only 500 state-owned enterprises. In addition to strategic military industries, this figure presumably included many, but not all, of the largest industrial firms in China, but it is unlikely that these firms accounted for more than 10 to 15 percent of industrial output.[3]

Whatever the intentions of China's industrial policymakers—whether they want to comply with the rules of the global economic system or not—they are not in a position to duplicate the kind of control over industrial development that President Park Chung Hee exercised in Korea in the 1970s. In Korea in the early 1970s, the 46 largest industrial conglomerates (*chaebol*) accounted for 37 percent of value added in manufacturing and 19 percent of all nonagricultural GDP. The top five *chaebol* alone accounted for 15 percent of manufacturing value added. State-owned enterprises in Korea at that time accounted for another 13 percent of nonagricultural GDP (Jones and Sakong 1980: 148, 260–66). Therefore, more than half of all manufacturing was in the hands of fewer than 200 firms. President Park and his ministers could meet regularly with the heads of these firms and could personally keep track of their progress in implementing national industrial policy.

The problem facing industrial policymakers in China is one facing policymakers in any number of areas—the huge size of the Chinese nation. The number of enterprises needed to account for half of Chinese industrial output is in the hundreds of thousands. If China were to try to reduce this number to a few hundred that accounted for a third or more of manufacturing value added, these consolidated enterprises would have to be 10 to 20 times the size of the Korean *chaebol* in the 1970s.

It is difficult to see how China could possibly carry out an activist industrial policy along the lines of the Korean heavy and chemical industry drive of the 1970s. In that Korean drive, the president's office designed how the entire heavy industry sector was to be developed, down to and including the scale of individual factories. The president's office then negotiated with the leaders of the *chaebol* to determine who would carry out the government's plans. In this manner, the Korean president, working with a committee of a few dozen specialists, was able to provide hands-on direction to the development of what soon accounted for more than half of all Korean manufacturing output and a comparable share of exports.[4]

If China's industrial policymakers were to attempt a similar effort, they would have to deal with several thousand firms, not several dozen. A small committee located in the office of the Chinese prime minister would be overwhelmed. Instead, China would have to create a large bureaucracy and give that bureaucracy the power to order firms to carry out its plans.

The industrial policy of Park Chung Hee's Korea was an extreme case of centralized decisionmaking. The Ministry of International Trade and Industry (MITI) in Japan played a similar role but relied somewhat less on centralized direction and more on coordination of and cooperation with a wide variety of private industry associations. This system is widely seen today as being a major contributor to the economic stagnation experienced by Japan throughout the 1990s, but a nation such as China that is at a much earlier stage of growth conceivably could make the system work as it did in Japan in the 1960s and 1970s. Thus it is possible that the MITI version of a government-led industrial effort would have worked better in China than the Korean version did or better than it worked in Japan itself in the 1990s. It is more probable, however, that the industrial policy bureaucracy in China would revert to China's own past and would operate in many ways like the old State Planning Commission. Certainly that would be the likely outcome if the implementers of Chinese industrial policy were mostly made up of officials from the old planning bureaucracy.

Vietnam's industrial policymakers did not and do not face China's problem of overwhelming numbers of industrial firms. The total number of state-owned firms fell from 3,020 in 1989 to 1,958 in 1995, largely because the Vietnamese closed many inefficient state firms managed by local governments. The number of firms directly controlled by the central government did not change much during the reform period, totaling 549 firms in 1995 (World Bank 1997: table 8.1; Vietnam, General Statistical Office 1994: 79). Even these figures somewhat overstate the total, because joint ventures between foreign and Vietnamese firms are mostly included in the state sector. The number of private enterprises came to just over 1,000; there were just over 5,000 industrial cooperatives (down from 21,900 in 1989) and an additional 368,000 household industrial establishments (in 1992). The state sector's share of gross value of industrial output, however, was much higher in Vietnam than in China. The state share of gross industrial output in 1992 was 71 percent, and this share rose during the reform period of the 1990s. Most of the rest of industrial output was accounted for by the household sector (24 percent in 1992).

The Vietnamese central government, therefore, had direct control of most industrial output even after a decade of reform. By controlling a few hundred enterprises, the government policymakers in Hanoi could, in principle, direct and supervise most of the industrial development that mattered. This small number of modern industrial enterprises, when compared with the situation in China, was due in part to the fact that Vietnam's population was only 6 percent of that of China and in part to Vietnam's much more limited industrial development as of the mid-1990s. Does it follow that Vietnam was in a position to carry out a 1970s Korean- or Japanese-style industrial policy?

Neoclassical economic purists assert that an efficient activist industrial policy is a contradiction in terms, and so their answer to the question posed is an unequivocal "no." The recent experience of Japan in the 1990s and Korea in the late 1990s also makes clear that an activist industrial policy can go awry. Long before the Asian financial crisis, economic decisionmakers in both Korea and Taiwan Province were expending considerable time and energy attempting to dismantle much of what they perceived to be the excessive regulatory overhang of the earlier activist era. But Asians, among others, also look at the experience of Korea and Japan in the 1960s and 1970s and conclude that those countries must have been doing something right. Economic historians have long pointed out that the state typically plays a much larger role in economic development in follower countries than in leading industrial countries. One of the "advantages of backwardness" is that a follower can learn from the leaders, and government officials are sometimes well placed to do the necessary learning (this view is stated most clearly in the works of Alexander Gerschenkron; see Gerschenkron 1962). Could Vietnamese government officials learn from the experience of Korea and Japan, adopting what worked in their industrial policies and revising or avoiding Korea's and Japan's more obvious mistakes? For that matter, could China do the same, provided that it confined government's role to a scope that was manageable?

There are three reasons, arising out of the recent past and current situation, why Vietnam and China would have great difficulty making a Korean- or Japanese-style industrial policy work efficiently even if the rules of the international economic system allowed such actions. The first is that the economic bureaucracy in both countries was built and trained to carry out a Soviet-style system of central planning, not the kind of strategic planning that existed in Korea and Japan. The latter system relied heavily on "guidance," market forces, and the private sector when it came to planning implementation. Soviet-style central planners rely on orders backed up by direct control of most inputs to enforce the plan. Vietnam and China could, of course, disband their current economic bureaucracy and, to a degree, already have done so. In 1998 China began a major reduction in the size of government. The two countries could then rebuild a new economic bureaucracy on the Korean or Japanese model. Such a restructuring is possible, but not very likely. Far more likely is that the decision to create a Korean- or Japanese-style strategic planning system would become an excuse to retain as much of the old planning bureaucracy as possible. Some of these people could be retrained for the new approach, but many would stick as well as they could to the old ways they know best.

The second and third reasons why it would be difficult to operate an efficient Korean- or Japanese-style industrial policy have to do with politics and with corruption. Korea and Japan in the 1960s and 1970s certainly had experience with corruption and with economic decisions that were made more on political than economic or technical criteria. But politics and corruption were not an important part of industrial policy decisions in the 1960s and 1970s. President Park Chung Hee in Korea insulated his Blue House heavy and chemical industry team from politics so that decisions could be made on technical criteria alone. When individual *chaebol* received a major task from the government, the main reason was that President Park thought they could do the job. Korean state enterprises were also expected to perform well in economic and financial terms, and that is the main reason why the giant steel firm POSCO did as well as it did. When politics did play a major role in economic and industrial decisions in Korea, as was the case in the 1990s, the result was the Hanbo steel bankruptcy and the debt crisis of 1997–98.

Japan's MITI, in its heyday, was also insulated from politics and corruption.[5] Politicians heavily influenced public works spending, but bureaucrats who were experts in the relevant industries made industrial policy; trade and financial policies were used to back up those technical decisions. The technical criteria used were not always the ideal or correct ones for achieving efficient industrial development, but the industrial policymakers were trying to do what was best for the country. They were not generating rents for themselves or for their political masters.

Politics and corruption were a frequent element in how economic decisions were made and implemented in both Vietnam and China in the 1990s. The international services that attempt to measure the degree of corruption affecting business decisions generally put China and Vietnam at the lower end of lists where the top is occupied by nations such as Singapore that are largely free of corruption in business.[6]

The customs services in both countries regularly require payoffs to get imports into the country. Politically based decisions that do not involve corruption can be just as damaging. A petrochemical plant placed in Central Vietnam far from sources of supply and far from markets can become an enormous drain on the country's limited investment resources. The Three Gorges Dam project in China was driven as much by political as economic criteria. If the costs of building that dam escalate well above initial estimates, the project could contribute to a slowdown in growth.

Political criteria are not suddenly going to be eliminated from government decisions affecting the economy in either China or Vietnam. Politics play a major role in most decisions by most governments around the world. The government of Korea's Park Chung Hee and Japan's MITI of the 1960s and 1970s are the outliers, as is the government of Singapore. Public works projects all over the world are built to get votes or other forms of political support as well as to provide needed infrastructure. In the United States, these are known as "pork barrel projects." China and Vietnam have authoritarian political systems, but the politicians who run those systems must build political support from various constituencies in order to make decisions. President Park Chung Hee relied mainly on a modern combat army plus rural farmers for his political support, and he had no need to buy the support of other politicians or industrialists. They were completely dependent on him.

There are ways of reducing the role of politics in economic decisionmaking. The most obvious way is to have the private sector make most of the decisions without government interference, but in China and Vietnam that is not likely to solve the problem of how to build the large amount of infrastructure needed. For both political and economic reasons, the government is likely to play the dominant role in infrastructure development for at least the next decade or two. Most infrastructure investments elsewhere in Asia, including in Japan in the first half of the twentieth century, were carried out by the state.[7] Efforts to minimize the political impact on efficiency in these projects will depend on measures such as the greater use of tendering procedures (open competitive bidding for projects) and greater transparency (for example, allowing the press to cover mistakes as well as successes).

A wide variety of measures can be used to keep corruption and rent seeking under control, but the most important measures involve reducing the opportunities for corruption and rent seeking. With fewer opportunities, it then becomes possible to police a more limited number of targets. Most opportunities for rent seeking come from government efforts to regulate the economy through licensing and similar procedures. When a business must obtain permission from an official, and that official has discretionary authority to give or withhold permission, an opportunity is created for an informal and usually illegal payment. Discretionary authority to negotiate taxes or to determine the classification of imports subject to duties also creates such opportunities. This list can be readily extended, but the main point is a simple one. To control rent-seeking behavior, a government needs to reduce its regulatory interventions to the minimum necessary to achieve important national goals. Where regulatory and tax interventions are necessary, discretionary authority on the part of government officials must be kept to a minimum.

Within East Asia, Singapore is as good a model as any of how to control corruption. Hong Kong has been equally effective. Both allow the market to govern most decisions and have law-based rules backed up by reasonably independent courts to oversee the regulation that remains. They also have vigorous anticorruption commissions, whose success is due in part to their ability to concentrate their efforts on the few remaining areas where opportunities for corruption continue to exist.

An activist industrial policy is the antithesis of an effort to reduce rent-seeking behavior. The tools used to enforce government industrial policy initiatives involve and even require various kinds of licenses, government control over critical imports, and government-directed loans at subsidized rates. Generally the officials who administer these interventions must be given a high degree of discretionary authority. Sometimes industrial policy subsidies can be made available across-the-board to whoever applies, but that is not the norm.

The implication of this discussion of politics and rent seeking for the industrial policies of China and Vietnam is straightforward. Barring a miraculous return to the revolutionary spirit of the 1950s in China or the 1960s and 1970s in Vietnam (and the very tight surveillance system), government decisionmaking in the two countries is going to be heavily influenced by politics. Rent-seeking behavior will also be widespread where opportunity allows. If the two nations attempt to introduce a MITI-style industrial policy, the results will frequently lead to investment and other economic decisions that are far below the optimum. Economic growth, as a result, would probably slow down, and rent seeking would undermine the very credibility of the government.

Something like this has already been occurring, not because China and Vietnam have introduced a version of the Korean and Japanese systems, but because many of the interventionist policies of the old command system have not yet been eradicated. The danger is that the appeal of the Korean and Japanese approaches will lead to decisions that effectively leave industrial development policy stuck in this twilight zone between a planning and a market system. The alternative is for China and Vietnam to eliminate most of the procedures that interfere with the operation of the market.

Does it follow that China and Vietnam must leave all industrial development decisions to market forces and confine government's role to the provision of roads, electric power, and a few other infrastructure investments that have traditionally been provided by government?[8] Certainly, the leaders of both China and Vietnam do not see it this way. Their approach remains highly interventionist, but they have not articulated where this approach is heading. Enthusiasm for the Korean and Japanese industrial policy models has waned a bit, and critics of these models have been emboldened by the perceived connection between these approaches and the Asian financial crisis of 1997–98.

Vietnam's industrial policymakers remain stuck to a significant degree in strategies based on import substitution and continued state dominance of all but the smallest firms and those controlled or managed by foreign investors. Many foreign investors began to withdraw from Vietnam in 1998 and 1999, in part because of crises at home, but also because of the difficulty of getting through the red tape of the government bureaucracy. As long as Vietnamese growth rates remain high—averaging roughly 9 percent a year from 1992 through 1997 before falling to between 4 and 5 percent a year in 1998 and 1999—a fundamental change in this approach to industrial development is not likely. If growth rates fall markedly, however, or even if they stay at the level achieved in 1998 and 1999, the debate over the future of industrial policy will become more active.

China is much further along in the debate over the appropriate role for government in industry than is Vietnam. The decision to push ahead vigorously with negotiations to enter the WTO is the best single piece of evidence that many Chinese economic leaders recognize the need to move decisively to implement the rules of the global economic system. The decision by the central government to directly control only 500 state-owned enterprises, or even 1,000, similarly can be seen as the abandonment of a broad-based direct role for the state in industrial development along Korean lines of the 1970s. The role of the centrally directed industrial intervention that remains in China has two more limited goals. One goal is to pick a single industrial sector, or at most several, and to use government support to bring that sector up to an internationally competitive position. The other goal is to provide time for the loss-making state enterprises either to return to profitability or to go out of business in a way that is not politically disruptive. The issue of loss-making state enterprises will be taken up in the next section of this chapter.

The Chinese government's efforts to develop one or several key industries can be seen as an infant-industry strategy, although some of these firms have been in existence for decades. Or the effort can be seen as a narrower version of MITI-style strategic planning. The automotive sector received most of the attention in the 1990s. Producing more than 1 million vehicles of all kinds a year, China had a large enough market to achieve economies of scale, and that market is growing rapidly. Many of the hundreds of Chinese firms in the industry are small and backward, and even the few large firms are struggling with high costs, usually in joint ventures with German, Japanese, or American companies. It took more than a decade for the automobile firms of Korea and Japan to become internationally competitive, and Malaysia's Proton is not yet internationally competitive after more than a decade since startup. China's automobile industry, therefore, may require state support for some time to come. It is all the more remarkable, therefore, that China went ahead with and signed the trade agreement with the United States even though that agreement set a timetable for the relatively rapid opening of the Chinese automobile market. Formal trade treaties on paper and actual implementation on the ground, to be sure, are not the same thing, and Chinese trade negotiators do not always have an easy time getting local authorities to comply with what they have signed. Still, there is little doubt that the push to join WTO signifies that many of China's leaders recognize the need to develop China's strategic industries in a way that is consistent with the rules of an open trading system, as spelled out in the international agreements governing the global system.

There are compelling reasons why China will remain under great pressure to move toward a full market economy with greatly reduced government intervention in development of the industrial sector. The sector is too large and made up of too many thousands of firms to be efficiently controlled from Beijing. There are too much politics and rent seeking in Chinese economic decisionmaking for industrial development decisions to be made mainly on the basis of appropriate economic and technical criteria. And the rules of the world trading system—rules on which China depends to continue developing its exports—are clearly in conflict with mercantilist policies similar to those pursued elsewhere in East Asia in the past.

Do these compelling reasons mean that China will abandon its efforts to maintain an activist industrial policy patterned on Korea and Japan or on some other model? However compelling these arguments may be to an economist-observer outside of China, it will be a long time before such arguments are fully accepted within China, particularly at the local level, where many of the decisions concerning implementation of the global rules will be played out. Many of the people running China today have experience in the central planning bureaucracy. On top of that, China has had centuries of centralized bureaucratic rule. Attitudes and ways of doing things that are as deeply embedded as these do not disappear overnight. But the forces of tradition do not determine everything. When tradition and personal experience conflict with the requirements of the present, tradition and experience usually give way. This process takes time, first to understand the nature of the problem and then to implement the changes necessary to make the problem disappear.

Many of these same arguments apply to Vietnam. The difference is that Vietnam has not yet committed itself to an export strategy based on manufactures and continues to rely heavily on an import-substituting path to industrialization. Vietnam's industrial sector and the number of its industrial firms are also much smaller than they are in China, so a policy of control from Hanoi is not as obviously impossible as in the case of China. Vietnam's initial refusal to sign a trade agreement with the United States, an agreement that its own officials had negotiated, is clear evidence of the reluctance of many officials, even in the top leadership, to accept the kind of industrial policy that is likely to be the most appropriate for their country.

The Path toward the Reform of State-Owned Enterprises

Up to this point, the discussion has focused on the role of government industrial policy in shaping the development of industrial enterprises in China and Vietnam. What choices face the individuals deciding how the enterprises themselves should be organized?

Most of the issues here deal with how China and Vietnam should go about completing the reform of state-owned enterprises. There are, to be sure, issues in this area that do not involve the state-owned enterprise problem. There is the question, for example, of whether the TVEs are the wave of China's industrial future, and, if so, how they will have to change in order to remain competitive. This issue, like a number of others, is likely to be determined first by market forces and only second by rules set in Beijing. The Chinese TVEs are also the subject of chapter 7, by Lin and Yao, in this volume.[9] The state-owned enterprise problem, however, is not one that can be left to market forces for a solution. Put differently, market forces alone could "solve" the state-owned enterprise problem if the Chinese and Vietnamese governments allowed them to, but both governments are unwilling to allow an unfettered market to impose a solution, for political and social reasons, among others.

There are many dimensions to the problem of state-owned enterprises. For years both China and Vietnam saw the issue as one of giving these enterprises limited autonomy. Bonuses were geared to the performance of the individual units, goods produced above government allocation quotas could be sold at higher prices on the market, and inputs could be bought on the market if they were not available through the state allocation system. As the state allocation system gradually disappeared, the government introduced what it called the "enterprise responsibility system," patterned in a vague way on the household responsibility system that had proved so successful in agriculture. But the degree of autonomy allowed state enterprises was always much less than that enjoyed by rural households. In critical respects, state-owned enterprises were still subunits of the central or provincial government bureaucracies that supervised them.

Some economists reject the notion that a state-owned enterprise can ever operate efficiently, but there are a number of highly efficient state enterprises in Asia. POSCO, the giant Korean steel producer, has already been mentioned. Singapore has established a great many successful state-owned enterprises, and these enterprises had total sales of S\$9.2 billion and profits of S\$2.1 billion in 1990 (Goh 1992). Singapore airlines—one of the best airlines in the world—is state-owned. Much of Taiwan Province's heavy industry in fields ranging from petrochemicals to steel was dominated initially by state firms, and many of these firms have yet to be privatized. These state firms were oriented mainly toward the domestic market and were not the source of Taiwan's dynamic export performance, but neither were they a major drag on that performance.

Stringent conditions were needed to achieve success with these state firms elsewhere in Asia. All enjoyed a high degree of autonomy. Management's performance was judged mainly or even solely on its ability to generate long-term profits for the company. The multiple objectives—so often imposed on state enterprises elsewhere in the world—were mostly absent. Autonomy and profit orientation were difficult to achieve. POSCO was run by an individual politically more powerful than most government ministers at the time. Singapore was able to isolate these enterprises completely from local politics.

What must China and Vietnam do to make their large state-owned firms successful, and is what is required feasible in the Chinese and Vietnamese contexts?[10] There is no secret as to what needs to be done. State-owned enterprises must be made fully autonomous and responsive primarily to market forces. The steps required to achieve that aim have been discussed at length in China and to a lesser degree in Vietnam. The critical issues involve the following.

First, these enterprises must stand on their own feet financially and face a hard budget constraint. Money borrowed should be paid back at market interest rates, and the failure to do so should lead to bankruptcy. Taxes should be based on fixed rates and rules and not subject to negotiation between the firm and the tax collector. Inputs should be paid for at market prices. Output should be sold on competitive markets where market entry is as easy as scale and financing requirements allow. China and Vietnam have gone most of the way to making state enterprises buy and sell on competitive markets. It has proved to be much more difficult to harden the soft budget constraint. Bankruptcy laws were passed in China in the latter half of the 1980s, but they were not applied with any vigor until the late 1990s. The government, as part of its campaign to control inflation, did make it much more difficult for state firms to get credits from the banking system, but firms simply forced their suppliers to extend them credit. In the absence of a willingness to force these firms into bankruptcy, the accounts receivable on enterprise books continued to pile up. Vietnam did close down many local state enterprises as part of its efforts to control inflation in the early 1990s, but then the effort to impose a hard budget constraint stalled. Many Vietnamese state firms are profitable only because they operate behind high walls of protection from imports and equally high walls of protection from a domestic private sector that is unable to get the licenses required to operate in fields where the state sector is heavily involved.

Second, management of state enterprises must be chosen by people whose sole or primary concern is with the profitability of the enterprise. In both China and Vietnam, managers are picked instead by government and party officials who apply a wide variety of criteria, only one of which is profits. One solution to this problem would be to privatize state enterprises, and, in the end, that may be the solution chosen. Formally, however, both countries have rejected outright privatization. In contrast, China's decision to remove the central government from responsibility for the fate of all but 500 of 2,000 state firms essentially allows extensive privatization in some form. The TVEs also enjoy most of the property rights that are enjoyed by private firms, although the owner who exercises those rights is often a township or village. Vietnam has not decided to privatize all but its larger state firms.

Both China and Vietnam have experimented with a shareholding system, or corporatization as distinct from privatization. In Vietnam, as of 1998, only a dozen state firms were corporatized, while the number in China was in the many thousands. Shareholding could become the vehicle for creating boards of directors who would ensure that plant managers concentrated mainly on making profits rather than on pleasing their government and party superiors. The shareholders would not necessarily even have to be private individuals or organizations. Other state enterprises and institutions such as public pension funds might serve as profit-oriented members of company boards of directors. In Vietnam, boards with the power to hire and fire management are possible, in principle, and that is one reason why managers of

Vietnam's state firms are so reluctant to corporatize. In China there is no such problem because the government has retained majority control and the power to hire and fire management. Shareholding, in its present form in China, is mainly a way of raising capital.

Third, if a fundamental restructuring of state enterprises is to succeed, the political cost of that restructuring must be kept at an acceptable level. One political cost is the loss of power and control by the government bureaucracy and the Communist Party. Conceivably both the bureaucracy and the party will decide that giving up control is too high a price, but both have surrendered considerable power in the past. The decollectivization of agriculture in China and Vietnam is the most dramatic example of a surrender of control. The government and party also gave up considerable power when they converted from an administrative system for the allocation of key inputs to a market system, and there are other examples. Thus there is no reason to believe that cutting the umbilical cord that attaches state enterprises to the government and the Communist Party will be resisted at all costs because of the fear of a loss of control.

Other kinds of social and political costs also are connected with state enterprise reform, however. The one that worries the Chinese leadership the most is that bankruptcy will lead to large-scale unemployment and social unrest. Millions of workers were laid off in 1997 through 1999, and there was some unrest. An unemployment insurance system did exist, but it was not yet nationwide in scope. The Vietnamese do not face a similar problem, in part because the government, once inflation was brought under control, ended the downsizing of state enterprises. In addition, state sector industrial employment in Vietnam involves only 700,000 workers as contrasted to the 42.8 million workers in state-owned industrial enterprises in China.

The political problems of state enterprise reform in China are compounded by the fact that these enterprises provide most of the housing, the pensions, and all of the health insurance to their employees. Overly generous pension liabilities are one reason why so many state enterprises are losing money. Health insurance was also more generous for state employees than for anyone else in China. Enterprise bankruptcy threatens these employees' health, their pensions, and their housing. Experiments designed to lead to national health and pension systems have been under way in China for many years. Subsidized housing is also being eliminated gradually, either through privatization or by charging commercial rents on state property. But the process in China has been painfully slow.

For all of the political problems surrounding China's efforts to substitute a national welfare and pension system for an enterprise-based system, those problems are small compared to the lavish national welfare systems found in Eastern Europe. In 1996, for example, social insurance and welfare funds for all state retirees in China, not just in industry, amounted to 2.2 percent of GDP.

Two other issues connected with industrial enterprise organization and ownership in China and Vietnam should be noted. First, both China and, to a lesser degree, Vietnam have been much more open to foreign direct investment than was ever the case in Japan, Korea, or even Taiwan Province. FDI started modestly in the early 1980s in China but averaged US$40 billion in the late 1990s. FDI is an integral and important part of China's industrial development strategy.[11] FDI firms are the source of a large share of the rapid rise in exports, and these enterprises also play a central role in the reform of industrial organization, technology, and management in key sectors such as automobiles. Joint ventures with both state and private firms have set standards of quality that have spread rapidly throughout Chinese industry. The gradually improving Chinese legal system also owes much of its progress to the need to provide a better legal framework for foreign investors.

Vietnam's support of FDI is more restrained than that of China, in part because Vietnam has not decided how it wants to deal with private enterprise more generally. For all of the problems of foreign investors in Vietnam—problems that led to declining FDI in 1998 and 1999—a case can be made that foreign investors are still treated better than private domestic firms. Vietnam's manufactured export sector, small as it is, is completely dependent on FDI.

Neither China nor Vietnam relies as heavily on FDI for development as Singapore and Hong Kong, nor will they even if they were to give unfettered national treatment in all sectors to foreign firms. There simply is not enough FDI in the world to do for a nation of 1.2 billion people what it has done for a nation of 2.8 million or a territory of 5.8 million. Hong Kong is part of China, and Hong Kong's economic system has had a large influence on the way business is handled in neighboring Guangdong Province and beyond.

Although China and Vietnam have not followed the Japanese or Korean approach to foreign direct investment, many in both China and Vietnam remain enamored of the large Japanese and Korean conglomerates (*chaebol* in Korea and *keiretsu* in Japan). Governments in both China and Vietnam, as a result, have set about creating large conglomerates of their own. Generally this involves bringing a number of enterprises together into one large unit. In some cases, government offices connected to these firms are also included in the new conglomerate. These larger units, it is believed, will be better able to compete internationally as well as domestically. Their brand names, it is hoped, might someday become as well known as Hitachi or Samsung.

There are serious problems with this approach to creating conglomerates. The government-directed approach, as it has been applied in Vietnam, often appears to be little more than a repackaging of existing arrangements. In Vietnam in the past, for example, the firms involved in the new, larger units worked closely together under the supervision of the relevant industrial bureau. The new arrangement simply formalizes these connections; it does not necessarily change behavior. Without a change in business behavior, it is hard to see what contribution these new, larger units will make to Vietnam's international competitiveness.

Initially, there was reason to believe that China's fascination with the Korean *chaebol* would also lead to government-directed reorganizations that would leave the government planning bureaucracy very much in tact and in control. But China's size, the decentralized nature of so many of its economic decisions, and the very diversity of enterprise forms of ownership, have led to mergers and acquisitions driven, more often than not, by the interests of particular firms or groups of firms. Almost all of the larger firms now appear to be part of one *jituan* (group) or another, but there are so many thousands of *jituan* that in no way do they resemble the Korean *chaebol* or the Japanese *keiretsu*; nor are they simply the Chinese planning bureaucracy in disguise. The mergers and acquisitions process in China, therefore, has begun to take on some of the characteristics of similar processes in market economies, although the government's role remains large.

There is nothing necessarily wrong with large conglomerates in either the Chinese or the Vietnamese context. The existing state enterprise structure was a product of the central planning system adopted from the Soviet Union and, in many instances, probably makes little sense under the current market-driven system. The question is whether government officials are the right people to decide to create a particular conglomerate or whether that decision should be left to market forces. But, if the process is left to market forces, are the state enterprises in a position to take the steps required in order to merge with other firms? A partial answer in the case of China is that the large state and nonstate firms are already well into the mergers and acquisitions process. If the process is to proceed smoothly and efficiently, however, the government will have to create the rules under which one firm can merge with or acquire another. As of the late 1990s, in both China and Vietnam, the government's role is more that of a discretionary decisionmaker than of a creator of the rules of the game. If the government does become mainly a setter of the rules, however, and the enterprises, both state and private, are run by able profit-oriented managers, the resulting new conglomerates are likely to be more effective than ones directly engineered by government officials.

China's structure of industrial organization and ownership is still evolving. The same is true of Vietnam, although Vietnam has barely started along the restructuring path. Neither country is likely to end up as a carbon copy of any other single Asian industrial economy. In terms of foreign ownership, China and Vietnam will be halfway along a spectrum with Japan and Korea at one end and Singapore at the other. Both China and Vietnam are likely to rely more heavily on this state ownership of industrial firms than other countries in Asia, but not all that much more heavily than Korea or Singapore in an earlier period. The dominant form of industrial enterprises will behave like privately owned firms, whatever their nominal mode of ownership.

Two related questions have to do with the size of industrial firms in the two nations and the degree of concentration in the various industrial sectors. Given China's enormous size, it is probably inevitable that the degree of concentration in particular industrial sectors will be substantially less than in a much smaller country at a similar stage of development. China, with an income per capita of US$2,000 in purchasing power parity terms, produced 124 million tons of steel in 1999, enough to allow China to have six 20-million-ton plants without taking exports into account. China had far more steel enterprises than this, but many of them were small. Korea's domestic market at the same stage of development could only support one plant of 2 million to 4 million tons.

Still, China's structure of industrial organization appears to be much less concentrated than China's size alone can explain. China is not a land of giant conglomerates on the model of Korea or of conglomerates supported by thousands of small dependent supplier firms, as in Japan. The TVE boom, together with tens of thousands of urban collectives and private firms, not to mention thousands of small joint ventures with firms from Hong Kong and Taiwan, has altered China's industrial structure probably for a very long time. If it had continued its Stalinist-style industrial development of the 1950s, with its emphasis on large heavy industries in the Northeast, China might have a very different organizational structure today. China instead deliberately set out on a different kind of development path, relying much more on small manufacturers scattered across the country. This small-scale industrialization program got off to a disastrous start with the "backyard" iron and steel program, but major adjustments were made, and these small firms have served China very well over the past two to three decades. China's experience has no precise analogy in Asia. The closest is Taiwan Province, which also built up its manufacturing sector by relying heavily on small producers, except in a few producer goods industries where large state enterprises dominated, at least at the outset.

Vietnam's structure of industrial organization is much less developed, and that makes it much harder to speculate about what that structure might look like in the future. The current structure is made up of a few large state firms—large relative to the size of Vietnam's market—a few thousand other state industrial enterprises, FDI firms producing mainly for export, and a small scattering of private industrial enterprises. There is nothing comparable to the TVE industries of China. If Vietnam stays with the institutions and policies that have created this structure, it may gradually become an inefficient version of the Singapore model of state enterprises together with an FDI-dominated industrial sector. Alternatively, Vietnam could free up the private sector, in which case it might get rapid development of small-scale domestic industrial firms not unlike what happened in Taiwan during the first decades of that island's development.

How China and Vietnam deal with these issues of industrial organization will have a large influence on whether their two economies continue to grow rapidly. One way or another, the two countries need to transform their enterprises into dynamic units that can compete both domestically and internationally. Enterprises that operate along bureaucratic lines or are weighed down by extensive government controls will not be able to provide the necessary leadership.

Financial Reform and Macroeconomic Policy

The problems facing reform in the financial sectors of China and Vietnam are in many ways similar to those facing the state-owned industrial sector. In fact, it is not possible to reform the financial sector unless one also does something about the state industrial sector; the reverse is also true. Similarly, it is not possible to move to a market-based macroeconomic policy unless China and Vietnam reform the state financial and industrial sectors.

The problems facing the Chinese and Vietnamese financial sectors also have many features in common with the crisis-hit financial sectors of Southeast Asia and Korea and for some of the same reasons. Both in China and Vietnam and in Southeast Asia and Korea, the weakness of the banking systems was a direct result of decades of government-directed bank lending. The banks themselves had little autonomy and did pretty much what their governments asked them to do. When government efforts led to healthy firms, the banks had strong loan portfolios. When government lent support to efforts that ended in failure, bank loan portfolios filled up with nonperforming assets.

The financial sector in China and Vietnam is dominated by a few large state-owned commercial banks. China also has a growing non-bank financial sector, but it is not discussed here. The state banks have the standard state enterprise problems, including soft budgets and management picked by higher-level government and party officials. In certain respects, the problems of the banks are worse than those of the state industrial enterprises. The banks are too large and too important to the national economy to be allowed to fail. These banks also face very little competition, except from a few small private banks and from the nonbank financial sector. Historically, under the Soviet command system, these banks were an integral part of the central bank, and their main role was to monitor compliance with the central plan. The normal service functions of a modern commercial bank were at best a sideline and were generally carried out in a highly bureaucratic manner. This inherited behavior has been slow to change.

If nonperforming loans were properly accounted for in their balance sheets, all of these banks would probably be classified as bankrupt.[12] Since most of the debt is owed domestically, however, the government can always step in and refinance these banks by using general revenues, by selling government bonds to the public, or by printing money. Bailing out the banks without reforming their behavior, however, will encourage those banks to continue making loans that will be classified as nonperforming, a problem that economists refer to as moral hazard. But, if the banks do not lend to state industrial enterprises, these firms will have to close down or stop paying their suppliers. Since many of these state industrial enterprises would be profitable if other enterprises paid their bills, simply cutting off bank loans to those who do not repay may lead to the bankruptcy of many potentially viable enterprises. Any real solution thus involves simultaneously sorting out the nonperforming assets of the banks and the accounts receivable that will never be received of industrial enterprises. Simultaneity in solving the problems of both sectors does not mean that the process has to be achieved overnight, but there has to be a concerted effort to change behavior in both sectors at the same time. Sequencing, where one deals first with only one sector and then the other, is not realistic in this context.

China in 1998 and 1999 began to come to grips with this complex problem of joint reform. One part of the solution was as much political as economic or administrative. Pressure on the banks to lend to losing state enterprises generally came from powerful political figures in the provinces. Provincial political leaders did not have to be concerned with the macroeconomic implications of excessive bank lending, so they used their power to support local firms. Bank officials in China traditionally were far down the ladder of political power and hence were in a weak position to resist these local political pressures. China, therefore, took steps to weaken the influence of politicians on the bankers. Earlier in the 1990s, when inflation was accelerating, this involved placing a powerful figure at the head of the banking system for the first time (Zhu Rongji). In the late 1990s, the jurisdiction of bank branches was made broad enough so that bank officials were not beholden to or under the thumb of only one local group of politicians. One way or another, China will have to get politicians out of the banking business if it wants to modernize the system.

The solution to the problem of the low quality of bank services in both China and Vietnam will probably only come through competition. Conceivably, domestic private banks could provide the necessary competition, but competition is more likely to be effective if it comes from established international banks. China's policy of allowing foreign banks first to set up full-service branches only in Pudong across the river from Shanghai and then to expand those privileges to a few other cities will have only a limited effect on the state banks. When China joins the WTO, however, one of the conditions of entry is the gradual movement of China to national treatment for all financial services, including banks.[13]

Reform of China's and Vietnam's banking system involves more than the improvement of commercial banking services or the efficient allocation of investment. Until the banking system is reformed, it will be difficult for China and Vietnam to implement a modern market-based system of macroeconomic management.

On paper, China and Vietnam appear to have modern banking systems much like those in the industrial nations. Both have central banks and a number of separate commercial banks, unlike the unitary banking system characteristic of the Soviet command system. The commercial banks lend to enterprises and charge interest, and the enterprises are required to pay back their loans. The problem with this picture is that it implies that the banks and enterprises behave the way they do in a market system. However, due to soft budgets and other reasons, neither the banks nor the enterprises behave in the appropriate manner.

As a result, the banking and monetary system runs in reverse. In a typical modern banking system, monetary policy begins with the central bank attempting to control the growth of high-powered money by buying or selling government bonds on the domestic market or by some other similar method. The high-powered money or the money base, together with the commercial bank reserve ratio, determines the money multiplier, which in turn determines the potential lending capacity of the commercial banks. The interest rate then brings the demand for credit in line with the actual or potential supply of credit.

When the growth of the money supply threatens to accelerate the rise in prices, the central bank cuts back on the growth of high-powered money, and the rest of the process follows more or less automatically.[14]

In China and Vietnam, however, higher interest rates do not easily deter lending because enterprises in many cases have no intention of paying back the loan in the first place. Backed by politicians, these enterprises pressure the banks to lend, and the banks often are too weak to resist. When the banks no longer have the funds to make further loans, they simply ask the central bank to provide them with whatever money they require. In the past, more often than not, the central bank complied.

When inflation accelerated, however, the top government leadership realized that something had to be done to rein in the growth in the money supply. Rather than try to control money growth indirectly by using market mechanisms to restrict the increase in the money base, the government simply set quotas on lending by the commercial banks. Each commercial bank was allowed to lend up to a certain limit and no more. As a method of controlling inflation, this procedure worked reasonably well. Twice in the case of China, first in 1990 and then again in 1995–96, price increases that had accelerated to more than 20 percent a year were brought down into the low single digits. But the procedure was also very inefficient. Any pretense of lending on the basis of commercial profitability criteria went out the window, and loans were allocated in accordance with administratively set quotas. This procedure did nothing to eliminate the underlying cause of inflationary pressure: the soft budget constraint of both the state enterprises and the commercial banks themselves.

The decisions to deal with both state enterprise and banking reform, therefore, are essential ingredients in China's efforts to move to a modern system of macroeconomic management based on indirect market mechanisms. Some of these mechanisms, a domestic government bond market for example, are already in place, at least in China. If the enterprise and commercial bank budget constraints can be hardened, open market operations on the government bond market should work in China, much as they do in other industrial countries.

The discussion to this point has assumed that macroeconomic policy in China would not have to deal with the problem of having complete capital account convertibility of the Chinese currency. Even in the face of the Asian currency crisis of 1997–98, it is likely that China could move to complete capital account convertibility without generating a run on the Chinese renminbi. China's huge foreign exchange reserves in 1998 and 1999 (US$154.7 billion at the end of 1999) and its large current account surpluses make it unlikely that China would default on its foreign loans, most of which are in long-term credits in any case. Even Vietnam, which had a large current account deficit and low foreign exchange reserves, did not feel the full brunt of the Asian financial crisis. One reason was that Vietnam had relatively little short-term foreign debt. The other reason was that the Vietnamese dong was not convertible on the capital account.

But if China at some future date had lower reserves, more short-term debt, and a substantial current account deficit, the danger of capital flight could be very real. In that context, the weaknesses of the Chinese banks and state enterprises could well support a full-fledged financial panic. The Chinese banking system has followed a path of government-directed lending and the accumulation of large portfolios of nonperforming assets, much like its counterparts in Korea and Southeast Asia. In many respects, reform of the Chinese banking system is little, if any, further along than was the case in Indonesia on the eve of the crisis. Reform of the Chinese banks and the state enterprises, therefore, is a prerequisite for full convertibility of the renminbi. Reforms of this sort are necessary in Vietnam as well, but Vietnam will also have to strengthen its current account situation before any consideration of capital account convertibility is possible.

The Impact of Reform on Economic Growth and Structure

Economic reform is not carried out for its own sake. The purpose of these reforms is to change the growth rate and structure of the economy. What can one say about the impact of reforms in China and Vietnam on the growth and structure of those two nations' economies? The data available make it possible to begin to answer this question for China. Data limitations and the relatively short reform period in Vietnam make judgments about the impact of the reforms more speculative.

The impact of the reforms on China's industrial structure can be seen from the data in figure 6.2. The Chinese decision to follow the

Soviet model led to a rapid rise in the share of heavy industry in the
1950s, a far greater rise than occurred elsewhere in East and Southeast Asia at a comparable level of per capita income. The mistakes of
the Great Leap Forward (1958–60) and the withdrawal of Soviet technical support in 1960 led paradoxically to an even larger rise in the
share of heavy industry.

With recovery from the Great Leap Forward completed, light industry recovered some of its pre–Great Leap share, and this share continued to rise slightly during the disruption of the Cultural Revolution in the late 1960s. Heavy industry's predominant position was then
restored during the calmer 1970s and lasted until the beginning of the
reform period. At the beginning of the reforms, a conscious effort was
made to shift more investment to light industry. During the first years
of the reform period, the light industry share rose again, but then
leveled off. From 1985 or 1986 onward, the shares of the two sectors
fluctuated only mildly, and the balance between the two presumably
reflected the influence of shifting market forces more than a centrally
directed effort to push one sector over the other. By 1998, when China's
per capita gross national product (GNP) reached or surpassed about
US$2,000 in purchasing power parity terms, the shares of light and

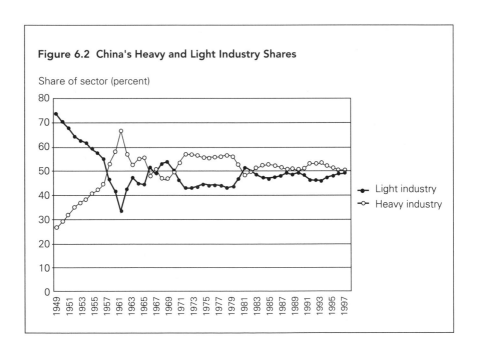

Figure 6.2 China's Heavy and Light Industry Shares

heavy industry were similar to the shares found elsewhere in the region at per capita income levels of US$2,000.[15]

As the country shifted toward a market economy, therefore, China's industrial structure changed to one much like that found in other market economies in the region. Correlation does not establish causation, but the increasing role of market forces in China is the most logical explanation for this result. In a market economy, it no longer made sense to produce steel and machinery for the main purpose of producing more steel and machinery. Ultimately, the consumer was supposed to benefit, and that meant more light industry products.

What was the impact of reform on efficiency? This chapter deals mainly with the modern industrial and service sector, but it is useful to begin a discussion of the impact of reform on productivity by looking at the whole economy. One important reason for beginning at this aggregate level is that available statistics allow one to say something reasonably systematic at this level, whereas more disaggregated figures are frequently not available. The relevant data are presented in table 6.2. The results of the growth-accounting calculations indicated that reforms brought about a major positive change and significantly raised the contribution of TFP to growth.

The other difference between the growth-accounting calculations in this chapter and those of most others who do calculations of this sort is that, here, an effort has been made to divide the periods into ones that reflect fundamental differences in policy and approach. In particular, I look at the performance of the economy in various prereform periods and then divide the post-1978 reform period into two separate decades. The first reform period begins with the agricultural and foreign trade reforms and includes the first efforts at industrial reform up through the onset of inflation in 1988. The second reform period starts with the conservative reaction to inflation and the Tiananmen student demonstrations and carries the story up through the first phases of the Asian financial crisis, with a major economic boom in between.

At the aggregate level, the post-1978 reforms had a dramatic and immediate impact on productivity growth. Total factor productivity rose from negative numbers to account for more than 4 percent of the annual increase in the GNP growth rate. As market-oriented reforms took hold, TFP continued to rise, particularly in the 1990s, when

Table 6.2 Sources of Growth in China, 1952–98

| Year | Growth rate | | | Share of national income[d] | | |
	Gross domestic product[a]	Capital[b]	Employment[c]	Total factor productivity	Labor	Capital
1952–57	6.2	4.81	2.78	2.608	0.6	0.4
1958–65	1.52	5.49	2.37	-2.098	0.6	0.4
1966–78	5	8.07	2.63	0.194	0.6	0.4
1979–88	9.9	10.1	3.07	4.018	0.6	0.4
1989–98 I	9.37	9.15	2.56	4.174	0.6	0.4
1989–98 II	9.08	9.15	2.56	3.884	0.6	0.4
1952–78	4.14	6.64	2.58	-0.064	0.6	0.4
1979–98	9.71	9.64	2.94	4.09	0.6	0.4

a. GDP growth rates are all derived from official data with the exception of estimate II for the 1989–98 period, which assumes a growth rate for GDP of 5 percent in 1978 because of the widespread belief that Chinese official GDP figures in 1998 exaggerate the growth rate and because some recent efforts to calculate an alternative rate suggest that the real rate may have been closer to 5 percent. The figures for growth rates in the other periods are not the same as one finds in the official handbooks because Chinese GDP by sector is recalculated in 1990 prices. This procedure eliminates the high growth rates for the prereform years that are produced by a price structure giving a very heavy weight to the faster-growing industrial sector. The 1990 prices are much closer to true market prices than the earlier prices used under the system of central planning.

b. Capital stock growth rates are estimated using the perpetual inventory method. Gross domestic capital formation in current prices is converted to constant prices using the ex-factory price index for industrial products for the years after 1978. For earlier years, the net material product price deflator for the industrial sector is used. A capital stock or gross capital formation deflator was not available. Deflation is a more serious problem for the post-1978 period, since prices prior to that changed very slowly.

c. Labor growth rates are the official estimates of the growth rate of employment. Data on hours actually worked are not available.

d. Labor and capital shares in national income are assumed on the basis of estimates from other economies with roughly similar levels of development. The results, particularly the changes in total factor productivity from one period to the next, are not very sensitive to the share estimates, although a higher labor share would raise total factor productivity in all periods and vice versa.

Source: The data are derived from official Chinese statistical sources with minor exceptions, which are detailed in the notes.

China's leaders finally committed themselves to creating a market economy. This result, obvious as it is from the data, is sufficiently controversial to warrant going behind these crude estimates to try to understand why one gets these results.

It has become conventional wisdom in some circles to argue that the East Asian experience was built not on productivity growth but on the rapid increase in inputs of capital and labor.[16] The extreme form of this argument is to state that East Asian growth is much like that of the Soviet Union in an earlier period and is likely to experience a similar fate. Is China the exception, or is China's experience much like that of the rest of East Asia? It is best to start with a review of what we know about possible refinements in these estimates for China that could moderate the conclusion reached about the impact of productivity on growth.[17]

To begin with, my estimates do not include improvements in the quality of the labor force. The data are available for estimating the growth rate of labor force quality, but such a task is well beyond the scope of this chapter. Education levels clearly have improved in China over the years, but much of the quantitative improvement occurred prior to 1978. The number of students enrolled in secondary school, for example, was the same in 1996 as in 1978 (the age cohort also declined as a result of the family planning program). Primary school enrollment tells a similar story. Only university-level enrollments expanded rapidly in the reform period, but such enrollments still accounted for less than 5 percent of the relevant age cohort in the mid-1990s. Any effort to attribute growth to improvements in labor force quality, therefore, must be based on an argument about improving educational quality. Such quality improvements clearly did occur, and in many respects they were the direct result of the economic reforms, but it is hard to measure quality improvements of this type.

The shift of labor from low-productivity jobs in agriculture to much higher-productivity work in urban areas and in township and village enterprises also can be seen as either an improvement in the quality of labor or, following the practice of Edward Dennison, as an explanation for the rise in TFP. In the two decades beginning in 1978 and ending in 1998, employment in agriculture fell from 71 to 50 percent of total employment.[18] Put differently, of the total increase in China's labor force of 298 million workers between 1978 and 1998, more than 230 million found jobs outside of agriculture. These industrial and service jobs may not appear to be high-productivity occupations to the casual observer. The alternative for these workers, however, was to share extremely low-productivity activities in agriculture, where there were already 100 million or more workers than were needed to maintain farm output.[19]

There is little question that there were major improvements in the quality of the capital stock, and some of these improvements may not be captured in the estimates used to calculate the figures in table 6.2.

One clear improvement was the switch to far greater reliance on imported machinery and equipment than was the case during the period of "self-reliance" prior to 1977. It is unlikely that the impact of these imported capital goods is fully captured because many such imports not only were of higher quality but also cost less to purchase once China had the necessary foreign exchange. But the great increase in imported capital goods was a major object of and a direct result of the reforms. It is at least as plausible to speak of these improvements as a source of productivity improvement than simply as an accumulation of more input.

Total factor productivity, with or without the adjustments, therefore, explains much of the rise in China's GNP growth in the reform period. The continual rise in the TFP rate is also notable and is different from the experience of either Korea or Taiwan Province. In Korea and Taiwan Province, the period of high growth began with a five- to seven-year spurt in productivity. TFP growth then fell, however, and much of the high growth in these two economies over the next decade or two is explained by the steady rise in the rate of gross capital formation.[20] Why was the Chinese experience apparently so different? China, Taiwan Province, and Korea did not conduct much research and development (R&D) in the first decades of rapid growth. Differences in the pattern of R&D expenditures, therefore, cannot be the explanation. One plausible explanation for the difference is that China during the period of Stalinist development had strayed far from the most-efficient development path. There were, therefore, far more opportunities for productivity improvement than was the case in Taiwan Province and Korea. TFP growth in China during the first six years of reform (1979–84) was carried by the spurt in agriculture that followed decollectivization. After 1984, agriculture slowed down, but efforts to reform industry began and resulted in a dramatic rise in the output of township and village enterprises. Beginning in 1992 with Deng Xiaoping's famous trip to Guangdong Province, China fully committed itself to completing the move to a market system. The reforms that followed sustained the growth in TFP at least until the onset of the Asian financial crisis and the overall slowdown in Chinese growth in 1998.

A different perspective on the same phenomenon begins from the fact that the rate of gross capital formation as a share of GDP was already extremely high in China in the decade prior to reform. In the years 1970 through 1978, China's rate of gross capital formation as a share of gross domestic product averaged 35 percent each year (China, National Bureau of Statistics 1999a: 6). The average gross capital formation rate over the next decade (1979–88) was 36 percent. Thus China, unlike Taiwan and Korea, through state efforts to hold down incomes and consumption, achieved very high rates of investment prior to beginning reform, but much of that investment was wasted. Taiwan and Korea, in contrast, had low rates of investment both before and immediately after the beginning of reform. Reforms led to higher productivity growth, which then stimulated a rise in the rate of investment.

Studies of the industrial sector based on more disaggregated data also suggest that at least part of the rise in TFP in the economy as a whole was explained by a rise in TFP in industry itself.[21] The weakness of all of these studies, from the point of view of this chapter, is that they deal only with the post-1978 reform period, largely because the required disaggregated input data do not exist for earlier periods. There is also a significant difference in the findings of at least two of the studies with respect to the performance of state-owned industry.

The main finding of Jefferson, Rawski, and Zheng (1992) is that all industrial sectors (classified by ownership) enjoyed positive TFP growth throughout the 1980–92 period. TFP growth among the TVEs and other collective enterprises, however, was much higher, more than double, the rate of TFP growth in state-owned industrial enterprises. Woo and others (1994) agree that TFP was high in the collective sector, but dispute the finding that state industrial enterprise TFP was positive.[22] Li's data only cover the years 1981–87, but they are disaggregated by industrial sector rather than by ownership (Li and others 1993). In these estimates, TFP for 18 of the 24 industrial sectors was positive, with machinery and transport equipment enjoying the highest rate of TFP growth.[23] The industries with sharply negative TFP growth included electric power, post and telecommunications, and tobacco products. The mining sectors experienced either no significant productivity growth or, in the case of petroleum and nonferrous metals, sharply negative rates. Finally, Xiao and his coauthors use a large survey of enterprises done in 1995–97 to measure TFP by both ownership and industrial sector categories (Xiao and others 1998).

Their survey shows that a higher percentage of foreign-invested and private enterprises had high TFP than either state-owned or collective enterprises, but in comparing sectors, the best-performing sectors were those dominated by large state monopolies such as petroleum and gas or tobacco.

These studies of industrial performance lend weak support to the view that reforms led to improvements in industrial performance. The best evidence for this view is the high productivity growth in the collective ownership sector as contrasted with that in the state-owned enterprises. Unfortunately, one cannot say anything about the change in productivity that came with the shift away from the Stalinist development strategy of the pre-1979 period because data at the necessary level of disaggregation do not yet exist.

Vietnam's reform period is much briefer than that of China, and the data needed to come up with reliable estimates of capital stock growth and total factor productivity growth are not available. The limited data that are available have been used to make the estimates reported in table 6.3. As the data in the table suggest, despite large-scale aid from the Soviet Union, Vietnamese economic growth in the period before the reforms was very slow, and total factor productivity growth was negligible. In per capita terms, with population growing at 2 percent a year (1976–90), real growth was barely over 1 percent a year, and that estimate may well be too high since it depends on the questionable reliability of the relatively high growth rates reported for the early 1980s. In the 1990s, as is well known, GDP growth accelerated to East Asian levels, but the larger share of this increase was accounted for by the even more rapid increase in the growth rate of capital stock. Total factor productivity growth did rise, as one would expect given the opening up of the economy and the greater reliance on market forces, but by a lesser amount than was the case during the first phase of reform in China.[24] If the analysis in this chapter is accurate, even this level of productivity growth might not be sustainable unless Vietnam moves much more decisively to reduce the barriers to investment outside of the state-owned sector. The growth rate in Vietnam in the years 1998 and 1999 was sharply lower than in the first years after reform, and it is likely that total factor productivity fell, but we do not have the necessary capital formation data with which to estimate TFP.

Productivity data, therefore, lend weak support to the qualitative analysis of economic reform in the modern industrial and service sectors of China and Vietnam. The reforms did make a large measurable difference. In China that difference shows up mainly as a rise in total factor productivity. In Vietnam, the opening of the economy to the hard-currency world led to higher investment levels from both domestic and foreign sources, but the improvements in efficiency, particularly outside of agriculture, were more modest.

Neither country, however, is in a position to rest on its past accomplishments if it wants to maintain the high growth rates of the 1990s. In Vietnam's case, the period of easy increases in national product may already be over. The period of easy increases in productivity may be over in China as well. The large spurt in agricultural productivity growth was a one-shot affair that ended after 1984. The TVEs then played the dominant role in sustaining high GDP growth over the next decade, and there was a further boost from the rapid acceleration of foreign direct investment in the early 1990s and very high rates of growth of exports. The acceleration of market reforms after Deng Xiaoping's trip to the South in 1992 may have temporarily boosted productivity growth even further. If many of these productivity-inducing reforms have largely spent their force, as is likely, where will the next burst in high productivity and GDP growth come from? It is not likely to come from state-led infrastructure development programs like those in 1998 and 1999, however desirable that new infrastructure may have been. It will have to come from within the enterprises themselves, but it is not clear whether China's industrial and financial sector enterprises are ready to take on this role.

CONCLUSIONS

Both China and Vietnam have made remarkable economic progress over the past decade or two, but a successful past does not ensure an equally successful future. If high rates of growth are to be sustained, it is likely that both countries will have to carry out a series of major reforms in how they develop their industrial and financial sectors. I would like to propose the following policy and institutional reforms:

Table 6.3 Sources of Growth in Vietnam, 1976–96

Period	Growth rate of net material product (1975–90) or gross domestic product (1990–96) or	Growth rate (percent)		
		Capital	Labor	Total factor productivity
1976–80	0.4	5.4	—	—
1980–86	6.4	1.9	—	—
1986–90	3.3	3.3	3.1	0.1
1990–96	8.4	10.4	2.7	2.6

— Not available.
Source: The Vietnamese data available for use in growth-accounting exercises of this sort are very limited. GDP data are available only for the period from 1990 in sources such as Vietnam, General Statistical Office (1997) and from World Bank publications. Data for earlier years are taken from Vietnam, General Statistical Office (1991), which also includes data for years prior to 1986. The data are for net material product and accumulation, however, not GDP and gross capital formation. The Vietnamese data on accumulation appear to materially understate the level of capital formation, so assumptions have been made to adjust the data. The shares of labor and capital in national income are assumed to be similar to the shares used in the calculations for China.

1. Both countries should resist the temptation to adopt a Korean- or Japanese-style industrial policy and should continue to reduce government intervention in industrial development, recognizing that government intervention will remain much larger than would be the case in some ideal free-market economy.

2. They will have to complete the process of transforming state-owned enterprises into fully autonomous firms facing hard budget constraints and no longer responsible for a wide range of worker housing and social welfare activities.

3. The state should abandon its role in the selection of enterprise managers and should turn that role over to enterprise shareholders and their elected representatives on company boards of directors.

4. They will have to complete the process of creating a modern independent banking system where government is not involved to any significant degree in lending decisions.

5. In the case of Vietnam, there should be recognition that the private sector is a vital part of any future development program and not just a sector to be vigilantly regulated and controlled. China has accomplished much in this regard, but still has a way to go.

6. While letting mergers and acquisitions happen in response to market considerations of enterprises themselves, government should do more to set the rules governing mergers and acquisitions.

7. Vietnam will have to make the economic changes required to arrive at a trade agreement with the United States and eventual membership in the World Trade Organization.

This list could be extended without difficulty, but the main point is clear. Even ignoring issues such as rural poverty, uneven regional development, and much else that is well beyond the scope of this chapter, China and Vietnam have a lot to do in the area of reform if they want the next decade or two to be as successful as the previous decades have been. Although both countries can learn from the experiences of their East Asian neighbors and from others, China and Vietnam face a situation that is different from that of their neighbors in several fundamental ways. First, the structure of their economies is different in important respects from that of their neighbors at a comparable stage of development, which inhibits or precludes the duplication of Korea's or Japan's industrial and financial policies of the 1960s and 1970s. Similarly, China and Vietnam do not have the political and social underpinnings of an efficient industrial policy that eschews politics and corruption. And, finally, the global economic system has changed from what it was as recently as the 1970s. The current rules of the international economic system as established in the 1990s give China and Vietnam a choice between adopting an activist industrial and financial policy on the model of Japan or Korea or participating fully in the WTO and the global economy. There is little doubt which of those choices is most likely to provide long-term benefits to the economies of China and Vietnam. If China and Vietnam are to take full advantage of the global economic system, they must devise paths that are consistent with their own conditions as well as with the requirements of the international economy.

NOTES

1. The formal definition includes requirements such as that they are established legally, are able to take civil liability, possess and use their assets independently, are entitled to sign contracts with other units, and are financially independent and compile their own balance sheets.
2. Village industrial enterprises prior to 1984 were included in agricultural output.

3. A good example of a firm that is likely to remain under state ownership is the Guizhou Aluminum Complex, which I visited in May 1999. The complex produced 1.87 million tons of aluminum products, owned a number of low-cost bauxite mines that provided most of its raw material, and was highly profitable, earning profits plus taxes of 2.5 billion yuan in 1998.

4. The Korean heavy and chemical industry drive of the 1970s was and is controversial. Studies that see the drive as an unqualified success include Amsden (1989). For a more mixed assessment, see Stern and others (1995).

5. The concept of corruption itself evolves over time. The Japanese practice of *amakudare*, whereby a government official, on retiring, often took a job in the industry that he had regulated, was long praised as being one reason for the close cooperation between business and government in Japan. By the late 1990s, Japanese increasingly saw this system as creating serious conflicts of interest among its government regulators, and the practice began to be phased out.

6. Of the 85 countries ranked in Transparency International's Corruption Perceptions Index, China was tied with Zambia in fifty-second place, and Vietnam was tied with Kenya for seventy-fourth place (number one, Denmark, had the least corruption). Indexes of this sort are highly subjective and not very reliable, since few people, if any, are qualified to make the kinds of comparisons called for, except in the crudest possible way. However, they do indicate where a country's corruption stands vis-à-vis the most- and least-corrupt nations.

7. In Japan, as elsewhere, roughly half of all gross capital formation was carried out by the state during the first decades of modern economic growth.

8. These infrastructure projects can also be provided by the private sector and are, in some cases, being provided by private investors in China and, to a much lesser degree, in Vietnam. It is highly unlikely, however, that the private sector will be the major provider of infrastructure in these two countries.

9. There is also, by now, a very large literature on the nature of TVE property rights, organization, and so forth. See, for example, Che and Qian (1998); Hai (1997); Huang and Cai (1998).

10. For a contrast with the way POSCO is run and a discussion of the way in which China runs its large state-owned enterprises in key sectors such as steel, see Steinfeld (1998); Otsuka, Liu, and Murakami (1998).

11. There is by now a very large literature on foreign direct investment in China. For one recent study, see Ishihara (1998).

12. For one discussion of the possible magnitude of nonperforming loans in China, see Lardy (1998).

13. If China were to move to a fully liberalized financial system with private banks and market-determined interest rates, one danger is that it would lose the seigniorage revenue that it now receives, not only from the issuance of currency but also from the below-market rates paid to depositors. One estimate puts this seigniorage revenue as equivalent to 5 percent of GDP in China (Fry 1998). I am indebted to Ronald McKinnon for pointing this out.

14. For a more in-depth study of the way inflation was generated in the banking and financial system of China in the early 1990s, see Yi (1994).

15. The division between heavy and light industry is not identical to the division between consumer and producer goods, but the two concepts are close enough for the purposes of this analysis.

16. World Bank (1993) also stresses the importance of productivity growth to the high rates of growth in East Asia.

17. There have been other growth-accounting estimates for China. One of the more careful is by Jingwen Li and his associates. Li's periodization is different from this study's, but, with a few notable exceptions, his results are similar to those here. Specifically, he gets a negative rate of TFP for the 1953–78 period (-0.8 percent) and a positive rate for 1979–90 (2.5 percent). His underlying labor force growth series is also very close to the one used in this study. His capital stock growth rate is very different from the one in this study for the 1950s and, to a lesser degree, the 1960s, but the differences in the two estimates are small thereafter. Basically, Li gets very high capital stock growth rates in the 1950s and 1960s. My estimates are much lower, probably because I have deflated the earlier capital stock figures by a price index that, in my opinion, takes better account of the very high relative prices of industrial products in those earlier periods. There may also be some difference between the assumptions made in this study and in Li's about the initial capital stock in 1952, and this would affect capital stock growth rates in the early period, but not in the later years. Li's GDP/NMP growth rate for the prereform period is also higher than the one used in this study, and that difference is mainly due to the fact that earlier year NMP in this study was deflated to take out the bias caused by very high relative industrial prices in the 1950s through the 1970s, whereas Li's figures are closer to the official estimates that retain this bias. Li and others (1993: 52–56).

18. These figures are for employment in the primary sector, which includes mining, but the overwhelming majority of workers in this sector are in agriculture.

19. In formal terms, this statement implies that the marginal product of labor in agriculture was zero, which was not the case. But marginal productivity was extremely low, well below what workers could earn in rural nonfarm occupations.

20. This conclusion is controversial because it appears to contradict the findings of Alwyn Young (1995) and Lawrence Lau (Kim and Lau 1994). But Young does not calculate the sources of growth for the initial years of high growth in Taiwan (1961–65). In Korea, calculations by myself and Lora Sabin suggest that Young may have made assumptions about the initial capital stock, among others, that result in too low a TFP estimate for these early years (Perkins and Sabin forthcoming). Lawrence Lau's very different methodology suggests that TFP in these two economies was negligible, but his estimates also indicate that there were substantial economies of scale at the aggregate level. Scale economies, in an aggregate production function, are not necessarily much different from increases in total factor productivity in a production function with no economies of scale, a finding that also goes back to Edward Dennison. These issues are argued further in a forthcoming study of Taiwan by Hsueh, Perkins, and Hsu.

21. The studies referred to here are Li and others (1993, ch. 3); Jefferson, Rawski, and Zheng (1992); Woo and others (1994). There has also been a subsequent

debate between the authors of the last two studies over the sources of differences in their estimates.

22. The difference is due to how the two sets of authors deflate industrial value added.

23. This statement refers to four sectors: machinery, electrical machinery, motor vehicles, and other transport equipment.

24. One can speculate about why the growth rate of TFP in Vietnam was relatively low during the first phase of reforms, but the data are so weak that one cannot put much weight on such speculation. It may have been the case, for example, that Vietnamese agriculture, particularly in the south, was not as distorted by the collectivization effort simply because it did not last long. Thus there were fewer productivity gains to be had from abandoning collectivization than was the case in China. The data are also consistent with a widespread view that much of Vietnam's growth in the 1990s, particularly in the industrial sector, was driven by a large influx of capital from abroad in the form of foreign direct investment and international and bilateral aid. This influx made high growth possible in industry, despite the slow pace of reform in that sector.

REFERENCES

The word "processed" describes informally reproduced works that may not be commonly available through library systems.

Amsden, Alice. 1989. *Asia's Next Giant: South Korea and Late Industrialization.* Oxford: Oxford University Press.

Che, Jiahua, and Yingyi Qian. 1998. "Institutional Environment, Community Government, and Corporate Governance: Understanding China's Township-Village Enterprises." *Journal of Law, Economics, and Organization* 14(1):1–23.

China, National Bureau of Statistics. 1999a. *Comprehensive Statistical Data and Materials on 50 Years of New China.* Beijing: China Statistics Press.

———. 1999b. *Statistical Communiqué of the People's Republic of China on the 1998 National Economic and Social Development.* Beijing: China Statistical Publishing House.

———. 2000. *Statistical Communiqué of the People's Republic of China on the 1999 National Economic and Social Development.* Beijing: China Statistical Publishing House.

China, State Statistical Bureau. 1997. *China Statistical Yearbook 1997.* Beijing: China Statistics Publishers.

———. 1998. *China Statistical Yearbook 1998.* Beijing: China Statistical Publishing House.

Fry, Maxwell J. 1998. "Can Seigniorage Revenue Keep China's Financial System Afloat?" In Donald J. S. Brean, ed., *Taxation in Modern China.* New York: Routledge.

Gerschenkron, Alexander. 1962. *Economic Backwardness in Historical Perspective*. Cambridge, Mass.: Harvard University Press.

Goh, Keng Swee. 1992. "Xinjiapo jingji fazhande jingyan ji qianying: zhanlueh busho ji shishi qingkuang." East Asian Institute Offprint. Singapore (July 27). Processed.

Hai, Wen, ed. 1997. *Zhongguo xiangzhen qiye yanjiu*. Beijing: China Industry and Commerce Publishers.

Hsueh, Li-Min, Dwight H. Perkins, and Chen-Kuo Hsu. 2000. *Industrial Development and the Role of the State in Taiwan* (forthcoming).

Huang, Yiping, and Fang Cai. 1998. "Myths and Realities of China's Rural Industrial Miracles." Paper presented at the Asia Pacific Economics Seminar, Australian National University, Canberra, Australia. July. Processed.

Ishihara, Kyoichi, ed. 1998. *Chugoku keizai to Gaishi [China's Economy and Foreign Investment]*. Tokyo: Institute of Developing Economies.

Jefferson, Gary, Thomas Rawski, and Yuxin Zheng. 1992. "Growth, Efficiency, and Convergence in China's State and Collective Industry." *Economic Development and Cultural Change* 40(January):239–66.

Jones, Leroy P., and Il Sakong. 1980. *Government, Business, and Entrepreneurship in Economic Development: The Korean Case*. Cambridge, U.K.: Council on East Asian Studies.

Kim, Jong-Il, and Lawrence J. Lau. 1994. "The Sources of Economics Growth of the East Asian Newly Industrialized Countries." *Journal of the Japanese and International Economies* 8:235–71.

Lardy, Nicholas. 1998. *China's Unfinished Economic Revolution*. Washington, D.C.: Brookings Institution.

Li, Jingwen, Dale W. Jorgenson, Zheng Youjing, and Masahiro Kuroda. 1993. *Productivity and Economic Growth in China, USA, and Japan [in Chinese]*. Beijing: Social Science Publishers.

Otsuka, Kenjiro, Deqiang Liu, and Naoki Murakami. 1998. *Industrial Reform in China: Past Performance and Future Prospects*. Oxford: Clarendon Press.

Steinfeld, Edward S. 1998. *Forging Reform in China: The Fate of State-Owned Industry*. Cambridge, U.K.: Cambridge University Press.

Stern, Joseph J., Ji-Hong Kim, Dwight H. Perkins, and Jung-ho Yoo. 1995. *Industrialization and the State: The Korean Heavy and Chemical Industry Drive*. Cambridge, Mass.: Harvard Institute for International Development.

Sun, Yun-Wing. 1991. *The China-Hong Kong Connection: The Key to China's Open-Door Policy*. Cambridge, U.K.: Cambridge University Press.

Vietnam, General Statistical Office. 1991. *Economy and Finance of Vietnam, 1986–1990*. Hanoi: Statistical Publishing House.

———. 1994. *Cong Nghiep Viet Nam*. Hanoi: Statistical Publishing House.

———. 1997. *Statistical Yearbook 1996*. Hanoi: Statistical Publishing House.

Woo, Wing Thye, Wen Hai, Yibiao Jin, and Gang Fan. 1994. "How Successful Has

Chinese Enterprise Reform Been? Pitfalls in Opposite Biases and Focus." *Journal of Comparative Economics* 18(June):410–37.

World Bank. 1993. *The East Asian Miracle: Economic Growth and Public Policy.* New York: Oxford University Press.

———. 1997. *Vietnam: Deepening Reform for Growth.* Washington, D.C.

Xiao, Geng, Liu Fujiang, Xing Junling, He Ping, and Yu Xiaoyuan. 1998. "Performance of China's Core Industrial Enterprises during the Period of Structural and Macroeconomic Adjustments: 1995–1997." (December 9). Processed.

Yi, Gang. 1994. *Money, Banking, and Financial Markets in China.* Boulder, Colo.: Westview Press.

Young, Alwyn. 1995. "The Tyranny of Numbers: Confronting the Statistical Realities of the East Asian Growth Experience." *Quarterly Journal of Economics* 110(August):651–80.

CHAPTER 7

GOVERNMENT CONTROL IN CORPORATE GOVERNANCE AS A TRANSITIONAL INSTITUTION: LESSONS FROM CHINA

Yingyi Qian

n East Asian economies, governments generally maintain a close relationship with business enterprises through formal or information channels. There are two prevailing views on these ties. In one view, the government helps business in the presence of market failure, and thus the close ties are one source of East Asia's miracle (the "market failure view"). In another view, the government's close ties with business result in corruption and crony capitalism and thus are one reason for East Asia's bubble (the "corrupt government view").

Although both views contain some truth, they also overlook important institutional realities of these economies at different stages of development. The market failure view focuses narrowly on explanations such as monopolies and externalities, missing other important institutional factors. The corrupt government view looks for a market system as it exists in the West, which is the result of hundreds of years of evolution and is not a realistic and immediate expectation for most other countries.

This chapter proposes a third view derived from examining China's experience in the past two decades of economic reform and development. China is an important part of the East Asian miracle, although it is not included in the original World Bank study on the subject (World Bank 1993). Between 1978 and 1998, China achieved about 9 percent growth, accounting for about two-thirds of all growth in the world's low-income countries. On a per capita basis, China's gross domestic product (GDP) grew about 8 percent a year and thus more than quadrupled in two decades. Clearly, China's economic performance is comparable with that of the original eight high-performing East Asian economies including Hong Kong, Indonesia, Japan, the Republic of Korea, Malaysia, Singapore, Taiwan (China), and Thailand. However, China has a population about three times that of all these economies combined, which makes achieving this performance even more impressive.

China differs from the other East Asian economies on one crucial institutional dimension. Two decades ago, when the current development started, China had a centrally planned system, similar to that of Eastern Europe and the former Soviet Union, in which public ownership dominated the means of production. China's high growth during the past two decades was closely associated with the profound and dynamic institutional reform that transformed China from a centrally planned to an emerging-market economy. China's institutional change played a more striking role in this transformation than did that in the other East Asian economies. Examining China's case can help us to rethink key aspects of development in East Asian economies.

China's transition from a planned to a market economy occurred in two stages: the first stage took place during the 15 years between 1978 and 1993, and the second stage began in 1994 (Qian 1999). In the first stage, reform was carried out incrementally to improve incentives and increase the scope of the market for resource allocation. Because the basic institutional framework of central planning remained, many institutional innovations were designed to respond to particular constraints in the planning system or to take advantage of loopholes in it. Beginning in 1994, China's reform entered the second stage. The milestone in the course of China's reform was the November 1993 decision of the Chinese Communist Party ("Decision on Issues Concerning the Establishment of a Socialist Market Economic Structure"). In essence, this decision recognizes the limits of previous reforms as the economy develops and seeks to establish a modern market system that eventually will incorporate international institutions recognized as "best practice."

The dynamics of government and business relationships are quite different in the two stages of reform. In the first stage, the government became more, rather than less, involved in enterprises. The government (especially the local government) was directly involved in corporate governance through its ownership and control. Indeed, in the first stage, because market and legal institutions were poorly developed, maintaining or even increasing government control in enterprises yielded certain advantages, albeit second-best ones. The miracle was that in spite of (or because of) pervasive government ownership and control of enterprises, the Chinese economy grew strongly and outperformed other transition economies.

However, in the second stage, building market-supporting institutions, including legal institutions, became the main focus of reform. As government's control over enterprises became more and more costly, the government started to retreat by means of privatization, corporatization, and securitization. Although China weathered the Asian financial crisis, the institutional reform and the government retreat from control over enterprises proceeded at a moderate pace and have not yet been implemented fully. The experience of the past few years has demonstrated that deeper institutional reforms are essential but can be very difficult to achieve.

This perspective leads us to the view that government control of firms can be a transitional institution during the process of economic development. The relationship between the government and business enterprises should be studied by considering the overall institutional environment at a particular stage of development. In China, the level of economic development and the institutional environment were quite different in the first and the second stages. Therefore, the relationship between government and business should be examined through a dynamic rather than a static perspective.

The view that government control in corporate governance is a transitional institution consists of three major arguments. First, based on the modern theory of firm and corporate governance and the empirical evidence in the past decades, economists generally agree that government ownership and control of firms do not have obvious advantages over private ownership and control under well-established market institutions and with reasonable assumptions about the government's behavior. However, government ownership and control of firms clearly have major disadvantages. The government not only is concerned with economic matters but often has political objectives as well. In some sense, we do not want to have a government that has strong profit motives because we may want it to act when the private sector has no incentives to do so. Another major problem with the government concerns its ability to make a commitment. A big difference between government and the private sector is its power: the more powerful the government is, the harder it is for it to make a credible commitment. Finally, even without the problems of objectives and commitment, there is still a problem of overload. If the government is overwhelmed with too many things, its efficiency declines quickly beyond its "core competence" of the provision and regulation of public goods.

Second, both government and market institutions are imperfect, and their development will take some time. Given these institutional failures, there are economic reasons (in addition to political reasons) for government control in corporate governance as a second-best response in the primitive stage of economic development. This is analyzed in this chapter from two perspectives. Government ownership and control may have comparative advantages over private control in an imperfect institutional environment, such as when there is a lack of rule of law in securing property rights, a lack of a functioning capital market, and a lack of adequate taxation and fiscal institutions. This argument explains why some types (but not others) of government ownership of firms, such as township-village enterprises, have been more successful than private ownership. Furthermore, even if government ownership and control are inefficient, there are still economic arguments for delaying the privatization of existing state firms, such as the lack of a social safety net, the lack of a legal framework for corporate governance, and the lack of regulatory institutions for special industries (such as banks).

Third, because government ownership and control of firms are not the first-best arrangement, the government should eventually exit corporate governance, as is happening in China in the second stage of reform. Indeed, the institutional and market environment changes over time, so the costs and benefits of government control of firms change accordingly. What is the mechanism to facilitate the government in exiting corporate governance and avoiding a trap in which the government, to defend its vested interests, resists moving away from corporate control? Two factors seem relevant to institutional changes: a flexible economy and the right government incentives. The incentives for privatization require harder budget constraints and increased competition. The recent emerging local government–driven privatization in China provides an example.

The rest of the chapter is organized as follows. First I examine the changing role of government in corporate governance in China during the past two decades in the context of two stages of development (Qian 1999). Then I argue that, although they have major disadvantages over the long run, government ownership and control in corporate governance can be a second-best response during the first stage of reform and development. This is followed by an investigation of reform in the second stage, focusing on the mechanisms needed to induce the government's exit from corporate governance in a smooth yet "incentive-compatible" way. The final section concludes that government ownership and control of corporate governance can be better understood as a transitional institution and draws lessons for other countries.

THE TWO-STAGE EVOLUTION OF GOVERNMENT CONTROL IN CORPORATE GOVERNANCE IN CHINA

China's economic reform has evolved in two stages. The first stage spanned about 15 years between 1979 and 1993, and the second stage began in 1994 and is ongoing. Unlike countries in Eastern Europe and the former Soviet Union, where incremental reforms and transition to markets were sharply divided by the events of political democratization, China has featured much political continuity in this reform period. Nevertheless, the division between the stages is clearly marked by the November 1993 decision (Qian 1999). This decision concerns many areas of economic reform, including the government-business relationship. The dynamics of the role of government in enterprises had quite different patterns in the first and second stages of reform, and it is useful to examine the two stages separately.

The First Stage (1979–93): Increasing Government Control in Corporate Governance

At the outset of economic reform in 1978, China was a centrally planned economy with state ownership dominating the nonagriculture sector.

Private ownership of the means of production was prohibited in all activities. During the next 15 years, China's industrial sector grew very fast and displayed three major features.

First, private ownership and control of firms played only a minor role. The prohibition of private ownership of firms was lifted after 1979, but by 1993, private enterprises only accounted for less than 15 percent of national industrial output. The remainder of national industrial output was contributed by firms that were involved with government ownership and control. During this stage of reform, private ownership mainly consisted of two types of firms: very small-scale "individual-ownership" firms, which are private firms employing less than eight employees, and foreign-invested firms.

Second, the growth engine of the economy did not come from old state-owned enterprises (SOEs) either. Rather, it came from new nonstate enterprises, especially rural "collective" enterprises known as township-village enterprises (TVEs). TVEs are essentially community (township or village) government-controlled enterprises, whose share in national industrial output increased from 9 percent in 1978 to 27 percent in 1993. In 1993 TVEs employed more than 50 million people. Other types of nonstate and nonprivate firms include joint ventures between the government and foreign investors and stock companies in which the government owns majority shares. In both cases, some government agencies exercise effective control in corporate governance.

Third, privatization of SOEs was delayed. In fact, there was no privatization or even layoffs of workers in SOEs in the first stage of reform. During this period, the state sector continued to expand in absolute size, including assets, investment, employment, and output, and in all industrial sectors. But the relative share of the state sector declined due to the growth of the nonstate sector. True, many reforms were carried out in the state sector for the purpose of expanding the autonomy of enterprises and increasing their profit incentives. Nevertheless, in most important dimensions, such as appointments and finance, the government still had the ultimate authority over enterprises through its sole ownership.

Except for its intervention in day-to-day decisions, government actually increased its control in enterprises during this stage through (a) the rapid expansion of TVEs and other enterprises controlled by local government and (b) the expansion of SOEs in absolute scale. There-fore, during the first 15 years, government control in corporate governance increased rather than decreased.

The Second Stage (1994 to the Present): Decreasing Government Control in Corporate Governance

During the first stage of reform, China's GDP grew rapidly, and the living standard of ordinary citizens improved significantly. For example, an average Chinese consumer increased his or her consumption about three times for edible vegetable oil, pork, and eggs. The number of people living in absolute poverty was substantially reduced from 250 million to less than 100 million. By the end of 1993, reform was supported by people in all walks of life simply because everybody benefited from it. This contrasted with the dismal performance in Eastern European reforming countries, such as Hungary and Poland, in the late 1980s.

By the end of 1993, China's economic landscape had changed dramatically. The state sector was no longer the dominant sector of the economy: the state's share of industrial output accounted for 43 percent of the national total in 1993, and the share of SOE employment in total nonagricultural employment was also down to about 30 percent. About 90 percent of prices (in terms of output values) were liberalized, and the economy became substantially more open to foreign competition. The change in economic fundamentals and the shift in the mind-set of China's leaders altered the costs and benefits of the government's role in corporate governance. Since 1994, the development of the government-business relationship has taken a new direction, as reflected in the following three areas.

First, small- and medium-size private enterprises emerged as the new engine of growth. By 1998, private enterprises accounted for 37 percent of total industrial output and for more than 50 percent of retail sales of consumer goods. In this respect, the most striking example is Zhejiang province. With a population the size of the Republic of Korea's, Zhejiang has been the star performer since 1994. Its outstanding economic performance is closely related to its extraordinarily fast development of privately owned enterprises, which accounted for 57 percent of its industrial output by 1998. In 1998,

Zhejiang became the first province in which private industry accounted for more than half of its industrial output.

Second, privatization of small- and medium-size SOEs and TVEs and massive layoffs of state employees began, driven mainly by local government initiatives. Unlike in Eastern Europe and Russia, in China privatization was driven not by ideology or political agenda, but by economic and financial realities. Privatization proceeded rapidly in 1996 and 1997, but slowed down in 1998 and 1999, partly because of the Asian financial crisis. Privatization also progressed unevenly across provinces. Some provinces (such as Zhejiang and Guangdong) moved quite fast, while others (such as the Northeast provinces) moved relatively slowly. In some cities (such as Shanghai) the majority of state enterprises in a particular industry (such as textiles) closed down.

Third, transforming large-size SOEs was very slow between 1994 and 1998, and the policy of "grasping the large and releasing the small" produced few results for large-size enterprises up to 1998. But the 1999 September decision on SOE reform may signal a breakthrough. This decision introduced three major new policies: (a) readjustment of the layout of the state economy to narrow dramatically its scope, (b) diversification of the ownership structure of those enterprises over which the state still wants to maintain control, and (c) establishment of effective corporate governance according to international standards. New development followed soon after this decision. For instance, the government regulatory body, the China Securities Regulatory Commission, was authorized to promulgate the regulations on selling state shares. Several large state enterprises were reorganized to seek listings abroad. For example, China Telecom (Hong Kong) was listed on the Hong Kong Stock Exchange, and PetroChina was listed in the West. The Legend Group, the largest maker of personal computers in China, distributed 35 percent of its shares to its managers and engineers in 1999.

A clear shift of direction is occurring. The emergence of private enterprises occurred rapidly, although the privatization of small- and medium-size SOEs and TVEs was uneven across provinces as well as over time. The transformation of large-size SOEs got off to a very slow start but showed signs of acceleration in early 2000.

INSTITUTIONAL ENVIRONMENT AND GOVERNMENT IN CORPORATE GOVERNANCE: A SECOND-BEST PERSPECTIVE

This section argues that government ownership and control of firms do not have obvious advantages over private ownership and control under well-established market institutions and with reasonable assumptions about the government's behavior. However, both government and market institutions are imperfect, and their development will take some time. Given these institutional failures, there are economic reasons (in addition to political reasons) for government control in corporate governance as a second-best response in the primitive stage of economic development. This is analyzed from two perspectives. Government ownership and control may have comparative advantages over private control in the imperfect institutional environment, such as when there is lack of rule of law in securing property rights, lack of a functioning capital market, and lack of adequate taxation and fiscal institutions. This argument explains why some types of government ownership of firms, such as township-village enterprises, have been more successful than private ownership. Furthermore, even if government ownership and control are inefficient, there still are economic arguments for delaying the privatization of existing state firms, such as lack of a social safety net, lack of a legal framework for corporate governance, and lack of regulatory institutions for special industries (for example, banks).

The Disadvantages of Government Control in Corporate Governance

In analyzing government versus private ownership of firms, the reference point is the Sappington and Stiglitz (1987) irrelevance result: even with asymmetric information, ownership does not matter if the government is benevolent and contracting is complete. This is because an appropriately designed public firm can mimic anything a private firm can achieve. This is a useful benchmark for our analysis; indeed, recent theoretical advances are based mostly on the notion that the irrelevance result no longer holds once one (or both) of the assumptions is relaxed.

The assumption of a benevolent government has received serious criticism (see, for example, Shleifer and Vishny 1994; Shleifer 1998). However, criticism of the assumption that the government is benevolent does not necessarily imply that one must assume that the government is malevolent. The government has its own agenda, which may or may not coincide with public interests. For example, maintaining political and social stability concerns the power of the ruling group, so preventing riots and crises is the government's first priority. But stability is also in the interests of the public. The government may be interested in increasing the amount of revenue at its disposal. Increasing government revenue can be in the public interests if it is spent on those interests, but it may not be. The government also needs to buy political support from members of the ruling group who should be compensated if reforms make them potential losers.

The second assumption is that contracts are complete. However, contracts are likely to be incomplete for a variety of reasons, such as transaction costs, measurement costs, and monitoring costs (Hart 1988). Contracting is also more likely to be incomplete in developing and transition economies as a result of imperfect government and market institutions. For example, in the absence of a rule of law and an independent judicial system, the enforcer of a contract (for example, the government) may be either corrupt or a party to the contract. Therefore, it is likely that an enforceable contract in a developed economy may become unenforceable in a developing or transitional economy (Che and Qian 1998a). Incomplete contracting is a more natural assumption in the study of government ownership and control in corporate governance (Schmidt 1996).

The lack of benevolence of government, together with incomplete contracting, constitutes the first disadvantage of government control of firms. When a contract is incomplete, the government as an owner would impose actions to achieve its objectives. Unlike private owners, the government may have political objectives other than maintaining the asset value of the firm, which could be very costly to economic efficiency. This leads to the following fundamental dilemma: maintaining the government's control over firms entails high political costs because of political interference, and expanding managerial autonomy also induces high agency costs when managers tend to experience a lack of accountability (Qian 1996).

The second disadvantage of government control in corporate governance concerns a lack of credible commitment, which can arise in situations regardless of whether the government is benevolent or not. The difference between the government and private sector is the enormous power of the former. Because of this power, the government often lacks a credible commitment to carry out its announced policy, and it may have difficulty making a credible commitment to either high-power incentives for managers or the imposition of hard budget constraints.

The third disadvantage of government control in corporate governance is that it may well overload the government. The government has many other things to do, such as regulation and the provision of public goods, and therefore, control of firms is likely to overburden it. The "core competence" of the government is regulation and the provision of public goods, not corporate governance.

If government control has many disadvantages, then what constitutes the relative success of some government-owned enterprises such as TVEs over private enterprises? And, why is there a delay in the privatization of SOEs? I argue that government ownership and control of firms (or the lack of private ownership) can be understood once we consider the institutional imperfections in developing and transition economies. In some cases, government control of firms can be understood as a "second-best" institutional arrangement given the unsympathetic institutional environment and the government's limited ability to make a commitment arising from, for instance, the absence of the rule of law to constrain the government. This analysis goes beyond the argument of market failure, because many institutional imperfections are due to the institutional failures of the government itself.

Why Does Government Control in Corporate Governance Have Comparative Advantages?

There are three reasons why government control has comparative advantages over private ownership in an imperfect institutional environment: the insecurity of property rights, the imperfection of capital markets, and the inadequacy of taxation systems.

Lack of rule of law in securing property rights. In studying the ownership of firms in rural industry, many scholars recognize the critical role that local government plays in protecting firms in an environment lacking a rule of law (Chang and Wang 1994; Li 1996; Che and Qian 1998a, 1998b). In China, private property rights are not secure. Indeed, the state has attacked private enterprises during several general political crackdowns, including the "anti-spiritual pollution campaign" of 1983, the "anti-bourgeois liberalization campaign" of 1987, and, most recently, political repression following the Tiananmen incident of 1989. Facing such uncertainties, private enterprises have reacted by withholding investments or seeking protection. For example, some private enterprises sought protection by becoming TVEs after 1989.

Che and Qian (1998a) explain why the property rights of local government-owned firms (such as TVEs) are more secure than those of private enterprises in China's institutional environment. They argue that because the local government engages in two activities—providing productive local public goods and controlling TVEs—it is more useful than private enterprises to higher-level government. At equilibrium, the higher-level government may optimally prey less on TVEs than on private enterprises, and the local government may be less worried than private firms that higher-level government will confiscate revenue. Thus TVEs hide less revenue than private enterprises, and local governments invest more in local public goods, both of which improve economic efficiency.

Indeed, the national government has stipulated that the after-tax profits of TVEs should be used for two purposes: reinvestment and provision of local public goods. Nationwide in 1985 about 46 percent of the after-tax profits of TVEs were reinvested, and 49 percent were used for local public expenditure. In 1992, 59 percent of the after-tax profits of TVEs were reinvested, and 40 percent were used for local public expenditure (China Statistics Publishing House 1992, 1993).

The cities of Wuxi in Jiangsu province and Wenzhou in Zhejiang province represent two extremes of ownership structure in rural industries. In Wuxi, TVEs are dominant, and private enterprises are extremely rare; in Wenzhou, private enterprises are dominant. As a result, in Wuxi, TVEs are the chief source of revenue for the township and village governments to invest in agricultural machinery, bridges, power stations, field terracing, and other agricultural improvements. In contrast, in Wenzhou, township and village governments are unable to perform their basic administrative functions. In a World Bank study, Song and Du (1990: 347) report that, in 1983, township governments in Wenzhou were "impotent in performing their administrative functions," and "basic facilities and public works in the townships of Wenzhou Prefecture were rather backward, considering the rate of capital accumulation. Farmers were building three- and four-story houses with kitchens and bathrooms, but their kitchen slops were running in the streets for lack of sewers. Cultural, public health, and other public undertakings were lagging behind other areas."

Lack of a functioning capital market. In transition and developing economies, capital is one of the most scarce resources, and its efficient use is a major source of growth. In particular, new firms have great difficulty obtaining capital to start or expand their businesses. One fundamental reason for capital constraint is the uncertainty and risk underlying new ventures: an information gap between investors (those who have capital) and entrepreneurs (those who have ideas) induces the problems of adverse selection and moral hazard. The problems become even worse than in developing and transition economies for two additional reasons: market institutions for monitoring behavior and enforcing contracts are poorly developed, and entrepreneurs lack the capital needed to make partial investments or to put up as collateral for a loan. As a result, credit is rationed in the sense that either loans are not available or they are available only for a smaller amount than is needed (the underinvestment problem). Thus new private enterprises are capital constrained and forced to start with small, less capital-intensive projects. Only after accumulating retained earnings over time are they able to raise more capital, increase the scale of projects, and shift to more capital-intensive technologies. This process can be slow.

TVEs have distinct advantages over private enterprises when it comes to financing investment. TVEs are able to access a larger pool of capital—in particular, bank loans—with the help of the local government. TVEs may have an advantage over private enterprises in financing investment because the local government can use its political connections with the state banks to channel loans to TVEs. The state banks are also more willing to lend to TVEs because ideological discrimination against private enterprises makes lending to them politically risky. TVEs may also have advantages in financing investment due to the underdevelopment of market financial institutions and imperfect capital markets. For example, local government can share risks by means of cross-subsidization among its many diversified enterprises, reducing the default risks borne by banks. The local government can also reduce agency costs in borrowing because it has a larger endowment of physical and financial assets (see, for example, Byrd 1990; Che and Qian 1998b).

Lack of adequate taxation and fiscal institutions. Also missing is an adequate taxation system for generating tax revenue for the government and a good fiscal system for allocating revenue. These two problems are related. On the revenue side, all transitional economies have been experiencing sharp shortfalls in government revenue because of the erosion of monopoly profits from SOEs and the great difficulty of taxing new private firms. In a centrally planned economy, taxation is simple: the government uses distorted prices to concentrate surpluses in the final industrial sectors and extracts revenues from there. After liberalization of prices and ownership, profits are distributed more equally among sectors, and the government loses its base of revenue, especially in enterprises it does not control (McKinnon 1991). Fiscal collapse is one of the major reasons behind the recent crisis in Russia.

On the expenditure side, for political economy reasons, the governments in developing countries often bias expenditures toward certain groups, such as urban residents (Bates 1987). This can be viewed as a commitment problem. After revenue is collected, the government is unable to commit itself credibly to spending some of it on local public goods in rural areas because political lobbying is stronger in urban than in rural areas.

Both problems hurt rural industrialization and development, and both are due to a lack of appropriate government institutions. Local government control in TVEs works to mitigate both problems. Several studies have emphasized the revenue goals of the local government in developing TVEs, but why are TVEs in a better position than private firms to achieve the revenue objectives of the local government? In essence, it is less costly for local government to extract revenues from firms it owns and controls than from private firms. For the same reason, it is harder for central government to extract revenue from firms owned and controlled by local government (rather than itself), and this makes it more likely that revenue will stay in the local areas.

Empirical evidence. Recent econometric studies on the data from China's rural industry have provided evidence to support these theoretical arguments. Using panel data from 28 provinces in China between 1986 and 1993, Jin and Qian (1998) investigate the share of TVEs relative to that of private enterprises and the impact on government revenues.

They find that local political strength to resist pressure from higher-level government (appropriately measured) played an important role in favoring TVEs (table 7.1). The relative share of TVEs in rural industry is also higher if the supply of credits from state banks is higher. With the help of local government, these loans are more likely to go to TVEs for both political and economic reasons.

Jin and Qian also find that the share of TVEs increased the revenue shares of both the national and especially the township-village governments, after controlling for the level of per capita income and other geographic and political variables (table 7.2). Therefore, local government ownership provides higher revenues to both national and local governments, and it also allows the local government to retain a larger share of revenues. The authors provide evidence on the fiscal incentives of the local governments in developing TVEs, and they show that government control plays an important role by substituting for the lack of adequate taxation institutions.

Why Has Privatization of Existing State-Owned Enterprises Been Delayed?

Delaying the privatization of existing state firms is partly due to the transitional advantages of government control of firms (tax considerations), but there are other reasons as well. Ideological commitment to state ownership is one reason, but that reason becomes less and less convincing. The vested interests furthered as a result of political control over SOEs is another reason, which has nothing to do with efficiency. On economic grounds, there are still several reasons for delaying the privatization of SOEs, especially large ones.

Table 7.1 The Institutional Environment and Government Control of Firms

Variable	Share of township and village enterprises in rural industrial employment			Share of township and village enterprises in rural industrial output		
Intercept	-2.076 (2.547)	-1.596 (2.217)	-2.195 (2.069)	-0.444 (0.455)	0.370 (0.592)	-0.577 (0.476)
State supply of credits	0.274 (5.200)	0.480 (4.687)		0.363 (3.650)	0.538 (4.365)	
Size of state industry	0.746 (1.324)	1.322 (2.170)	1.487 (2.902)	1.866 (2.529)	2.957 (3.972)	2.846 (4.523)
Log of initial collective assets	0.698 (3.838)	0.563 (3.318)	0.690 (2.929)	0.522 (2.444)	0.292 (1.625)	0.506 (1.928)
Local political strength	1.532 (3.739)	2.062 (4.049)	1.356 (3.732)	2.319 (4.679)	2.902 (4.329)	2.079 (4.065)
Private financial assets	-0.009 (0.006)	-2.785 (2.375)		-0.102 (0.057)	-2.506 (1.507)	
Product market development	-7.476 (5.782)	-5.452 (2.998)	-6.586 (4.536)	-7.503 (4.441)	-5.155 (2.439)	-6.375 (3.247)
Share of urban population	-1.977 (2.627)	-1.636 (1.605)	-1.574 (1.938)	-3.440 (2.855)	-3.137 (2.220)	-2.913 (2.285)
Region dummy for huge cities	0.568 (2.057)		0.788 (2.525)	0.509 (1.070)		0.806 (1.483)
Region dummy for coastal	0.391 (3.177)		0.572 (3.737)	0.283 (1.426)		0.520 (2.259)
Region dummy for Southwest	0.253 (1.751)		0.251 (1.411)	0.312 (1.457)		0.307 (1.332)
Region dummy for Northwest	-0.243 (1.730)		-0.208 (2.456)	-0.201 (1.024)		-0.164 (1.049)
Region dummy for North	-0.349 (2.181)		-0.308 (1.875)	-0.482 (2.530)		-0.433 (2.130)
R^2	0.929	0.875	0.911	0.847	0.782	0.815

Note: A full set of year dummies is included in each specification. Sample size is 224. The t-statistics are in parentheses, which are based on Huber-White robust standard errors allowing for group errors by provinces.
Source: Jin and Qian (1998).

Table 7.2 Government Control of Firms and Government Revenue

Variable	Ordinary least squares estimations		Instrumental variable estimations	
	State share	Community government share	State share	Community government share
Intercept	-0.066 (3.879)	0.001 (0.042)	-0.098 (7.356)	-0.074 (3.255)
Share of TVES in rural enterprise employment	0.108 (3.690)	0.112 (4.292)	0.114 (3.896)	0.242 (4.316)
Net rural income per capita	0.181 (3.741)	-0.055 (0.957)	0.285 (7.742)	-0.006 (0.108)
Local political strength	-0.073 (2.819)	0.026 (0.966)	-0.095 (5.468)	-0.095 (0.811)
Region dummy for huge cities	0.048 (3.197)	0.126 (4.426)	0.019 (1.679)	0.056 (2.549)
Region dummy for Coastal	0.003 (0.267)	0.039 (2.497)	-0.010 (1.795)	0.008 (0.639)
Region dummy for Southwest	0.008 (1.002)	-0.010 (1.278)	0.013 (1.496)	-0.002 (0.144)
Region dummy for Northwest	0.003 (0.458)	0.002 (0.212)	0.008 (1.193)	0.004 (0.423)
Region dummy for North	0.014 (2.376)	0.032 (4.615)	0.015 (2.779)	0.039 (3.897)
Standard errors	0.015	0.021	0.016	0.024

Note: A full set of year dummies is included in each specification. Endogenous variables are the share of TVEs in rural enterprise employment and net rural income. Instruments are local political strength, regional dummies, year dummies, state supply of credit, size of state industry, private financial assets, product market development, share of urban population, log of initial collective assets, and cultivated land per capita. Sample size is 224. The t-statistics are in parentheses, which are based on Huber-White robust standard errors allowing for group errors by provinces.

Source: Jin and Qian (1998).

Privatization is delayed not only in China but also in Eastern Europe, for example, in Poland and Hungary. This is because a quick privatization may incur high costs due to the absence of supporting institutions.

Lack of the social safety net. The lack of a social safety net other than what is provided by state enterprises is an important reason why their privatization has been delayed. SOEs in socialist countries do not just generate profits; they serve many other purposes as well, including the provision of social welfare, such as housing, health care, and retirement benefits. Without a social safety net independent of state enterprises, protests by laid-off workers could directly threaten the ruling group's power. Indirectly, an unstable social environment adversely affects the development of the rest of the economy. In this sense, maintaining social order is a public good. Private owners of a firm do not take this externality into consideration when making their decisions. Therefore, there is a second-best argument for favoring government control of firms in the absence of a social safety net.

The fact that SOEs are charged with two tasks—production and provision of a social safety net—has several implications. First, although profit figures tend to overstate the social contribution of SOEs because of cheap credit, they may also understate their ability to provide social stability. Second, in the multiple-task framework, if profit is easier to measure than social stability, it may become necessary to provide fewer incentives to the managers of SOEs and to strengthen the link between reward and profits (Bai and others 1997).

Lack of a legal framework for corporate governance. The agency problem arises from the separation of ownership and control or, more precisely, the separation of management and finance. This is a particularly serious problem for large firms. When managers have considerable discretion over the use of funds, how can investors be sure that they will get what they are due and that their funds will not be expropriated? There are several ways to align the interests of investors and managers. One way is to draw up incentive contracts based on measurements such as earnings and stock prices; another is to tie these to managerial reputations and career concerns.

Corporate governance provides another important mechanism. Successful corporate governance systems, such as those in the United States, Germany, and Japan, combine significant legal protection for investors with an important role for large shareholders or creditors (Shleifer and Vishny 1997). Corporate governance is a set of institutional arrangements governing the relationships among investors (shareholders and creditors), boards of directors, and managers. The structure of corporate governance concerns (a) how control rights are allocated and exercised, (b) how boards of directors and top managers are selected and monitored, and (c) how incentives are designed and enforced. Specifically, shareholders have the right to select boards of directors and the right to access information and to make strategic decisions. Creditors have priority of payments and have the right to grab collateral and take over the firm's assets after bankruptcy. Boards of directors have fiduciary duty—the duty of loyalty—toward shareholders, and members of the board can be sued for breach of fiduciary duty. In transition and developing economies, all of these safeguards for investors are very weak because the legal system is weak, and legal protection usually does not give enough control rights to small investors because of the well-known free-rider problem.

For all of these reasons, large shareholders or creditors have a special role in addressing the agency problem. If control rights are concentrated among a few large investors, a concerted action by them is much easier than when control rights are split among many small investors. In transition economies, for the time being, it is unlikely that there will be many large domestic private investors for large enterprises. Privatization without legal protection and the existence of large external investors have led to the problem known as "insider control," such as that experienced in Russia. This creates two problems. First, managers find it easy to divert resources from firms, and second, incompetent managers are not removed because they have control over the firm. This in turn makes it difficult for firms to obtain external financing.

A natural candidate for a large investor is the government or government-owned institutions, such as state investment companies or state banks. Although government control may incur high political costs, the government can act as a large investor to balance the insider control problem of managers. Li (1997) suggests that the government can play the role of a large shareholder because it takes a large share of profits as tax revenue. Wang and Xu (1997) have studied the role of institutional shareholders ("legal person shares") in corporate perfor-mance of publicly listed firms in China. They find that the presence of these institutional shares, although most of them are still ultimately controlled by the government, plays a positive role in firm perfor-mance. There is a positive and significant correlation between owner-ship concentration and profitability. The effect of ownership concen-tration is stronger for companies dominated by legal person shares than for those dominated by the state. A firm's profitability is posi-tively correlated with the proportion of legal person shares; it is either negatively correlated or uncorrelated with the proportion of state shares and of individuals' shares. Wang and Xu also find that legal person owners are able to monitor management effectively through their con-trol over the board of directors, the selection of corporate officers, and the compensation of chief corporate officers.

Lack of regulatory institutions for special industries. Some special industries require sophisticated government regulation even in devel-oped economies because of potential market failure. For example, the financial and banking industry requires prudential regulations because the potential moral hazard problem of the banks under deposit insur-ance can cripple the banking system. In the telecommunications in-dustry, a government competition policy is needed to prevent a mo-nopoly. But in most developing and transition economies, these regulations and their enforcement either do not exist or perform poorly. Although the ultimate goal is to set up such a regulatory framework, it is not realistic to expect this to work in the short run. In this case, there is a second-best justification for the government's direct control over firms in industries where an unregulated situation is considered harmful to the economy.

    For example, in China, the government owns all major com-mercial banks. With the government in full control, it can appoint and dismiss top bank managers directly and force banks to take certain actions. For example, the government fired the head of Ever Bright Financial Group in 1999 and rotated the heads of the four major state commercial banks in early 2000. Other things being equal, with con-trol rights the government can obtain better information about the operation of banks. If a good regulatory framework is lacking, private firms have no incentive to disclose crucial information to the government, and the government has limited ways to punish private firms.

GOVERNMENT EXIT FROM CORPORATE GOVERNANCE: FLEXIBILITY AND INCENTIVES FOR INSTITUTIONAL CHANGE

The benefits of government control of firms tend to decline or disappear with the creation of market-supporting institutions. Indeed, when the rule of law is established, taxation institutions are functioning well, the social safety net is in place, and the legal framework of corporate governance and the regulatory regime are set up and well enforced, the private ownership of firms is more advantageous than government control. The benefits of government control of firms are also declining as a result of increased competition, especially international competition.

A fundamental issue is how the government can remove itself from corporate governance in a timely manner. International pressure for reform, such as that seen in Indonesia and Korea, is one possibility. China has demonstrated another possibility through internal mechanisms. Since 1994 China has been pursuing the quiet privatization of its small- and medium-size SOEs and TVEs. This reform was initiated and implemented by local governments. In this section, I analyze how this happened, drawing attention to two relevant factors: the flexibility of the institutional structure of an economy in initiating changes without major disturbances and the incentives of local governments to make such changes.

The Flexibility of an Economy for Institutional Changes

The flexibility of a system has been studied in the context of polyarchies versus hierarchies (Sah and Stiglitz 1986), M-form versus U-form (Qian, Roland, and Xu 1998), and federalist versus unitary state (Qian and Weingast 1996). The basic idea is that consideration should be given to the architecture of the economy and political systems of a country in order to understand how the system accommodates changes such as innovation and reform. It is argued that the advantage of polyarchies, the M-form organization, and federalism is that they can facilitate such changes with smaller costs because their parallel decisionmaking procedures allow experimentation in different units or because the potential disturbances from changes can be localized. This is compared with the more rigid institutional framework of hierarchies, the U-form, and the unitary state.

From these perspectives, we can see the virtues of China's relatively flexible institutional structures. Even without a central program, local governments successfully experimented with reforms without incurring major disruptions to the rest of the economy. Consider the pioneering example of Shunde county in Guangdong province. Located near Hong Kong, Shunde is a fast-growing area and is famous for its TVEs. In the late 1980s, Shunde had more than half of the top 10 TVEs in the country, and its consumer electronics and gas ranges comprised one-tenth and one-third of the national market share for those products, respectively. Qian and Stiglitz (1996) describe a range of innovations in Shunde, based on a visit in 1992. At that time there was no effort to privatize SOEs and TVEs.

Beginning in 1993, the Shunde government decided to make major changes in the ownership structures of firms in the region. By 1994, out of about 1,000 state and collectively owned enterprises (including TVEs), 69 percent of firms changed their form of ownership. Among them, 23 percent of firms were sold to the public, and 31 percent were sold to employees inside the firms. The county or township government maintained minority shares in 1.9 percent of the profitable firms and had controlling shares in 13 percent of firms, mainly in public utilities, highways, real estate, and foreign trade. Simultaneously, the county government replaced a dozen bureaus with three comprehensive development bureaus in industry, agriculture, and trade. These bureaus no longer supervised firms, but instead regulated the local economy. As a result, the county government was able to reduce the number of its bureaus from 56 to 29 and to reduce its staff by a third. Now the county government concentrates on the provision of local public goods and other social services (Cao, Qian, and Weingast 1999).

This dramatic exit of the government from corporate governance was supported by the Guangdong provincial government, but without approval from the central government. Shunde did it on its own, and other regions later followed suit. An alternative system requiring central government approval, which is subject to national politics, undoubtedly would have delayed the change considerably.

The Incentives of Government for Privatization

Even if the system is flexible, government incentives continue to determine if the change will actually take place. The government's vested interests in the control of firms could prevent economically efficient changes from happening. China's recent experiences offer two major sources of incentives for local governments to undertake privatization: harder budget constraints and increased market competition (Cao, Qian, and Weingast 1999; Li, Li, and Zhang 1997).

First, recent reforms in fiscal, monetary, and banking systems in China have substantially hardened the budget constraints of local governments in both the fiscal and financial channels. After centralizing the operation of the central bank and state commercial banks, the influence of local governments on credit allocation and their access to cheap credits were severely curtailed. This is a dramatic change from the 1980s, when local governments effectively controlled the state banking system and had access to unlimited credit.

Second, increased competition from the nonstate sector and within the state sector has raised the competitive pressure on existing SOEs. After 15 years of successful reform, the nonstate sector has become a major force in the economy. For example, foreign firms and rural enterprises alone account for more than half of national industrial output. Regional trade barriers seem to have been reduced, simply because it is harder to enforce local protection.

Harder budget constraints, together with increased competition, have altered the costs and benefits to local governments of keeping SOEs. In recent years, the performance of many SOEs, especially small- and medium-size firms in a competitive industry, have deteriorated quickly. Under a hard budget constraint, this declining performance implies that enterprises are imposing increasingly heavy fiscal burdens on local government. Financing these losses crowds out other expenditures, providing local governments with an incentive to privatize and restructure their SOEs. In the case of Shunde county, the government decided to privatize because it needed funds for infrastructure investment to attract more foreign investment.

CONCLUDING REMARKS

Both the market failure view and the corrupt government view of the close ties between government and business have taken a static perspective and missed some important institutional realities at different stages of development in most developing and transition economies. During the past two decades of reform in China—the largest developing and transition economy—government control in corporate governance has evolved in two stages. In the first 15 years, government control in enterprises increased and arguably played a positive role. Since 1994, the focus of reform has shifted to building market and legal institutions, and the government began to exit corporate governance. This chapter argues that a dynamic perspective of the role of government control in corporate governance is needed in order to better understand this historic process of change.

In some sense, the corporate form of TVE is special to China. Nevertheless, we can draw general lessons from the analysis in this chapter.

First, one needs to pay attention to the details of the institutional environment. Private ownership and control work well in an environment with good supporting institutions of both market and state. The institutional realities of developing and transition economies are often far from perfect. Although these economies should make an effort to build conventional market-supporting institutions such as the rule of law, they cannot expect these institutions to function as well as those in developed economies in the short run. The second-best principle tells us that removing one distortion may not improve efficiency in the presence of other ones. As this chapter shows, there are circumstances in which government control in corporate governance can work better than private control.

Second, because government control in corporate governance involves many costs and is not the first-best arrangement, mechanisms are needed to encourage the government to exit corporate governance. Therefore, one should also pay attention to the institutional framework that makes it less costly for government to move away from corporate governance. An economic system should be flexible in order to induce institutional change and avoid stagnation or crisis. Furthermore, the institutional framework should provide incentives for the government to relinquish corporate governance. Hard budget constraints and competition are two mechanisms capable of providing the necessary incentives for government to make changes.

Third, analyzing the role of government control in corporate governance from a dynamic perspective addresses the important issue of the sequencing of reform. This chapter demonstrates that a determining factor in the sequencing of reform is the changing institutional environment. In the early stage of reform, the conventional market-supporting institutions (such as the rule of law) are lacking and so are the people and human capital to operate them (such as law enforcement). Both usually take years to develop. During this period, some forms of local government control of firms and some delay in privatizing existing state firms can improve economic performance, contrary to conventional wisdom. As reform deepens, conventional market-supporting institutions are being built, and human capital is being accumulated. Consequently, the institutional environment becomes more sympathetic to private ownership and control. At that time, the disadvantage of government control becomes a dominant effect. Then further reform requires the government to exit corporate governance.

Finally, although the principles underlying reform and institutional changes are general, a good path of reform has to accommodate country-specific conditions. Because institutional transformation is complicated and our understanding of it remains very limited, policy recommendations should not seek to impose one specific model on all countries.

The author is grateful to Shahid Yusuf for helpful comments and discussions.

REFERENCES

The word "processed" describes informally reproduced works that may not be commonly available through library systems.

Bai, Chong-en, David D. Li, Zhigang Tao, and Yijiang Wang. 1997. "State-Owned Enterprise in Transition: A Multi-Task Perspective." Boston College, Department of Economics, Boston, Mass. Processed.

Bates, Robert. 1987. *Essays on the Political Economy of Rural Africa.* Berkeley: University of California Press.

Byrd, William. 1990. "Entrepreneurship, Capital, and Ownership." In William Byrd and Qingsong Lin, eds., *China's Rural Industry: Structure, Development, and Reform*. New York: Oxford University Press.

Cao, Yuanzheng, Yingyi Qian, and Barry Weingast. 1999. "From Federalism, Chinese Style, to Privatization, Chinese Style." *Economics of Transition* 7(March):103–31.

Chang, Chun, and Yijiang Wang. 1994. "The Nature of the Township Enterprises." *Journal of Comparative Economics* 19(December):434–52.

Che, Jiahua, and Yingyi Qian. 1998a. "Insecure Property Rights and Government Ownership of Firms." *Quarterly Journal of Economics* 113(May):467–96.

———. 1998b. "Institutional Environment, Community Government, and Corporate Governance: Understanding China's Township-Village Enterprises." *Journal of Law, Economics, and Organization* 14(April):1–23.

China Statistics Publishing House. 1992. *A Statistical Survey of China 1992*. Beijing.

———. 1993. *A Statistical Survey of China 1993*. Beijing.

Hart, Oliver. 1988. "Incomplete Contracts and the Theory of the Firm." *Journal of Law, Economics, and Organization* 4(1):119–39.

Jin, Hehui, and Yingyi Qian. 1998. "Public versus Private Ownership of Firms: Evidence from Rural China." *Quarterly Journal of Economics* 113(August):773–808.

Li, David D. 1996. "A Theory of Ambiguous Property Rights in Transition Economies." *Journal of Comparative Economics* 23(March):1–19.

———. 1997. "Government Control of State Enterprise: Evidence from China." University of Michigan, Department of Economics, Ann Arbor. Processed.

Li, Shaomin, Shuhe Li, and Weiying Zhang. 1997. "Competition and Institutional Change: Privatization in China." City University of Hong Kong, Department of Economics. Processed.

McKinnon, Ronald. 1991. "Financial Control in the Transition to a Market Economy from Classical Socialism." In Christopher Clague, ed., *The Emergence of Market Economies in Eastern Europe*. Oxford: Basil Blackwell.

Qian, Yingyi. 1996. "Enterprise Reform in China: Agency Problems and Political Control." *Economics of Transition* 4(October):427–47.

———. 1999. "The Institutional Foundations of China's Market Transition." Paper presented at the World Bank's Annual Conference on Development Economics 1999. Online at http://www-econ.stanford.edu/faculty/workp/swp99011.html.

Qian, Yingyi, Gerard Roland, and Chenggang Xu. 1998. "Coordinating Changes in M-form and U-form Organizations." Stanford University, Department of Economics, Stanford, Calif. Processed.

Qian, Yingyi, and Joseph Stiglitz. 1996. "Institutional Innovations and the Role of Local Government in Transition Economies: The Case of Guangdong Province of China." In John McMillan and Barry Naughton, eds., *Reforming Asian Socialism: The Growth of Market Institutions*. Ann Arbor: University of Michigan Press.

Qian, Yingyi, and Barry Weingast. 1996. "China's Transition to Markets: Market-Preserving Federalism, Chinese Style." *Journal of Policy Reform* 1(2):149–86.

Sah, Rajiv, and Joseph Stiglitz. 1986. "The Architecture of Economic Systems: Hierarchies and Polyarchies." *American Economic Review* 76(September):716–27.

Sappington, David, and Joseph Stiglitz. 1987. "Privatization, Information, and Incentives." *Journal of Policy Analysis and Management* 6:567–82.

Schmidt, Klaus. 1996. "The Costs and Benefits of Privatization: An Incomplete Contracts Approach." *Journal of Law, Economics, and Organization* 12(April):1–24.

Shleifer, Andrei. 1998. "State versus Private Ownership." *Journal of Economic Perspectives* 12(Fall):133–50.

Shleifer, Andrei, and Robert W. Vishny. 1994. "Politicians and Firms." *Quarterly Journal of Economics* 109(November):995–1025.

———. 1997. "A Survey of Corporate Governance." *Journal of Finance* 52(June):737–83.

Song, Lina, and He Du. 1990. "The Role of Township Governments in Rural Industrialization." In William Byrd and Lin Qingsong, eds., *China's Rural Industry: Structure, Development, and Reform.* New York: Oxford University Press.

Wang, Yan, and Xiaonian Xu. 1997. "Ownership Structure, Corporate Governance, and Firms Performance: The Case of Chinese Stock Companies." Policy Research Working Paper 1794. World Bank, Economic Development Institute, Washington, D.C. Processed.

World Bank. 1993. *The East Asian Miracle: Economic Growth and Public Policy.* New York: Oxford University Press.

CHAPTER 8

THE GOVERNMENT-FIRM RELATIONSHIP IN POSTWAR JAPAN: THE SUCCESS AND FAILURE OF BUREAU PLURALISM

Tetsuji Okazaki

The Japanese economy has been attracting the attention of economists and practitioners for the past decade. In the early 1990s, its success was regarded as a core ingredient of the East Asian Miracle, and experts were inspired to revise the orthodox neoclassical view of development policy (World Bank 1993). Industrial policy was granted legitimacy , while the deliberative council was seen as a device to facilitate the exchange of information between the government and the private sector. In the late 1990s, after years of economic depression and financial crisis, Japan's economic system faced severe criticism. Government intervention and regulation were regarded as sources of inefficiency, and the deliberative council was considered a linchpin of the notorious iron triangle, composed of the political, bureaucratic, and business sectors.

However, events in the 1990s should not negate East Asia's long experience with high growth (Stiglitz 1999). We need to devise a consistent framework capable of explaining both the high growth until the 1980s and the stagnation in the 1990s. In this chapter, I clarify the common organizational and institutional factors behind the success and failure of the Japanese economy, focusing on industrial policy and the government-firm relationship.

The key concept is "bureau pluralism" (Aoki 1988: ch. 7). In the bureau-pluralistic state, private interests are primarily aggregated into an industrial association and then transmitted to its counterpart in the bureaucracy, namely the "original bureau" (*genkyoku*), which is in charge of the industry. The original bureau bargains inside the government, representing the interests of the industry under its jurisdiction. The bargaining is carried out first within each ministry and then across ministries. This system is pluralistic in the sense that the people participate in policymaking. At the same time, it is bureaucratic, in the sense that bureaucrats represent the interests of the people. The efficacy of bureau pluralism depends on environmental conditions, and a change in environmental conditions is one of the major factors explaining the success and failure of the Japanese economy.

The chapter is organized as follows. The first section characterizes the organizational aspects of the Japanese government-firm relationship, focusing on the composition and historical origin of the deliberative councils. The next section describes the function of bureau pluralism in the early 1950s and the high-growth era, focusing on industrial rationalization and the provision of industrial infrastructure. This is followed by a discussion of the conditions that enabled bureau pluralism to perform so well until the high-growth era and an examination of the changes occurring in the 1980s, with a focus on the information and telecommunications industry. A final section concludes.

ORGANIZATIONAL ASPECTS AND HISTORICAL ORIGIN OF BUREAU PLURALISM

The bureau-pluralistic nature of Japan's political economy is reflected in the organization and composition of the deliberative council. To examine it, I focus on the Industrial Structure Council, under the Ministry of International Trade and Industry (MITI). The Industrial Structure Council was established in 1964 as a successor to the Council for Industrial Rationalization. The Industrial Structure Council is "a permanent organization which investigates and deliberates on basic issues related to Japan's industrial structure" (MITI 1994: 182).

The Industrial Structure Council in 1970, a year close to the end of the high-growth era, was organized into 19 branches, seven of which were organized by industry (figure 8.1). That same year, committee members were classified according to their position as written in the council's membership list, which reflected MITI's perception at that time (table 8.1). The Industrial Structure Council was a large deliberative council with 505 members. Of these, 108 (21.3 percent) were representatives of industrial associations. Most of them participated in the branches of the council that related to their industry. For example, representatives of the Japan Iron and Steel Association and the Japan Machinery Industry Federation were also members of the Heavy Industries Branch.

Industrial associations were organized in most Japanese industries. MITI (1970b) listed all of the industrial associations under its jurisdiction, and these numbered as many as 528 (table 8.2). Bureaus that were in charge of individual industries—the original bureaus—controlled a large number of industrial associations.

Bureau pluralism does not have historically deep roots in Japan's political economy. Although there were deliberative councils before the war, the number and composition of their membership were substantially different than they were after the war. Table 8.3 shows the membership of the Economic Council, the Council of Commerce and Industry, and the Temporary Industrial Council, the three major deliberative councils in the prewar period. The number of council members was much smaller before the war than after, and the composition was different as well. First, before the war the councils included few representatives of industrial associations. Second, a high ratio of council members represented organizations that crossed industries, such as networks based on ownership (*zaibatsu*) and chambers of commerce. Third, many members also belonged to the diet.

The first two characteristics suggest that the mode of aggregating private interests in the prewar period differed from that in the postwar period. Interests were mainly aggregated by geographic area (chambers of commerce) or by *zaibatsu*. The third characteristic suggests that politicians had a larger role in prewar than in postwar Japan. In postwar Japan, coordination has been carried out largely by bureaucrats as opposed to politicians.

The government-firm relationship in Japan was deeply affected by World War II (Okazaki 1993a; Okazaki and Okuno-Fujiwara 1999). The Sino-Japanese War, which broke out in 1937, forced the government to mobilize huge resources. The government intended to do this by means of government planning and control. In 1939 a system of economic plans was established that encompassed the Materials

Figure 8.1 Organization of the Industrial Structure Council

Coordination Branch ———————— Basic Problems Special Committee

Distribution Branch ————————— Local Vision Subcommittee
                                              Cost Sharing Subcommittee

Industrial Pollution Branch ———— Industrial Waste Matters Subcommittee
                                              Subcommittee of Countermeasure against
                                                  Automobile Pollution

Industrial Fund Branch

Management Branch ———————— Corporate Finance Subcommittee
                                              Production Management Subcommitttee

International Economy Branch ———— Import Subcommittee

Industrial Finance Branch

Consumption Branch

Industrial Labor Branch

Industrial Location Branch ————— Large-scale Industry Base Subcommittee
                                              Rural Industrialzation Subcommittee
                                              Subcommittee of Direct Investment to Okinawa

Industrial Technology Branch

Heavy Industry Branch ————————— Machinery Policy Subcommittee
                                              Export Subcommittee

Iron and Steel Branch ————————— Special Steel Subcommittee
                                              Open Hearth and Electric Hearth Subcommittee

Inftormation Industry Branch

Chemical Industry Branch ————— Chemical Goods Export Subcommittee
                                              Automobile Tire Subcommittee

Textile Branch ———————————— Distribution Subcommittee
                                              First Industrial Organization Subcommittee
                                              Second Industrial Organization Subcommittee

Miscellaneous Goods Branch ——— Miscellaneous Goods Distribution Subcommittee
                                              Miscellaneous Goods Export Subcommittee
                                              Miscellaneous Goods Basic Policy Subcommittee

Housing Industry Branch ————— Aggregate Subcommittee

Source: MITI (1970a).

Table 8.1 Membership of the Industrial Structure Council (1970)

Total	505
General association	13
Industrial association	108
Financial institution	24
Industrial company	179
Public company	39
Journalist	19
Labor union	0
Academic	53
Diet member	0
Bureaucrat	4
Others	66

Source: MITI (1970a).

Table 8.2 Number of Industrial Associations under MITI's Jurisdiction (1970)

Total	528
Minister's Secretariat	1
International Trade Bureau	14
Trade and Development Bureau	76
Enterprise Bureau	20
Heavy Industry Bureau	137
Chemical Industry Bureau	74
Textile and Miscellaneous Industries Bureau	123
Mine and Coal Bureau	40
Mine Safety Bureau	2
Public Utilities Bureau	20
Patent Office	5
Smaller Enterprise Agency	9
Agency of Industrial Science and Technology	7

Source: MITI (1970b).

Mobilization Plan, the Foreign Trade Plan, the Fund Control Plan, the Labor Mobilization Plan, and the Production Capacity Expansion Plan. Unlike Japan's postwar long-term economic plans, these wartime plans were implemented according to economic controls endorsed by laws such as the National Mobilization Law.

In order to manage the planned economy, the government made heavy use of industrial associations. From 1941 to 1942, industry established 22 control associations (*toseikai*; see table 8.4). Okazaki (1988) details the function of the Iron and Steel Control Association, using association and government documents. The Iron and Steel Control

Table 8.3 Membership of the Prewar Deliberative Councils

	Economic Council		Commerce and Industry Council		Temporary Industrial Council	
Total	72	20	25	9	16	5
General association	13	1	4	1	5	1
Industrial association	1	1	0	0	2	0
Zaibatsu	6	0	3	1	2	1
Financial institution	3	1	1	1	2	1
Industrial company	16	6	3	1	3	0
Public company	3	1	1	1	0	0
Journalist	2	0	5	0	0	0
Labor union	0	0	0	0	0	0
Academic	7	0	3	1	2	2
Diet member	10	10	3	3	0	0
Bureaucrat	9	0	0	0	0	0
Others	2	0	2	0	0	0

Note: The numbers in the second column of each council denote the persons who were the diet members at the same time.
Source: MITI (1961).

Association, in cooperation with the Planning Board, participated in making the Materials Mobilization Plan, the short-term plan for allocating resources.

In drawing up the Materials Mobilization Plan, the Planning Board instructed that a single strategic variable—the bottom of ships—be allocated by the Control Association. The bottom of ships was the most binding condition determining the level of production (Hara 1989). The Planning Board controlled this single variable, and the Control Association drew up concrete production plans based on that variable.

In this procedure, local information specific to each industry was processed exclusively by the Control Association, and the Control Association's draft plans were reflected in the government's plan. This mechanism is similar to the Material Balance Method of the Socialist Soviet Union (Aoki 1970). The capability and position of the industrial associations rose substantially as they gained experience during the war, and this experience was an important element of Japan's postwar political economy.

When the war ended in 1945, the Japanese government intended to cede a major part of its power to the control associations or their successors. Although this scheme was not realized, because of the an-

Table 8.4 Control Associations and their Successors

Name of Control Association established	Month and year established	Successor	Month and year
Iron and Steel Control Association	11/1941	Japan Iron and Steel Council	12/1945
Coal Control Association	11/1941	Japan Coal Association	5/1946
Mine Control Association	12/1941	National Mine Association	3/1946
Cement Control Association	12/1941	Cement Industry Association	—
Rolling Stock Control Association	12/1941	Rolling Stock Industry Association	11/1945
Automobile Control Association	12/1941	Automobile Council	11/1945
Precision Machine Control Association	1/1942	Japan Machine Tool Association	1/1946
Electric Machinery Control Association	1/1942	Japan Electric Machinery Association	2/1946
Industrial Machine Control Association	1/1942	Industrial Machinery Association	3/1946
Metal Industry Control Association	1/1942	Japan Cable Association	11/1945
International Trade Control Association	1/1942	Japan International Trade Association	—
Shipbuilding Control Association	1/1942	Federation of Shipbuilding Associations	10/1945
Railways Control Association	5/1942	Japan Railways Association	12/1945
Light Metal Control Association	9/1942	Light Metal Council	10/1946
Wool Control Association	9/1942	Japan Textile Association	12/1945
Leather Control Association	9/1942	Leather Association	12/1945
Hemp Control Association	9/1942	Japan Textile Association	12/1945
Silk and Rayon Control Association	10/1942	Japan Textile Association	12/1945
Cotton and Staple Fiber Control Association	10/1942	Japan Textile Association	12/1945
Oils and Fats Control Association	10/1942	Oils and Fats Processing Association	1/1946
Chemical Industry Control Association	10/1942	Chemical Industry Federation	3/1946
Rubber Control Association	1/1943	Rubber Association	12/1945

— not available.

Source: Nakamura and Hara (1972); MITI and others (1991, 1992).

timonopoly policy of the U.S. occupation authority, the successors of the control associations continued to support planning and control by the government in the late 1940s. It is notable that many of the executives of the control associations came to be the executives of the postwar associations (Yonekura 1999: 195–96). The early stage of Japan's postwar recovery was achieved through the system of planning and control, which maintained a role for the industrial associations. The well-known Priority Production Policy was carried out through this system.

In 1948, the Japanese government started to examine the long-term strategy for making the transition to a market economy and for achieving economic recovery. For this purpose, the government established the Committee for the Economic Recovery Plan, the first major deliberative council created after the war (see figure 8.2 for the organization of the committee). There were four branches organized by industry: mining and manufacturing, food and necessities, international trade, and transportation. Each of the first two branches was composed of several subcommittees, which also were organized by industry.

Figure 8.2 Organization of the Economic Recovery Committee

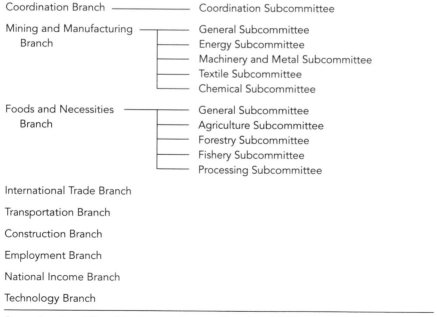

Coordination Branch —————————— Coordination Subcommittee

Mining and Manufacturing ————— General Subcommittee
    Branch   Energy Subcommittee
                                    Machinery and Metal Subcommittee
                                    Textile Subcommittee
                                    Chemical Subcommittee

Foods and Necessities ———————— General Subcommittee
    Branch   Agriculture Subcommittee
                                    Forestry Subcommittee
                                    Fishery Subcommittee
                                    Processing Subcommittee

International Trade Branch

Transportation Branch

Construction Branch

Employment Branch

National Income Branch

Technology Branch

Source: Secretary, Office of the Economic Recovery Committee (1948).

In many cases, the chairmen of the industrial associations appointed the chairmen of the branches and subcommittees. For example, the chairmen of the Energy, Machinery and Metal, Textile, and Chemical subcommittees appointed the chairmen of the Japan Coal Association, the Japan Iron and Steel Association, the Japan Cotton Spinning Association, and the Japan Chemical Industries Association.

The representatives of the industrial associations constituted almost 20 percent of all members of the council, second only to the bureaucrats (table 8.5). This committee's organizational structure was similar to that of the Industrial Structure Council in 1970.

COORDINATION OF ECONOMIC GROWTH

After the war, government coordination focused on two areas: industrial rationalization and supply of basic materials and infrastructure. I deal with each in turn.

Industrial Rationalization

In 1949 the Japanese economy was transformed into a market economy in accordance with the instructions of the American occupation authority. Most economic controls and subsidies were abolished. Still,

Table 8.5 Membership of the Economic Recovery Committee and the Council for Industrial Rationalization

	Economic Recovery Committee	Council for Industrial Rationalization
Total	377	118
General association	8	3
Industrial association	77	30
Financial institution	2	0
Industrial company	46	48
Public company	28	8
Journalist	0	0
Labor union	3	0
Academic	39	4
Diet member	10	0
Bureaucrat	141	18
Others	23	7

Source: Secretary, Office of the Economic Recovery Committee (1948); MITI (1949).

the government continued to play a substantial role in the economy (Okazaki 1996).

The Japanese economy, just after the transformation, had to contend with serious coordination failure. In those days, a wide consensus had already formed concerning the long-term prospects of the Japanese economy. This was achieved, for example, through discussions of the Committee for the Economic Recovery Plan. The consensus was that the major driving force of the Japanese economy would be the growth of an export-oriented machinery industry. It was thought that newly developing Asian countries would catch up in the textile industry, which had been Japan's leading industry in the prewar period, and that the machinery industry would absorb redundant labor forces and earn foreign currencies. However, the Japanese machinery industry at that time was not competitive in the international market. The major reason was the high price of iron and steel, which, in turn, resulted partly from the high price of coal and iron ore and partly from the small scale of iron and steel production. Furthermore, the high price of iron ore resulted from the high cost of freight, which, in turn, was caused by the high price of ships, a kind of machinery. Also, iron and steel were being produced on a small scale because the machinery industry was poorly developed.

In short, the machinery industry, the leading industry of the future, was not competitive because of factors affecting several industries. Therefore, the machinery industry, either as individual companies or as a whole, could not become competitive on its own, and its lack of competitiveness, in turn, checked the development of the iron and steel industry. This vicious cycle is what is known as a coordination failure.

The Council for Industrial Rationalization, established under MITI in 1949, was the second major deliberative council established after the war. It was created to resolve this coordination failure. The council was composed of 29 industry branches that reported to the Coordination Branch and the General Branch. The industry branches reported to the Coordination Branch, which coordinated them. As in the Committee for the Economic Recovery Plan, the representatives of the industrial associations constituted a large part of the council members: 30 of the council's 118 members (25 percent) were the chairmen, secretaries, and other representatives of industrial associations (table 8.5).

In 1949 and 1950, the council concentrated the discussion of coordination failure in the Iron and Steel Branch and the Coal Branch. The Iron and Steel Branch examined the price of coal necessary to make the iron and steel industry competitive, on the condition that the iron and steel industry itself carried out new investment to enhance efficiency. It thought that the price of coking coal should be lower than 2,800 yen per ton. At the same time, the Coal Branch examined the prospect of a decrease in the price of coal, which would be achieved by the new investment in coal mines. It was thought that the cost of running a coal mine could be cut 18 percent. However, the price of coking coal would still be 3,700 yen per ton. The interim conclusions were pessimistic.

The two branches reported their interim conclusions to the Coordination Branch, which reexamined them. It found that the upper price limit of coking coal could be raised to 3,200–3,300 yen per ton, if iron and steel production was concentrated into relatively efficient plants and crude oil was used as fuel. Another condition was that coal production had to be concentrated in relatively efficient mines and the interest rate on the loan of the Reconversion Finance Bank, a public financial institution for economic recovery, had to be lower. The Coordination Branch included this conclusion in its final report to the minister of international trade and industry, who was appointed by the cabinet in August 1950.

Meanwhile, the Ministry of Transportation (MOT), which was in charge of the shipbuilding industry, organized the Research Committee on Steel for Shipbuilding, with the Economic Stabilization Board. It specified that, in order for Japanese ships to be competitive with European ships, the price of steel for shipbuilding would have to fall below 27,000 yen per ton. According to the committee, this condition could be met, if the price of steel plates became 24,090 yen per ton. A thorough examination by the Iron and Steel Branch of the Industrial Rationalization Council showed that, with rationalization, the price of steel plates would fall to that approximate level. In other words, along with the rationalization of the steel and coal industry, rationalization of the shipbuilding industry would create the prospect of an internationally competitive industry.

In this case, a certain amount of simultaneous new investment supported by government policies constituted the path out of a coordination failure, and the government committed itself to that policy at the cabinet level. This induced the aggressive investment plans of the iron and steel companies in 1950 and 1951. These plans were compiled by MITI and issued as the First Iron and Steel Rationalization Plan. Table 8.6 shows investment by industry. It is remarkable that total investment increased in 1950 and that the share of the mining, metal, and machinery industries in total investment rose sharply. The increase in 1950 partly reflected the effect of the Korean War, but the level of investment continued to be high after the armistice in 1951 (table 8.6).

Supply of Basic Materials and Industrial Infrastructure

The industrial rationalization in early 1950s boosted the Japanese economy. However, soon after high economic growth was initiated in 1955, basic materials and services, such as the steel, electricity, and transportation, experienced bottlenecks. In particular, the shortage of steel impeded the export of machinery. This problem was resolved through the cooperation of MITI and the related industrial associations. Deliberating with these industrial associations, MITI determined the measures to secure steel for machinery for export at the end of 1956 (MITI 1956). It aimed at "securing steel for exporting machinery at the stable price, through the voluntary organization, based on cooperation between the steel industry and the machinery industry." It prescribed that the steel industry should supply 25,000 tons of steel on preferential terms to the machinery export industry every quarter. This steel would be allocated to each machinery company, based on the decision of the Screening Committee of Steel for Exporting Ma-

Table 8.6 Investment by Industry

	Million yen Total	Mining	Metal	Machinery
1949	44,150	(2,720)	1,930	(2,071)
1950	544,358	4,470	61,470	27,251
1951	637,933	58,638	39,563	42,097
1952	485,280	25,429	48,591	34,072
1953	601,269	29,094	57,108	43,061
1954	—	46,229	72,652	94,940
1955	523,662	9,544	41,787	56,899

— not available.

Source: Ministry of Finance, Hojin Kigyo Tokei Nenpo (Year Book of Company Statistics), various issues.

chinery, which was composed of MITI bureaucrats and the representatives of industrial associations.

Meanwhile, the iron and steel companies drew up their own plans for expanding equipment, referring to the Five-Year Plan for Economic Independence, which was determined by the cabinet in December 1955. MITI compiled these company plans issued them as the Second Iron and Steel Rationalization Plan. The focus of the Second Iron and Steel Rationalization Plan was to introduce basic oxygen furnaces and renovating blast furnaces (Lynn 1982). Thus Japan's steel industry would substitute iron ore for scrap, on which it had depended heavily since before the war. In order to make the plan effective, infrastructure such as ore carriers and port facilities for unloading the iron ore had to be provided simultaneously.

This coordination was achieved in the bureau-pluralistic manner. In early 1956, MITI drew up a document that stressed the need to invest in overseas iron ore mines, ore carriers, and port facilities (MITI, Heavy Industry Bureau 1963: 60–61). Responding to MITI's proposal, the Committee of the Overseas Iron Raw Materials, a private committee of the major iron and steel companies, requested that the Ministry of Transportation construct 15 ore carriers in the 15,000-gross ton class within five years.

However, because the ore carriers specialized in iron ore, a typical holdup problem took place. Once the ore carriers were built, the iron and steel companies could hold up the shipping companies, and the shipping companies, expecting the holdup, delayed building the ore carriers. This problem was resolved through negotiations among the industrial associations of the steel and shipping industries, MITI, and the MOT. The iron and steel companies established the Japan Ore Transportation Company, which shared the ore carriers with the shipping companies (Tekko Shinbunsha 1957: 84–85; 1959: 8, 69; MITI, Heavy Industry Bureau 1963: 323).

Meanwhile, the Japan Iron and Steel Association established the Committee for Port Preparation and petitioned government authorities and the parties to set up the Special Account for Emergent Preparation of the Ports for the Specific Industries (Japan Iron and Steel Association 1957). MOT came to share the idea. MOT's Bureau of Ports considered that the level of port capacity was restricting economic growth and determined that the ports had to be prepared for industries such as iron and steel, petroleum, and coal (Japan Iron and Steel Association 1957). In August 1958, the cabinet decided to set up a special account for preparing the ports to ship iron, steel, and petroleum (Tekko Shinbunsha 1959:178–80; MITI, Heavy Industry Bureau 1963: 324–25).

Owing to the Second Iron and Steel Rationalization Plan, the production costs of Japan's iron and steel industry declined to a level below those of the U.S. iron and steel industry in the late 1950s (Yamawaki 1984: 263). This enabled Japan's machinery industry to become internationally competitive. The system of bureau-pluralistic coordination resolved the bottlenecks in basic materials and infrastructure, which sustained the economy's high growth.

TRANSITION OF ENVIRONMENTAL CONDITIONS AND POLICY MISMANAGEMENT

The bureau-pluralistic system worked to coordinate Japanese economic growth after the 1950s. What conditions enabled the solid performance of bureau pluralism? How did those conditions evolve? These questions are fundamental to understanding the success and failure of the Japanese economy from the 1950s to the 1990s.

Bureau pluralism is a highly decentralized system. First, the power of decisionmaking is distributed to each bureau, which is in charge of an industry, and its counterpart in the business sector. Second, a substantial part of the coordination among the original bureaus is executed horizontally. In other words, there is no powerful central unit (headquarters) to coordinate the activities of the units on the lower level of the hierarchy.

These characteristics are both an advantage and a disadvantage of bureau pluralism. The advantage is that local information scattered around the industries can be incorporated quickly into government policy (Aoki 1988: 284–85). In the early 1950s, the coordination failure in the coal, steel, and machinery industries was recognized precisely, and the appropriate coordination measures were taken to resolve it. In the high-growth era, various bottlenecks were detected quickly and resolved.

The disadvantage is that bureau pluralism tends to be conservative. Because decisionmaking is decentralized in each original bureau, it is

difficult to draw up and implement a radical policy against the interests of the original bureau and the industry under its jurisdiction. In
other words, bureau pluralism is inclined to protect the vested interests of existing industries and bureaucrats.

The efficacy of bureau pluralism depends on the relative importance of these advantages and disadvantages, which, in turn, depends
on environmental conditions. The environmental conditions in Japan
in the 1950s and 1960s were favorable for bureau pluralism. Complementarity among industries was pervasive in this period. In the early
1950s, the coal, steel, and machinery industries were highly complementary to one another, and in the late 1950s, steel, machinery, and
transportation were complementary. One industry's interests were also
the other industries' interests. There were few serious conflicts among
industries, and the vested interests were not especially harmful to economic growth. It is true that declining industries such as coal mining
and agriculture (rice) were protected by the government, but the protection could be easily bypassed by importing substitutive goods,
namely petroleum and wheat. In fact, the share of coal in the total
energy supply and that of rice in the total food supply declined sharply
in the 1950s and 1960s.

At the same time, in the process of economic growth, numerous
small problems related to coordination failures, and bottlenecks
continuously arose. In order to cope with these problems quickly, bureau pluralism, with its decentralized decisionmaking, was an efficient
system.

However, the conditions have changed substantially since the 1980s.
These changes are well illustrated by the case of the information and
telecommunications industry. It is widely recognized that the major
force driving the rapid growth of the U.S. economy in the 1990s was
the advanced use of information technology in wide-ranging areas of
the economy. Japan has lagged far behind the United States in this
respect, as shown in table 8.7 (Oniki 1996: 18; Kokuryo 1998: 353;
Japan Federation of Economic Organizations 2000).

The information and telecommunications industry emerged in the
1980s, fusing the computer, telecommunications, and broadcasting
industries (Higashi 1999: 31–32). In Japan, the computer has been
under the jurisdiction of MITI, and telecommunications and broadcasting have been under the jurisdiction of the Ministry of Postal Ser-

Table 8.7 Comparison of the Utilization of Information Technology for Industry
between Japan and the United States (1993–94)

Total	Ratios (United States/Japan)
Equipment ratio of personal computers	4.7
Networking ratio of personal computers	3.9
Subscription ratio of computer telecommunications	1.3
Number of internet hosts	12.5
Equipment ratio of data bases	1.4

Source: Ministry of Postal Services, Tsushin Hakusho (Telecommunication White Paper), 1996, p. 264.

vices (MPS). When the information and telecommunications industry started to develop, the two ministries struggled severely over its
jurisdiction. This struggle retarded the provision of institutional and
physical infrastructure for the information and telecommunications
industry in Japan.

In 1984, MITI drew up a draft of the Law for Facilitating Information Processing, which aimed to achieve advanced use of the computer, security of the computer, standardization of the information
apparatus, and protection of privacy. At the same time, the MPS drew
up a draft of the Law for Providing Infrastructure of Advanced Telecommunications, which closely resembled MITI's draft. MITI and the
MPS made efforts to adjust the two drafts, but eventually neither of
them was realized (Kawakita 1985: 123–26). In general, the struggle
over jurisdiction between MITI and MPS made it difficult for the
Japanese government to implement consistent policies regarding the
information and telecommunications industry (Itami 1996: 210).

Bureau-pluralistic coordination assumes clear demarcation and jurisdiction over industry. If this condition is not met, ministries tend to
struggle for jurisdiction, as occurred in the information and telecommunications industry, because the expansion of jurisdiction is connected
directly to the interests of the bureaucrats, through the allocation of
budget and former bureaucrats to the industries (*amakudari*). The industry demarcation problem is serious, because new fields, such as
biotechnology and environmental protection, cross the borders of existing industries (Aoki 1999: 24).

Besides the struggle for jurisdiction between MITI and MPS, another
disadvantage of bureau pluralism retarded the development of Japan's
information and telecommunications industry. As a result of the tele-

communications reform in 1985, the Telecommunication and Telephone Corporation was privatized and became NTT, and three new common carriers were established. Although path-breaking, subsequent reform was terribly slow (Suzumura 1997: 31; Takigawa 1999: 178–81).

After the reform in 1985, the discussion of telecommunications reform focused on the reorganization of NTT. More than 10 years passed before MPS decided to divide NTT into two local companies and one long-distance company. Until 1996, telecommunications reform hardly progressed, and MPS continued to exercise discretionary control over various aspects of the industry, including fees, new entries, and competition among NTT and the new common carriers.

The slow pace of reform caused substantial problems. According to the MPS's survey in 1997, the fee for using an exclusive circuit (1.5 Mbps) was 4.7 times as high in Tokyo as in New York. The high fee checked the use of information technology by Japanese companies. Higashi (1999: 69) mentions the case of Kao Company, which is a major chemical company and famous for its progressive strategy to use information technology. In 1998, Kao Company announced that it had given up its plan to exercise remote control over all of its plants, which were scattered throughout Japan, because of the high cost of telecommunications. According to Higashi (1999), if the cost had been the same in Japan as in the United States, Kao's plan would have been feasible.

The reason why telecommunications reform was so slow lies in bureau-pluralistic decisionmaking. The basic telecommunications policy was deliberated by the Telecommunication Council under MPS. The deliberation concerning telecommunications reform was very time-consuming, because the reform would directly affect the vested interests of existing companies and of MPS itself. In this sense, the nature of the policy issues was different from that in the 1950s and 1960s, making the conservative bias of bureau pluralism harmful to the economy.

CONCLUDING REMARKS

We can identify the common institutional and organizational factors, namely bureau pluralism, behind the success and failure of the Japanese economy from the 1950s to the 1990s. Bureau pluralism in Japan is an outcome of a path-dependent evolution of the economic system.

The bureau-pluralistic system, including deliberative councils and industrial associations, evolved from experiences during World War II. This system worked efficiently to coordinate economic growth in the 1950s and the high-growth era.

It was effective in this era because industries were highly complementary. Consequently, on the one hand, there were few serious conflicts among industries and their counterparts in the bureaucracy, which made it possible to avoid the conservative bias due to the vested interests of existing industries. On the other hand, this complementarity was a source of numerous failures to coordinate various aspects of the economy. The decentralized decisionmaking and horizontal coordination of bureau pluralism worked efficiently and quickly to detect and resolve these coordination failures.

The same attribute of bureau pluralism impeded the Japanese economy from adapting to changes in the global economy since the 1980s. First, the newly growing industries of information and telecommunications crossed the borders of existing industries and therefore the borders of bureaucratic jurisdiction, which caused serious disputes among ministries. Second, the reforms necessary to adapt to the global changes collided with the interests of existing industries and ministries. Bureau pluralism is not adept at resolving disputes over jurisdiction and conflicts with vested interests. In this sense, the success and failure of the Japanese economy resulted from the same source.

I would like to thank Yingyi Qian, Ha-Joon Chang, Meredith Woo-Cumings, Shahid Yasuf, Shujiro Urata, and other participants of the World Bank Workshop on Rethinking the East Asian Miracle, for helpful comments.

REFERENCES

Aoki, Masahiko. 1970. *Soshiki to Keikaku no Keizai Riron [Economic Theory of Organization and Planning]*. Tokyo: Iwanami Shoten.

———. 1988. *Information, Incentives, and Bargaining in the Japanese Economy*. New York: Cambridge University Press.

———. 1999. "Kanryosei Tagenshugi Kokka to Sangyo Soshiki no Kyoshinka [Co-evolution of the Bureau-Pluralistic State and Industrial Organization]." In Masahiko Aoki, M. Okuno-Fujiwara, and T. Okazaki, eds., *Shijo no Yakuwari, Kokka no Yakuwari [Role of Market, Role of State]*. Toyo Keizai.

Economic Planning Agency. 1996. *Chokisokyu Syuyo Keiretsu Kokumin Keizai Keisan Hokoku: Heisei 2nen Kijun [Report on National Accounts from 1955 to 1994].* Tokyo: Printing Bureau of the Ministry of Finance.

Hara, A. 1989. "Senji Tosei." In T. Nakamura, ed., *Keikakuka to Minshuka [Planning and Democratization].* Tokyo: Iwanami Shoten.

Heavy Industry Bureau, MITI. 1963. *Tekkogyo no Gorika to sono Seika: Dainiji Gorika Keikaku wo Chushintoshite [Rationalization of the Iron and Steel Industry].* Tokyo: Kogyo Tosho Shuppan.

Higashi. 1999. "Joho Tsushin Kodoka Jidai no Kozu to Senryaku [Perspectives and Strategy of the Age of Advanced Information and Telecommunication]." In I. Shirakawa, ed., *Gurobaruka to Shintensuru Joho Tsuhin Sangyo [Globalization and Development of the Information and Telecommunication Industry].* Tokyo: Tsusho Sangyo Chosakai.

Itami, H.. 1996. *Nihon no Konpyuta Sangyo [Japan's Computer Industry].* Tokyo: NTT Shuppan.

Japan Federation of Economic Organizations. 2000. "Proposals for Realization of a Free, Fair, and Transparent Information and Telecommunication Market." http://www.keidanren.or.jp/english/policy/pol078/index.html.

Japan Iron and Steel Association. 1957. "Un'ei Iinkai Shiryo [Materials of the Management Committee]." Tokyo. Processed.

———. 1959. *Postwar History of Iron and Steel.* Tokyo.

Kawakita, T. 1985. *Tsusan Yusei Senso [The War between MITI and MPS].* Tokyo: Kyoikusha.

Kokuryo, J. 1998. "Johoka ni yoru Purattofomugata Keiei Senryaku no Tenkai to Nihon Kigyo. [Platform Strategy by Information Technology and the Japanese Firm]." In R. Komiya and M. Okuno-Fujiwara, eds., *The Japanese Economy: Agenda for 21st Century.* Tokyo: Toyo Keizai Shinposha.

Komiya, R. 1998. *Nihon Sangyo Boeki no Keizai Bunseki [Economic Analysis of the Japanese Industry and International Trade].* Tokyo: Toyo Kiezai Shinposha.

Lynn, L. 1982. *How Japan Innovates: A Comparison with U.S. in the Case of Oxygen Steelmaking.* Boulder, Colo.: Westview Press.

MITI (Ministry of International Trade and Industry). 1949. "Sangyo Gorika Shingikai Iin [Membership List of the Council for Industrial Rationalization]." Tokyo. Processed.

———. 1956. "Yushutsu Kikai-yo Futsuko Kozai Kakuhosochi Yoko [Measures to Secure Steel for Machinery for Export]." *Nihon Kikai Yushutsu Kumiai [Japan Machinery Exporters' Association]* 4(9).

———. 1961. *Shoko Seisakushi [History of Commercial and Industrial Policy].* Vol. 4. Tokyo: Association for Publishing History of Commercial and Industrial Policy.

———. 1970a. "Sangyo Kozo Shingikai Iin Meibo [Membership List of the Industrial Structure Council]." Tokyo. Processed.

———. 1970b. *Tsusan Handobukku [MITI Handbook].* Tokyo: Shoko Kaikan.

———. 1994. *MITI Handbook.* Tokyo.

Nippon Steel Company. 1981. *Hono to Tomoni: Yawata Seitetsu Kabushikigaisha Shashi [History of Yawata Steel Company]*. Tokyo.

Okazaki, Tetsuji. 1988. "Dainiji Sekaitaisenki Niokeru Senji Keikaku Keizai no Kozo to Unko [Structure and Working of the Japanese Wartime Planned Economy in WWII]." *Shakai Kagaku Kenkyu* 40(4).

———. 1993a. "The Japanese Firm under the Wartime Planned Economy." *Journal of the Japanese and International Economies* 7:175–203.

———. 1993b. "Nihon no Seifu Kigyo kan Kankei: Gyokaidantai-Shingikai Shisutemu no Keisei ni Kansuru Oboegaki [Government-Firm Relationship in Japan: A Note on the Evolution of the System of Industrial Associations and Deliberative Councils]." *Soshiki Kagaku* 26 (4).

———. 1996. "The Government-Firm Relationship in Postwar Japanese Economic Recovery: Resolving the Coordination Failure by Coordination in Industrial Rationalization." In Masahiko Aoki, Hyung-Ki Kim, and Masahiro Okuno-Fujiwara, eds., *The Role of Government in East Asian Economic Development: Comparative Institutional Analysis*. New York: Oxford University Press.

Okazaki, Tetsuji, and M. Okuno-Fujiwara. 1999. "Japan's Present-Day Economic System and Its Historical Origins." In T. Okazaki and M. Okuno-Fujiwara, eds., *The Japanese Economic System and Its Historical Origins*. New York: Oxford University Press.

Oniki, H. 1996. "Joho Tsuhin Sangyo ni okeru Kyoso to Kisei [Competition and Regulation in the Information and Telecommunication Industry]." *Jurist* 1099.

Secretary, Office of the Council of the Economic Recovery Plan. 1948. "The Membership List of the Council of the Economic Recovery Plan." Tokyo. Processed.

Stiglitz, Joseph. 1999. "Lessons from East Asia." *Journal of Policy Modeling* 21(3):283–87.

Suzumura, K. 1996. "Joho Tsushin no Seido Kaikaku to Sangyo Seisaku [Institutional Reform and Industrial Policy in Information and Telecommunication]." *Business Review* 44(1).

———. 1997. "Kyoso ni Hitsuyo na Dokuritsu Referi Kikan [Competiton Needs an Independent Referee Institution]." *Nihon Keizai Kenkyu Senta Kaiho* (June).

Takigawa, T. 1999. "Tsushin Sangyo no Jiyuka to Kisei Kaikaku [Liberalization of Telecommunications Industry and Reform of Regulation]." In I. Shirakawa, ed., *Gurobaruka to Shintensuru Joho Tsuhin Sangyo [Globalization and Development of the Information and Telecommunication Industry]*. Tokyo: Tsusho Sangyo Chosakai.

Tekko Shinbunsha. 1957. *Tekko Nenkan [Iron and Steel Year Book]*. Tokyo.

———. 1959. *Tekko Nenkan [Iron and Steel Year Book]*. Tokyo.

World Bank. 1993. *The East Asian Miracle: Economic Growth and Public Policy*. New York: Oxford University Press.

Yamawaki. 1984. "Tekko Gyo [Iron and Steel Industry]." In R. Komiya, M. Okuno-Fujiwara, and K. Suzumura, eds., *Nihon no Sangyo Seisaku [The Japanese Industrial Policy]*. Tokyo: Daigaku Shuppankai.

Yonekura, S. 1999. "The Functions of Industrial Associations." In T. Okazaki and M. Okuno-Fujiwara, eds., *The Japanese Economic System and Its Historical Origins*. New York: Oxford University Press.

CHAPTER 9

MIRACLE AS PROLOGUE:
THE STATE AND THE REFORM OF
THE CORPORATE SECTOR IN KOREA

Meredith Woo-Cumings

T
he owl of Minerva, it is said, stretches its wings at the fall of dusk. The Asian financial crisis began in the region four years ago, profoundly altering the political and social landscape in places like Indonesia and Korea and exacting a huge economic toll. The crisis has finally come full circle. Growth has resumed in the area, obviating dark worries that the "miracle" in East Asia would end in the kind of "lost decade" that beset much of Latin America and Africa in the 1980s. In the comfort of such knowledge, this volume seeks to ask what lessons we might derive from the experience of the past three years and thus revise our understanding of economic growth in East Asia.

In one sense, the rapid resumption of growth would seem to vindicate the analysis in *The East Asian Miracle* (World Bank 1993) that the region had indeed achieved its growth on the basis of superior accumulation of physical and human capital as well as sound macroeconomic fundamentals. As the introductory chapter to this volume suggests, the V-shaped recovery does restore some faith in the region's underlying competitive strength. But *The East Asian Miracle*, for all its discussions about the basics and fundamentals, failed to explore the true basics: the social and political underpinnings that have propelled economic growth in East Asia. There was precious little in the book that anticipated the charges of "crony capitalism" that were immediately raised in the wake of the Asian crisis or to suggest, on the basis of real and profound knowledge about the countries concerned, the kind of social and economic reforms that could be enacted to address issues like crony capitalism.

This chapter seeks to examine the social and political relationships that have determined the conduct of economic policy in East Asia by examining the relationship between the state and the private sector. The focus is primarily on Korea, but I frame the Korean situation against the backdrop of Southeast Asia to underscore the vast regional differences in state-business relationships that were not appreciated sufficiently in *The East Asian Miracle*, not to mention the problem in issuing one-size-fits-all policy recommendations regarding corporate sector restructuring.

This chapter is organized as follows. First, I discuss the state-business relationship that emerged in Korea as the result of industrial policy. The debate on industrial policy, including the one in *The East Asian Miracle*, was concerned mostly with economic outcomes, missing the important point that industrial policy can lead to profound structural corruption. One of the most powerful arguments against industrial policy is not that it supplants the market but that it is commonly used to protect vested interests.[1] This form of structural corruption is different, however, from the Southeast Asian "crony capitalism" that K. S. Jomo discusses in chapter 12 of this volume. I argue that the financial crisis in Korea was born, in part, by the inability of government to resolve the long-standing dilemma of its industrial policy—the existence of a high-leverage economy, binding the state together with a weak banking sector and a hugely indebted corporate sector in a kind of co-insurance scheme. The government's best effort to resolve this dilemma, mostly by monitoring the corporate sector and limiting its access to capital, was often defeated by the politicians. In the 1990s the government shifted gears and reduced its oversight of banks and the corporate sector, hoping for the market to discipline firms. In the end, neither the intensification nor the reduction of government regulation worked to remedy the problem of highly leveraged firms and a weak banking sector.

Second, I discuss the experience of private sector restructuring in Korea in the aftermath of the Asian crisis. I argue that the reform in Korea does not signify a retreat of the state from the market. The Korean leadership is deeply committed to increasing transparency and market discipline in the private sector, but to do so, it has had to intervene in the market even more deeply than before the crisis, reinvigorating the developmental bureaucracy. In other words, the Asian crisis has contributed to reinventing the developmental state in Korea, which seemed to be in retreat for much of the 1990s. In that sense, Korean growth in the past decades—the "miracle"—is but a prologue for the future.

Finally, I discuss the lessons for other countries from Korea's experience in restructuring the corporate sector. This experience is especially relevant for China, which has occasionally expressed an interest in developing Korean-type conglomerates and where the relationship between the state and state-owned enterprises (SOEs) seems to contain elements of the Korean-like developmental dilemma. The Korean experience may also shed light on Japan's effort to restructure the banking sector. Japan has provided Korea with a political and economic template for rapid growth but is now mired in a similar developmental quandary.

Before proceeding with the discussion of Korea and, to a more limited extent, Southeast Asia, I offer some preliminary remarks to explain my preference for thinking about corporate sector reform in terms of the state-business relationship rather than in terms of corporate governance.

CORPORATE GOVERNANCE AND THE FORMATION OF THE STATE-BUSINESS RELATIONSHIP IN KOREA AND SOUTHEAST ASIA

The traditional discourse of corporate governance was predicated on the long-standing practice in the United States of separating corporate ownership from control. In the context of "modern" enterprise, good governance is really about holding corporate management accountable to the interests of shareholders or reducing *agency costs* (meaning the costs to shareholders of managerial behavior not consistent with their interests). The methods for achieving this accountability are often formal and legalistic and, according to some, idiosyncratic to Anglo-American traditions. In this sense, corporate governance can be thought of as a separate taxonomic entity from, say, "contractual governance," which is said to characterize the "Nippo-Rhenish" model of business organization. In the latter, good governance is a matter of reducing *transaction costs* by building and investing in stable and long-term commercial relationships among transacting companies (Gourevitch 1996).

To avoid equating corporate governance with the ideal type of Anglo-American business practice (which would have limited utility as a template for countries with substantially different legal norms and traditions), we can seek a broader conceptualization that transcends the regional specificity of governance models and refer to it simply as "the entire set of incentives, safeguards, and dispute-resolution processes used to order the activities of various corporate stakeholders, each seeking to improve its welfare through coordinated economic activity with others" (Kester 1996: 109). In this rendering, both the Anglo-American and Nippo-Rhenish systems of governance are economically rational attempts to resolve problems of coordination and control among corporate stakeholders, and no a priori judgment can be made about the ultimate superiority of either national configuration. This catholic definition of corporate governance is still, however, predicated on the highly evolved structure of the modern corporation, with a whole panoply of legal or otherwise regularized sets of norms that dictate the behavior of transacting parties.

Furthermore, the debate on corporate governance in the context of global competition has been particularly fickle and prone to revaluations. In the 1980s and well into the 1990s, for instance, it was fashionable to argue that the Anglo-American style of corporate governance (and various corporate restructuring movements in particular) reduced investment and forced American managers to think short term. In contrast, Japanese corporate managers were thought to enjoy certain freedoms in retaining excess capital (rather than returning it to shareholders) and in determining long-term investment strategies (without oversight of shareholders). This used to be viewed as the core of Japan's competitive edge.

Today this historical verdict has been completely reversed, as Japan completes what Tetsuji Okazaki in chapter 8 of this volume calls its most stagnant decade since the late nineteenth century and as scholars reassess the legacy of the 1980s. In periods of industrial transformation, rapid technological and organizational change encourages lower production costs and higher average productivity of labor. But rapid change also results in widespread excess capacity and lower rates of growth in labor income, causing corporate downsizing and exit. The result was the mergers-and-acquisitions wave of the 1980s that ended up sharply reducing capacity; that, combined with leveraged takeovers and buyouts, represented "healthy adjustments" to the overcapacity that burdened many sectors of the U.S. economy (Jensen 1997). Corporate raiders turned out to be the ephors, or overseers, of modern capitalism. Likewise, the decline in the Japanese economy was viewed as the result of structural overcapacity, fueled by lax investment criteria employed by Japanese companies and the failure to pay out excess capital in the form of higher dividends or share repurchases.

Such periodic revaluation reflects profound (or at least shifting) uncertainty about what constitutes a good system of corporate governance. We all agree that good corporate governance is important, as are motherhood, the flag, peace, and goodwill to humanity. But what exactly constitutes truly *good* governance, and how is it obtained?

In the context of East Asia, I sharply distinguish Northeast Asia from Southeast Asia and find two highly distinctive patterns of corporate governance. The first is a Japan-shaped model that influences Taiwan (China) and the current leadership in China, but is best exemplified by the Republic of Korea (hereafter Korea). The second is a Chinese business practice having roots at least 150 years old that is market-adaptive and efficient enough to need little reform of corporate practice or perhaps, from an Anglo-Saxon standpoint, to need so *much* reform as to make the task impossible. This is the model that is widely used in Southeast Asia.

The Korean model of corporate governance resembles the Nippo-Rhenish model, in that it is essentially controlled by insiders, rather than outside investors, and is accomplished through the mechanism of intragroup shareholding, against the backdrop of a corporate law, until 1998, banning hostile takeover. The difference, however, is in the relational monitoring agent: unlike in Japan or Germany, the main monitoring agent is the state, which exercises strong influences on corporate investment decisions and mediates the process of changes in corporate control (Chang, Park, and Yoo 1998).

The reason for this has to do with history, from the colonial through the postindependence period. The template for Korea's big-business firm, called the *chaebol*, was the wartime Japanese *zaibatsu*. (In fact, they mean the same thing in Chinese characters.) The term *zaibatsu* refers to family-dominated combines that developed following World War I, using holding organizations to maintain control over their industries and expanding rapidly in the heavy industrialization drives and wartime conditions of the 1930s and 1940s (Hadley 1970: 21). Keiichiro Nakagawa, a business historian at the University of Tokyo, sees the *zaibatsu* as "a major economic entity established in a developing country, whose fundamental social structure is based on [an] instinctive gregarious group expressed as [a] family, to pursue an industrialization process in [the] face of international competition against industrialized countries" (Keiichiro Nakagawa, quoted in Hattori 1989: 80). In other words, an extraordinary family-based combination of wealth and power at home is necessary to fight more weighty and competitive foreign corporations that arrived in the world economy earlier. From Professor Nakagawa's developmental perspective, it is not so surprising that the Korean *chaebol* of today is an atavism of the prewar *zaibatsu*. When the *chaebol* is defined as a "large multicompany which operates in different markets under common financial and management control and maintains relationships of long-lasting trust, loyalty, and cooperation among group members," we see the parallel with the *zaibatsu* of the prewar years (Kim 1987: 6).

The goal of the *zaibatsu* was not high-market occupancy of one, two, or a few related markets, but an oligopolistic position running the gamut of the modern sector of the economy. And because these firms emphasized corporate unity through family ties and coordination of subsidiaries by the holding company, they achieved tight control over the astonishing market breadth of the combines.[2] The prewar *zaibatsu* also represented a means of extending control far beyond the controller's corporate (or partnership) limits, thus denying independence of action to businesses within the network. The techniques to bring this about included ownership, personnel, credit, and centralized buying and selling. This system of enterprise worked more for market share than solely for the company's profit; companies often operated at a loss (and, of course, during the war they produced everything under government dictate; Hadley 1970: 37–41).

Korea's military leaders who served in the Pacific War were familiar with this model, and the extensive wartime coordination between the Japanese state and big business, with highly centralized finance as the linchpin, appealed to them. State control over finance not only made the implementation of industrial policy possible but also bolstered the power base of the state by creating a whole entrepreneurial class beholden to the political leadership. This was no small consideration for a postcolonial state with a military regime at the helm that was perennially struggling for legitimacy. The idea was to graft the *zaibatsu* onto Korea; the only question was how to create the Korean *zaibatsu* out of the ravages of colonialism and war. The answer was industrial policy, with financial repression as the core mechanism for shifting resources from savers to producers, which created hugely leveraged firms as the carriers of Korean capitalism.[3]

The state created the *chaebol* by using a credit-based system of industrial finance. In a nation with a dearth of accumulated capital, business had to rely on credits from banks controlled and (until the 1980s) owned by the state. Since the firms were highly leveraged, much more so than they were in Latin America or Southeast Asia, business had to maintain good relations with the state so as to avert the possibility of default (through the severance of friendly credits). For its part, the state manipulated Korea's credit-based system of industrial financing so that it could influence the economy's investment pattern and guide sectoral mobility. The highly leveraged nature of business firms in Korea—the norm throughout Korean history—meant that even small changes in the discount rate or in concessional credit rates between sectors could dramatically affect resource allocation, because the effect of such instruments on the firms' cash flow position was so much greater given their high debt/equity ratios. For that reason, Korean firms closely conformed to the macroeconomic policy goals of the state (for detailed discussion, see Woo 1991).

In Southeast Asia, in contrast, the relationship between the state and big business is forged not through industrial policy, but through an ethnic division of labor in managing politics and the economy in the context of ethnic apartheid between political and economic powers. Because Southeast Asian states are bereft of industrial policy, except where it is a device to buttress the economically disadvantaged ethnic majority, they have had a (relatively) free market, punctuated by economic affirmative action of sorts. The upshot is that family businesses in Southeast Asia rely less on the ethnically alien government and, of course, less on government-mediated capital. Thus the business class in the heterogeneous Southeast Asia was forced into self-sufficiency and onto the market.

The differences were determined from the days of colonialism. If Japanese colonialism bequeathed to the Koreans the template of the authoritarian interventionist state and the *zaibatsu*, European colonialism bequeathed the opposite: minimal taxation, strict avoidance of deficits, and an unprotected market. K. S. Jomo attributes the habits and practices of Chinese businesses in Southeast Asia to their historical inability to rely on the colonial government. Even when the state and the legal system became more accessible to Chinese business interests, a "Chinese business idiom" persisted that abjured close association with the government (Jomo 1997: 251). Colonial governments also left a legacy of an ethnic division of labor and a cobbled-together concept of the nation—best exemplified by Malaysia.

Malaysia had its origins in an explicitly negotiated "bargain" that set the stage for a peaceful transfer of power from the British in 1957. This bargain, reached between ethnic political parties representing the Malay, Chinese, and Indians, became the basis for a coalition that has ruled Malaysia since independence. Malaysia has practiced the most pronounced policy of "apartheid," because it was also the last to be independent from British rule. Elsewhere, ethnic compacts occurred more haphazardly, but the generalization—cobbled-together nations, ethnic divisions of labor—holds for most of Southeast Asia. (For detailed discussions, see Bowie 1991; McVey 1992; Lim and Gosling 1983; Jesudason 1989.)

Notwithstanding wide variations from country to country, the general sociological trend in Southeast Asia after independence was for upwardly mobile "natives" to claim positions in the political realm (state bureaucracies, military, and police), especially in Malaysia and Indonesia; the people of Chinese ancestry were relegated to the private commercial sector.[4] Benedict Anderson reminds us that from 1966 to 1998 not a single person of known Chinese descent became a cabinet minister, senior civil servant, general, admiral, or air marshal in Indonesia. Yet the Chinese in Indonesia have been called "the race that counts," according to Adam Schwarz, and almost all of the biggest "crony capitalists" around Suharto came from this group (Anderson 1998; Schwarz 1995). Unlike industrial leaders in Korea or Japan who have stuck with one big idea (industrial policy), Chinese "pariah" capitalists have quickly adapted themselves to policy decisions made by the alien ethnic elites, whose single advantage over the Chinese is that they hold state power.

Chinese businesses have thrived in all milieus, under both protectionist *and* liberal regimes. For instance, occasional nationalist restrictions on foreign-owned enterprises tended to help the Chinese by limiting competition, and when foreign firms were localized, the Chinese often were the logical partners. With import-substitution industrialization, the local-ownership requirement often helped the Chinese to acquire foreign technology, and "local-content" requirements in industries such as automobiles also created new business opportunities for local Chinese enterprises. But the Chinese have also done well with structural adjustment and liberal market-oriented economic reform programs (involving trade and investment regimes, financial reforms, deregulation, and privatization of state-owned enterprises), which frequently hurt the local private sector. These policies are more readily effected in Southeast Asia than in other developing countries because of the political weakness of the Chinese-dominated local private sector. Instead of resisting the state, the Chinese just made the best of their opportunities, as usual. The Chinese were also protected against the tight monetary policies, credit rationing, and high interest rates characteristic of macroeconomic stabilization policies. This is because they have disproportionate access to alternative sources of capital abroad, including informal ethnic-based credit networks at home, internal financing in Chinese conglomerates (many of which own their own banks), and preferred-customer status among other local banks (most of which are Chinese owned; see Lim and Gosling 1997: 287–88).

When Chinese family firms engage in "opportunistic diversification," they use the retained profits of existing firms (unlike the Korean *chaebol*) under the management of a family member or another highly trusted close associate. And even when they grow and diversify (as, say, in Hong Kong), they tend to think in terms of their long experience in, say, the textile industry, and their major managerial skills and commitments reflect it. Where investment requirements are too great or political and business connections are needed, the families enter into alliances with trusted partners to set up new businesses, thus forming the Chinese "business groups" that operate in a variety of industries.

Large Chinese family businesses span a number of fields and are in-
terconnected through a network of alliances and ties between family
heads. In contrast to the Korean *chaebol*, Chinese businesses combine
managerial specialization with entrepreneurial diversification. The
strategic preferences of the Chinese family firm include reliance on
price and cost competition, short payback periods for new investments,
the intensive use of resources, and a reluctance to share control or
responsibility. Risks are managed largely by restricting commitments
and maximizing resource flexibility. These firms are not integrated
through a central administrative hierarchy like the Korean *chaebol*; instead, they operate as partnerships united by common
investments and mutual trust. The critical locus of decisionmaking and
control remains the individual family business (Whitley 1992: 54–55).

In Hong Kong, where there are many public companies, the typical
Chinese-run family business invites outside equity participation by
offering a minority stake in a public company within the network of
family firms. Control of public companies stays within the family
through direct investment in the equity by other family companies
and family members, cross-holdings and cross-directorships with
related companies associated with the family group, and other
arrangements yielding an element of control with related parties. The
familism of the Chinese firm also points to the pervasiveness of the
so-called Buddenbrooks phenomenon: the typical successful Chinese
family business is said to go through four distinct phases—emergent,
centralized, segmented, and disintegrative—in about three generations.

To some, like Francis Fukuyama, this pattern is the Chinese
counterpart to the cycle that the Irish call "from shirtsleeves to
shirtsleeves," attesting to the Chinese reluctance to develop and use
professional management. It indicates a real problem with forward
integration, especially in unfamiliar markets (Fukuyama 1995: 78–80).
But to the Schumpeterian mind-set, the Chinese Buddenbrooks
indicates something else—a world of perpetual destruction and
creation, where flexibility and innovation count (as they should) and
the families involved cannot rely on the state or some other political
benefactor to bail them out. In any case, it is a world far apart from
Northeast Asia. The reform of corporate governance in Southeast Asia
toward ideal-typical western standards seems tantamount to asking
Chinese businesses to stop being, well, Chinese.

KOREA'S CAPITALIST ENTERPRISES: GROWTH, CONTROL, INDEBTEDNESS, PROFITABILITY

Almost all the *chaebol* groups began when Korea was in the phase of export-led, light industrial production. Lucky made toothpaste, Goldstar made radios, Samsung made clothes, and Hyundai began with U.S. military contracts during the Korean War to transport goods and people around in war-surplus trucks and buses. Daewoo was founded only in 1967, just over 30 years ago. The *chaebol* acquired their typical large and diversified structure even more recently, during the Third Five-Year Plan in the early 1970s, which developed heavy industries: steel, chemicals, machine tools, automobiles, shipbuilding, and power generation. By the 1980s, electronics had also become a huge part of the *chaebol* repertoire.

The expansion of these firms was stupendous: between 1970 and 1975, the three fastest-growing *chaebol* (Hyundai, Daewoo, Ssangyong) grew at an annual rate of 33, 35, and 34 percent, respectively. This breakneck rate of growth, combined with reliance on politically mediated debt, encouraged high risk taking and competitive overinvestment in various industries—like integrated petrochemicals, which more than doubled the output of ethylene at a time when world prices were declining and surplus capacity was widely anticipated (Whitley 1992: 43). The same was often true of sectors like semiconductors, ships, steel, and cars, so that excess capacity bulked large as an explanation of Korea's serious economic downturn in 1979, leading to a loss of 6 percent of gross national product (GNP) in 1980.[5]

Still, there were great advantages to the state-directed heavy industrialization of the 1970s. The experience with managing complex technologies in heavy and capital-intensive industries, requiring effective coordination and integration of separate independent components, became the basis for generalizable managerial skills—skills transferable to other kinds of manufacturing. The largest firm, Hyundai, has carried out globe-ranging operations in automobiles, shipbuilding, construction, electronics, aircraft, machine building, and many other sectors. This organizational aspect has not received much scrutiny, but the fact that the *chaebol* kept increasing their market share at home and abroad attests to their organizational ability. The effective presence of Korean firms today in the fledgling markets of Eastern

Europe, the Central Asian republics, and other emerging areas is testimony to the advantage that accrues to having an internal organization that is vast, flexible, and well coordinated. This success should be considered alongside the well-known inefficiencies of the so-called convoy system, whereby even the most inefficient unit of the *chaebol* group is kept afloat through intricate cross-subsidiary financing agreements.

The Korean *chaebol* is also known for the concentration of control in the hands of owner families. Yet compared with other East Asian countries, Korea stands somewhere in the middle regarding the concentration of family control. If we look at the percentage of total market capitalization controlled by the top five families, the figure is 29 percent in Korea, whereas it is much higher in Indonesia (41 percent), the Philippines (43 percent), and Thailand (32 percent). The percentage is considerably lower in Singapore (20 percent), Taiwan (15 percent), and Malaysia (17 percent) and is stunningly low in Japan (less than 2 percent). The comparative ranking is about the same for the top 15 families as well. It is only when we look at the share of the top family that Korea begins to look more like Indonesia or the Philippines: Hyundai's Chung Ju-Yung family is the biggest family holder not only in Korea but in all of East Asia, with holdings worth $48 billion.

The manner in which family control is assured is fairly common throughout East Asia, as it is in some industrial countries—the use of pyramid schemes (owning a majority of the stock of one corporation, which in turn holds a majority of the stock of another—a process that can be repeated a number of times), deviations from one-share-one-vote rules, cross-holdings, and the appointment of managers and directors who are related to the controlling family (Claessens, Djankov, and Lang 1998b). In Korea, the disparity between control and actual ownership rights can be gleaned from the fact that the controlling shareholders of the largest 30 conglomerates own less than 10 percent of total ownership on average, but they exert disproportionate control by exploiting the structure of interlocking institutional ownership.[6] This is because most shareholders are small individual shareholders owning less than 1 percent of total shares, and large shareholders are either nonfinancial corporations or nonbank financial corporations that are linked to controlling shareholders through cross-holding or interlocking ownership. (Banks, however, hold about 10 percent of the shares of listed firms and are controlled by the government.)

The pattern of institutional interlocking ownership can be Byzantine to avoid regulations on ownership, which include bans on holding companies (which were only recently lifted) and direct interlocking ownership (in which firm A owns firm B, which in turn owns firm A), as well as various ceilings on equity investment by the *chaebol*. The upshot is a circular pattern, where several de facto holding companies own a large portion of the affiliated firms' stocks (Joh 1999).

For the top 30 Korean *chaebol*, family ownership (defined as the share held by family members as well as by affiliated firms) came to 43 percent in 1997 (combining the family share of 8.5 percent and the affiliated firms' share of 34.5 percent). This figure for 1997 reflected a long trend toward a decline in family ownership. (In 1987, for instance, the figure was 56 percent.) In the midst of the Asian financial crisis and the Korean government's decision to allow hostile takeover of firms, the *chaebol* groups tightened the family control of firms. In 1998, combined family ownership bucked the historical trend by reaching 44.5 percent, and in 1999, it jumped to 50.5 percent (Republic of Korea Fair Trade Commission 1999).

These family-controlled firms are also highly diversified compared with those in advanced western countries. In 1994, the number of affiliated firms for the top five *chaebol* averaged about 40, with a total of 210 firms; and the top 30 *chaebol* had some 616 affiliated firms (Yu 1996: 24). This extraordinary diversification was achieved primarily by establishing new subsidiaries: the mammoth and extraordinarily diversified structure of the *chaebol* and an open call on state-mediated loans were essential to Korea's success in gaining market share around the world, because losses in one subsidiary could be made up by gains in another. This extensive diversification has been the main staple of public criticism of the *chaebol*, but perhaps the criticism needs to be weighed against at least three considerations.

The first consideration is the obvious point that while the *chaebol* have been criticized for failing to nurture "core competence," in order to exploit more fully the gains from economies of scale, diversification into many different sectors can be justified through the gains from the economies of *scope* (as opposed to scale), dynamic back-and-forth synergy among firms, and of course portfolio diversification to reduce risk. The second and often forgotten point is that diversification goes hand in hand with specialization. In 1994, out of Samsung's 50 affiliated firms, Hyundai's 49 affiliated firms, LG's 53, Daewoo's 25, and Sunkyung's 33, only a select few firms in a few sectors were responsible for the bulk of total sales. In the case of Samsung, only three firms were responsible for 67 percent of sales, and even in the case of Hyundai, which is evenly spread out in many different manufacturing sectors, five affiliated firms accounted for 70 percent of total sales; as for Daewoo, four firms accounted for 85 percent of total sales (Yu 1996: 39). The third and last point about the merits and demerits of diversification again has to do with corporate governance: whenever the structure of a given *chaebol* changes as firms become detached from the group, the firm is instantly "specialized." Over the years, the government has tried to use its elaborate system of credit control to curtail the *chaebol* tendency toward diversification and to coax the groups to "specialize" in a few sectors, but to little avail.

These diversified firms were also heavily indebted, to the point where some large firms were sustaining, on the eve of the 1997–98 crisis, debt of more than 1,000 percent of their equity. Of the top 30 firms, five were sustaining debts over 1,000 percent of their equity. Of the top five, Hyundai and LG Group sustained debts over 500 percent of their equity, with others being not far below.[7] This, combined with low profitability, especially in the 1990s, pointed to inevitable and massive insolvencies on the eve of the Asian crisis.

The conventional wisdom is that the *chaebol* are not profitable and indeed are not even interested in profit. Their activity, it is said, has rarely been driven by ordinary market concerns of price or supply and demand; instead they have allegedly long pursued market share, not just operating at a loss in doing so, but courting a kind of habitual bankruptcy, should anyone call them to account on a given day. The data for the decade before the crisis seem to validate such impressions.

In a comparative study of corporate profits in East Asia, Stijn Claessens, Simeon Djankov, and Larry Lang show that in 1988–96, profitability, as measured by real return on assets in local currency, was lower in Korea than in nine other East Asian economies as well as Germany and the United States.[8] The rate for Korea was 3.7 percent, whereas it was 4.6 percent for Hong Kong, 4.1 percent for Japan, 4.4 percent for Singapore, 7.1 percent for Indonesia, 7.9 percent for the

Philippines, 6.7 percent for Taiwan, 6.3 percent for Malaysia, and 9.8 percent for Thailand. All Southeast Asian economies and Taiwan had rates higher than those recorded in Germany (4.7 percent) and the United States (5.3 percent). Likewise, the return on assets in U.S. dollars, adjusted for the effects of currency movements, shows that, for the same period, Korea again recorded relatively low rates (9.2 percent), compared with the Philippines (17.2 percent) and Thailand (14.7 percent), although its rates were higher than those of Japan (6.6 percent); see Claessens, Djankov, and Lang (1998a).

If profits were low, real sales were rising. In the same study, Claessens, Djankov, and Lang show that real sales growth, year-on-year, for the 1988–96 period, was 8.2 percent for Korea compared with 3.7 percent for the United States and 2.6 percent for Germany. Capital investments were also growing briskly. Korea, along with Thailand, had the highest rate of capital investment among the nine East Asian economies under study, at 13.6 and 13.8 percent, respectively. The rates were 3.4 percent for the United States and 2.5 percent for Germany. Japan had a relatively low rate—8 percent—compared with other East Asian economies, reflecting continuing recession.

By 1996 Korea was sustaining one of the lowest profit rates and one of the highest capital investment rates in East Asia, meaning that external financing had to be huge to make up for the very limited retained earnings. For the period of 1988–96, the corporate indebtedness of Korean firms was greater than that of practically any other firms in the world. A comparison of corporate leverage—total debt over equity—in some 50 countries shows that in 1988–96 Korean firms had the highest ratio of leverage *by far*, at 348 percent, followed by Japan, at 230 percent. The leverage ratio in Taiwan was only 82 percent, less than one-quarter of that in Korea. The ratio in the United States and Germany for the same time period was 103 and 151 percent, respectively (Claessens, Djankov, and Lang 1998a). Still, this is not so different from the situation prevailing in the 1970s when Korean firms had leverage ratios anywhere between 300 and 400 percent; in Mexico and Brazil, firms had ratios between 100 and 120 percent; in Taiwan, firms had ratios between 160 and 200 percent (Woo 1991: 12). If the corporate leverage ratio remained the same, the manner in which it came about remained the same as well. Banks in Korea allocated credit to the large corporations, relying on real collateral for repayment, a very complex system of cross-guarantees from the various subsidiaries and affiliates of the group, and personal guarantees from the group chairman and directors. Little attention was paid to the earnings performance and cash flow of borrowers. Finally, the pattern of financial crisis in Korea also remained more or less the same: low return on assets, declining sales growth, excess capacity, stiff price competition, and high leverage. In many ways, 1997 was a rerun of the crisis of 1979.

By late 1997, the sharp rise in interest rates (used to defend the won) pushed the *chaebol* over the brink. According to some analysts, the combination of interest rate and currency shocks left up to 49 percent of Korean firms illiquid and 40 percent technically insolvent. This situation of massive bankruptcies was unprecedented. Until 1997, large-scale bankruptcy was a rare phenomenon in Korea, where the government, fearing financial instability and chain bankruptcies involving suppliers, routinely bailed out ailing firms through debt reduction and deferrals. In 1997, however, five major groups—with a combined work force of more than 100,000 employees and 26.7 trillion won in assets—failed in quick succession, unable to pay their debts. And more than half of the 30 largest *chaebol* (with combined employment of more than a quarter million people and liabilities of 103.4 trillion won) were at risk of falling into bankruptcy (Lieberman and Mako 1998). These failures significantly weakened the financial institutions and suddenly frightened foreign investors, who demanded repayment of the short-term loans given to Korea's financial institutions. In that sense, foreign banks and investors exacerbated the crisis, but they did not cause it. The cause of the crisis has to be sought in the failure of the reform efforts in Korea.

ANTINOMIES OF THE DEVELOPMENTAL STATE

Why has economic reform proven so difficult in Korea? To the extent that economic reform lagged in Korea, it was owing to the complex and highly involuted dynamics between the state and the entrepreneurs, which in turn deeply prejudiced the emergence of the rule of law and transparency in corporate accounting. In this section, I reflect on the nature and quality of the bureaucratic state in Korea and the difficulties it has encountered in its efforts at reform.

In one sense, the dilemma of the developmental state in Korea is straightforward. In Korea development has provided a far greater trickle-down effect than any Reaganite ever imagined, yielding an egalitarian payoff at the end of the developmental tunnel. The critical part in this equation has been the corporations, most of which are in industry. Industry constitutes 42.9 percent of Korean gross domestic product (GDP), compared with approximately 30 percent for the Organisation for Economic Co-operation and Development (OECD) countries as a whole. The five largest *chaebol* alone employ more than 600,000 workers, even without counting suppliers. These large firms perform an indispensable welfare function in a society largely bereft of a social safety net. Layoffs as a result of bankruptcy, therefore, affect a large proportion of the work force, as Korea lacks the cushion against unemployment provided by the large agricultural sector of Southeast Asia and the service sector of the OECD countries (Lieberman and Mako 1998). Even as the *chaebol* in Korea courted habitual bankruptcy, it was difficult to sever the credit that sustained them and allow them to go bankrupt. Lowi (1975) calls this the "state of permanent receivership."

In Korea, politics were hostage to economics—and more. A developmental state like Korea's creates a permanent bind for itself with regard to big business. On the one hand, the state has had to intervene to rescue the *chaebol* in distress, in order to prevent the collapse of the banking system as well as massive unemployment. This is what the Korean government did during the debt crisis in 1972, when it placed a moratorium on corporate debt repayment and provided firms with bailout loans; again in 1979 to 1993 when it provided financial subsidies to firms in the heavy and chemical industry; and again in 1984–88 when it restructured the debts of firms in overseas construction, shipping, textiles, and machinery. The government became insurers and underwriters, guaranteeing the *chaebol* and their investments.

For its part, the developmental bureaucracy seeks to rein in and tame the *chaebol*, through regulatory means, creating an endless number of rules. By all accounts, the Korean state has been a relentless nag, trying to force firms to reform. For instance, in the aftermath of the financial crisis in 1972 and the bailout of big business through a sudden moratorium on corporate repayments of loans to the curb market, the government selected what it considered "blue chip" firms (based on profitability, equity, and asset position) and forced them to go public, threatening to slap the recalcitrants with a 40 percent corporate tax (rather than the usual 27 percent). Overnight, new public stock offerings inundated the Seoul Stock Exchange, valued at $48 million, and the number of companies listed jumped 50 percent. The stock market received a further boost in 1974, when a special presidential decree tightened the audit and supervision of bank credit for all nonlisted (but listable, according to government standards) firms. Many more measures like these followed in the 1970s. Finding themselves between the state's punitive measures, on the one hand, and the costs of going public (losing autonomy and cheap credit, the high costs of raising undervalued equity capital), on the other, the *chaebol* responded predictably. Some firms decided that it was better to resist the government order, pay the tax, and bypass the government palliatives offered to listed firms. Others obeyed the government, but without really complying: the owners themselves absorbed much of the newly issued stock (Woo 1991: 174–75). The equity market in Korea thus remained relatively small.

The state also tried to limit *chaebol* access to bank credit, through what surely must be one of the most arcane and intractable sets of "credit controls" (*yoshin kwalli*) that the world has known. The system of credit controls had its origins in the era of industrial policy. In a system where bank credit was extended not on the basis of economic viability, but on the exigencies of state economic policy, the only way to prevent default was a system of incessant supervision and control, including ubiquitous surveillance over the use of credit (to prevent speculation, for instance), supervision of the reform of corporate financing structures, and the creation of a web of credit ceilings. Attempting to prevent the concentration of credit, the government devised complex rules limiting credit to the same borrower, limiting credit per individual bank for large borrowers, and establishing credit ceilings for *chaebol*-affiliated firms. To prevent default, the government developed a series of guidelines for "early warning," procedures for "modernizing" credit evaluation, as well as intricate rules for default management. A special set of decrees applying only to the *chaebol* sought to regulate the ratio between equity and debt in various industrial sectors and gave fiscal incentives for going public. Since 1980, the government closely monitored *chaebol* use of bank credit and expanded external audits; by the middle of the 1980s, the state also instituted a consistent policy package based on fair trade laws. In 1992 the fair trade law was again fortified, the use of intersubsidiary loan guarantees was restricted, and relaxation of the loan ceiling was offered as an incentive for some *chaebol* to develop their "core" industries. The result was a regulatory albatross that, in the end, did not achieve its purpose. But the state had to proliferate regulations to stem the worst effects of its own developmental strategy.

For much of the 1980s, the state chose bureaucratic—and not market—means to rein in the *chaebol*, allowing regulations to hypertrophy. Why did this happen, especially in light of three decades of the best advice of liberal economists in and out of Korea that the only effective solution to the *chaebol* problem was to reform and liberalize the banking sector? Part of the answer may be political (cronyism!), but the bigger reason has to do with the habits of "late" development, of being "results-oriented" rather than rule-oriented. Korea may have grown very fast over the past four decades, but it did not overcome the fear of real competition and the free market. Even reformers are drawn to the use of discretionary measures by the government because Korea, after all, has one of the oldest and finest traditions of civil service. In times of crisis, the temptation grows strong to use this ubiquitous state structure to force industrial reorganization. The bureaucrats—who come from the best universities and constitute a respected and experienced elite—always think that around the next corner is the regulation that will finally achieve real reform. Thus almost all major reforms—import liberalization, financial liberalization, privatization—not only moved at a snail's pace but also went hand in hand with the proliferation of more regulations in order to obtain an economically desirable outcome.

This picture changed substantially in the 1990s, as the first civilian government (1993–97) sought to break the stasis caused by the state's dual requirement to be both the guarantor and the regulator of the *chaebol*. So the government decided to downplay its role as regulator. The government substantially relaxed its supervision of the banking sector and of its lending practices. There were many reasons for this, including pressures from international organizations for more comprehensive and rapid financial deregulation. At home, the *chaebol* also pressed hard to lift various barriers to entry into the financial sector. These factors, combined with the government's desire to become the second Asian nation to join the OECD, led to the opening of domestic financial markets in 1993–94 and to the abrupt elimination of the Ministry of Finance's direct intervention in credit allocation as well as its prerogative in the appointment of bank management. The financial supervisory authority became compartmentalized between the Ministry of Finance and the Bank of Korea, creating a big lacuna in regulatory oversight. In other words, the pendulum had swung excessively in the other direction.

If the bureaucrats receded to the background in the 1990s, the politicians did not. The appointment of the presidents of commercial banks could still be vetoed by the politically powerful, such as key party members or close associates of the president, and bank management often succumbed to the pressures of politicians who sought approval of the projects of their campaign donors. The government also moved to lift entry barriers and other restrictions on the compartmentalized financial sectors and, at the behest of the *chaebol*, eliminated asset restrictions and reduced reporting requirements for banks and nonbank financial intermediaries, which had been introduced for prudential purposes. The upshot was that the nonbank financial intermediaries became rapidly deregulated, outside of the state's supervision and under the control of the *chaebol*. The reckless lending behavior of these nonbank financial intermediaries was partly responsible for the financial crisis that beset Korea in 1997 (Cho 1999).

The dilemma in Korea is that the state had to both guarantee and discipline the *chaebol*. The true "miracle" in Korea in the three decades since the 1960s was that it juggled these conflicting roles. But in the early 1990s the government abandoned its juggling act, without putting in place prudential regulations to rein in the behavior of the nonbank financial intermediaries, which were increasingly providing an internal capital market for the *chaebol*. This sudden auto-da-fé in favor of the "markets" left Korea defenseless in the face of a massive financial crisis.

Given the history and structure of Korean developmentalism in the past, the Korean government should have built on its strength—its formidable bureaucratic organizational know-how—to bolster the regulatory capacity of the state, while ensuring great transparency and discipline in the marketplace. In the end, this task was shifted over to the democratic regime that was inaugurated in 1998, as it embarked on a highly unusual reform that aimed at liberalizing the economy, while reinvigorating the state's economic decisionmaking power.

DEMOCRACY AND CORPORATE REFORM

Corporate restructuring is still under way in Korea, but a confluence of three factors has made the current reform effective thus far. First was the magnitude of the crisis that afflicted Korea, drawing international financial institutions into the reform process. Second was the inauguration of a reform leadership long committed to the project of severing state-business ties and abiding by the rule of law to which the corporations and the government are both subject. Third was continuing use of the tools of industrial policy in order to bring about a more liberal economic order. Most important, liberal economic reform in Korea has not meant the retreat of the state from the market, as it might have in the earlier administration; on the contrary, it has meant a deep intervention by the state, using the tried-and-true method of industrial swaps and mergers dictated or brokered from above. This heterodox mix of policies, backed by the vast power and prestige of a centralized polity, is giving momentum to the reforms today.

The crisis of 1997–98 was a disaster waiting to happen, given the highly leveraged nature of the *chaebol*. Without it the resolution of the bad debt problem in the Korean banking system would again have been postponed, as it had been for decades. The crisis and the subsequent bailout also inserted international financial institutions, mainly the International Monetary Fund (IMF) and the World Bank, deeply into the reform process in Korea, greatly raising the stakes of reform. The virtue of this was that the international financial institutions could run political interference for the new regime, with every unpopular policy and outcome being blamed on the IMF—from legalizing layoffs and sky-rocketing unemployment to massive corporate bankruptcy. (Indeed the Koreans dubbed the crisis the "IMF crisis," making the nature and cause of the event deliberately ambiguous.) The international financial institutions thus reduced the political perils of reform and provided a shield for the regime.

The relationship between democratization and financial reform and liberalization is difficult to establish. General Pinochet's Chile and Suharto's Indonesia brooked financial liberalization, but not democracy; and Japan in the 1950s brooked democracy, but not financial liberalization. In the minds of Korean democrats, however, the two are inextricably connected. The most prominent Korean democrat to have articulated this position was Kim Dae Jung, going back to the late 1960s. The policy of financial repression, he argued, went hand in hand with political repression. The power of military authoritarianism was based not only on the coercive capacity of the state, but also on its capacity, through financial repression, to control the business class. Businessmen then kicked back political funds to the dictators. For 30 years Kim advocated financial liberalization, not because he subsumed everything in the name of allocative efficiency, but because this was the most effective way to cut the Gordian knot between the repressive state and the *chaebol*.

In the trials of two former presidents, held in the mid-1990s, one after another *chaebol* leader was brought into the dock and shown to have lined the pockets of all the leading politicians going back to the 1960s. If the image of the flagship firms that made the Korean miracle was deeply tarnished, this nonetheless was a hugely important phenomenon: it signaled the arrival, finally, of democratic politics in Korea, and it was only through democratic means that the deep nexus between the *chaebol* and the authoritarian state could be broken. The best news for those interested in *chaebol* reform is simply that real reform is now possible, given the election of two successive civilian presidents (Kim Young Sam in 1992 and Kim Dae Jung in 1997) and an economic crisis unparalleled since the Korean War.

In the middle of an analogous crisis, President Franklin Roosevelt in his message to Congress in 1938 called for an investigation of concentrated economic power: "The liberty of a democracy," he said, "is not safe if the people tolerate the growth of private power to a point where it becomes stronger than their democratic state itself" (quoted in Hadley 1970: 455). In Korea the problem of private power is as President Roosevelt described it, but much more so: politicians and political parties extracted funds from the *chaebol*, offering in return loan guarantees to sustain these highly leveraged firms. No firm could avoid paying out one day, lest it be declared "bankrupt" the following day. The mid-1990s investigations, ultimately leading to the incarceration of two previous presidents and several big-business leaders, revealed to the Korean people the operational method of patronage. Korea, Inc. proved to be far more arbitrary than Japan, Inc.: especially in the 1980s, a racketeering state was the flip side of the much-touted developmental state, as the earlier, more systemic pattern of *chaebol* support for the ruling groups changed into a kind of mad extortionism.

President Kim Dae Jung, long a dissident who was the object of *chaebol*-provisioned political funding (he nearly won his first presidential campaign in 1971 in spite of widespread irregularities and munificent support for Park Chung Hee, whereupon there were no more elections until 1987), needs no tutoring in the politics or the economic liabilities of the state-*chaebol* relationship. He wrote, "The Korean economy ... has been plagued by inefficient allocation of valuable resources ... [which is] the result of government interference in almost every aspect of market functions, including pricing, credit allocation, industrial location decisions, and labor-management relations. This interference has left the Korean economy in a state of serious imbalance" (Kim 1985: 3). The economic crisis gave him the leverage needed to pursue real reform of the Korean system for the first time since the 1960s.

The new Korean government issued a number of measures to force corporate reform, including ending the system of intersubsidiary loan guarantees among the *chaebol* affiliates, enhancing overall management transparency and accountability, and posting deadlines to lower corporate debt/equity ratios and improve capital structures. Kim Dae Jung also demanded a "Big Deal," meaning a swap of key subsidiaries so that each of the top *chaebol* would emerge stronger in the areas of their core competence. This would reduce overlapping investments and allow firms to close down surplus production capacity. Some of these measures were critically important departures from the past (such as the decisive ending of intersubsidiary loans), helped along by the demands of the International Monetary Fund. Others were not departures, but continuations of past government policy, if with more teeth.

The main difference from the past was the simultaneity of the banking and corporate restructuring. Since individual Korean banks made a substantial percentage of their loans to specific *chaebol*, there was an incentive for banks to prop up groups with fresh loans rather than let them collapse, bringing the banks down with them. This situation, in which banks were de facto quasi-equity holders in corporations, highlights the need to undertake simultaneous corporate and financial sector restructuring in Korea. Hence, corporate restructuring has been closely linked to bank restructuring and recapitalization and to the resolution of bad loans in the banking sector; this is happening in tandem with the push to increase the equity and cash flows of the *chaebol* and extend the maturity profile of their debt.

To do this, the government created the Financial Supervisory Commission (FSC), an independent agency reporting directly to the prime minister, with the mandate to restructure both the corporate sector and the financial institutions. The FSC has taken a step-by-step approach, focusing first on voluntary workouts for the "6 to 64" *chaebol*. The idea behind the prioritization of these medium-size *chaebol* (ranked numbers 6 to 64) was that they were in deepest distress, and a large number of insolvencies in this group could bring severe social distress and political pressure on the government to abandon its reform program. A series of defaults, it was feared, could provoke another crisis. If the restructuring of the medium-size *chaebol* worked, the recipe could then be applied to the Big Five *chaebol* (Lieberman and Mako 1998).

The government produced, in rapid succession, a set of legal and regulatory policies to restructure the "6 to 64." Foreign direct investment was genuinely liberalized to permit takeovers of nonstrategic companies by foreign investors, and the ceiling was raised on foreign ownership of stock. The securities exchange was also overhauled to facilitate mergers and acquisitions by increasing the portion of shares that could be acquired without board approval. The government also bolstered the antitrust and fair trade acts, prohibited any new intersubsidiary debt guarantees, and pledged to eliminate all existing guarantees by the year 2000. There were tax breaks for restructuring firms.

To provide infrastructural support, the FSC promoted the Corporate Restructuring Accord and formed a committee to assess the viability of corporate candidates for restructuring and arbitrating differences among creditors and, if necessary, modifying "workout" plans proposed by participating creditors. While there were six lead banks in charge of restructuring the 64 corporate groups, all commercial banks had their internal workout groups. A workout could involve debt/equity conversions, term extensions, deferred payment of principal or interest, reduction of interest rates, waiver of indebtedness, provision of new credits, cancellation of existing guarantee obligations, sale of noncore businesses, and new equity issues (Lieberman and Mako 1998).

As for the five largest *chaebol*, the government was clearly thinking long term, with an eye to producing internationally competitive enterprises, even if that involved stiff-arming the Big Five into business swaps, mergers, and acquisitions among themselves. Thus in spite of the pledges from the *chaebol* to improve their financial structure voluntarily, the state was singularly insistent on a Big Deal designed to streamline business lines and reduce overcapacity. Threatening to cut off credit, the government brokered a series of high-profile business swaps. Daewoo, for instance, agreed to give up its electronics firm to Samsung in exchange for Samsung's automobile firm. This meant that Samsung would dominate Korea's consumer electronics market with 60 percent of market share. Internationally, Samsung would control production of about 30 percent of microwave ovens, about 18 percent of videocassette recorders, and more than 10 percent of television sets (*Wall Street Journal*, December 17, 1998). Daewoo would have become the only Korean automobile maker other than Hyundai, now that the industry had been consolidated from a five-player to a two-player field. (This deal floundered, however, as the result of Daewoo's bankruptcy.) The government also brokered a merger between the memory chip companies of Hyundai Group and LG Group to create the world's second-largest maker of dynamic random access memory (DRAM) chips. (The world's largest DRAM chip maker is Samsung.) Hailed as the centerpiece of the restructuring drive, this effort was aimed at creating a national champion, with a global market share of almost 16 percent.

The democratic government of Kim Dae Jung did not shy away from using strong-arm tactics to bring about the desired results. When LG Group decided to pull out in the midst of merger negotiations, objecting to Hyundai taking the controlling share, the Financial Supervisory Commission immediately called in LG Group's creditors to discuss punitive measures, including immediate suspension of credit and recall of existing loans. On top of that, the government threatened to conduct a tax probe. In the end, LG Group finally agreed to the merger, relinquishing management control to Hyundai Electronics. In June 1999, the government also embarked on a massive tax probe into the affiliates of the Hanjin Business Group (sixth largest), using a 150-strong tax audit team, as a warning to the top five to maintain their pledges to restructure. But the Big Deal was not all sticks, of course: it also offered incentives including reduced swap-related taxes, deferred capital gains, deferred corporate taxes, and reduced individual taxes.

The corporate restructuring effort was a success in many ways. The big firms clearly did improve their capital structures, with the top five lowering their debt/equity rate below 200 percent. The number of group affiliates also dropped from some 232 firms at the end of 1997 to 165 as of December 1999.

There were also improvements in the governance of corporations. Big firms are now required to produce combined financial statements covering all affiliated companies, and all listed companies are obligated to appoint outside directors and auditing committees to their boards. (In reality, these outside directors, who must comprise more than 25 percent of the total number of directors, are but "friends" of the corporations. They are not experts in corporate matters and are often burdened with multiple directorships. Still, the focus on outside directors is a step in the right direction.) The government also enacted a law enabling class action suits to be brought by minority shareholders representing just 0.01 percent of total outstanding shares. The law notwithstanding, it is still the case that minority rights are often violated, and valuations of firms controlled by inside shareholders are far below those of comparable firms, suggesting large-scale expropriation by the principals. There is also said to be large-scale financial transfer between affiliated firms—for instance, the channeling of SK Telecom profits to loss-making affiliates rather than to shareholders (Root 2000: 19).

However, the twin tendencies in Kim's reform policy—neoliberalism and openness with regard to the outside world as well as selective continuation of industrial policy in the form of business swaps—have produced curious results. As the government lifted all bans against mergers, acquisitions, and hostile takeovers, the *chaebol* groups chose to counter with increasing insider ownership. The share of insider ownership, which had been 33 percent in the mid-1990s, rose to 44 percent in 1999. This situation is somewhat akin to what happened in Japan in the mid-1960s, as firms sought to insulate themselves from hostile takeovers (often by foreigners) by developing the system of mutual shareholding between companies and financial institutions, notably city banks (Aoki 1989: 269–73). This was one of the milestones that eventually gave birth to the postwar structure known as the *keiretsu*.

Corporate restructuring of this scope wreaks havoc on labor. The current regime has sought in a variety of ways to share the pain of the IMF bailout fairly throughout society, but the restructuring-related layoffs have continued. By the end of 1998 the Big Five firms had slashed some 10 percent of their labor force and threatened to do more. Labor, in turn, protested against corporate restructuring, but the sheer magnitude of the financial crisis dealt it a poor hand to play. Moreover, for the first time in Korean history the current regime has given labor a strong voice at the bargaining table with business and government—certainly a major achievement of reform and one that has generally kept labor from (truly) major strikes and disruptions in the face of unemployment that tripled in one year (from 2 percent in mid-1997 to more than 7 percent in late 1998).

LESSONS FROM THE KOREAN CASE

What does this discussion of Korea's corporate restructuring suggest about reform in other East Asian countries? Indonesia could certainly take note of the way in which democratization has aided economic reform in Korea, Malaysia could observe the benefits of trying to accommodate legitimate western demands for reform (rather than posturing about western imperialism and "Asian values"), and Thailand could learn from Seoul's efforts at achieving financial transparency and working with organized labor. Still, the main lessons will relate to Korea's big neighbors—China and Japan.

China is saddled with the kind of massive problem of bad debt in the banking sector that plagued Korea. From Korea's example, it might take two—albeit contradictory—lessons: either (a) Korea's bad debt problem cannot be as bad as western observers make it out to be, since Korea had far worse levels of bad debt in relation to GNP, yet grew at

spectacular rates for three decades, against the advice of leading western economists or (b) given the magnitude of the Asian financial crisis
and Korea's disastrous past two years, delayed reform makes the problem potentially that much more unmanageable. Chinese policy responses suggest that the second lesson has had an effect: in early 1999
Premier Zhu Rongji cited the need for decisive and quick resolution,
within the next three years, of the problems in the state-owned enterprises and the banking sector. The rub will come in actually doing this
in such a way that the efficiency gains of accelerated reform and job
creation can mitigate the social disasters spawned by reform-related
unemployment.

There is also a rough and important parallel between the Korean
chaebol and the Chinese state-owned enterprises. With a small or non-
existent social safety net in both countries, the *chaebol* and the SOEs
provide crucial welfare for their workers. It is well known that the
SOEs provide an "iron rice bowl" of supports to their multitude of
workers, including low-cost housing, health care, and retirement
stipends. Less appreciated are the "company town" features of the
big Korean firms. *Chaebol* firms provide for their employees' needs
in every way. The typical Hyundai worker drives a Hyundai car, lives
in a Hyundai apartment, gets his mortgage from Hyundai credit, gets
health care from a Hyundai hospital, sends his children to school on
Hyundai loans or scholarships, and eats his meals at Hyundai cafete-
rias. If his son graduates out of the blue-collar work force and enters
the ranks of well-educated technocratic professionals (which is the goal
of every Korean parent), he may well work for Hyundai research and
development. The extreme form is seen in the construction teams that
Hyundai has long sent to the Middle East: every worker departs in
a Hyundai T-shirt and cap and carrying a Hyundai bag, lives and eats
in Hyundai dormitories, and uses Hyundai tools and equipment to
build Hyundai cities in the desert. In the same way that Kim Il Sung
built a Confucian-influenced hereditary family-state in North Korea
and called it communism, the *chaebol* built large family-run hereditary
corporate estates in South Korea and called it capitalism (Cumings 1997).

Such practices, of course, show why it has been and continues to be
so difficult to truly reform Korean corporations: it is like asking a giant cruise ship to change course abruptly, while throwing 10 or 20
percent of its work force overboard. Clearly, the situation in China is

analogous—the SOEs provision more than 100 million people. How then to reform? It cannot be done overnight, or perhaps even in three years, but it can be done. Both Korea and Taiwan inherited large state-owned enterprises from Japanese colonialism but managed to dismantle or privatize many of them over the years. The tradeoff between accumulation and distribution (or employment) is always difficult, but Kim Dae Jung has shown that it is possible to mitigate the worse abuses by severing nefarious ties between the state and big enterprises.

A less dispiriting example can also be drawn from the Korean case. As we have seen, the reform of financial and banking structures may be aided by the very state that promoted these structures in the first place—a strong, interventionist state capable not only of restructuring the state-corporate nexus but also of maintaining a steady hand in dampening the shocks of social dislocation. Kim Dae Jung arranged for the state to play the role of broker between labor and business, with labor trading economic gains for the rights of political representation. China has sought to solve the SOE problem by quickening the pace of job creation in the private sector, through Keynesian demand management. It has done well to date, but Korean-style "peak bargaining" between the state, business, and national unions might be necessary when private sector job creation inevitably lags. But does China have a strong, efficacious state that could learn from the Korean state's role in the reform process?

The traditional conundrum of China has been the "modernization" of its central state, which—whether in the imperial, the nationalist, or the communist era—was both too centralized and too decentralized, simultaneously hyper-statized and yet politically parceled. The resolution of this problem evaded Mao and Deng Xiaoping, even if Deng nudged the state to begin shedding its hypertrophied central responsibilities after 1978, while deepening its provincial penetration. In this sense, some observers have interpreted the reforms in the Deng era and after as increasing the "reach of the state" (this term is used by Shue [1988]).

Just what constitutes an effective state with "a long reach" is a difficult question; clearly the Communist Party–run Chinese state is both penetrative and remarkably (and often self-defeatingly) intrusive. Citizens have no inalienable rights in the face of state prerogatives. But that was also true (if in a lesser way) of the military dictatorships in

Korea. This problem cannot be settled in the manner of the World Bank's *World Development Report 1997* on reforming the state, which developed an admirable if very long laundry list of how to make the state efficient, with little idea how the list might actually be implemented (World Bank 1997). Successful reform in Korea also built on the long tradition of civil service statecraft; since China was the original source of this tradition and has no lack of bureaucrats, this background still might be the source of bureaucratic renewal.

What about the lessons for Japan? On several counts, it is more the other way around: Korea is finally adopting measures that have been prevalent in Japan since the 1950s, like peak bargaining with labor unions, structural reform of the *zaibatsu*, and the provision of a wide social safety net. That Japan needs reform—especially in its banking system, which seemed so dominant just a decade ago—is not in doubt. In the face of years of recession Japan's leaders have been unable to summon the will to do anything more than muddle along, vegetating in the teeth of a rather remarkable economic and political malaise that only seems to grow worse as time passes. Korea's relatively successful reform has come because of the depth of the financial crisis occurring simultaneously with a defining presidential election, such that Kim Dae Jung had Korea's strong state dropped in his lap so to speak. As we have seen, he has used the full panoply of executive powers to push through serious reform. If Japan's political system is so often described as "a web with no spider" (Lockwood 1965:503), Korea's is the opposite—and since Kim's inauguration, the spider has been moving rapidly through the web. This fundamental difference helps to explain the dynamism of Korea's reform effort compared with Japan's political dithering.

Therefore, reform in Japan is and no doubt will continue to be a vastly slower process. If in Korea the regime of political economy collapsed of its own weight through the crisis in 1997–99, in Japan the "regime shift" has continued in subtle ways since the early 1980s, involving a transformation in socioeconomic alliances, political and economic institutions, and public policy, making Japanese politics far different than the stable regime of the 1960s and 1970s (Pempel 1998). The relationship among corporations, banks, and the state is far more legitimate and far less brittle in Japan than in Korea. (In part this is because Korea wanted to do what Japan did, but in half the time it took Japan to do it.) But to ask Japan to find a strong, accountable executive like President Kim and proceed with the business of reform is like asking Americans to adopt a parliamentary system of no-confidence voting in the middle of President Clinton's 1998–99 intern scandal. Japanese reform will come, but it is impossible to predict when. Most likely, it will move along the twisting and evolving paths of the past 20 years rather than the "developmental state" model it pioneered 70 years ago.

CONCLUSION

I suggested at the outset of this chapter that *The East Asian Miracle* leaves unexplored the basic social and political underpinnings that propelled growth in East Asia. Even when it deals with the question of the role of the state in economic development, it approaches the question ideologically, acknowledging that some East Asian states engaged in industrial policy to promote growth, but asserting that it was not possible to establish any direct causal relationship between state policy and growth. At the same time, the authors endeavor to show that industrial policy aimed at infant-industry promotion does not *always* work. By and large, the book betrays great ambivalence on the part of the World Bank regarding the role of the state in economic development.

The Korean experience with restructuring its highly leveraged corporate sector shows the pitfalls of black-and-white views about the state's role in the economy. The Korean case shows that, in an economy where growth was led by massively indebted firms, the challenge of creating a healthy financial sector cannot be met through simple measures. The Korean government tried both the regulatory and the laissez-faire route to meet the challenge, as this chapter shows. For the most part since the mid-1970s the Korean government allowed regulatory measures to proliferate in order to contain the preponderance of the *chaebol*-incurred debt in the banking system, but to little avail. Then in the 1990s, the government opted for "laissez-faire," hoping that the markets would discipline the *chaebol*, even if that meant allowing massive bankruptcies that threatened the health of the banking sector, thus contributing to the crisis in November of 1997.

The reform effort of Kim Dae Jung's administration is anything but ideological. It is not based on any stylized understanding of the state's role in the economy. It is bereft of the innocent exuberance often found in the proponents of industrial policy, extolling the virtues of developmental coordination between the state and the enterprises. But it is also bereft of innocence with regard to laissez-faire. Instead, the thrust of the reform has been profoundly practical, mixing the exigency of liberal reform with heavy-handed industrial reorganization to force private sector restructuring.

In the course of managing the financial crisis and restructuring the corporate sector, the economic bureaucracies in Korea have regained their vitality and authority. The Korean "miracle," made possible by an authoritarian developmental state, appears in this sense to have been but a prologue to a democratic future where the state still has a central role to play in the economic advancement of the Korean people.

NOTES

1. This argument is contained in Woo-Cumings (1999: ch. 1). Peter Evans (1995: 234) puts it like this, "For developmental states, connections with society are connections to industrial capital" (and hardly anyone else).

2. Even when the companies were "opened," two features made family control of the *zaibatsu* possible. One was that stock did not have to be paid up equally, meaning that the families and the holding companies could increase the "stretch" of their capital. The other was the implicit understanding that the will of the family and the holding company would prevail, regardless of actual ownership position. Indeed, the historian Eleanor Hadley points to numerous instances in core companies at the end of the war when *zaibatsu* ownership (defined as the sum of top holding company ownership, family holdings, and cross-subsidiary ties) fell short of majority control. One might think of it as a remarkable instance of the personalistic—even feudal—basis of mutual trust in corporate power. See Hadley (1970: 24–25).

3. This is not to imply that Korea's *chaebol* have functioned politically like the old *zaibatsu*, supporting aggression and huge armaments expenditures. But an examination of the similar corporate structure in Korea helps to clarify the relationship between authoritarianism and its legacy, on the one hand, and the type of big business, on the other. It also underlines the extent and enormous complexity of contemporary reform efforts, in that the war hero of the Pacific campaigns, General Douglas MacArthur, could not decisively break the power of the *zaibatsu*. They hunkered down and waited when they could, restructured when they had to, and transmogrified into the post-occupation *keiretsu*—a defi-

nite improvement, but by no means the thorough breakup and reform that MacArthur had planned.

4. The modern diaspora was peopled by the millions of young, mostly male, mostly illiterate people, who, between the Opium Wars in the 1840s and the onset of the Sino-Japanese War in the 1890s, left the coastal districts of Fukien and Kwangtung for the labor-hungry European colonies in Southeast Asia and independent Thailand. In Thailand and Malaysia, they formed the bulk of the working class, but significant numbers also worked their way up the occupational ladder to become small traders, entrepreneurs, and professionals. Particularly in the Dutch East Indies, such people came to form a middle tier between the colonial administrative apparatus and the peasant bulk of the indigenous population. The Chinese used their position as intermediaries between western big business and the local economy to gain knowledge of modern trade, manufacturing techniques, and the local market. They also were the interlocutors when Japanese firms sought to reestablish their presence in Southeast Asia after World War II. In the early stages of development, Chinese immigrants were excluded from peasant production by lack of access to land and were concentrated in wage labor, while indigenous peasants were excluded from commercial activity by lack of access to capital and market outlets. Because they were denied access to land, the Chinese tended to keep their assets in liquid form and to invest in economic activities that generated quick returns. This racial divide quickly became a vertical division of labor, as upwardly mobile Chinese entered into commercial activity, often as intermediaries between indigenous peasant producers and the world market, and obtained higher returns from their investments of capital and labor. Soon the indigenes shook loose from the land and joined wage labor at the bottom of the economic hierarchy.

5. In other words, 1998 was not the first year that Korea recorded a minus 6 percent growth, nor was the 1997–98 crisis the worst since the Korean War, as is often reported in the press. The economic crisis of 1979 was worse in terms of its social and political consequences and was followed by a military coup.

6. According to the Republic of Korea Fair Trade Commission, the weighted average ownership of the controlling shareholder families was 10.3 percent in 1993, 9.7 percent in 1994, 10.5 percent in 1995, 10.3 percent in 1996, and 8.3 percent in 1997. See Joh (1999).

7. These figures are from the Republic of Korea Fair Trade Commission.

8. This is calculated at the firm level as the earnings before interest and taxes in local currency over total assets minus the annual inflation rate in the country.

REFERENCES

The word "processed" describes informally reproduced works that may not be commonly available through library systems.

Anderson, Benedict. 1998. "From Miracle to Crash." *London Review of Books.* April. 27.

Aoki, Masahiko. 1989. "The Japanese Firm in Transition." In Kozo Yamamura and Yasukichi Yasuba, ed., *The Political Economy of Japan*. Stanford, Calif.: Stanford University Press.

Bowie, Alasdair. 1991. *Crossing the Industrial Divide: State, Society, and the Politics of Economic Transformation in Malaysia*. New York: Columbia University Press.

Chang, Ha-Joon, H. J. Park, and C. G. Yoo. 1998. "Interpreting the Korean Crisis: Financial Liberalization, Industrial Policy, and Corporate Governance." *Cambridge Journal of Economics* 22(6):735–46.

Cho, Yoon Je. 1999. "The Political Economy of the Financial Liberalization and Crisis in Korea." Paper prepared for the conference "Comparative Study of Financial Liberalization in Asia," East-West Center, Honolulu, September 23–24. Processed.

Claessens, Stijn, Simon Djankov, and Larry Lang. 1998a. "East Asian Corporates: Growth, Financing, and Risks over the Last Decade." Policy Research Working Paper 2017. World Bank, Policy Research Department, Washington, D.C. Processed.

———. 1998b. "Who Controls East Asian Corporations?" Policy Research Working Paper 2054. World Bank, Policy Research Department, Washington, D.C. Processed.

Cumings, Bruce. 1997. *Korea's Place in the Sun*. New York: W. W. Norton.

Evans, Peter. 1995. *Embedded Autonomy*. Princeton, N.J.: Princeton University Press.

Fukuyama, Francis. 1995. *Trust: The Social Virtues and the Creation of Prosperity*. New York: Simon and Schuster.

Gourevitch, Peter. 1996. "The Macropolitics of Microinstitutional Differences in the Analysis of Comparative Capitalism." In Suzanne Berger and Ronald Dore, eds., *National Diversity and Global Capitalism*. Ithaca, N.Y.: Cornell University Press.

Hadley, Eleanor. 1970. *Antitrust in Japan*. Princeton, N.J.: Princeton University Press.

Hattori, Tamio. 1989. "Japanese *Zaibatsu* and Korean *Chaebol*." In Kae H. Chung and Hank Chong Lee, eds., *Korean Managerial Dynamics*. New York: Praeger.

Jensen, Michael. 1997. "The Modern Industrial Revolution." In Donald Chew, ed., *Studies in Corporate Governance and Governance Systems: A Comparison of the U.S., Japan, and Europe*. New York: Oxford University Press.

Jesudason, James V. 1989. *Ethnicity and the Economy: The State, Chinese Business, and Multinationals in Malaysia*. Singapore: Oxford University Press.

Joh, Sung Wook. 1999. "Control, Ownership, and Firm Performance: The Case of Korea." Working Paper. Korea Development Institute, Seoul. Processed.

Jomo, K. S. 1997. "A Specific Idiom of Chinese Capitalism in Southeast Asia: Sino-Malaysian Capital Accumulation in the Face of State Hostility." In Daniel Chirot and Anthony Reid, eds., *Essential Outsiders: Chinese and Jews in the Modern Transformation of Southeast Asia and Central Europe*. Seattle: University of Washington Press.

Kester, Carl. 1996. "American and Japanese Corporate Governance: Convergence to Best Practice?" In Suzanne Berger and Ronald Dore, eds., *National Diversity and Global Capitalism*. Ithaca, N.Y.: Cornell University Press.

Kim, Dae Jung. 1985. *Mass Participatory Economy*. Cambridge, Mass.: Harvard University, Harvard East Asian Center.

Kim, Seok Ki. 1987. "Business Concentration and Government Policy: A Study of a Phenomenon of Business Groups in the Republic of Korea, 1945–1985." Ph.D. diss. Harvard University, Harvard Business School, Cambridge, Mass.

Lieberman, Ira, and William Mako. 1998. "Korea's Corporate Crisis." World Bank, Private Sector Development Department, Washington, D.C. Processed.

Lim, Linda Y. C., and L. A. Peter Gosling. 1997. "Strengths and Weaknesses of Minority Status for Southeast Asian Chinese at a Time of Economic Growth and Liberalization." In Daniel Chirot and Anthony Reid, eds., *Essential Outsiders: Chinese and Jews in the Modern Transformation of Southeast Asia and Central Europe*. Seattle: University of Washington Press.

Lim, Linda Y. C., and L. A. Peter Gosling, eds. 1983. *The Chinese in Southeast Asia*. Singapore: Maruzen.

Lockwood, William. 1965. "Japan's New Capitalism." In William Lockwood, ed., *The State and Economic Enterprise*. Princeton, N.J.: Princeton University Press.

Lowi, Ted. 1975. "Toward a Politics of Economics: The State of Permanent Receivership." In Leon Lindberg, ed., *Stress and Contraction in Modern Capitalism*. Lexington, Mass.: D. C. Heath.

McVey, Ruth, ed. 1992. *Southeast Asian Capitalists*. Ithaca, N.Y.: Cornell University, Southeast Asia Center.

Pempel, T. J. 1998. *Regime Shift: Comparative Dynamics of the Japanese Political Economy*. Ithaca, N.Y.: Cornell University Press.

Republic of Korea Fair Trade Commission. 1999. "In-Group Ownership Trends in the Largest Thirty *Chaebol*s." Kwanchon. Processed.

Root, Hilton. 2000. "Korea's Recovery." *The Milken Institute Report, 2000*. Santa Monica, Calif.: Milken Institute.

Schwarz, Adam. 1995. *A Nation in Waiting*. Boulder, Colo.: Westview.

Shue, Vivienne. 1988. *The Reach of the State: Sketches of the Chinese Body Politic*. Stanford, Calif.: Stanford University Press.

Whitley, Richard. 1992. *Business Systems in East Asia: Firms, Markets, and Societies*. New York: Sage Publications.

Woo, Jung-en (Meredith Woo-Cumings). 1991. *Race to the Swift: State and Finance in the Industrialization of Korea*. New York: Columbia University Press.

Woo-Cumings, Meredith, ed. 1999. *The Developmental State*. Ithaca: Cornell University Press.

World Bank. 1993. *The East Asian Miracle: Economic Growth and Public Policy*. New York: Oxford University Press.

———. 1997. *World Development Report 1997: The State in a Changing World*. New York: Oxford University Press.

Yu, Sungmin. 1996. *Nanumyonso k'oganda [Growth and Sharing]*. Seoul: Mirae Media.

CHAPTER 10

TRADE AND GROWTH: IMPORT LED OR EXPORT LED? EVIDENCE FROM JAPAN AND KOREA

Robert Z. Lawrence and David E. Weinstein

Interpretations of the contributions that international trade and competition have made to East Asian growth differ widely. First, there is the view associated with authors such as Balassa (1971), Krueger (1993), and Hughes (1992) that openness to trade was a crucial source of East Asia's rapid growth and that government's principal contribution was to limit protection and ensure that incentives were largely neutral. This stands in sharp contrast to a second position, exemplified by authors such as Amsden (1989) and Wade (1988), that, while seeing trade performance as having a vital role, emphasizes the impact of interventionist policies that changed the comparative advantage by "getting prices wrong." Another view questions the particular emphasis placed on trade policies. According to Rodrik (1995), for example, industrial policies played the most important role by creating a particularly favorable environment for domestic investment.

The East Asian Miracle (World Bank 1993a) stakes out an intermediate position. The study puts strong emphasis on the importance of performance in manufactured goods exports. The study goes beyond simply arguing that rapid export growth played an important role in permitting East Asian economies to avoid foreign exchange constraints. It suggests that exports and export policies played a crucial role in stimulating growth. The authors challenge the view that simply striving for a neutral incentive structure was adequate. Instead, they advocate broad government support for exports as a "highly effective way of enhancing absorption of international best practice technology [and] thus boosting productivity and output growth."[1] Exporting is an effective means of introducing new technologies both to the exporting firms in particular and to the rest of the economy.[2] However, the World Bank study does not advocate intervention to promote the export competitiveness of particular sectors. In general, it remains skeptical of selective industrial policies—"policies to alter the industrial structure to promote productivity-based growth"—although it does find evidence that these policies had positive effects in the case of Japan. Although the study emphasizes exports as a channel for learning and technological advancement, conspicuously absent is a discussion of the role of imports and import competition in providing similar benefits.

In addition to considering Korea, in this chapter we analyze the determinants of Japanese productivity growth at the sectoral level. Japan is an important case. There are some who support the view that Japanese growth was "export led." (On export-led growth, see Blumenthal 1972.) By contrast, others suggest that Japanese export success merely reflected favorable domestic conditions. Porter (1990), for example, maintains that highly competitive domestic conditions led to innovation in both products and management techniques. He adds that demanding consumers and unusual demand conditions also played a key role, as did the availability of factors of production, particularly physical and human capital. In this view, Japanese export prowess was the result of—rather than the reason for—strong domestic productivity growth.[3] There is a related controversy over the contribution of Japanese industrial policies. Some argue that Japanese interventionist policies were crucial for trade performance and growth, while others believe that Japan grew despite these policies, which were not particularly effective.[4]

In this chapter, we challenge three central conclusions of the World Bank study. First, we are unable to find support for the view that exporting was a particularly beneficial conduit for faster productivity growth in Japan. The positive association between exports and productivity growth appears due to the impact of productivity growth on exports rather than the reverse. Second, with the exception of selective corporate tax rates, we find no support for the view that direct subsidies or other industrial policies stimulated productivity. In this case, we support the Bank's general conclusion that selective industrial policies were ineffective, rather than its particular conclusion that these policies may have achieved some success in the case of Japan. And third, our results suggest that the World Bank study neglected an important channel of growth—imports. We find that imports and lower tariffs did stimulate productivity. This suggests that the Japanese economy would have grown even faster than it did if it had reduced domestic protection and imported more.

There is, of course, a long-standing debate as to whether the Japanese economy remains protected by unusually high invisible barriers, but there is widespread consensus that the Japanese economy was highly protectionist in the 1960s. Although many in Japan today might agree that reducing trade barriers could raise Japanese living standards, it is commonly thought that trade barriers in the 1960s contributed positively to Japanese development. Therefore, our finding that less import protection could have been beneficial during the earlier phases of Japan's development is particularly noteworthy.

In fact, one of the problems in trying to explain why East Asian growth was miraculous is that we are tempted to ignore ways in which it might have been even faster and more durable. Although our findings on the effects of imports may not explain why Japan grew rapidly, they may have important policy implications for other countries.[5] In particular, this evidence calls into question the view that Japanese sectoral productivity growth benefited from mercantilism. In the rest of this chapter, we demonstrate how we reach these conclusions. Before doing so, however, we consider briefly the theory and evidence on the links between international competition and productivity growth.

TRADE AND GROWTH: THEORY AND EVIDENCE

The starting point for understanding the link between trade and growth is the realization that, as international trade theory suggests, trade can have both static and dynamic effects. Traditional arguments about why countries gain from trade are typically static in nature. If a country moves from autarky to trade, theory tells us that production and consumption will change in such a way as to raise overall gross national product (GNP). These gains are static in the sense that once a country has opened to trade, all of the benefits from trade will be obtained on liberalization. Although traditional trade theory provides strong arguments for reducing trade barriers, these are essentially seen as one-time gains. Once these gains have been achieved, this theory has little to tell us about future performance.

Other considerations point to dynamic effects that could operate through their impact on competition and profitability. However, it is not obvious whether these effects will be positive or negative. Opening an economy up to trade will increase competition, and this could affect innovation, but economists are divided on the relationship between innovation and competition. On the one hand, there are those, like Hicks, who believe that competition is good for innovation because monopoly leads to lethargy and a search for "the quiet life"; on the other hand, there are those, like Schumpeter, who believe that some degree of monopoly is required to stimulate innovation. In fact, it is likely that neither perfect competition nor monopoly is particularly conducive to innovation and that intermediate market structures that combine rents to innovation with competitive pressures will be more stimulative.[6] The effects of increased international competition could depend, therefore, on the degree to which it generates this combination.

In general, investment in technological change and innovation will be stimulated by anticipated profits. This might lead us to expect that trade would reduce innovation in import-competing industries and increase it in export sectors. If import competition depresses the returns in certain industries, we might expect *less* rather than more spending and effort on innovation.[7] However, under conditions of imperfect competition, as Baldwin (1992) shows, firms may have an incentive not to innovate if they derive high profits from existing technologies. Under these circumstances, import competition could actually stimulate innovation by reducing the monopoly profits derived from not innovating.

In addition, scale is often an important factor in the returns to research and development (R&D) spending because research has a substantial fixed-cost component. Again, we might expect *less* R&D spending in import-competing sectors, whose scale of activity is reduced by trade, and more spending in export sectors, whose scale of activity is enlarged because the gains from innovation in global markets are likely to be larger than the gains in local markets.[8] Similarly, as Lucas (1988) has suggested, if one of the reasons why sectors grow is because of learning-by-doing, then we might expect sectors that produce a lot to grow faster than sectors that produce less. Trade is likely to cause the output of industries with comparative advantage (export sectors) to expand as workers and firms become more proficient at producing particular products. By contrast, import-competing sectors might be adversely affected.

Emulation is another channel by which trade could stimulate productivity growth in both export and import-competing industries. Competition with and exposure to superior foreign firms could also speed up technological acquisition and thus lead to faster technological change. Since it is easier to copy or absorb technology than to innovate, we might expect more technologically backward countries to grow faster than advanced countries (see Gerschenkron 1952). Firms that export, such as semiconductor firms in Korea, are more likely to have contacts abroad and could have higher rates of productivity growth because they can learn more easily than firms that principally sell in a domestic market. However, firms in import-competing industries tend to be further behind and may have more room to learn.

The work of Grossman and Helpman (1991), among others, points to another important mechanism by which trade can enhance growth. In a world in which firm output depends not only on the quantity but also on the variety of intermediates, access to imports can improve productivity by increasing the variety of intermediates. This may be important in sectors like electronics with a large number of specialized inputs. Alternatively, intermediate inputs may enhance productivity by providing domestic firms with access to technologies that are embodied in foreign capital goods not available domestically (see, for example, Bayoumi, Coe, and Helpman 1999).

There are paradigms that are different from those of traditional profit maximization in which managers may be stimulated to innovate when international competition threatens their rents (for example, Nelson and Winter 1974). This involves the existence of managers who satisfice rather than maximize and behave under conditions of what is sometimes termed bounded rationality. Basically, they do not innovate continuously; rather they only innovate when subject to an unusual stimulus. In this world, import competition could spur competition, while the greater profitability of exports could do the reverse.

Overall, therefore, theory is quite ambiguous on the dynamic effects of trade. There are reasons to expect that increased international competition could accelerate productivity growth, but also reasons to expect the reverse. "Sometimes" as the saying goes, "a kick in the pants gets you going, and sometimes it just hurts you." Given this ambiguity, it is perhaps not surprising that views on the likely impact of trade on growth remain widely divided.

For a 30-year period, starting in the 1950s, many saw import substitution as a crucial element for development, and protectionist policies were adopted not only in Japan but also in much of the developing world. Those favoring these policies typically argued that in order to achieve economic growth, countries had to protect infant industries. Various development experts often advised developing countries that, although static efficiency losses may be associated with protection, the gains from increasing domestic production and moving down the cost curve would more than offset the static inefficiencies arising from protection.

Over the past two decades, however, a considerable amount of empirical evidence has tended to contradict the notion that more protectionist regimes grow faster. In the early 1970s, Balassa (1971) and others began exploring the links between trade and growth. Over the next 20 years, a large number of studies found that export growth and export levels were highly correlated with GNP growth (see Edwards 1993 for a survey of the literature). Although there was a clear link between exports and development, the literature was sharply divided on whether countries that grow faster tend to export more or whether exporting more leads to faster growth.[9] In addition, countries that have rapid export growth also tend to have rapid import growth, so the association between exports and growth could actually be picking up a connection between imports and gross domestic product growth.

In a second generation of studies, Barro and Sala-i-Martin (1992), Beason and Weinstein (1996), Dollar (1992), Edwards (1992), and Krishna and Mitra (1998) explore the relationship between protection and either growth or productivity growth. Beason and Weinstein, examining the case of Japan, and Krishna and Mitra, examining the case of India, find that protection was not positively associated with productivity growth within various industries. Similarly, Barro and Sala-i-Martin, Dollar, and Edwards examine aggregate GNP data and find that countries that followed more protective policies typically grew more slowly. Lawrence (1999) finds that import competition stimulated total factor productivity (TFP) growth in the United States. Therefore, the evidence suggests that protection tended to reduce, or at best to leave unaffected, productivity and output growth.

The literature on the productivity-enhancing effects of exports is more ambivalent. Clerides and others (1998) find that relatively efficient firms become exporters, but that unit costs are not affected by the firm's previous participation in the export market. Although they find some evidence that exporters reduce the costs of breaking into foreign markets for other firms, they do not help those firms become more efficient. Similarly, Bernard and Jensen (1999a, 1999b) find that in the United States, firms with high levels of productivity become exporters, but that exporters do not have superior productivity and wage growth. Rodrik (1999) provocatively concludes, from his survey of the literature, that there is no evidence that a dollar of exports contributes any more, or any less, to an economy than a dollar of some other kind of productive activity. He suggests, however, that imports of capital goods and intermediate goods may impart additional benefits by supplying inputs that otherwise would not be available.[10]

Important questions remain unresolved in the literature. To what degree is the positive association between trade and growth due to the fact that trade is disproportionately stimulative of growth, and to what degree does it reflect the fact that growth leads to trade? Second, to the degree that trade induces rapid growth, what are the channels by which this effect operates? Is rapid growth primarily due to the impact of exporting or import-competing activity? If it is due to importing or exporting, is it primarily due to effects that stimulate productivity within sectors directly engaged in international competition or to indirect spillover effects such as the diffusion of technologies acquired through exporting to nonexport sectors or the use of superior imported machinery and other inputs in such sectors?

The focus of this chapter is too narrow to answer all of these questions. In particular, we concentrate only on the effects that are evident at the level of individual sectors and therefore do not explore the indirect channels through which trade might operate. Nonetheless, we hope to improve our understanding of the links between trade and growth and to explain the role that trade played in East Asian growth.

EMPIRICAL ANALYSIS

Our modeling strategy in this chapter is to control for several determinants of TFP growth at the sectoral level and then to test for the effects of trade and industrial policy. On theoretical grounds, we are led to include several variables. First, it seems reasonable to expect that the degree of technological backwardness is important. In particular, we might expect a process of convergence in which sectors that are relatively backward tend to have relatively faster TFP growth. To measure this effect, we use the estimates of TFP levels made by Jorgenson and Kuroda (1990) for Japan and for the United States, the latter being representative of the global technological frontier.[11] Second, as emphasized by Lucas (1988), we might expect that learning-by-doing could be important. In particular, we might expect experience to generate improvements in productive efficiency. To measure this effect, we aggregate the cumulative output growth in each sector starting in 1960. Third, we expect spending on research and development to be important. To measure this, we include a variable measuring the ratio of R&D to sales. In addition to these three control variables, we also include industry and time dummies to capture cycle and sector-specific determinants of productivity growth. Finally, we add in the variables that measure trade involvement, trade policy, and industrial policies. These include the share of imports in domestic demand, the share of exports in total output, the level of tariff protection, and several industrial policy measures. We also distinguish between imported inputs and those that compete directly with final production.

Data

All of our productivity data, unless otherwise noted, are taken from Jorgenson and Kuroda (1990). This data set is especially constructed to allow for comparisons of the United States and Japan on a variety of industry variables including TFP levels. Our trade variables are all taken from the STAN database of the Organisation for Economic Co-operation and Development (OECD) or from OECD trade statistics. Research and development data for the United States are taken from the National Science Foundation, *Research and Development in Industry* (various years). R&D data for Japan are taken from the Survey of Research and Development.

Preliminary Observations

Before we proceed with our regression analysis, it is useful to examine, in a preliminary way, the relationships between trade and TFP growth and between relative productivity levels.

Trade. Figure 10.1 shows a positive relationship between the average ratio of exports to sales over the period 1964 to 1985 and average TFP growth over the same time period. Similarly, figure 10.2 shows a negative correlation between average import penetration and average TFP growth. This evidence is consistent with the idea that Japanese growth was export led. First, TFP growth was relatively higher in sectors with larger export shares. There is, of course, an expectation that a country will export products in which it has relatively high TFP. Thus the association between export growth and TFP growth could mean that faster TFP growth leads to exports. However, one crude way to control for the causal effects of TFP is to plot export shares in 1964 against TFP growth over the following 20 years. As shown in figure 10.3, the association between exports and TFP growth remains.

Convergence. As figure 10.4 shows, there appears to have been some convergence in some sectors. The two tradable nonmanufacturing sectors—agriculture and mining—were heavily targeted by the Japanese government and exhibit radical movements in their productivity levels. Because we want to focus on manufacturing sectors rather than resource-intensive sectors, we drop these industries from subsequent analysis. Of the remaining sectors, about half exhibit convergence, and half exhibit divergence. Indeed, in some sectors, Japan overtook the United States. These results contrast sharply with the findings of Dollar and Wolff (1994), who find fast rates of convergence within the Japanese manufacturing sector. This highlights the sensitivity of TFP

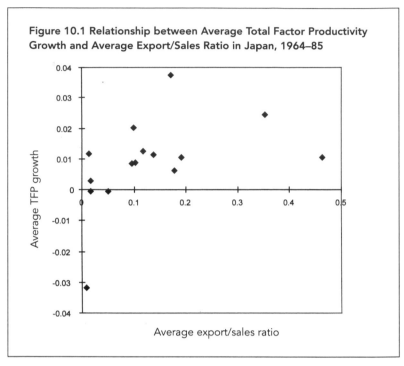

Figure 10.1 Relationship between Average Total Factor Productivity Growth and Average Export/Sales Ratio in Japan, 1964–85

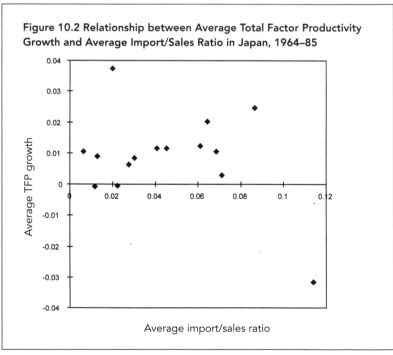

Figure 10.2 Relationship between Average Total Factor Productivity Growth and Average Import/Sales Ratio in Japan, 1964–85

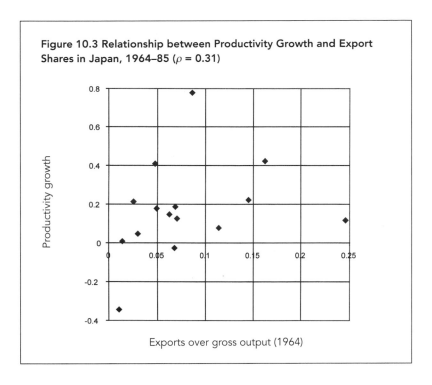

Figure 10.3 Relationship between Productivity Growth and Export Shares in Japan, 1964–85 (ρ = 0.31)

numbers to data construction issues. We use the Jorgenson and Kuroda (1990) data that were constructed and compiled to ensure compatibility, while other studies use OECD data that have greater compatibility problems.

In sum, the raw data suggest a positive association between export shares and TFP growth and a negative association between import shares and TFP growth. However, regression analysis shows that drawing causal implications from this evidence can be highly misleading.

HYPOTHESES

In the regression analysis, we use the annual growth rate in Japanese industry (TFPJ) as the dependent variable. In all regressions we enter the lagged dependent variable and a set of industry dummies. This means that we are obtaining estimates that are within (fixed-effects) estimates. In addition, we include the ratio of the level of Japanese TFP to U.S. TFP in each industry; the change in the log of cumula-

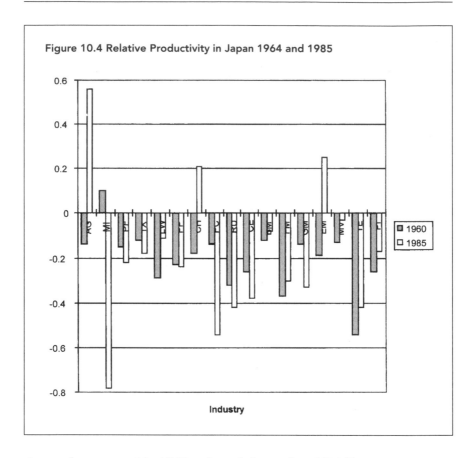

Figure 10.4 Relative Productivity in Japan 1964 and 1985

tive real output with 1960 = 1; and the ratio of R&D to output over the previous three years. We then add various variables representing trade and industrial policy. Precise definitions of the variables are reported in table 10.1.

As reported in table 10.2, in most of the regressions the three control variables are significant. When Japan is behind, the relative productivity variable is less than 1, so a negative coefficient implies that relative backwardness has a positive impact on TFP growth. This is exactly what one would expect from a neoclassical growth model. Moreover, cumulative output growth and R&D spending all boost TFP growth, presumably for conventional reasons. However, neither exports as a share of output (column 1) nor imports (column 2) nor net trade (column 3) nor exports and imports entered separately are statistically significant. These results imply that trade per se does not have a positive (or negative) impact on sectoral TFP.

These results are modified in the case of the import variable, however, both when we enter the trade variables in interaction with relative backwardness and when we enter dummy variables that split the sample period into two periods. As reported in table 10.3, when the export (column 1) and net trade (column 2) variables interact with relative backwardness, they continue not to be significant. However, the variable that interacts import share with relative backwardness is now significant and positive, while the coefficient on the average import share is negative and almost significant. This means that, for sectors whose relative TFP level is just over half that of the United States, *higher levels of imports actually cause faster rates of convergence.* This runs

Table 10.1 Variable Definitions

Variable	Definition
GROWTFP	Growth rate of total factor productivity
TFPJ(-1)	Japanese total factor productivity level lagged one year
RELTFP	Lag of level of Japanese total factor productivity relative to the U.S. level
CUMOUT	Change in log cumulative real output (1960 real output = 1)
AVERD	Average R&D expenditures divided by output over the past three years
AVEX	Average exports to output ratio over the past three years
AVENET	Average net trade to output ratio over the past three years
COMPIM	Average competing imports over the past three years
NCOMPIM	Average noncompeting imports over the past three years
AVIM	Average imports to output ratio over the past three years
RELTFP*AVEX	Interaction of average RELTFP over the past three years with AVEX
RELTFP*AVENET	Interaction of average RELTFP over the past three years with AVENET
RELTFP*AVEIMP	Interaction of average RELTFP over the past three years with AVEIMP
RELTFP*CUMOUT	Interaction of RELTFP with CUMOUT
RELTFP*AVERD	Interaction of average RELTFP over the past three years with AVERD
TAX	Average corporate tax rate less tax rate for the industry
LOAN	Japan Development Bank loans divided by total loans for industry less manufacturing average
DELTAERP	Effective rate of protection less industry average
SUBSIDY	Subsidies less taxes divided by sales for industry less manufacturing average
ERP	Effective rate of protection
LOGOUT	Log of output
EXOUT	Exports divided by output

Table 10.2 Basic Trade and Growth Results

Variable	Exports as a share of output	Imports	Net trade	Imports and exports entered separately
TFPJ(-1)	-0.083	-0.082	-0.070	-0.077
	(-0.077)	(0.077)	(0.0763)	(0.078)
RELTFP(-1)	-0.274**	-0.273**	-0.283**	-0.277**
	(0.098)	(0.097)	(0.097)	(0.098)
CUMOUT	0.263**	0.267**	0.276**	0.272**
	(0.093)	(0.094)	(0.094)	(0.095)
AVERD	5.105**	4.989**	3.586**	4.327*
	(2.114)	(1.788)	(1.500)	(2.402)
AVEX	-0.092			-0.057
	(0.133)			(0.143)
AVENET		-0.095		
		(0.109)		
AVEIMP			0.266	0.221
			(0.300)	(0.143)
Adjusted R^2	0.151	0.152	0.152	0.149

Note: * Significant at the 1 percent level; ** significant at the 5 percent level.
Source: Jorgenson and Kuroda (1990).

contrary to the notion that protection from imports tends to enhance the ability of sectors to catch up.

We also have some evidence that extremely backward sectors, those with TFP levels that are less than half that of the United States, seem to not benefit from or even be harmed by higher import levels. This arises because the negative coefficient on the average import share variable dominates the positive coefficient on the interaction term when relative TFP levels are low. However, one should be cautious about reading too much into this effect for a number of reasons. First, the negative impact of imports on productivity growth for very backward sectors is not statistically significant. Hence, one must be very cautious about interpreting this result in terms of an infant industry–style argument. Second, most sectors in Japan never fell into the range in which productivity levels were so low that imports were actually harmful. Indeed, the three sectors that at times did have relative TFP levels below 0.5—petroleum and coal products, rubber products not elsewhere classified, and transportation equipment excluding motor vehicles—are not sectors that are usually thought of as potentially benefiting from infant-industry protection.

Table 10.3 Interreaction between Convergence and Growth

Variable	Exports as a share of output	Net trade	Imports	Average
TFPJ(-1)	-0.075	-0.064	-0.066	-0.077
	(0.075)	(0.073)	(0.078)	(0.075)
RELTFP(-1)	-0.210**	-0.200**	-0.298**	-0.309**
	(0.089)	(0.087)	(0.098)	(0.098)
CUMOUT	0.225**	0.226**	0.214**	0.215**
	(0.73)	(0.073)	(0.095)	(0.075)
AVERD	2.975*	3.286**	1.775	1.519
	(1.686)	(1.457)	(2.402)	(1.866)
AVEX	-0.197			-0.169
	(0.275)			(0.273)
AVEIMP			-0.956	-0.169
			(0.687)	(0.689)
AVENET		-0.070		
		(0.253)		
RELTFP*AVEX	0.176			0.220
	(0.312)			(0.309)
RELTFP *AVEIMP			1.760**	1.773**
			(0.848)	(0.852)
RELTFP*AVENET		-0.020		
		(0.292)		
Adjusted R^2	0.151	0.153	0.171	0.167

Note: * Significant at the 1 percent level; ** significant at the 5 percent level.
Source: Jorgenson and Kuroda (1990).

In table 10.4, we introduce a dummy variable that takes the value of 1 for the period after 1973. In this regression, the control variables have lower levels of significance, suggesting that they could be capturing a pre-1973 effect rather than what we think they capture. Relative backwardness still matters, but less powerfully (and is not significant), and neither cumulative output nor R&D variables are significant. The first regression indicates an appreciable slowdown in productivity growth after 1973 by an annual average of 3.8 percent. In the early period, exporting has a negative impact, which becomes even larger after 1973. This certainly does not suggest that exports have stimulated TFP. By contrast, we find that imports have a positive impact in the early period and, in the specification with imports, the R&D variable becomes significant. In the second half of the period, the impact of imports continues to be significant, but it is now cut by about half. These results clearly suggest a positive role for imports. Furthermore, they suggest that import liberalization in the early period had an even more important positive impact on productivity growth than later liberalization. Since Japanese industries tended to be relatively further behind during the earlier period, this result contrasts with that obtained earlier.

We have seen that exporting does not cause productivity growth, but it would be very distressing if, in our data, higher productivity levels were not associated with greater levels of exports and production. In a Ricardian model, one would expect to find that higher levels of productivity result in both higher levels of output and greater exports. We explore this conjecture explicitly in table 10.5. Here we regress the log of output and the export to output ratio on TFP levels as well as lagged dependent variables to assess the relationship between productivity and exports. We find that contemporaneous TFP is very

Table 10.4 Testing for Sample Breaks

Variable	Late interacted with exports	Late interacted with net exports	Late interacted with imports	Late interacted with exports & imports	Late
TFPJ(-1)	-0.144	-0.167	-0.129	-0.145	-0.099
	(0.069)	(0.069)	(0.067)	(0.069)	(0.067)
RELTFP(-1)	-0.110	-0.111	-0.118	-0.121	-0.119
	(0.076)	(0.075)	(0.076)	(0.075)	(0.077)
CUMOUT	0.023	0.038	0.119	0.072	0.103
	(0.115)	(0.112)	(0.112)	(0.115)	(0.113)
AVERD	2.021	2.661*	2.751**	0.649	2.772**
	(1.812)	(1.577)	(1.313)	(1.947)	(1.302)
AVEX	-0.309*			-0.032	
	(0.182)			(0.218)	
AVEIMP			0.949**	0.943**	
			(0.322)	(0.376)	
AVENET		-0.346			
		(0.131)			
LATE	-0.038**	-0.025*	0.008	0.943**	-0.008
	(0.016)	(0.013)	(0.016)	(0.376)	(0.012)
LATE*AVEX	0.322**			0.196	
	(0.115)			(0.127)	
LATE*AVEIMP			-0.449**	-0.467**	
			(0.224)	(0.229)	
LATE*AVENET		0.324			
		(0.096)			
Adjusted R^2	0.210	0.221	0.211	0.226	0.226

Note: * Significant at the 1 percent level; ** significant at the 5 percent level.
Source: Jorgenson and Kuroda (1990).

tightly correlated with both output and exports and that lagged TFP is also strongly associated with exports. These results strongly suggest that the direction of causality is from TFP to exports and not the reverse.

It is also instructive to ask if effective tariff protection promoted or inhibited productivity growth. In table 10.6, we explore the effects of a number of industrial policy variables. We add to our basic specification variables that include average corporate taxes, the proportion of loans granted by the Japan Development Bank, the effective rate of protection less the industry average, and subsidies less taxes. Among these variables, only the tax rate variable is significant. Once again, when export and import shares are introduced into this specification, the import variable is significant and positive, while the export variable is not. Hence, even controlling for various industrial policy tools, we find that imports are important for productivity growth, but exports are not.

In table 10.7, we test the robustness of our contention that effective rates of protection are not associated with greater productivity growth. In particular, it is often alleged that during the 1960s, protection was an important part of Japan's industrial policy. To see if protection was

Table 10.5 Riccardian Regressions

Variable	Relative TFP	Lagged relative TFP
Dependent variable: LOGOUT		
LOGOUT(-1)	0.754**	0.788**
	(0.024)	(0.027)
RELTFP	0.494**	
	(0.097)	
RELTFP(-1)		0.089
		(0.104)
Adjusted R^2	0.986	0.984
Dependent variable: EXOUT		
EXOUT(-1)	0.834**	0.845**
	(0.030)	(0.029)
RELTFP		0.067**
		(0.022)
RELTFP(-1)	0.070**	
	(0.022)	
Adjusted R^2	0.962	0.962

Note: * Significant at the 1 percent level; ** significant at the 5 percent level.
Source: Jorgenson and Kuroda (1990).

Table 10.6 Industrial Policy Regressions

Variable	Exports	Standard control	Net trade	Imports
GROWTFP	-0.117	-0.116	-0.120	-0.116
	(0.069)	(0.071)	(0.070)	(0.069)
RELTFP(-1)	-0.127*	-0.128*	-0.126	-0.129*
	(0.077)	(0.077)	(0.077)	(0.076)
CUMOUT	0.263**	0.266**	0.262**	0.294**
	(0.085)	(0.085)	(0.085)	(0.085)
AVERD	2.932*	2.582	3.419**	1.094
	(1.422)	(1.854)	(1.642)	(1.958)
AVEX	0.038			0.136
	(1.855)			(0.137)
AVEIMP				0.561
				(0.255)
AVENET			0.061	
			(0.102)	
TAX(-1)	0.012**	0.012**	0.012**	0.012**
	(0.004)	(0.004)	(0.004)	(0.004)
LOAN(-1)	-0.001	-0.002	-0.002	0.000
	(0.003)	(0.003)	(0.003)	(0.003)
DELTAERP(-1)	0.000	0.000	0.000	0.000
	(0.001)	(0.001)	(0.001)	(0.001)
SUBSIDY(-1)	0.000	0.000	0.000	0.002
	(0.002)	(0.002)	(0.002)	(0.003)
ERP(-1)	0.000	0.000	0.000	0.000
	(0.001)	(0.001)	(0.001)	(0.001)
Adjusted R^2	0.221	0.217	0.232	0.232

Note: * Significant at the 1 percent level; ** significant at the 5 percent level.
Source: Jorgenson and Kuroda (1990).

more important in the early period, we once again introduce our LATE dummy and interact it with the relative level of protection. Contrary to conventional wisdom, we find that increasing protection in the early period was associated with lower rates of productivity growth and that higher protection had virtually no impact after 1973.

It might be argued that Japan only lowered its tariffs once industries were sufficiently productive, so the negative relationship between tariffs and TFP growth could actually reflect reverse causation. However, this concern would result in a negative relationship between productivity levels and tariffs and not between tariff levels and productivity growth rates. Therefore, this interpretation of our results is not plausible. Finally, in table 10.8 we examine whether the protection of more backward sectors improved productivity growth. The data militate against this view. No matter how we specify our regressions, we find no impact or negative impacts from protection.

Table 10.7 Protection and Growth Regressions

Variable	Control	Exports
TFPJ(-1)	-0.088	-0.085
	(0.067)	(0.068)
RELTFP(-1)	-0.149**	-0.149**
	(0.078)	(0.078)
CUMOUT	0.080	0.079
	(0.113)	(0.113)
AVERD	2.685**	2.026
	(1.384)	(1.829)
AVEX		0.071
		(0.129)
DELTAERP(-1)	-0.002**	-0.002**
	(0.001)	(0.001)
LATE	-0.012	-0.012
	(0.012)	(0.013)
LATE*DELTAERP(-1)	0.0014**	0.0014
	(0.0006)	(0.0006)
Adjusted R^2	0.198	0.195

Note: * Significant at the 1 percent level; ** significant at the 5 percent level.
Source: Jorgenson and Kuroda (1990).

Table 10.8 Backwardness, Protection, and Growth

Variable	Control	Exports	Net trade	Imports and Exports	Imports
TFPJ(-1)	-0.113	-0.112	-0.117	-0.116	-0.111
	(0.69)	(0.069)	(0.069)	(0.069)	(0.069)
RELTFP(-1)	-0.147	-0.147	-0.145	-0.146	-0.147
	(0.077)	(0.077)	(0.077)	(0.077)	(0.077)
CUMOUT	0.258	0.258	0.259	0.274	0.278
	(0.077)	(0.077)	(0.077)	(0.077)	(0.077)
AVERD	2.283	2.105	2.828	1.796	0.764
	(1.458)	(1.862)	(1.666)	(1.471)	(1.954)
AVEX		0.019		0.107	
		(0.128)		(0.133)	
AVEIMP				0.466	0.529
				(0.240)	(0.253)
AVENET			0.068		
			(0.100)		
TAX(-1)	0.014	0.014	0.014	0.014	0.013
	(0.004)	(0.004)	(0.004)	(0.004)	(0.004)
LOAN(-1)	0.000	0.000	0.000	0.000	0.000
	(0.003)	(0.003)	(.003)	(0.003)	(0.003)
DELTAERP(-1)	0.003	0.003	0.003	0.003	0.002
	(0.002)	(0.002)	(0.002)	(0.002)	(0.002)
SUBSIDY(-1)	-0.002	-0.002	-0.002	-0.003	-0.003
	(0.003)	(0.003)	(0.003)	(0.003)	(0.003)
RELTFP*DELTAERP(-1)	-0.004	-0.004	-0.004	-0.003	-0.003
	(0.002)	(0.002)	(0.002)	(0.002)	(0.002)
Adjusted R^2	0.221	0.228	0.229	0.241	0.241

Note: * Significant at the 1 percent level; ** significant at the 5 percent level.
Source: Jorgenson and Kuroda (1990).

In sum, this analysis suggests that, although exporting did not promote TFP growth, import protection actually retarded productivity growth and imports enhanced it.

WHY DO IMPORTS MATTER?

One major issue that remains is the mechanism by which imports affect TFP growth. Our results show a positive relationship between import shares and productivity growth, but we have not shown why this is the case. We have suggested two possible mechanisms by which this is likely to occur. The first is that the quality of firms in the industry might rise because of the added competition from foreign firms. This might occur because domestic firms learn by examining foreign imports or because foreign competition spurs innovation. Alternatively, it may be access to better intermediates that is important. For example, Japanese apparel producers may benefit from importing higher-quality cotton from abroad. This would be an example of superior intermediates in the same sector spurring productivity growth.

In order to separate these two hypotheses, we need to separate imports within a sector that compete with the output of firms in that sector from imports that are used as intermediates. Fortunately, it is possible to achieve that dichotomy by using the import input-output tables of Japan. We obtained these tables from the OECD input-output database for the years 1970, 1975, and 1980. Using these tables, we estimate the share of imports into a sector that were used by firms in that sector (noncompeting imports) and the share of imports that were sold to other sectors (competing imports). We then run our basic regression again separating competing from noncompeting imports.

The results are presented in table 10.9. The impact of noncompeting imports on productivity growth is extremely small and statistically insignificant. Competing imports, however, have a significant impact. The magnitudes of the coefficients indicate that for most sectors and time periods in our sample, higher past levels of competing imports are associated with more rapid productivity growth. It is important to remember that this result is not a product of the fact that sectors that import more have lower initial levels of productivity because we are already controlling for the initial level of relative productivity. Rather, it appears that higher import levels have an independent effect.

In addition to being statistically significant, the impact of competing imports is economically significant as well. In order to assess the economic significance of competing imports, for each sector we first calculate the standard deviation in competing imports as a share of total imports. For a sector that is 80 percent as productive as a U.S. sector, the median 1 standard deviation increase in the share of competing imports would raise TFP by about 3 percentage points. This understates the importance of competing imports in some sectors. For example, in electrical machinery, progressive liberalization caused competing imports to rise from 68 percent of imports in 1970 to 99 percent in 1985. This increased competition from imports raised productivity in electrical machinery by about 35 percent, which suggests that competing imports are very important in understanding the success of that sector.

Table 10.9 Competing versus Noncompeting Imports

Variable	Competing and noncompeting imports alone	Full specification	Competing imports alone
TFPJ(-1)	-0.087	-0.101	-0.094
	(0.077)	(0.082)	(0.072)
RELTFP(-1)	-0.292	-0.297	-0.289
	(0.097)	(0.010)	(0.092)
CUMOUT	0.202	0.200	0.195
	(0.077)	(0.079)	(0.073)
AVERD	1.694	1.690	1.727
	(1.254)	(1.889)	(1.229)
AVEX		-0.167	
		(0.287)	
AVEX*RELTFP		0.193	
		(0.331)	
NCOMPIM	-0.063	-0.089	
	(1.207)	(1.227)	
COMPIM	-1.808	-1.692	-1.909
	(1.157)	(1.207)	(1.081)
NCOMPIM*RELTFP	0.285	0.250	
	(1.995)	(2.048)	
COMPIM*RELTFP	2.939	2.835	3.081
	(1.518)	(1.554)	(1.363)
Adjusted R^2	0.168	0.163	0.175

Source: Jorgenson and Kuroda (1990).

The effect of competition is larger for sectors that have converged than for sectors that are further behind. When competing imports enter a sector that is technologically backward, there is relatively little impact on productivity growth. This may be due to the inability of backward firms to compete with their more sophisticated foreign counterparts. However, as sectors converge, the importance of imports rises. As we suggested in the beginning, "sometimes a kick in the pants gets you going, and sometimes it just hurts." This lesson is particularly relevant for the more developed economies such as Hong Kong, Korea, Singapore, and Taiwan (China), which now have productivity gaps that are on par with or smaller than Japan's gap in the 1970s. The lesser-developed economies still may be at levels where protection is less costly in terms of its impact on productivity growth.

RESULTS FROM OTHER COUNTRIES

It would be interesting to see if our results for Japan are applicable to those for other economies as well. Thus we present information on productivity in Korea and the United States.

Korea

Korea is the third largest East Asian economy in GNP terms. Unfortunately, data problems preclude making as careful an analysis of Korea as we performed for Japan. TFP indexes are considerably more crude, and we had difficult finding sectoral trade data for Korea prior to 1970. However, Lee (1995) has performed a similar analysis on Korean data, and we are able to use some of his data to replicate parts of our experiments on Japan.

Table 10.10 presents the results of Lee's attempt to assess the impact of industrial policy on productivity growth in Korea. The results are quite similar to those reported in Beason and Weinstein (1996) and in this chapter. Practically all forms of industrial policy had either negative or insignificant impacts on Korean productivity growth. Hence there appears to be little systematic evidence that greater levels of targeting improved productivity growth in Korea.

Table 10.10 Regression Results for the Impact of Industrial Policy and Trade on
Productivity Growth in Korea, 1963–83

Variable	Lee's results 1963–83	Imports, no fixed effect 1968–83	Imports, fixed effect 1968–83	Exports, no fixed effect 1968–83	Exports, fixed effect 1968–83
Fixed effects	Yes	No	Yes	No	Yes
Log (initial value added)	-0.144				
	(0.146)				
Log (initial capital)	0.071**				
	(0.017)				
Nontariff barrier	-0.072**				
	(0.032)				
Tariff	-0.079				
	(0.069)				
Tax incentive	0.044				
	(0.110)				
Bank loans	-0.019				
	(0.138)				
Imports/gross output		0.032	0.077		
		(0.021)	(0.064)		
Exports/gross output				-0.007	-0.203**
				(0.041)	(0.097)
Number of observations	146	69	69	69	69

Note: * Significant at the 1 percent level; ** significant at the 5 percent level.
Source: Lee (1995).

Lee does not examine the impact of trade per se. Therefore, we use
import and export data from the World Trade database (see Feenstra,
Lipsey, and Bowen 1997) and production data from the STAN database to calculate ratios of imports and exports to production. We then
merge these numbers with Lee's database. Lee provides data on productivity growth rates for three five-year periods (1968–73, 1973–78,
and 1978–83). For each of the sectors in Lee's analysis we match the
ratio of imports to production for the year at the start of the period
with productivity and other data for the remaining years. Since our
trade data start in 1970, we are forced to match trade data for this year
with the earlier sample. Unfortunately, the data for Korea are more
limited than those for Japan, and we are only able to use 69 observations and cannot calculate relative productivity levels.

Table 10.11 presents results from two simple specifications regressing productivity growth against import and export shares. The results

reveal that, as in the Japanese data, higher levels of imports are associated with greater productivity growth. Although the results are not statistically significant, the signs are consistent with the Japanese results.

Turning to exports, we find the reverse of export-led growth. Sectors that started by exporting more recorded lower rates of productivity growth. When we add in several trade policy measures, tariffs, and nontariff barriers, our results do not change much. We find a positive, but not statistically significant, impact from imports and a negative but not significant impact from exports. We find a negative relationship between protection and productivity growth in Korea. Higher tariffs have a statistically significant negative impact on TFP. As in the case of Japan, it appears that tariff protection in Korea retarded TFP.

United States

Lawrence (1999) estimates the impact of international competition on total factor productivity in more than 100 U.S. manufacturing industries in the 1980s. After controlling for spending on research and development and the degree of industry concentration, he finds that a higher share of imports in domestic consumption is associated with a

Table 10.11 Integrated Trade and Industrial Policy Regressions for Korea, 1968–83

Variable	Imports and Exports	Imports only
Fixed effects	Yes	Yes
Nontariff barrier	0.137*	0.140*
	(0.085)	(0.084)
Tariff	-0.230**	-0.253**
	(0.107)	(0.104)
Imports/gross output ratio	0.053	0.057
	(0.064)	(0.064)
Exports/gross output ratio	-0.102	
	(0.102)	
Number of observations	69	69
Adjusted R^2	0.038	0.040

Note: * Significant at the 1 percent level; ** significant at the 5 percent level.
Source: Lee (1995).

statistically significant positive effect on subsequent total factor productivity growth. These effects are apparent for imports from both industrial and developing countries. Lawrence similarly finds no evidence of a positive association between the share of exports in domestic production and subsequent productivity growth. Thus the evidence for the United States appears consistent with that found for Japan and Korea. Imports stimulate domestic productivity growth, while exports apparently do not.

CONCLUSION

Neoclassical arguments about free trade have convinced many developing countries to liberalize unilaterally. In addition, there is a growing view within Japan itself that more liberalization and deregulation are called for. But revisionist critics argue that Japan's spectacular growth was not achieved by following laissez-faire precepts. On the contrary, Japan officially maintained high levels of protection during the 1950s and 1960s when its growth was most rapid, and even though official barriers were lowered considerably in the 1970s and 1980s, Japan continued its mercantilist practices through more subtle mechanisms (Lawrence 1993). In the revisionist view, Japanese trade protection enabled the nurturing and development of internationally competitive firms—a lesson that developing countries ignore at their peril.[12] Moreover, since its domestic protection promotes growth, foreigners advocating a more open, market-oriented Japanese market today are suggesting that Japan should take steps that are not in its domestic interest.

In fact, the results in this chapter suggest that, when it comes to TFP growth, this view of Japan is seriously erroneous.[13] We find that lower tariffs and higher import volumes would have been particularly beneficial for Japan during the period from 1964 to 1973. Our results also lead us to question whether Japanese exports were a particularly important source of productivity growth. We support the conclusion of Rodrik (1999) that export fetishism is unwarranted. However, our findings on Japan suggest that the salutary impact of imports stems more from their contribution to competition than to intermediate inputs. Instead, this chapter suggests that Japan's performance was even more of a miracle than we thought, since it occurred despite the maintenance of protectionist barriers.

Furthermore, our results suggest a reason why imports are important. Greater imports of competing products spur innovation, and competitive pressures and learning from foreign rivals are important conduits for growth. These channels are even more important as industries converge with the market leader. Thus further liberalization by Japan and other East Asian countries may result in future dynamic gains.

Although our analysis has focused principally on Japan, we also have provided corroborating evidence suggesting that our conclusions apply more broadly. Imports into the United States seem to be an important factor in promoting productivity growth. The evidence for Korea suggests similar impacts from imports and tariffs and no evidence that exports promoted productivity. Our results call into question the views of both the World Bank and the revisionists and provide support for those who advocate more liberal trade policies.

Even so, the experience of East Asia must be seen within the international trading environment and the changing rules of the General Agreement on Tariffs and Trade and the World Trade Organization from the 1960s through the 1990s. The enlightened approaches to development in the late 1970s through the late 1980s argued for export-led growth but did not press for liberalizing imports, and the rules of international trade were quite forbearing for East Asian countries. Basic international economics teaches us that an import tariff has identical effects as an export tax. Put another way, to the extent that East Asian countries subsidized exports, they were in effect subsidizing imports.

The pressure to liberalize imports intensified dramatically after completion of the Uruguay Round. Given the relatively low level of productivity in many Asian countries, one interpretation of our results is that many East Asian countries could have moved more quickly in the latter half of the 1990s to scale down import barriers, but that the impact of these barriers may not have been that important in the 1970s and 1980s. Several Asian countries have made impressive steps toward dismantling trade barriers, and our analysis suggests that these may improve the long-run performance of their economies. The experience of Japan and the United States, however, argues for a more venturesome position on the part of the more developed East Asian economies with regard to unilateral or multilateral reductions in tariffs.

NOTES

The authors would like to thank Donald Davis, Richard Katz, Howard Pack, Jungsoo Park, Joseph Stiglitz, and participants at the World Bank workshop on rethinking the East Asian miracle for comments on earlier drafts of this chapter. David Weinstein would also like to thank the Japan Advanced Research Grant Program at the Social Science Research Council Japan and the Nippon Telephone and Telegraph Fellowship Program at the University of Michigan Business School for providing research support for this project. In addition, this chapter could not have been written without the excellent research assistance of Pao-Li Chang and Carolyn Evans.

1. World Bank (1993a:357). The emphasis on exports in general is interesting because, in some places, it also voices skepticism that selective industrial policy was effective and, in others, it seems to argue that exports played an important role in making industrial policies effective. See Rodrik (1994).
2. The study also argues that by making access to credit, industrial licensing, and sometimes foreign exchange contingent on export performance, policymakers in Japan and in other East Asian economies were able to create contests that led to rapid growth.
3. According to Michael Porter, "In nearly every industry we studied, exports increased substantially *only* when the domestic market became mature" (Porter 1990: 402).
4. For the first view, see Ito (1992); Dore (1986); Boltho (1985); Fallows (1994); Itoh and others (1988); for the second view, see Beason and Weinstein (1996).
5. According to Porter (1990: 708), "Japan must import more if vibrant productivity growth is to continue. Imports stimulate domestic productivity growth."
6. The literature suggests that the impact of competition on managerial slack could be positive or negative. See Scharfstein (1988).
7. In the conventional formal theory of trade and growth, import competition has an antigrowth bias since it reduces the profitability of innovation. See, for example, Grossman and Helpman (1991).
8. In the presence of imperfect competition, increased trade could reduce aggregate output in import-competing industries, but it also could increase capacity utilization of individual firms, thus raising the scale at which they operate.
9. Frankel, Romer, and Cyrus (1996) use simultaneous equation estimation to show that trade stimulates growth rather than the reverse.
10. Rodrik is similarly skeptical of the role of foreign direct investment (FDI). We would expect, however, that FDI would provide similar opportunities for competition and the increased availability of technology and inputs to imports of

goods, making the case for liberalization of FDI similar to that for the liberalization of goods. Nonetheless, exploring this impact is an important topic for further research. A similar argument could be made for services.

11. One problem with the Jorgenson and Kuroda data is that they are constructed under the assumption of constant returns to scale, perfect product and factor markets, and so forth. Although we would have liked to implement a methodology that would have allowed for these real-world phenomena, data limitations precluded that option in this study.

12. Protection did not mean eliminating competition. While external competition was blocked, internally there was fierce competition between rivals. See World Bank (1993b: 22).

13. There are, of course, reasons for protection other than the promotion of productivity growth. Protection may reduce income inequality and income volatility and may serve important political interests as well.

REFERENCES

The word "processed" describes informally reproduced works that may not be commonly available through library systems.

Amsden, Alice. 1989. *Asia's Next Giant: South Korea and Late Industrialization.* New York: Oxford University Press.

Balassa, Bela. 1971. *The Structure of Protection in Developing Countries.* Baltimore, Md.: Johns Hopkins University Press.

Baldwin, Richard. 1992. "On the Growth Effects of Import Competition." NBER Working Paper 4045. National Bureau of Economic Research, Cambridge, Mass. Processed.

Barro, Robert, and Xavier Sala-i-Martin. 1992. "Convergence." *Journal of Political Economy* 100(April):223–51.

Bayoumi, Tamim., David T. Coe, and Elhanan Helpman. 1999. "R&D Spillovers and Global Growth." *Journal of International Economics* 47(2):399–428.

Beason, Richard., and David Weinstein. 1996. "Growth, Economies of Scale, and Targeting in Japan (1955–1990)." *Review of Economics and Statistics* (May):286–95.

Bernard, Andrew. B., and J. Bradford Jensen. 1999a. "Exceptional Exporter Performance: Cause, Effect, or Both?" *Journal of International Economics* 47(1):1–26.

———. 1999b. "Exporting and Productivity." Yale University, Economics Department, New Haven, Conn. (March). Processed.

Blumenthal, Tuvia. 1972. "Exports and Economic Growth: The Case of Postwar Japan." *Quarterly Journal of Economics* 86(4):617–31.

Boltho, Andrea. 1985. "Was Japan's Industrial Policy Successful." *Cambridge Journal of Economics* 9(June):187–201.

Clerides, Sofronis, Saul Lach, and James Tybout 1998. "Is Learning by Exporting Important? Micro-Dynamic Evidence from Colombia, Mexico, and Morocco." *Quarterly Journal of Economics* 113(August):903–47.

Denison, Edward, and William Chung. 1976. "Economic Growth and Its Sources." In Hugh Patrick and Henry Rosovsky, eds., *Asia's New Giant*. Washington, D.C.: Brookings Institution.

Dollar, David. 1992. "Outward-Oriented Developing Economies Really Do Grow More Rapidly: Evidence from 95 LDC's, 1976–1985." *Economic Development and Cultural Change* 40(April):523–44.

Dollar, David, and Edward N. Wolff. 1994. "Capital Intensity and TFP Convergence by Industry in Manufacturing, 1963–1985." In William. J. Baumol, Richard R. Nelson, and Edward N. Wolff, eds., *Convergence of Productivity*. New York: Oxford University Press.

Dore, Ronald. 1986. *Flexible Rigidities: Industrial Policy and Structural Adjustment in the Japanese Economy*. Stanford, Calif.: Stanford University Press.

Edwards, Sebastian. 1992. "Trade Orientation, Distortions, and Growth in Developing Countries." *Journal of Development Economics* 39(July):31–57.

————. 1993. "Openness, Trade Liberalization, and Growth in Developing Countries." *Journal of Economic Literature* 31(September):1358–93.

Fallows, James. 1994. *Looking at the Sun*. New York: Pantheon Books.

Feenstra, Robert, Robert Lipsey, and Harry Bowen. 1997. "World Trade Flows, 1970–1992, with Production and Tariff Data." NBER Working Paper 5910. National Bureau of Economic Research, Cambridge, Mass. Processed.

Frankel, Jeffrey, David Romer, and Teresa Cyrus. 1996. "Trade and Growth in East Asian Countries: Cause and Effect?" NBER Working Paper 5732. National Bureau of Economic Research, Cambridge, Mass. Processed.

Gerschenkron, Alexander. 1952. "Economic Backwardness in Historical Perspective." In B. F. Hoselitz, ed., *The Progress of Underdeveloped Areas*, pp. 3–29. Chicago: University of Chicago Press.

Grossman, Gene, and Elhanan Helpman. 1991. *Innovation and Growth in the Global Economy*. Cambridge, Mass.: MIT Press.

Hughes, Helen. 1992. "Explaining the Differences between the Growth of Developing Countries in Asia and Latin America in the 1980s." In R. Adhikari, C. Kirkpatrick, and J. Weiss, eds., *Industrial and Trade Policy Reform in Developing Countries*, pp. 15–31. New York: St. Martin's Press.

Ito, Takatoshi. 1992. *The Japanese Economy*. Cambridge, Mass.: MIT Press.

Itoh, M., M. Okuno, and others. 1988. "Foreign Trade and Direct Investment." In R. Komiya, M. Okuno, and K. Suzumura, eds., *Industrial Policy of Japan*. San Diego: Academic Press.

Jorgenson, D., and M. Kuroda. 1990. "Productivity and International Competitiveness in Japan and the United States, 1960–1985." In C. Hulten, ed., *Productivity Growth in Japan and the United States*. Chicago: University of Chicago Press.

Krishna, Pravin, and Devashish Mitra. 1998. "Trade Liberalization, Market Discipline, and Productivity Growth: New Evidence from India." *Journal of Development Economics* 56(2):447–62.

Krueger, Anne. 1993. "American Bilateral Trading Arrangements and East Asian Interests." In Takatoshi Ito and Anne O. Krueger, eds., *Trade and Protectionism*, pp. 25–40. Chicago: University of Chicago Press.

Lawrence, Robert Z. 1993. "Japan's Different Trade Regime: An Analysis with Particular Reference to Keiretsu." *Journal of Economic Perspectives* 7(3):3–19.

———. 1999. "Does a Kick in the Pants Get You Going or Does It Just Hurt? The Impact of International Competition on Technological Change in U.S. Manufacturing." In Robert Feenstra, ed., *Globalization and Wages*. Chicago: University of Chicago Press.

Lee, Jongwha. 1995. "Government Interventions and Productivity Growth in Korean Manufacturing Industries." NBER Working Paper 5060. National Bureau of Economic Research, Cambridge, Mass. Processed.

Lucas, Robert. 1988. "On the Mechanics of Economic Development." *Journal of Monetary Economics* 22(July):3-42.

National Science Foundation. Various years. *Research and Development in Industry*. Washington, D.C.

Nelson, Richard., and S. Winter. 1974. "Neoclassical vs. Evolutionary Theories of Economic Growth: Critique and Prospectus." *Economic Journal* 84(December):886–905.

Porter, Michael E. 1990. *The Competitive Advantage of Nations*. Detroit: Free Press.

Rodrik, Dani. 1994. "King Kong vs. Godzilla: The World Bank and the East Asian Miracle." In A. Fishlow, C. Gwin, S. Haggard, Dani Rodrik, and Robert Wade, eds., *Miracle or Design? Lessons for the East Asian Experience*. Washington, D.C.: Overseas Development Council.

———. 1995. "Getting Interventions Right: How South Korea and Taiwan Grew Rich." *Economic Policy* (April):55–107.

———. 1999. *The New Global Economy and Developing Countries: Making Openness Work*. Washington, D.C.: Overseas Development Council.

Scharfstein, David. 1988. "Product-Market Competition and Managerial Slack." *Rand Journal of Economics* 19(Spring):147–55.

Wade, Robert. 1988. "The Role of Government in Overcoming Market Failure: Taiwan, Republic of Korea, and Japan." In Helen Hughes, ed., *Achieving Industrialization in East Asia*, pp. 129–63. Cambridge, U.K.: Cambridge University Press.

World Bank. 1993a. *The East Asian Miracle*. New York: Oxford University Press.

———. 1993b. "The East Asian Miracle: Proceedings." World Bank and the Overseas Economic Cooperation Fund, Washington, D.C. Processed.

CHAPTER 11

EMERGENCE OF AN FDI-TRADE NEXUS AND ECONOMIC GROWTH IN EAST ASIA

Shujiro Urata

One notable and common characteristic of the developing East Asian economies in recent years has been their increasing exposure to international economic activities such as international trade and foreign direct investment (FDI).[1] The World Bank (1993) study on the East Asian miracle finds that in the late 1980s the share of foreign trade in gross domestic product (GDP) was significantly higher for developing economies in East Asia than for developing economies in other parts of the world. Moreover, between 1970 and 1988 their share of foreign trade in GDP increased at significantly greater rates as well.

The 1980s also saw new developments in the international economic activities taking place in East Asian economies. In particular, developing East Asia took part in the rapid expansion of FDI, and FDI joined foreign trade as a means for conducting international business.[2] Indeed, between 1980 and 1998, world FDI grew at an annual average rate of 16 percent, significantly higher than the corresponding rate of 6 percent for world trade. Since FDI promoted foreign trade, large inflows of FDI to developing East Asia further increased the region's exposure to international economic activities.

This chapter examines the changing structure of foreign trade and FDI in East Asia and its impact on economic growth. It attempts to shed light on the interaction between foreign trade and FDI, which is a special characteristic of developments in the region.

The analysis in this chapter documents the increase in intraregional dependence on foreign trade and FDI, reflecting the formation of a

FDI-trade nexus in East Asia. The expansion of foreign trade and FDI is argued to have contributed to economic growth through various channels. For example, it has enabled the economies to obtain foreign exchange, which they can use to purchase capital goods and technologies that support economic growth. What is remarkable in East Asia is the formation of regional production networks by multinational corporations. The construction of these networks has promoted the specialization of production in East Asia and thus improved efficiency. Although strong intraregional dependence spread the unfavorable impacts of the economic crisis throughout the region in the late 1990s, this network also aided the region's economic recovery from the crisis. Indeed, it is argued that further expansion of foreign trade and FDI is necessary to promote economic growth in the region.

RAPID EXPANSION OF FOREIGN TRADE AND FOREIGN DIRECT INVESTMENT

Foreign trade and foreign direct investment of the East Asian economies expanded rapidly beginning in the mid-1980s (tables 11.1 and 11.2). Between 1986 and 1997, East Asian exports expanded steadily to register an almost fivefold increase, before declining in 1998 as a result of the currency and economic crisis in East Asia. The rate of expansion was particularly high from 1986 to 1988, when the annual rate of growth exceeded 20 percent. The 1990s saw fluctuations in the annual rates of growth, with a peak at 22 percent in 1995 followed by a decline, resulting in negative growth in 1998. The patterns of export growth for the 1986–98 period are similar for all developing economies in East Asia, with few exceptions. Compared with the newly industrializing economies (NIEs) and Association of Southeast Asian Nations (ASEAN) economies (Indonesia, Malaysia, Philippines, Singapore, and Thailand), China registered a significantly higher growth rate in 1994 and in 1997. Relatively high growth in 1994 is attributable to the devaluation of the Chinese yuan, while that in 1997 is attributable to China's escape from the unfavorable impact of the currency and economic crisis. As the result of rapid export expansion, East Asia increased its share of world exports from 9 percent in 1980–85 to almost 18 percent in 1997, before declining in 1998. As a group, the NIEs expanded their share from 4 percent in 1980–85 to 8 percent in 1997. China became the largest exporter among the developing East Asian economies in 1998, accounting for 3 percent of world exports. One notable development was the rapid expansion of manufactured exports. Specifically, the share of manufactured products in total exports for the NIEs and ASEAN increased from 71 and 18 percent, respectively, in 1980 to 87 and 60 percent in 1995.[3] For China, the corresponding share increased from 67 percent in 1990 to 79 percent in 1995.

FDI inflows to developing East Asian economies grew at a remarkably high rate from the mid-1980s to 1998, significantly faster than exports. Indeed, FDI inflows increased more than 12 times in the 12 years from 1986 to 1998. Unlike exports, FDI inflows continued to grow throughout the period. In terms of annual growth, FDI inflows peaked twice during the period, once in 1987 and once in 1993. For both years, the rate of growth was higher than 70 percent. After peaking in 1993, the annual rate of growth declined to 2 percent in 1998. Particularly high growth rates are observed in several cases: Korea in 1986, Hong Kong in 1987 and 1992, China in 1986, 1992, and 1993, and the Philippines in 1986, 1987, 1988, and 1993. These growth rates are largely due to the implementation of large FDI projects. As result of this rapid expansion, the share of developing East Asian economies in world FDI inflows increased from 8 percent in 1986 to 20 percent in the mid-1990s, before declining sharply to 12 percent in 1998. China increased its share in world FDI inflows from 2 percent in 1986 to 7 percent in 1998. Indeed, China was the largest recipient of FDI among developing economies and the third largest recipient in the world, behind the United States and the United Kingdom, in 1998.

Two developments are important concerning recent FDI in developing East Asia. One is its resilience even during the period of economic crisis. Compared with other forms of international capital flows such as bank lending, which declined precipitously before and after the crisis, FDI inflows remained relatively stable in developing East Asia, particularly in economies seriously affected by the crisis. Another important development is the increase in mergers and acquisitions (M&A) as a mode of entry, particularly after the economic crisis (United Nations 1999). Developing East Asian economies with a keen interest in attracting FDI relaxed the restrictions on FDI. Coupled

Table 11.1 Exports of East Asian Developing Economies, 1980–98

Indicator and region	1980–85	1986	1987	1988	1989	1990	1991	1992	1993	1994	1995	1996	1997	1998
Value (billions of U.S. dollars)														
World	1,829.6	2,045.3	2,405.7	2,750.5	2,991.2	3,405.0	3,201.4	3,743.2	3,744.1	4,260.0	5,122.9	5,352.3	5,534.8	5,444.9
Developed economies	1,223.4	1,488.4	1,736.1	1,986.1	2,127.7	2,453.5	2,503.3	2,649.1	2,592.1	2,917.3	3,470.4	3,560.8	3,640.5	3,656.7
Developing economies	606.3	556.9	669.6	764.4	863.4	951.5	998.1	1,094.2	1,152.0	1,342.7	1,652.5	1,791.4	1,894.3	1,788.2
East Asia	165.5	205.4	269.7	334.5	373.9	415.4	478.2	542.8	598.9	715.5	870.9	906.7	968.2	914.1
China	23.0	30.9	39.4	47.5	52.5	62.1	71.9	84.9	91.0	121.0	148.8	151.2	182.9	183.6
Newly industrializing economies	73.0	109.8	149.2	184.4	201.6	214.3	246.6	277.5	302.2	340.3	410.4	426.2	445.5	416.8
Hong Kong (China)	23.8	35.4	48.5	63.2	73.1	82.2	98.6	119.5	135.2	151.4	173.8	180.8	188.1	174.0
Korea, Rep. of	24.1	34.7	47.3	60.7	62.4	65.0	71.9	76.6	82.2	96.0	125.1	129.7	136.2	132.3
Taiwan (China)	25.1	39.6	53.5	60.5	66.1	67.1	76.1	81.4	84.7	92.8	111.6	115.7	121.3	110.5
ASEAN	69.4	64.7	81.1	102.6	119.7	139.0	159.7	180.4	205.8	254.2	311.7	329.3	339.8	313.8
Indonesia	21.8	14.8	17.1	19.2	22.2	25.7	29.1	34.0	36.8	40.1	45.4	49.8	53.4	48.8
Malaysia	13.8	13.8	17.9	21.1	25.1	29.4	34.3	40.7	47.1	58.8	74.0	78.3	78.7	73.3
Philippines	5.2	4.8	5.6	7.0	7.8	8.1	8.8	9.8	11.1	13.3	17.5	20.4	25.1	27.8
Singapore	21.6	22.5	28.7	39.3	44.7	52.8	59.0	63.5	74.0	96.8	118.3	125.0	125.0	109.4
Thailand	6.9	8.9	11.7	16.0	20.1	23.1	28.4	32.5	36.8	45.3	56.4	55.7	57.5	54.5
Change from previous year (percent)														
World	n.a.	1.12	1.18	1.14	1.09	1.14	0.94	1.17	1.00	1.14	1.20	1.04	1.03	0.98
Developed economies	n.a.	1.22	1.17	1.14	1.07	1.15	1.02	1.06	0.98	1.13	1.19	1.03	1.02	1.00
Developing economies	n.a.	0.92	1.20	1.14	1.13	1.10	1.05	1.10	1.05	1.17	1.23	1.08	1.06	0.94
East Asia	n.a.	1.24	1.31	1.24	1.12	1.11	1.15	1.14	1.10	1.19	1.22	1.04	1.07	0.94
China	n.a.	1.34	1.27	1.20	1.11	1.18	1.16	1.18	1.07	1.33	1.23	1.02	1.21	1.00
Newly industrializing economies	n.a.	1.50	1.36	1.24	1.09	1.06	1.15	1.13	1.09	1.13	1.21	1.04	1.05	0.94
Hong Kong (China)	n.a.	1.49	1.37	1.30	1.16	1.12	1.20	1.21	1.13	1.12	1.15	1.04	1.04	0.93
Korea, Rep. of	n.a.	1.44	1.36	1.28	1.03	1.04	1.11	1.07	1.07	1.17	1.30	1.04	1.05	0.97
Taiwan (China)	n.a.	1.58	1.35	1.13	1.09	1.02	1.13	1.07	1.04	1.10	1.20	1.04	1.05	0.91

ASEAN	n.a.	0.93	1.25	1.27	1.17	1.16	1.15	1.13	1.14	1.24	1.23	1.06	1.03	0.92
Indonesia	n.a.	0.68	1.16	1.12	1.15	1.16	1.14	1.17	1.08	1.09	1.13	1.10	1.07	0.91
Malaysia	n.a.	1.00	1.30	1.18	1.19	1.17	1.17	1.19	1.16	1.25	1.26	1.06	1.01	0.93
Philippines	n.a.	0.92	1.18	1.24	1.10	1.04	1.09	1.11	1.14	1.20	1.32	1.17	1.23	1.11
Singapore	n.a.	1.04	1.28	1.37	1.14	1.18	1.12	1.08	1.17	1.31	1.22	1.06	1.00	0.88
Thailand	n.a.	1.29	1.31	1.37	1.26	1.15	1.23	1.14	1.13	1.23	1.25	0.99	1.03	0.95

Geographic distribution (percent)

World	100.0	100.0	100.0	100.0	100.0	100.0	100.0	100.0	100.0	100.0	100.0	100.0	100.0	100.0
Developed economies	66.9	72.8	72.2	72.2	71.1	72.1	78.2	70.8	69.2	68.5	67.7	66.5	65.8	67.2
Developing economies	33.1	27.2	27.8	27.8	28.9	27.9	31.2	29.2	30.8	31.5	32.3	33.5	34.2	32.8
East Asia	9.0	10.0	11.2	12.2	12.5	12.2	14.9	14.5	16.0	16.8	17.0	16.9	17.5	16.8
China	1.3	1.5	1.6	1.7	1.8	1.8	2.2	2.3	2.4	2.8	2.9	2.8	3.3	3.4
Newly industrializing economies	4.0	5.4	6.2	6.7	6.7	6.3	7.7	7.4	8.1	8.0	8.0	8.0	8.0	7.7
Hong Kong (China)	1.3	1.7	2.0	2.3	2.4	2.4	3.1	3.2	3.6	3.6	3.4	3.4	3.4	3.2
Korea, Rep. of	1.3	1.7	2.0	2.2	2.1	1.9	2.2	2.0	2.2	2.3	2.4	2.4	2.5	2.4
Taiwan (China)	1.4	1.9	2.2	2.2	2.2	2.0	2.4	2.2	2.3	2.2	2.2	2.2	2.2	2.0
ASEAN	3.8	3.2	3.4	3.7	4.0	4.1	5.0	4.8	5.5	6.0	6.1	6.2	6.1	5.8
Indonesia	1.2	0.7	0.7	0.7	0.7	0.8	0.9	0.9	1.0	0.9	0.9	0.9	1.0	0.9
Malaysia	0.8	0.7	0.7	0.8	0.8	0.9	1.1	1.1	1.3	1.4	1.4	1.5	1.4	1.3
Philippines	0.3	0.2	0.2	0.3	0.3	0.2	0.3	0.3	0.3	0.3	0.3	0.4	0.5	0.5
Singapore	1.2	1.1	1.2	1.4	1.5	1.5	1.8	1.7	2.0	2.3	2.3	2.3	2.3	2.0
Thailand	0.4	0.4	0.5	0.6	0.7	0.7	0.9	0.9	1.0	1.1	1.1	1.0	1.0	1.0

n.a. Not applicable.
Source: IMF (1999).

Table 11.2 Inflows of Foreign Direct Investment, 1980–98

Indicator and region	1980–85	1986	1987	1988	1989	1990	1991	1992	1993	1994	1995	1996	1997	1998
Value (billions of U.S. dollars)														
World	49.8	78.3	132.9	158.3	195.2	183.8	158.9	173.8	219.4	253.5	328.9	358.9	464.3	643.9
Developed economies	37.2	64.1	107.9	128.6	165.4	152.0	114.8	119.7	133.9	146.4	208.4	211.1	273.3	460.4
Developing economies	12.6	14.2	25.0	29.7	29.8	31.8	41.7	49.6	78.8	101.2	106.2	135.3	172.5	165.9
East Asia	4.5	6.5	11.2	14.7	15.7	17.9	20.3	26.3	45.4	52.8	60.2	72.9	77.0	78.2
China	0.7	1.9	2.3	3.2	3.4	3.5	4.4	11.2	27.5	33.8	35.8	40.2	44.2	45.5
Newly industrializing economies	0.8	1.8	4.6	4.5	3.4	2.8	3.0	3.7	5.2	6.3	6.6	9.7	11.1	7.0
Hong Kong (China)	0.5	1.0	3.3	2.7	1.1	0.8	0.5	2.1	3.7	4.1	3.3	5.5	6.0	1.6
Korea, Rep. of	0.1	0.4	0.6	0.9	0.8	0.7	1.2	0.7	0.6	0.8	1.8	2.3	2.8	5.1
Taiwan (China)	0.2	0.3	0.7	1.0	1.6	1.3	1.3	0.9	0.9	1.4	1.6	1.9	2.2	0.2
ASEAN	2.9	2.8	4.3	7.0	8.9	11.6	12.9	11.5	14.7	18.0	19.3	23.0	24.4	19.3
Indonesia	0.2	0.3	0.4	0.6	0.7	1.0	1.5	1.8	2.0	2.1	4.3	6.2	4.7	-0.4
Malaysia	1.1	0.5	0.4	0.7	1.7	2.9	4.0	5.2	5.0	4.3	4.2	5.1	5.1	3.7
Philippines	0.0	0.1	0.3	0.9	0.6	0.5	0.5	0.2	1.2	1.6	1.5	1.5	1.2	1.7
Singapore	1.3	1.7	2.8	3.6	4.2	4.8	4.9	2.2	4.7	8.6	7.2	7.9	9.7	7.2
Thailand	0.3	0.3	0.4	1.1	1.8	2.4	2.0	2.1	1.8	1.4	2.1	2.3	3.7	7.0
Change from previous year (percent)														
World	n.a.	1.57	1.70	1.19	1.23	0.94	0.86	1.09	1.26	1.16	1.30	1.09	1.29	1.39
Developed economies	n.a.	1.72	1.68	1.19	1.29	0.92	0.76	1.04	1.12	1.09	1.42	1.01	1.29	1.68
Developing economies	n.a.	1.12	1.76	1.19	1.00	1.07	1.31	1.19	1.59	1.28	1.05	1.27	1.27	0.96
East Asia	n.a.	1.45	1.73	1.31	1.07	1.14	1.13	1.30	1.72	1.16	1.14	1.21	1.06	1.02
China	n.a.	2.61	1.23	1.38	1.06	1.03	1.25	2.56	2.47	1.23	1.06	1.12	1.10	1.03
Newly industrializing economies	n.a.	2.13	2.63	0.98	0.76	0.82	1.06	1.22	1.41	1.22	1.05	1.47	1.14	0.63
Hong Kong (China)	n.a.	1.84	3.31	0.81	0.40	0.73	0.69	3.81	1.78	1.13	0.79	1.68	1.09	0.27
Korea, Rep. of	n.a.	4.44	1.38	1.45	0.87	0.94	1.65	0.62	0.81	1.38	2.20	1.31	1.22	1.81
Taiwan (China)	n.a.	1.76	2.19	1.34	1.67	0.83	0.96	0.69	1.04	1.50	1.13	1.20	1.21	0.10

ASEAN	n.a.	0.98	1.51	1.62	1.27	1.30	1.12	0.89	1.28	1.22	1.07	1.19	1.06	0.79
Indonesia	n.a.	1.14	1.49	1.50	1.18	1.41	1.54	1.20	1.13	1.05	2.06	1.43	0.76	-0.08
Malaysia	n.a.	0.46	0.87	1.70	2.32	1.74	1.38	1.30	0.97	0.87	0.96	1.22	1.01	0.73
Philippines	n.a.	3.63	2.42	3.05	0.60	0.94	1.03	0.42	5.43	1.29	0.93	1.03	0.81	1.40
Singapore	n.a.	1.29	1.66	1.29	1.15	1.14	1.02	0.45	2.13	1.82	0.84	1.09	1.23	0.74
Thailand	n.a.	1.00	1.34	3.14	1.61	1.34	0.85	1.05	0.85	0.76	1.52	1.13	1.60	1.87

Geographic distribution (percent)

World	100.0	100.0	100.0	100.0	100.0	100.0	100.0	100.0	100.0	100.0	100.0	100.0	100.0	100.0
Developed economies	74.6	81.9	81.2	81.2	84.7	82.7	72.2	68.9	61.0	57.7	63.4	58.8	58.9	71.5
Developing economies	25.4	18.1	18.8	18.8	15.2	17.3	26.2	28.6	35.9	39.9	32.3	37.7	37.2	25.8
East Asia	8.9	8.3	8.4	9.3	8.1	9.7	12.8	15.1	20.7	20.8	18.3	20.3	16.6	12.1
China	1.4	2.4	1.7	2.0	1.7	1.9	2.7	6.4	12.5	13.3	10.9	11.2	9.5	7.1
Newly industrializing economies	1.7	2.2	3.5	2.8	1.8	1.5	1.9	2.1	2.4	2.5	2.0	2.7	2.4	1.1
Hong Kong (China)	1.1	1.3	2.5	1.7	0.6	0.4	0.3	1.2	1.7	1.6	1.0	1.5	1.3	0.2
Korea, Rep. of	0.2	0.6	0.5	0.6	0.4	0.4	0.7	0.4	0.3	0.3	0.5	0.6	0.6	0.8
Taiwan (China)	0.4	0.4	0.5	0.6	0.8	0.7	0.8	0.5	0.4	0.5	0.5	0.5	0.5	0.0
ASEAN	5.8	3.6	3.2	4.4	4.6	6.3	8.1	6.6	6.7	7.1	5.9	6.4	5.3	3.0
Indonesia	0.5	0.3	0.3	0.4	0.3	0.5	0.9	1.0	0.9	0.8	1.3	1.7	1.0	-0.1
Malaysia	2.1	0.6	0.3	0.5	0.9	1.6	2.5	3.0	2.3	1.7	1.3	1.4	1.1	0.6
Philippines	0.1	0.2	0.2	0.6	0.3	0.3	0.3	0.1	0.6	0.6	0.4	0.4	0.3	0.3
Singapore	2.7	2.2	2.1	2.3	2.2	2.6	3.1	1.3	2.1	3.4	2.2	2.2	2.1	1.1
Thailand	0.5	0.3	0.3	0.7	0.9	1.3	1.3	1.2	0.8	0.5	0.6	0.7	0.8	1.1

n.a. Not applicable.
Source: United Nations (various issues).

with relaxation of the FDI regime, the huge depreciation of East Asian currencies, which reduced the value of assets in foreign currency, encouraged multinationals to undertake M&A.

Exports and FDI inflows became increasingly important in the economies of developing East Asia (table 11.3). All of the economies except China and Indonesia registered a ratio of exports to GDP exceeding 30 percent, significantly higher than the average ratio of approximately 23 percent for the developing economies in 1997 (World Bank 1999). Hong Kong and Singapore had extremely high values, which are attributable to their engagement in entrepôt trade. Although high, the values for Korea and Taiwan (China) declined from the mid-1980s to the mid-1990s because of the rapid increase in GDP. ASEAN-4 countries, consisting of Indonesia, Malaysia, Philippines, and Thailand, exhibited an increase in the ratio of exports to GDP, reflecting faster growth of exports compared with GDP. Considering that large countries tend to be less dependent on foreign trade than small countries, it is notable that China's and Indonesia's ratio of exports to GDP exceeded 20 percent.

Although increasing steadily for most developing East Asian economies, the ratio of FDI to GDP was significantly smaller than the ratio of exports to GDP and varied widely within the region. Singapore had the highest ratio, around 10 percent, while Korea and Taiwan had the lowest, around 0.5–1.0 percent. China and Malaysia registered a rapid increase in the ratio, each reaching about 5 percent in 1997. The role of FDI in economic activities is even more important because the foreign affiliates of multinationals engage in various activities, including foreign trade, in the FDI-recipient economies.

FACTORS CONTRIBUTING TO THE RAPID EXPANSION OF TRADE AND FDI

The factors behind the significant expansion in foreign trade and FDI inflows in East Asia fall into two groups, one concerning internal factors and the other concerning external factors. As for the internal factors, the liberalization of both trade and FDI was one of the most important. In addition, a stable macroeconomic environment, reflected in relatively stable price levels and an abundant supply of well-

Table 11.3 Ratio of Exports and of Foreign Direct Investment to Gross Domestic Product in East Asia, 1986–97 (percent)

Indicator and economy	1986	1987	1988	1989	1990	1991	1992	1993	1994	1995	1996	1997
Ratio of exports to GDP												
China	10.5	14.7	15.5	15.3	17.5	19.1	20.3	21.1	22.3	21.3	18.5	20.3
Hong Kong (China)	88.5	98.3	108.4	108.9	109.9	114.6	118.7	116.6	115.7	124.8	117.2	109.7
Korea, Rep. of	32.0	34.7	33.3	28.1	25.6	24.4	24.9	24.7	25.2	27.4	26.8	30.8
Taiwan (China)	52.5	52.4	49.1	44.3	41.9	42.4	38.4	38.0	38.5	42.9	42.5	42.8
Indonesia	18.5	22.6	21.6	21.8	22.4	22.7	24.4	23.3	22.6	22.5	21.9	24.9
Malaysia	49.6	56.8	60.8	66.2	68.8	73.0	69.8	73.4	81.0	84.8	78.9	80.0
Philippines	16.0	17.0	18.6	18.2	18.2	19.3	18.4	20.4	20.7	23.6	24.6	30.5
Singapore	124.7	138.7	153.2	146.8	140.9	135.0	127.8	126.8	136.7	138.9	134.8	129.8
Thailand	20.6	23.1	25.9	27.8	27.0	28.9	29.1	29.4	31.4	33.6	30.7	37.4
Ratio of FDI inflow to GDP												
China	0.6	0.9	1.0	1.0	1.0	1.2	2.7	6.4	6.2	5.1	4.9	4.9
Hong Kong (China)	2.5	6.7	4.6	1.6	1.0	0.6	2.0	3.2	3.2	2.4	3.6	3.5
Korea, Rep. of	0.4	0.4	0.5	0.3	0.3	0.4	0.2	0.2	0.2	0.4	0.5	0.6
Taiwan (China)	0.4	0.7	0.8	1.1	0.8	0.7	0.4	0.4	0.6	0.6	0.7	0.8
Indonesia	0.3	0.5	0.6	0.7	0.8	1.2	1.3	1.3	1.2	2.2	2.7	2.2
Malaysia	1.8	1.3	2.1	4.4	6.8	8.5	8.9	7.8	6.0	4.8	5.1	5.2
Philippines	0.4	0.9	2.5	1.3	1.2	1.2	0.4	2.3	2.5	2.0	1.8	1.5
Singapore	9.5	13.7	14.2	13.8	12.8	11.2	4.4	8.0	12.1	8.5	8.5	10.1
Thailand	0.6	0.7	1.8	2.5	2.8	2.1	1.9	1.4	0.9	1.2	1.3	2.4

Source: For the ratio of exports to gross domestic product, IMF (1999); World Bank (1999); Asian Development Bank (1999) *Taiwan Statistical Yearbook 1999.* For the ratio of foreign direct investment inflows to gross domestic product, United Nations (various issues); World Bank (1999); Asian Development Bank (1999); *Taiwan Statistical Yearbook 1999.*

disciplined, low-wage labor, contributed to the expansion of exports and the attraction of FDI inflows.[4] As for the external factors, the substantial realignment of exchange rates, particularly the yen-dollar exchange rate, was important, as was the remarkable technical progress achieved in information technology, which reduced the cost of communications. Finally, increased competition among multinational firms, which resulted partly from liberalization and deregulation in various sectors in many countries of the world, promoted foreign trade and FDI.

Liberalization of Trade and FDI

After their favorable economic performance in the 1970s, a number of developing economies in East Asia experienced an economic slowdown in the early 1980s. The second oil crisis in the late 1970s and its aftermath were major factors behind the slowdown, as were inward-looking import substitution policies and active public investment.

The sharp rise in oil prices resulted in worldwide recession, as a number of countries pursued tight macroeconomic policies to deal with the inflation triggered by the increase. In particular, the growth rates of many industrial economies turned negative in 1982. The slowdown in the world economy exerted a negative influence on the economic performance of developing East Asian economies, mainly by reducing the demand for their products.

Several internal problems also contributed to the slowdown in economic growth. Import substitution policies, which had been pursued for some time in most economies in the region, caused various problems.[5] A protected market provided opportunities for local businesses that led to reasonable economic growth in the 1970s. However, by the 1980s the industries with potential for import substitution had become more or less exhausted. Moreover, import substitution policies gave rise to the inefficient use of available resources in three ways. First, they encouraged noncompetitive import-substituting production at the expense of competitive export production. Second, the absence of competition from foreign sources enabled local firms to enjoy a lucrative protected market, retarding the efficient use of resources and technological progress. Third, they promoted rent-seeking activities, encouraging the misuse of available resources.

The large volume of public investment undertaken by a number of developing East Asian economies in the 1970s was another factor in the slowdown in economic growth in the early 1980s. Encouraged by favorable economic growth in the early to mid-1970s and recognizing the underdevelopment of infrastructure, the governments of developing East Asian economies expanded public investment aggressively in the second half of the 1970s. Coupled with the reduction in government revenue as a result of the slowdown in economic activities, the expansion in public expenditure resulted in large public sector current account deficits, which in turn increased foreign debt. These twin deficits forced the governments to reduce expenditure, worsening the economic slowdown.

To deal with the serious economic situation in the early 1980s, developing East Asian economies adopted structural adjustment policies consisting mainly of liberalization in foreign trade and FDI and deregulation in domestic economic activities. The change in policy from inward-looking protection to outward-looking liberalization was attributable to the recommendations of donors, such as the World Bank and the International Monetary Fund. Such policy changes were also due to the realization that liberalization would promote economic growth. The liberalization of trade and FDI led to the expansion of exports and inward FDI because it shifted the incentives from import-substituting production to export production and increased the attractiveness of these economies to foreign investors. This section examines the liberalization of trade and FDI in East Asian economies from the 1980s through the 1990s.[6]

As can be seen from table 11.4, developing East Asian economies liberalized their import regimes by lowering tariff rates and nontariff barriers from the early 1980s through the early 1990s. The notable exceptions were Hong Kong and Singapore, which adopted virtually free trade regimes. China and Indonesia significantly reduced their average tariff rates during the period under study, while Malaysia and Thailand slightly increased their average tariff rates. The incidence of nontariff barriers declined in many East Asian economies. Indeed, China is the only economy in the sample that increased the incidence of nontariff barriers during the period under study. The most remarkable is Indonesia, which reduced nontariff barriers from 95 percent in 1984–87 to less than 3 percent in 1991–93. Although not included in

**Table 11.4 Tariffs and Nontariff Barriers for Select East Asian Economies, 1980–93
(unweighted averages in percentages)**

Economy and indicator	Primary products	Manufactured products	All products
China			
Mean tariffs			
1980–83	46.5	50.5	49.5
1984–87	33.1	41.9	39.5
1988–90	34.1	42.7	40.3
1991–93	31.7	39.7	37.5
Incidence of nontariff bariers			
1984–87	17.8	7.9	10.6
1988–90	27.2	21.9	23.2
1991–93	11.5	11.3	11.3
Hong Kong (China)			
Mean tariffs			
1984–87	0.0	0.0	0.0
1988–90	0.0	0.0	0.0
1991–93	0.0	0.0	0.0
Incidence of nontariff barriers			
1984–87	6.9	2.1	3.4
1988–90	0.8	0.3	0.5
1991–93	0.8	0.3	0.5
Indonesia			
Mean tariffs			
1980–83	23.0	31.3	29.0
1984–87	14.7	19.4	18.1
1988–90	14.8	22.5	20.3
1991–93	13.6	18.3	17.0
Incidence of nontariff barriers			
1984–87	98.9	93.1	94.7
1988–90	15.7	7.0	9.4
1991–93	4.6	2.0	2.7
Malaysia			
Mean tariffs			
1980–83	4.3	12.7	10.6
1984–87	8.6	15.4	13.6
1988–90	7.7	14.8	13.0
1991–93	7.3	14.7	12.8
Incidence of nontariff barriers			
1984–87	4.5	3.2	3.7
1988–90	1.6	3.0	2.8
1991–93	1.2	2.4	2.1

Table 11.4, *continued*
(unweighted averages in percentages)

Economy and indicator	Primary products	Manufactured products	All products
Singapore			
Mean tariffs			
1980–83	0.1	0.4	0.3
1984–87	0.1	0.4	0.3
1988–90	0.2	0.4	0.4
1991–93	0.3	0.4	0.4
Incidence of nontariff barriers			
1984–87	15.3	14.1	14.7
1988–90	3.0	0.2	1.0
1991–93	1.2	0.0	0.3
Thailand			
Mean tariffs			
1980–83	26.3	34.6	32.3
1984–87	28.0	32.5	31.2
1988–90	33.4	43.7	40.8
1991–93	26.2	41.8	37.8
Incidence of nontariff barriers			
1984–87	24.4	7.8	12.4
1988–90	7.9	8.8	8.5
1991–93	8.8	4.2	5.5

Source: Pacific Economic Cooperation Council (1995).

the table because of a lack of comparable data, Korea is reported to have reduced both its tariff rates and the incidence of nontariff barriers during the period from 1988 to 1993.[7]

Inward FDI policies were liberalized in the mid-1980s, as East Asian economies began to realize that FDI would promote economic growth. Although it is difficult to quantify the restrictiveness of an FDI regime, it is clear that many developing East Asian economies have liberalized their FDI policies since the mid-1980s. Restrictions on FDI take various forms, including restrictions on market access, most-favored-nation treatment, and national treatment. Many developing East Asian economies reduced the restrictions on market access by reducing the number of sectors and industries for which FDI was prohibited and by relaxing the limits on foreign equity ownership (see Pacific Economic Cooperation Council 1995; United Nations various years). Among the developing East Asian economies, in particular, the five economies most seriously affected by the crisis in 1997—Indone-

sia, Korea, Malaysia, Philippines, and Thailand—adopted substantial
FDI liberalization measures in an effort to attract FDI (United Nations 1998 provides a list of liberalization measures adopted by the
five economies). Furthermore, recognizing the important contribution that FDI may make toward economic growth, a number of economies introduced incentives such as tax breaks to attract FDI. Indeed,
there has been stiff competition among East Asian economies to attract FDI by reducing barriers and providing incentives.

Liberalization of trade and FDI also progressed under the regional
and global frameworks. The members of the ASEAN formed the
ASEAN Free Trade Area (AFTA) in 1992, the only formal regional
trade arrangement in East Asia (see Chia 2000 for a detailed discussion of ASEAN and its trade and FDI policies). The 1992 agreement
provided for the liberalization of tariff and nontariff measures under
the Common Effective Preferential Tariffs. The target year for achieving tariff and nontariff liberalization was originally set for 2008, but
was later moved forward to 2002. FDI liberalization in the ASEAN
has been scheduled for implementation. In 1998 the ASEAN Investment Area was created to provide coordinated investment cooperation and facilitation programs, market access, and national treatment
of all industries, with target dates for the original ASEAN-5 members, Brunei, and Myanmar to be 2003 and for Vietnam, Cambodia,
and Laos to be 2010.

APEC, whose members include not only East Asian economies but
also countries in North and South America and Oceania, contributed
to the liberalization and facilitation of trade and FDI for developing
East Asian economies (see Morrison 1998 for an insightful analysis of
the evolution of APEC and its functions). One important characteristic of APEC is its inclusion of China and Taiwan as members. Indeed,
APEC is the only regional or international economic forum in which
China and Taiwan participate, because neither is a member of the World
Trade Organization. Following the Bogor declaration in 1994 calling
for full liberalization of trade and FDI by 2010 for developed-country
members and by 2020 for developing-country members, APEC member economies agreed to prepare and implement individual action plans
specifying near- and medium-term liberalization measures. Peer pressure is expected to play a crucial role in implementation. Although it
is not clear how effective the APEC process has been for promoting

the liberalization of trade and FDI, all the APEC members have made significant progress toward freer trade and FDI regimes.[8]

The Uruguay Round of multilateral trade negotiations under the GATT started in 1986 and ended in 1994. Although the negotiations lasted eight years, the Uruguay Round made substantial progress toward liberalizing trade and FDI. The achievements include a reduction in tariff rates, a framework agreement on trade in services, agreements on intellectual property rights and trade-related investment measures, a timetable for phasing out all quantitative restrictions on trade, first steps toward bringing agriculture more firmly under a multilateral discipline, a stronger dispute settlement mechanism, and the establishment of the World Trade Organization (Krueger 1998 contains a number of useful articles on the GATT/WTO). The impacts of these achievements are difficult to estimate because liberalization of trade and FDI is carried out not only as a result of the commitments made in the GATT/WTO but also as a result of factors such as bilateral pressures and regional commitments. Nevertheless, there is no doubt that the GATT/WTO has promoted trade and FDI liberalization in East Asia.

Exchange Rate Adjustments and the Bubble Economy

In addition to trade and FDI liberalization policies, several external developments in the mid-1980s precipitated the expansion of exports from and of FDI inflows to the developing East Asian economies. One is the substantial realignment of the exchange rates of major currencies, notably the appreciation of the Japanese yen vis-à-vis the U.S. dollar and other currencies. In September 1985, to correct the imbalances in the current accounts among major industrial countries—a huge current account surplus in Japan and Germany and a huge current account deficit in the United States were major causes of instability of the world economy—the G-5 countries agreed to realign the exchange rates of their currencies. As a result, the Japanese yen and the Deutsche mark appreciated in value vis-à-vis the U.S. dollar and other currencies.

The yen appreciation contributed to the expansion of exports from developing East Asian economies and the expansion of inflows of FDI to these economies through several channels.[9] The yen appreciation increased the price of Japanese products vis-à-vis the price of products produced in the economies experiencing the currency depreciation. These changes in relative prices led to the expansion of exports from developing East Asian economies, not only to Japan but also to other economies, at the cost of exports from Japan.

The drastic yen appreciation stimulated Japanese FDI to developing East Asian economies in two ways (see Kawai and Urata 1998 for a detailed discussion). To cope with the loss in international price competitiveness, many Japanese firms moved their base of production from Japan to foreign economies where production costs were lower. The yen appreciation also had a positive impact on outflows of Japanese FDI through the "liquidity" or "wealth" effect. To the extent that yen appreciation made Japanese firms relatively more wealthy by increasing their collateral and liquidity, it enabled them to finance outward FDI relatively more cheaply than their foreign competitors. In addition, liquidity was injected into the economy in the second half of the 1980s, with the objective of reactivating the Japanese economy from a recession caused by a decline in exports, pushing up the prices of shares and land and creating the so-called bubble economy. Such an increase in liquidity and the subsequent asset-price inflation further promoted Japan's FDI by making it easier for Japanese firms to obtain loans. The bubble economy contributed to the expansion of exports from developing East Asian economies to Japan by increasing Japan's demand for imports.

Japan's trade friction with developed economies such as the United States and the European Union and the protectionist sentiment in these economies discouraged Japan's exports to these regions, creating opportunities for other economies, including those in developing East Asia. It had the effect of promoting Japanese FDI as well. In order to secure their markets in developed economies, a number of Japanese firms invested not only in those developed economies but also in other economies, most notably in East Asia, setting up export platforms to enable them to get around the import barriers in developed economies (Kawai and Urata 1996 present evidence of such behavior).

Thus Japan contributed to the rapid expansion of exports and FDI in East Asia in the second half of the 1980s, while the Asian NIEs did so in the 1990s. Facing a similar set of problems such as currency appreciation, the bubble economy, and trade friction with developed economies, firms from the NIEs undertook FDI in other developing

East Asian economies in search of low-cost production. They invested heavily in ASEAN countries, China, and other parts of East Asia.[10]

The depreciation of the Japanese yen vis-à-vis the U.S. dollar and the bursting of the bubble in the late 1980s and early 1990s not only resulted in a decline in Japanese FDI to developing East Asia but also discouraged exports from developing East Asia.[11] A gradual, but steady, appreciation of the yen started in the early 1990s and lasted until 1995, promoting Japanese FDI in developing East Asian economies and exports from these economies. A quick turnaround of the Japanese yen from appreciation to depreciation vis-à-vis the U.S. dollar in 1995 did not discourage Japanese FDI, but it did discourage exports from developing East Asian economies by reducing the international competitiveness of their products. Indeed, the sizable fluctuations in the yen-dollar exchange rate in the 1990s had a destabilizing impact on developing East Asian economies, contributing to the currency crisis in 1997.[12]

THE EMERGENCE OF AN INTRAREGIONAL PRODUCTION SYSTEM IN EAST ASIA

In this section I analyze the emerging patterns of an intraregional production system that has been promoted by the expansion of foreign trade and FDI. First, I examine the changing patterns of intraregional trade and FDI in East Asia. This analysis sheds light on the impact of an economic shock in one economy, such as the Asian economic crisis in 1997, on other economies in the region through trade and FDI flows. Second, I turn to the link between foreign trade and FDI, examining whether FDI promotes foreign trade. Third, I investigate the changing importance of intraregional dependence by explicitly considering interindustry relations among East Asian economies. Finally, I examine the patterns of sales and procurements by multinationals and their impact on intraregional links in East Asia.

Increasing Intraregional Dependence

Several studies have examined the changes in intraregional dependence in foreign trade in East Asia. Computing three sets of measures, Petri (1993) finds that intraregional dependence on foreign trade in East

Asia increased steadily in the post–World War II period, after declining in the pre–World War II period, and that intraregional bias declined in the post–World War II period. Frankel (1993) also finds a decline in intraregional bias in foreign trade in the 1980s by estimating the magnitude of the bias in the gravity model framework. This subsection investigates the changing patterns of intraregional trade and FDI in East Asia from the early 1980s to the mid-1990s. Following Petri (1993), the following three measures are computed: absolute measures, relative measures, and double-relative measures.

- Absolute measure (A): $A = Xij / X..$

- Relative measure (B): $B = A / (Xi. / X..) = Xij / Xi.$

- Double-relative measure (C): $C = A / [(Xi. / X..) (X.j / X..)] =$
$$Xij^*X.. / Xi.^*X.j,$$

where Xij represents exports (or outward FDI) from region i to region j, and "." indicates the summation across all i or j. Therefore, $Xi.$ represents total exports (or outward FDI) of region i, $X.j$ represents total imports (or inward FDI) of region j, and $X..$ represents world trade (or FDI).

The absolute measure compares the scale of a particular bilateral trading (or FDI) relationship to world trade (or world FDI), while the relative measure compares it to trade (or FDI) of one or the other of the two partners participating in the relationship. The double-relative measure, which is commonly described as gravity coefficients, indicates the intensity or bias of the bilateral trading (or FDI) relationship by taking into account its importance in world trade (or world FDI). The value of unity for the double-relative measure can be interpreted so that the bilateral relationship is neutral, while the relationship is more (or less) biased when the measure is greater (or less) than unity.

Table 11.5 shows the estimated values of the three measures of foreign trade and FDI for three regions—East Asia, the North American Free Trade Agreement (NAFTA), and the European Union. The results indicate that intraregional trade in East Asia became more important not only in world trade but also in regional trade. However, intraregional bias became smaller over time.

The importance of intra–East Asian trade in world trade increased significantly from 5 percent in 1980 to 12 percent in 1997. The share of intra-NAFTA trade in world trade also increased over the same period, but the share was smaller, at 9 percent in 1997. The corresponding share for the European Union was significantly greater, at 22 percent in 1997, although the share had declined sharply from 29 percent in 1990.

A significant part of intra–East Asian trade takes place between Japan and other East Asian economies (or developing East Asian economies). This can be seen from the observation that the share of intraregional trade among developing East Asian economies (7 percent) amounts to only slightly more than half of the level observed for East Asia as a whole (12 percent). The magnitude of intraregional trade for the Asian NIEs and for ASEAN is still quite small in world trade, amounting to 0.9 and 1.3 percent of world trade in 1997, respectively.

Intra–East Asian trade increased its importance for East Asian trade over time, as shown in the increase in the relative measure from 34 percent in 1980 to 50 percent in 1997. The comparable figures for developing East Asia were 22 and 40 percent in 1980 and 1997, respectively. The importance of intraregional trade in regional trade also increased for the members of NAFTA from 33 to 46 percent during the same period, but it declined for the European Union from 66 percent in 1990 to 62 percent in 1997, after increasing between 1980 and 1990. Among the subgroups in East Asia, intragroup trade among the NIEs was quite small, amounting to only 12 percent of total trade, while intra-ASEAN trade was larger, at 21 percent.

An analysis of the relative measures computed for exports and for imports shows that intra–East Asian trade is more important as a source of imports than as a destination for exports. This finding indicates a trading pattern in which East Asian economies procure imports within the region and sell exports outside the region. This appears to reflect the behavior of multinationals. Many multinationals use East Asia as an export platform, in which they assemble export products for regions outside of East Asia by importing parts and components from inside the region. In contrast, intra-NAFTA trade is more important for NAFTA's exports than for its imports.

The results of the double-relative measure reveal an interesting contrast concerning the intraregional trade bias for East Asia, on the one hand, and the NAFTA and the European Union, on the other hand. Specifically, intraregional bias declined in East Asia from 2.43 in 1980

Table 11.5 Intraregional Dependence for Foreign Trade and Foreign Direct Investment, Various Years, 1980–94

Indicator and year	East Asia				North American Free Trade Agreement	European Union
	All East Asia	East Asia excluding Japan	Newly industrializing economies	ASEAN		
Absolute measure (percent)						
Trade						
1980	4.9	1.7	0.2	0.6	5.4	24.2
1990	8.2	3.9	0.5	0.8	6.7	29.1
1997	12.1	6.8	0.9	1.3	9.1	22.3
Foreign direct investment						
1980	3.5	1.5	0.1	0.5	13.6	12.9
1994	8.4	5.5	0.1	0.8	5.3	19.3
Relative measure (percent)						
Trade (exports plus imports)						
1980	34.4	22.2	5.7	16.8	33.1	58.8
1990	42.9	32.9	8.9	18.9	37.9	66.3
1997	50.4	39.5	11.9	21.3	45.8	61.5
Foreign direct investment (outward plus inward)						
1980	40.0	32.1	5.6	17.9	33.0	37.3
1994	42.5	53.1	3.5	18.8	19.9	51.2
Exports						
1980	33.9	22.1	5.7	16.7	33.6	61.0
1990	39.5	31.7	8.5	19.1	41.4	66.0
1997	47.6	38.7	11.5	21.3	49.1	59.6
Outward foreign direct investment						
1980	38.1	86.8	8.6	73.2	27.5	38.6
1994	35.0	86.6	2.8	56.5	18.7	47.9

Imports						
1980	34.8	22.2	5.7	17.0	32.6	56.9
1990	46.8	34.1	9.3	18.7	35.0	66.5
1997	53.5	40.2	12.2	21.3	43.0	63.5
Inward foreign direct investment						
1980	42.0	19.7	4.1	10.2	41.5	36.2
1994	54.0	38.3	4.6	11.3	21.2	55.0
Double relative measure (gravity coefficients)						
Trade						
1980	2.43	2.97	1.91	4.83	2.03	1.43
1990	2.25	2.77	1.47	4.54	2.16	1.51
1997	2.11	2.28	1.51	3.42	2.33	1.70
Foreign direct investment						
1980	4.59	11.36	4.20	14.09	0.84	1.08
1994	2.25	6.08	0.98	7.59	0.74	1.37

Note: Definitions are described in the main text.

Source: For trade data, computed from JETRO; for foreign direct investment data, from Industry Canada.

to 2.11 in 1997, while the corresponding values for the NAFTA and the European Union increased from 2.03 and 1.43 to 2.33 and 1.70, respectively, over the same period.[13] Among East Asian subgroups, intraregional trade bias is very high for ASEAN, with the double-relative measure at 3.42 in 1997, although the size of the bias has declined over time.

The estimated values for the measures of intraregional dependence reveal that the importance of intraregional trade in East Asia increased not only in world trade but also in regional trade over time. However, extraregional trade also expanded rapidly. Indeed, intraregional trade bias declined in East Asia, while it increased in the NAFTA and the European Union. One may attribute these differences partly to differences in the institutional arrangements. Both the NAFTA and the European Union have trade arrangements that give preferential treatment to their members, possibly leading to an increasing regional bias.[14] In East Asia, a preferential trading arrangement has been set up only for the ASEAN members that make up a small portion of intra–East Asian trade, and other economies do not have any discriminatory arrangements. The absence of discriminatory trade measures may have been responsible for the decline in trade bias. Unilateral trade liberalization without discriminatory treatment among trading partners contributed to a decline in regional trade bias in East Asia. Furthermore, a decline in the cost of communications and transportation services, resulting from technological progress and liberalization, contributed to the diversification of trading partners. Rapid industrialization centered on similar industries such as textiles and electric machinery has forced many East Asian economies to look outside the region for markets for their products, diminishing the intraregional trade bias (see Petri 1993 on this point).

Similar to the changing patterns of foreign trade, intraregional FDI in East Asia increased from 4 percent of world FDI in 1980 to 8 percent in 1994. The corresponding share for the European Union also increased from 13 to 19 percent, while it declined for the NAFTA from 14 to 5 percent. Among the East Asian subgroups, the stock of intraregional FDI among the developing economies registered relatively high growth, increasing from 2 to 6 percent of world FDI during the 1980–94 period.

Intraregional FDI in East Asia increased from 40 percent in 1980 to 43 percent in 1994. Among the subgroups, intraregional FDI became particularly important for developing East Asian economies. Coupled with this observation, the relatively small shares of intraregional FDI for ASEAN and NIEs indicate the importance of FDI between these subgroups. Intraregional FDI is particularly important because 87 percent of outward FDI has been undertaken in developing East Asian economies. The share of inward FDI has increased in East Asia, which means that an increasing share of inward FDI originates inside the region. However, the share of intraregional FDI in regional FDI is substantially smaller for developing East Asian economies, reflecting the importance of Japan as a source of FDI.

The results of double-relative measures show an interesting contrast between East Asia and the European Union. Although the magnitude of the bias is higher for East Asia than for the European Union, the magnitude of the bias declined for East Asia, while it increased for the European Union. The extent of the bias remained more or less the same for the NAFTA. These observations are consistent with those made for foreign trade, and differences in the direction of bias for East Asia and for the European Union may reflect differences in institutional arrangements, as argued for foreign trade.

From 1980 to 1997 the importance of intraregional trade in East Asia increased not only in world trade but also in overall trade in East Asia. However, a regional bias declined during the 1980–97 period. Similar patterns are found for intraregional FDI in East Asia. These findings indicate that the increasing importance of intraregional trade and FDI is attributable largely to the rapid expansion of overall trade and FDI in the region through market forces. This contrasts with the case in the European Union or the NAFTA, where intraregional bias in foreign trade and FDI increased possibly because of discriminatory institutional arrangements under which regional members get preferential treatment, worsening resource allocation.

The Emergence of an FDI-Trade Nexus: An Application of the Gravity Model

In the analysis in the previous section, foreign trade and FDI are analyzed separately. However, in reality foreign trade and FDI appear to have a close relationship. For example, an increasing proportion of world trade is conducted by multinational enterprises, which are active in undertaking FDI. A multinational enterprise may export capital goods and intermediate goods from its home office to its overseas affiliates to assist its overseas affiliates and may import products from its overseas affiliates to serve its home market. Such activities promote the linkage between FDI and foreign trade. In this section I use the gravity model to examine empirically the link between foreign trade and FDI in East Asia.

The gravity model has been applied extensively to investigate the determinants of bilateral trade flows. In its basic formulation, the geographic distance between the two economies and their economic size are included to explain bilateral trade flows. It is postulated that the shorter is the distance between the two economies and the bigger their economies, the larger are the bilateral trade flows between them. Indeed, many empirical studies have found such a relationship. For example, Frankel (1993) finds in his study of bilateral trade flows among 63 countries for 1980, 1985, and 1990 that economic size denoted by gross national product (GNP) and geographic distance have positive and negative effects on bilateral trade flows, respectively.

In addition to these two basic variables, several other factors have been introduced in the gravity equation that would influence bilateral trade flows. Frankel (1993) adds per capita GNP and regional dummies. Per capita GNP is included to capture the factors associated with the level of economic development. One may argue that industrial countries tend to specialize in production, leading to greater dependence on foreign trade. Furthermore, the residents of high-income countries tend to desire greater variety in their consumption, leading to greater dependence on trade. Regional dummies are included to test the existence of special regional bias in some regions such as East Asia and the European Community. Frankel finds a positive effect of per capita GNP, as expected. As to regional dummies, he finds that for regional groups in the western hemisphere, the European Community, and East Asia dummy variables are positive and statistically significant, indicating the presence of regional bias in bilateral trade. He also finds that the regional bias in East Asia declined as the estimated coefficients on the East Asia dummy became smaller over time. Boisso and Ferrantino (1997) introduce "economic and cultural distance" and the characteristics of trade regime as factors influencing bilateral trade flows. They find the deterrent effect of economic and cultural distance and inward-looking trade regime on international trade.

To examine the link between FDI and foreign trade in East Asia, we modify the basic gravity equation by introducing an FDI variable as one of the explanatory variables. We assume that FDI causes foreign trade, but the causation may go the other way as well. The justification for our specification is that we use FDI stock, which may be interpreted as a predetermined variable because it represents the accumulated value of past FDI, not FDI flows (Kawai and Urata 1998 test the two alternative specifications). Although a number of studies have suggested the existence of a link between FDI and trade, very few studies have examined this link empirically. Kawai and Urata (1998) examine the case of Japan and find a strong link between them. I estimate the following three equations to test the presence of FDI-trade linkage.

(11.1) $\ln Xij + \ln Xji = a0 + a1 \ln \text{DISTANCE}ij + a2 (\ln \text{GNP}i + \ln \text{GNP}j)$
$+ a3 [\ln(\text{GNP/POP})I + \ln \text{GNP/POP})j]$
$+ a4 (\ln \text{FDI}ij + \ln \text{FDI}ji) + a5 \text{ East Asia}$

(11.2) $\ln Xij = a0 + a1 \ln \text{DISTANCE}ij + a2 \ln \text{GNP}i + a3 \ln \text{GNP}j + a4$
$\ln (\text{GNP/POP})i + a5 [\ln(\text{GNP/POP})j]$
$+ a6 \ln \text{FDI}ij + a7 \text{ East Asia}$

(11.3) $\ln Xji = a0 + a1 \ln \text{DISTANCE}ij + a2 \ln \text{GNP}i + a3 \ln \text{GNP}j +$
$a4 \ln(\text{GNP/POP})i + a5$
$[\ln(\text{GNP/POP})j] + a6 \ln \text{FDI}ij + a7 \text{ East Asia}$

Xij indicates i's exports to j, and Xji indicates j's exports to i, or i's imports from j; where DISTANCEij indicates geographic distance between i and j; GNPi and (GNP/POP)i indicate i's GNP and GNP per capita, respectively; FDIij indicates FDI stock in j from i; and East Asia represents an East Asia dummy variable. Data on distance are taken from Fitzpatrick and Modlin (1986), data on trade and FDI stock are taken from JETRO and Industry Canada, respectively, and data on other variables are taken from the World Bank and Asian Development Bank. The East Asia dummy is applied to trade among 10 East Asian economies—China, Hong Kong, Indonesia, Japan, Korea, Malaysia, the Philippines, Singapore, Taiwan, and Thailand. In addition to these 10 economies, Canada, Chile, Mexico, the United States, Australia, and New Zealand also are included in the analysis.[15]

The coefficients in the three equations are estimated for 1980 and 1994 by ordinary least squares. The results are shown in table 11.6. The estimates on distance are negative and statistically significant in most cases, as expected. One exception is the case for East Asian economies in 1980. One possible reason for this anomaly may be due to the presence of trade-distorting restrictions. However, distance came to play an expected role of restraining foreign trade in 1994, as the result of substantial trade liberalization adopted in the 1980s. Both economic size and level of economic development show a positive impact, indicating that the volume of trade increases with the size and economic level of the economies involved in bilateral trade.

FDI promotes foreign trade, as expected. The effect of FDI on foreign trade was greater in 1980 than in 1994, possibly indicating that multinationals had diversified their trading partners by 1994. In an early stage of foreign operation, the link between foreign affiliates and parent company was strong, because foreign affiliates depended on their parent for inputs and capital goods. As the procurement and sales networks of foreign affiliates expanded with the length of operation, the link between FDI and foreign trade diminished. This observation can be supported by the following statistics for the overseas affiliates of Japanese firms. For manufacturing as a whole, in 1980, the shares of Japan in total export sales and the import procurement of overseas affiliates of Japanese firms were 40 and 73 percent, respectively. The corresponding values in 1995 were lower at 32 and 71 percent, indicating that reliance on Japan—the home economy in this case—for sales and procurement declined from 1980 to 1995.[16] Although the impact of FDI on bilateral trade fell between 1980 and 1994, it is still significant, supporting an argument that the increase in intraregional FDI played a role in increasing intraregional trade in East Asia. The results on exports and imports reveal that outward FDI has a greater impact on imports of the home economy than on its exports. This has an important implication for the trade balance of the home and host economies. Specifically, according to our results, FDI would lead to a trade deficit for the home economy, while it would lead to a trade surplus for the host economy.

Finally, the estimated coefficients on the East Asian dummy indicate the presence of intraregional bias in foreign trade for East Asia, but such bias is shown to decline from 1980 to 1994. This finding is consistent with the observations made in the previous section and in Frankel (1993).

Creation of an Intraregional Production System in East Asia

So far the changing patterns of foreign trade and FDI in East Asia have been examined without considering their relations with the economic structures of the East Asian economies. My earlier observation that foreign trade of the East Asian economies—in particular, intraregional trade in East Asia—expanded rapidly in the 1980s and 1990s may indicate a substantial impact on economic structures of the East Asian region as well as those of the individual economies. This section explicitly relates intraregional trade patterns in East Asia to procurement sources of the inputs for production and those of products for final demand by using international input-output tables. The analysis is intended to discern the changing characteristics of intraregional, interindustry relationships in East Asia.

The Institute of Developing Economies in Japan has constructed international input-output tables covering East Asian economies and the United States for 1985 and 1990. The international input-output tables are constructed by explicitly specifying the import sources and export destinations of the products of the individual economies. The international input-output tables show the sources of inputs for production—that is, inputs from the domestic market and inputs imported from other economies. Similarly, the table shows the sources of products purchased for final demand—that is, the products procured from the domestic market and those imported from foreign economies. Just as input-output tables, the international input-output tables show destinations of outputs—that is, outputs sold in the domestic market and those exported to other economies. I examine mainly the sources of inputs for production in the East Asian economies, because my main interest is to examine the interindustry, intraregional production relationship in East Asia.

Table 11.7 shows the changes in production (input) structures of East Asian economies from 1985 to 1990. During the period, the importance of imported inputs in production increased for the East Asian economies excluding Japan.[17] For Japan dependence on imported in-

Table 11.6 The Determinants of Bilateral Trade Flows: Links between Foreign Trade and Foreign Direct Investment, 1980 and 1994

| | Total | | | | East Asia | | | |
| | 1980 | | 1994 | | 1980 | | 1994 | |
Explanatory variables	Estimates	t-value	Estimates	t-value	Estimates	t-value	Estimates	t-value
Dependent variable: $\ln X_{ij} + \ln X_{ji}$ (total trade between i and j)								
$\ln$Distance(i,j)	-0.221	-0.866	-0.686*	-4.992	0.194	0.608	-0.371**	-2.190
$\ln$GNPi + $\ln$GNPj	0.305*	3.573	0.473*	10.315	0.144	1.211	0.312*	4.514
$\ln$(GNP / POP)i + $\ln$(GNP / POP)j	0.267**	2.315	0.277*	6.360	0.320***	1.924	0.338*	6.400
$\ln$FDIij + $\ln$FDIji	0.397*	5.574	0.152*	5.275	0.401*	3.752	0.140*	3.117
East Asia dummy	0.918***	1.916	0.457***	1.935				
Constant	-4.910	-1.517	-4.267*	-2.727	-4.285	-1.228	-3.114***	-1.807
R^2	0.680		0.850		0.626		0.781	
F-statistic	42.172*		112.489*		16.730*		35.659*	
Number of observations	105		105		45		45	
Dependent variable: $\ln X_{ij}$ (exports from i to j)								
$\ln$Distance(i,j)	-0.917*	-5.974	-0.881*	-10.158	0.023	0.089	-0.369**	-2.297
$\ln$GNPi	0.455*	5.270	0.511*	9.907	0.270**	2.136	0.479*	6.002
$\ln$GNPj	0.546*	7.413	0.590*	12.417	0.256**	2.066	0.269*	3.430
$\ln$(GNP / POP)i	0.519*	4.003	0.264*	4.407	0.420**	2.243	0.265*	3.185
$\ln$(GNP / POP)j	0.386*	4.336	0.278*	5.653	0.793*	6.247	0.405*	5.940
$\ln$FDIij	0.211*	3.760	0.118*	4.637	0.225**	2.386	0.073***	1.731
East Asia dummy	0.805*	2.641	0.540*	3.456				
Constant	-6.705*	-3.587	-5.077*	-4.615	-9.708*	-3.718	-4.766*	-2.979
R^2	0.599		0.778		0.518		0.653	
F-statistic	43.194*		100.950*		14.871*		25.996*	
Number of observations	210		210		90		90	

Dependent variable: lnXji (imports of i from j)

	Coef.	t	Coef.	t	Coef.	t	Coef.	t
lnDistance(i,j)	-0.877*	-5.783	-0.943*	-10.898	0.136	0.543	-0.285***	-1.920
lnGNPi	0.446*	5.217	0.512*	9.960	0.034	0.285	0.216*	2.922
lnGNPj	0.487*	6.684	0.539*	11.383	0.480*	4.065	0.489*	6.738
ln(GNP / POP)i	0.219***	1.710	0.103***	1.724	0.313***	1.752	0.172**	2.229
lnFDIij	0.273*	4.917	0.155*	6.123	0.340*	3.784	0.163*	4.165
East Asia dummy	0.495	1.643	0.012	0.075				
Constant	-5.082*	-2.749	-3.004*	-2.738	-9.378*	-3.761	-4.722*	-3.188
R^2	0.608		0.779		0.561		0.702	
F-statistic	44.833*		101.6297*		17.664*		32.641*	
Number of observations	210		210		90		90	

* Significant at the 1 percent level.
** Significant at the 5 percent level.
*** Significant at the 10 percent level.
Source: Authors' calculations.

Table 11.7 Sources of Inputs in Production for East Asian Economies, 1985–90 (percent)

Inputs and year	Newly industrializing economies	ASEAN	China	East Asia, excluding Japan	Japan	All East Asia	East Asia (millions of U.S. dollars)
Domestic inputs							
1985	45.1	35.8	50.1	44.8	47.4	46.5	1,935,141
1990	44.3	35.7	55.4	46.0	46.0	46.0	3,854,918
Imported inputs to total							
1985	11.9	11.1	3.6	7.9	4.5	5.7	236,726
1990	11.3	14.2	4.2	9.5	3.5	5.3	443,403
From newly industrializing economies							
1985	0.2	0.6	0.3	0.4	0.2	0.3	11,888
1990	0.4	1.2	1.5	1.0	0.2	0.5	39,199
From ASEAN							
1985	0.9	1.8	0.1	0.8	0.6	0.7	29,178
1990	0.8	1.8	0.3	0.9	0.4	0.5	45,508
From Japan							
1985	2.4	1.7	0.9	1.5	0.0	0.6	23,221
1990	2.5	2.9	0.5	1.9	0.0	0.6	49,850
From East Asia							
1985	3.6	4.7	1.4	2.9	1.0	1.6	67,998
1990	3.7	6.4	2.3	3.9	0.7	1.7	140,760
From the rest of the world							
1985	8.3	6.4	2.3	5.0	3.6	4.1	170,713
1990	7.6	7.8	1.9	5.6	2.8	3.6	304,633

Total inputs							
1985	58.3	48.0	54.3	53.6	52.2	52.7	2,189,897
1990	56.5	51.3	59.9	56.4	49.8	51.7	4,334,424
Value added							
1985	41.7	52.0	45.7	46.4	47.8	47.4	1,970,726
1990	43.5	48.7	40.1	43.6	50.2	48.3	4,043,535
Output							
1985	100.0	100.0	100.0	100.0	100.0	100.0	4,158,637
1990	100.0	100.0	100.0	100.0	100.0	100.0	8,375,969

Note: Total inputs include domestic and imported inputs, freight and insurance, and import duties. Therefore, domestic inputs and imported inputs do not add to total inputs.

Source: Author's calculations based on the international input-output tables of the Institute of Developing Economies.

puts in production not only was low compared with that of other economies, but also declined from 1985 to 1990. A closer look at the figures reveals variations in the changes in the proportions of imported inputs in output (the sum of total inputs and value added) for different groups of East Asian economies. Specifically, the proportion of imported inputs in output increased for ASEAN and China from 1985 to 1990, but declined for the NIEs. The ratio of imported inputs to output for the NIEs and ASEAN is significantly higher than the ratio for China, indicating significantly greater dependence on imported inputs in production. Dependence on imported inputs from East Asia increased for the NIEs, ASEAN, and China, while it declined for Japan. Dependence on production inputs imported from outside East Asia increased from 1985 to 1990, excluding Japan, because of inputs for ASEAN. Indeed, for the NIEs and China, along with Japan, dependence on production inputs imported from outside East Asia declined. ASEAN's increasingly high dependence on imported inputs from East Asia appears to have resulted from a substantial increase in FDI inflows from East Asia, notably Japan and the NIEs, which led to an increase in imported inputs from these economies. I return to the patterns of procurement by multinationals later.

Domestic sources of products for final demand (the sum of consumption and investment) have a dominant position over foreign sources in all East Asian economies (table 11.8). Indeed, the degree of dependence on domestic products for final demand is significantly greater for many East Asian economies than it is for intermediate inputs; for East Asia as a whole, the shares of imported products in total final demand and in total intermediate inputs were, respectively, 5.3 and 10.3 percent (5.3 / [46.0 + 5.3]) in 1990. Despite high dependence on domestic products and low dependence on imported products in final demand, the importance of imported products increased from 1985 to 1990 for East Asia except China. The rate of increase was particularly high for ASEAN, as reflected in a 6.1-percentage-point increase in the share of imported products in total products for final demand. East Asia increased the importance of imported products from other countries in East Asia as a source of supply for final demand, contributing to an increase in intraregional trade. However, the rest of the world increased their importance as a source of inputs for East Asia by a greater magnitude than did East Asia itself. This finding on the pattern of final

Table 11.8 Sources of Final Demand for East Asian Economies, 1985 and 1990 (percentages except where noted)

Source	Newly industrializing economies	ASEAN	China	East Asia, excluding Japan	Japan	All East Asia	East Asia (millions of U.S. dollars)
Domestic sources							
1985	91.3	89.3	91.9	91.0	98.1	95.7	1,852,100
1990	90.7	82.7	94.9	89.6	96.8	94.9	3,828,553
Imported sources							
1985	7.6	9.3	6.4	7.5	1.7	3.7	71,483
1990	8.2	15.4	4.7	9.3	2.9	4.6	187,251
From newly industrializing economies							
1985	0.2	0.6	1.2	0.8	0.2	0.4	8,131
1990	0.3	1.5	1.2	0.9	0.3	0.5	19,262
From ASEAN							
1985	0.0	0.9	0.0	0.3	0.1	0.1	2,584
1990	0.2	1.6	0.1	0.6	0.1	0.3	10,472
From Japan							
1985	2.5	1.8	2.6	2.3	0.0	0.8	15,237
1990	2.3	4.1	0.8	2.4	0.0	0.6	25,832
From East Asia							
1985	2.8	3.4	3.8	3.5	0.4	1.4	27,175
1990	2.8	7.5	2.0	4.0	0.6	1.5	60,570
From the rest of the world							
1985	4.8	5.9	2.6	4.1	1.4	2.3	44,308
1990	5.5	7.9	2.7	5.3	2.3	3.1	126,681
Total							
1985	100.0	100.0	100.0	100.0	100.0	100.0	1,935,285
1990	100.0	100.0	100.0	100.0	100.0	100.0	4,035,203

Note: Total includes final demand from domestic and imported sources, freight and insurance, and import duties. Therefore, final demand from domestic and imported sources does not add to total.

Source: Author's calculations based on the international input-output tables of the Institute of Developing Economies.

demand contrasts with the earlier finding on the pattern of intermediate demand, for which intraregional dependence in East Asia increased faster than dependence on the rest of the world.

To what extent did intraregional dependence in production intensify over time? To see this, I compute the magnitude of output being induced by a unit increase in final demand in a particular economy, and the results are shown in table 11.9. For example, in 1985 a one unit increase in final demand in Indonesia increased Indonesia's output by 1.532 units.[18] It also increased the output of Korea and Taiwan by 0.018 in the same year. The computed figures incorporate not only interindustry relationships inside the economy but also those with other East Asian economies.

Intraregional, interindustry relationships deepened from 1985 to 1990, because East Asia obtained a higher level of output in 1990 (16.632 units) than in 1985 (16.275 units) as the result of a simultaneous unit increase in final demand for all East Asian economies. Although a large part of induced production was realized in the economy registering an increase in final demand, the output of other economies also increased. Indeed, the induced level of output in other East Asian economies, excluding output induced in an economy having an increase in final demand, increased from 1.291 in 1985 to 1.443 in 1990, indicating a net deepening in the intraregional, interindustry relationship. However, the magnitude of the contribution to the deepening was not uniform among East Asian economies. Indonesia, Malaysia, the Philippines, China, Taiwan, and Korea contributed to deepening of the relationship, whereas Singapore, Thailand, and Japan did not. An examination of the magnitude of output induced in East Asia shows a strong dependence on Japan for the supply of intermediate inputs, since Japan experienced the largest increase in output as a result of an increase in final demand in all the developing East Asian economies. This finding may indicate that a large amount of FDI from Japan promoted imports of inputs from Japan.

Multinationals in East Asia: Promoters of Greater Intraregional Dependence

In light of the findings that interindustry, intraregional trade in intermediate goods intensified in East Asia and that FDI promoted foreign trade, in this section I examine the trading patterns of multinationals in order to see the influence of FDI.

FDI seems to have played an important role in promoting the exports of host countries. The contribution of FDI to export expansion has been particularly large for the second-tier exporting economies—that is, ASEAN members and China—in contrast to the first-tier exporting economies—Hong Kong, Korea, and Taiwan. Specifically, around 1990 the share of foreign affiliates in total manufactured exports was approximately 20 percent for the first-tier economies and 30–90 percent for the second-tier economies.[19] The large contribution that foreign firms made to the export expansion of the host economies can be explained by their FDI strategy, which in turn was strongly influenced by the trade and FDI regimes of the host economies. Foreign firms seeking efficient production in order to export their products were attracted to East Asian economies where outward-oriented policies have been applied. Among various outward-oriented policies, the establishment of export-processing zones has contributed much to the creation of an FDI-trade nexus. In addition, the abundance of disciplined and low-wage labor has attracted export-oriented, efficiency-seeking FDI, leading to the export expansion of foreign firms.

It would be of interest to see whether foreign firms actually contributed to the deepening of intraregional dependence. However, the data needed to carry out such an analysis are not available for foreign firms of all origins in East Asia. In this section, I use information on Japanese multinationals to examine this issue. Although limited in its coverage, the data provide us with useful information because Japanese multinationals account for a large portion of multinationals operating in East Asia.

Table 11.10 presents the procurement and sales patterns of Japanese manufacturing multinationals in Asia in 1986 and 1995. For the Asian affiliates of Japanese firms, dependence on Asia as a source of intermediate goods and as a sales destination of products increased from 1986 to 1995. Specifically, the shares of Asia in total procurement and total sales of Asian affiliates increased from 51 and 29 percent, respectively, in 1986 to 55 and 32 percent in 1995. A similar pattern may be found for ASEAN affiliates. The importance of other Asian economies as a procurement source increased significantly, as did the importance of Japan as a sales destination, from 1986 to 1995. Asia

Table 11.9 Intereconomy, Interindustry Linkages in East Asia, 1985–90

Increase in production	An increase in final demand in									
	Indonesia	Malaysia	Philippines	Singapore	Thailand	China	Taiwan	Korea	Japan	Total
Domestic production										
1985	1.532	1.478	1.569	1.424	1.618	1.893	1.790	1.716	1.963	14.984
1990	1.574	1.586	1.518	1.357	1.534	2.195	1.767	1.747	1.910	15.189
1985–90	0.042	0.108	-0.051	-0.068	-0.083	0.302	-0.023	0.031	-0.053	0.205
Korea and Taiwan (China)										
1985	0.018	0.022	0.019	0.047	0.018	0.003	0.003	0.005	0.007	0.141
1990	0.024	0.035	0.048	0.043	0.029	0.011	0.008	0.007	0.008	0.212
1985–90	0.006	0.013	0.029	-0.005	0.011	0.008	0.006	0.002	0.002	0.070
ASEAN										
1985	0.019	0.079	0.030	0.141	0.040	0.007	0.032	0.039	0.028	0.414
1990	0.016	0.061	0.034	0.118	0.048	0.015	0.035	0.033	0.019	0.379
1985–90	-0.003	-0.017	0.004	-0.023	0.007	0.008	0.003	-0.006	-0.009	-0.035
Japan										
1985	0.073	0.117	0.033	0.110	0.077	0.038	0.079	0.090	0.000	0.618
1990	0.065	0.124	0.099	0.170	0.100	0.026	0.094	0.073	0.000	0.750
1985–90	-0.008	0.007	0.066	0.059	0.022	-0.012	0.015	-0.018	0.000	0.132
China										
1985	0.006	0.018	0.021	0.051	0.009	0.000	0.001	0.001	0.011	0.118
1990	0.009	0.017	0.008	0.039	0.019	0.000	0.001	0.001	0.009	0.103
1985–90	0.003	-0.001	-0.013	-0.012	0.010	0.000	0.000	0.000	-0.002	-0.016

East Asia excluding own domestic production

1985	0.116	0.236	0.102	0.349	0.145	0.047	0.115	0.135	0.046	1.291
1990	0.115	0.237	0.189	0.369	0.195	0.051	0.138	0.113	0.036	1.443
1985–90	-0.001	0.001	0.087	0.020	0.050	0.004	0.024	-0.022	-0.010	0.152

Total East Asia

1985	1.648	1.714	1.671	1.774	1.763	1.940	1.904	1.851	2.009	16.275
1990	1.689	1.823	1.707	1.726	1.729	2.246	1.905	1.860	1.947	16.632
1985–90	0.041	0.109	0.036	-0.048	-0.033	0.305	0.001	0.009	-0.062	0.357

Note: The figures indicate the amount of production induced in an economy shown in a row by a unit increase in final demand in an economy shown in the column. East Asia includes Korea and Taiwan, ASEAN-5 (Indonesia, Malaysia, Philippines, Singapore, and Thailand), China, and Japan. East Asia, Korea and Taiwan, and ASEAN -5 do not include an economy appearing in the column. For example, an increase in production in Indonesia (column) is not included in ASEAN -5 (row).

Source: Institute of Developing Economies, international input-output tables for Asian economies.

also became more important for Asian affiliates of Japanese firms, both as a source of imports and as a destination for exports. In proportion to total imports and exports of Asian affiliates of Japanese firms, imports from and exports to Asia increased from 88 and 63 percent, respectively, in 1986 to 92 and 77 percent in 1995.

Two interesting observations may be made from the findings on procurement and sales of Japanese multinationals. First, Japanese multinationals have contributed to deepening intraregional dependence through their import and export activities, as Asia increased its importance as a procurement source and as a sales destination for Japanese multinationals in Asia.[20] Second, an increase in the shares of Asia in the total procurement of Japanese multinationals from 1986 to 1995 tends to indicate that Japanese multinationals have become more active in pursuing intraregional, interprocess division of labor.

A large number of multinationals in East Asia seek efficiency rather than markets. As such, they locate themselves in an economy where they can perform their operation most efficiently or at the least cost. Japanese multinationals in machinery sectors such as electronics, which account for a large part of Japanese multinationals in East Asia, break up their production process into several subprocesses and locate each subprocess in an economy where it may be carried out most efficiently. For example, some television-producing Japanese multinationals break up the production process into subprocesses such as parts production and assembly operation, and they locate parts production in an economy where high-skilled workers are available and locate assembly operation in an economy where low-wage labor is available. The television producers export parts to an economy where final assembly is conducted and then export the assembled televisions to various economies. The high share of intrafirm trade in total trade for Japanese multinationals (shown in table 11.10) tends to support the argument that Japanese multinationals conduct interprocess division of labor. A closer look at the statistics shows that intrafirm trade is prevalent in machinery sectors, where a number of different components are used for production (see Urata 1993). These findings show that multinationals have set up a regional production system in East Asia.

U.S. firms also have been active in setting up production networks in East Asia. Unlike the more or less closed production systems constructed by Japanese firms, production networks constructed by U.S.

Table 11.10 Patterns of Transactions by Japanese Multinationals in Manufacturing in Asia, 1986 and 1995 (percent)

Indicator	Procurement					Sales				
	Local market	Imports from			Share of all Asia in total imports	Local market	Exports to			Share of all Asia in total exports
		Japan	Other Asia	All Asia			Japan	Other Asia	All Asia	
Geographical distribution of total procurements and sales										
1986										
Asia	42.2	45.3	5.6	50.9	88.1	54.7	15.8	12.8	28.6	63.1
ASEAN	47.4	38.7	7.0	45.7	86.8	59.3	10.0	18.6	28.6	70.3
1995										
Asia	40.3	40.3	14.4	54.7	91.6	58.4	18.8	13.4	32.2	77.3
ASEAN	37.9	44.3	13.4	57.7	93.0	60.1	18.9	11.7	30.6	76.7
Intrafirm transactions as a proportion of total transactions										
1986										
Asia	6.8	66.6	47.6	—	—	8.9	76.5	20.1	—	—
ASEAN	8.2	66.7	43.5	—	—	9.2	78.5	24.2	—	—
1995										
Asia	15.3	77.4	44.9	—	—	15.8	84.5	49.9	—	—
ASEAN	18.4	77.2	29.0	—	—	21.5	84.5	48.5	—	—

— Not available.
Source: MITI (1989, 1998).

firms are more open to firms from other economies such as Taiwan, Korea, and Singapore. Indeed, the basic strategy of the U.S. firms is to link up with the most efficient producers, regardless of nationality (see Borrus 1999 for the case of U.S. electronics firms in East Asia). Many firms from the NIEs also set up production networks in various parts of the world, particularly in East Asia. One of the industries that have actively pursued such globalization strategy is textiles. All of these production systems and networks clearly have contributed to greater intraregional dependence in East Asia (Gereffi 1999 presents an interesting analysis of an apparel commodity chain developed by firms from the NIEs).

TRADE-LED AND FDI-LED ECONOMIC GROWTH IN EAST ASIA

This section investigates the impact of the rapid expansion in trade and FDI and the resultant regional production networks on economic growth in East Asia.

Foreign trade and FDI may contribute to economic growth through various channels (Caves 1996 and Blomstrom and Kokko 1997 present good surveys on the impact of FDI on the host economies). These channels may be divided into those related to supply and those related to demand. Supply-side factors can be divided further into those leading to an expansion of productive capacity and those leading to an improvement in the efficient use of productive capacity. I examine each in turn.

I begin with the impact of trade and FDI on productive capacity. Both exports and FDI contribute to the expansion of productive capacity because they bring in foreign exchange, which the economy can use to import foreign items necessary for the expansion of productive capacity such as high-quality foreign capital goods, intermediate goods, and technologies. Since the ratio of exports and of FDI to GDP increased significantly for a number of East Asian economies from the mid-1980s to the 1990s, the contribution of export expansion and FDI inflows to the expansion of productive capacity is likely to have been significant.

Foreign trade provides an economy with an opportunity to improve the use of its productive resources or to improve its resource allocation. The improvement in resource allocation obtained by removing protection has been estimated to be rather small. For example, the inefficient resource allocation due to tariff and nontariff protection was only 0.6 percent of Japan's GDP in 1989 (Sazanami, Urata, and Kawai [1994] use a partial general equilibrium model to estimate the effect of tariff and nontariff protection measures for Japan).

A greater benefit from trade expansion appears to come from the improvement of technical efficiency or the increase in productivity. Export expansion may lead to greater productivity for a variety of reasons: greater capacity use in industries in which the minimum efficient scale of plants is large relative to the domestic market; increasing familiarity with and absorption of new technologies; greater learning-by-doing insofar as this is a function of cumulative output and exports permit greater output in an industry; and the stimulative effects of the need to achieve internationally competitive prices and quality. (Pack 1988 presents a good survey of the impact of foreign trade on economic growth and development.) The World Bank (1993) study of 69 countries for the 1960–89 period finds that the high share of manufactured exports in total exports increased the growth rate of total factor productivity. A case study of Korean firms by Rhee, Ross-Larson, and Pursell (1984) finds that exporting firms achieved higher productivity by obtaining technologies through contact with foreign firms, supporting the assertion that exports increase productivity.

An expansion in imports is also likely to improve the technical efficiency of domestic firms as imports create competitive pressures. In order to survive under competitive pressures, domestic firms have to improve their productivity by adopting strategies such as the introduction of new technologies and new products. Several studies have found that greater imports have an impact on productivity. In their study of trade policy and its impact on productivity for Japan in the post–World War II period, Lawrence and Weinstein (chapter 10 of this volume) find that the expansion of imports improved productivity in Japan.

FDI is likely to improve the productivity of the recipient economy because it brings technologies and managerial know-how, which are in short supply in developing economies. The transfer of technology and managerial know-how from the multinationals to the recipient or host economy takes two different forms. In intrafirm technology transfer, technology is transferred from a parent company of a multinational to its foreign affiliate, and in technology spillover, technology is transferred from a foreign affiliate to local firms. Intrafirm technology transfer takes the form of on-the-job training, training at parent companies, and others. Technology spillover is realized through various means. For example, it takes place when local workers, who acquired technology and managerial know-how by working at foreign affiliates, use these skills at local companies. Technology spillover may also be realized when local firms imitate the technology and managerial know-how used at foreign affiliates. FDI also improves the technical efficiency of local firms by generating competition.

Several studies have identified intrafirm technology transfer. Using the results of a survey conducted on the East Asian affiliates of Japanese firms, Urata (1999) finds that relatively simple technologies such as the maintenance and repair of production lines have been transferred from parent companies to foreign affiliates, while relatively sophisticated new technologies and new products have not been transferred (Yamashita 1991 finds a similar pattern in his study of Japanese firms in the ASEAN countries). Analyzing the determinants of the extent of intrafirm technology transfer achieved by Japanese multinationals, Urata and Kawai (2000) find that the capability of absorbing technologies, reflected in level of education, plays a key role in enabling host economies to benefit from intrafirm technology transfer. Their study also emphasizes the time and experience needed to transfer technology within a firm, suggesting the importance of maintaining a stable economic environment, so that multinationals may stay for a long period of time.

The results of the analyses on the presence of technology spillover are mixed. Using industry-level data, Caves (1974) finds the presence of technology spillover in his study of the Australian manufacturing sector, but not in his study of the Canadian manufacturing sector. Using a similar methodology, Globerman (1979) finds the presence of the spillover effect of FDI in the Canadian manufacturing sector. Blomstrom and Persson (1983) and Blomstrom and Wolff (1994) also detect technology spillover in their studies of the Mexican manufacturing sector. One problem common to these earlier studies is that they do not take into account the differences in productivity across domestic industries. Controlling for differences in productivity across industries using firm-level data, Haddad and Harrison (1993) and Aitken and Harrison (1994) do not find spillover effects in their studies of Morocco and Venezuela. One possible reason is the limited presence of foreign firms in these countries.

In addition to supply-side factors, exports and FDI contribute to economic growth by influencing demand-side factors. Export expansion increases the foreign demand for domestic products, and FDI increases the demand for domestically produced investment and intermediate goods, because the funds transferred through FDI are used mainly for investments and production. The increase in the demand for domestic goods, in turn, leads to an expansion of output.

Very few studies have examined the impact of FDI inflow on economic growth. Borensztein, de Gregorio, and Lee (1998) find that FDI does not have a significantly positive impact on economic growth unless it is interacted with the educational level of the host country, in which case it has a significantly positive impact.[21] Their finding may be interpreted to mean that education becomes more effective when it is associated with foreign knowledge. Because educational levels in East Asia are higher than in other developing economies, it is reasonable to assert that substantial FDI inflows contributed to economic growth in East Asia.

Exports and FDI interacted with each other to reinforce their individual impact on economic growth by forming virtuous spirals of economic growth in East Asia. In response to the increased incentive given to exports by trade liberalization, foreign firms set up export platforms through FDI. As a result, FDI and exports expanded. The economies that succeeded in expanding exports attracted FDI, because they were seen as capable of providing an environment conducive to competitive production. In this way, virtuous spirals of export expansion and FDI expansion, or the FDI-trade nexus, were formed. These spirals are closely associated with the formation of intraregional production networks by multinationals. Such production networks enable multinationals to improve technical efficiency by exploiting greater division of labor, and it is probable that production networks will continue to emerge and to contribute to economic growth in East Asia.

CONCLUSIONS: IS EXPORT-LED AND FDI-LED GROWTH SUSTAINABLE?

Developing East Asian economies had been outperforming the rest of the world for several decades until they were struck by a currency and economic crisis in 1997. Their economic performance was particularly remarkable from the mid-1980s until the crisis. According to World Bank (1993), various factors such as sound fundamentals, including stable macroeconomic environment, human capital, and limited price distortions explain East Asia's high economic growth during the 1970s and 1980s. In addition to these factors, large inflows of FDI played a key role in the latter half of the 1980s and the 1990s.

The analysis in this chapter showed that foreign trade and FDI in East Asia expanded rapidly in the 1980s and 1990s largely due to unilateral liberalization of trade and FDI and to rapid economic growth. Intraregional economic dependence increased in East Asia through foreign trade and FDI, mainly as a result of rapid economic growth in the region rather than any discriminatory measures against other regions. Moreover, an FDI-trade nexus emerged, partly as a result of regional production and trade networks created by multinationals. Indeed, some multinationals intensively and extensively pursued a strategy of intraregional division of labor by forming regional production networks.

FDI inflows transferred not only the funds for fixed investment but also technology and managerial know-how, both of which contributed to the expansion and improvement of productive capabilities. In addition, FDI inflows enabled economies to use the extensive sales networks developed by multinationals. What has been remarkable in East Asia is the interaction and simultaneous expansion of FDI inflows and exports, which reinforced the favorable impacts of each. The regional production and trade networks established by multinationals through FDI contributed to economic growth by enabling multinationals and regional economies to improve their technical efficiency and achieve greater division of labor. The experience of East Asia should prove useful for the developing economies in other parts of the world. In particular, countries wishing to emulate East Asia's success will have to provide a liberalized environment, under which domestic as well as foreign firms can achieve efficient operations.

In response to the recent currency and economic crisis in East Asia, some observers have cast doubt on the desirability of deepening intraregional trade and FDI relations. They argue that intensified intraregional trade and FDI relations transmitted harmful economic impacts among the East Asian economies, creating a vicious cycle of unfavorable economic repercussions. Policymakers sympathetic to this view advocate a shift from outward-oriented policies to inward-oriented policies in order to insulate the economy from negative external impacts. Such a policy is clearly incorrect, once one realizes that the inward-oriented protectionist policies adopted by a number of countries with the aim of protecting their own markets deepened the world depression in the 1930s. The application of inward-oriented policies would worsen a crisis of this kind by reducing the demand for products produced by trading partners. Moreover, recent research indicates that crises are more likely to be transmitted through financial links.

With a few exceptions, developing economies in East Asia have not reversed the liberalization of their trade and FDI regimes. Rapid export expansion, which resulted largely from substantial depreciation of the currencies of the crisis-stricken economies with support by liberalized export and FDI regimes, contributed significantly to the speedy recovery of these economies. Indeed, many economies liberalized their FDI regimes in an effort to boost economic recovery and growth. FDI inflows in East Asia have remained strong, maintaining more or less the level achieved before the crisis.[22]

Globalization of economic activities is expected to strengthen in the future, mainly because of technological progress in information technologies. Under these circumstances, developing East Asian economies should try to increase FDI and foreign trade to achieve economic growth, as they did in the past. To increase FDI and foreign trade, developing East Asian economies have to overcome a number of challenges. They have to lower and remove the barriers to trade and FDI not only by pursuing unilateral liberalization but also by participating in regional liberalization schemes such as APEC and AFTA and multilateral liberalization under the World Trade Organization. In addition to liberalization, they will have to overcome other obstacles such as the underdevelopment of infrastructure—both hard infrastructure such as transportation and communication facilities and soft infrastructure such as the governance system—and the shortage of skilled human resources.[23] Furthermore, one cannot overemphasize some lessons from East Asia's experience, stressing the importance of maintaining a stable macroeconomic environment with low inflation, sound fiscal policy, and a stable exchange rate.

Finally, recipient economies will have to assimilate foreign technologies transferred via FDI or other means if they are to achieve a sustainable economic growth. The efficient assimilation of foreign technologies has become more important in recent years because mergers and acquisitions rather than green-field operations are an increasingly important vehicle of FDI.[24] Under mergers and acquisitions, physical productive capacity does not increase. For efficient and effective assimilation of technologies, a number of studies have pointed out the importance of absorptive capability such as high educational and technical capabilities in the recipient economies (for example, see Urata and Kawai 2000). To improve the quality of infrastructure and educational and technical capabilities, East Asian governments can play an important role by shifting resources into these areas and by using economic and technical assistance obtained from international development agencies and donor economies.

NOTES

The author would like to thank Stephen Parker, David Weinstein, Shahid Yusuf, and other participants of the project for helpful comments and discussions.

1. For the purposes of this chapter, East Asia includes the following economies: China, Hong Kong, Indonesia, Japan, the Republic of Korea, Malaysia, Philippines, Singapore, Taiwan (China), and Thailand; developing East Asia excludes Japan.

2. It is important to note that World Bank (1993) does not examine the issues related to FDI in detail, because the rapid growth in FDI began after completion of the study. In addition to FDI, which involves equity participation, various types of international alliances without equity participation such as joint research and development (R&D) and original equipment manufacturing (OEM) have also increased in recent years. However, I do not analyze international alliances mainly because reliable data are lacking. Oman (1984) is one of the pioneering works on international alliances.

3. This information was obtained from the Institute of Developing Economies in Tokyo.

4. For the factors that induce FDI and for the case of U.S. FDI, see Wheeler and Mody (1992); for the case of Japanese FDI, see Urata and Kawai (1998).

5. Different economies adopted different types of trade policies. The degree of outward orientation of these economies can be ranked generally in the following descending order: the NIEs, ASEAN, and China. Hong Kong and Singapore were two exceptions in that they pursued very open trade policies. Many economies applied import substitution policies in certain sectors and export promotion policies in others. However, the developing economies in East Asia adopted trade policies with a greater outward orientation than developing economies in other regions, such as Latin America.

6. The liberalization of trade and FDI was pursued in many sectors, while restrictions remained in some sectors, generally in heavy manufacturing industries and services. See Pacific Economic Cooperation Council (1995) for detailed information.

7. For Korea the unweighted average of tariff rates declined from 19 to 12 percent from 1988 to 1993, while the incidence of nontariff barriers declined from 9 to 2 percent (Pacific Economic Cooperation Council 1995).

8. Yamazawa and Urata (2000) emphasize the need for a mechanism for evaluating the performance of the APEC members in their pursuit of liberalization and present the result of their assessment.

9. As cited in McKinnon (chapter 5 of this volume), Kwan (1998) shows the positive impact of the yen appreciation on the economic performance of developing East Asian economies through its positive impact on Japanese FDI in the region.

10. Hill and Athukorala (1998) provide a good survey of foreign direct investment in East Asia. Their discussions include the basic trends of FDI and their impact on exports and technology transfer.

11. The values of most Asian currencies were basically pegged to the U.S. dollar, and the depreciation (appreciation) of the Japanese yen vis-à-vis the U.S. dollar meant the appreciation (depreciation) of their currencies vis-à-vis the Japanese yen. See McKinnon (chapter 5 of this volume) for the movements of the Asian currencies in recent years.

12. See McKinnon (chapter 5 of this volume). Several studies have found that exchange rate volatility inhibits foreign trade and FDI. See Thursby and Thursby (1987) and Cushman (1988) for the case of trade and Urata and Kawai (1999) for the case of FDI.

13. Petri (1993) also finds a downward trend of regional bias for East Asia up to the mid-1980s. Unlike my finding here, he observes a turnaround in the mid-1980s and an increase of regional bias in the 1990s.

14. The NAFTA was established in 1994 by extending the U.S.-Canadian Free Trade Agreement, which had been in effect since 1989, to include Mexico. As such, the figures computed for FDI reflect mainly the impact of the U.S.-Canadian Free Trade Agreement rather than the NAFTA, while those for trade reflect the impact of the NAFTA.

15. Country coverage is constrained by the availability of the data on FDI.

16. The data are taken from MITI (1983, 1989).

17. This observation is consistent with Yeats (1999), who finds that the components trade expanded rapidly in East Asia in the period 1984–96, reflecting the expansion of intraregional division of labor since the mid-1980s.

18. The figures are computed as follows. The analysis uses international input-output tables with 24-sector disaggregation and 10 economies. To derive the amount of output induced by an increase in final demand, the Leontief inverse matrix is multiplied by a final demand vector consisting of unity for 24 sectors. The resulting output is divided by 24 to obtain the level of output induced by a one unit increase in final demand.

19. Hill and Athukorala (1998: table 3). Although the discussions in the text only refer to the contribution of FDI to export expansion of the recipient economies, FDI also has contributed much to the expansion of imports of the recipient economies. Indeed, some observers claim that foreign firms contribute negatively to the trade balance of the recipient economies, because they expand imports more than exports. The analysis here refutes this argument. The statistics in MITI (1994) also show that the trade balance of the recipients of Japanese FDI tends to be positive.

20. In Urata (1993), I observe that Japanese multinationals contribute to deepening intraregional dependence through trade in East Asia. Compared with overall trade, Japanese multinationals tend more toward intraregional trade in East Asia, because the share of intraregional trade in overall trade is significantly smaller than the corresponding share for Japanese multinationals.

21. United Nations (1999) presents similar findings. Blomstrom, Lipsey, and Zejan (1994) find a significantly positive relationship between the ratio of FDI to GDP and the growth of GDP per capita for industrial countries, but not for developing countries.

22. See United Nations (1999) for FDI developments after the crisis. The report emphasizes the importance of FDI in economic recovery and growth because FDI flows were significantly less volatile than other types of capital flows such as portfolio investments.

23. The importance of infrastructure and economic and political stability for attracting FDI is found in the study of U.S. FDI by Wheeler and Mody (1992) and in the study of Japanese FDI by Urata and Kawai (1998).

24. United Nations (1999) reports the increase in mergers and acquisitions in East Asia after the economic crisis.

REFERENCES

The word "processed" describes informally reproduced works that may not be commonly available through library systems.

Aitken, Brian, and Ann Harrison. 1994. "Do Domestic Firms Benefit from Foreign Direct Investment? Evidence from Panel Data." Policy Research Working Paper 1248. World Bank, Policy Research Department, Washington, D.C. Processed.

Asian Development Bank. 1999, *Key Indicators of Developing Asian and Pacific Countries 1999*. Manila, Philippines.

Blomstrom, Magnus, and Ari Kokko. 1997. "How Foreign Investment Affects Host Countries." Policy Research Working Paper 1745. World Bank, Policy Research Department, Washington, D.C. Processed.

Blomstrom, Magnus, Robert E. Lipsey, and Mario Zejan. 1994. "What Explains Developing Country Growth?" NBER Working Paper 4132. National Bureau of Economic Research, Cambridge, Mass. Processed.

Blomstrom, Magnus, and Hakan Persson. 1983. "Foreign Investment and Spillover Efficiency in an Underdeveloped Economy: Evidence from the Mexican Manufacturing Industry." *World Development* 11(6):493–501.

Blomstrom, Magnus, and Edward N. Wolff. 1994. "Multinational Corporations and Productivity Convergence in Mexico." In William Baumol, Richard Nelson, and Edward N. Wolff, eds., *Convergence of Productivity: Cross-national Studies and Historical Evidence*. New York: Oxford University Press.

Boisso, Dale, and Michael Ferrantino. 1997. "Economic Distance, Cultural Distance, and Openness in International Trade: Empirical Puzzles." *Journal of Economic Integration* 12(4), December:456-84.

Borensztein, Eduardo, José de Gregorio, and Jong-Wha Lee. 1998. "How Does Foreign Direct Investment Affect Economic Growth?" *Journal of International Economics* 45(June):115–35.

Borrus, Michael. 1999. "Exploiting Asia to Beat Japan." In Dennis J. Encarnation, ed., *Japanese Multinationals in Asia*. New York: Oxford University Press.

Caves, Richard E. 1974. "Multinational Firms, Competition, and Productivity in Host-Country Industries." *Economica* 41(May):176-93.

———. 1996. *Multinational Enterprise and Economic Analysis*, 2d ed. Cambridge, U.K.: Cambridge University Press.

Chia, Siow Yue. 2000. "Regional Economic Integration in East Asia: Developments, Issues, and Challenges." In Koichi Hamada, Mitsuo Matsushita, and Chikara Komura, eds., *Dreams and Dilemmas*. Singapore: Institute of Southeast Asian Studies.

Cushman, David O. 1988. "U.S. Bilateral Trade Flows and Exchange Risk during the Floating Period." *Journal of International Economics* 24(May):317-30.

Fitzpatrick, Gary L., and Marilyn J. Modlin. 1986. *Direct Line Distances*. Lanham, Md.: Scarecrow Press.

Frankel, Jeffrey A. 1993. "Is Japan Creating a Yen Bloc in East Asia and the Pacific?" In Jeffrey A. Frankel and Miles Kahler, eds., *Regionalism and Rivalry: Japan and the United States in Pacific Asia*. Chicago: University of Chicago Press.

Gereffi, Gary. 1999. "International Trade and Industrial Upgrading in the Apparel Commodity Chain." *Journal of International Economics* 48(1)June:37–70.

Globerman, Steven. 1979. "Foreign Direct Investment and 'Spillover' Efficiency Benefits in Canadian Manufacturing Industries." *Canadian Journal of Economics* 12(1):42–56.

Haddad, Mona, and Ann Harrison. 1993. "Are There Positive Spillovers from Direct Investment? Evidence from Panel Data for Morocco." *Journal of Development Economics* 42(1)October:51–74.

Hill, Hal, and Prema-chandra Athukorala. 1998. "Foreign Direct Investment in East Asia: A Survey." *Asia-Pacific Economic Literature* 12(November):23–50.

IMF (International Monetary Fund). 1999. *International Financial Statistics Yearbook.* Washington, D.C.

Kawai, Masahiro, and Shujiro Urata. 1996. "Trade Imbalances and Japanese Foreign Direct Investment: Bilateral and Triangular Issues." Discussion Paper Series F-52. University of Tokyo, Institute of Social Sciences, Tokyo. Processed.

———. 1998. "Are Trade and Direct Investment Substitutes or Complements? An Empirical Analysis of Japanese Manufacturing Industries." In Hiro Lee and D. W. Roland-Holst, eds., *Economic Development and Cooperation in the Pacific Basin: Trade, Investment, and Environmental Issues.* Cambridge, U.K.: Cambridge University Press.

Krueger, Anne O., ed. 1998. *The WTO as an International Organization.* Chicago: University of Chicago Press.

Kwan, C. H. 1998. "The Yen, the Yuan, and the Asian Currency Crisis: Changing Fortune between Japan and China." Nomura Research Institute Tokyo. Processed.

MITI (Ministry of International Trade and Industry) (1983, 1989, 1998) *Kaigai Jigyo Katsudo Kihon Chosa [Comprehensive Survey of Overseas Activities of Japanese Firms],* nos. 1, 3, 6. Tokyo, Japan

MITI (Ministry of International Trade and Industry) (1994) *Kigyo Katsudo Kihon Chosa [Comprehensive Statistics on Japanese Firms' Activities].* 1992 version. Tokyo, Japan.

Morrison, Charles E. 1998. "APEC: The Evolution of an Institution." In Vinod K. Aggarwal and Charles E. Morrison, eds., *Asia-Pacific Crossroads: Regime Creation and the Future of APEC.* New York: St. Martin's Press.

Oman, Charles. 1984. *New Forms of International Investment in Developing Countries.* Paris: Organisation for Economic Co-operation and Development.

Pacific Economic Cooperation Council. 1995. *Survey of Impediments to Trade and Investment in the APEC Region.* Singapore.

Pack, Howard. 1988. "Industrialization and Trade." In Hollis Chenery and T. N. Srinivasan, eds., *Handbook of Development Economics.* Vol. 1. Amsterdam: North-Holland.

Petri, Peter A. 1993. "The East Asian Trading Bloc: An Analytical History." In Jeffrey A. Frankel and Miles Kahler, eds., *Regionalism and Rivalry: Japan and the United States in Pacific Asia.* Chicago: University of Chicago Press.

Rhee, Y. W., Bruce Ross-Larson, and Gary Pursell. 1984. *Korea's Competitive Edge: Managing Entry to World Markets.* Baltimore, Md.: Johns Hopkins University Press.

Sazanami, Yoko, Shujiro Urata, and Hiroki Kawai. 1994. *Measuring the Costs of Protection in Japan.* Washington, D.C.: Institute for International Economics.

Taiwan Council for Economic Planning and Development 1999. *Taiwan Statistical Data Book 1999.* Taipei, Republic of China.

Thursby, Jerry G., and Marie C. Thursby. 1987. "Bilateral Trade Flows, the Linder Hypothesis, and Exchange Risk." *Review of Economics and Statistics* 60(August) 488-95.

United Nations. Various years. *World Investment Report.* New York.

Urata, Shujiro. 1993. "Japanese Foreign Direct Investment and Its Effect on Foreign Trade in Asia." In Takatoshi Ito and Anne O. Krueger, eds., *Trade and Protectionism.* Chicago: University of Chicago Press for National Bureau for Economic Research.

————. 1998. "Regionalization and the Formation of Regional Institutions in East Asia." In Kiichiro Fukasaku, Fukunari Kimura, and Shujiro Urata, eds., *Asia and Europe: Beyond Competing Regionalism.* Sussex: Academic Press.

————. 1999. "Intrafirm Technology Transfer by Japanese Multinationals." In Dennis J. Encarnation, ed., *Japanese Multinationals in Asia: Regional Operations in Comparative Perspective.* New York: Oxford University Press.

Urata, Shujiro, and Hiroki Kawai. 1998. "Governance and the Flow of Japanese Foreign Direct Investment." Paper prepared for the World Bank project "Governance and Private Investment." World Bank, Economic Development Institute Washington, D.C. Processed.

————. 1999. "The Determinants of the Location of Foreign Direct Investment by Japanese Small and Medium-sized Enterprises." Forthcoming in Small Business Economics.

————. 2000. "Intrafirm Technology Transfer by Japanese Manufacturing Firms in Asia." Forthcoming in Takatoshi Ito and Anne O. Krueger, eds., *The Role of Foreign Direct Investment in Economic Development.* Chicago: University of Chicago Press for National Bureau for Economic Research.

Wheeler, David, and Ashoka Mody. 1992. "International Investment Location Decisions: The Case of U.S. Firms." *Journal of International Economics* 33(1/2)August:57–76.

World Bank. 1993. *The East Asian Miracle: Economic Growth and Public Policy.* New York: Oxford University Press.

————. 1999. *World Development Indicators 1999: Data on Diskette.* Washington, D.C.

Yamashita, Shoichi. 1991. "Economic Development of the ASEAN Countries and the Role of Japanese Direct Investment." In Shoichi Yamashita, ed., *Transfer of Japanese Technology and Management to the ASEAN Countries.* Tokyo: University of Tokyo Press.

Yamazawa, Ippei, and Shujiro Urata. 2000. "Trade and Investment Liberalization and Facilitation." Forthcoming in Ippei Yamazawa, ed. *Asia Pacific Economic Cooperation (APEC).* London: Routledge.

Yeats, Alexander J. 1999. "The East Asian Economic Crisis, Was the Region's Export Performance a Factor?" Paper presented at ASEM Regional Economists' Workshop in Bali, Indonesia, September 15–17. Processed.

CHAPTER 12

RETHINKING THE ROLE OF GOVERNMENT POLICY IN SOUTHEAST ASIA

K. S. Jomo

I n September 1993, the World Bank published *The East Asian Miracle: Economic Growth and Public Policy*. The study was commissioned at the insistence of the Japanese government to gain greater recognition and appreciation of Japanese and other East Asian experiences. For years, the Japanese government had been frustrated with the neoclassical economic orthodoxy and free market conservatism that had come to dominate World Bank thinking, operations, and policy recommendations, especially with the resurgence of neoliberal economic fundamentalism in the 1980s.

The World Bank study's argument can be summed up as follows. It identifies eight economies—Japan; the four Northeast Asian economies of the Republic of Korea, Taiwan (China); the island city-state of Singapore, and the then–British Crown colony of Hong Kong; as well as the three Southeast Asian economies of Malaysia, Thailand, and Indonesia—as high-performing Asian economies (HPAEs). These eight economies achieved the highest growth rates in the world between 1965 and 1990. In the early 1980s, China joined their number. According to the World Bank study, the statistical chance of such success on a regional scale is extremely remote: "In large measure, the HPAEs achieved high growth by getting the basics right. . . . In this sense there is little that is 'miraculous' about the HPAEs' superior record of growth; it is largely due to superior accumulation of physical and human capital" (World Bank 1993: 5).

At the time of its publication, the book was deemed important for explicitly incorporating some of the arguments made by proponents of industrial policy and for acknowledging a position previously considered beyond the pale of World Bank economic orthodoxy. However, in many respects, the publication does not go far enough in seeking to reconcile the undeniable achievements of state intervention with the neoliberal thrust of the dominant Washington consensus.

The study emphasizes the difficulty of getting industrial policy right as well as the special historical, political, and cultural circumstances of the Northeast Asian economic miracle, which enabled competent, meritocratic, and insulated technocracies to pursue industrial policy and thus strengthen legitimacy of the regime. It points instead to the Southeast Asian HPAEs' record of rapid growth and industrialization without industrial policy as more desirable and worthy of emulation than the model pursued by the Northeast Asian countries. Most important for the purposes of this chapter, the Bank study claims that, besides Hong Kong and perhaps Singapore, the Southeast Asian HPAEs achieved rapid growth and industrialization without resorting to industrial policy (Thailand) or by abandoning it in the mid-1980s (Malaysia and Indonesia).

The World Bank study concedes that directed credit contributed to the success of the Northeast Asian economies (Japan, Korea, and Taiwan). Some observers suggest that this was due to Joseph Stiglitz's authorship of the section on financing. Others claim that it was a necessary concession to the financiers of the World Bank study, namely Japan's Ministry of Finance.[1] In contrast, the report is more disparaging of the contribution made by trade-related industrial policy under the jurisdiction of Japan's Ministry of International Trade and Industry, a rival of the Ministry of Finance.[2]

The results of industrial policy in Northeast Asia are mixed, and the economic miracle cannot be attributed to other kinds of state intervention, such as government promotion of strategic industries. Using an extremely restrictive definition of industrial policy translated into a dubious methodology (see Chang 1994a), the Bank study concludes that the results of industrial policy in East Asia were limited and ambiguous at best.

The study thus argues that Indonesia, Malaysia, and Thailand "may show the way for the next generation of developing economies to follow export-push strategies" (World Bank 1993: 25). Unlike the Northeast Asian economies, the three Southeast Asian economies courted foreign direct investment (FDI) and created a favorable environment for exporters without resorting to financial repression and industrial targeting. Thus, the World Bank study claims, the Southeast Asian HPAEs grew rapidly by relying on market forces and minimal, but appropriate and generally supportive, functional interventions (mainly in the areas of primary education and infrastructure provision) without, or despite, bad strategic or selective interventions involving trade, finance, technology, and human resources to promote particular industries. The success of Malaysia, Indonesia, and Thailand is presented as proof that other developing countries do not need industrial policy to achieve rapid growth, industrialization, and structural change.

Southeast Asia is, of course, quite different from Northeast Asia (also see Booth 2001). The historical circumstances of Southeast Asia are different from those of post–Meiji Restoration Japan and its colonies of Korea and Taiwan. Certain industrial, educational, and administrative developments in the first half of this century were conducive to rapid industrialization and were quite distinct from those experienced in other former colonies. For example, more manufacturing activity developed in Japanese than in other colonies. With the possible exception of the Philippines under the United States, tertiary education developed much more in the Japanese colonies than in the European colonies. Also, the administrative ethos that evolved was meritocratic, nationalistic, and potentially pro-development.

Industrial relocation within the East Asian region contributed tremendously to the export-oriented manufacturing boom in the Southeast Asian HPAEs for almost a decade beginning in the mid-1980s. Much of this was driven by firm responses to changing domestic and regional conditions, including labor and other production costs as well as environmental, occupational health, and pollution regulation. There is considerable evidence that the pattern and pace of regional industrial restructuring in East Asia were not simply firm- or market-driven, but also very much influenced by Japanese, Taiwanese, Korean, and Singaporean industrial policies, which encouraged industries to relocate in Southeast Asia and China.

This chapter offers a different interpretation of the experiences of newly industrializing economies in Southeast Asia. It disputes some, though not all, of the World Bank's explanations for rapid growth and structural change in the region. It also reviews the historical and contemporary factors contributing to rapid economic development. There is little disagreement about the broad macroeconomic and other trends noted in the World Bank study. However, this chapter seeks to offer a more nuanced explanation, focusing on the nature of business-government relations and their implications for industrial policy, industrial capabilities, and the financial crises beginning in mid-1997.

DIFFERENCES WITHIN EAST ASIA

Before the more recent booms in Southeast Asia and China, attention focused on Japan and the newly industrializing economies of Hong Kong, Korea, Singapore, and Taiwan. With rapid economic growth in most of the economies in the Association of Southeast Asian Nations (ASEAN) since the 1970s, and in Vietnam as well since the late 1980s, there has been increased interest in the second-generation HPAEs (Indonesia, Malaysia, and Thailand) and further speculation and debate about the crucial factors responsible for the economic miracles in East Asia, including Southeast Asia.

The key question for other developing countries is whether the experience of the Southeast Asian HPAEs offers an attractive alternative to the strategy pursued by the Northeast Asian HPAEs. Has the development of certain manufacturing industries in the Southeast Asian economies resulted in the accumulation of local managerial and technological capabilities? Are their manufacturing sectors economic enclaves with little technological and managerial capabilities outside of foreign subsidiaries? If so, are they going to remain so in the future? Are the technological and managerial capabilities accumulated in foreign firms adequate to ensure continued industrial progress, whether or not foreign investors stay? What are the governments and the domestically controlled firms doing to ensure sustained growth and technological progress? If foreign investors move elsewhere (for example, to China and Vietnam), will the Southeast Asian economies be able to continue progressing industrially, especially technologically, particularly if they are still heavily reliant on foreign investors for capital, technology, and market access? It is quite possible that these countries are already accumulating adequate capabilities. If this is the case, it is crucial to ascertain the relative contributions that market processes and specific government policies are making to the development of these capabilities.

The Historical Context

The indexes of manufacturing sector growth in the Southeast Asian HPAEs conceal important differences with those of Northeast Asian economies (Chandrasekhar and Ghosh 2001). Besides having relatively lower economic growth, Southeast Asian HPAEs also have had relatively higher population growth, meaning that average living standards have risen more slowly. In the contribution of manufacturing to gross domestic product, the Southeast Asian HPAEs have performed well, but not as well as the Northeast Asian HPAEs. The share of primary commodities in exports has declined significantly. At least in gross aggregate terms, the Southeast Asian HPAEs seem to be progressing well on the path of industrialization, although somewhat behind the Northeast Asian HPAEs. However, these figures do not tell us much about the nature and process of industrialization, which requires closer scrutiny of the manufacturing firms, products, and processes involved.

Besides some raw material–processing and food-processing industries for which transport costs and related considerations are important, Malaysia and Indonesia had little experience with manufacturing during the colonial period. Korea and Taiwan experienced far greater industrialization under Japanese colonialism, which encouraged the growth of manufacturing. Also, Singapore's (limited) industrialization under colonialism preempted parallel developments in its Malaysian hinterland.

During the cold war, both Korea and Taiwan were strategically very important for the United States in its postwar confrontation with communist forces. Besides military support, successive authoritarian pro-U.S. regimes enjoyed tremendous economic support, which lowered the costs of food and wages, helped to develop human resources, and compensated somewhat for the huge costs of war and military preparedness. The cold war also stimulated rapid growth and industrialization, ostensibly to build an economic base against the communist threat.

The legacy of Japanese colonialism, the preeminence of refugee capital not based on landed interests, and the U.S. presence facilitated agrarian reforms in both Taiwan and Korea in the early 1950s. These reforms ensured more equitable distribution of land and agricultural income, raised agricultural productivity, and consolidated land-owning peasantries critical to maintaining stable regimes in what were still predominantly agrarian societies. Both Hong Kong and Singapore are urban societies, with negligible rural hinterlands. Hong Kong has long enjoyed the benefits of cheap food and other agricultural produce from China. Singapore has had a similarly beneficial relationship with the hinterland in other Southeast Asian economies. The absence of a rural hinterland within these economies has kept administrative, infrastructural, and other costs low.

The Southeast Asian HPAEs have not experienced major land reforms despite considerable investments in agricultural expansion and rural development. Peasants are hungry for land. Although expanding employment outside the peasant economy and rising agricultural productivity have reduced poverty, inequalities have continued in ownership as well as in access to land and incomes. Labor costs are low largely as a result of cheap rice prices.

It used to be presumed that an economy blessed with abundant natural resources would be more likely to develop. This view has been turned on its head to explain the success of the Northeast Asian HPAEs. Although they have strategic locations and deep-water natural harbors, both Singapore and Hong Kong lack significant hinterlands of their own. The natural resource endowments of Korea and Taiwan are also modest. So the view that natural resources constitute an advantage has been inverted to argue that since countries lack significant natural resources, their imperative to industrialize is that much greater. Consequently, the Southeast Asian HPAEs lagged behind because they lacked this sense of urgency. Southeast Asia's success at export agriculture and mining is said to have compounded this sense of complacency.

The contribution of resources to Southeast Asian growth cannot be overstated, even in Indonesia and Thailand, with their large populations. Resources have not only made important contributions to the accumulation of wealth as well as export growth but have also been crucial for fiscal viability. Governments have used the rents captured from resources to develop infrastructure, finance essential social services, and enhance the legitimacy and capacity of the regimes. These rents circulate within the national economy and contribute to national savings, accumulation, and investment.

Unfortunately, much of the natural resource wealth captured by states in Southeast Asia has been deployed inefficiently due to soft budget constraints, especially in Malaysia and Indonesia. The populations of Indonesia and Thailand are also large in relation to the resource rents captured. The expenditures on social welfare are minimal.

It is often maintained that the Northeast Asian economies have progressed because of deliberate government policies in education and training that are supported by cultural values. In contrast, although Malaysia has invested a great deal in education, much of this has been spent on tertiary education, especially abroad, with little emphasis on innovation, adaptation, and the development of skills at intermediate levels. The achievements of both Thailand and Indonesia have been far more modest than those of the Northeast Asian economies, as reflected in comparative literacy rates and levels of tertiary education.

Favorable economic conditions in the postwar "golden age" also contributed to the industrialization of the Northeast Asian HPAEs. During the 1950s and 1960s the expansion of international trade created tremendous opportunities for export-led growth. The transnationalization of manufacturing also created opportunities for industrialization. The General Agreement on Tariffs and Trade (GATT) created an international environment conducive to industrialization and the expansion of trade. Under the Generalized System of Preferences, exports from developing countries were subject to lower import duties and fewer restrictions in industrial countries (Aslam and Jomo 2001). Although world economic growth has slowed since the 1970s, global conditions have remained favorable to industrialization.

However, the resurgence of protectionism and the emergence of new international economic governance are creating less favorable circumstances. The extension of GATT's jurisdiction to foreign investments, the international trade in services and intellectual property rights, as well as the establishment of the World Trade Organization (WTO) have strengthened transnational corporate hegemony and imposed additional costs on new industrialization efforts, especially under the auspices of domestic capital. However, opportunities still exist within the emerging global economic environment. After the Southeast Asian recessions of the mid-1980s, recoveries were initially buoyed by improved prices for primary commodities, marked depreciations of their currencies, and foreign investments, especially in export-oriented manufacturing. However, the recent export growth of China, India, and other economies is constraining the options for all economies seeking to grow and industrialize on a similar basis (Rowthorn 2001).

There is, of course, an important pan–East Asian dimension (see Borrego, Bejar, and Jomo 1996) to much of the recent economic growth. Much of the region coincides with Japan's wartime Greater East Asian Co-Prosperity Sphere and perceived postwar sphere of influence. Rapid and sustained growth in much of East Asia also suggests significant economies of location. Besides transport and communication costs, as well as (mainly Chinese and Japanese) transborder business networks, less tangible considerations such as shared historical and cultural commonalities seem to be at work.

East Asia came to be perceived as the obvious external market for Japanese goods as its industry became more sophisticated and internationally competitive. Subsequent trade barriers set up by European colonial powers unwittingly encouraged subsequent military expansion. After the war, Japanese industrial recovery eventually sought external markets in the region, and Japanese firms sought to take advantage of the import-substituting industrialization strategies of most postcolonial regimes, especially in the 1960s. The subsequent relocation abroad of manufacturing by Japanese firms was accelerated by the yen appreciations occurring in the mid-1980s. Japanese firms increasingly became part of the export-oriented industrialization strategies of East, especially Southeast, Asia.

Foreign Direct Investment

Although the World Bank has been very concerned that economies remain open to foreign investment, the 1993 study does not address the significance, pattern, and consequences of foreign investment in the HPAEs. Restrictions on foreign investment have allowed internationally competitive domestic manufacturing firms to emerge in some

East Asian economies, often with state support. Such regulation also has increased the gains and reduced the losses to the national economy from the presence of foreign investment. The contribution of FDI to gross domestic capital formation among the HPAEs has been varied (see table 12.1). Of the eight HPAEs, only Malaysia and Singapore have relied extensively on foreign direct investment.[3] The role of FDI grew in both Singapore and Malaysia in the 1990s, as it did in China and India, where the contributions of FDI still are much closer to the East Asian average.

The greater use of FDI may be a transitory phenomenon characteristic of a relatively early phase of development, when domestic capital accumulation, technological capacity, and external market access are weak. For example, Korea relied less on FDI in the 1980s and 1990s than it did up to the early 1970s (Chang 1994b). Also, the importance of FDI at a particular historical moment may be largely due to the interests of foreign investors. For example, Indonesian efforts to adjust to the 1986 petroleum price collapse occurred just when Japan and the Northeast Asian economies were experiencing declines in their international competitiveness and were seeking to relocate their more labor-intensive and environmentally less acceptable industries. Such industrial relocation within the East Asian region can be seen as consistent with product-cycle explanations of FDI as well as the Japanese "flying geese" theory. However, the pattern and pace of regional industrial restructuring in East Asia has not been simply market-driven; it also has been very much affected by home- as well as host-country industrial policies that have encouraged industries to relocate abroad.

As shown in table 12.2, the currencies of all three Southeast Asian economies depreciated against the U.S. dollar around 1985, when the U.S. dollar depreciated dramatically against the Japanese yen and the currencies of the other Northeast Asian HPAEs (except Hong Kong, whose currency has been tied to the U.S. dollar since 1983). These currency depreciations reduced the relative costs of production, especially labor costs, in Southeast Asia as the more advanced East Asian economies experienced higher production costs (due to their currency appreciations), tight domestic labor market conditions, and other cost-raising domestic developments (high mandatory contributions to the Central Provident Fund in Singapore, growing industrial unrest in Korea, and increasing environmental protests in Taiwan).

Table 12.1 Foreign Direct Investment as a Share of Gross Domestic Capital Formation in the High-Performing Asian Economies, 1991–97 (annual averages)

Country	1991	1992	1993	1994	1995	1996	1997
Indonesia	3.3	3.6	4.3	3.8	6.7	8.8	6.9
Korea, Rep. of	1.0	0.6	0.5	0.6	1.1	1.3	1.8
Malaysia	22.8	26.0	20.3	14.9	11.0	n.a.	n.a.
Philippines	6.0	2.1	9.6	10.5	9.0	7.8	6.2
Singapore	33.7	12.4	23.0	35.0	26.0	21.7	n.a.
Thailand	4.9	4.8	3.7	2.4	3.0	3.2	7.2

n.a. Not available.

Note: Foreign direct investment includes equity capital, reinvested earnings, and other capital associated with various intercompany transactions between affiliated enterprises. Excluded are flows of direct investment capital for exceptional financing such as debt.

Source: Jomo and others (1997: table 2.1).

Table 12.2 Exchange Rate Movements in Select High-Performing Asian Economies, 1973–97 (national currency unit per U.S. dollar)

Year	Thailand	Malaysia	Indonesia	Japan	Republic of Korea	Singapore
1973	20.119	2.443	415.000	271.702	398.322	2.457
1974	20.374	2.407	415.000	292.082	404.472	2.437
1975	20.391	2.402	415.000	296.787	484.000	2.371
1976	20.399	2.542	415.000	296.552	484.000	2.471
1977	20.399	2.461	415.000	268.510	484.000	2.439
1978	20.265	2.316	442.050	210.442	484.000	2.274
1979	20.422	2.188	623.060	219.140	484.000	2.175
1980	20.587	2.177	626.990	226.741	607.432	2.141
1981	22.999	2.304	631.760	220.536	681.028	2.113
1982	22.999	2.335	661.420	249.077	731.084	2.140
1983	22.999	2.321	909.260	237.512	775.748	2.113
1984	25.556	2.344	1,025.900	237.522	805.976	2.113
1985	26.469	2.483	1,110.600	238.536	870.020	2.200
1986	26.199	2.581	1,282.600	168.520	881.454	2.177
1987	25.487	2.520	1,643.800	144.637	822.567	2.106
1988	25.209	2.619	1,685.700	128.152	731.468	2.012
1989	25.816	2.709	1,770.060	137.964	671.456	1.950
1990	25.114	2.705	1,842.810	144.792	707.764	1.813
1991	25.465	2.750	1,950.300	134.707	733.353	1.728
1992	25.387	2.547	2,029.920	126.651	780.651	1.629
1993	25.354	2.574	2,087.100	111.198	802.671	1.614
1994	25.011	2.624	2,160.800	102.210	803.450	1.527
1995	25.141	2.504	2,248.600	94.060	771.270	1.417
1996	25.487	2.516	2,342.300	108.780	804.450	1.141
1997	40.662	2.813	2,909.400	120.990	951.290	1.485

Source: World Bank, with the International Monetary Fund (various years).

Industrial Policies

Gerschenkron (1962) recognizes and emphasizes the role of the state in late industrialization in Europe in the nineteenth century. List (1841) and other theorists of the national economy recognize the implications of unlimited exposure to the international economy. Kalecki (1967) recognizes the nationalist potential of "intermediate regimes" established by anticolonial movements led by the middle class. Of course, economic nationalism, in itself, is no guarantee of political success. However, industrial policy can be an instrument of economic nationalism (Wade 1991), quite different from the usual focus on national ownership, management, or control of productive assets, especially those considered important for the international exercise of power (Johnson 1982). The states of East Asia have undertaken late industrialization as a nationalist economic project. Ethnic and cultural homogeneity has probably rendered nationalism a potent force in Northeast Asia. In contrast, in Southeast Asia, as in much of Africa and Latin America, nation-states were often the unintended by-products of European colonialism, and the resulting ethnic and religious heterogeneity weakened nationalist impulses and national capacities.

The elaboration of industrial policy in Northeast Asia was not shaped primarily by business interests. The Northeast Asian states have been credited with having capacity, coherence, and competence, particularly the ability to coordinate and discipline private firms and otherwise intervene in market processes without causing serious government failure. Effective decisionmaking depended on good consultation (see chapter 8, by Okazaki).

It is often claimed that success was due to the avoidance of capture or diversion of rents by rentier interests; however, there is considerable, mainly anecdotal, evidence of a great deal of corruption and rent seeking. A coordinating role by the state can overcome many collective action dilemmas. Governments capable of making and implementing appropriate proactive economic policies are able to create, deploy, and allocate rents to induce investments in state-designated priority areas. The prospect of capturing further rents has ensured that captured rents are invested in line with industrial targets set by the state (but see the elucidation of the Northeast Asian experience by Woo-Cumings in chapter 9).

The conditions for the emergence of such "relatively autonomous" states also have existed in Southeast Asia. Such circumstances have made it possible for regimes to undertake industrial policy. In Thailand, despite frequent changes in political regime, bureaucratic capacity and autonomy have facilitated some modest but fairly effective industrial policies by Southeast Asian standards, often compromised by the rentier activities of the military and politicians. In Malaysia, state intervention has been especially pronounced, particularly from the 1970s up to the mid-1980s, but much of it has been motivated or compromised by the priority given to interethnic economic redistribution exacerbated by rent-seeking activity of the politically influential (Jomo 1990; Gomez and Jomo 1999; Jomo and Gomez 1997, 2000). Unlike in Thailand, political continuity in Malaysia and Indonesia has been more pronounced in recent decades, facilitating more ambitious industrial policies. Unfortunately, these often have been motivated by grandiose ambitions rather than careful consideration. In Indonesia, government intervention seems to have been more influenced by rentier considerations, and this has undermined industrial policy initiatives.

Good intentions are not enough, and the possibility of getting industrial policy "wrong" is very real. Industrial policy instruments have been deployed more extensively in Northeast Asia than in Southeast Asia, so the issue is not really one of more or less industrial policy. Perhaps most important is that much state intervention in Southeast Asia has been for reasons other than industrial policy, mainly at the behest of politically influential business interests and interethnic redistribution. This is true primarily in Malaysia, but also in Indonesia. Insofar as such state intervention involves the manufacturing sector and many of the instruments, rationale, and rhetoric of industrial policy, it is easy to (wrongly) associate state intervention with, say, selective industrial targeting policies.

There also have been important recent instances of almost capricious selective industrial policy by the executive, with the technocracy having little say in its elaboration. This was the case with heavy industrialization in Malaysia in the early and mid-1980s (Edwards and Jomo 1993) and with high-tech heavy industrialization in Indonesia in the 1990s. Such efforts did not attempt to achieve international competitiveness or to provide support for other industries seeking to achieve international competitiveness, even in the long run. Such apparently arbitrary interventions have given industrial policy in Southeast Asia a bad reputation and have obscured other industrial policy interventions that have been conceived and sometimes implemented on more considered bases, such as the two (10-year) Malaysian Industrial Master Plans of 1986 and 1996 or the 1990 technology development policy.

Cultural Policies

In East Asia, cultural practices have consolidated and promoted trust as well as other social relations conducive to business coordination, cooperation, collaboration, or even collusion. These seem to have been crucial for the development of culturally distinctive business networks and industrial organizations that do not rely on the state. An example is the development of credit relations. The culturally distinctive business idioms that have developed appear to have reduced some transaction costs (legal documentation), while introducing others (entertainment, mutual help, and other expenses to reinforce links of obligation and reciprocity), generally reducing overall transaction costs, often by circumventing or evading state-designated requirements and procedures. More important, such cultural capital appears to have been crucial for promoting capital accumulation, especially in the face of uncertainty.

Thai, Malaysian, and Indonesian economic performance has been attributed to Chinese minorities (Yoshihara 1988), while Filipino underdevelopment has been blamed on official repression of the country's ethnic Chinese minority (Yoshihara 1995). This makes it difficult to explain recent Malaysian and Indonesian growth. Others have taken this view even further, arguing that ethnic discrimination against Chinese minorities has motivated much economic policy, affecting growth and industrialization in particular (Jesudason 1989; Bowie 1991; Yoshihara 1988, 1995). Such ethnic goals have undermined the ability of Southeast Asian states to assume the kind of leading role played by other East Asian economies. Thus the politically dominant indigenous ethnic elites have emphasized interethnic economic redistribution at the expense of policy agendas more conducive to late industrialization.

Chinese business networks are believed to have played a crucial role in much of the economic dynamism of Hong Kong, Taiwan, and the economies of Southeast Asia (Jomo 1997). This suggests the possibility that contemporary Chinese capitalism, at least in Southeast Asia, has distinctive institutions, norms, and practices. It is possible that such networks—often based on trust, despite Fukuyama's (1995) assertions to the contrary, and other noncontractual relations ostensibly based on fictive as well as real kinship—have reduced some transaction, information, and other costs as well as risks, and resolved some coordination and collective action problems not satisfactorily addressed by state intervention. Although there undoubtedly are statist rentiers among Chinese businessmen—the infamous bureaucrat capitalists in the Maoist lexicon—such wealth does not necessarily detract from or undermine further capital accumulation, especially if the state regulatory or corporate governance frameworks are conducive to further investment and accumulation. Capital accumulation by the Chinese is proceeding regardless of, or even despite, rather than because of state intervention. Consequently, the seemingly ethnically exclusive Chinese business networks are believed to be responsible for the success of Chinese business in Southeast Asia and elsewhere.

Business uncertainty in much of the region has been accentuated by the presence of hostile, alien, or simply unsupportive or unreliable states, whether colonial, nationalist, ethnically discriminatory, communist party–led, or predatory. Hence, a distinctly Chinese capitalism seems to have developed in response to perceived, if not real, hostility by the states in Malaysia and Indonesia. Even in Thailand, which was never formally colonized by any European power and where Buddhism is said to have allowed a greater degree of Chinese assimilation into the host society, anti-Chinese sentiment has been reflected in discriminatory economic policies. This was especially true during the early 1950s.

Some of the features of this Chinese capitalism, which have enabled it to thrive in adverse circumstances, also have limited the development of Chinese business enterprises. Business uncertainty stemming from such insecurity tends to encourage short-term commitments, which are generally inimical to the long-term commitments required for most productive investments, especially in heavy industry, high technology, and research and development (R&D), as well as for long-term investments such as brand-name promotion. Economic liberalization opens up new opportunities for capital outflows, encouraging capital flight in adverse circumstances. It is not surprising that Indonesian and other Southeast Asian Chinese buy real estate and otherwise invest in Singapore and elsewhere, not because the rates of return are particularly attractive, but because they want to balance their own investment portfolios.

The dominant role of ethnic Chinese business minorities in most Southeast Asian economies and the sustained boom in China since the 1980s have encouraged talk of a Chinese economic zone and renewed emphasis on Confucian ethical explanations of Chinese business success. This discussion ignores the often modest (and hence, unschooled and "uncultured") social origins of most first-generation immigrant Chinese businessmen in Southeast Asia and the clear anti-Confucian intellectual thrust of progressive Chinese intelligentsia since the May

Fourth Movement of 1919.[4] The blatant encouragement and privileging of "overseas Chinese" investments by the Chinese authorities have resulted in increased investments by Southeast Asian Chinese, leading to official disapproval as well as popular resentments—encouraged by ethnopopulist politicians—against Chinese economic dominance in Southeast Asia.

SOUTHEAST ASIAN FLYING GEESE?

Sustained growth and rapid industrialization in the eight high-performing Asian economies and deepening economic relations among them have encouraged notions of an East Asian model as well as growth process. In contrast, the World Bank (1993: vi) dismisses the notion of an East Asian model of development, positing instead that "rapid growth in each economy was primarily due to the application of a set of common, market-friendly economic policies."

Akamatsu's "flying geese" model was the development orthodoxy among Japanese economists and intellectuals in the early and mid-1990s (Akamatsu 1962). The basic idea is as follows. A "follower" country first imports a product from a more "advanced" country, then it produces the good for itself, and finally, it exports the product to other countries. A follower country ascends the technology ladder sequentially, learning to produce goods of increasing value, sophistication, and complexity. In trying to do so, it may protect infant industries and encourage new exports. The ranking of geese within this hierarchy may change as different national economies progress at different rates by developing new capabilities and new comparative advantages, creating a hierarchical, yet fluid, division of labor among economies.

The flying geese theory incorporates a product cycle theory emphasizing national location rather than firm control. It represents an alternative perspective to both the fairly static versions of vertical international divisions of labor (associated with nineteenth- and twentieth-century economic colonialism) as well as the horizontal divisions of labor involving specialization among economies ostensibly determined by comparative advantage. The competitors' positions shift constantly as each upgrades its industrial capacity and capabilities, although at different rates.

In the late 1950s and with U.S. encouragement, Japan's foreign policy in East Asia used war reparations, aid, and investment to secure a stable supply of resources for Japanese industry as well as to gain and expand market shares. In the 1960s, the flying geese theory came to be associated both with domestic industrial policy—phasing out sunset industries and supporting sunrise industries and technologies—as well as with Japan's East Asia policy (Korhonen 1994: 102). When external shocks, such as the two oil shocks of 1973–74 and 1978–79 and the later yen shocks of the 1980s and 1990s, forced Japanese industries to relocate abroad, the Japanese government worked with other governments to facilitate this transfer, changing the division of labor in East Asia.

Japan's East Asia policy increasingly influenced industrial policy in the region as Japan actively promoted industrial policy among its East Asian neighbors, often suggesting which industries to target. Japan's success also had a demonstration effect by showing that it is possible to industrialize and catch up technologically. East Asian governments were inspired to promote capital accumulation, industrialization, and productivity enhancement (Amsden 1995).

One of the great paradoxes of the flying geese theory is that if other Asian countries truly imitated Japan, they would limit foreign investment and keep domestic markets closed as long as desirable. As Nakatani Iwao argues, "If the entire world were to adopt the Japanese system, the world's markets would be closed and Japan's economic expansion would be stopped right there" (in Fallows 1994: 207). To the extent that East Asian governments have pursued protectionist policies for economic development, Japanese businesses also have been constrained in the region. To the extent that Japan has continued to keep its own market closed to Asian imports, it has failed to offer the external engine for East Asian development.

The World Bank's 1993 study cites openness to foreign direct investment as one feature that sets apart the economies of the southern tier of high-performing East Asian economies from those of the northern tier. Although extraordinarily important in Singapore and Malaysia, FDI has been closer to the developing-country norm both in Thailand and Indonesia and in the Northeast Asian economies (Chang 1994a). The World Bank study does not consider either the sources of foreign direct investment or its consequences for regional economic integration. Instead, it looks at the FDI policies of the Southeast Asian HPAEs as one aspect of their willingness and ability to conform to global trade regimes. Although it was possible for the Northeast Asian economies to use "unfair" tactics 20 or 30 years ago during their high-growth phases, such practices are no longer feasible, as the industrial countries are insisting that developing-country exporters play by the rules of the General Agreement on Tariffs and Trade and its successor, the WTO.

Since the 1960s, the Japanese government has played a leading role by informing, advising, supporting, and even coordinating the efforts of investors. Both the government and private sector agreed that East Asia could supply crucial raw materials, lower manufacturing costs, and rapidly growing new markets for Japanese industry. For Japan, then, regional investments and growth have been an extension of national industrial policy. The result has been regional economic integration, especially between the Japanese and other East Asian economies—a highly asymmetrical relationship (Rowthorn 2001).

Japanese investment has been a major factor in Southeast Asian growth since the late 1980s. As wages and other costs rose, investors in Japan and the other newly industrializing economies moved rapidly to their cheaper neighbors. After relatively weak growth in the early 1980s, all three Southeast Asian economies experienced rapid increases in gross domestic product and manufacturing growth after 1986. Meanwhile, Japanese investment in manufacturing soared in each of the economies. By 1991 Asia had surpassed the United States as Japan's major export destination. By 1993 Asia accounted for more of Japan's trade surplus than the United States. In 1994 Japanese investment in Asia grew to almost $10 billion, overtaking Europe to make Asia Japan's second-largest investment destination, after the United States.

Japanese corporations abroad, both big and small, keep in close touch with their government after they move offshore. Such collaboration seems to be particularly influential in East Asia. As Unger (1993: 159) puts it, "Ministry of International Trade and Industry officials in Southeast Asia have attempted to reproduce some of the instruments of industrial policy as practiced in Japan. It is consistent with the general Japanese perception regarding its economic assistance that in Japanese usage the term 'economic cooperation' encompasses not only grant aid and concessionary loans, but private loans and investment flows as well."

Phongpaichit (1990: 66–99) has documented the role that host-government policy played in attracting Japanese investment to Southeast

Asia in the late 1980s. In the 1990s host-government policies continued to adjust to new circumstances, problems, and opportunities. Authorities in Thailand and Malaysia made conscious efforts to be more selective in approving new foreign investments to cope with infrastructure bottlenecks, labor shortages, and the widespread impression that foreign investments were overheating their economies (Felker 2000). Indonesia, which did not experience quite the same overall increases in foreign investment as Malaysia and Thailand, launched a program in June 1994 to attract more foreign investment.

Host-government policies toward FDI have been very important. Since much FDI in Southeast Asia has sought lower labor costs, the pattern of FDI in these countries has been greatly influenced by labor market conditions, including wage and immigrant labor policies. Structural changes in Northeast Asia, including labor market conditions, also have been important for the changing pattern of FDI in Southeast Asia. Of course, other factors have influenced FDI inflows, such as the growth prospects of host-country markets, trade barriers, overall returns to capital, and exchange rate fluctuations. Japanese firms thus have played a key role in organizing regional production networks and in increasing intraregional trade flows. Since the second half of the 1980s, there has been increased product specialization in different locations—and countries—with the formation of closely knit regional supply networks involving flows of parts and components. East Asia has become a geographically distinct region in the global strategies of many Japanese transnational corporations.

Japanese and other Northeast Asian investments in Southeast Asia after 1985 gave a tremendous boost to the three newly industrializing economies in ASEAN—Indonesia, Malaysia, and Thailand. By the late 1980s, investment in the region from the four Northeast Asian HPAEs had collectively overtaken Japanese investment in quantity. However, since the early 1990s, Northeast Asian investors have been reducing new investments in ASEAN in favor of China and Vietnam. By the mid-1990s, Japanese investors did not seem to be investing much more in ASEAN than in the higher-labor-cost newly industrializing economies of Northeast Asia.

Have Japanese and other Northeast Asian firms replicated their national business practices and environments in their Southeast Asian host countries? There is very little evidence that Japanese companies have introduced more than superficial elements of Japanese industrial culture in their local subsidiaries (Jomo 1994). Many Japanese sub-contractors, who initially moved to Southeast Asia in response to requests or pressures from their *keiretsu* (linked-company) clients, have subsequently developed new business relations independent of the *keiretsu* system. The same seems to be true of Taiwanese and Korean firms in the region, for whom such relationships were not as strong in the first place.

In Southeast Asia, FDI in the 1970s was dominated by resource-oriented and labor-intensive industries. However, changes since the 1980s have significantly transformed the character of FDI. Currency appreciation, trade conflicts, as well as structural changes, such as in labor markets, have significantly changed the nature of Northeast Asian FDI in Southeast Asia. As FDI in Southeast Asia remains largely labor-intensive, it is no longer complementary to the factor endowments of host economies such as Malaysia and Thailand, which have been experiencing growing labor shortages and labor immigration from abroad.

Japanese government policies were formulated with an eye to widening Japanese influence and supporting Japanese capital. The Japanese government has become more assertive and self-confident in recommending industrial policy to Southeast Asian governments. The end of the *endaka* era—the era of the high yen—has seen a deepened and extended regional division of labor under corporate and government auspices, but formal regional integration has remained weak. Attempts to reproduce Japanese-style institutions and practices have had a mixed record. Although Akamatsu's original version of the flying geese hypothesis acknowledged the likelihood of bitter struggles over declining industries and import penetration, its latter-day reformulations often imply or even claim that for Japan's "followers" to catch up, they should privilege "benevolent" Japanese FDI and official development assistance, which are seen as purely complementary to domestic investments. These harmonious versions tend to ignore the contentious conflicts over key issues such as the terms of FDI as well as the upgrading of production activities and transfer of technology.

INDUSTRIAL POLICIES IN SOUTHEAST ASIA

The role of industrial policy instruments in the development of the Southeast Asian HPAEs, especially in the past three decades, is undeniable, although often problematic (Jomo and others 1997; Rock 2001a, 2001b). The role of governments in promoting industrialization beyond what would have been possible and likely without intervention is illustrated by the contrasts between the economies of Malaysia and Indonesia in the late colonial period and today. There is little doubt that the structural transformation and industrialization of these economies have gone well beyond what would have been achieved by relying exclusively on market forces and private sector initiatives.

In Thailand, Malaysia, and even Indonesia, government intervention was crucial for much of the successful development of agriculture and agroprocessing (Timmer 1991, 1993; Jomo and Rock 1997; Jomo and others 1997; Rock 2001a, 2001b). In Malaysia, for instance, the imposition of higher duties on exports of crude palm oil in the mid-1970s stimulated massive investments in refining capacity. Intense competition, specialization, and excess refining capacity soon resulted in rapid technical progress, taking Malaysian palm oil refining to the world technological frontier in barely a decade (Gopal 1999). Effective collective action with government support and coordination has seen rapid development of the Thai gem and jewelry industry (Siroros and Wannitikul 2001). Although problematic in economic welfare terms and grossly abused by Soeharto cronies, the mid-1980s' ban on log exports enabled Indonesia's plywood industry to break into the Japanese import market by the early 1990s (Jomo and others 1997).

Without government leadership, it is unlikely that Malaysia would have emerged from the 1970s as a major offshore site for electronics assembly. The state (federal and state governments) has played a crucial role in attracting foreign direct investments to particular locations by providing facilities and improving them in response to changing needs and requirements. Various incentives have been used to encourage foreign investors to transfer technology to Malaysian suppliers, who have gone on to develop their own capabilities (Rasiah 1999). The state government set up the very successful Penang Skills Development Centre, which helps employers to develop the technical capabilities of their employees, allaying their fear of worker poaching and free-rider problems. A well-connected Malaysian engineering firm that enjoyed privileged access to government-disbursed business opportunities appears to have used the rents so captured to enable it to compete internationally in new product markets (Alavi 1999).

Although Thailand carefully avoided the Malaysian national car development strategy (later emulated by the Soeharto government in Indonesia), the Thai government used government investments to foster the development of an automotive parts industry in the late 1980s. Whereas the Malaysian national car industry failed to become internationally competitive after more than a decade and a half of very high protection (at great cost to Malaysian car buyers), Thai automotive parts industries made more gradual, but nonetheless significant, gains in producing parts for assembly by the subsidiaries of foreign firms located in Thailand. Clearly then, the key issue should not be government intervention or not, although this is the current preoccupation. Instead, analytical concern should focus on appropriate government interventions in light of specific conditions and policy goals.

Conflicting or rival policy objectives are likely to undermine the commitment to and efficacy of industrial policy. Also, particular policies have specific consequences, some of which may be more compatible with industrial policy than others. For example, heavy investments by the Malaysian government in the 1970s to improve the quality of ethnic Malay human resources have contributed much more to enhancing industrial productivity than, say, the 1975 Industrial Coordination Act's requirement of at least 30 percent ethnic Malay ownership of enterprises beyond a certain size.[5]

Furthermore, the successful industrial policy experiences of Northeast Asia and Singapore were obscured from international attention by their political alignment with the West (particularly the United States), their continued reliance on price signals (including international markets), their export orientation, the limited role or profile of state-owned enterprises, and the greater earlier tolerance for, if not appreciation of, state intervention before the resurgence of neoliberal economic ideologies in the 1980s.

The initial recognition of these counterfactuals resulted in an almost euphoric reaction, reflected in slogans such as "getting prices wrong" (as opposed to the neoliberal insistence on "getting prices right"), blind faith in state intervention, and a tendency to see the late-industrializing East Asian economies as following a well-trodden path pioneered by Japan or some variation thereof. While emphasizing the common policies ostensibly practiced in East Asia, the World Bank (1993) study fails to recognize interconnectedness, as if geography, location, proximity, investment patterns, and trade partners do not matter. The study also fails to recognize the diversity of the HPAEs' experiences and policies (see Perkins 1994).

While agreeing that there is no single East Asian model of development, the World Bank report suggests that industrial policy has not contributed positively to the economic performance of the Southeast Asian HPAEs. This view is erroneous. Although the consequences of state intervention in the Northeast Asian HPAEs have been mixed, this is largely because much of that intervention has sought to accomplish goals other than accelerating late industrialization (see the discussion of Korea by Woo-Cumings in chapter 9). Such state interventions should be judged on their own terms, and specific negative consequences should not be taken to indict all state intervention nor all industrial policy.

The experiences of the Southeast Asian HPAEs with industrial policy offer several important lessons for other developing countries. Many such efforts may be constrained by the small initial size of domestic markets; the weaknesses of national industrial entrepreneurial communities, managerial expertise, technological capacity and capability, and international marketing networks; as well as domestic and external pressures to liberalize. Foreign investments and the temporary use of foreign human resources (such as consultants) have allowed Southeast Asian HPAEs to compensate for their own resource inadequacies. Host governments have a role to play in attracting foreign investments that maximize gains for the national economy, for example, investments that increase wages and enhance technology transfer. The leverage and bargaining power of host governments can often be enhanced by the presence of foreign investors from varied sources, in both different as well as competitive activities.

Most economies rely on existing comparative advantages to secure export earnings for industrialization, including primary commodity exports, resource-based manufacturing, tourism, and simple labor-intensive manufactures. But static considerations of comparative advantage may limit the options for pursuing a late-industrialization strategy. Precisely because static considerations only acknowledge gains from specialization given existing factor endowments, a more dynamic perspective is required to identify the factors needed to develop an economy over time. Nevertheless, static considerations of comparative advantage often require late industrializers to limit both the size and the duration of current welfare losses due to infant-industry protection, even though such losses may be recognized as a necessary and unavoidable price to pay.

During the early stages of industrialization, strengthening exports is usually better achieved with government support—in the form of information, coordination, marketing, finance, and incentives—rather than through market forces alone (Doraisami and Rasiah 2001). Sustaining export growth requires constantly acquiring greater technological capabilities—the main challenge of late industrialization. Although technological capacity may often be obtained through foreign investments or even foreign aid, foreign exchange earnings from exports are usually crucial for securing foreign technology (in the form of equipment, licenses, and training). This is necessary to accelerate industrialization through long-term technology acquisition, capacity building, and capability enhancement.

Developing international competitiveness requires continued—although changing and possibly diminishing—government protection and support, as suggested by the infant-industry argument. A well-designed infant-industry program—including temporary tariff protection, subsidies, human resource training, and other government support or mutual cooperation—should provide temporary support to an industry conditional on achieving realistic objectives—lowering unit costs and increasing exports—while gradually shifting such support to more sophisticated sunrise industries. This may involve a sequential process of infant-industry protection conditional on export promotion. Such gradual exposure to the international market has been important in Southeast Asia for ensuring productive efficiency, cost competitiveness, as well as product quality improvements. Although such sequential technological capability building is key to learning-by-doing, it does not negate the possibility that unnecessary steps or stages can be bypassed in the process of upgrading or enhancing technology.

In the Southeast Asian HPAEs, export-oriented labor-intensive manufacturing by foreign investors has not developed spontaneously with the availability of cheap labor, free trade, and foreign capital. Besides the provision of infrastructure and primary education, other supportive conditions and policies often have been decisive in attracting the foreign investments desired. Intervention is most likely to be needed in the following areas:

1. ***Trade.*** Companies may prefer not to compete in international markets if they can enjoy highly profitable domestic sales with protection. A company's optimum profit-maximizing level of output may require temporary costs and losses instead of a lower (but acceptable) rate of profit with less effort, cost, or risk. With market imperfections due to economies of scale, uncertainties, or both, it may be socially beneficial for the state to impose export targets in return for temporary protection in the domestic market. Thailand's Board of Investments restructured its investment incentives to favor export-oriented manufacturers by providing effective protection contingent on export promotion. Such conditional protection is critically different from the experiences of other countries with import-substituting protection in which infant industries were never able to compete internationally.

2. ***Finance.*** Companies tend to make insufficient long-term investments in production facilities since they require a higher profit rate than society (Chin 2001; Chin and Jomo 2001). Owing to market imperfections stemming from risk and uncertainty, long-term investment is likely to be smaller than socially desired unless the state underwrites it (Chin and Jomo 2001). While foreign investments, borrowings, and aid can augment investments, over the long run, national savings are generally the primary determinant of national investments (Matthias 2001). This poses problems in poor societies that consume most of their output, leaving very little for investment. As long as real interest rates are positive, the actual interest rate is less important for raising investment rates than are macroeconomic stability, rapid income growth, and restraints on luxury consumption. In East Asia, corporate savings are more important to investments than household savings (Akyuz and Gore 1994), suggesting that an environment conducive to reinvestment of firm profits would enhance the accumulation of savings.

3. ***Human resources.*** Because companies that spend money on training may not be able to recoup their costs, training is likely to be underfunded without state coordination. Although there is little dispute over recommendations for universal primary education, much more can and should be done to strengthen human resource development. The government often plays a major role in providing tech-

nical and vocational training as well as relevant secondary and tertiary education. Often, only the government is in a position to influence and coordinate the supply of and demand for different skills
and to anticipate human resource requirements in the medium and
long term.[6] Incentives should be offered to encourage in-house training, but when firms are reluctant to make such investments (for fear
that other firms will free ride on them), government will have to
step in, as the Malaysian authorities did with some success in the
1990s.

4. *Technology and marketing.* There is a strong chance that society
as a whole will gain if the state pays some of the costs of getting and
sharing information on technology (Jomo and Felker 1999). This
would reduce the likelihood that the cost of gaining information
about technology will be high relative to the benefits. Owing to
market imperfections, there are likely to be significant economies
of scale in the acquisition and dissemination of such information
(see Pack and Westphal 1986). Similar considerations are likely to
be important for international marketing, especially in the penetration of distant new markets, such as the market for generic products. An example is the marketing of Malaysian palm oil in India,
Russia, and China (Jomo, Felker and Rasiah 1999, especially Gopal
1999).

Furthermore, the government's supportive role should be ongoing
and not limited to initiating the industrialization process. An ongoing
role must be flexible enough to address new problems of market as
well as state failures and to adjust constantly to changing international
conditions. Market failures are usually understood in a static neoclassical sense, but the inability of markets to bring about desirable structural transformations—for example, to build new dynamic comparative advantage—is the most important reason for industrial policy.

After the mid-1980s, governments in Southeast Asia used industrial policy to respond to the new industrial policies of Northeast Asia.
This industrial policy responsiveness was probably more critical than
the supposedly "neutral" economic liberalization measures undertaken
in attracting the massive Northeast Asian industrial investments to
the region in the first place. Liberalization alone cannot explain the
upsurge of Northeast Asian—rather than other—industrial investments

in Southeast Asia because other parts of the world, such as Latin America and Eastern Europe, were pursuing industrialization as well.

The proliferation of growth triangles in Southeast Asia in the 1990s suggests that regionally coordinated industrial policy initiatives recognized and sought to gain advantage from economies of proximity and agglomeration as well as from international divisions of labor. Firms responded to new opportunities offered by regional rather than national comparative advantages by locating different processes in different neighboring countries. Such regional integration also was attractive to firms that stood to gain from regional economic cooperation, such as the ASEAN Free Trade Area. Small countries also gained by coordinating their industrial policy efforts so as not to undermine one another's efforts and not to reduce their leverage vis-à-vis external investors.

Industrial policy should favor and develop national capacities, especially human resources. Many social investments—such as education, housing, transport, and health—enhance labor productivity and contribute to industrial development by socializing costs and promoting social and political stability. Employers also should be induced to improve worker skills and working conditions as well as remuneration. Government can enhance the nation's capacity to absorb technology by supporting education and training. Malaysia's new Human Resources Development Fund—funded by employer contributions to be disbursed for employee training—is worthy of emulation if managed more effectively.

It is widely believed that Singapore's Central Provident Fund and Malaysia's Employees Provident Fund—both compulsory employee savings schemes—have raised national savings rates, especially household savings. Elsewhere among the high-performing East Asian economies, corporate savings have been more significant (Akyuz 1999). Although such high levels of forced savings have been widely criticized, they probably have reduced the social demands on governments to provide welfare facilities for retired workers (World Bank 1994). Both provident funds have provided governments, especially Singapore's government, with sources of relatively cheap funds with which to finance public development projects.

Hence, with the inflow of FDI to supplement the high domestic savings rates, the financing needs of both public and private sectors were largely met without resorting to foreign bank borrowings or portfolio capital inflows, until liberalization in the late 1980s led to considerable net inflows in the 1990s. The availability of such funds proved especially tempting for Thailand and Malaysia, which began running sizable current account deficits, increasingly financed by foreign portfolio investment and bank borrowing.

State capacities need to be improved even if the role of the state is to be trimmed. Despite the self-interested behavior of politicians, military officers, and bureaucrats in general, the contribution of competent and dedicated technocrats should not be dismissed prematurely. Unfortunately, criticisms of the role of government since the 1980s have demoralized state personnel in much of Southeast Asia. These criticisms have come largely from abroad, especially from the Anglophone world after the election of Margaret Thatcher in 1979 and Ronald Reagan in 1990 (for Malaysian examples, see Jomo 1995). Countries responded by reducing, but not eliminating, the role of government, with considerable deregulation, on the one hand, and privatization of state-owned enterprises, on the other.

State coordination of and support for concurrent investments in different, but related, industries may well be crucial to ensuring that a "big push" industrialization effort gets off to a viable start (Jomo, Khoo, and Chang 1997; Krongkaew forthcoming). Such industries would provide inputs and markets for one another. Although many government interventions have been abused and numerous state-owned enterprises have been badly run, privatization and deregulation have been problematic solutions, as suggested by the Malaysian experience (Jomo 1995). Harder budget constraints and managerial reforms are often desperately needed, but shock treatment privatization (as in Russia) is rarely necessary and often undesirable.[7] In both Singapore and Taiwan, the public sectors have not been significantly privatized, although their private sectors have grown ahead of the national economy, reducing the role of state-owned enterprises over time.

Following British tradition, the civil service is not as specialized in Malaysia as it is in Thailand and Indonesia. Calling for specialization should not be misunderstood as a plea that only economists should be involved in economic affairs. For example, the regular rotation of civil servants in Malaysia has undermined the accumulation of relevant experience and expertise, which comes with specialized career paths. The organization and efficiency of bureaucracies are also very important.

Poor planning and organization can adversely affect implementation, enforcement, and efficiency. Government bureaucracies tend to become moribund and resistant to change, which partly explains the popular enthusiasm for the organizational and managerial reforms usually accompanying privatization.

The argument for a more balanced assessment of the contribution of industrial policy to late industrialization in the Southeast Asian HPAEs does not suggest that all industrial policy in the region has been the best possible or even consistently desirable. There have been many instances of bad industrial policy, but the existence of bad industrial policy is not proof that all industrial policy has been bad. Many of the structural transformations occurring in the region would not have taken place without industrial policy. Good industrial policy is needed. The circumstances in which industrial policy may have been bad also offer important lessons for how industrial policy should and should not be developed. Such lessons can be learned by the governments of other developing countries, most of which are sufficiently accountable and constrained by fiscal and other resources to want to avoid "heroic" failures.

Many mistakes were made in the past, and many industrial policy interventions had objectives other than industrial promotion. Indeed, some interventions clearly were in the interests of or were "captured" (abused) by politically influential groups or individuals. Ill-conceived industrial policy has at least some of the following characteristics:

- It is not based on a sound analysis of the market failures it was supposed to overcome.
- It does not address specific market failures or maximize the positive externalities from developing certain strategic industries.
- It ignores market signals in trying to achieve efficiency.
- It underestimates the information needed for effective interventions
- It overlooks the limited capacities, competencies, and capabilities of the government.
- It overestimates the human and other resources available to build efficient industries.
- It disregards efficiency, scale, and other considerations.

State interventions should address specific problems of market failure in realizing long-term industrial objectives. Careful analysis—detailed cost-benefit evaluations of industrial incentives—is a prerequisite for formulating efficient and effective industrial policy. It is important to analyze and understand not just the effective levels of protection but also the activities that take place behind protective barriers. Detailed analysis is essential because state intervention may be a necessary, but is certainly not a sufficient, condition for rapid industrial growth.

Industrial policy in East Asia has placed less emphasis than the old-style postcolonial economics of the intermediate regimes on state ownership and central planning, although the size of the public sector in Taiwan, Singapore, Malaysia, and Indonesia is considerable by international standards. Many instruments of industrial policy deployed in the region have used market mechanisms and signals. Rather than strive for "perfect competition," they have held private monopolies in check by ensuring intense oligopolistic or imperfect competition ("contests") or by disciplining exposure to the international market. Some East Asian governments also have been concerned with achieving economies of scale or scope and avoiding excessive or wasteful cutthroat competition.[8] For example, as Korea liberalized in an effort to secure entry into the prestigious Organisation of Economic Co-operation and Development (OECD), such regulation was undermined, resulting in significant buildup of excess capacity in certain manufacturing sectors. This would have been avoided under the regime of limited contests acknowledged by the World Bank volume (Chang 1999).

The discussion in this section has highlighted important differences between the HPAEs in the two East Asian regions, especially regarding the motivations for and nature of government interventions. These differences have significant implications for the sustainability of growth and structural change, particularly industrialization, in Southeast Asia. They also call into question the characterization of the Southeast Asian experience as one of high growth with minimal industrial policy. Ultimately, it challenges the claim that economic liberalization is a more desirable, more feasible, and more easily emulated alternative for other developing and transitional economies than the Northeast Asian experience of rapid growth and structural change accelerated by industrial policy.

INVESTMENT POLICIES IN SOUTHEAST ASIA

The economic crises of 1997–98 have led to significant changes in economic policy in Southeast Asia (Montes 1998; Jomo 1998). Although short-term considerations (International Monetary Fund [IMF] emergency credit conditionalities, efforts to restore market confidence, and the urgent desire to stimulate recovery) have shaped many recent reforms, the inexorable thrust toward economic liberalization has been bolstered by an expanding corpus of multilateral rules and policy directions promoted under the auspices of the WTO, APEC (Asia Pacific Economic Cooperation), and ASEAN. To many observers, these changes signify the demise of government intervention. However, such pronouncements may be premature, as there is still considerable evidence that crisis-affected governments are continuing to promote and shape economic growth, development, and industrialization (for example, NEAC 1998). The following brief review of some recent trends in investment policy (drawn heavily from Felker and Jomo 1999) suggests that government interventions continue to be important. Parallel policy adjustments have occurred in the areas of international trade, finance, infrastructure, and human resource development.

The aftermath of the crisis has seen the reduction—if not the elimination—of barriers to foreign investment in previously protected sectors. Having surrendered some of their discretionary powers to regulate entry into key economic sectors, Southeast Asian governments must now let global markets reshape their industrial sectors according to their (inherent) comparative advantages. Although the scope in Southeast Asia for old-style industrial policy has been greatly reduced, the region's governments do not necessarily have to stop trying to influence investment trends. Governments have been paying more attention to the nature and quality of investments and encouraging the development of domestic technological capabilities and skills.

Seen against the policy priorities of the 1990s, the postcrisis investment policy reforms are less drastic than they may seem. The Thai, Malaysian, Filipino, and Indonesian governments began to liberalize investment gradually during the decade-long boom preceding the collapse of 1997–98; arguably, some even developed new approaches to investment promotion (UNCTAD 1998). In this period, Southeast Asian governments balanced infant-industry policies in certain sectors while promoting new export industries, usually with foreign direct investment. They promoted FDI inflows into export-processing zones and licensed manufacturing warehouses by providing special exemptions from tariff protection for inputs and investment rules for sectors not for export (Rasiah 1995). The authorities also tried to foster linkages with the domestic economy and to enhance transfers of technology from transnational corporations to domestic producers.

Undoubtedly, the crises forced most governments to put on hold policies to upgrade industrial technologies. For the time being, all kinds of investments are being used to accelerate economic recovery. Changes are more evident in some countries than in others, but adjustments in the immediate aftermath of the crises are likely to give way to further reforms as recovery is consolidated and governments pay greater attention to sustaining development in the medium term.

To a greater or lesser extent, investment policies before the crisis embraced new priorities, instruments, and institutional frameworks. Two major themes became important for policy. First, investment policies recognized the growing globalization of production involving international operations by transnational corporations themselves. Instead of aiming for nationally integrated and controlled industries, governments sought to position national economies to maximum feasible advantage within the corporations' own international divisions of labor. Infrastructure and policy support were oriented to ensuring locational attractiveness, as governments modified their incentives to attract particular activities, such as management, procurement, logistics, R&D, and design.

The shift from policies to support infant industry toward policies to attract export-oriented transnational corporations had earlier distinguished the Southeast Asian HPAEs from the other high-performing Asian economies as well as other developing countries. Acceptance of transnational corporation–led integration into regional and global systems of production distinguished the ASEAN-4 from their late-industrializing predecessors, Japan and Korea. Meanwhile, Taiwan's industrial capabilities enabled it to define unique terms of engagement with transnational corporations. Although the other East Asian HPAEs also have drawn heavily on foreign technology, they have done so on terms in line with limiting foreign ownership of industry to promote domestic industrial capital. Both Korea and Taiwan initially invited foreign investment in order to enter new export-oriented industries such as electronics, but they restricted FDI over time while accessing foreign technology through licensing (Mardon 1990; Dahlman and Sananikone 1990).

Southeast Asian efforts to promote indigenous industrialization have been more limited and generally less successful. Thailand, Malaysia, and Indonesia all have resource-based industries that can compete internationally, while Thailand probably has the most internationally competitive light manufacturing industries. But Southeast Asia's export-led growth boom before the crisis was driven mainly by massive foreign investments from Japan and the other first-generation newly industrializing economies in East Asia, with North American and European investors joining later (Jomo and others 1997: ch. 3). Alarmist predictions that footloose FDI would render the region's growth ephemeral have proven to be largely unfounded, except in the case of relatively small Taiwanese investments during the early 1990s. However, passive reliance on foreign capital and technology inflows will generate little more than direct employment.

Consequently, greater attention has been given to the dynamic effects of new investment projects, even extending to matters such as market access, technology transfer, and human resource development. Such considerations for evaluating investment performance became far more important during the decade-long boom before the 1997–98 crises. While capital formation, employment generation, and foreign exchange earnings did not become irrelevant, governments did become more selective in their efforts to promote investment, largely with a view to maximizing value added and positive externalities over time. The new emphasis on investment externalities has, in some countries, shifted the objective of investment promotion policies from particular industries to industrial clusters of complementary assembly, component production, and producer-service activities. Emphasis has shifted from maximizing new green-field FDI in export-oriented industries to encouraging reinvestment by established producers in deepening their local operations, upgrading skills, forming domestic economy linkages, and gaining a larger share of their parent companies' global operations.

To varying degrees, the other Southeast Asian HPAEs have sought to emulate their regional neighbor, Singapore, which initiated its "second industrial revolution" after achieving full employment in the late 1970s and, beginning in 1986, sought to establish itself as the best location for the regional headquarters of transnational corporations (Rodan 1989). Unlike Taiwan and Korea, Singapore adopted an FDI-led path to export-oriented industrialization in the late 1960s, partly for political reasons (Rodan 1989). Yet, despite its desire for foreign investment, Singapore is not opposed to government intervention. The Singaporean state has shaped the investment environment by providing a range of facilities, infrastructure, subsidies, and complementary public investments (Low 2001; Wong and others forthcoming). Although its circumstances are very different from those of its neighbors, Singapore's experience clearly demonstrates that the scope for proactive investment policy in a liberal ownership regime is much greater than commonly presumed.

As investment policy goals have shifted, policy instruments have changed accordingly. Negative restrictions, such as foreign ownership limits and local content requirements, have been or are currently being phased out in most sectors, although significant exceptions remain. Tax holidays also have become less important insofar as most governments offer them to varying degrees. Instead, some governments have begun providing infrastructure and services designed to enhance their investment environments, attract desired investments, and induce positive externalities such as (a) one-stop facilitation of administrative approvals, (b) provision of specialized physical, customs-related, and technical infrastructure, (c) support for labor procurement and skills development, (d) matching of investors with local suppliers, and (e) other services relating to investors' routine operations, such as immigration, customs, other tax services, and the trouble-shooting of administrative problems with other government bureaucracies.

Implementation of these new investment policies has involved daunting political and administrative challenges, requiring government investment agencies to develop *greater* expertise and flexibility rather than a sector-neutral and passive policy stance. Reshaping national investment environments in line with new investor demands requires understanding the great variation within particular industries, the logistical needs and strategic concerns of transnational businesses, and the rapidly changing international investment environment.

Changing the main task of investment policy from *regulation* to *promotion* and now *service* requires changing often deeply entrenched institutions and organizational cultures within the relevant bureaucracies. Hence, new investment policies have often involved creating new specialized agencies, authorities, and administrative zones.

The new investment policy direction has had to respond to and cope with important challenges. Most important, the operations of relatively sophisticated transnational corporations have had limited impacts on the production linkages, skill formation, and other externalities of host economies, ostensibly because of limited domestic "absorptive capacity," resulting in the inadequacy of skills and other technological capabilities. Clearly, FDI alone cannot ensure the development of capabilities, as is often presumed. Instead, dynamic externalities from foreign investment are more likely in host environments with appropriate skills, infrastructure, and supplier and technical capacities. In less-conducive investment environments, export-manufacturing FDI may not generate the desired consequences, remaining primarily low-skill, import-dependent enclaves, as in Mexico.

This situation poses difficult challenges for countries with weak skill endowments, particularly related to engineering. For them, foreign investment is expected to catalyze industrial development, but these countries have limited complementary capabilities to offer. They have few technologically advanced producers able to integrate easily into the international supply chains of transnational corporations. Similarly, the efforts of transnational corporations to develop internationally integrated production specializations may constrain host-country efforts to promote domestic linkages and spillovers. Although some transnational corporations have begun to devolve functions like procurement, marketing, design, and even R&D to their Southeast Asian operations, certain functions remain centralized in regional headquarters in Singapore or Hong Kong. Most subsidiaries in other Southeast Asian countries lack the authority to make important decisions in close proximity to a regional headquarters. As a consequence, they may not even have the independence to develop new supply sources for anything other than the simplest components. These challenges point to the potential scope for policy initiative by governments and private entrepreneurs in enhancing the gains from FDI under a liberal investment regime. However, government efforts to foster linkages, skill formation, and technology spillovers have met with considerable difficulties thus far.

Investment policy regimes are usually seen as lying somewhere along a continuum from the restrictive to the more liberal and incentive-neutral, with the analytical focus on regulations that shape entry barriers. From this perspective, the main trend since the mid-1980s has been the relaxation of restrictive regulations on foreign ownership. So-called trade-related investment measures—like local content, foreign exchange balancing, and technology transfer requirements—also have been relaxed. However, three issues have compromised this regional trend toward open investment regimes.

First, liberalization has occurred unevenly across sectors and countries. Although general investment barriers have been relaxed, the remaining restrictions have become more significant, sending clearer signals about policy priorities and concerns. Next to Singapore, Malaysia has the most open investment regime, allowing wholly foreign-owned firms to operate in the export-oriented manufacturing sector with minimal restrictions. However, following the crises, Thailand and Indonesia have opened their financial and other services to foreign mergers and acquisitions, while Malaysia has liberalized more cautiously in this regard.

Second, exemptions from (national) equity ownership requirements in the Southeast Asian HPAEs usually have been tied to exports and sometimes to other more specific policy goals. For example, unlimited foreign ownership was allowed in export-oriented industries, but not for import-substituting production. Integration into the global economy in the 1980s and 1990s did not involve incentive neutrality and market-determined specialization. Instead, government initiatives responded to new opportunities offered by new strategies of firms responding to the globalization of industrial production.

Third, Southeast Asian HPAEs have used investment *subsidies* such as tax holidays, exemptions, and deductions rather than entry restrictions (Felker and Jomo 1999). Incentives have been used to promote particular industries or to impose specific performance requirements. Such subsidies have been conventionally viewed as due to (socially inefficient) competition among prospective host governments. Nevertheless, they have enabled host economies to promote certain industries to some advantage if investment externalities exceed subsidy costs, for example, due to scale or agglomeration economies. It also has been argued that investment incentives compensate transnational corporations for their search costs and extra risks involved in transferring advanced production activities to new locations (UNCTAD 1998: 97–106). Generally, governments in the region have used investment incentives to signal their commitment to attracting and retaining investors. Unlike investment restrictions and direct export subsidies, many investment subsidies are not proscribed by existing WTO provisions.

Investment subsidies have been addressed in recent years by the prospect of a multilateral investment policy regime. First mooted unsuccessfully as part of the GATT Uruguay Round initiative on trade-related investment measures, another unsuccessful attempt was made through the OECD's Multilateral Agreement on Investment. The WTO's Working Group on the Relationship between Trade and Investment is drafting a Multilateral Investment Agreement. If successful, such discretionary investment subsidies and other promotional measures will deprive developing countries of crucial policy tools in an increasingly challenging globalized investment environment. Current reform programs, as prescribed by the IMF, exclude a priori the possibility that government investment policies can encourage technology transfer, linkage formation, skill development, and other externalities. An important requirement for sustainable recovery is stronger expertise and more flexibility in public agencies overseeing industrial development. In the wake of the East Asian crises, the IMF has urged or even required countries to dismantle or reduce such subsidies. However, as they lose some policy instruments for promoting and shaping industrialization, Southeast Asian countries will need to retain and hone the remaining instruments in order to cope with new challenges.

A country's comparative advantage as a location for production linked to transnational corporations increasingly depends on factors that affect those corporations' costs and competitive advantages. Besides political stability and investment security, transnational corporations are increasingly concerned about the quality of physical infrastructure and administrative systems, skill endowments, and proximity to quality suppliers. Host governments require considerable public expertise, institutional flexibility, and judicious investments in skill and technical capacities to ensure a mutually advantageous investment environment.

Authorities will undoubtedly continue to seek new ways of encouraging industrial and technological progress. Overcapacity in several manufacturing sectors and slow recovery in Japan probably mean that the new manufacturing FDI will not quickly resume the dizzying rates in the decade before the crisis. More worrying is the shift in FDI flows toward mergers and acquisitions and away from new green-field investments or even reinvestments of profits. Such trends have important implications for the development of industrial and technological capabilities. While facilitating investments has become central to recovery throughout the region, the new situation also poses significant downside risks. For example, opportunities for more value added activities, such as design and R&D, may be constrained by the new strategies and internal organization of transnational corporations.

It is unlikely that nuanced proactive investment policies will continue to shape new investment trends for other reasons as well (Ernst 1998). The region's opening to export-oriented FDI in the past did not result in the same sort of industrial linkages and technology development found in Taiwan and Korea because of poorer policy, weaker institutional support, and fewer capabilities. Whatever the potential advantages of mergers and acquisitions, it is unlikely that these will be fully realized without appropriate institutional support, skills, policy incentives, and the ability to extract and capture rents.

Building new investment-management capabilities continues to face formidable difficulties. Assisting governments to regulate foreign investment is low on the agenda of the powerful international financial institutions as well as most domestic reformers. In Indonesia, the desire to restore investor confidence is likely to constrain government policy activism for some time. Although there are some signs of emerging public-private coordination in fostering skills and technology development in Thailand, some of the indigenous industrial capacities built up in recent years have been lost with the financial liquidation of many manufacturers. Mahathir's rejection of orthodox prescriptions for economic restructuring in Malaysia has mainly protected financial and other nonmanufacturing interests. Although the government retains important policy instruments, efforts to revive growth in the short term have forced Malaysia to liberalize its de facto investment policy regime.

Prospects for rebuilding investment-management capacities also have been clouded by current multilateral efforts to proscribe discretionary government interventions and regulations affecting investment flows. Establishing a multilateral investment regime even more restrictive of national government initiative may reduce the potential for abuses of investment policy. The main effect will be the loss of an important tool for fostering long-term industrial development.

PROSPECTS

Since mid-1997, the sustainability of the growth and industrialization processes in Southeast Asia has been in grave doubt. Unlike the Northeast Asian economies, the Southeast Asian HPAEs have been far more dependent on foreign investment. Although only Singapore and Malaysia stand out statistically in the proportion of FDI in total investment, much of the export-oriented, nonresource-based, export-oriented manufacturing in all three Northeast Asian HPAEs is owned and controlled by foreigners. Although the Northeast Asian economies of Japan, Korea, and Taiwan also have foreign investment, their governments have been far more selective and restrictive. Their levels of foreign direct investment are well below the average for developing countries (around 5 percent). Instead, these economies have emphasized the development of national (not necessarily state-owned, except perhaps in Taiwan) industrial, technological, marketing, and related capacities. In contrast, most rentier entrepreneurs in Southeast Asia have continued to capture rentier opportunities (often based on political and other connections), rather than develop the new capabilities desperately needed to accelerate late industrialization.

There is a real danger that Southeast Asian economies will lose their earlier attractiveness as sites for foreign direct investment, and their indigenous capabilities seem to be inadequate to sustain internationally competitive export-oriented industrialization in its absence. Foreign investors can choose among alternative investment sites in line with overall firm strategies, domestic market prospects, infrastructure and other support facilities, incentive and tax regimes, relative resource endowments, comparative production costs in the short and medium term, as well as other considerations of likely competitive advantage.

With limited indigenous capabilities and the irrepressible industrial-ization of China and, more recently, India, the Southeast Asian HPAEs, including Malaysia and Thailand, are less attractive than they used to be.

There is little evidence that the massive devaluation of the crisis-affected Southeast Asian economies will support sustained growth. For some analysts, the crisis was precipitated by the collapse of Thai ex-port growth (and the related slowdown in output growth) after the Chinese renminbi devaluation in 1994 and the U.S. dollar apprecia-tion in mid-1995. The crisis beginning in mid-1997 saw the deprecia-tion of all crisis-affected currencies, leaving Southeast Asian econo-mies (including Thailand's) a little more cost-competitive, but only in relation to those economies that did not experience currency depre-ciations. They did not become more competitive in comparison with their neighbors, often their main competitors.

In the immediate aftermath of the crisis, palm oil prices rose, help-ing to alleviate the worst impact of the crisis. However, vegetable oil prices generally collapsed with the bumper soybean harvest of mid-1999. Fortunately for Malaysia and Indonesia, petroleum prices rose strongly in 1999 and into 2000, but again, there is no evidence that commodity prices increased as a result of the depreciated currencies. The strong upswing in the electronics business cycle since 1998 also has helped the region, especially Malaysia, with the share of electron-ics in Malaysian manufactured exports rising from below 60 percent before the crisis to more than 70 percent. But again, there is little evidence that higher demand for electronics is mainly due to lower production costs owing to the weaker currencies. On the contrary, some observers have argued that increases in Malaysian electronics output and exports have been below those of the industry as a whole, and even below those of neighboring Singapore, which experienced less drastic currency depreciation.

More worrying, there is considerable evidence that commodity prices have decreased in recent years, including the prices of most primary as well as manufactured commodities. There is now consid-erable evidence of significant price deflation for generic manufactured goods, which are subject to ineffective entry barriers, in contrast with industries that are subject to effective entry barriers as a result of en-forceable intellectual property rights. This divide is characterized by a race to the bottom for the former as lower prices (and cheaper currencies) transfer economic gains from the producers (workers and contract suppliers) to the oligopolies commanding market shares and to consumers (in the form of lower consumer prices; Kaplinsky 1999).

Before the 1997–98 crises, Thailand and Malaysia were already experiencing full employment with significant labor shortages; estimates of the presence of foreign workers in both economies in the late 1990s ran into the millions. It is widely believed that this presence was tolerated, if not encouraged, by the authorities, especially in Malaysia, as the governments wanted to remain competitive in low-wage economic activities such as plantation agriculture. Thus labor immigration discouraged industrial upgrading and limited indigenous Malaysian technological capabilities, further exacerbating the problem of inadequate industrial capabilities to sustain more rapid industrialization and technological progress (Edwards 1999).

Although the first phase of economic recovery in the region may be rapid as existing capacity is more fully utilized, the decline of new, especially green-field, investments in the crisis-affected economies since the mid-1990s is cause for concern. Malaysia, for example, has experienced three consecutive years of declines in investment approvals since 1996, although investment approvals have exceeded applications in recent years (Jomo 2001a). Also of concern is the apparent shift of investments from manufacturing for export to production for domestic consumption, particularly of nontradables, contributing to asset price bubbles and increasing the vulnerability of the financial sector as a whole. Malaysia has successfully held down interest rates since September 1998, but loan growth has fallen far short of the central bank's target of 8 percent for 1998 as well as 1999. The share of bank credit going to manufacturing, agriculture, and mining also has declined significantly, while loans for property and share purchases have been encouraged once again and now account for even larger shares of new loans than before the crisis.

There is a real possibility that, while economic recovery during 1999 will continue into 2000 and beyond (World Bank 1998), growth may begin to sputter as existing capacity becomes fully utilized and new investments are not forthcoming, at least at the same levels as those preceding the crisis (Rasiah 2001; Yoshihara 1999). The changed international situation does not augur well for the Southeast Asian

HPAEs, which have grown rapidly in recent decades but have been unable to sustain the momentum of manufacturing growth.

NOTES

1. The report pays surprisingly little attention to the mobilization and deployment of savings, which have been primarily responsible for the region's high investment rates, rapid growth, and structural transformation. As Akyuz and Gore (1994) have pointed out, the high savings rates in East Asia primarily involve corporate—rather than household—savings, that is, savings out of profits. This suggests the existence of regulatory and institutional frameworks that encourage such savings and investment behavior—instead of, say, high levels of dividend payments to shareholders.

2. The study claims that Northeast Asian success was largely due to their ability to switch from distorting import substitution to allegedly nondistorting export-oriented industrialization. Wade (1991) has described an interesting variation of this "free market" argument as the "simulated free market" thesis (Little 1981; Bhagwati 1988). According to this view, the distorting effects of import substitution in Korea were sufficiently negated by, and hence compensated for by, the same government's export promotion and subsidization efforts.

3. After seceding from Malaysia in 1965, the Singapore authorities deemed it crucial to attract foreign investment to ensure a continued international stake in the security and future of Singapore, even at the expense of discriminating against predominantly ethnic Chinese domestic capital (Rodan 1989). In Malaysia, influential elements in the ethnic Malay–dominated regimes have favored foreign investment to limit and circumvent the expansion and accompanying influence of ethnic Chinese Malaysian capital (Jesudason 1989; Bowie 1991).

4. Progressive Eastern modernizers (the Chinese May Fourth Movement of 1919) as well as Western analysts favoring cultural explanations, among others, have blamed Confucianism for the past economic backwardness of the Chinese. Western anthropologists, sociologists, and others used to explain East Asian—and particularly Chinese—poverty in terms of Confucian and other supposedly regressive values. By the 1980s, however, the situation had been reversed, with an almost naive celebration of the ostensibly Confucian basis for the Japanese miracle and the success of the East Asian economies (Morishima 1982). Culturalist explanations have since been touting Confucianism as the common cultural element responsible for the economic miracle in East Asia. Most Chinese have never reduced their mixed cultural heritage, including Daoism, Buddhism, and other influences, to Confucianism, often considered a reified Western culturalist construct. Also, while acknowledging the profound impact of Chinese culture on their own cultures, few Japanese and Koreans have reduced this influence to Confucianism. Nevertheless, with the hegemonic influence of Western academia, a generation of culturalists has been engaged in rediscovering Confucianist influences throughout East Asia, often to the bemusement of East Asians themselves.

5. This finding is especially relevant to developing economies seeking to reconcile redistribution policies with growth objectives.

6. Governments, however, have a tendency to overemphasize formal education, while neglecting the significance of work experience and training on the job.

7. Organizational flexibility and incentive reform have been important in ensuring the good performance of public enterprises in Singapore and elsewhere.

8. In this regard, important negative lessons can be drawn from Malaysia's failure to regulate the market entry of firms into the rubber latex gloves and condoms markets in response to the AIDS scare in the late 1980s and the licensing of nine cellular telephone companies in the mid-1990s. In both instances, the result was wasteful excessive competition.

REFERENCES

Akamatsu, K. 1962. "A Historical Pattern of Economic Growth in Developing Countries." *Developing Economies* 1(March-August):3–25.

Akyuz, Yilmaz, ed. 1999. *East Asian Development: New Perspectives*. London: Cass.

Akyuz, Yilmaz, and Charles Gore. 1994. *The Investment-Profits Nexus in East Asian Industrialization.* Discussion Paper 91. Geneva: United Nations Conference on Trade and Development.

Alavi, Rokiah. 1999. "Rents, Technological Innovation, and Firm Competitiveness in a Bumiputra Malaysian Firm." In K. S. Jomo, Greg Felker, and Rajah Rasiah, eds., *Industrial Technology Development in Malaysia*, pp. 329–59. London: Routledge.

Amsden, A. H. 1995. "Like the Rest: Southeast Asia's 'Late' Industrialization." *Journal of International Development* 7(5):791–99.

Aslam, Mohamed G. H., and K. S. Jomo. 2001. "Implications of the GATT Uruguay Round for the Malaysian Economy." In K. S. Jomo and Shyamala Nagaraj, eds., *Globalisation versus Development: Heterodox Perspectives*. Basingstoke: Palgrave.

Bhagwati, Jagdish. 1988. "Export-Promoting Trade Strategy: Issues and Evidence." *The World Bank Research Observer* 3(January):27–57.

Booth, Anne. 2001. "Initial Conditions and Miraculous Growth: Why Is Southeast Asia Different from Taiwan and South Korea?" In K. S. Jomo, ed., *Southeast Asia's Industrialisation*. Basingstoke: Palgrave.

Borrego, John, A. Alvarez Bejar, and K. S. Jomo, eds. 1996. *Capital, the State, and Late Industrialization: Comparative Perspectives from the Pacific Rim*. Boulder, Colo.: Westview Press.

Bowie, Alasdair. 1991. *Crossing the Industrial Divide: State, Society, and the Politics of Economic Transformation in Malaysia*. New York: Columbia University Press.

Chandrasekhar, C. P., and Jayati Ghosh. 2001. "The Fragile Foundations of the Southeast Asian Miracle: Relocative Capital, the Proliferation of Capitalism, and Industrial Growth." In K. S. Jomo, ed., *Southeast Asia's Industrialisation*. Basingstoke: Palgrave.

Chang, Ha-Joon. 1994a. "Explaining 'Flexible Rigidities' in East Asia." In Tony Killick, ed., *The Flexible Economy.* London: Routledge.

————. 1994b. *The Political Economy of Industrial Policy.* London: Macmillan.

————. 1999. "Industrial Policy and East Asia: The Miracle, the Crisis, and the Future." Workshop on Rethinking the East Asian Miracle, World Bank, San Francisco, February 16–17. Processed.

Chin, K. F. 2001. "Financing Manufacturing in Malaysia: Experience, Issues, and Challenges." In K. S. Jomo, ed., *Southeast Industrialisation.* Basingstoke: Palgrave.

Chin, K. F., and K. S. Jomo. 2000. "Financial Sector Rents in Malaysia." In K. S. Jomo and Mushtaq Khan, eds., *Rents, Rent-Seeking, and Development.* New York: Cambridge University Press.

————. 2001. "Industrial Financing Options: Lessons for Malaysia." In K. S. Jomo and Shyamala Nagaraj, eds., *Globalisation versus Development.* Basingstoke: Macmillan.

Dahlman, C. J., and O. Sananikone. 1990. "Technology Strategy in the Economy of Taiwan: Exploiting Foreign Linkages and Investing in Local Capabilities." World Bank, Washington, D.C. (December). Processed.

Doraisami, Anita, and Rajah Rasiah. 2001. "Fiscal Incentives for Promotion of Manufactured Exports in Malaysia." In K. S. Jomo, ed., *Southeast Asia's Industrialisation.* Basingstoke: Palgrave.

Edwards, C. B. 1999. "Skilled and Unskilled Foreign Labour in Malaysian Development—A Strategic Shift?" In K. S. Jomo and Greg Felker, eds., *Technology, Competitiveness, and the State,* pp. 235–66. London: Routledge.

Edwards, C. B., and K. S. Jomo. 1993. "Malaysian Industrialisation: Performance, Problems, Prospects." In K. S. Jomo, ed., *Industrialising Malaysia.* London: Routledge.

Ernst, Dieter. 1998. "Catching-Up, Crisis, and Truncated Industrial Upgrading: Evolutionary Aspects of Technological Learning in East Asia's Electronics Industry." Paper presented at Intech conference, Lisbon, September 21. Processed.

Fallows, James. 1994. *Looking at the Sun: The Rise of the New East Asian Economic and Political System.* New York: Pantheon Books.

Felker, Greg. 2000. "Industrial Policy and Industrialisation in Malaysia and Thailand." In K. S. Jomo, ed., *Southeast Asia's Ersatz Industrialisation.* Basingstoke: Macmillan.

Felker, Greg, and K. S. Jomo. 1999. "New Approaches to Investment Policy in the Asean 4." Paper presented at the first anniversary conference, Asian Development Bank Institute, Tokyo, December 10. Processed.

Fukuyama, Francis. 1995. *Trust.* New York: Free Press.

Gerschenkron, Alexander. 1962. *Economic Backwardness in Historical Perspective.* Cambridge, Mass.: Harvard University Press.

Gomez, E. T., and K. S. Jomo. 1999. *Malaysia's Political Economy,* rev. ed. New York: Cambridge University Press.

Gopal, Jaya. 1999. "Malaysia's Palm Oil Refining Industry: Policy, Growth, Technical Change, and Competitiveness." In K. S. Jomo, Greg Felker, and Rajah Rasiah, eds., *Industrial Technology Development in Malaysia*, pp. 360–95. London: Routledge.

Jesudason, James V. 1989. *Ethnicity and the Economy: The State, Chinese Business, and Multinationals in Malaysia*. Singapore: Oxford University Press.

Johnson, Chalmers. 1982. *MITI and the Japanese Miracle*. Stanford, Calif.: Stanford University Press.

Jomo, K. S. 1990. *Growth and Structural Change in the Malaysian Economy*. London: Macmillan.

———. 1997. "A Distinct Chinese Idiom of Business in Malaysia." In Anthony Reid and Daniel Chirot, eds., *Entrepreneurial Minorities in Central Europe and Southeast Asia*, pp. 237–57. Seattle: University of Washington Press.

———. 2001a. "Growth and Structural Change in the Second-tier Southeast Asian NICs." In K. S. Jomo, ed., *Southeast Asia's Industrialisation*. Basingstoke: Palgrave.

———. 2001b. "The Southeast Asian Difference: An Introduction." In K. S. Jomo, ed., *Southeast Asia's Industrialisation*. Basingstoke: Palgrave.

Jomo, K. S., ed. 1994. *Japan and Malaysian Development*. London: Routledge.

———. 1995. *Privatizing Malaysia*. Boulder, Colo.: Westview Press.

———. 1998. *Tigers in Trouble: Financial Governance, Liberalisation, and Crises in East Asia*. London: Zed Books.

Jomo, K. S., with Chen Yun Chung, Brian C. Folk, Irfan ul-Haque, Pasuk Phongpaichit, Batara Simatupang, and Mayuri Tateishi. 1997. *Southeast Asia's Misunderstood Miracle: Industrial Policy and Economic Development in Thailand, Malaysia, and Indonesia*. Boulder, Colo.: Westview Press.

Jomo, K. S., and Greg Felker, eds. 1999. *Technology, Competitiveness, and the State*. London: Routledge.

Jomo, K. S., Greg Felker, and Rajah Rasiah, eds. 1999. *Industrial Technology Development in Malaysia*. London: Routledge.

Jomo, K. S., and E. T. Gomez. 1997. "Rents and Development in Multiethnic Malaysia." In M. Aoki, H.-K. Kim, and M. Okuno-Fujiwara, eds., *The Role of Government in East Asian Economic Development: Comparative Institutional Analysis*, pp. 342–72. Oxford: Clarendon Press.

———. 2000. "Creating Efficient Rent-seeking Rights for Development: The Malaysian Dilemma." In Mushtaq Khan and K. S. Jomo, eds., *Rents, Rent-Seeking, and Development*. Cambridge, U.K.: Cambridge University Press.

Jomo, K. S., B. T. Khoo, and Y. T. Chang. 1997. "Vision, Policy, and Governance in Malaysia." In Leila Frischtak and Izak Atiyas, eds., *Governance, Leadership, and Communication: Building Constituencies for Economic Reform*, pp. 65–90. Washington, D.C.: World Bank.

Jomo, K. S., and Michael Rock. 1997. "Economic Diversification and Primary Commodity Processing in the Southeast Asian Newly Industrializing Countries (NICs)." United Nations Conference on Trade and Development, Geneva. Processed.

Kalecki, Michal. 1967. "Observations on Social and Economic Aspects of Interme-
    diate Regimes." *Coexistence* 4.

Kaplinsky, Raphael. 1999. "'If You Want to Get Somewhere Else, You Must Run at
    Least Twice as Fast as That': The Roots of the East Asian Crisis." *Competition
    and Change* 4(1):1–30.

Korhonen, Pekka. 1994. "The Theory of the Flying Geese Pattern of Development
    and Its Implications." *Journal of Peace Research* 31(1):93–108.

Krongkaew, Medhi. forthcoming. "Economic Policy Determination in Thailand: The
    Interplay of Bureaucracy, Political Power, and Private Business." In K. S. Jomo,
    ed., *Manufacturing Competitiveness: How Internationally Competitive National Firms
    and Industries Developed in East Asia*. Cambridge, U.K.: Cambridge University
    Press.

List, Friedrich. 1841. *The National System of Political Economy* [English translation by
    Sampson Lloyd]. London: Longman [1904].

Little, Ian M. D. 1981. "The Experience and Causes of Rapid Labour-Intensive
    Development in Korea, Taiwan Province, Hong Kong, and Singapore and the
    Possibilities of Emulation." In Eddy Lee, ed., *Export-led Industrialization and
    Development*. Geneva: International Labour Organisation, Asian Employment
    Programme.

Low, Linda. 2001. "The Role of the Government in Singapore's Industrialisation."
    In K. S. Jomo, ed., *Southeast Asia's Industrialisation*. Basingstoke: Palgrave.

Mardon, R. 1990. "The State and Effective Control of Foreign Capital: The Case of
    South Korea." *World Politics* 43(1):111–38.

Matthias, Rudolph. 2001. "Corporate Financing and the Systems of Industrial Fi-
    nance: A Comparative Analysis of Malaysia, Thailand, and Selected Industrialised
    Countries." In K. S. Jomo, ed., *Southeast Asia's Industrialisation*. Basingstoke:
    Palgrave.

Montes, Manuel. 1998. *The Currency Crisis in South East Asia*. Singapore: Institute of
    South East Asian Studies.

Morishima Michio. 1982. *Why Has Japan "Succeeded"? Western Technology and the Japa-
    nese Ethos*. Cambridge, U.K.: Cambridge University Press.

NEAC (National Economic Action Council). 1998. *National Economic Recovery Plan:
    Agenda for Action*. National Economic Action Council, Economic Planning Unit,
    Prime Minister's Department, Kuala Lumpur (August).

Pack, Howard, and Larry Westphal. 1986. "Industrial Strategy and Technological
    Change: Theory vs. Reality." *Journal of Development Economics* 22:87–128.

Perkins, Dwight. 1994. "There Are at Least Three Models of East Asian Develop-
    ment." *World Development* 2(4):655–61.

Phongpaichit, Pasuk. 1990. *The Recent Wave of Japanese Investment in Southeast Asia*.
    Singapore: ISEAS.

Rasiah, Rajah. 1995. *Foreign Investment and Industrialization in Malaysia*. Basingstoke:
    Macmillan.

————. 1999. "Government-Business Co-ordination and the Development of Eng Hardware." In K. S. Jomo, Greg Felker, and Rajah Rasiah, eds., *Industrial Technology Development in Malaysia*, pp. 231–46. London: Routledge.

————. 2001. "Southeast Asia's Ersatz Miracle: The Dubious Sustainability of Its Growth and Industrialisation." In K. S. Jomo, ed., *Southeast Asia's Industrialisation*. Basingstoke: Palgrave.

Rasiah, Rajah, Ishak Shari, and K. S. Jomo. 1996. "Globalization and Liberalization in East and South East Asia: Implications for Growth, Inequality, and Poverty." In *Globalization and Liberalization: Effects of International Economic Relations on Poverty*, pp. 191–200. New York and Geneva: United Nations Conference on Trade and Development.

Rock, Michael. 2001a. "Making the Case for the Success of Industrial Policy in Indonesia." In K. S. Jomo, ed., *Southeast Asia's Industrialisation*. Basingstoke: Palgrave.

————. 2001b. "Selective Industrial Policy and Manufacturing Export Success in Thailand." In K. S. Jomo, ed., *Southeast Asia's Industrialisation*. Basingstoke: Palgrave.

Rodan, Garry. 1989. *The Political Economy of Singapore's Industrialization*. London: Macmillan.

Rowthorn, Robert. 2001. "Replicating the Experience of the NIEs on a Large Scale." In K. S. Jomo and Shyamala Nagaraj, eds., *Globalisation versus Development: Heterodox Perspectives*. Basingstoke: Macmillan.

Siroros, Patcharee, and Wilaiwan Wannitikul. 2001. "The Thai Gems and Jewellery Industry and the Siam Cement Group." In K. S. Jomo, ed., *Manufacturing Competitiveness: How Internationally Competitive National Firms and Industries Developed in East Asia*. Cambridge, U.K.: Cambridge University Press.

Timmer, Peter. 1991. "Agricultural Employment and Poverty Alleviation in Asia." In Peter Timmer, ed., *Agriculture and the State*. Ithaca, N.Y.: Cornell University Press.

————. 1993. "Rural Bias in East and Southeast Asian Rice Economies." *Journal of Development Studies* 29(July):149–76.

UNCTAD (United Nations Conference on Trade and Development). 1998. *Trade and Development Report 1998*. Geneva.

Unger, Danny. 1993. "Japan's Capital Exports: Moulding East Asia." In Danny Unger and Paul Blackburn, eds., *Japan's Emerging Global Role*. Boulder, Colo.: Lynne Rienner.

Wade, Robert. 1991. *Governing the Market*. Princeton, N. J.: Princeton University Press.

Wong, P. K., M-K Chng, S-Y Phang, and J-S Yong. Forthcoming. "Government Policy in Singapore's Manufacturing Development." In K. S. Jomo, ed., *Manufacturing Competitiveness: How Internationally Competitive National Firms and Industries Developed in East Asia*. Cambridge, U.K.: Cambridge University Press.

World Bank. 1993. *The East Asian Miracle: Economic Growth and Public Policy*. New York: Oxford University Press.

————. 1994. *Averting the Old Age Crisis*. New York: Oxford University Press.

————. 1998. *East Asia: The Road to Recovery*. Washington, D.C.

World Bank (with the International Monetary Fund). Various years. *World Debt Tables* [now *Global Development Finance*]. Washington, D.C.

————. Various years. *Global Development Finance* [formerly *World Debt Tables*]. Washington, D.C.

Yoshihara, Kunio. 1988. *The Rise of Ersatz Capitalism in Southeast Asia*. Singapore: Oxford University Press.

————. 1995. *The Nation and Economic Growth: The Philippines and Thailand*. Kuala Lumpur: Oxford University Press.

————. 1999. *Building a Prosperous Southeast Asia*. Richmond, Surrey: Curzon.

CHAPTER 13

FROM MIRACLE TO CRISIS TO RECOVERY: LESSONS FROM FOUR DECADES OF EAST ASIAN EXPERIENCE

Joseph E. Stiglitz

There has been much debate about whether there was or was not an East Asia miracle, and if there was, what contributed to it, and whether there are lessons that are applicable to other regions. By the same token, there has been much debate about what caused the East Asian crisis, what lessons should be drawn from that experience, and what insights the crisis itself sheds on the economic developments of the preceding three decades. As countries have recovered from the crisis—some more quickly than others—the debate has not diminished. Some have viewed the quick recovery as evidence of these countries' long-standing strengths, others as bearing testimony to the wisdom of the reforms that had been urged upon them in the midst of the crisis. The distinguished authors who have contributed to this volume, all with a long-standing interest in the region, have analyzed different facets of the East Asian experience refracted through the two years of crisis and with the benefit of nearly a decade of scholarship that has deepened our understanding of the miracle.

Instead of attempting to provide an overview of the volume and a synthesis of the findings that would go over ground already covered by Shahid Yusuf in chapter 1, I will indicate how my own thinking on East Asia has evolved since I contributed to the World Bank's miracle study, *The East Asian Miracle* (World Bank 1993), almost a decade ago. In doing so I will be at times complementing and at other times providing a counterpoint to the views of the other authors.

WAS THERE A MIRACLE?

As Shahid Yusuf has suggested, the debate as to whether what happened in East Asia deserves the appellation of a miracle is just a matter of semantics: whether we call it a miracle or not, the fact of the matter is that the increases in living standards were virtually unprecedented. Only a tiny number of other countries have succeeded in achieving comparable rates of saving on a voluntary basis, over an extended period of time, and even countries with considerably lower savings rates have found it difficult to invest comparable amounts (relative to gross domestic product) efficiently, with high and sustained incremental output capital ratios. A large part of the *real* debate on East Asia's development prowess revolves around explaining these high savings rates and the relative efficiency of investment.

There is another aspect of the miracle that has received all too little attention but plays a role in the sequel: capitalism has always been plagued by fluctuations, including financial panics. What is remarkable about East Asia is not that it experienced a crisis in 1997, but that it had experienced so few crises over the preceding three decades—two of the countries had not had one year of downturn and two had had one year of recession, a better record than any of the supposedly advanced and well-managed Organisation for Economic Co-operation and Development (OECD) countries. This experience naturally raises several questions: Were there features of the "miracle" that led both to growth and to relative stability? Did the crisis of 1997 represent a manifestation of weaknesses that had long been latent, a change in the world, with a failure of the region to make concomitant adaptations, or an abandonment—partly under the influence of outsiders—of long-standing policies? I will argue below that while there are elements of all three explanations, the last almost surely was pivotal.

THE TOTAL FACTOR PRODUCTIVITY DEBATE

Whether one can explain increases in East Asian incomes largely as a result of changes in inputs turns on technical issues discussed by Pack (see chapter 3 of this volume), Kim and Lau (1994), and Lau (1998). These have not been, and are not likely to be, ever cleanly sorted out: in effect, there is a problem of underidentification. Some now claim that "all" one has to do in order to attain rapid growth is to reach East Asian levels of saving and ensure that the funds are well invested. According to this view, there was little evidence of a "miracle" in the sense that the pace of total factor productivity (TFP) increase was not large at all. In fact the estimates by Kim and Lau (1994) suggest that TFP made no contribution to the growth of the newly industrializing East Asian economies. They underscore the significance of investments in physical capital, human capital, and research and development. The East Asian countries still lag far behind the major industrial countries in terms of TFP.

However, I remain skeptical as to the robustness of the results generated by growth accounting. As Rodriguez-Clare has pointed out, slight (and plausible) changes in how human capital is measured can lead to markedly different results (Rodriguez-Clare 1996). The difficulties of aggregating capital are well known. Moreover, the standard Solow methodology for measuring TFP (based on the residual method) assumes that factors get paid their marginal product (as they would in fully competitive markets). But there is overwhelming evidence that, especially in many of the markets in East Asian countries, competition is far from perfect. Governments intervene in wage setting. This is important: because of the high rate of increase in capital, *if* a large weight is assigned to capital in measuring inputs, then, not surprisingly, the amount of TFP is low. The purported share of capital, say, in Singapore, is 50 percent—twice the figure of more developed countries. Thus, *if* the maintained hypothesis is that the industrial and developing countries are on the same production function, and differ only in capital per capita, one must assume that the elasticity of substitution is markedly less than unity—a hypothesis that is inconsistent with the longer-term historical data, which suggest an elasticity of substitution much closer to unity. This maintained hypothesis looks weaker still when we note that even today, with Singapore's per capita income comparable to that of more industrialized countries, the share of capital is considerably greater.

The unreliability of the Solow methodology has long been recognized: it is as if the distance between Newark and New York were to be determined by using a 12-inch rule to measure the distance between New York and Los Angeles and Newark and Los Angeles, and subtracting the difference. The errors in measurement of each of the components are likely to determine the outcome.

Alwyn Young's (1992) often-cited study arguing that the freedom of markets in Hong Kong, China, can explain the relatively rapid increase in its total factor productivity illustrates how the Solow technique can yield erroneous results. Not only is it the case that the measurement of total factor productivity increases can be unreliable, as we have just suggested, but the interpretation of the residual, what is left over after measuring inputs, is highly ambiguous. Assume that one could feel confident that Hong Kong's residual was greater than that of Singapore. Is it because of better economic policies? Or is it because Hong Kong was the entrepôt for the mainland of China, and as the mainland's economy grew, so did the demand for Hong Kong's services? In this interpretation, Young's explanation of Hong Kong's higher TFP relative to Singapore is turned on its head: Hong Kong's success actually was a result of the growth of perhaps the least free-market regime of the region.

In a sense, the total factor productivity debate is much ado about nothing. There has been a narrowing of the technology gap—and there is every reason to believe that this will continue. Those who argue for little TFP are not denying the decrease in the technology gap, but only that the technological gains were "purchased." But the key policy issue facing all developing countries remains: how to close the knowledge gap. It may be reassuring to know that technology can be acquired at a price. But money alone will not do the trick, or else many other countries would have narrowed the technology gap as well. At the very least, we have to allow for the possibility that governments in some Asian countries provided the preconditions, through a variety of channels, most notably their support for technical education. While the closing of the knowledge gap *may* have been a by-product of the high levels of investment, the successful countries made deliberate efforts to enhance the transfer of technology, including foreign direct investment.

SAVINGS

Similar issues surround many of the other components of the "miracle." Several governments deliberately promoted savings. In Japan, postal savings banks made it easier (and more secure) for those in the rural sector to save, while in Singapore the National Provident Fund, in effect, imposed a 42 percent savings rate on workers. There is a debate: Can the high savings rate be "simply" explained by characteristics of the economy, such as the high growth rate? If increases in consumption lag behind increases in income, then a high growth rate will be associated with a high savings rate. There may then be multiple equilibria in the short run—one with high savings and high growth, the other with low savings and low growth. But that leaves unanswered the key question: Why did East Asia gravitate toward one equilibrium, the rest of the world the other? Government action may have been a key determinant. Indeed, as in other multiple equilibria models, government actions, which move the economy from one equilibrium to another, can be self-sustaining; once the economy has moved to the new equilibrium, the intervention is no longer needed. Thus it may be the case that after Singapore succeeded in moving to the high growth/high savings equilibrium, there was no longer any need to "force" savings, and the government interventions made little further difference to total savings.

FINANCIAL MARKETS

When financial depth is measured by the ratio of money to gross domestic product, financial markets appear deeper in East Asia than in most of the rest of the developing world. To be sure, security markets emerged slowly, but broad-based equities markets require strong legal protections for minority shareholders—of a kind that relatively few industrial countries have succeeded in providing. Moreover, asymmetries of information imply that even in industrial countries, a very small percentage of new investment is financed by equity issues, in spite of their greater virtues in risk diversification. It is thus not surprising that East Asia relied heavily on bank-financed debt. There was always a risk with debt finance: with high, fixed obligations, an economic downturn could lead to firms facing cash constraints. But the countries of the region (especially the Republic of Korea) addressed the problem through a system of *flexible bank finance*, which had distinct advantages over securitized debt instruments. Bank finance is *infor-*

mation intensive, entailing, in principle, close monitoring of the borrower. So long as the firm's net worth remains sufficiently positive, a
cash flow shortage need not be a problem: the bank can roll over loans
and make good on any shortfalls, *provided the bank itself is in a position to
make loans.* Thus, it is largely when there are macroeconomic problems, which make it difficult or unattractive for banks to lend, that the
high leverage becomes problematic. But one can argue that government has a responsibility not only to maintain macrostability, but to
mitigate the consequences of any residual volatility. It can do this in
several ways: for example, regulatory forbearance (on capital adequacy
standards) or capital injections into the banking system. In East Asia,
the rationale for government interventions was even stronger: given
the state of development of the capital market, there was, as we have
noted, less reliance on equity than in more developed countries. Hence,
there was a need for alternative mechanisms for societal risk sharing—
to compensate for the market failure. The government "bailouts" *in
the face of macroeconomic instability* were a form of risk sharing (in effect,
converting the debt into partial equity), with limited adverse incentive
effects. If the government restricted itself to bailouts associated with
macro-instability, it avoided any incentive for excessive risk taking,
other than investments that were excessively correlated with the
economy as a whole. In principle, good supervision could mitigate
this risk, though in practice it does not seem to have done so, at least
in Thailand and Korea.

A number of East Asian governments played a large role both in
helping create financial institutions and in maintaining their capacity
to lend. Historically, financial institutions in most countries have lent
largely for trade credit and collateralized real estate. Development lending (long-term investment lending) by banks is limited. But in countries such as Korea, the government helped create a number of banks
and encouraged them (through a variety of mechanisms) to go beyond
these traditional lending avenues. *Financial restraint* (as opposed to
financial repression) led to faster economic growth as well as the growth
of the banking sector. By limiting competition and lowering deposit
rates, governments in some East Asian countries increased the profitability of banking, and thus both the net worth and the franchise value.
Some of the benefits were passed on to borrowers in the form of lower
lending rates. The lower rates at which both firms and financial insti-

tutions had access to funds enhanced bank and corporate equity—especially important in an environment where directly raising new equity was difficult. The higher level of bank and corporate equity enabled firms to undertake riskier—and higher-return—investments. Moreover, since the marginal propensity to save of corporations was higher than that of individuals, and the interest elasticity of household savings was very low, the effective transfer of funds from the household to the corporate and banking sector led to higher national savings, again enhancing economic growth.

As noted above, given the almost inevitable limitations on equity markets as a source of finance, growth could have been sustained only by a high debt policy. The alternative would have been to limit expansion to what could be financed by retained earnings. East Asian countries thus faced two challenges: finding alternative ways of enhancing equity and managing the risks associated with high debt.

The financial restraint described in the previous paragraph represented the most important way that governments helped strengthen the equity bases of firms. To be sure, some of the governments recognized the importance of the legal reforms that would facilitate the creation of a deeper equity market; at the same time they realized that even in the most advanced of the industrial countries, well-established firms financed only a small percentage of their investment by new equity issues.

Accordingly, much of the burden of risk management was placed on the banking system, which, often under government pressure, rolled over loans in the face of macroeconomic shocks. However, in such cases the government often tacitly or explicitly underwrote the risks incurred. This risk absorption mechanism, while it allowed countries like Korea to weather some of the macroeconomic shocks (like the oil price increases of the 1970s) far better than other countries, was put under stress in the 1990s from several sources. First, the countries of the region liberalized their capital markets quickly, under pressure from the International Monetary Fund (IMF) and the U.S. Treasury (and the decision to seek OECD membership), before the appropriate regulatory structures were in place. The pressure for rapid liberalization also meant that the gradualist strategy of the early 1990s was set aside. With the focus on rapid liberalization, and insufficient attention to the details, what appeared in hindsight as mistakes were almost inevitable.

While the reduced extent of government involvement in banking—presumably with less policy (and "connected") lending—should have strengthened the banking system, liberalization increased the scope for risk taking (for example, by eliminating the restrictions on speculative real estate lending that had been a hallmark of Thailand's policies in the miracle period) and the incentives for doing so (greater competition reduced the franchise value, and therefore the incentive for prudential behavior) at the same time that it increased the risks that the banking systems were exposed to. Compounding these problems was the fact that just at the time that *better* regulation was required, government regulators found it virtually impossible to keep their best and brightest, who were lured away by higher salaries offered by the private sector. Finally, the strictures against the risk-sharing mechanisms that had been customary under the earlier regime in some countries meant that firms had to fend for themselves to a greater degree—though their financial structures did not have time to adapt.

The criticism from the West compounded these problems, and not only in contributing to the massive flight of capital. It was not clear to what extent cronyism had played a role or to what extent cronyism Asian-style was different from cronyism American-style. Certainly, the publicly orchestrated, privately financed bailout of LTCM (Long-Term Capital Management), where CEOs seemed to use their corporate positions to bail out their private positions, raised questions about crony capitalism, corporate governance, *and* financial regulation even in the most advanced of the industrial countries. The fact that the *marginal* lenders in Korea were Western banks suggested bad judgment might be playing a more important role in bank lending policy than hidden government influence. Nonetheless, Korea took to heart the criticism of the government/banking/industrial nexus of the *chaebol*, and these concerns played a key role in the restructuring of the Korean economy, and indeed, are likely to play an important role in the rebalancing of political power as well.

These reforms are likely to lead an economic system that, while it exposes the country to greater risks[1], is better able to manage risks than the one that it replaced, and one that is likely to suffer less from political influence in resource allocation. Whether they will lead to an economic system better able to manage risks than the one that prevailed before liberalization is a moot question; the process of integration into the global economy has advanced to the point where it would have been hard, at best, to adapt that system to today's world. But it is also surely the case that the reforms, including the limitations on debt-equity ratios (as a result of both government pressure and the recognition of the huge risks that the high volatility in interest rates that mark IMF macromanagement strategies impose on highly levered companies) will imply that future long-term growth rates will almost surely be lower than they otherwise would have been.

INDUSTRIAL POLICY AND THE ROLE OF GOVERNMENT

Those who put their faith in the market tend to downplay the role of government during the miracle period, particularly in the northeast Asian countries—but they can, at times, elevate its role when it comes to the crisis of 1997–98. Evidently, according to this view, during the period of success, markets drove the efficient allocation of resources, and more recently, it is government that has been the source of the problem. But again, the evidence is to the contrary: over time, the role of government in resource allocation has diminished in the 1990s, not increased.

Earlier, I noted the wide array of government programs, for example, to promote savings, strengthen and expand financial institutions, enhance education, and ensure macrostability. I also touched upon some of the controversies surrounding the role of government in promoting savings and in strengthening and broadening financial institutions. Perhaps the most contentious issue of all relates to the role of industrial policies, which several contributors to this volume have critically assessed.

It is clear that the government intervened in the allocation of resources. For instance, some governments promoted exports by making credits more available to successful exporters and by directing credit to selected sectors. Where such policy was subject to strict rules, the corruption and distortions associated with more ad hoc policies was avoided or at least kept relatively limited. It is also clear that the sectors that were supported grew and, in many cases, have become the foundations of these countries' economies as they enter the new millennium.

Part of the success of the leading East Asian economies relates to the closing of the technology/knowledge gap. Of this, there can be little doubt. The externalities and public goods aspects of knowledge provide a theoretical rationale for a role of government. In other countries that have implemented successful growth strategies, governments have pursued active policies promoting the production and dissemination of knowledge and technology, going well beyond just the protection of intellectual property through patent and copyright laws. In the United States, the increases in productivity in agriculture in the 19th century were promoted by the land grant colleges, with their research and extension services. The U.S. telecommunications industry was promoted by government, by establishing the first telegraph line, between Baltimore and Washington, in 1842, and, more recently, by creating the Internet. Moreover, industrialization occurred within the United States behind the protection afforded by industrial tariffs. Would the countries in the East Asian region have succeeded in closing the knowledge and technology gap had they limited themselves simply to education? Possibly, but there is little historical precedent for such an achievement.[2]

Still, the subject of industrial policy remains highly controversial. The controversy surrounds two questions—the counterfactual and the aggregative *quantitative* significance of these interventions, that is, what would have happened otherwise, did they work and did they make much difference? The more extreme critics argue that, by and large, they were distortive and thereby counterproductive. A few failures, such as Japan's attempt to "rationalize" the automobile industry and inhibit the entry of Honda into car production, are cited time and time again. In my view, some of the criticism is misplaced. These arguments suggest that these countries would have grown even faster but for the interventions—possible, but not very probable. Today, as Korea has joined the OECD and become a major player in some of the key electronics industries, one hears less criticism of Korea's high-technology strategy.

The more subtle criticism is that while there was considerable fanfare surrounding the industrial policies, they really were not of much quantitative significance. To be sure, they affected *particular* industries; but did they make much difference *in the aggregate?* (Interestingly, there is a parallel argument *against* the critics; the Harberger triangles associated with most price distortions are of second-order importance.) The controversy remains unresolved: How much credence can be put in the admittedly flawed econometric techniques that sometimes seem to suggest that these interventions played a limited role, versus the broader analysis, which links these policies to the sectors that are playing key roles in the economies in the region today?

To understand the central features that contributed to the rapid growth in the region one can look across countries for *common* policies. That is, the countries in the region shared some policies in common, while they differed in others. Most have high savings rates, though the *particular* policies they used to achieve that high savings rate differed. They have differed in their attitudes toward foreign direct investment. While foreign direct investment was at the center of Singapore's and Malaysia's strategies, Korea and Japan relied on investment by their own firms.

The fact that almost *all* of the economies in the region had industrial policies (with the exception of Hong Kong, which benefited from the industrial policies of its neighbor, mainland China) *suggests* that such policies were an important part of their growth strategies, whether or not the highly imperfect econometric techniques for quantifying such impacts succeeded in verifying such claims.

One of the principal ways that industrial policies were pursued was through interventions in financial markets. As I have noted, government both encouraged some forms of lending (for exports, to small and medium-size enterprises, to particular sectors) and, at times, in a few countries, discouraged other forms of lending (for speculative investment in real estate). These interventions in the capital market too have been widely criticized, both for their potential for corruption and for their distortions in resource allocation. But again, the relevant question concerns the counterfactual. One can argue that the interventions were helping to address market failures that are endemic in capital markets. Again, other successful "market" economies, like the United States, have massively intervened in the capital market—quite recently, more than a quarter of all loans in the United States either were intermediated by government or government-sponsored enterprises or had government guarantees. Governments, like any human institution, are fallible, and so one should not expect *perfection* in resource allocation. The question is, given the imperfections, would growth have been higher had governments intervened far less in their financial markets? This question is even harder to answer than the previous one, since in every country, governments intervene in financial markets, if only to ensure the safety and soundness of the financial system and to protect consumers against fraud.

In retrospect, perhaps the criticism that should have been leveled is that the government did not take strong enough actions, not that it intervened too much: it deregulated the financial sector when it should have been asking what was the *appropriate* set of regulations, and it did not do enough to ensure good corporate governance, which would have been necessary to create an effective stock market.

A third area of contention is the role of cooperation between business and government, which is also examined by several authors in this volume. The coordination provided by Japan, Inc., or Malaysia, Inc., was, at one time, widely lauded. In effect, it was argued that market prices do not convey all the relevant information. However, even while it was lauded, many warned of the risks: cooperation could become capture and lead to corruption. It is hard to assess the *relative* importance of corruption—both relative to what occurs in other countries and relative to the benefits that accrued from cooperation. There is corruption in every society. Campaign contributions lead to corporate welfare, including special tax benefits for housing, large subsidies for agriculture, and a host of other tax expenditures and direct subsidies. Were the distortions in Korea, say, larger than those in the United States? There is no way of ascertaining the answer to that question. And were the costs of the distortions greater than the benefits that accrued from the cooperation? The fact of the matter is that we simply do not have tools with which we can answer these questions with any degree of certitude.

This poses both easy and hard policy questions. It is easy enough to say that the government should do everything it can to reduce corruption, and that government interventions should be designed in such a way as to mitigate the risk of corruption. It is easy enough to explain why corruption has adverse effects on economic growth. It is harder to design and implement corruption-resistant strategies. It is even harder to assess with any precision the impact of the particular level and forms of corruption on the growth of the economy.[3]

Reducing the scope for rent seeking is clearly one aspect of corruption-resistant policies. But in many countries, reforms intended to reduce rent seeking, in particular, privatizations, have themselves been highly corrupted. In the light of *market* and *government* failures, there are two alternative strategies: to focus on one and ignore the other or to try to address the weaknesses in each, viewing the public and private sectors as *complementary*. Singapore illustrates nicely the advantages of the latter approach. It undertook great efforts in reducing public corruption and, by most accounts, succeeded remarkably well. In doing so, it employed, in part, what have now become standard efficiency wage/incentive approaches. It relied heavily on the private sector but did not shy away from an active government role, not only in social policy but also in industrial policy. It developed a highly effective financial regulatory system, earning its marks when it excluded BCCI (the Bank of Credit and Commerce International), which succeeded in duping the United States' regulatory authorities. And partly because of the soundness and credibility of its financial system—based on effective regulation—it has become a regional financial center.

CONCLUDING REMARKS

Whether one calls it a miracle or not, the increases in income and reductions in poverty in East Asia were real and impressive. They showed that development is possible and that rapid development could be associated with egalitarian policies that greatly reduced poverty. And the contrasting experiences in the rest of the world showed not only that development was not inevitable but indeed that there seemed something very unusual about what had occurred in East Asia, the most populous region of the world. The crisis has tarnished that record only slightly and, if anything, together with the strong recovery in several of the countries, may have reinforced the conclusion that there is something very special about these countries. At the same time, the rapid growth in India over the past decade (especially if one looks at *particular* states within India) shows that East Asia has no monopoly on growth. India's success suggests that other countries too can achieve rapid economic growth and, at the very least, reinforces the need to understand the ingredients that contribute to success.

At one level, the problem of interpreting the miracle, crisis, and recovery is that we have an underidentified system: we do not have the controlled experiments that would allow us to assess what would have happened *but for.* If, say, the governments had simply had good macromanagement but not liberalized markets earlier, would growth have been even faster, and would the crisis not have occurred? We have a wealth of countries in other regions that followed different policies. On the basis of this juxtaposing their experience with that of East Asia, we can offer a few suggestions for the future.

All of the countries in the East Asian region will need to reexamine their *risk management* strategies: as their economies have become increasingly open, they are more exposed to the vagaries of international markets. For instance, as noted by Ito in chapter 2 of this volume, currency and term mismatching poses severe risks to banks in the management of their portfolios. East Asian countries will need to determine how to reduce their exposure, how to reduce their overall sensitivity to the risks that remain, and how to insulate the most vulnerable elements of their population. Some of these changes will likely result in a slowing down of growth, while some of the changes will actually enhance their ability to grow more rapidly, by becoming more integrated into the global economy. For instance, Korea's rapid growth, as noted, has been based on a high debt policy. Without debt finance, firms would have had to rely on retained earnings, and growth would inevitably have been slower. Lowering debt equity ratios *may* thus lead to lower growth. But institutional reforms may lead to a strengthened equity market—although I must repeat that even in the most advanced industrial countries, relatively little new investment is financed through equity issues, and few countries have managed to create equity markets with dispersed ownership. But the reforms under way in Korea may strengthen equity markets, and so the country will be in a better position to both sustain growth momentum and manage shocks at the same time.

The weakness of safety nets is not a surprise, given that prior to the recent crisis the countries in the region had faced few economic downturns. But even in this area, some of the countries have shown an impressive level of institutional creativity: Singapore's provident fund has integrated the various social insurance programs and, in a relatively short span of time, improved housing, health, and income security.[4]

The countries of the region face enormous challenges going forward. They have fundamental strengths on which to build, but they will have to adapt in numerous ways to the changing global environment and the changes in their own economies. The role of government will have to be redefined. Just as before they were misled by the chimera of deregulation—they should have asked instead what is the *right* regulatory structure for their current situation—so too in the future, they will have to resist accepting without question the current mantras of the global marketplace of ideas. There will have to be *strengthened* regulation of securities markets and an improved overall legal environment, especially in areas such as corporate governance and bankruptcy. The legal structures will have to comport with international standards, yet be adapted to their own special situations; wholesale borrowing will not work. The countries have moved toward democracy; democratic institutions and processes will need to be strengthened. Progress on all these fronts in most of the countries has already been impressive. Transparency is being increased, with Thailand even incorporating a right-to-know within its constitution.

Each of the countries faces its own individual challenges: Thailand needs to strengthen its secondary and tertiary education; in Korea, there is widespread support for reducing the role of the *chaebol*; in Indonesia, the difficult and delicate process of decentralization will have to be addressed. But while each of the countries faces different challenges, most of the countries are well poised to take advantage of many of the opportunities that are afforded by globalization and the new economy: the government-led strategies of closing the technology gap and investing heavily in human capital have placed several of the countries in a position not only to avail themselves of the new technologies, but even to become leaders in their exploitation.

Gazing through our cloudy crystal ball into the future, we can see prospects for continued robust growth—probably at a somewhat more muted pace, but still fast enough to continue the process of closing the gap between the countries in the region and the more advanced industrial countries. There are reasons for expecting a slowdown:

- Diminishing returns eventually set in. There are diminishing returns not only to capital but to investments in knowledge as well. It is almost surely easier to close the gap in knowledge (by a given amount) when the gap is moderate than when the gap is small.

- The export-oriented strategy may encounter difficulties, as such policies become widely imitated, and the world becomes saturated with the goods that represented the traditional comparative advantage of East Asian economies, and more broadly, as they become larger relative to the rest of the world. This can be a problem especially for China. Clearly, East Asia will again have to develop new sources of dynamic comparative advantage—just as the countries in the region have repeatedly adjusted over the past four decades.

- The larger countries will face concern about growing regional inequalities. These concerns will drive strategies that focus more attention on these regions. The successes achieved in some areas imply that it may be possible to sustain high growth rates even as the benefits are broadened out, but many of the poorer regions face severe geographical disadvantages.

- Even with new safeguards, the increased openness to volatile foreign capital flows will make it difficult to manage the economies with debt-driven growth. But even with substantial legal reforms, such as those related to corporate governance, it will be difficult to channel efficiently the high savings into the corporate sector through equity markets. Thus, firms will have to rely more on retained earnings, and this will slow down growth.

The growth slowdown itself will present a challenge: Many economic structures have become adapted to high-growth scenarios, and the moderation of growth will, accordingly, require potentially serious adjustments.

But beyond these economic challenges are the broader challenges: increases in gross domestic product are a means to an end, not an end in itself. Elsewhere I have spoken of the broader mandate for democratic, equitable, sustainable development and traced out some of the implications for the countries in the region in the coming decades (Stiglitz 1998, 1999). Here, I emphasize two aspects: First, the development of the region has been accompanied by enormous urbanization. The cities that have expanded need to be made more livable—with better public transportation systems, improved environments, and public amenities, such as parks. Second, the success of the region has been based in part on building on existing social capital, reaching broad social consensus, maintaining reasonable levels of social cohesion, and fostering a broader sense of community. In some cases, doing so has not been easy: the societies are highly ethnically fractionated. The most successful governments have realized the importance of these *social* policies (including egalitarian income distribution and education policies), not only as ends in themselves but even as *necessary* for long-term economic growth. The challenge going forward is to maintain these traditional values as the process of globalization and market development continues; there will be strong forces leading to greater inequality and undermining traditional cultural norms.

NOTES

1. The argument that some advocates of capital market liberalization for East Asia (where high savings rates meant that there was little need for additional outside capital) put forward, that such capital would help stabilize the economies, never had any empirical support—even before the East Asia crisis; short-term capital flows tend to be procyclical, not countercyclical.

2. In this respect, the controversy, discussed earlier, about whether closing of the technology gap was a result of "investments" is not the central issue.

3. Many rankings show China at the high end of the corruption scale. Does this suggest that but for the corruption, the economy would have grown *significantly* faster? Interestingly, most of the regression studies showing that corruption has an adverse effect on growth (such as the 1997 *World Development Report* [World Bank 1997]) do not include China. If China was included, weighted appropriately by its size, to what extent would the standard cross-country regressions be changed? There are good theoretical arguments for believing that corruption does have adverse effects. The question being raised is that there are severe problems in assessing with any precision the *magnitude* of those impacts.

4. One can show that there are distinct advantages to be gained from integration of social insurance programs, allowing for greater risk mitigation with less attenuation of incentives.

REFERENCES

Kim, J-I, and Lawrence J. Lau. 1994. "The Sources of Growth in East Asian Newly Industrializing Economies." *Economics* 8(1):235–71.

Lau, Lawrence J. 1998. "The Sources of East Asian Economic Growth." In F. Gerard Adams and Shinichi Ichimura, eds., *East Asian development: Will the East Asian Growth Miracle Survive?* Westport, Conn.: Praeger.

Stiglitz, Joseph E. 1998. "Second Generation Strategies for Reform for China." Paper presented to Beijing University, Beijing, China, July 20.

———. 1999. "Back to Basics: Policies and Strategies for Enhanced Growth and Equity in Post-Crisis East Asia." Bangkok, Thailand. July 29.

Rodriguez-Clare, Andrés. 1996. "Multinationals, Linkages, and Economic Development." *American Economic Review*, 86:4(September):852–73.

World Bank. 1993. *The East Asian Miracle*. New York: Oxford University Press.

———. 1997. World Development Report 1997: The State in a Changing World. World Bank, Washington, DC

Young, Alwyn. 1992. "A Tale of Two Cities: Factor Accumulation and Technological Change in Hong Kong and Singapore." *NBER Macroeconomics Annual 1992*. Cambridge, Mass.: MIT Press.